The Role of the Court of Justice in EU Labour Law

Bulletin of Comparative Labour Relations

VOLUME 112

Founding Editor

The series started in 1970 under the dynamic editorship of Professor Roger Blanpain (Belgium), former President of the International Industrial Relations Association. Professor Blanpain, Professor Emeritus of Labour Law, Universities of Leuven and Tilburg, was also General Editor of the International Encyclopedia of Laws (with more than 1,600 collaborators worldwide) and President of the Association of Educative and Scientific Authors Authors. He passed away in October 2016.

General Editor

In 2015 Frank Hendrickx, Professor of labour law at the Faculty of Law of the University of Leuven (Belgium) joined as a co-Editor. Frank Hendrickx has published numerous articles and books and regularly advises governments, international institutions and private organisations in the area of labour law as well as in sports law. He is the Editor-in-Chief of the European Labour Law Journal and General Editor of the International Encyclopaedia of Laws.

Introduction

The Bulletins constitute a unique source of information and thought-provoking discussion, laying the groundwork for studies of employment relations in the 21st century, involving among much else the effects of globalization, new technologies, migration, and the greying of the population.

Contents/Subjects

Amongst other subjects the Bulletins frequently include the proceedings of international or regional conferences; reports from comparative projects devoted to salient issues in industrial relations, human resources management, and/or labour law; and specific issues underlying the multicultural aspects of our industrial societies.

Objective

The Bulletins offer a platform of expression and discussion on labour relations to scholars and practitioners worldwide, often featuring special guest editors.

The titles published in this series are listed at the end of this volume.

The Role of the Court of Justice in EU Labour Law

A Case Study on the Transfer of Undertakings Directive

Silvia Rainone

General Editor
Frank Hendrickx

Founding Editor
Roger Blanpain

Wolters Kluwer

Published by:
Kluwer Law International B.V.
PO Box 316
2400 AH Alphen aan den Rijn
The Netherlands
E-mail: lrs-sales@wolterskluwer.com
Website: www.wolterskluwer.com/en/solutions/kluwerlawinternational

Sold and distributed by:
Wolters Kluwer Legal & Regulatory U.S.
920 Links Avenue
Landisville, PA 17538
United States of America
E-mail: customer.service@wolterskluwer.com

ISBN 978-94-035-2896-0

e-Book: ISBN 978-94-035-3006-2
web-PDF: ISBN 978-94-035-3016-1

Table of Contents

Preface xi
Acknowledgements xiii

Introduction 1
1 Exploring the Role of the Court of Justice in Defining Labour Law 1
2 The First Analytical Layer: The Court from a Labour Law's Doctrinal Perspective 3
3 The Second Analytical Layer: The Court from a Judicial Lawmaking Perspective 6
4 Research Questions, Methodology and Structure 8
4.1 Research Aim and Questions 8
4.2 Structure 10
4.3 Methodology 12
4.4 The Limitations of the Research 13

CHAPTER 1
Theoretical and Normative Framework 19
1 Introduction 19
2 Labour Law's Origins and Its Transformation 20
2.1 Three Fundamental Principles of Labour Law 20
2.1.1 Fundamental Principle 1: Addressing the Uneven Distribution in the Bargaining Power 20
2.1.2 Fundamental Principle 2: Labour Law Is Not (Just) a Commodity 21
2.1.3 Fundamental Principle 3: Workers' Rights Shall Coexist with the Market Economy 22
2.2 The Functions of Labour Law 24
2.2.1 The Protective Function 24

2.2.2 Uplifting Workers' Bargaining Power 25
2.2.3 Reconciling Economic and Social Progress 26
2.2.4 Labour Law as Labour Market Regulation 29
3 The Court of Justice and the Purposive Approach to Labour Law: Myth or Reality? 31
3.1 The *Alemo-Herron* Case 33
3.2 The *Aget Iraklis* Case 38
4 Concluding Remarks 41

CHAPTER 2
Labour Law in EU Policymaking 43
1 Introduction 43
2 Historical Overview of the EU's Approach to Labour Law 45
2.1 The Origins: Dual Polity 45
2.2 Parenthesis of Upward Harmonisation 47
2.3 New Challenges and Completion of the Internal Market 49
2.4 Labour Policy Consolidates as a Dimension of the Internal Market 52
2.5 The Role of Labour Law in the Modern 'Social Market Economy' 55
2.6 EU Social Policy in Time of Economic Crisis 58
2.6.1 The EU Strategy for a Deeper EMU 58
2.6.2 'Social Triple A' as an Economic Necessity 60
3 The EPSR: A Paradigm Shift? 64
3.1 Again a Social Agenda for Economic Growth? 65
3.2 Structure and Content of the EPSR 66
3.3 The Implementation of the EPSR 70
3.3.1 Implementation Through the European Semester 70
3.3.2 Implementation Through EU Law 73
4 The EU Response to COVID-19: A Game Changer? 77
4.1 The Immediate Reaction to the COVID-19 Outbreak 78
4.2 The Next Generation EU 81
5 Concluding Remarks 84

CHAPTER 3
The Court of Justice and Labour Law: A Case Study on the Transfer of Undertakings Directive 87
1 Introduction 87
2 Directive 2001/23/EC on Acquired Rights in Case of Transfer of Undertaking 88
3 Margin of Generalisation of the Case Study 92
3.1 The Court Can 'Choose' Between Different Functions 92
3.2 Normative Indeterminacy 94
3.3 A Rich Body of Case Law 94
3.4 Debate on the Purposive Approach by the Court 95
4 Case Study's Structure and Methodology 98
5 The Case Studies 100

5.1 The Scope of Application 100
5.1.1 Legal Transfer 103
5.1.2 Transfer of a Business 110
5.2 Workers' Rights 122
6 The Court's Approach to Labour Law 136
7 Concluding Considerations: A First Definition of the Role of the Court 142

CHAPTER 4
The Court of Justice as a Judicial Policymaker 147
1 Introduction 147
1.1 Judicial Activism and EU Policymaking 148
1.2 Structure and Goals 151
2 Political Inclination and Neofunctionalist Theory 152
2.1 The Two Postulates of Neofunctionalism 153
2.1.1 Enforcing EU Law Through Individuals and National Courts 154
2.1.2 Development of Non-internal Market-Related Policies 158
2.2 The Relevance of a Collaborative Relationship with National Courts 160
2.3 Limits of the Neofunctionalist Theory 163
3 The Court of Justice as the Trustee of EU Integration: The Integrationalist Theory 166
3.1 The Court as the Guardian of the Treaties 167
3.2 Integrationalism in the Court of Justice's Reasoning 169
3.2.1 The Creation of a Sui Generis Legal System 169
3.2.2 Widening the EU Competences 171
3.2.2.1 The Deepening of the Internal Market via Negative Integration 172
3.2.2.2 The Expansive Approach to the Principle of Non-discrimination 174
3.3 Informal Partnership with the European Commission 177
3.4 Weak Aspects of the Integrationalist Theory 181
4 Concluding Remarks 184

CHAPTER 5
The Relevance of the National Context in the Reasoning of the Court 187
1 Introduction 187
2 Intergovernmentalism 189
2.1 The Realist and the Neorational Variants 190
2.2 Member States' Interests in the Court's Reasoning 191
2.3 Amicus Briefs 193
2.4 The Ability of National Governments to Redirect the Court's Jurisprudence 195
2.5 Weaknesses of the Intergovernmental Theory 197
3 The Relevance of National Legal Systems in the Court's Reasoning 201

3.1 The Common Constitutional Traditions of the Member States 202
3.2 The Majoritarian Approach 205
3.2.1 Examples of the Majoritarian Approach 207
3.2.2 Implications of the Majoritarian Approach for the Court's Policymaking 210
3.2.3 The Critical Aspects of the Majoritarian Theory 211
3.3 The Pluralistic Approach 212
3.3.1 The Heterarchical Understanding of the EU Legal Order 213
3.3.2 The Origins of the Pluralist Approach 213
3.3.3 Constitutional Pluralism in the Court of Justice's Case Law 216
3.3.4 But How Pluralistic Is the Court Really? 221
4 Trans-judicial Dialogue 225
4.1 The Trans-judicial Dialogue as an Instrument of Contamination Between European and National Legal Systems 226
4.2 The Preliminary Ruling Procedure 228
4.2.1 The Establishment of the Dialogical Relationship and the 'Hidden Dialogue' 229
4.2.2 Superior and Lower Courts: A Different Kind of Dialogue 231
4.2.3 Establishing the Dialogue and 'Preemptive Opinions' of National Courts 233
4.3 The Limits of the Court's Discretion 235
4.3.1 Limits from Within the EU Legal System 236
4.3.2 Dialectical Limits 237
4.4 The Counter-Limits 239
4.4.1 The Inviolable Constitutional Principles of the National Legal System 239
4.4.1.1 Italy 239
4.4.1.2 Germany 240
4.4.1.3 The Court's Reactions and National Counteractions 241
4.4.1.4 The Normalisation of the Counter-Limits 243
4.4.2 *Kompetenz-Kompetenz* 244
4.4.3 The Spread of Counter-Limits in National Constitutional Jurisprudence 248
4.5 Trans-judicial Dialogue in Action 254
4.5.1 The Judicial Activism of the Court of Justice 254
4.5.2 The Reaction of National Courts 257
4.5.3 The Effects of Trans-judicial Dialogue on the Court of Justice's Reasoning 259
4.5.4 Case Law Challenging the Trans-judicial Dialogue Narrative 263
5 Concluding Remarks 265

CHAPTER 6
What's Behind the Decision-Making of the Court of Justice? A Case Study on Directive 2001/23/EC 267
1 Introduction 267
2 Objects, Structure and Methodology of the Case Study 270
2.1 Objects 270
2.2 Structure 271
2.3 Methodology 271
3 A Purposive Approach Behind Labour Law Adjudication 273
3.1 Neofunctionalism 273
3.2 Integrationalism 279
4 Influences from the National Context 287
4.1 Intergovernmentalism 288
4.2 Influence of National Legal Traditions 293
4.3 Trans-judicial Dialogue 297
4.3.1 Preemptive Opinions 298
4.3.2 Margin of Appreciation 302
4.3.3 The Court's Approach to National Jurisprudence 304
5 Concluding Remarks on the Judicial Lawmaking Logics 307
5.1 The Prevailing Judicial Lawmaking Logics 307
5.2 Concluding Remarks 314

Conclusion 317
1 Introduction 317
2 The Main Findings 318
3 Reshaping the Perception of the Court of Justice in Relation to Labour Law 323

Annex: Case Study Figures for Chapter 6 325

Bibliography 355

Table of Cases 385

Table of AG Opinions 395

Table of Policy Documents 401

Index 407

Preface

This book seeks to answer the following research question: *What role does the Court of Justice play in relation to the normative model underlying EU labour law?*

The relevance of this question should be seen in the light of two premises that relate to different aspects of European Union (EU) labour law studies. The first is that labour law was originally conceived with social, emancipatory features. This emancipatory rationale and the ability to pursue the ideal of social justice is, however, seriously jeopardised when labour law is seen foremost as a labour market instrument. The vulnerable nature of the social and emancipatory dimension of labour law constitutes the theoretical embedding of the research.

The second premise coincides with the dogmatic assumption whereby the Court of Justice of the European Union (hereinafter also 'CJEU' or 'the Court') approaches labour law in a purposive manner and contributes to the marginalisation of its emancipatory component. This assumption is grounded on a widespread perception in the labour law discipline and is challenged throughout the research outlined in the book. When relying solely on the labour law doctrinal perspective, the rule-making activity of the Court indeed risks being reduced to its positioning in the 'social versus economic' tension. By adopting a multidisciplinary approach and including judicial lawmaking studies into its analytical lenses, the research conducted in the book instead shows that the Court's decision-making is populated by a range of dynamics that transcend the balancing of values underpinning the rules that the Court is asked to interpret.

The analysis is conducted by means of two series of case studies on the directive on acquired rights in case of transfer of undertakings. The first set of case studies, conducted through the dogmatic lenses of labour law, shows that the normative model pursued by the Court coincides with an understanding of labour law that seeks to reconcile economic and social progress. A certain degree of convergence between the Court's approach and EU institutional policymaking was identified. In both cases, there has been a sharpening of the economic dimension in the 1990s and in the Euro crisis years and, only recently, signs of rehabilitation of the emancipatory function. However, it is important to note that in the Court's case law, there has not been such a radical compression of the emancipatory component as there has been in EU policy-making, with the exception of a few judgments. In light of these findings, the role that was assumed by the Court appears to not oppose the normative model emerging from institutional policymaking.

Then, the book turns to the examination of the Court's lawmaking logics that characterise its reasoning. Here, the second set of case studies shows that it is not possible to identify a clearly dominant decision-making dynamic in the Court's approach, but that integrationalism, trans-judicial dialogue and intergovernmentalism are the most plausible theories. In particular, the case studies suggest that the Court's decision-making is characterised by a logic of synthesis with respect to the normative claims made by multiple actors, institutional or otherwise, involved in the proceedings.

Ultimately, the book demonstrates the importance of broadening the doctrinal and analytical lenses through which the Court's approach to labour law is assessed. A deeper understanding of judicial lawmaking logics is shown to be highly valuable for EU labour law studies and enriches the perception of the Court's role in relation to labour norms.

Acknowledgements

I would like to deeply thank my PhD supervisors, Professors Mijke Houwerzijl and Frank Hendrickx, for their guidance, patience, help, and kindness throughout all these years.

I would also like to thank the following people, without whom writing this thesis would have been much harder:

Joost, for your understanding and full support. My family, who perhaps won't even believe that my PhD thesis is actually over. My colleagues and friends, near and far, Samiha, Ilda, Charalampos, Antonio, Valerio, Beth, Zane, Aude, Sara, Mariya, Sophie, Erica, Sergio, Martina, Elisa, Lorenzo and Elena, for always being there. Carla, for the patience and the technical support. Philippe Pochet, Nicola Countouris and Aline Hoffmann, for having granted me the flexibility to work on this dissertation. My Tilburg colleagues, for having been so welcoming.

Finally, I would like to show my appreciation to Arthur Dyevre, Zef Even, Luca Ratti, Paul Schoukens and Nuna Zekić for their willingness to step in as members of the PhD committee, and for their clear and expert comments which helped me in turning my PhD dissertation into a book.

Introduction

1 EXPLORING THE ROLE OF THE COURT OF JUSTICE IN DEFINING LABOUR LAW

Along with the evolving world of work, labour law has been going through a transformative phase for a long time. A series of circumstances, such as globalisation, the emergence of neoliberal ideology, digitalisation, and the creation of the European single market, has led to the gradual adaptation of labour norms.[1] In this context, a general perception has developed in the field of European labour law that the European Union (EU) has limited ability to effectively promote labour standards.[2] Within the overall stream of critical thought, the CJEU is often included among those institutional actors who bear responsibility for the declining condition of labour law in the Union.[3]

1. B. Hepple, 'Factor Influencing the Making and Transformation of Labour Law in Europe' in G. Davidov & B. Langille (eds), *The Idea of Labour Law*, Oxford University Press, Oxford, 2011, pp. 30-42; K.W. Stone, 'Flexibilisation, Globalization and Privatization: Three Challenges to Labour Rights in Out Time', Public Law and Legal Theory Research Paper Series, UCLA School of Law, 2005; A. Figueroa, 'Labour Market Theories and Labour Standards' in Werner Sengenberger & Duncan Campbell (eds), *International Labour Standards and Economic Interdependence*, International Institute for Labour Studies, Geneva, 1994; A. Figueroa, 'Labour Market Theories and Labour Standards' in *International Labour Standards and Economic Interdependence*, International Institute for Labour Studies, Geneva, 1994, pp. 57-65; R. Blanpain, 'The End of Labour Law', Bulletin of Comparative Labour Law, 65, pp. 3-13, 2008; L. Wedderburn, 'Labour Standards, Global Markets and Labour Law in Europe' in *International Labour Standards and Economic Interdependence*, International Institute for Labour Studies, Geneva, 1994, pp. 247-253. Some scholars have suggested revisiting the normative model of labour law to ensure its relevance even in changing times: R. Dukes, 'Hugo Sinzheimer and the Constitutional Function of Labour Law' in G. Davidov & B. Langille (eds), *The Idea of Labour Law*, Oxford University Press, Oxford, 2011, pp. 57-68; M. Weiss, 'Re-inventing Labour Law?' in G. Davidov & B. Langille (eds), *The Idea of Labour Law*, Oxford University Press, Oxford, 2011, pp. 43-56.
2. There are countless academic contributions that have looked critically at the approach of EU policymaking towards labour rights. Among the authors who have addressed this topic, without any claim to completeness, Kilpatrick, Garben, Dawson, Hendrickx, Weiss, Barbard, Syrpis, Vanhercke, Bruun, Veneziani, Bercusson, Houwerzijl, Giubboni, Dorssemont, Countouris.
3. S. Giubboni, 'The Rise and Fall of EU Labour Law', European Law Journal, 24(1), pp. 7-20, 2018; G. Orlandini, 'Libertà di stabilimento versus diritto al lavoro: ancora un bilanciamento "sbilanciato" tra libertà economiche e diritti dei lavoratori', Giornale Di Diritto Del Lavoro e di Relazioni

Reference can be made to the Court's case law arising from judgments such as the *Laval* and *Viking* judgments and,[4] in more recent times, also *Alemo-Herron*, *Aget Iraklis*, or *Achbita* and *Bougnaoui*.[5]

This book addresses these considerations, which constitute its theoretical and normative embedding, by proposing a reflection on the role of the CJEU with respect to EU labour law.

It should be stressed that the academic debate on the CJEU's contribution to the development of EU labour law is by no means new. It is at least since the *Defrenne II* case (1976)[6] that the policymaking of the Court has been discussed from a labour law's disciplinary perspective.[7] This book engages with this stream of studies but does so through an innovative angle. It does not only take into account the impact of the Court's rulings on the scope and substance of labour law but also considers the wider judicial lawmaking context. The 'classical' labour law perspective on the Court's impact on EU policymaking is certainly valuable to frame the doctrinal discussion. However, it is here contended that to obtain a fuller understanding of the role of the Court with respect to labour law, focusing only on the normative orientation of its rulings might not be sufficient. The specific hypothesis explored in this research is that when the Court's case law is approached from a sole and specialised point of view, as labour lawyers tend to do, relevant elements risk escaping the analysis. There is in fact a danger of overlooking that the Court's interpretative activity is embedded in a multitude of dialectical processes, whereby the Court interacts with national legislatures, EU political institutions,[8] and national courts.[9] As Weatherill rightly argued, 'any

---

Industriali, 153(1), pp. 203-217, 2017; N. Countouris & A. Koukiadaki, 'The Glass Half Full: Collective Redundancies, Public Interest, and the (unfulfilled) Potential of Europe's "Highly Competitive Social Market Economy"', Giornale di Diritto del Lavoro e di Relazioni Industriali, 153(1), pp. 193-201, 2017; S. Weatherill, 'Use and Abuse of the EU's Charter of Fundamental Rights: on the Improper Veneration of "Freedom of Contract"', European Review of Contract Law, 10(1), pp. 167-182, 2014.

4. Judgment of 18 December 2007, *Laval un Partneri Ltd v. Svenska Byggnadsarbetareförbundet, Svenska Byggnadsarbetareförbundets avdelning 1, Byggettan and Svenska Elektrikerförbundet*, C-341/05, ECLI:EU:C:2007:809; judgment of 11 December 2007, *International Transport Workers' Federation and Finnish Seamen's Union v. Viking Line ABP and OÜ Viking Line Eesti*, C-438/05, ECLI:EU:C:2007:772.
5. Judgment of 18 July 2013, *Mark Alemo-Herron and Others v. Parkwood Leisure Ltd*, C-426/11, ECLI:EU:C:2013:521; judgment of 21 December 2016, *Anonymi Geniki Etairia Tsimenton Iraklis (AGET Iraklis) v. Ypourgos Ergasias, Koinonikis Asfalisis kai Koinonikis Allilengyis*, C-201/15, ECLI:EU:C:2016:972; judgment of 14 March 2017, *Samira Achbita and Centrum voor gelijkheid van kansen en voor racismebestrijding v. G4S Secure Solutions NV*, C-157/15, ECLI:EU:C:2017:203; judgment of 14 March 2017, *Asma Bougnaoui and Association de défense des droits de l'homme (ADDH) v. Micropole SA*, C-188/15, ECLI:EU:C:2017:204.
6. Judgment of 8 April 1976, *Gabrielle Defrenne v. Société anonyme belge de navigation aérienne Sabena*, C-43/75, ECLI:EU:C:1976:56.
7. C. Barnard, 'EU Employment law and the European Social Model: The Past, the Present and the Future', Current Legal Problems, 67, pp. 199-237, 2014.
8. P. Eeckhout, 'The European Court of Justice and the Legislature', Yearbook of European Law, 18(1), pp. 1-28, 1998.
9. L.B. Tremblay, 'The Legitimacy of Judicial Review: The Limits of Dialogue Between Courts and Legislatures', International Journal of Constitutional Law, 3(4), pp. 617-648, 2005; R. Van Gestel & J. De Poorter, *In the Court We Trust: Cooperation, Coordination and Collaboration Between the ECJ and Supreme Administrative Courts*, Cambridge University Press, Cambridge, 2019.

attempt to present one-dimensional accounts of [the Court's] activity is doomed to failure'.[10] Similarly, O'Leary noted that critiques of the Court's work often neglect the procedural or structural factors which determine the context in which the Court operates.[11]

By taking this direction, this book seeks to overcome what can be considered a limitation of sectoral studies on the Court's case law. In fact, this research aims to fill the void resulting from the lack of adequate integration of two different but complementary disciplinary perspectives. On the one hand, the EU labour law discipline tends to assess the Court on the basis of the normative orientation of its rulings. On the other hand, there are judicial lawmaking studies, which, instead of looking at the normative outcomes of the rulings, focus on interpreting the Court's behaviour and that of the other actors involved in the judicial process. These include the possible influence exerted by the Commission, by the Member State governments, and by national courts. This stream of judicial lawmaking studies could potentially be able to validate, nuance, or refute the association between the policy implications of the judgments and (possible) normative preferences of the Court. However, the two disciplines very rarely talk to each other. For instance, empirical studies measuring the impact of the EU judiciaries' ideological bias on case law in the labour law field have not yet been carried out.[12] And labour law studies have so far considered only limited aspects pertaining to the context in which the Court elaborates its reasonings.

This book takes a first step to connect both disciplines by embedding the inquiry on the role of the CJEU in relation to EU labour law in the context of judicial lawmaking dynamics. The exploration of the Court's approach to judicial adjudication in the labour law field is in fact conducted on two successive layers of analysis: at first, the dissertation addresses the CJEU as a labour court and, subsequently, as a judicial lawmaking authority.

2 THE FIRST ANALYTICAL LAYER: THE COURT FROM A LABOUR LAW'S DOCTRINAL PERSPECTIVE

A first layer of analysis consists in approaching the case law of the Court through the epistemological lenses typical of the labour law's disciplinary perspective. The Court's rulings will thus be examined through the same evaluation standards that could be used for political policymakers. It involves looking at the way the Court approaches labour law and interacts with its normative underpinnings and rationales. Does the Court tend to value the economic or social component of labour law? And how does its interpretative approach stand in relation to the transformation processes that regulators are imposing on labour law? Is the Court's approach consistent with that promoted

10. S. Weatherill, 'The Common Market: Mission Accomplished?' in V. Heiskanen & K. Kulovesi (eds), *Function and future of European Law*, Helsinki University Press, Helsinki, 1999, pp. 33-57.
11. S. O'Leary, *Employment Law at the European Court of Justice: Judicial Structures, Policies, and Processes*, Hart Publishing, Oxford, 2002, p. 26.
12. W. Wijtvliet & A. Dyevre, 'Judicial Ideology in Economic Cases: Evidence from the General Court of the European Union', European Union Politics, 22(1), 2021, pp. 25-45.

by political institutions, or is it perhaps more protective of workers or, conversely, more business-friendly?

This kind of analysis allows proposing a preliminary definition of the Court's role vis-à-vis labour norms. This definition is essentially embedded in the evaluative paradigms that belong to the discipline of labour law and is therefore calibrated on how the Court's interpretation relates to the social and economic dimensions of the norms. It should be noted that this definition is formulated in relational terms with the policies pursued by the other (rulemaking) institutions of the Union. It essentially consists of an assessment on whether the Court reinforces or rather limits the normative model pursued by the EU lawmakers. Using EU policymaking as a term of reference makes it easier to situate the Court's normative approach in relation to the analysed labour norms. EU lawmakers in fact are the main regulatory source of labour law and it is therefore in relation to the policy preferences that they express that the Court's role can be better appraised.

Up to this point, the book follows an already covered ground. It suffices to refer to the rich academic literature that has pervaded European labour law following pivotal rulings such as *Viking* and *Laval*. Several commentators have identified in those rulings the same deregulatory approach exhibited by EU policymakers in the context of the EU employment policy and flexicurity agenda, and have recognised the Court as a complicit policy-driven actor, promoting the same neoliberal-inspired vision.[13]

Although this critical engagement from a labour law perspective has contributed a great deal to placing the Court's rulings within the 'social versus economic' tension, the risk is, as already mentioned, to consider only part of the picture.[14] It is indeed

13. J. Hunt, 'The Court of Justice as a Policy Actor: The Case of the Acquired Rights Directive', Legal Studies, 18(3), pp. 336-359, 1998, where Hunt identifies the Court as significant driver of European integration, with a specific normative approach towards labour law; A.C.L. Davies, A. Bogg & C. Costello, 'The Role of the Court of Justice in Labour Law' in A. Bogg, C. Costello & A.C.L. Davies (eds), *Research Handbook on EU Labour Law*, Edward Elgar Publishing, Cheltenham, 2016, pp. 114-149: the authors address Viking and Laval as yardstick for the EU's approach to the 'social v economic' debate, p. 129; M. Freedland & J. Prassl, 'Viking, Laval and Beyond: An Introduction' in M. Freedland & J. Prassl (eds), *Viking, Laval and Beyond*, Hart Publishing, London, 2014, pp. 1-20: Prassl and Freedland have collected national reports illustrating the implications at Member States' level of the Laval and Viking judgment and, in doing so, have also expertly represented the great impact that the underlying issue of balancing economic freedom and fundamental labour rights has had in the European academic debate. These cases prompted the authors to outline different models which represent the relation or intersection between fundamental labour freedoms and economic rights: exclusionary (absence of interference of internal market logics in the sphere of collective and individual labour relations), reconciliation (economic freedoms and labour rights coexist in tandem), supersession (internal market law is superimposed upon labour relations). Viking and Laval tended to reflect the supersession, since 'the appearance of balanced neutrality in the Viking and Laval case law is a deceptive one in various sense. […] The normative positions which have been established by or under the protection of European labour law are systemically exposed to scrutiny by reference to EU internal market law, but this is almost entirely one-way traffic – if is not as if the normative positions of EU internal market law are being scrutinised by reference to those of European labour law', p. 18.
14. C. Barnard, 'The Calm after the Storm: Time to Reflect on EU (Labour) Law Scholarship Following the Decisions in Viking and Laval' in A. Bogg, C. Costello & A.C.L. Davies (eds), *Research Handbook on EU Labour Law*, Edward Elgar Publishing, Cheltenham, 2016, pp. 337-362: while reviewing the academic literature on Viking and Laval, Barnard noted that 'there

highly unlikely that in performing its interpretative activity, the Court is solely guided by a purposive approach in relation to a specific normative model of labour rights. It suffices to point out that *Viking* and *Laval* have triggered a rich academic debate also in disciplines other than labour law. Conway, for example, interpreted those rulings as an expression of the competence creep tendency of the Court, which led to a widening of the scope of EU law to the detriment of national legal systems.[15] Weatherill, moreover, argued that *Viking* and *Laval* 'are not only out of line with the expectation of labour lawyers; they are out of line with the expectations of internal market lawyers too'.[16] It is also interesting to note that Maduro, who was the Advocate General in the *Viking* case, is also an academic who, even prior to his appointment to the CJEU, elaborated a theoretical framework for the harmonious coexistence of the European and national constitutional orders.[17] It is thus presumable that the Court's reasoning in the *Viking* ruling might have also been influenced by considerations that are not necessarily connected to the 'labour rights versus economic freedom' tension.[18]

are a number of pieces written by left-leaning academics [...] close to the hegemonic view with little or no engagement with alternative perspectives', p. 347.

15. G. Conway, 'Conflicts of Competence Norm in EU Law and the Legal Reasoning of the ECJ', German Law Journal, 11(9), 2010, pp. 966-1005. G. Conway, *The Limits of Legal Reasoning and the European Court of Justice*, Cambridge University Press, Cambridge, 2012, p. 49.
16. S. Weatherill, 'Viking and Laval: The Internal Market Perspective' in M. Freedland & J. Prassl (eds), *Viking, Laval and Beyond*, Hart Publishing, London, 2014, pp. 23-40.
17. M. Poiares Maduro, 'Contrapunctual Law: Europe's Constitutional Pluralism in Action' in N. Walker (ed.), *Sovereignty in Transition*, Hart Publishing, Portland, 2003, pp. 501-537.
18. One could also bring as examples other judgments which, although inherent from a substantive point of view to labour standards, have also been analysed by commentators from other disciplines. Mattli and Slaughter have identified an integrationist logic in the *Defrenne II* judgment, W. Mattli & A. M. Slaughter, 'The Role of National Courts in the Process of European Integration' in A.M. Slaughter, A. Stone Sweet & J. Weiler (eds), *The European Court and National Court – Doctrine and Jurisprudence: Legal Change in Its Social Context*, Hart Publishing, Oxford, 1998, pp. 253-276. Another example is from Lenaerts, who refers to the *Maruko* case (judgment of 1 April 2008, *Tadao Maruko v. Versorgungsanstalt der deutschen Bühnen*, C-267/06, ECLI:EU:C:2008:179), dealing with non-discrimination on sexual orientation and access to social protection, to illustrate the impact of the comparative approach in the Court's decision-making, in K. Lenaerts, 'Discovering the Law of the EU: the European Court of Justice and the Comparative Law Method' in E. Perisin & S. Rodin (eds), *The Transformation or Reconstitution of Europe: The Critical Legal Studies Perspective on the Role of the Courts in the European Union*, Hart Publishing, Oxford, 2018, pp. 61-87. Or, again in the context of the principle of non-discrimination in the employment context, one may recall the *Mangold* (judgment of 22 November 2005, *Werner Mangold v. Rüdiger Helm*, C-144/04, ECLI: EU:C:2005:709) or *Kücükdeveci* (judgment of 19 January 2010, *Seda Kücükdeveci gegen Swedex GmbH & Co. KG.*, C-555/07, ECLI:EU:C:2010:21) cases in which the Court's reasoning has been interpreted as 'activist' from the point of view of accelerating the integration of the Union's legal system by recognising the direct effect of directives whose implementation period had not yet been completed, for instance, in O. Pollicino, *Allargamento dell'Europa a est e rapporto tra Corti costituzionali e Corti europee*, Giuffrè, Milano, 2010. Or, once again on the principle of non-discrimination on grounds of age, the *Ajos* case (judgment of 19 April 2016, *Dansk Industri (DI), acting on behalf of Ajos A/S v. Estate of Karsten Eigil Rasmussen*, C-441/14, ECLI: EU:C:2016:278), which has been analysed by observers mainly from the point of view of the dynamics of trans-judicial cooperation: H. Krunke & S. Kinge, 'The Danish Ajos Case and the Danish Approach to International Law', European Public Law, 24(2), pp. 183-193, 2018.

3 THE SECOND ANALYTICAL LAYER: THE COURT FROM A JUDICIAL LAWMAKING PERSPECTIVE

The second analytical layer of this book consists in approaching the CJEU not merely as an EU labour law interpreter but, first and foremost, as a judicial authority that operates in a multilevel and complex framework. Accordingly, the Court is no longer observed in relation to the normative outcomes of its rulings. Instead, a broader perspective is taken, so to consider the different judicial lawmaking dynamics that might underpin the Court's case law.

It should come as no surprise that the Court may be animated by other logics than those inherent to the interpretation of the actual norms at stake. This is, indeed, also the case with the other lawmaking institution of the EU. The importance of the context and institutional structure in which institutional actors define their regulatory choices has been brilliantly illustrated by Sharpf with reference to the policies that led to the expansion of the single market.[19] Similarly, Vanhercke and Verdun have illustrated that the social dimension of EU policies largely depends on the processes in which those policies are defined and on the actors involved.[20] If EU regulatory developments are also determined by logics which are not related to the actual object of the policymaking activity, it is reasonable to assume that this would occur even more frequently in the context of the Court's reasoning. Unlike other rule-making institutions, the Court is in fact devoid of a political mandate and its activity is not oriented towards the achievement of the socioeconomic objectives set by the Treaties.[21]

To address this second analytical layer, the book engages with two different types of judicial lawmaking theories. The first type describes the CJEU as an EU policymaker, capable of pursuing a specific vision with respect to the evolution of the EU legal system. From this point of view, the Court tends to approach EU labour law in a purposive manner, although not necessarily with the intention of enhancing the inherent social or economic dimension of the law. The second type of theory instead contends that EU judgments are the result of an effort on the part of the Court to meet the different demands emerging from the national context. This implies that a bias towards the social or economic component of labour law should not be read as the expression of a normative preference of the Court. It is instead (at least partly) the result of other dynamics, such as the pressure from national governments, the inclination to comply with national legal practices, and trans-judicial interactions.

19. F. Scharpf, 'The Asymmetry of European Integration, or Why the EU Cannot Be a "Social Market Economy"', Socio-Economic Review, 8(2), pp. 211-250, 2009.
20. B. Vanhercke & B. Verdun, 'From the European Semester to the Recovery and Resilience Facility – Some Social Actors Are (Not) Resurfacing', Working Paper, 13, ETUI, Brussels, 2021.
21. *Inter alia*, W. Mattli & A.-M. Slaughter, 'Revisiting the European Court of Justice', International Organization, 52(1), pp. 177-209, 1998; A. Stone Sweet & T. Brunell, 'Constructing a Supranational Constitution' in *The Judicial Construction of Europe*, Oxford University Press, New York, 2004.

The exploration of these judicial lawmaking logics consents to formulate a refined definition of the Court's role in relation to labour law. This wider epistemological framework in fact allows to nuance or enrich what emerged from the investigation embedded in the first analytical layer, focused on the Court's normative preferences. By examining the various possible judicial lawmaking mechanisms, it may in fact be possible to unpack the origins of the judicial reasoning and identify relevant dynamics besides an eventual normative bias of the Court.

It is worth noting that other legal researchers have already conducted analyses of the Court's case law on labour norms while also considering the judicial lawmaking context. It is, thus, not an entirely unexplored ground. However, these studies have either focused on a particular aspect of judicial lawmaking (for instance, the interaction between courts, or the relationship between institutions) or have conducted the analysis on a non-systematic selection of cases. These works, although seminal, therefore do not fill the disciplinary void referred to in the first introductory pages of this book.

Among the most important and comprehensive examples is the collective volume 'Labour law in the Courts' (2001) edited by Sciarra, in which the authors examined the evolution of the EU case law in relation to a series of EU labour law directives from the perspective of the trans-judicial dialogue between the CJEU and the national judiciary.[22] Similarly, O'Leary, in the book *Employment law at the European Court of Justice: Judicial Structures, Policies and Process* showed that the context and decision-making processes in which the Court adjudicates have a considerable impact on its reasoning. Differently from Sciarra's volume, O'Leary paid attention not only to the relationship between courts but also to the possible influence of the institutional policymaking developed by the European Commission and the Council.[23] The importance of placing and interpreting the CJEU's case law also emerges from the contributions of other prominent labour lawyers, such as Prassl, Davies, Bogg and Costello. In their collective work *Research Handbook on EU Labour Law*, the authors illustrated how the Court is by no means immune to national sensitivities while approaching labour law.[24] Eventually, they identified a predominant integrationalist inclination in the Court's reasoning, coinciding with the adoption of an expansive reading of the

22. S. Sciarra (ed.), *Labour Law in the Courts: National Judges and the European Court of Justice*, Hart Publishing, Oxford, 2001.
23. S. O'Leary, *Employment Law at the European Court of Justice: Judicial Structures, Policies, and Processes*, Hart Publishing, Oxford, 2002. O'Leary looked at the context in which the CJEU exercises its interpretative activity and reflected on how this context may affect the judicial reasoning and outcome; the author stated that criticising the Court without a full understanding of its limits and constraints leads to only a partial picture, p. 12.
24. J. Prassl, 'The interaction of EU Law and National Law: Between Myth and Reality' in A. Bogg, C. Costello & A.C.L. Davies (eds), *Research Handbook on EU Labour Law*, Edward Elgar Publishing, Cheltenham, 2016, pp. 42-63; Prassl argued that, 'Court of Justice did, in fact, take account of domestic sensitivities in its case law, introducing a series of doctrines to mollify the impact of EU law and its interaction with national law', p. 50.

Union's competences, especially when inherent to the fundamental economic freedoms.[25] Finally, the work of Hunt should be mentioned, with specific reference to the journal article 'The Court of Justice as a Policy Actor: The Case of the Acquired Rights Directive'. There, Hunt carried out a case study on the directive on acquired rights in case of transfers of undertakings – the same directive that will be analysed in this book – and showed that it cannot be excluded that the case law of the Court reflects the political pressures of the Council and the European Commission.[26]

These academic contributions, along with others not mentioned for reasons of space, have all been a source of inspiration for this book, both from the point of view of the objective and methodology. The intention of this research is to take an extra step and explore the interaction between judicial lawmaking dynamics and EU labour law in a more encompassing and, as far as possible, empirical way. This book in fact explores the major doctrines on judicial lawmaking, thus adopting a broader analytical lens than the mentioned studies. In addition, the salience of the different doctrines is measured through a series of case studies, conducted on the case law of the Court on a specific directive, namely the EU Directive on transfer of undertakings (Directive 77/187/EEC and then Directive 2001/23/EC), thereby limiting the risk of drawing conclusions on an anecdotal basis.

4 RESEARCH QUESTIONS, METHODOLOGY AND STRUCTURE

4.1 Research Aim and Questions

Having identified the underlying themes that constitute the starting point of this research, this section proceeds with positioning the research questions and methodological and structural indications.

The aim of the research is to broaden the understanding of the role of the CJEU in relation to the definition of labour law. It is sought to understand to what extent the Court can be considered a purposive policymaking actor, committed to advancing a specific narrative and promoting a specific hierarchy of values, or whether there are other dynamics that influence its decision-making.

The central research question of this research can be formulated as follows:

What role does the CJEU play in relation to the normative model underlying EU labour law?

As mentioned, the exploration of the Court's role is approached through two analytical layers. Through the first analytical layer, the Court is observed from the labour law's disciplinary perspective and the case law is appraised in terms of the underlying

25. A.C.L. Davies, A. Bogg & C. Costello, 'The Role of the Court of Justice in Labour Law' in A. Bogg, C. Costello & A.C.L. Davies (eds), *Research Handbook on EU Labour Law*, Edward Elgar Publishing, Cheltenham, 2016, pp. 114-149.
26. J. Hunt, 'The Court of Justice as a Policy Actor: The Case of the Acquired Rights Directive', Legal Studies, 18(3), pp. 336-359, 1998; Hunt designed the case study 'to reveal the possible contours of the interrelation between the different institutional actors who together create and develop EU policies', p. 25.

balancing of the social and economic interests. In the second layer, the Court's activity is instead placed in a broader analytical context, where other factors, foreign to the typical labour law discourse, come into play. Here, the case law is analysed in light of the different possible judicial lawmaking dynamics. An investigation on the relevance of these logics is functional to eventually nuance the definition of the role of the Court which would instead emerge from assessments that are fully and solely embedded in the labour law discipline.

The central research question can be further divided into three sub-questions:

- *RQ1: What (prevailing) normative model(s) is(are) underlying the approaches of EU institutional policymakers with respect to labour law?*

This first research question aims at determining how EU rule-makers have, over the years, approached labour law and how, in doing so, have addressed its underlying economic and social rationales. The objective is to provide a contextual framework in order to, then, be able to assess the Court's case law. As mentioned, in the context of the first analytical layer, the definition of the role of the Court is largely dependent on its positioning with respect to the normative model pursued by the political and rule-making institutions of the Union.

- *RQ2: Is it possible to identify an underlying normative model in the case law of the CJEU with respect to labour law?*

This second research question is functional to outline a preliminary definition of the role that the Court plays in relation to labour law. The adopted perspective, which is inevitably reflected in this definition, is that of labour law studies. The exploration is intended to expose the Court's approach towards the functions and the normative rationales of labour norms. This definition of the Court's role considers whether the case law has contributed to enhance or rather weaken workers' rights established in the law. It is thus formulated in relational terms with the broader policymaking context of the Union emerging from the analysis carried out in relation to RQ1.

The research conducted to address RQ2 has a significant empirical component. The analysis of the Court's approach vis-à-vis the rationale of labour law is in fact carried through a series of case studies on the case law of Directive 2001/23/EC on acquired rights in case of transfer of undertakings.

- *RQ3: What are the logics that determine the Court's approach with respect to labour law, taking into account judicial lawmaking theories?*

In addressing this third question, the book broadens the exploration beyond a purely labour law perspective. The research thus enters the second analytical layer and engages with judicial lawmaking theories. This wider analytical framework is then tested on the same group of judgments on transfer of undertakings, so as to bring to light possible judicial lawmaking dynamics that had not emerged during the previous case studies.

4.2 Structure

The book engages with the central research question and the three sub-questions throughout six chapters.

Chapter 1 is dedicated to theoretical and normative embedding. This book has a twofold dogmatic foundation, which provides for the premises of the research. The first concerns the evolution of the functions pursued by labour law and the erosion of its social (or emancipatory) dimension. A theoretical discussion on the origins and purpose of labour law consents to contextualise and better appraise the development in institutional policymaking and the CJEU's reasonings. The second dogmatic foundation coincides with the assumption that the CJEU tends to approach labour norms as a purposive and policy-oriented actor. This assumption draws from a rather diffuse perception in the labour law discipline, as the academic debate surrounding certain judgments (for instance, *Alemo-Herron* and *Aget Iraklis*) shows. In this book, this assumption is first explored and then challenged.

In Chapter 2, the EU policymakers' approach towards labour law throughout the different stages of European integration, from the late 1950s until 2021, is discussed. The focus is on how the EU rule-makers have been engaging with the emancipatory and the economic underpinnings of labour law. This chapter addresses RQ1 (*What (prevailing) normative model(s) is(are) underlying the approaches of EU institutional policymakers with respect to labour law?*) as it explores the extent to which EU policymaking imposed a transformative pressure on the nature of labour law. The analysis of the Union's regulatory framework provides the regulatory background with which the Court's case law inevitably interacts and in relation to which can be evaluated.

In Chapter 3, the first series of case studies on the directive on transfer of undertakings is presented. This legal empirical analysis explores the Court's normative approach to labour law. In consideration of the findings of the case studies, RQ2 is answered (*Is it possible to identify an underlying normative model in the case law of the CJEU with respect to labour law?*). This analysis, combined with the research conducted in Chapter 2, consents to propose a first definition of the role of the Court in relation to labour law. As explained above, this definition reflects the constraints of a purely labour law perspective and is formulated in relational terms with respect to the policymaking of the institutional rule-makers.

Chapters 4 to 6 address RQ3 (*What are the logics that determine the Court's approach with respect to labour law, taking into account judicial lawmaking theories?*). Determining the logics underpinning the Court's approach to labour law is not an easy task and requires several analytical steps. In Chapters 4 and 5, the book moves away from the labour law narrative and delves into the doctrines on judicial lawmaking that have been developed over the past decades by EU law scholars and political scientists. The main innovative contribution of this book precisely derives from the epistemological tools offered by those doctrines, as they consent to a deeper insight into the Court's reasoning.

Chapter 4 describes the judicial decision-making of the Court through a first set of theories, which consider the Court as a quasi-political and autonomous actor in the normative evolution of the EU. The first is the neofunctional theory, according to which the Court has its own vision of the socioeconomic model to which the Union should adhere, as well as the central normative role that the Court itself should play to facilitate the pursuit of such model. Then, integrationalism is discussed. According to this theory, the Court tends to opt for reasonings that expand the scope of EU law and strengthen the autonomy of the EU legal system vis-à-vis the national legal systems.

Chapter 5 outlines alternative theoretical models whereby the Court is not presented as an autonomous policymaker. Instead, these theories share the view that the Court's judgments reflect the interests and normative solutions that emerge from the national context (either as they are put forward by national judges, or because they are inherent in the normative and constitutional practices of the Member States, or because they are supported by national governments). The first theory that is addressed is intergovernmentalism, which considers the Court as particularly attentive to the preferences expressed by national governments, especially those from the most politically influential states. Then, the focus moves to those theories that depict the Court as cautious to maintain a harmonious coexistence between the EU and the national legal orders. Finally, the chapter turns to the possible relevance of trans-judicial dynamics between the Court and national courts.

Chapter 6 presents the second series of case studies, focusing on the same group of judgments already analysed in Chapter 3. While in Chapter 3 this selection of judgments was approached with the aim of identifying the policy orientations of the Court, this time the rulings are examined with the intention of testing the doctrines explored in Chapters 4 and 5. Particular consideration is given to those judgments that have generated the perception in academics and observers that the Court is moved by a specific ideological preference. The goal of these case studies is to provide a picture of the judicial lawmaking dynamics that might have guided the Court's interpretation and might have contributed to informing its approach towards labour law.

This second empirical component of the research consents to collect elements and 'evidence' through which eventually nuance the definition of the role of the Court in relation to labour law as formulated in Chapter 3. For example, if the case studies would show that the Court is particularly sensitive to the preferences expressed in the proceedings by national governments, this is an indication that the policy implications of the case law might not (or at least not exclusively) be an expression of the Court's own normative inclinations. If, on the other hand, the case studies were to suggest that the Court is guided by a policy-driven agenda, then this might indicate that the Court approaches its interpretative function in view of steering and shaping EU (labour) law and policies. The Court may, for example, wish to accommodate the enhancement of the economic dimension over the social one, or it may have an even broader objective, such as strengthening the EU legal system and promoting a specific normative model for EU integration.

Finally, the book finishes with concluding observations. The central research question is answered by reviewing what has emerged from the research on the role of the Court in relation to labour law. Then, constructive reflections are offered on how a fuller understanding of the judicial lawmaking dynamics would be helpful to any (litigation) strategy aiming to use the case law of the CJEU as a vehicle for strengthening the emancipatory component of labour law.

4.3 Methodology

This book is a result of legal research which combines different methodologies.

First of all, the research is divided into two parts, each relying on two legal theoretical perspectives, namely those provided by labour law doctrine and by judicial lawmaking studies. Chapters 2 and 3 engage with typical labour law doctrine, as they address the normative implications of EU policymaking and of the CJEU's case law. What emerges from this analysis is thus informed by labour law 'lenses', meaning that the CJEU's reasoning is evaluated on the basis of its impact on the labour law provisions enshrined in the directive on transfer of undertakings. The scope of this analysis has two different levels of comprehensiveness. Chapter 2 provides a broad perspective on the policymaking framework and on the general normative position of the EU (and especially of the Commission) towards labour and social policies. The scope of the case study presented in Chapter 3 is instead more specific as it focuses on a single legal instrument, namely the directive on transfer of undertakings. It is worth anticipating that the narrow scope of the case law constitutes a limitation to the possibility of generalising the findings of the research. However, this limitation has been circumscribed by the selection of a directive that presents characteristics allowing a relatively high degree of abstraction, as is further elaborated below in section 4.4.

Chapters 4 to 6 engage with a field of study different from labour law. The focus is on judicial lawmaking theories and on how these might explain the logics underpinning the CJEU's decision-making. This means that in the second part of the book, the case law is considered from a broader dogmatic framework, eventually enabling a more articulated definition of the role of the Court with respect to the normative model pursued by labour law. Here too, the analysis varies in scope. Chapters 4 and 5 illustrate theories proposed over time by scholars in an attempt to explain the dynamics underlying the Court's judicial activity, without addressing any specific field of law. Then, once again, the case studies bring the book into a narrower dimension, where the focus is back on the case law on the directive on transfer of undertakings.

Furthermore, the book mixes different research methodologies also inasmuch as it combines analytical (Chapters 2, 4 and 5) and empirical approaches (Chapters 3 and 6). In Chapter 2, the appraisal of the predominant normative model of institutional policymaking in regard to labour law is conducted through the study of a wide range of policy documents and communications adopted primarily by the European Commission. The idea is to draw a picture of the broader socioeconomic direction that has been pursued by the political institutions of the Union since the late 1950s and in which context EU labour law has developed. Among the various institutional documents, specific consideration has been given to the various Social Action Plans, the main White and Green Papers of the Commission on the economic, social and labour policy agenda of the Community, and other Commission Communications and policy instruments, including the European Pillar of Social Rights (hereinafter 'Pillar' or 'EPSR').

Chapters 4 and 5 share a similar analytical approach even if, this time, the focus is not on institutional policy documents but on academic literature and doctrinal research. In these chapters, the work of EU law scholars and political scientists who have developed theories on the role of the Court in the context of EU integration is explored.[27]

The insights from Chapters 2, 4 and 5 are then used as analytical framework for the empirical part of the research, in Chapters 3 and 6. In Chapter 3, the case studies aim to identify how the Court's reasoning is positioned in the context of the legal framework developed by EU rule-makers. While the entire case law on transfer of undertakings has been considered (72 judgments, from 1983 to mid-2022), the analysis has specifically focused on those cases addressing the scope of the directive, its normative purpose, and the definition of the rights conferred to the workers. In doing so, the different legal arguments that the Court has developed over the years have been mapped and classified according to their affinity with the various labour law functions underlying the analysed rules. Finally, the Court's jurisprudential evolution is assessed in relation to the workers' rights set out in the directive. The Court's approach is also compared to the prevailing normative model emerging from EU policymaking, in order to formulate a first definition of the Court's role in relation to labour law.

The case law on the directive on transfer of undertakings is then, again, the subject of an empirical study in Chapter 6. This time, however, the case studies don't consider the policy implications of the Court's reasoning. The emphasis is, instead, on those elements which, in light of the doctrines analysed in Chapters 4 and 5, might indicate the presence of specific judicial lawmaking logics. Those elements have been traced through a combined analysis of the Court's judgments and the Advocate General's opinions, where present. Often, either the Court or the Advocate General make reference to the legal opinion of the Commission and to those of the national governments, as well as to the eventual positioning of the national referring court in relation to the interpretation of EU law.

4.4 The Limitations of the Research

Before concluding the introductory chapter, it is important to acknowledge the limitations of the research conducted in this book, especially its empirical components.

Starting with the case studies in Chapter 3, the first limitation concerns their limited scope. These case studies are designed to identify the Court's approach in relation to labour law but the picture that derives is inevitably narrow. Chapter 3 in fact only considers the case law on the directive on acquired rights in case of transfer of undertakings, and not a plurality of legislative instruments, which would provide a more holistic narrative. Moreover, the case studies focus on specific judicial reasonings relating only to certain aspects of the directive, namely the scope of application and the rights conferred on workers regarding the continuation of the employment relationship following a transfer. Reasoning concerning, for example, Article 5 of Directive

27. Stone Sweet, Mattli, Slaughter, Weiler, Garrett, Weinsteing, Maduro, Pollicino, Cartabia, Nyikos, De Witte, Van Gestel, Hertely and Tridimas, just to mention a few. Extensive references to their work are made throughout Chapters 4 and 5.

2001/23/EC, which exempts the application of protections to employees in the event that the transferor is subject to bankruptcy proceedings or any analogous insolvency proceedings, have not been analysed.

However, it is also important to note that, to mitigate this limitation, the choice of the directive was made on account of the relatively high degree of generalisation of the insights emerging from its analysis. This is further discussed in Chapter 3, section 3, but it is already worth anticipating the reasons that led to select the directive on transfer of undertakings. First, the directive is underpinned by both a social and an economic rationale[28] and the examination of the case law consents to get a sense, susceptible to a certain degree of abstraction, of the manner in which the Court positions itself with regard to the social and economic components of labour law.[29] In addition, the directive on transfer of undertaking was selected because of its rather vague and imprecise wording. While interpreting it, the Court thus enjoys a margin of creativity and room to give expression to possible policymaking preferences or other judicial lawmaking logics.[30] Another reason for basing the case studies on this directive is that it first entered into force in 1977 and has since been the subject of a rich jurisprudence on the part of the Court. This allows a broad temporal spectrum of analysis and identification of chronological variations in the Court's approach. Finally, the case law on this directive has been extensively commented on from a labour law's disciplinary perspective. The Court's inclination towards a specific normative preference – whether protective for the workers or in favour of the employers' interests – has in fact attracted a vivid academic debate.[31] By exploring the Court's role in relation to the transfer of undertakings directive, this book thus engages with a rather rich

28. On the Court's approach to the social and economic dimension of Directive 2001/23/EC, see two different opinions in J. Prassl, 'Freedom of Contract as a General Principle of EU Law? Transfers of Undertakings and the Protection of Employer Rights in EU Labour Law', Industrial Law Journal, 42(4), pp. 434-446, 2013 and E. Brameshuber, 'Balancing vs. Preservation of Rights under the Acquired Rights Directive', Industrial Law Journal, 45(3), pp. 443-454, 2016.
29. *See* Chapter 3, section 3.1.
30. A. Barak, 'The Nature of Judicial Discretion and Its Significance for the Administration of Justice' in O. Wiklund (ed.), *Judicial Discretion in European Perspective*, Norstedts Juridik, Stockholm, 2003, pp. 11-28; O. Wiklund, 'Taking the World View of the European Judge Seriously' in O. Wiklund (ed.), *Judicial Discretion in European Perspective*, Norstedts Juridik, Stockholm, 2003, pp. 29-47, where the author argues that 'the forces that trigger the on-going transformation of the EU polities are hard to pin down'; A. Stone Sweet & M. McCown, 'Discretion and Precedent in European Law' in O. Wiklund (ed.), *Judicial Discretion in European Perspective*, Norstedts Juridik, Stockholm, 2003, p. 84; where the authors identify the zone of discretion of the Court of Justice as relatively vast, being the sum of the powers delegated to or possessed by the Court minus the sum of the control mechanisms of the Member States. Compared with most courts in the world, the Court operates in a zone of discretion that is unusually large when it interprets the Treaty. In some domains, its discretionary powers are close to unlimited. In this sense, M. Shapiro, 'The European Court of Justice: Of Institutions and Democracy', Israel Law Review, 32(1), pp. 3-50, 1998: 'Courts acquire the virtues of neutrality and independence by announcing that their decisions are based on a legal rule that pre-existed the conflict. In reality, because a legal rule that would yield a clear choice of winner and loser in a particular conflict does not always pre-exist, courts will necessarily make legal rules from time to time and pretend they pre-existed the conflict which they are actually invented to resolve.'
31. A.C.L. Davies, A. Bogg & C. Costello, 'The Role of the Court of Justice in Labour Law', 2016, p. 121.

literature. The above-mentioned limitation on the circumscribed nature of the case studies in Chapter 3 thus remains, but it should not be overemphasised.

A second limitation of the case studies in Chapter 3 concerns the criteria on the basis of which the case law of the Court is assessed. The case studies use criteria that emerged from the Court's reasoning and that were selected in order to identify the judicial approach towards the labour norms. However, it is admittedly conceivable that other researchers might have preferred to choose other criteria. In that case, perhaps, the picture that emerges from the case studies would be somewhat different.

Passing now to the empirical analysis conducted in Chapter 6, three additional limitations can be identified. First, it should be considered that, here too, the case studies are based on criteria whose selection is characterised by a certain degree of subjectivity. The different indicators were chosen because deemed instrumental to identify the judicial lawmaking techniques of the Court. Despite the attempt to elaborate neutral and theory-based filters, it cannot be excluded that the research could also have been carried out on the basis of (slightly) different indicators.

A second limitation is then connected to the first and relates to the fact that the manner in which the theory is brought to the data reflects the background of the author, which is primarily rooted in legal and labour law studies. This has a couple of implications. The effort to interface with another discipline has certainly contributed to enriching the research. At the same time, it has also been a challenge that may in fact have led to an unintended bending of the methodologies through which empirical analyses are generally conducted in judicial behavioural and lawmaking studies. This may be reflected in the vocabulary used in relation to the judicial lawmaking sections,[32] as well as in the choice of criteria for the evaluation of the Court's reasoning and in the measurement of the results of the studies. The other implication is that when specific decision-making dynamics of the Court are covered by both legal and social science studies, the chosen approach of the book has been to engage primarily with the legal perspective and to rely on the theoretical framework pertaining to legal studies. A pertinent example concerns the trans-judicial interaction between the CJEU and national judges. There is very interesting social science research that focuses on the reasons behind national judges' choice to request a preliminary ruling and on the geographical distribution of preliminary references.[33] Or, there are also research

32. For instance, instead of 'criteria', social science studies on judicial behaviour would rather talk about 'codes'.
33. K. Alter, 'Explaining National Court Acceptance of European Court Jurisprudence: A Critical Evaluation of Theories of Legal Integration' in A.M. Slaughter, A. Stone Sweet & J. Weiler (eds), *The European Court and National Court – Doctrine and Jurisprudence: Legal Change in Its Social Context*, Hart Publishing, Oxford, 1998, pp. 227-252; S.A. Nyikos, 'The European Court of Justice and National Courts: Strategic Interaction Within the EU Judicial Process', University of Virginia, 2000; A. Dyevre, N. Lampach & M. Glavina, 'Chilling or Learning? The Effect of Negative Feedback on Interjudicial Cooperation in Nonhierarchical Referral Regimes', Journal of Law and Courts, 10(1), pp. 87-112, 2022; M. Glavina, 'Judicial Hierarchy in the Preliminary Ruling Procedure: Exploring the Relationship Between the First and the Second Instance Courts', European Papers, 5(2), 2020, pp. 799-823, 2022; A. Dyevre, M. Glavina & A. Atanasova, 'Who Refers Most? Institutional Incentives and Judicial Participation in the Preliminary Ruling System', Journal of European Public Policy, 27(6), pp. 912-930, 2019, among others.

workers that assess the propensity of national judges to formulate preliminary questions in such a way as to obtain a certain type of response from the Court.[34] References to these studies and to their contribution to exposing behavioural correlation can be found in the section on 'trans-judicial dialogue' in Chapter 5, but it should be stressed that they have been considered in a rather complementary manner to other aspects that are more often covered by the legal literature. These are, for instance, the margin of discretion that the CJEU leaves to the referring judge and the way the Court engages with national jurisprudence.

The other limitation concerns the exhaustivity of this second set of case studies. The empirical exploration of the different judicial lawmaking techniques in the case law in fact faces the limited accessibility of the judicial documents and the opacity of the CJEU's adjudication procedure. The Court's decisions are indeed the result of a dialectic process among several judges, articulated throughout a composite procedure.[35] Except for the Court's judgment and the Advocate General's opinion, none of the documents that pertain to the deliberation (such as the pleas of the parties, the

34. S.A. Nyikos, 'Strategic Interaction among Courts Within the Preliminary Reference Process – Stage 1: National Court Preemptive Opinions', European Journal of Political Research, 45, pp. 527-550, 2006.
35. The deliberations are indeed governed by the principle of collegiality, meaning that judgments are reached by consensus and that dissenting opinions are not revealed in the final judgment. Both Article 35 of the Statute and Article 32(1) Rules of Procedures establish that 'The deliberations of the Court shall be and shall remain secret.' As Rodin described (in T. Ćapeta, 'Ideology and Legal Reasoning at the European Court of Justice' in E. Perisin & S. Rodin (eds), *The Transformation or Reconstitution of Europe: The Critical Legal Studies Perspective on the Role of the Courts in the European Union*, Hart Publishing, Oxford, 2018, pp. 89-120), the Court adopts its judgments following a 'pyramidal' approach, on account of the fact that the final decision is adopted after a series of steps established in order to progressively narrow down and fine-tune the reasoning. When a new case arrives, the President of the Court allocates it to a reporting judge (*judge rapporteur*), who is in charge of preparing a preliminary report and of proposing the appropriate decision-making chamber. The chamber's composition can vary and, depending on the complexity of the case, it can be a three- or five-judges chamber, the Grand Chamber (15 judges), or the full Court (Article 60(1) RoP). Article 16(4) of the Statute disposes that the Court shall sit in a Grand Chamber also when a Member State or an institution of the Union that is party to the proceedings so requests. The Court shall sit as a full Court where cases are brought before it pursuant to Article 228(2) (dismissals of the Ombudsman), Article 245(2) (breach of obligations by Members of the Commission), 247 (serious misconduct of Members of the Commission) or Article 286(6) (relinquishment of pension's rights by Court of Justice's judges) of the Treaty on the Functioning of the European Union (TFEU) (Article 16(4) of the Statute). Furthermore, the Court shall sit as a full Court also where it considers that a case before it is of exceptional importance, after hearing the Advocate General. Once the decision-making chamber is established, the judge rapporteur presents the preliminary report and the suggestion regarding the chamber during the weekly general meeting (*réunion générale*), where all judges and advocates general can participate to a first round of discussion. At this *réunion générale* a decision is also taken on whether an advocate general will provide an opinion on the case (Article 59 RoP). The oral part of the proceeding (the hearing) usually follows, unless the information resulting from the written part of the procedure are sufficient to give a ruling (Article 76 RoP). The Advocate General delivers his Opinion shortly after the hearing (Article 82(1) RoP). The judge rapporteur then submits a draft decision, to which the other judges of the chamber can react with observation on the main reasoning or on specific parts of the argumentation (Article 32(3) RoP). In that case, a discussion (*tour de table*) will follow, where the judge rapporteur can decide to reformulate the decision to take into consideration the inputs received. After that, the draft judgment is presented and deliberated behind closed doors. (Article 32(4) RoP). Sometimes

submission of the referring judge, the report of the hearings, and the minutes of the meetings) is accessible to the public.[36] This entails a lack of information regarding the votes cast by the individual judges, as well as regarding dissenting opinions and the actual legal argumentation submitted by the various actors involved in the procedure. These include amicus briefs, legal opinions of the European Commission and the full text of the national court's request for a preliminary ruling. It is therefore quite hard to retrace the precise origins of the legal arguments that compose the Court's rulings.

In the absence of access to the acts of the judicial proceedings, an attempt has been made to reconstruct the decision-making process on the basis of what emerges from the judgments of the Court and the opinions of the Advocate General, when present. Often these contain a reference to the legal position of the different intervening parties. However, this entails that the resulting empirical analysis does not draw a full and detailed picture of all the elements that concur to shape the Court's final decision. In view of the limited resources available, the book has thus only considered those judicial lawmaking theories that can, to some extent, be validated on the basis of the information that can be extracted from an analysis of the text of the judgments and of the Advocate General's opinions. This approach excludes other judicial lawmaking theories that are currently rather dominant in the social science field. For instance, studies that elaborate on the role of ideology in the behaviour of the individual judges that compose the deciding chamber of the Court[37] are beyond the scope of this book (although this aspect is briefly touched upon in Chapter 6, section 5.1).[38]

---

the *judge rapporteur* can be asked to re-draft the judgment, and this will lead to a second round of deliberation. Finally, a consensus is reached, and the ruling is made public and published in the Official Journal.

36. Article 35 Statute and Article 32(1) Rules of Procedures.
37. A. Bonica & M. Sen, 'Estimating Judicial Ideology', The Journal of Economic Perspectives, 35(1), pp. 97-118, 2021.
38. Although disclosing the impact of judicial ideologies of the members of the Court could have been potentially significant to the research question, the lack of information on the voting patterns or on their political preferences led to the exclusion of this aspect from the research. (On the importance to consider voting patterns and the judges' behaviour in non-judicial activities: J.B. Fischman & D.S. Law, 'What Is Judicial Ideology, and How Should We Measure It?', Washington University Journal of Law & Policy, 29, pp. 133-214, 2009 and A. Bonica & M. Sen, 'Estimating Judicial Ideology', 2021). Admittedly, Wijtvliet and Dyevre showed that it is not impossible to identify judges' ideologies even in the absence of information on voting patterns and other common proxies (W. Wijtvliet & A. Dyevre, 'Judicial Ideology in Economic Cases: Evidence from the General Court of the European Union', 2021). However, their analysis made use of information on professional attributes of the judges, which is an aspect that is not covered by this book.

CHAPTER 1
Theoretical and Normative Framework

1 INTRODUCTION

This chapter sets the dogmatic foundations of the research. As mentioned in the introduction, the normative embedding of the book relies on two premises.

The first premise coincides with the question of the transformation of labour law, which over the decades has shown an increased sensitivity to economic objectives. In order to contextualise the research on the role of the Court with respect to the normative model underlying labour law, it is first important to define the original nature of labour law and to clarify the implications of a change in its main regulatory functions. These aspects are addressed in section 2 of the chapter.

The second dogmatic premise coincides with the assumption that the Court expresses a normative bias when ruling on labour norms, in favour of their economic rationale. This would imply that the CJEU is, in effect, complicit in the transformation and distortion of labour law. This assumption draws from a perception that has emerged in the labour law discipline and is explored throughout the book. Section 3 engages with this perception, its reasons and implications, relying on the example of two judgments (*Alemo-Herron* and *Aget Iraklis*) that have instigated a vivid academic debate.

These premises provide the dogmatic embedding in which the central research question took shape. By asking '*What role does the CJEU play in relation to the normative model underlying EU labour law?*', the book engages with both. First, it sheds light on the transformative pressure that the Court's case law exercises on the normative functions of labour law. Then, it challenges the accuracy of dogmatic assumption whereby the case law reflects a normative bias of the Court.

2 LABOUR LAW'S ORIGINS AND ITS TRANSFORMATION

The first premise on which this book is based is that labour law was initially conceived as a branch of law with a strong social component, expressed in its emancipatory rationale vis-à-vis workers. This section defines the emancipatory dimension of labour law and discusses how this has been, through time, sidelined by EU policymakers. The emancipatory features are in fact linked to fundamental principles on which labour norms are grounded. If those principles do not find expression in labour policies, it is a significant indication that the nature of labour law has changed.

2.1 Three Fundamental Principles of Labour Law

Looking back at its origins, labour law can be conceived as the expression of three fundamental principles, two of which have a pronounced emancipatory rationale. The first principle is that labour law shall address the uneven distribution of bargaining power that characterises the labour relationship. The second is that labour shall not be treated as a commodity. The third fundamental principle has an economic underpinning and it coincides with the assumption that labour law shall find expression in a market economy, where the economic freedoms of the employer must be guaranteed.

2.1.1 Fundamental Principle 1: Addressing the Uneven Distribution in the Bargaining Power

Labour law was conceived as a remedy to the disproportionate bargaining power that the employer would otherwise exercise over the employee.[39]

Since the French Revolution, the exaltation of the freedom of contract and self-determination has characterised the regulatory approach to a wide spectrum of human interactions, including labour relations.[40] The parties stipulating a (labour) contract were deemed to be equally free before the law, and labour was governed by civil law principles since it fell within the normative framework of the provision of services (*locatio conductio operarum*).[41] However, even at the time, freedom of contract was not actually enjoyed equally by the parties. The employer, on the one hand, because of his greater availability of resources, always had greater bargaining power and hence the possibility of dictating the terms and conditions of employment to

39. B. Veneziani, 'The Employment Relationship' in B.A. Hepple & B. Veneziani (eds), *The Transformation of Labour Law in Europe: A Comparative Study of 15 Countries, 1945-2004*, Hart Publishing, Oxford, 2009, pp. 99-128.
40. C. Watrin, 'The Social Market Economy: The Main Ideas and Their Influence on Economic Policy' in P. Koslowski (ed.), *The Social Market Economy*, Springer, Berlin, 1998, pp. 13-28.
41. R. Knegt, 'Recovering the Impact of Normative Regimes on Labour Relations Practices: A Socio-Historical View of Institutional Requirements' in A. Blackham, M. Kullmann & A. Zbyszewska (eds), *Theorising Labour Law in a Changing World: Towards Inclusive Labour Law*, Bloomsbury Publishing, London, 2019, pp. 19-36; B. Veneziani, 'The Employment Relationship', 2009.

his counterpart.[42] The worker, on the other hand, was, from the negotiating point of view, the weaker party in the contractual relationship and did not have the means to substantially intervene in the determination of the contractual terms and conditions relating to his work.

Before the creation of a body of law dedicated to regulating labour relationships, the parties to the labour relationship were thus only nominally equal, since the employer enjoyed a position of authority and domination over the worker.[43] Labour law began to be developed when the legal systems came to recognise the opportunity to remedy the prevalence of the contractual power of the employer over that of the employee.[44] The imbalance in bargaining power had indeed become more palpable during the first industrial revolution. The creation of factories and the increasing distance between those owning the means of production and those working to produce emphasised the employer's authority and the employee's subordination, which became central aspects of the employment relation.[45]

From the point of view of the distribution of bargaining power, labour law can thus be conceived as the instrument designed to *emancipate* the worker by limiting the contractual power of the employer.

2.1.2 *Fundamental Principle 2: Labour Law Is Not (Just) a Commodity*

Going beyond mere contractual aspects, labour law derives also from the consideration that labour is not (just) a commodity.[46] When labour law was first introduced into national legal systems, work was predominantly performed in the form of personal labour, and this made the regulation of working conditions closely intertwined with the preservation of human dignity.[47] If labour were to be valued as a commodity, it would dehumanise workers which would be treated as another element of production, like costs and assets.[48] It would mean approaching labour in the same way as the elements that contribute to the comparative advantage of one company over another or – if a

42. S. Sciarra, 'Market Freedom and Fundamental Social Rights', Working Paper, European University Institute, Florence, 2002.
43. L. Wedderburn, 'Labour Standards, Global Markets and Labour Law in Europe' in *International Labour Standards and Economic Interdependence,* International Institute for Labour Studies, Geneva, 1994, pp. 247-253; K. Polanyi, *Great Transformation: The Political and Economic Origins of Our Time,* Beacon Press, Boston, 2001, pp. 50 ff.
44. B. Veneziani, 'The Evolution of the Contract of Employment' in B. Hepple (ed.), *The Making of Labour Law in Europe,* Mansell Publishing Limited, London, 1986, pp. 31-70.
45. *Ibid.*; A. Neal, 'Comparative Labour Law and Industrial Relations: "A Major Discipline? – Who Cares?"' in R. Blanpain, C. Engels, M. Weiss & B. Aaron (eds), *Labour Law and Industrial Relations at the Turn of the Century: Liber Amicorum in Honour of Roger Blanpain,* Kluwer Law International, The Hague, 1998.
46. R. Dukes, 'Hugo Sinzheimer and the Constitutional Function of Labour Law' in G. Davidov & B. Langille (eds), *The Idea of Labour Law,* Oxford University Press, Oxford, 2011, pp. 57-68.
47. B.A. Hepple, 'Factor Influencing the Making and Transformation of Labour Law in Europe', 2011.
48. R. Dukes, 'Hugo Sinzheimer and the Constitutional Function of Labour Law', 2011, p. 65.

supranational perspective is adopted – to the competitiveness of one country's economy over another.[49]

Considering labour as a commodity would thus risk leading to a downward spiral of labour cost-reduction reforms triggered by global competition, with direct repercussions on working conditions.[50] The prevention of this downward competition (or social dumping) is also one of the reasons that prompted states to agree on minimum standards in relation to working conditions. This eventually also brought to the establishment of the International Labour Organization (ILO) and the definition of the first (admittedly scarce) labour provisions in the Treaty of Rome.[51]

Labour law therefore also finds its origin in the necessity to shield labour from being perceived as an element of production and from being dominated by market dynamics. This implies preserving labour relations from being subsumed into market efficiency logics and competitiveness discourse, as that is deemed incompatible with the realisation of social justice.[52]

By proposing a narrative whereby labour is not a commodity, labour law enables workers from being disenfranchised from the logic of productivity and deregulatory competition. Hence, as in fundamental principle 1, also fundamental principle 2 expresses an emancipatory rationale.

2.1.3 *Fundamental Principle 3: Workers' Rights Shall Coexist with the Market Economy*

The third fundamental principle of the labour law 'of the origins' is that workers' rights shall coexist with the economic freedom of the employer. In this respect, it is worth noting that Hendrickx includes the market economy among the foundations of EU labour law and Deakin identifies economic growth as one of the two main priorities of labour law, besides that of human development.[53]

49. B. Langille, 'Labour Law Is Not a Commodity', The Industrial Law Journal, 19, 1998.
50. H. Feis, 'International Labour Legislation in the Light of Economic Theory' in W. Sengenberger and D. Campbell (eds), *International Labour Standards and Economic Interdependence*, International Institute for Labour Studies, Geneva, 1994, pp. 29-57.
51. Article 119 TCEE; Declaration of Philadelphia concerning the aims and purposes of the ILO, in Article 1, l. a) states that labour law is not a commodity; M. Weiss, 'Re-inventing Labour Law?' in G. Davidov & B. Langille (eds), *The Idea of Labour Law*, Oxford University Press, Oxford, 2011, pp. 43-56.
52. M. Hansenne, 'The European Social Model and Globalization of the Economy' in R. Blanpain, C. Engels, M. Weiss & B. Aaron (eds), *Labour Law and Industrial Relations at the Turn of the Century: Liber Amicorum in Honour of Roger Blanpain*, Kluwer Law International, The Hague, 1998; M.E. Streit, 'Has the Market Economy Still a Chance? On the Lack of a Discipline Challenge' in P. Koslowski (ed.), *The Social Market Economy*, Springer, Berlin, 1998, pp. 50-63.
53. S. Deakin, 'The Contribution of Labour Law to Economic and Human Development' in G. Davidov & B. Langille (eds), *The Idea of Labour Law*, Oxford University Press, Oxford, 2011, pp. 156-175, p. 156; F. Hendrickx, 'Foundations and Functions of Contemporary Labour Law', European Labour Law Journal, 3(2), pp. 108-129, 2012.

Labour law has developed as a pillar of capitalist economies and was deemed to complement and not jeopardise economic freedoms and free market principles.[54] Depending on the scope recognised to labour rights, the market principles may either dominate above social considerations or, instead, find in labour law a substantial compression. A minimalist approach to labour law is typical of classical neoliberalism, where the preference is to invest in the inclusive capacity of the labour market rather than in the enhancement of the individual and collective prerogatives of the workers.[55] In fact, neoclassical thinking contends that the employment protection legislation will eventually stiffen the labour market and thus produce social exclusion.[56] However, the market economy principles can also coexist with the establishment of rather substantial labour rights. An example is the socioeconomic model of the 'social market economy', which was developed in the first half of the 20th century as a declination of German ordoliberalism.[57] The social market economy envisaged social re-equilibration policies to be implemented in both the social and labour spheres. These included minimum wages, worker participation in the management of the undertaking and forms of social security.[58] From the 1950s to the 1970s, in various national legal systems - including Western Germany, where this socioeconomic model was originally theorised - the social market economy concept was expanded to encompass more markedly social reforms inspired by the idea of the social state while keeping the fundamentals of the market economy intact.[59]

Even if the market economy tolerates and at times promotes labour standards and social protection mechanisms, the emancipatory, solidaristic and redistributive functions expressed by the welfare state and labour norms cannot go so far as to substantially compromise the existence of free market.[60] Labour law thus has an economic underpinning that should not be set aside. At the same time, it is important to note that if this economic dimension takes over the social rationale, labour law may end up losing its emancipatory rationale.[61] If this were the case, the very nature of

54. M. Albert, *Capitalism vs. Capitalism: How America's Obsession with Individual Achievement and Short-Term Profit Has Led It to the Brink of Collapse*, Four Wall Eight Windows, New York, 1993; R. Dukes, *The Labour Constitution – The Enduring Idea of Labour Law*, Oxford University Press, Oxford, 2014, where Dukes explains that also for Sinzheimer labour law was an essential component of the 'economic constitution' he theorised for the Weimar Republic, p. 15.
55. G. Dale & N. El-Enany, 'The Limits of Social Europe: EU Law and the Ordoliberal Agenda', German Law Journal, 14, pp. 613-649, 2013.
56. B. E. Kaufman, 'Labour Law and Employment Regulation: Neoclassical and Institutional Perspectives', UWRG Working Paper, 24, Georgia State University, 2008.
57. C. Joerges & F. Roedl, 'The "Social Market Economy" as Europe's Social Model?', Working Paper, European University Institute, Florence, 2004.
58. A. Müller-Armack, 'The Principles of the Social Market Economy' in Peter Koslowski (ed.), *The Social Market Economy: Theory and Ethics of the Economic Order*, Springer, Berlin, 1998.
59. A. Ebner, 'The Intellectual Foundations of the Social Market Economy', Journal of Economic Studies, 33(3), pp. 206-223, 2006.
60. F. Hendrickx, 'Foundations and Functions of Contemporary Labour Law', 2012.
61. On this assumption, *see* N. Bruun & B.A. Hepple, 'Economic Policy and Labour Law' in B.A. Hepple & B. Veneziani (eds), *The Transformation of Labour Law in Europe: A Comparative Study of 15 Countries, 1945-2004*, Hart Publishing, Oxford, 2009, pp. 31-57; B.A. Hepple, 'Factor Influencing the Making and Transformation of Labour Law in Europe' in G. Davidov & B. Langille (eds), *The Idea of Labour Law*, Oxford University Press, Oxford, 2011, pp. 30-42; S.

labour law would be altered, as there would be no room for fundamental principles 1 and 2 and their social underpinning. In other words, the norms governing the world of work would no longer comply with labour law's original (social and emancipatory) premises.

2.2 The Functions of Labour Law

The three fundamental principles of labour law can find expression in different normative models and each of those models can be linked to a specific function pursued by labour norms. However, not all models embody in equal measure the social (and more precisely, the emancipatory) dimension of labour law.

2.2.1 The Protective Function

Firstly, labour law can have a protective function with regard to workers. This is especially the case in the conception of labour law originally developed by Sinzheimer, the founding father of German labour law. According to Sinzheimer, labour law should establish minimum standards of protection of workers, to shield them from the employer's stronger contractual authority.[62] To this end, the legislature is entitled to introduce rules establishing substantive limits to the contractual and entrepreneurial freedom of the employer.

This model is based on the assumption that state intervention is guided by the realisation of the public interest, and that it is necessary to curb the bargaining freedom of the employer in order to guarantee an inalienable core of workers' rights.[63] At the same time, the state has a duty to promote, by institutionalising it, the participation of the social partners in the decision-making process leading to the drafting of rules on working conditions and the management of the enterprise.[64]

The protective function of labour law is therefore mainly translated into prescriptive rules that impose minimum guarantees to safeguard workers, such as provisions on minimum wage, working time, and dismissal protection. The fact that this labour law model finds expression in the adoption of minimum statutory standards does not exclude forms of codetermination and industrial democracy. It indeed provides for legal norms to consent and regulate the exercise of collective rights and workers' representation, information and consultation.[65]

Deakin, 'The Contribution of Labour Law to Economic and Human Development' in G. Davidov & B. Langille (eds), *The Idea of Labour Law*, Oxford University Press, Oxford, 2011, pp. 156-175.

62. R. Dukes, 'Hugo Sinzheimer and the Constitutional Function of Labour Law', 2011; M. Weiss, 'Re-inventing Labour Law?', 2011.
63. R. Dukes, *The Labour Constitution – The Enduring Idea of Labour Law*, 2014, where Dukes compares the different approach of Kahn Freud on this point, p. 32.
64. *Ibid.*, p. 17.
65. F. Mestitz, 'Hugo Sinzheimer e il diritto del lavoro: ieri e oggi', Scienza e Politica, 9(5), pp. 57-83, 2013.

When the normative model pursues a protective function, labour law clearly expresses an emancipatory dimension. The statutory imposition of minimum standards is intended to remedy the unequal distribution of bargaining power between the parties (fundamental principle 1).[66] In addition, the protective model prevents working conditions from being subject to excessive cost-cutting and deregulatory competition.[67] By imposing minimum labour standards, the legislation preserves labour conditions from being subject to market considerations, thus avoiding the commodification of labour (fundamental principle 2). It is also important to note that the pursuit of a protective function is compatible with the fundamental principle 3 and thus with the economic underpinning of labour law, inasmuch as workers' rights do not go so far as to deny the employer's contractual freedom and freedom to conduct a business in their entirety. And this is the case as long as the employer is granted basic freedoms, such as the right to dismiss workers, restructure its business, and renegotiate labour contracts.[68]

2.2.2 *Uplifting Workers' Bargaining Power*

Another function that labour law can pursue is to enhance the bargaining position of workers, who – as it was mentioned – find their vulnerability in the weaker contractual standing in the relationship with the employer. This is realised through the establishment and exercise of collective rights, such as the right to trade union representation and the right to collective bargaining, as vehicles to strengthen the contractual power of workers vis-à-vis the business side.[69]

This normative position reflects the paradigm first elaborated by Kahn-Freund, the father of the so-called common law approach, in which labour law is predominantly conceived from the point of view of the distribution of (bargaining) power.[70] According to Kahn-Freund, balancing the inequality inherent in the contractual position of employee and employer is intrinsically connected with the ideal of social justice. Equilibrating the power dynamics thus consents to introduce the values of dignity and freedom in labour relations.[71]

In Kahn-Freund's vision, the workers' power lies in collective power.[72] Workers' rights advancement shall be pursued by way of direct confrontation between the

66. A. Lyon-Caen, 'Italie' in *Droit du travail, démocratie et crise en Europe occidentale et en Amérique: Canada, Espagne, Etats-Unis d'Amérique, France, Grande Bretagne, Italie, Mexique, Pérou, République fédérale d'Allemagne: essai comparatif*, Actes Sud, Arles, 1986.
67. On the relation between labour standards and cost cutting competition: P. Syrpis, *EU Intervention in Domestic Labour Law*, Oxford University Press, Oxford, 2007, pp. 41, 42, among others.
68. R. Dukes, *The Labour Constitution – The Enduring Idea of Labour Law*, 2014, pp. 15-17.
69. R. Lewis, 'Kahn-Freund and Labour Law: An Outline Critique', Industrial Law Journal, 8(4), pp. 202-221, 1979, p. 217.
70. A. Neal, 'Comparative Labour Law and Industrial Relations: "A Major Discipline? – Who Cares?"', 1998.
71. P. Davies & M. Freedland, 'Changing Perspectives upon the Employment Relationship in British Labour Law' in C. Barnard, S. Deakin & G.S. Morris (eds), *The Future of Labour Law: Liber Amicorum Bob Hepple QC*, Hart Publishing, Portland, Oregon, 2004, pp. 129-159.
72. R. Dukes, 'Hugo Sinzheimer and the Constitutional Function of Labour Law', 2011. Similar concerns are also expressed in A. Bogg, 'Beyond Neo-Liberalism: The Trade Union Act 2016 and

collective representations of workers (trade unions) and employers (professional associations). To ensure that the outcome of collective bargaining leads to fairness and social justice, it is important that the legal systems support the creation of a pluralist, effective and inclusive industrial relations system.[73] Contrary to paradigms in which labour law is predominantly conceived in relation to a protective function (as in section 2.2.1), this function requires that the state essentially refrains from interfering in the collective labour standards-setting mechanism and from imposing minimum protective standards.[74] Instead, the functioning of the industrial relations system and the conditions under which collective bargaining takes place should be self-regulatory. This paradigm can be referred to as 'collective laissez-faire'.[75]

Similar to the protective model, here too the three fundamental principles on which labour law was originally conceived are expressed. The collective laissez-faire system was designed to remedy the bargaining gap between employer and workers and to enable the social partners to negotiate fair working conditions (fundamental principle 1). Moreover, it prevents the commodification of labour (fundamental principle 2) by establishing a collectively regulated system for the definition of the working conditions, involving workers' representatives and trade unions. This entails that the employer cannot unilaterally decide to adjust the labour costs to competitiveness or productivity objectives. The emancipatory nature of labour law is thus preserved.

At the same time, labour law respects its original economic underpinning as it still reflects fundamental principle 3, whereby workers' rights (and the processes leading to their definition) should be compatible with the functioning of the market economy. While expressed in a mediated form, the contractual freedom of the employer is not jeopardised. On the contrary, the institutionalisation of social dialogue between management and the workforce reduces moments of conflict and offers functional dialogue tools to solve complex situations such as business restructuring.[76]

2.2.3 *Reconciling Economic and Social Progress*

Another function that labour law can pursue is that of ensuring that workers' rights adapt to the evolution of society and the economy. In other words, labour law can be geared to reconcile economic and social interests and to provide that workers' rights go

---

the Authoritarian State', Industrial Law Journal, 45(3), pp. 299-336, 2016 and L. Wedderburn, 'Labour Standards, Global Markets and Labour Law in Europe', 1994.

73. B.A. Hepple, 'Factor Influencing the Making and Transformation of Labour Law in Europe', 2011; R. Lewis, 'Kahn-Freund and Labour Law: An Outline Critique', 1979, p. 208; J. Gardner, 'The Contractualisation of Labour Law' in H. Collins, G. Lester & V. Mantouvalou (eds), *Philosophical Foundations of Labour Law*, Oxford University Press, Oxford, 2019, pp. 33-47.
74. R. Dukes, 'Hugo Sinzheimer and the Constitutional Function of Labour Law', 2011.
75. A. Jacobs, 'Collective Self-Regulation' in B. Hepple (ed.), *The Making of Labour Law in Europe*, Mansell Publishing Limited, London, 1986, pp. 193-240; B. A. Hepple, 'Introduction' in B.A. Hepple (ed.), *Social and Labour Rights in a Global Context: International and Comparative Perspectives*, Cambridge University Press, Cambridge, 2002, pp. 1-18.
76. D. Grimshaw, A. Koukiadaki & I. Tavora, 'Social Dialogue and Economic Performance', Conditions of Work and Employment Series, 89, ILO, Geneva, 2017.

hand in hand with productivity. This means that labour law must not stand in the way of socioeconomic change, but should adapt and be resilient without, however, renouncing its emancipatory nature.

Over the past 150 years, labour law has accompanied the transformation of society and the evolution of business models and, therefore, of the world of work. For example, since the late 1970s, economic crises, globalisation, the deepening of European economic integration, and the impact of technology have put labour law systems under considerable pressure.[77] The global race for economic growth required businesses to be more responsive, productive and fit for competition. This led to a reconsideration of existing labour law paradigms and to the emersion of new forms of labour relationships, such as fixed-term contracts or part-time contracts.[78] This reconsideration did not concern the whole body of labour law; social - but also macroeconomic - concerns required the preservation of some of the original protective aspects of labour law as well as the institutions of collective bargaining.[79] Still, it was recognised that certain labour law norms, such as employment protection rules and certain aspects of the collective bargaining systems had a constraining effect on labour market inclusivity, occupational targets and economic growth. This narrative reflected the idea that, while keeping safeguarding workers' rights, labour law could also become more responsive to the demands of the changing business world.

There is no single paradigm to pursue this goal. In fact, the process of adaptation of labour law has resulted in various regulatory options. An interesting solution was proposed by Giugni, who was one of the founding fathers of Italian labour law. He was convinced that strong cooperation between the state and the social partners was the way forward and promoted a paradigm somewhat intermediate between the Sinzheimer and Kahn-Freund models.[80] Giugni proposed a collective effort to revise labour law, in which both the state and representatives of workers and the business world would be involved. Given the centrality of social dialogue, both at central and enterprise levels, this model can be described as a form of 'negotiated flexibilisation'. This collective effort ought to be geared towards a de-construction of labour law, in which the most obsolete features and rigidities are set aside, and, at the same time, towards a reconstruction, by extending protection also to workers not traditionally covered by labour law and social protection systems.[81] The result would be a neocorporatist and, in principle, sustainable model of flexibilisation of labour law.

77. T. Treu, 'The Role of a European Social Model' in R. Blanpain, C. Engels, M. Weiss & B. Aaron (eds), *Labour Law and Industrial Relations at the Turn of the Century: Liber Amicorum in Honour of Roger Blanpain*, Kluwer Law International, The Hague, 1998.
78. A. Ojeda Avilés & A.J. Garcia Vina, 'Regulation of the Labour Market' in B.A. Hepple & B. Veneziani (eds), *The Transformation of Labour Law in Europe: A Comparative Study of 15 Countries, 1945-2004*, Hart Publishing, Oxford, 2009, pp. 59-98.
79. B. Veneziani, 'The Employment Relationship' in B.A. Hepple & B. Veneziani (eds), *The Transformation of Labour Law in Europe: A Comparative Study of 15 Countries, 1945-2004*, Hart Publishing, Oxford, 2009, pp. 99-128.
80. A. Lyon-Caen, 'Italie', 1986.
81. G.P. Cella, 'Il Cammino Del Pluralismo: Giugni E Le Relazioni Industriali', Giornale Di Diritto Del Lavoro E Di Relazioni Industriali, Xxix(114), pp. 273-291, 2007; F. Liso, 'Appunti per un profilo di Gino Giugni dagli anni '50 allo Statuto dei lavoratori', Working Paper, Centre for the Study of

Other theoretical frameworks are certainly possible.[82] Bruun argued that this 'modernisation' of labour law could also be realised by opening labour law to labour market considerations. In particular, Bruun suggested that labour law should no longer be understood as a two-dimensional but a four-dimensional field of law.[83] Alongside the individual and collective meaning of labour law (two-dimensional conception), the legal systems should also adopt a human rights approach to labour as well as an access justice approach in relation to the labour market.[84] It is worth noticing that while facilitating labour market inclusivity would lead to a reduction of social exclusion, it also requires labour law to become more adaptable and responsive to the economic context.[85] In order to ensure that the economic rationale inherent in access justice policies does not override the social dimension of labour law, Bruun suggested that lawmakers should pursue balanced and holistic labour policies. In particular, Bruun argued that 'there must be some minimum elements of the two traditional labour law dimensions (individual and collective labour law) present in order for us to label a regulatory regime or governance model as a labour law system'.[86]

An alternative paradigm has been proposed also by Kullmann, Blackham and Zybszewska. They contended that while adapting to socioeconomic development, labour law should be refocused to promote inclusiveness, not only in relation to the labour market but in all its normative expressions.[87] This implies adopting minimum wages and income support, broadening the scope of labour law, and ensuring that the functioning of the labour market is based not only on access justice but also on substantive justice.[88]

Beyond what the specific paradigms may look like, it is worth noting that when labour law pursues the function of adapting labour rights to the economic context it can still embody its original fundamental principles. And this is the case, as Davidov observed, as long as the reforms of labour law 'have a view of what the law is supposed

European Labour Law 'Massimo D'Antona', Catania, 2016; R. Cosio, R. Foglia, *Il Diritto del Lavoro nell'Unione Europea*, Giuffrè, Milano, 2011, p. 420.

82. R. De Luca Tamajo, 'Flexicurity: Un Improbabile Ossimoro O Un'utile Mediazione?', Il Foro Italiano, 132(4), pp. 194-197, 2009.
83. N. Bruun, 'The Old and New Foundations of Labour Law' in K. Ahlberg & N. Bruun (eds), *The New Foundations of Labour Law*, Peter Lang, Frankfurt am Main, 2017, pp. 17.
84. N. Bruun, 'The Old and New Foundations of Labour Law', 2017; on this *see also* C. Stylogiannis, 'Freedom of Association and Collective Bargaining in the Platform Economy: A Human Rights-Based Approach and an Over Increasing Mobilisation of Workers', International Labour Review, 138(1), pp. 1-24, 2021.
85. The term 'access justice' is borrowed from H-W. Micklitz, 'Social Justice and Access Justice in Private Law', Working Paper, 2, European University Institute, Florence, 2011.
86. N. Bruun, 'The Old and New Foundations of Labour Law', 2017, p. 35.
87. A. Blackham, M. Kullman & A. Zbyszewska, 'Introduction' in A. Blackham, M. Kullmann & A. Zbyszewska (eds), *Theorising Labour Law in a Changing World: Towards Inclusive Labour Law*, Bloomsbury Publishing, Oxford, 2019, pp. 1-16.
88. A. Blackham, M. Kullman & A. Zbyszewska, 'Introduction', 2019, 'inclusive labour law eschews exclusion by remaining open to a multiplicity of regulatory approaches, which are capable of addressing different problems, rather than seeking one size fits all solutions. [...] Inclusive labour law rejects co-optation by economic rationalities and political agendas that seek to weaken protections and fragment solidarity under the guides of inclusivity', p. 5.

to achieve, i.e., what are its goals'.[89] Thus, the fact that labour law adapts to the macroeconomic agenda does not per se imply the abandonment of its social objectives. The emancipatory rationale is present if labour law, alongside market considerations, is still concerned with the improvement of working conditions. Undoubtedly, however, when labour policies begin to have a predominant focus on the labour market and economic growth, the emancipatory dimension will partially retreat in favour of the economic one.[90]

2.2.4 Labour Law as Labour Market Regulation

The original (emancipatory) nature of labour law is not, however, preserved in those normative models that are predominantly concerned with the regulation of the labour market.[91] According to mainstream (neoliberal) economics, a flexible and dynamic labour market is deemed of fundamental importance for the pursuit of economic growth, high employment rates and the promotion of entrepreneurship. When these become the main priorities of labour policies, labour law becomes subsumed into the labour market functioning discourse. It is thus re-oriented towards the pursuit of productivity and competitiveness objectives and is no longer able to realise its original main objective of improving working conditions.[92]

This approach gained ground in the United Kingdom (UK) from the 1980s onwards, during the Thatcher administration. Davies and Freedland pointed out that, in that period, labour law was invested by the generalised effort to implement and advance a free market economy.[93] As also reported by Dukes, labour policies were refocused towards the functioning of the labour market, with the objective to support economic growth.[94] The emphasis on the functioning of the labour market and the myth of full employment was then progressively accepted even outside the neoliberal

89. G. Davidov & B. Langille (eds), *The Idea of Labour Law*, Oxford University Press, Oxford, 2011, pp. 14, 15.
90. N. Bruun, 'The Old and New Foundations of Labour Law', 2017: 'Access justice forms a hybrid between social welfare law (labour law) and its traditional values, and market law and its economic rationale', p. 28.
91. F. Vergis, 'Back to the Future: Rediscovering the Non-economic Role, Value and Scope of Labour Law and Collective Labour Institutions in a Changing World' in A. Blackham, M. Kullmann & A. Zbyszewska (eds), *Theorising Labour Law in a Changing World: Towards Inclusive Labour Law*, Bloomsbury Publishing, Oxford, 2019, pp. 81-106; M. Weiss, 'Re-inventing Labour Law?', 2011; H.S. Giubboni, 'The Rise and Fall of EU Labour Law', European Law Journal, 24(1), pp. 7-20, 2018; P. Davies & M. Freedland, *Towards a Flexible Labour Market: Labour Legislation and Regulation since the 1990s*, Oxford University Press, Oxford, 2007, pp. 5, 6.
92. Neoliberal conception of labour law, for example *see* L. Rodgers, 'Theorising Labour Law in the State of Exception: Political and Judicial Responses to Crisis' in A. Blackham, M. Kullmann & A. Zbyszewska (eds), *Theorising Labour Law in a Changing World: Towards Inclusive Labour Law*, Bloomsbury Publishing, London, 2019, pp. 37-54; A. Bogg, 'Brexit, Labour Law and the Twilight of Liberalism' in K. Ahlberg & N. Bruun (eds), *The New Foundations of Labour Law*, Peter Lang, Frankfurt am Main, 2017.
93. P. Davies & M. Freedland, 'Changing Perspectives upon the Employment Relationship in British Labour Law' in C. Barnard, S. Deakin & G.S. Morris (eds), *The Future of Labour Law: Liber Amicorum Bob Hepple QC*, Hart Publishing, Portland, Oregon, 2004, pp. 129-159.
94. R. Dukes, *The Labour Constitution – The Enduring Idea of Labour Law*, 2014, p. 99.

narrative of the Thatcher government.[95] It became part of the so-called third-way paradigm advocated by the Blair administration and was also endorsed by distinguished labour scholars, such as H. Collins.[96] The pursuit of social progress was more and more presented as a responsibility of social welfare policies, and the idea that labour law shall enable business competitiveness was somewhat normalised.[97]

This evolution in the priorities of labour law expanded in other national legal systems and can also be detected in EU policymaking. A significant and still relevant example in which labour law has been conceived more as 'law of the labour market' than as 'law of the employment relationship' is the so-called flexicurity' model.[98] The flexicurity paradigm appeared in EU policymaking at the end of the 1990s and was promoted during the Barroso I and Barroso II Commission.[99] Flexicurity required labour policies to have strong functionality with respect to the achievement of higher employment rate and economic growth.[100] This found expression in the shift from the objective of job security to that of employability and employment security.[101] There was a reinforcement of the idea that some of the labour protection standards and norms

95. W. Kok, 'Jobs, Jobs, Jobs – Creating More Employment in Europe', Report of the Employment Taskforce Chaired by Wim Kok, Directorate General for Employment, Social Affairs and Inclusion (European Commission), Brussels, 2003.
96. H. Collins, 'Regulating the Employment Relation for Competitiveness', Industrial Law Journal, 30(1), pp. 17-48, 2001; J. Gardner, 'The Contractualisation of Labour Law' in H. Collins, G. Lester & V. Mantouvalou (eds), *Philosophical Foundations of Labour Law*, Oxford University Press, Oxford, 2019, pp. 33-47.
97. N. Bruun & B.A. Hepple, 'Economic Policy and Labour Law', 2009, pp. 50-52: 'Emphasis was turned to the concept of civil responsibility, to indicate that social welfare (to a limited extent) and progressive taxation should not be seen as favours or surrenders on the part of business. Indeed, the amelioration of the conditions of society as a whole have positive repercussions also on business.' 'In common with neoliberalism, there is the primacy of the freedom of conducting business, and the adoption of a functionalistic rhetoric with respect to labour standards.' *See also* P. Davies & M. Freedland, *Towards a Flexible Labour Market: Labour Legislation and Regulation since the 1990s*, Oxford University Press, Oxford, 2007, p. 5: 'labour law and the regulation of employment relations were viewed, in a much more pronounced and overt way than they had previously been, as instrumental to the securing and maintaining of a political equilibrium constructed around the key notions of full employment, carefully controlled inflation, taxation and social security expenditure, and financially efficient provision of public services'. In a way, the emerging paradigm was inspired by the Nordic model, where a flexible labour market is coupled with a strong social welfare system. In the 'third way' model, emphasis was placed on the dynamics of employment relations more than on social protection, however.
98. C. Barnard, 'Internal Market v Labour Market: A Brief History' in M. de Vos (ed.), *European Union Internal Market and Labour Law: Friends or Foes?*, Social Europe Series, 2009, pp. 19-45.
99. European Commission, Social Policy Agenda, COM(2000) 379 final, Brussels, 28 June 2000, European Commission, Social Agenda, COM(2005) 33 final, Brussels, 9 February 2005, Lisbon European Council, Presidency Conclusion, March 2000.
100. L. Burroni & M. Keune, 'Flexicurity: A Conceptual Critique', European Journal of Industrial Relations, 17(1), pp. 75-91, 2011; A.C.J.M. Wilthagen, 'Flexicurity Pathways: Turning Hurdles into Stepping-Stones', Expert Report for the European Commission, Tilburg Flexicurity Research Programme, Tilburg, 2007; P. Davies & M. Freedland, 'Changing Perspectives upon the Employment Relationship in British Labour Law', 2004, p. 249; R. Dukes, *The Labour Constitution – The Enduring Idea of Labour Law*, 2014, p. 102; L. Rodgers, 'Theorising Labour Law in the State of Exception: Political and Judicial Responses to Crisis', 2019; S.F. Deakin & F. Wilkinson, *The Law of the Labour Market: Industrialization, Employment, and Legal Evolution*, Oxford University Press, Oxford, 2005, pp. 277, 290-294.
101. S. Bekker, 'Flexicurity in the European Semester: Still a Relevant Policy Concept?', Journal of European Public Policy, 25(2), pp. 175-192, 2018.

addressing working conditions (i.e., dismissal protection, working time) constituted barriers to the proper functioning of the labour market and fostered tension between insiders and outsiders.[102] At the same time, it was recognised that the lifting of these labour standards would lead to higher precariousness and, to minimise this risk, regulators turned to the safety nets provided by social protection and welfare systems. Reforms were announced (although often not completely realised) to make these systems more responsive and inclusive, to combat social exclusion and promote reintegration into the labour market.[103]

In this understanding of labour law, the emancipatory dimension is profoundly eroded. The centrality of labour market regulation is an expression of the prevalence of the economic rationale over the social one. On the one hand, it is clear that this paradigm responds to the fundamental principle whereby labour law must be consistent with the tenets of the market economy (fundamental principle 3). It is instead less evident how a focus on labour market flexibility and on the 'lightening' of employment protection can adequately give expression to the more social components underlying the other two founding principles of labour law. By concentrating on 'access justice' – meaning the inclusivity of the labour market – labour law fails to prevent labour from being addressed as a commodity (fundamental principle 2). Similarly, labour law abdicates its responsibility to prevent the employer's stronger bargaining position from translating into unfair working conditions (fundamental principle 1).

It is worth recalling that, when describing principle 3 (section 2.1.3), it was noted that if this economic underpinning would end up prevailing over the emancipatory one, the nature of labour law would have to be considered transformed. This is exactly what might occur when labour law is designed to pursue labour market functioning instead of addressing labour conditions.

3 THE COURT OF JUSTICE AND THE PURPOSIVE APPROACH TO LABOUR LAW: MYTH OR REALITY?

The second premise of the study conducted in this book is the assumption that the CJEU approaches labour norms with a normative inclination. This assumption is taken as a starting point for the exploration of the CJEU's role vis-à-vis labour law and later tested through empirical analysis. While not uniformly acknowledged in the labour law literature, a significant number of legal scholars share the perception that the Court is moved by a purposive attitude towards labour norms. These views are explored in this section with reference to two rulings where labour rights have been weighed against the freedom to conduct a business of the employer, and that have been the subject of vivid academic debate.

It is worth noting that the CJEU has undoubtedly proven able to exercise substantial interference with policymaking and has played an important role in the

102. This precept is explained and challenged by: O. van Vliet & H. Nijboer, 'Flexicurity in the European Union: Flexibility for Outsiders, Security for Insiders', Research Memorandum n. 2, Department of Economics, 2012.
103. N. Bruun, 'The Old and New Foundations of Labour Law', 2017.

most crucial stages of European integration. Textbook examples are the *Van Gend en Loos* and *Costa v. Enel* judgments,[104] in which the Court instilled the idea that the European Community was something more than a system based on international law.[105] Or, another example is the expansive interpretation of certain Treaties articles that made the EU case law a point of reference both for the widening of the European internal market and for gender equality policies.[106]

Clearly, the Court's interpretative creativity finds also expression in the field of labour law.[107] The Court has indeed not shied away from influencing the regulatory models of labour law in place at the national level and, in some cases, added pressure to its transformation.[108] Mention has already been made of the *Viking* and *Laval* rulings, on which much has been written about the arguably biased approach of the Court towards the balancing of the interests at stake.[109] More recent examples are the *Alemo-Herron* and *Aget Iraklis* judgments discussed in this section. There, the Court established that (protective) labour norms and practices had to be lifted as they excessively restricted the employers' freedom to conduct business.[110] By placing the

104. Judgment of 5 February 1963, *NV Algemene Transport- en Expeditie Onderneming van Gend & Loos v. Netherlands Inland Revenue Administration*, C-26/62, ECLI:EU:C:1963:1; judgment of 15 July 1964, *Flaminio Costa v. E.N.E.L.*, C-6/64, ECLI:EU:C:1964:66.
105. J.H.H. Weiler, 'Van Gend En Loos: The Individual as Subject and Object and the Dilemma of European Legitimacy', International Journal of Constitutional Law, 12(1), pp. 94-103, 2014; G.F. Mancini, 'The Making of a Constitution for Europe', Common Market Law Review, 26(4), pp. 595-614, 1989: S. Bardutzky & E. Gahey, 'The Subjects and Objects of EU Law: Exploring a Research Platform' in S. Bardutzky & E. Fahey (eds), *Framing the Subjects and Objects of Contemporary EU Law*, Edward Elgar Publishing, Cheltenham, 2017, pp. 1-30.
106. O. Pollicino, *Discriminazione sulla Base del Sesso e Trattamento Preferenziale nel Diritto Comunitario*, Giuffrè, Milano, 2005; M.P. Maduro, *We the Court: The European Court of Justice and the European Economic Constitution: A Critical Reading of Article 30 of the EC Treaty*, Hart Publishing, Oxford, 1998; A. Stone Sweet & T. Brunell, 'Constructing a Supranational Constitution' in *The Judicial Construction of Europe*, Oxford University Press, New York, 2004.
107. I already referred to the rich literature on the *Viking* and *Laval* cases (footnotes 14 and 15). Among others, also A.C.L. Davies, 'One Step Forward, Two Steps Back? The Viking and Laval Cases in the ECJ', Industrial Law Journal, 37(2), pp. 126-148, 2008; L. Azoulai, 'The Court of Justice and the Social Market Economy: The Emergence of an Ideal and the Conditions for Its Realization', Common Market Law Review, 45, pp. 1335-1356, 2008; S. Deakin, 'Regulatory Competition After Laval', CYELS (2007-2008), 10, pp. 581 ff; C. Barnard, 'Social Dumping or Dumping Socialism', Cambridge Law Journal, 67, pp. 262-280, 2008.
108. E. Pataut, 'The Aftermath of the Laval Affair: The Swedish Lex Laval Before the Committee of Social Rights' in H. Muir Watt et al. (eds), *Global Private International Law – Adjudication without Frontiers*, Edward Elgar Publishing, Northampton, 2019, pp. 484-492.
109. Z. Rasnača, *First or One among Equals? The CJEU and the Construction of EU Social Policy*, European University Institute, Florence, 2017.
110. Judgment of 18 July 2013, *Mark Alemo-Herron and Others v. Parkwood Leisure Ltd*, C-426/11, ECLI:EU:C:2013:521; judgment of 21 December 2016, *Anonymi Geniki Etairia Tsimenton Iraklis (AGET Iraklis) v. Ypourgos Ergasias, Koinonikis Asfalisis kai Koinonikis Allilengyis*, C-201/15, ECLI:EU:C:2016:972. More extensive references to the academic debate on these rulings will be more extensively referred in sections 3.1 and 3.2 and in Chapter 3, section 3.4. *Inter alia*: C. Wynn-Evans, 'TUPE, Collective Agreements and the Static-Dynamic Debate', Industrial Law Journal, 39(3), pp. 275-279, 2010; S. Giubboni, 'Freedom to Conduct a Business and EU Labour Law', European Constitutional Law Review, 14, pp. 172-190, 2018; N. Countouris & A. Koukiadaki, 'The Glass Half Full: Collective Redundancies, Public Interest, and the (Unfulfilled) Potential of Europe's "Highly Competitive Social Market Economy"', Giornale di Diritto del Lavoro e di Relazioni Industriali, 153(1), pp. 193-201, 2017; V. Papa, 'The Dark Side of Fundamental Rights Adjudication? The Court, the Charter and the Asymmetric

emphasis on the economic interests of the employer, these rulings had the effect of marginalising the emancipatory rationale of labour law.[111] It is precisely because of this disruptive effect that observers and academic writers have looked critically at those rulings. The predominance of economic freedom over workers' rights can indeed be perceived as an expression of the Court's tendency to purposively intervene in the balance of interests underpinning labour law systems.[112]

The interpretation of these judgments as the result of a normative inclination of the Court is certainly justified. At the same time, the assumption that they are an expression of the Court's socioeconomic and ideological preferences risks diverting attention from exploring whether there might be other logics steering the reasoning of the Court. It also risks attributing a too simplistic characterisation of the Court, in contrast with the principle whereby dogmatic assertions should not be made on the basis of anecdotal, unsystematic studies. The danger is, indeed, to draw a potentially biased picture of the Court's role in shaping labour law, a bias that this research aims to bring to light and nuance.

3.1 The *Alemo-Herron* Case

The *Alemo-Herron* judgment concerns the interpretation of Directive 2001/23/EC on workers' acquired rights in case of transfers of undertakings. Directive 2001/23/EC provides that when an undertaking or business is transferred from one employer (transferor) to another (transferee), the transferee shall take over the employment contract of the workers that, prior to the transfer, were employed in the transferred economic entity.[113] Moreover, the transferee is compelled to observe the terms and conditions that were applicable to the transferor, regardless of the fact that such terms and conditions originate from the individual employment contract or from the collective agreement in force before the transfer.[114]

In the *Alemo-Herron* case,[115] the Court was addressed with a preliminary ruling request from the UK Supreme Court (the House of Lords). The legal issue at stake concerned a transfer of an undertaking where the transferee found himself bound by a collective agreement whose terms were subject to periodic and automatic adjustment. This is because of a clause in the individual contract of employment of the transferred

Interpretation of Fundamental Rights in the AMS Case and Beyond', European Labour Law Journal, 6(3), pp. 190-214, 2015.

111. On the evolution of the perception of the freedom of contract within the EU: E. Gill-Pedro, 'Freedom to Conduct Business in EU Law: Freedom from Interference or Freedom from Domination?', European Journal of Legal Studies, 9(2), pp. 103-134, 2017; S. Rainone, 'Workers' Involvement in Collective Redundancies in EU Law – What For? A Case Study', Bulletin of Comparative Labour Relations, 107, pp. 207-220, 2019.
112. *Supra* n. 3.
113. R.M. Beltzer, 'The Transfer of Undertakings and the Importance of Taking Over Personnel: A Vicious Circle', International Journal of Comparative Labour Law and Industrial Relations, 23(1), pp. 139-155, 2007; G. Santoro-Passarelli, 'The Transfer of Undertakings: Striking a Balance Between Individual Workers' Rights and Business Needs', International Journal of Comparative Labour Law and Industrial Relations, 23(3), pp. 311-334, 2007.
114. Article 3(1) and 3(3) of Directive 2001/23/EC.
115. C-426/11, *Alemo-Herron*.

workers which indicated that 'during your employment with [name of the employer], your terms and conditions of employment will be in accordance with the collective agreement negotiated from time to time by [name of the collective body]'.[116]

This type of clause is generally referred to as a 'dynamic clause'. In such cases, the agreements periodically concluded by the social partners in the framework of collective bargaining directly become part of individual employment contracts that include these clauses.[117] Dynamic clauses are a consolidated practice in the UK legal system, to remedy the absence of generally applicable (*erga omnes*) collective agreements.[118] A reference to the employment contract is indeed the only way to give collective agreements legal effect in the employment relationship.[119]

It is worth noting that, in the specific situation in the *Alemo-Herron* dispute, it was not possible for either the transferor or the transferee to join the collective body that periodically negotiated the employment conditions referred to by the dynamic clause. The reason was that both employers operated in the private sector, whereas the collective negotiating body represented only the public sector. This implied that the transferee was not in a position to participate in the collective negotiation of the terms of the collective agreement which was referred to in the employment contract of the transferred workers.[120]

By a preliminary reference to the CJEU, the referring court brought the issue of whether the national legal practice of dynamic clauses, and their applicability in case of transfer of undertakings, was compatible with EU law and, specifically, with Directive 2001/23/EC. The CJEU ruled that by mandating the transferee to comply with collective agreements negotiated after the transfer, the essence of his freedom of contract and freedom to conduct his business is adversely affected. The Court held that those freedoms found protection in Article 16 of the Charter of Fundamental Rights (CFR) of the European Union (hereinafter CFREU). This implies that neither the provision of the directive requiring the transferee to respect the rights arising from the contract of employment (Article 3.1) nor that requiring the transferee to continue to observe the terms and conditions laid down in the collective agreement applicable before the transfer (Article 3.3) could be invoked by the employee to obtain the wage increase mentioned in the dynamic clause.[121]

116. *Ibid.* (para. 10).
117. C. Wynn-Evans, 'TUPE, Collective Agreements and the Static-Dynamic Debate', 2010.
118. Opinion of Advocate General Cruz Villalon of 19 February 2013, *Mark Alemo-Herron and Others v. Parkwood Leisure Ltd*, C-426/11, ECLI:EU:C:2013:521 (para. 5).
119. J. Prassl, 'Freedom of Contract as a General Principle of EU Law? Transfers of Undertakings and the Protection of Employer Rights in EU Labour Law', Industrial Law Journal, 42(4), pp. 434-446, 2013; M. Bartl & C. Leone, 'Minimum Harmonisation after Alemo-Herron: The Janus Face of the EU Fundamental Rights Review', European Constitutional Law Review, 11(1), pp. 140-154, 2015.
120. C-426/11, *Alemo-Herron* (para. 34); J. Prassl, 'Freedom of Contract as a General Principle of EU Law? Transfers of Undertakings and the Protection of Employer Rights in EU Labour Law', 2013; R. Zahn, 'The Court of Justice of the European Union and Transfers of Undertakings: Implications for Collective Labour Rights', European Labour Law Journal, 6(1), pp. 72-85, 2015.
121. In *Alemo-Herron* the Court did not specify whether its reasoning was grounded on Article 3(1) or Article 3(3) or on a combined reading of the two.

To underpin its reasoning, the Court stated that the aim of the directive was to strike a fair balance between the interests of the employees and those of the employers. According to the Court, this balance would be disrupted if the transferee is required to observe dynamic clauses such as those at stake in the proceeding, inasmuch as these lead to an excessive limitation of his bargaining autonomy.[122] It is interesting to note that the Court's assertion that the objective of the directive is to strike a balance between the economic freedom of the employer and the need for protection of the workers did not derive from a literal interpretation of EU law. It rather was the result of the Court's creative interpretation. The text of the directive makes no reference neither to the preservation of the transferee's contractual freedom nor to such a balancing requirement. On the contrary, the preamble mentions that the purpose of the directive is to provide 'for the protection of employees in the event of a change of employer, in particular, to ensure that better rights are safeguarded'. The sole other objective that can be identified in the directive is that of reducing the differences which 'still remain in the Member States as regards the extent of the protection of employees in this respect'.[123] Moreover, the Court reached its decisions regarding the excessive compression of the employer's freedom to conduct a business without recurring to proportionality test or a balancing exercise between the conflicting interests.[124] Also, the Court did not leave any interpretative discretion to the referring judge.[125] And, perhaps most strikingly, the fact that Article 8 of the directive makes express reference to the possibility for Member States to adopt measures that are more protective than the minimum standards established in EU law seemed not to bear any significance.[126]

These elements suggest that the Court purposively reinterpreted the directive and, by doing so, it marginalised its protective function. The *Alemo-Herron* reasoning showed a preference for the normative model whereby labour law ought to adapt to labour market logics, towards the flexibilisation of the employment protection standards (discussed in section 2.2.4 above). This perception is strengthened when noting that the Court did not follow the opinion of Advocate General (AG) Villalòn, according to whom there were no reasons to retain that the compression of the transferee's

122. C-426/11, *Alemo-Herron* (paras 25 and 35).
123. Recitals 3 and 4 Directive 2001/23/EC.
124. It should be considered that proportionality tests is a rather common feature of the Court's reasoning when assessing the compatibility of rights established in national law with EU fundamental economic freedoms. Examples can be found in: judgment of 18 December 2007, *Laval un Partneri Ltd v. Svenska Byggnadsarbetareförbundet, Svenska Byggnadsarbetareförbundets avdelning 1, Byggettan and Svenska Elektrikerförbundet*, C-341/05, ECLI:EU:C:2007:809; judgment of 11 December 2007, *International Transport Workers' Federation and Finnish Seamen's Union v. Viking Line ABP and OÜ Viking Line Eesti*, C-438/05, ECLI:EU:C:2007:772; judgment of 12 June 2003, *Eugen Schmidberger, Internationale Transporte und Planzüge v. Republik Österreich*, C-112/00, ECLI:EU:C:2003:333; judgment of 14 October 2004, *Omega Spielhallen- und Automatenaufstellungs-GmbH v. Oberbürgermeisterin der Bundesstadt Bonn*, C-36/02, ECLI:EU:C:2004:614.
125. C-426/11, *Alemo-Herron* (para. 37).
126. Article 8 of Directive 2001/23/EC establishes that 'This directive shall not affect the right of Member States to apply or introduce laws, regulations or administrative provisions which are more favourable to employees or to promote or permit collective agreements or agreements between social partners more favourable to employees.'

freedom was excessive.[127] AG Villalòn argued that the effect of dynamic clauses was in no way permanent: in due time and following the relevant procedures, the transferee could renegotiate the terms and conditions of employment of his employees. Accordingly, the clauses incorporating collective agreements into individual employment contracts offer a rather weak protection to the workers. To overthrow the legal effects of these clauses, it is sufficient that the employer re-negotiates the individual employment contracts.[128] Moreover, as noted by Wynn-Evans and Prassl, the *Alemo-Herron* judgment leads to a paradoxical situation. The terms defined through collective bargaining are in fact now more likely to be overlooked by the transferee than if those terms were stated in the individual employment contract.[129]

To comply with this judgment, the UK had to reform the domestic rules on transfers of undertaking, and the result is that now dynamic clauses do not apply to the transferee who is not a member of the trade association which negotiated the collective agreement to which the clause refers.[130] The *Alemo-Herron* ruling, through its broad interpretation of the employer's freedom of contract, thus induced a reduction in the safeguards afforded to employees under the national regime. It is therefore not surprising that several labour scholars have expressed concern for the Court's seemingly clear normative position. Davies, Boggs and Costello wrote that in *Alemo-Herron*, 'the Court has deployed the Charter [of Fundamental Rights of the EU] in an aggressive fashion to support a deregulatory reading of the Acquired Rights Directive'.[131] Rémy expressed his dismay by observing that 'there was no desire on the part of the CJEU to spare English law or to take account of its specificities. But rather that of giving precedence to the freedom of enterprise and the contractual obligation over the directive transfer', and wondered 'whether the case law of the ECJ should still be taken so seriously'.[132] On the same lines, Weatherill picturesquely stated that 'on occasion a decision of the CJEU is so down-right odd that it deserves to be locked into a secure container, plunged into the icy waters of a deep lake and forgotten about. Such a decision is that of the Third Chamber in *Alemo-Herron*, in which the Court [...] tales a

127. Opinion of Advocate General Cruz Villalon, C-426/11, *Alemo-Herron* (para. 9).
128. P. Rémy, 'L'arrêt "Alemo-Herron" de la CJUE et la directive transfert: faut-il encore prendre au sérieux la Cour de justice?', Revue de droit du travail, 12, pp. 789-797, 2013.
129. C. Wynn-Evans, 'TUPE, Collective Agreements and the Static-Dynamic Debate', 2010; Wynn-Evans noted that 'it is not clear, for example, why an NJC arrangement such as that considered in Alemo-Herron should be frozen at the point of transfer, while a pay review mechanism based on an external determination, such a governmentally assessed inflation rate, would still apply on an ongoing basis'.
130. Regulation 7, The Collective redundancies and Transfer of Undertaking (Protection of Employment) (Amendment) Regulation 2014, in force since 31 January 2014.
131. A.C.L. Davies, A. Bogg & C. Costello, 'The Role of the Court of Justice in Labour Law' in A. Bogg, C. Costello & A.C.L. Davies (eds), *Research Handbook on EU Labour Law*, Edward Elgar Publishing, Cheltenham, 2016, pp. 114-149, p. 133.
132. P. Rémy, 'L'arrêt "Alemo-Herron" de la CJUE et la directive transfert: faut-il encore prendre au sérieux la Cour de justice?', 2013, free translation by the author; original: 'Nulle volonté donc pour la Court e Justice de ménager en l'espèce le droit anglais ou de tenir compte de ses spécificités, mais plutôt bel et bien celle de faire prévaloir la liberté d'entreprendre et la liberté contractuelle sur la directive transfert [...] Autant de considérations qui amènent nécessairement à se demander in fine s'il faut encore prendre avec autant de sérieux la jurisprudence de la ECJ?'.

mystifyingly aggressive approach to promote employer flexibility and, moreover, one which is quite out of line with existing EU law'.[133] Allusions that the Court has overstepped its role to delve into that of a policymaker have also been made by Bartl and Leone, who wrote that 'if a particular fundamental right has so little intrinsic essence as the freedom to contract does, the mobilisation of constitutional authority of the Court seems to be instrumental to pursuing a purely political or redistributive aim'.[134] And these are just a few of the critical remarks addressed to the Court on account of its judicial activism in favour of a market-centred view of labour law.

Overall, the critics that have been addressed to the Court in relation to *Alemo-Herron* are mostly focused on the Court's business-oriented reading of the legal matter, and on the lack of proper balancing of the interests at stake. Instead of conducting an assessment of the actual impact of the dynamic clauses practice on the employer's freedom to conduct a business, the Court hastily traced this practice to a violation of Article 16 CFREU. The weak argumentation, coupled with the markedly regressive implications of the ruling for UK workers, have legitimately led many to suspect an ideological bias on the part of the Court.

Other academic observers dissent, however.[135] Brameshuber and Martins, for instance, held that in *Alemo-Herron*, the Court legitimately gave expression to the economic dimension underlying the directive.[136] This view is also shared by AG Bot, in his opinion on the subsequent case *Asklepios*.[137] In Bot's analysis, in *Alemo-Herron* the Court provided a balanced interpretation of the directive by reading the workers' rights in light of the business safeguards set out in Article 3(3) of the directive. According to Bot, Article 3(3) reflects the intention of EU lawmakers to reconcile the transferred workers' rights with the transferee's legitimate interests not to be bound by collective agreements without *erga omnes* effect.[138] Despite the divergence of views, it is quite interesting to note that even from this second, and more positive perspective, the reasoning of the Court emerges as embedded in a conflict of values and interests (those of the workers versus those of the employers). From this perspective, by determining which interest should prevail in a given situation, the Court is inevitably perceived as

133. S. Weatherill, 'Use and Abuse of the EU's Charter of Fundamental Rights: On the Improper Veneration of "Freedom of Contract"', European Review of Contract Law, 10(1), pp. 167-182, 2014.
134. M. Bartl & C. Leone, 'Minimum Harmonisation after Alemo-Herron: The Janus Face of the EU Fundamental Rights Review', European Constitutional Law Review, 11(1), pp. 140-154, 2015.
135. Section 3.4.
136. E. Brameshuber, 'Balancing vs. Preservation of Rights under the Acquired Rights Directive', Industrial Law Journal, 45(3), 2016, pp. 443-454, 2015; D. Carvalho Martins, 'Transfer of an Economic Unit: Requirements, Effects and Recent CJEU Ruling', European Labour Law Journal, 9(1), pp. 24-49, 2018.
137. Opinion of Advocate General Bot of 19 January 2017, *Asklepios Kliniken Langen-Seligenstadt GmbH v. Ivan Felja and Asklepios Dienstleistungsgesellschaft mbH v. Vittoria Graf*, C-680/15, ECLI:EU:C:2017:30 (paras 75 and 77).
138. Advocate General Bot referred to the Commission's proposal from 1974 in which reference is made to the fact that the directive seeks to accommodate the prerogatives of the transferee: European Commission, Proposal for a Directive of the Council on harmonisation of the legislation of Member States on the retention of the rights and advantages of employees in the case of mergers, takeovers and amalgamations, COM(74)351 Final/2, Brussels, 29 May 1974.

leaning in favour of a normative model of labour law (protective, or instead more economically oriented) over the other.

3.2 The *Aget Iraklis* Case

In *Aget Iraklis*, the CJEU ruled on the rights and protection conferred on workers by Directive 98/59/EC on collective redundancies.[139] This directive provides that when the employer is contemplating collective redundancies, he has to observe two sets of rules. The first mandates that the employees must be granted information and consultation rights. The second imposes on the employer to notify the competent public authority which, from that moment, will monitor the consultation process between the employer and the workers' representatives.[140]

The CJEU was addressed by the Greek Council of State with a series of preliminary questions on whether Directive 98/59/EC, read in conjunction with Article 49 of the Treaty on the Functioning of the European Union (TFEU) on freedom of establishment and Article 16 CFREU on the freedom to conduct a business, precluded Greek legislation on collective dismissals.[141] It is important to note that, in transposing the EU rules on collective dismissals, Greek law went beyond the minimum standards established in the directive, a possibility explicitly provided for in Article 5 of the directive: 'This Directive shall not affect the right of Member States to apply or to introduce laws, regulations or administrative provisions which are more favourable to workers or to promote or to allow the application of collective agreements more favourable to workers.'

Greek law was more protective than the directive in that it gave the national authority (the Minister of Labour) broader powers than the mere monitoring function provided for under EU law. Basically, after assessing the factual circumstances and the reasons put forward by the employer to justify its decision to carry out collective redundancies, the Minister of Labour could refuse to authorise the dismissals.[142] More

139. Judgment of 21 December 2016, *Anonymi Geniki Etairia Tsimenton Iraklis (AGET Iraklis) v. Ypourgos Ergasias, Koinonikis Asfalisis kai Koinonikis Allilengyis*, C-201/15, ECLI: EU:C:2016:972.
140. S. Rainone, 'Workers' Involvement in Collective Redundancies in EU Law – What For? A Case Study', Bulletin of Comparative Labour Relations, 107, pp. 207-220, 2019; M.R. Freedland, 'Employment Protection: Redundancy Procedures and the EEC', Industrial Law Journal, 5(1), pp. 24-34, 1976; judgment of 25 January 2005, *Irmtraud Junk v. Wolfgang Kühnel*, C-188/03, ECLI:EU:C:2005:59 (para. 23), where the Court held that the consultation rights of the workers correspond to an obligation of the employer to negotiate; *see also* L. Ratti, 'The European Economic Constitution and the Constitution of a Social Europe: Gleanings from the CJEU's Collective Redundancies Cases' in H.C.H. Hofmann et al. (ed.), *The Metamorphosis of the European Economic Constitution*, Edward Elgar Publishing, Cheltenham, 2019, pp. 154-176.
141. It is worth noting that Greek law on collective dismissal was brought to the attention of the Court in judgment of 15 February 2007, *Athinaïki Chartopoiïa AE v. L. Panagiotidis and Others*, C-270/05, ECLI:EU:C:2007:101, but in that case, the referring judge did not explicitly refer a question on that matter (para. 37).
142. Article 5(3) of Law 1387/1983. Interestingly, Greek legislation on collective dismissals, and especially Article 5(3) thereof, had been a rather thorny matter of discussion between the Greek government and its international creditors in the context of the negotiations which accompanied the Greek economic and financial crisis; *see* I. Antonaki, 'Collective Redundancies in

specifically, the Minister could base its refusal on three grounds: the situation of the labour market, national economic interests, and the situation of the business or of the establishment.

In assessing the compatibility with EU law, the CJEU determined that Greek law had gone too far. This conclusion was drawn on the basis of a proportionality test from which emerged that national legislation went beyond what was necessary to attain the (legitimate) goal of protecting workers. At first, the Court held that the criteria on which the Ministry performed its assessment reflected a public interest objective, namely the safeguard of workers and employment.[143] Therefore, these criteria could in principle be a valid limitation of the freedom of establishment.[144] However, the Court also held that since the criteria implied limitations to an economic freedom enshrined in the EU Treaties, they had to be compatible with the CFREU. This descends from the *ERT* judgment, where the Court had established that it has the competence to assess whether national legislation derogating from the fundamental economic freedoms respects the fundamental rights protected by EU law.[145]

It was at that point of the reasoning that the Court found that the Minister of Labour's veto power collided with Article 16 CFREU on the right to conduct a business. The Court observed that the rights enshrined in the CFREU can only be limited if the restrictions, 'in accordance with the principle of proportionality, are necessary and genuinely meet objectives of general interest recognised by the European Union'.[146] As mentioned, the proportionality test eventually resulted in a negative outcome and the Court decided that the Greek law imposed an excessive limitation on the freedom to conduct the business of the employer. The criteria used by the Ministry to deliberate on the authorisation of the redundancies were found to be formulated imprecisely, granting too wide a discretion to the public authority, and making its decision hard to review.[147]

Following the Court's decision, the Greek legislation was reformed and the power of the Ministry of Labour not to authorise the collective redundancies was removed.[148]

Greece: AGET Iraklis', Common Market Law Review, 54(5), pp. 1513-1534, 2017 and N. Countouris, A. Koukiadaki, 'The Glass Half Full: Collective Redundancies, Public Interest, and the (unfulfilled) Potential of Europe's "Highly Competitive Social Market Economy"', Giornale di Diritto del Lavoro e di Relazioni Industriali, 153(1), pp. 193-201, 2017.

143. C-201/15, *AGET Iraklis*; the criterion on the interest of the national economy was considered not adequate: the Court established that 'purely economic grounds, such as, in particular, promotion of the national economy or its proper functioning, cannot serve as a justification for obstacles prohibited by the Treaty' (para. 72). The Court therefore conducted the proportionality test only in relation to the other two criteria laid down by Greek law (the conditions of the labour market and the situation of the undertaking).
144. C-201/15, *AGET Iraklis* (paras 57, 83).
145. *Ibid.* (paras 62, 63); judgment of 18 June 1991, *Elliniki Radiophonia Tiléorassi AE and Panellinia Omospondia Syllogon Prossopikou v. Dimotiki Etairia Pliroforissis and Sotirios Kouvelas and Nicolaos Avdellas and others*, C-260/89, ECLI:EU:C:1991:254.
146. C-201/15, *AGET Iraklis* (para. 70).
147. *Ibid.* (paras 99 and 100). D. Schiek, 'Constitutional Principles and Horizontal Effect: Kücükdeveci Revisited', European Labour Law Journal, 1(3), pp. 368-379, 2010.
148. Law 4472/2017. I. Antonaki, 'Collective Redundancies in Greece: AGET Iraklis', Common Market Law Review, 54(5), pp. 1513-1534, 2017.

The *Aget Iraklis* judgment thus had the result of preventing Greek law to transpose Directive 98/59/EC in a manner that would enhance its protective function.[149] The Court's reasoning expressed an attitude towards labour law similar to that which emerged in *Alemo-Herron*. In both cases, national labour rules were weighed and assessed against the freedom of the employer to conduct a business and were deprived of their emancipatory function.[150] Just like *Alemo-Herron*, *Aget Iraklis* reflects a preference for the labour law's fundamental principle 3 (on the coexistence with the market economy) over the fundamental principles 1 and 2, according to which labour law shall prevent the commodification of labour and should reduce the bargaining gap between workers and employer.[151]

As to be expected, also the *Aget Iraklis* ruling provoked a lively academic debate. Most commentators perceived this judgment as the result of an ideological inclination of the Court. The Court was seen again as playing the role of a policymaking actor, using its judicial and interpretative authority to pursue a specific socioeconomic model. For instance, Schieck stated without equivocation that, in relation to the *Aget Iraklis* case, 'the Court must be viewed as a political actor'.[152] Similarly, although in a more nuanced way, Ratti wrote that 'the CJEU's judgments in *Alemo Herron* and *Aget Iraklis* must be regarded as the cornerstone of its position on the relative balance to be struck between [economic] freedoms and workers' rights'.[153]

At the same time, certain observers tended to be milder and less bleak about the potential impact of this judgment on the future of labour law than they were in relation to *Alemo-Herron*.[154] This is largely due to the fact that in *Aget Iraklis*, the Court adopted

149. L. Ratti, 'The European Economic Constitution and the Constitution of a Social Europe: Gleanings from the CJEUs Collective Redundancies Cases' in H.C.H. Hofmann et al. (eds), *The Metamorphosis of the European Economic Constitution*, Edward Elgar Publishing, Cheltenham, 2019, pp. 154-176, p. 172.

150. S. Giubboni, 'The Rise and Fall of EU Labour Law', European Law Journal, 24(1), pp. 7-20, 2018; E. Gill-Pedro, 'Freedom to Conduct Business in EU Law: Freedom from Interference or Freedom from Domination?', European Journal of Legal Studies, 9(2), pp. 103-134, 2017.

151. It is interesting to note that the Court gears its reasoning to the Union's objective of 'creating a highly competitive social market economy'. From this reference, it could be inferred that the assessment in *Aget Iraklis* corresponds to what, according to the Court, should be the ideal of 'social and economic interests advancing hand in hand' and, therefore, to the 'reconciling' function of labour law, outlined in section 2.2.3. However, despite the reference to the social market economy, the broad interpretation of the scope of Article 16 CFREU seems to indicate that the Court's decision does not reflect an effectively balanced view of the interests at stake, but rather a predominantly economic understanding of labour law. *See also* N. Countouris & A. Koukiadaki, 'The Glass Half Full: Collective Redundancies, Public Interest, and the (Unfulfilled) Potential of Europe's "Highly Competitive Social Market Economy"', 2017; K.A. Polomarkakis, 'A Tale of Two Approaches to Social Europe: The CJEU and the Advocate General Drifting Apart in Case C-201/15 AGET Iraklis', Maastricht Journal of European and Comparative Law, 24(3), pp. 424-437, 2017.

152. D. Schiek, 'Constitutional Principles and Horizontal Effect: Kücükdeveci Revisited', European Labour Law Journal, 1(3), pp. 368-379, 2010.

153. L. Ratti, 'The European Economic Constitution and the Constitution of a Social Europe: Gleanings from the CJEUs Collective Redundancies Cases', 2019.

154. *Ibid.*; M. Markakis, 'Can Governments Control Mass Layoffs by Employers? Economic Freedoms vs Labour Rights in Case C-201/15 AGET Iraklis', European Constitutional Law Review, 13, pp. 724-743, 2017; K.A. Polomarkakis, 'A Tale of Two Approaches to Social Europe: The CJEU and the Advocate General Drifting Apart in Case C-201/15 AGET Iraklis', 2017.

a less blatantly biased reasoning leaning towards the prevalence of economic freedoms over labour protection rules, especially if one considers the reasoning proposed by AG Wahl. Suffice it to consider that the opening sentence of AG Wahl was the following: 'The European Union is based on a free market economy, which implies that undertakings must have the freedom to conduct their business as they see fit.'[155] Moreover, the Court enriched its reasoning with a digression on the social market economy (one of the objectives of the Union according to Article 2 of the Treaty on European Union (TEU)) and on how it requires to take social concerns and labour rights into greater account.[156] This led, for example, Polomarkakis to consider that 'if social Europe is to emerge in a more substantial way following the latest reforms, then it is partially the CJEU's task to contribute to its development. Until such ambitions fully materialise, however, one can only hope that the CJEU will not digress from this aim'.[157]

Regardless of the divergent views on the effective direction in which the *Aget Iraklis* might have steered EU social policies, it is important to stress that scholars seemed to share the perception of the Court as a normatively driven institution. The Court emerged again as a purposive actor, whose normative inclination contributed to shaping the social dimension of the Union.

4 CONCLUDING REMARKS

In this chapter, the theoretical and normative embedding of the book were outlined and the two main premises of the research were presented.

Section 2 provided an overview of the foundations of labour law and how certain normative models lead to the erosion of the emancipatory nature of labour norms. It was seen that when labour law widely coincides with labour market regulation, it fails to express its social and emancipatory dimension. Labour law instead pursues an economic narrative and is distanced from the ideal of social justice, which is assigned to other branches of the legal system (social welfare policies *in primis*).

These considerations on the nature of labour law and its emancipatory nature accompany the rest of the book. They inform the analysis in Chapter 2, where the EU institutional policymaking approach to labour law and social policies is illustrated. They come back in Chapter 3 and in the case studies on the CJEU case law on the directive on transfer of undertakings. Finally, the transformation of (the normative functions of) labour law underpins Chapter 6. There, the case studies especially

155. Opinion of Advocate General Wahl of 9 June 2016, *Anonymi Geniki Etairia Tsimenton Iraklis (AGET Iraklis) v. Ypourgos Ergasias, Koinonikis Asfalisis kai Koinonikis Allilengyis*, C-201/15, ECLI:EU:C:2016:972.
156. C-201/15, *AGET Iraklis* (para. 76). *See also* N. Countouris & A. Koukiadaki, 'The Glass Half Full: Collective Redundancies, Public Interest, and the (Unfulfilled) Potential of Europe's "Highly Competitive Social Market Economy"', 2017; M. Markakis, 'Can Governments Control Mass Layoffs by Employers? Economic Freedoms vs Labour Rights in Case C-201/15 AGET Iraklis', 2017.
157. K.A. Polomarkakis, 'A Tale of Two Approaches to Social Europe: The CJEU and the Advocate General Drifting Apart in Case C-201/15 AGET Iraklis', 2017.

address those judgments that marked a change of approach with respect to the emancipatory rationale of the directive.

The second dogmatic premise of this work was presented in section 3, where it was seen that, from a labour law perspective, the CJEU can legitimately be perceived as a policy-driven actor. The *Alemo-Herron* and *Aget Iraklis* judgments are significant examples of how the Court can rely on a creative interpretation of EU law to interfere with (and marginalise) the emancipatory component of labour law. And it is with this perception that the research presented in this book engages. On the one hand, these judgments justify a characterisation of the Court as a policy actor. On the other hand, the risk of such a characterisation is to promote a stereotypical view of the Court as a political institution, which conveys its ideological preferences in the interpretation of EU labour law.

In Chapter 3, the case law on the directive on transfer of undertakings is analysed through 'labour policy lenses', which admittedly offer grounds for a perception of the Court as a purposive actor. This perception is then challenged through what, in the Introduction (section 3), was defined as the 'second analytical layer' of the research. Chapters 4 and 5 discuss various judicial lawmaking theories and, in doing so, provide additional epistemological tools to observe and evaluate the Court's judgments. Chapter 6 is then dedicated to a series of case studies through which the significance of the different judicial lawmaking theories is tested. By considering those theories, the book opens up to the possibility that the Court's judgments, even those that had a disruptive impact on the emancipatory dimension of labour law, are not (only) an expression of a purposive approach.

The overall normative framework is then again addressed in the concluding chapter, where the two initial dogmatic premises are discussed in consideration of the findings that have emerged from the research.

CHAPTER 2

Labour Law in EU Policymaking

1 INTRODUCTION

This chapter is collocated in the first analytical layer of the research that is conducted in this book. It addresses RQ1 (*What (prevailing) normative model(s) is(are) underlying the approaches of EU institutional policymakers with respect to labour law?*). The exploration is rooted in the labour law discourse as it concerns the policymaking framework that governs EU labour policies. In particular, the objective is to reconstruct the evolution of the social and labour policy spheres in the process of European integration. To do so, the analysis is based on a wide range of policy documents and institutional communications, mainly from the European Commission, through which it is possible to map the approach of the EC (European Communities) and EU institutional actors.

It is clear that, since its creation in 1957, the European Communities have undergone a profound process of maturation. Established as a tariff and custom-free space, the European project turned into a single market and monetary union with ramifications in other policy fields, including social and labour policies. This maturation is clearly reflected in the evolution of the Treaties and the policymaking documents. While initially the European institutions had no ambition to intervene in the labour and social policies of Member States, with the expansion of economic integration the policy agenda of the European Economic Community (EEC; and of the EC and the EU afterwards) became more pervasive.[158] Employment and social policy matters got progressively attracted into the sphere of competence of European policymakers.

The initial paradigm based essentially on a dual polity (economic integration at the European level, and social progress reserved for the national level) evolved into a

158. D. Collins, *Social Policy of the European Economic Community*, Halsted Press, New York, 1975, p. 21; B. Bercusson, *European Labour Law*, Cambridge University Press, Leiden, 2009, pp. 99-126; D. Chalmers, C. Hadijemmanuil & G. Monti, *European Union Law*, Cambridge University Press, Cambridge, 2006, pp. 465-470.

more ubiquitous model, in which the EU intervened in the definition of an increasing number of national policy areas.[159] The result was an increasingly expansive EU approach to labour issues, which, around the 2000s, substantially influenced domestic labour policies.[160] The discretion of national legislators was thus reduced, as pressure grew from EU policymaking to implement reforms that would streamline labour law and make the labour market more dynamic and flexible. Labour law models pursuing a purely protective function, as well as those based on strong industrial relations traditions, began to suffer an inexorable erosion.[161]

This deregulatory tendency seemed to slow down at the end of the Barroso II Commission, when the European Commission moved towards a greater enhancement, even if at times just rhetorical, of social dialogue, the social market economy and, more generally, the social dimension of European integration. It is in this context that, by the Commission Juncker, the European Pillar of Social Rights was adopted. Although the Pillar proposes a vision of labour law which is in substantial continuity with the policymaking of previous years, at the same time, its implementation is revealing potential for a revival of the Union's social dimension.[162] In 2020, the COVID-19 pandemic broke out in Europe with devastating social and economic consequences. Interestingly, even from such a dramatic event it is possible to identify a positive spillover. The crisis induced by the spread of COVID-19 has in fact led to the relaxation of the fiscal rules and European macroeconomic surveillance over the national economic and fiscal situations. This gave some leeway to national legislators to implement the necessary spending programmes, including in the healthcare sector, and to strengthen their social and labour protection policies.

Overall, the picture that emerges is complex and in constant evolution. This makes it quite hard to identify an overall prevailing normative model regarding labour law in EU policymaking. It is for this reason that in section 2, the analysis develops in consideration of different historical periods. This consents to highlight that policymakers have changed over time their approach to the relationship between the economic and social dimensions of EU integration. Section 3 is dedicated to the EPSR and to an examination of its origins, the macroeconomic and regulatory context in which it was conceived and its implications for labour law. The Pillar is one of the most recent

159. R.D. Collins, *Social Policy of the European Economic Community*, Halsted Press, New York, 1975, pp. 186-201; R.R. Geyer, *Exploring European Social Policy*, Polity Press, Cambridge, 2000, pp. 34-56; C. Barnard, *EU Employment Law*, Oxford University Press, Oxford, 2012, pp. 3-47.
160. R.R. Geyer, *Exploring European Social Policy*, 2000, pp. 81-98; B. Bercusson, *European Labour Law*, 2009, pp. 454-466.
161. F. Dorssemont, 'The Right to Take Collective Action v Fundamental Economic Freedoms in the Aftermath of Laval and Viking. Foes Are Forever!' in M. de Vos (ed.), *European Union Internal Market and Labour Law: Friends or Foes?*, Intersentia, Cambridge, 2009, pp. 45-105.
162. European Commission, Speech by M. Thyssen, European Commissioner for Eurostat and Employment, Social Affairs, Skills and Labour Mobility, First outline of the European Pillar of Social Rights and reform of the Posting of Workers Directive, SPEECH/16/682, Brussels, 8 March 2016, where the social dimension of the EU was presented as strongly linked to the completion of the European economic and monetary union; S. Rainone, 'The European Pillar of Social Rights – Tell Me Where You Come from and I Will Tell You Who You Are', Zbornik Znanstvenih Razprav Letnik LXXX, Perspective on the European Pillar of Social Rights, pp. 133-178, 2020.

Union's structural interventions in labour law and has provoked curiosity and hope in the world of labour law and social policy experts.[163] Next, in section 4 the measures that have been taken so far at the EU level to react to the COVID-19 crisis are briefly outlined. Their possible implications for future EU labour policies are also highlighted. Finally, section 5 explicitly addresses RQ1 and provides a reflection on the normative model that prevails in EU policymaking vis-à-vis labour law.

2 HISTORICAL OVERVIEW OF THE EU'S APPROACH TO LABOUR LAW

Labour and employment matters were originally not included among the competences of the European Communities, the prevailing objective being the creation of a single European market. It was in fact believed that the pursuit of social cohesion would be realised at the national level as a spillover effect of market integration.[164] However, things turned out differently and labour policies began to take shape also at the European level.

2.1 The Origins: Dual Polity

The Treaty of Rome of 1957 leaves no doubts about its prevailing (if not exclusive) market-oriented nature. Its main objective was the creation of a customs-free space and, in the second stage, a single market.[165] Still, it would be incorrect not to acknowledge the broader societal design that the six original Member States had in mind. As stated in the Preamble of the Treaty of Rome and in Article 117 of the original version of that Treaty, the founding fathers of the European Community intended to link the establishment of the common market with the constant improvement of living and working conditions.[166]

It is meaningful to note that Petrilli, Commissioner in charge of the social affairs in the first Hallstein Commission, indicated that, despite the scarcity of explicit social references in the Treaty, the Community had a *raison d'etre* beyond mere economic interests. Certainly, the Community policy agenda was focused on economic integration, balanced and liberalised trade, monetary stability, fair competition and freedom

163. *See, inter alia*: F. Hendrickx, 'European Labour Law and the Millenium Shift: From Post to (Social) Pillar' in F. Hendrickx & V. De Stefano (eds), *Game Changers in Labour Law: Shaping the Future of Work*, Wolters Kluwer, Alphen aan den Rijn, 2018, pp. 49-63; F. Bonciu, 'The European Pillar of Social Rights: Too Little, Too Late?', Romanian Journal of European Affairs, 18(1), pp. 60-70, 2018; Z. Rasnača, 'Bridging the Gaps or Falling Short? The European Pillar of Social Rights and What It Can Bring to EU-Level Policymaking', Working Paper, ETUI, Brussels, 2017.

164. P. Syrpis, *EU Intervention in Domestic Labour Law*, Oxford University Press, 2007, pp. 51-60.

165. Bulletin of the European Communities, 'The First Milestone: Common Market Reaching End of First Stage', 50, 1961.

166. The Treaty of Rome, in its Preamble established that the signatory parties were 'Affirming as the essential objective of their efforts the constant improvement of the living and working conditions of their people.'

of movement.[167] However, the idea was that these policies would lead to economic growth and, in turn, to social progress. Trade intensification and the EEC economic policy were thus not to be considered in isolation from social implications. This thinking reflected Monnet's functional interpretation of European integration, where social welfare was expected to constitute a spillover effect of the correct functioning of the common market.[168]

The abstention from Community intervention in social and labour matters was also not absolute. It was recognised that, in some cases, social progress would not descend automatically from economic expansion. At the same time, convergence of specific labour standards was considered to have a potentially positive impact on the creation of the single market.[169] In those areas, it was for the Community to promote the upward harmonisation of living and working conditions.[170] This led the European Commission to advocate a more coordinated effort to achieve greater harmonisation.[171] Far from aiming at depriving the Member States of their autonomy and competences in social and labour policy areas, the Commission aimed at a reconciliation of national divergences through the establishment of 'equivalent guarantees'.[172] The Commission thus began to promote the definition of common social policy objectives, oriented at preserving working and living conditions from the deregulatory risks deriving from market integration.[173]

The creation of a balanced relationship between economic progress and social values was also central for Levi Sandri, Commissioner for Social Affairs between 1961 and 1970 and who succeeded Petrilli. For instance, his view was that Article 118 of the Treaty Establishing the European Economic Community (TEEC) – prescribing a close collaboration between Member States in the social field – called for joint efforts to achieve harmonisation of national legal systems.[174]

So, this first period of European integration is overall characterised by a dual polity: market integration at the Community level, while the social and labour policy spheres were left to national legislatures. The interventions that the Commission

167. European Commission, Speech by G. Petrilli, Member of the Commission of the European Economic Community, The Social Tasks Facing the EEC, X/2613/60-E, April 1960.
168. C.G. Anta, 'The Europe of Jean Monnet: The Road to Functionalism', History of European Ideas, 47(5), pp. 773-784, 2021.
169. European Commission, Speech by G. Petrilli, Member of the Commission of the European Economic Community, The Social Tasks Facing the EEC, X/2613/60-E, April 1960; Levi Sandri, Member of the Commission of the European Economic Community, Interview sur les objectives de la Communauté Européenne, February 1963.
170. *Ibid.*
171. Bulletin of the European Communities, 'The First Milestone: Common Market Reaching End of First Stage', 1961.
172. Levi Sandri, Member of the Commission of the European Economic Community, Interview sur les objectives de la Communauté Européenne, February 1963; European Commission, Speech by L. Levi Sandri, Member of the Commission of the European Economic Community, to the General Meeting of the Belgian Association for Social Progress on The Role of Social Policy in European Integration, 1820/PP/64-E, 10 February 1964.
173. European Commission, Speech by Lionello Levi Sandri, EEC Commissioner, at the 47th International Labour Conference, IP (63) 109, Brussels, 14 June 1964.
174. Levi Sandri, Member of the Commission of the European Economic Community, Interview sur les objectives de la Communauté Européenne, February 1963.

envisaged in relation to national labour policies were mostly aimed at coordination. The absence of substantial interference allowed national legislators to continue pursuing autonomous strategies aiming at the improvement of working and living conditions.

It is worth noting that this division of policy areas recalls the 'social market economy' paradigm, developed by Muller Armack as a variant of ordoliberalism.[175] To provide some context, ordoliberalism was the predominant socioeconomic theory among economists in the post-war period in West Germany.[176] In simplified terms, according to the ordoliberal view, economy should be regulated only to the extent necessary to prevent market failure. Muller Armack partially departed from this principle and argued that the market is just one - although essential - of the elements that govern society. Accordingly, social progress can be attained only if the functioning of the market and the exercise of individual (economic) freedoms are counterbalanced by policies directed at social redistribution and equilibration.[177] Referring to Muller Armack's own words: 'The Social Market Economy seems to me to be synonymous with the conviction that it is possible to attempt to overcome the antithesis of social progress and free enterprise [...] in the wider context of society as a whole.'[178]

While it is possible to identify an influence of the social market economy paradigm in early EC policymaking, it is not clear whether the European Communities, at that time, aimed at a specific model concerning labour law. Looking at the different functions of labour law outlined in Chapter 1 (section 2), no specific approach emerges at this stage of the evolution of European integration. The main focus was the creation of a single market, meaning that the EEC left broad autonomy to the Member States to develop their regulatory paradigm. National legislature thus had ample latitude to adopt labour legislation to uplift the workers' bargaining power and protect them against the employers' stronger contractual position. In this respect, the European Communities did not prevent, but actually indirectly supported, the emancipatory rationale of labour policies.[179]

2.2 Parenthesis of Upward Harmonisation

Soon, however, the division of policymaking spheres (economic integration at the European level and social progress at the national level) began to reveal its limits. It became clear that the realisation of social progress would not automatically descend

175. A. Ebner, 'The Intellectual Foundations of the Social Market Economy', Journal of Economic Studies, 33(3), pp. 206-223, 2006.
176. C. Joerges & F. Roedl, 'The "Social Market Economy" as Europe's Social Model?', Working Paper, European University Institute, Florence, 2004.
177. A. Müller-Armack, 'The Principles of the Social Market Economy' in *The Social Market Economy: Theory and Ethics of the Economic Order*, Springer, Berlin, 1998.
178. *Ibid.*; G. Dale & N. El-Enany, 'The Limits of Social Europe: EU Law and the Ordoliberal Agenda', German Law Journal, 14, pp. 613-649, 2013.
179. The emancipatory component of labour law has been discussed in Chapter 1, section 2.1.

from the advancement of the market integration process and that Member States' policies would not converge as the Commission wished.[180]

During the Paris Summit of October 1972, the heads of state and government of the Member States decided on a structural change. After declaring that economic expansion was not an end in itself, they confided to the Commission the mandate to define a common strategy in the social and labour policies.[181] The result was the drafting of a Social Action Programme delineating an agenda aimed at realising harmonisation on the way of progress.[182] In the Resolution adopting the 1974-1976 Social Action Programme, the rule-making institutions of the European Community committed to the future adoption of binding measures directed at creating convergence in an upward direction in certain social and labour policy areas.[183]

It was during this period that the directives on workers' acquired rights in case of transfers of undertakings and on information and consultation rights in case of collective redundancies (already discussed in Chapter 1, sections 3.1 and 3.2) were adopted.[184] Together with the directive on insolvency of the employer, these measures are the most remarkable expressions of the so-called golden period of European labour law.[185] Not least, they are still today among the most progressive rules adopted at the EU level. They clearly embody an emancipatory component as, besides pursuing the function of harmonising the internal market, provide for protective rules and confer collective rights enhancing the workers' bargaining position.

The 1974-1976 Social Action Programme was underpinned by a twofold purpose. First, it intended to promote upward convergence in labour standards, especially in the context of business restructurings, which had become more common as a result of market integration.[186] Moreover, the harmonisation of working conditions pursued the objective to reduce the regulatory differences among Member States and proceed with the expansion of the internal market. Economic integration and social development

180. European Commission, Preliminary guidelines for a community social policy programme, SEC (71) 600 final, Brussels, 17 March 1971; European Parliament, Opinion of the European Parliament on the 1972 Report of the Commission on the development of the social situation in the Community, 30 April 1973.
181. European Parliament, Report, Rapport fait au nom de la commission politique sur les résultats de la Conférence au sommet des Chefs d'État ou de gouvernement des Etats membres de la Communauté élargie, Paris, 19 October 1972.
182. European Commission, Social Action Programme, COM(73) 1600, Brussels, 25 October 1973.
183. European Council, Resolution concerning a Social Action Programme, Brussels, 21 January 1974.
184. Council Directive 77/187/EEC of 14 February 1977 on the approximation of the laws of the Member States relating to the safeguarding of employees' rights in the event of transfers of undertakings, businesses or parts of businesses *OJ L 61, 5.3.1977, pp. 26-28*; Council Directive 75/129/EEC of 17 February 1975 on the approximation of the laws of the Member States relating to collective redundancies *OJ L 48, 22.2.1975, pp. 29-30*.
185. R. Blanpain, *European Labour Law*, Kluwer Law International, The Hague, 2008, p. 208.
186. Eurofound, Monitoring and managing restructuring in the 21st century, Publications Office of the European Union, Luxembourg, 2013.

were thus strictly interwoven.[187] Actual progress on both sides was deemed necessary to reach the socioeconomic objectives of the Rome Treaty and to obtain social justice.[188]

In this period, the original dualism between market integration (allocated at the Community level) and the pursuit of social objectives (reserved for the national legislature) were disrupted. The European Community made a tangible step towards the realisation of a fair balance between economic growth and the safeguarding of social prerogatives. This brief parenthesis of upward convergence in labour standards appears quite coherent with Muller Armack's social market economy theory. In fact, this socioeconomic model required labour and social policies to offset the societal impact of economic integration and to pursue social re-equilibration.[189]

With respect to the normative approach towards labour law, all three fundamental principles described in Chapter 1 section 2.1 were clearly present in this period.[190] The legislation adopted to implement the Social Action Plan of 1974 expressed both the protective function (most markedly present in the directive on transfer of undertakings) as well as the function of uplifting the workers' bargaining power (which characterises the directive on collective redundancies). The emancipatory rationale of the labour norms adopted in this period is thus rather prominent.

2.3 New Challenges and Completion of the Internal Market

During the mid-1970s, Europe entered into a period of economic stagnation. Price inflation and wages went up, triggering concerns about the rising unemployment rate and social stability.[191] Moreover, new challenges, such as fast technological changes, increased competitiveness[192] and rapid rearrangement of industrial production,

187. European Commission, Speech by M. Shanks, Director-General for Social Affairs at the European Commission, to the European Institute for Social Security, Towards a Community social action programme, X/417/73-E, Cambridge, 10 September 1973.
188. Economic and Social Committee, Opinion on a draft Council Resolution on a Social Action Programme, 74/C 37/09, Strasbourg, 29 November 1973; European Commission, Speech by P.J. Hillery, Vice-President of the Commission of the European Communities, to the Financial Times and Irish Times conference 'Europe after the Referendum', Does the Community need a social policy?, Dublin, 24 July 1975.
189. A. Müller-Armack, 'The Principles of the Social Market Economy' in *The Social Market Economy: Theory and Ethics of the Economic Order*, Springer, Berlin, 1998.
190. European policymaking in the labour area in fact reflected genuinely social principles, such as the requilibration of bargaining power between workers and principals and the decommodification of labour, as well as awareness for the importance of the smooth functioning of the market economy.
191. M. Albert, *Capitalism vs. Capitalism: How America's Obsession with Individual Achievement and Short-Term Profit Has Led It to the Brink of Collapse*, Four Wall Eight Windows, New York, 1993; European Commission, Speech by H. Vredeling, Vice-President of the Commission of the European Communities, to the London Europe Society and Confederation of British Industry, The Community role in the field of social and employment policy, London, 9 February 1979.
192. European Commission, 'The European Community's Social Policy', European Documentation, 1978/2, Brussels.

resulted in disruptive business restructurings[193] and worsened a situation already aggravated by global recession.[194]

This led EEC policymakers to strive for restoring more favourable market conditions (price stability, full employment and economic growth).[195] That being the priority, social and labour policies appeared to assume a new, different relevance. As Hillery – Commissioner for Social Affairs from 1973 to 1976 – argued, 'future social and economic policies must be closely linked if they are to be effective' as 'in general terms, the only sound framework for future social and economic progress must surely be based on the development of social institutions'.[196] Similarly, his successor Vredeling, maintained that labour policies should be developed in a way that takes more account of economic policy objectives, so as to foster economic growth in the Community.[197] The result was that the Community began to look at social and labour policy through the narrative of economic dynamism and competitiveness. This led, for instance, to consider for the first time the introduction of income guarantees and flexible labour contracts to support productivity and employability.[198] Perhaps not surprisingly, from the mid-1970s onwards references to upward social convergence and the realisation of social justice became rarer in the policy documents of the Commission. Labour and social policies were instead presented as somehow subordinate and functional to economic growth and competitiveness.

The transformed economic and social context and the need for adaptation of labour policies induced the Commission and the Council to adopt in 1984 a new Medium Term Social Action Programme.[199] Even if this programmatic document mentioned the importance to ensure high-quality working conditions, the tone and substance were remarkably different from the 1974-1976 Social Action Programme. This time the objective was to develop a strategy to revive the economy, although in a socially sustainable manner. The emphasis was placed on the importance to develop social and labour policy measures that are not only compatible with, but also supportive of economic targets. The salience of labour policies was thus mainly determined from a market perspective. For instance, the 1984 Action Programme recommended that national labour policies should be reformed to increase their

193. European Commission, Speech by H. Vredeling, Vice-President of the Commission of the European Communities, to the London Europe Society and Confederation of British Industry, The Community role in the field of social and employment policy, London, 9 February 1979.
194. European Commission, 'The European Community's Social Policy', European Documentation, 1978/2, Brussels.
195. European Commission, Speech by P.J. Hillery, Vice-President of the Commission of the European Communities, to the Royal Irish Academy, European social policies: problems and prospects, 98/75, Dublin, 28 April 1975; European Commission, Speech by P.J. Hillery, Vice-President of the Commission of the European Communities, to the Financial Times and Irish Times conference 'Europe after the Referendum', Does the Community need a social policy?, Dublin, 24 July 1975.
196. *Ibid.*
197. European Commission, Speech by H. Vredeling, Vice-President of the Commission of the European Communities, to the London Europe Society and Confederation of British Industry, The Community role in the field of social and employment policy, London, 9 February 1979.
198. *Ibid.*
199. European Council, Concerning a Community Medium Term Social Action Programme, 84/C 175/01, 22 June 1984.

efficiency and 'contribute to the strengthening of competitiveness of European economies in the face of international competition'.[200] Quite evidently, this approach valorised the economic dimension of labour law (expressed in the fundamental principle 3 presented in Chapter 1, section 2.1.3).[201] The same rhetoric is present also in the 1985 White Paper for completing the internal market adopted by the Delors Commission.[202] The White Paper announced the full liberalisation of the European economic space by the end of 1992 and, stated that the European Communities would substantially limit legislative interventions in the social and labour policy fields.[203] When, in 1986, the Single European Act (SEA) reformed the Rome Treaty, it basically transposed the White Paper into primary law and, while the advancement of the Economic and Monetary Union marked a further stage in the process of European integration, the Community's limited competences in social matters remained unaltered.

The parenthesis of upward harmonisation of labour standards that had characterised the second half of the 1970s was thus officially over.[204] The European Commission renounced to develop a concrete labour policy agenda at the European level.[205] The analysis of the policy documents adopted in the 1980s indicates that labour and social standards were predominantly approached through the lens of a market-oriented perspective, and depicted as a possible threat to optimal competition, especially in relation to the freedom to provide services.[206] Labour norms were appraised primarily in relation to their compatibility with the Community economic agenda, and not for their adequacy to realise social re-equilibration.[207]

As for the predominant normative model regarding labour law, its main function appeared to be that of adapting labour rights to the changing economic environment. The more market-oriented approach of the EC institutions was not (yet) reflected in an actual weakening of the existing body of labour law, neither at the European nor at the national level, which could preserve its emancipatory rationale. The main difference from the previous period is that this rationale is no longer actively pursued.

200. *Ibid.* The Council specified that in the labour policy field the European Community would only adopt harmonization instruments regarding occupation health and safety standards.
201. According to this fundamental principle workers' rights shall coexist with the market economy.
202. European Commission, Completing the Internal Market, White Paper, COM(85) 310 final, Brussels, 14 June 1985.
203. *Ibid.*, p. 19.
204. *See* judgment of 29 September 1987, *Giménez Zaera v. Instituto Nacional de la Seguridad Social and Tesorería General de la Seguridad Social*, C-126/86, ECLI:EU:C:1987:395 (para. 18): 'neither Article 2 or Article 117 and 118 of the EEC Treaty prevent the introduction by national legislation of a rule which prohibits the overlapping of a retirement pension with the emoluments due to a public servant and reduces the income of the pension concerned'.
205. European Commission, Completing the Internal Market, White Paper, COM(85) 310 final, Brussels, 14 June 1985, pp. 23, 25-30.
206. W. Sauter & H. Schepel, *State and Market in European Union Law: The Public and Private Spheres of the Internal Market Before the EU Courts*, Cambridge University Press, Leiden, 2009, pp. 2-26.
207. P. Syrpis, *EU Intervention in Domestic Labour Law*, Oxford University Press, Oxford, 2007, pp. 72-75; S. Giubboni, 'Social Rights and Market Freedom in the European Constitution: A Re-appraisal', European Labour Law Journal, 1(2), pp. 161-184, 2010.

2.4 Labour Policy Consolidates as a Dimension of the Internal Market

During the end of the 1980s and throughout the 1990s, the acceleration in the completion of the internal market brought about the consolidation of labour policy as a dimension of the Community's economic strategy. In policymaking documents, the adaptation of the labour legislation was consistently addressed as crucial for the deepening of the single market and for the realisation of a common monetary policy.[208] This clearly appears from the 1988 Working Paper on the social dimension of the Community,[209] where the Commission opened a reflection on the 'Social policy measures for the realisation of the internal market'. There, the Commission plainly stated that an effort to define a Community's social dimension would help maximise the economic gain of market integration.[210] There was no consideration for the protective function or of the function of raising the bargaining power of workers. Clearly, the economic component of labour law came first.

As in the previous years, arguments were made against the legislative pursuit of upwards harmonisation of labour standards. EU rule-makers feared that stricter labour rules would lead to less investment in Europe and at the same time would push companies to close or relocate. Basically, as the Commission put it, the concern was to prevent labour law from 'slowing down the completion of the market'.[211] This underlying approach could also be detected in the 1989 Community Charter of Fundamental Social Rights of Workers.[212] Formally, the main intent of the Charter was to ensure that the social and economic dimensions could develop in a balanced manner. It listed a series of workers' rights embodying a protecting function and an ideal of industrial democracy. However, it also clarified that labour rights should not hamper market integration and specified that 'the completion of the internal market is the most effective means of creating employment and ensuring maximum well-being in the Community' and that it 'is for the Community to take up the challenges of the future with regard to economic competitiveness'.[213] Moreover, the Charter was adopted as a non-binding instrument, lacking any enforcement mechanisms. The main policymaking initiative that followed the Charter, and that was geared towards its implementation, was a Social Action Programme (1989). Here too, there was no reference to measures that could actually strengthen working conditions.[214] Priority was rather given to the objectives of reaching a high employment level, and the emphasis was

208. N. Kyriazis, 'The Economic and Social Cohesion of the Community', Economic Series, European Parliament Directorate General for Research, Brussels, 1988.
209. European Commission, Social Dimension of the Internal Market, Working Paper, SEC (88) 1148 final, Brussels, 14 September 1988.
210. *Ibid.*, p. 6, 'the social dimension of the internal market must therefore help to maximize the gains derived from the single market, by helping of making full use of the human resources and preparing for changes which will come about'.
211. *Ibid.*, p. 7.
212. European Commission, Community Charter of Fundamental Social Rights, COM(89) 471 final, Brussels, 2 October 1989.
213. European Commission, Social Dimension of the Internal Market, Working Paper, SEC (88) 1148 final, Brussels, 14 September 1988.
214. B.A. Hepple, 'Fundamental Social Rights Since the Lisbon Treaty', European Labour Law Journal, 2(2), pp. 150-154, 2011.

again placed on the functioning of the labour market and supporting firms' competitiveness.[215] One of the few (non-legislative) initiatives thereby announced was the promotion of the convergence of objectives of national social security systems, with the aim of reducing the obstacles to free movements.

Then, in 1992, the adoption of the Maastricht Treaty extended the Union's competences in the social policy area and, at the same time, reinforced the overall progress towards the Economic and Monetary Union. The more central role that social concerns had acquired in EU primary law was again rooted in an understanding of social and labour matters as functional to the realisation of economic growth. In the same year, in fact, the Commission published a Green Paper on European Social Policy, where the advancement of social standards was addressed purely from a market-oriented perspective.[216] Quite openly, the Commission stated that 'high social standards are a vital part of building a competitive economy'.[217]

The new Medium Term Social Action Programme 1995-1997 continued in the same direction, by creating stronger links between employment policies and the Union's growth strategy. In the Social Action Programme, the Commission advocated stronger coordination of national policies to promote the flexibilisation of the labour market.[218] This implied the establishment of a common set of minimum standards in areas such as part-time, fixed-term and temporary work, individual dismissal and working time. In this period, the EU also turned to the mechanisms of 'soft law' or 'governance' to intervene in the national labour policy area. These mechanisms consisted of institutional processes for the coordination and monitoring of national policies. In contrast to the bland convergence objectives that had characterised the early stages of the European Community, these surveillance mechanisms were now rather stringent. The main objective was to direct national governments towards the progressive flexibilisation of workers' protection legislation.

The emergence of these governance processes corresponded to a new, critical trend concerning labour policies. On the one hand, the Union supported those national reforms aimed at 'softening' employment protections and creating a more flexible and inclusive labour market.[219] On the other hand, the EU rule-makers did not develop adequate social re-equilibration mechanisms to counterbalance this deregulatory

215. European Commission, Communication on the action programme relating to the implementation of the Community Charter of Basic Social Rights for Workers, COM(89) 568 final, Brussels, 29 November 1989, p. 6.
216. European Commission, Green Paper – European Social Policy, Options for the Future, COM(93) 551, Brussels, 17 November 1993.
217. *Ibid.*
218. European Commission, Medium Term Social Action Programme 1995-1997, COM(95) 134 final, Brussels, 12 April 1995.
219. R. Blanpain, 'The European Social Model (ESM): Myth or Reality?', European Labour Law Journal, 2(2), pp. 142-149, 2011; O. Oladeinde, 'Global Capitalism and Rise of Non-standard Employment: Challenges to Industrial Relations' in R. Blanpain (ed.), *The Global Labour Market: From Globalization to Flexicurity*, Wolters Kluwer, Alphen aan den Rijn, 2008, pp. 53-61; F. Hendrickx, S. Giubboni, 'European Union Labour Law and the European Social Model: A Critical Appraisal' in M.W. Finkin and G. Mundlak (eds), *Comparative Labour Law*, Edward Elgar Publishing, Cheltenham, 2015, pp. 379-402.

wave.[220] This approach was nevertheless further institutionalised in the Amsterdam Treaty[221] and with the launch of the Luxembourg process in 2000.[222] Central to the Luxemburg strategy was the so-called Open method of coordination (OMC),[223] consisting of institutionalised exchanges between EU and Member States' officials in view to assist national legislators in modernising their labour policies.[224] Through the social OMC, national governments were provided with guidelines, benchmarks, and best practices, in order to realise the social objectives defined by the Union.[225]

It was in this context that the Commission developed the 'flexicurity' agenda.[226] As mentioned in Chapter 1 section 2.2.4, the flexicurity model sought to ensure that labour law could adapt to the growth objectives while ensuring high social welfare standards.[227] Part of the strategy was to make the labour market more accessible, so as to attract those who traditionally are outsiders. To achieve this, employment protection legislation had to be relaxed; EU lawmakers thus supported a distancing of labour law from its original emancipatory component.[228] The social rationale originally pervading labour norms was reallocated (more or less effectively) to other policy areas, i.e., welfare systems.[229]

It is in those years, that the flexicurity strategy compromised labour law capacity to reflect fundamental principles 1 (repairing the bargaining gap) and 2 (labour law is

220. M. Daly, 'The Dynamics of European Union Social Policy' in N. Lendvai-Bainton (ed.), *Handbook of European Social Policy*, Edward Elgar Publishing, Cheltenham, 2017, pp. 93-107.
221. Title VII of the TEC following the reform brought by the Treaty of Amsterdam.
222. European Council, Presidency Conclusions, Lisbon strategy, Lisbon, 23 March 2000.
223. B. ter Haar, 'Open Method of Coordination: A New Stepping Stone in the Legal Order of International and European Relations', Nordin Journal of International Law, 77(3), pp. 235-251, 2008; M. De Vos, 'Flexicurity and the European Globalisation Adjustment Fund: Propaganda or Panacea?' in M. de Vos (ed.), *European Union Internal Market and Labour Law: Friends or Foes?*, Intersentia, Cambridge, 2009, pp. 105-133.
224. European Commission, Medium Term Social Action Programme 1995-1997, COM(95) 134 final, Brussels, 12 April 1995, p. 7.
225. Policy coordination in the field of employment was introduced by the Treaty of Amsterdam, in the context of the European Employment Strategy, currently in Title IX TFEU.
226. S. O'Leary, *Employment Law at the European Court of Justice: Judicial Structures, Policies, and Processes*, Hart Publishing, Oxford, 2002, p. 126; S. Deakin & H. Reed, 'The Contested Meaning of Labour Market Flexibility: Economic Theory and the Discourse of European Integration' in J. Shaw (ed.), *Social Law and Policy in an Evolving European Union*, Hart Publishing, London, 2000, pp. 71-100; C. Barnard, 'EU Employment law and the European Social Model: The Past, the Present and the Future', Current Legal Problems, 67, pp. 199-237, 2014.
227. European Commission, Towards Common Principles of Flexicurity: More and Better Jobs Through Flexicurity and Security, Communication, COM(2007) 359 final, Brussels, 27 June 2007; N. Zekic, 'Job Security or Employment Security: What's in a Name', European Labour Law Journal, 7(4), pp. 548-575, 2016; A.C.J.M. Wilthagen, 'Flexicurity Pathways: Turning Hurdles into Stepping-Stones', Expert Report for the European Commission, Tilburg Flexicurity Research Programme, Tilburg, 2007.
228. N. Zekic, 'Job Security or Employment Security: What's in a Name', European Labour Law Journal, 7(4), pp. 548-575, 2016, where it was noted that the flexicurity paradigm overlooked the importance of legal instruments providing job security (i.e., dismissal law) in order to ensure fairness in the labour market; P. Syrpis, *EU Intervention in Domestic Labour Law*, Oxford University Press, Oxford, 2007, p. 136.
229. L. Burroni & M. Keune, 'Flexicurity: A Conceptual Critique', European Journal of Industrial Relations, 17(1), pp. 75-91, 2011.

not a commodity).[230] By favouring the economic rationale over the emancipatory one, the EU thus favoured a transformation process of the actual nature of labour law, resulting in the erosion of its emancipatory component.[231]

2.5 The Role of Labour Law in the Modern 'Social Market Economy'

The years 2000-2010 were particularly intense for the institutional and constitutional development of European integration. One can think of the 2000 Nice Charter on Fundamental Rights (hereinafter 'CFREU'), the enlargement of the Union towards the East, the failed attempt to ratify the Treaty establishing a Constitution for Europe, the adoption of the Lisbon Treaty and the attribution of binding legal force to the CFREU. Much has been written about the potential implications of these developments for the social dimension of the Union.[232] This section focuses mainly on the policy documents that have been directly addressing EU labour policy. In this regard, it is important to observe that, despite the constitutional maturation of the Union and the greater valorisation of social values in the Treaties, the overall approach to labour law did not change. EU policymakers continued to 'normalise' the role of labour policies as a variable of economic growth and to pursue the flexicurity paradigm by means of governance instruments.[233] In other words, the Union continued to promote the transformation of labour law, to the detriment of its original emancipatory nature.

In 2000, at the Lisbon European Council, the heads of state and government agreed to a new political agenda (the Lisbon Strategy) whose aim was to transform the EU into 'the most competitive and dynamic knowledge-based economy in the world capable of sustainable economic growth with more and better jobs and greater social cohesion'.[234] Ambitious employment and poverty eradication targets were set, for the achievement of which the flexicurity paradigm was central.[235] In section 2.4 above it was explained that the flexibilisation of employment protection was a central point of the flexicurity agenda. It was also mentioned that, despite the ambitious social

230. Chapter 1, sections 2.1.1 and 2.1.2.
231. N. Bruun, 'The Old and New Foundations of Labour Law' in K. Ahlberg and N. Bruun (eds), *The New Foundations of Labour Law*, Peter Lang, Frankfurt am Main, 2017, pp. 17-27, p. 26.
232. *Inter alia*, A. Jacobs, 'The Janus Head of the European Union: The Social Market Economy Versus Ultraliberal Policies' in J. Wouters, L. Verhey & P. Kiiver (eds), *European Constitutionalism Beyond Lisbon*, Intersentia, 2009; S. Deakin, 'In Search of the EU's Social Constitution: Using the Charter to Recalibrate Social and Economic Rights' in F. Dorssemont, K. Lörcher, S. Clauwaert & M. Schmitt (eds), Hart Publishing, 2019, pp. 53-80; O. De Schutter, 'The CFREU and Its Specific Role to Protect Fundamental Social Rights' in F. Dorssemont, K. Lörcher, S. Clauwaert & M. Schmitt (eds), Hart Publishing, 2019, pp. 9-38.
233. N. Zekic, 'Job Security or Employment Security: What's in a Name', European Labour Law Journal, 7(4), pp. 548-575, 2016; S. Bekker, 'Flexicurity in the European Semester: Still a Relevant Policy Concept?', Journal of European Public Policy, 25(2), pp. 175-192, 2018.
234. European Council, Presidency Conclusions, Lisbon strategy, Lisbon strategy, Lisbon, 23 March 2000.
235. *Ibid.*

objectives, EU policymaking promoted a deregulatory effect on national labour systems, not offset by an equal valorisation of social policies.[236]

In an attempt to remedy the initial underwhelming results, in 2005, the Lisbon Strategy was re-energised. The European Commission and the Council adopted a new set of integrated economic and employment guidelines deemed to inform the whole EU as well as national agendas.[237] The effect was to reinforce the tie between employment policies and macroeconomic objectives. The employment guidelines thus streamlined policy objectives responding to the flexicurity agenda, such as the 'modernisation' of employment contracts, the reduction of fiscal, administrative and labour burdens on business and the adaptation of social welfare systems.[238] The economic rationale was by far predominant also across other EU policy documents. The 2006 Green Paper on 'Modernising Labour Law to Meet the Challenges of the 21st Century' addressed labour policies predominantly in terms of an economic factor.[239] Similarly, in the 2010 Communication 'Towards a single market act for a highly competitive social market economy', the Commission stated that a 'highly competitive social market economy [...] requires us to adopt a more all-embracing view of the single market by putting business and Europeans back at the heart of the single market in order to restore confidence'.[240]

Curiously, however, a novelty was introduced in relation to the vocabulary of EU institutional documents addressing the social dimension of European integration.[241] Significant rhetorical emphasis was now placed on social policies as central to the growth strategy of the Union. More media exposure was in fact given to social themes and social objectives. A significant example is the appearance of the notion of 'social market economy' in the institutional vocabulary of the Union.[242] As explained in

236. The Lisbon Strategy aimed at raising the employment rate in the 15-64 age group from an average of 61% to 70% by 2010. Employment rate objective in the Lisbon Strategy; S. Rainone & A. Aloisi, 'Time to Deliver? Assessing the Action Plan on the European Pillar of Social Rights', Policy Brief, ETUI, Brussels, 2021.
237. European Commission, Integrated Guidelines for Growth and Jobs (2005-2008), Communication, COM(2005) 141 final, Brussels, 12 April 2005.
238. *Ibid.*, 'The modernisation of social protection systems is also necessary to ensure their adequacy, financial sustainability and responsiveness to changing needs in society and to support lasting economic and employment growth.'
239. European Commission, Modernising Labour Law to Meet the Challenges of the 21st Century, COM(2006) 708 final, Brussels, 22 November 2006.
240. European Commission, Towards a Single Market Act for a Highly Competitive Social Market Economy (50 Proposals for Improving our Work, Business and Exchange with One Another), Communication, COM(2010) 608 final, Brussels, 27 October 2010: 'By availing of non-standard contractual arrangements, businesses seek to remain competitive in the globalised economy by avoiding inter alia the cost of compliance with employment protection rules, notice periods and the costs of associated social security contributions.'
241. European Commission, The Social Dimension of Globalisation – The EU's Policy Contribution on extending the benefits to all, Communication, COM(2004) 383 final, Brussels, 18 May 2004; European Commission, Strengthening the Social Dimension of the Economic and Monetary Union, Communication, COM(2013) 690 final, Brussels, 2 October 2013; European Commission, Towards a Single Market Act for a Highly Competitive Social Market Economy (50 Proposals for Improving our Work, Business and Exchange with One Another), Communication, COM(2010) 608 final, Brussels, 27 October 2010.
242. European Commission, Towards a Single Market Act for a Highly Competitive Social Market Economy (50 Proposals for Improving our Work, Business and Exchange with One Another),

sections 2.1 and 2.2, 'social market economy' refers to a socioeconomic model whereby the economic agenda is accompanied by regulatory initiatives in the social and labour policy areas, designed to counterbalance the social consequences of the expansion of the market economy.[243] However, as mentioned, EU policymaking failed at valorising social re-equilibration policies that could compensate for the weakening of the emancipatory effect of labour law.[244] Nevertheless, the reference to 'social market economy' in the Commission documents gave the (misleading) impression of an overall greater focus on the social dimension.

The economic underpinning of EU labour policies became even more pronounced following the Euro crisis of 2011. The EU policymakers reacted to the economic recession by adopting the Europe 2020 agenda (which substituted the Lisbon strategy), which strengthened European governance mechanisms, and by launching the so-called European Semester.[245] The European Semester is a governance (or soft law) process consisting of an institutionalised dialogue between the EU executive (the Commission and the Council) and national governments. Through the European Semester, the Union intended to achieve the goals set in the Europe 2020 macroeconomic agenda, where labour law was, once again, presented as a mere variable of the economic strategy.[246] The overall objective was to push national governments to undertake reforms to reduce public debt and lower labour costs while supporting businesses and productivity.[247] The sense of urgency caused by the Euro crisis had indeed caused the neoliberal narrative to gain more ground.[248] This led to further marginalisation of the social and emancipatory scope of labour law.[249] Moreover, unlike the OMC, the European Semester was endowed with a more stringent and pervasive force, as it was associated with possible punitive repercussions, especially for those Member States that had availed of bail-out programmes.[250]

Communication, COM(2010) 608 final, Brussels, 27 October 2010; A. Jacobs, 'The Janus Head of the European Union: The Social Market Economy Versus Ultraliberal Policies' in J. Wouters, L. Verhey & P. Kiiver (eds), *European Constitutionalism Beyond Lisbon*, Intersentia, 2009.

243. A. Müller-Armack, 'The Principles of the Social Market Economy' in *The Social Market Economy: Theory and Ethics of the Economic Order*, Springer, Berlin, 1998, *see* above section 2.1.
244. *See* section 2.4.
245. European Commission, Europe 2020: A Strategy for Smart, Sustainable and Inclusive Growth, COM(2010) 2020, Brussels, 3 March 2010.
246. M.S. Houwerzijl & T. Wilkinson, 'The Effects of EU Law on the Social and Economic Goals of Europe 2020: A Decision Theoretic Approach to Wage Liability Regimes in Modern Europe', German Law Journal, 14(10), pp. 1981-2001, 2013; P. Schoukens & J.B. Smets, 'Fighting Social Exclusion under EU Horizon 2020: Enhancing the Legal Enforceability of the Social Inclusion Recommendations?', European Journal of Social Security, 16(1), pp. 51-72, 2014.
247. C. Degryse, 'The New European Economic Governance', Working Paper, 14, ETUI, Brussels, 2012.
248. F. Costamagna, 'National Social Spaces as Adjustment Variables in the EMU: A Critical Legal Appraisal', European Law Journal, 23(2), pp. 163-190, 2018; C. Degryse, M. Jepsen & P. Pochet, 'The Eurocrisis and Its Impact on National and European Social Policies', Working Paper, 5, ETUI, Brussels, 2013.
249. S. Giubboni, 'The Rise and Fall of EU Labour Law', European Law Journal, 24(1), pp. 7-20, 2018.
250. C. Degryse, 'The New European Economic Governance', Working Paper, 14, ETUI, Brussels, 2012; and Clauwaert; M.S. Houwerzijl & T. Wilkinson, 'The Effects of EU Law on the Social and

It goes without saying that neither the protective function of labour law nor that of lifting the workers' bargaining position was reflected in EU policymaking. The same applies also to the third original function of labour law, that of reconciling social and economic interests. The balance appears too in favour of the economic dimension. Instead of exploring ways to readjust labour standards to the changing economic environment, the EU official documents reflect the perceptions that protective employment standards are incompatible with economic goals. Hence, they are addressed as mere economic factors and as costs. In this period, the erosion of the emancipatory rationale of labour law undoubtedly accelerated, leading to a transformation in the nature of labour law.

2.6 EU Social Policy in Time of Economic Crisis

The legacy of the Euro crisis was a prolonged period of economic stagnation, rising unemployment and worsening social exclusion. In this context, the Juncker Commission (2014-2019) promoted a new growth-enhancing strategy, whose social dimension would eventually be expressed by the EPSR.

2.6.1 The EU Strategy for a Deeper EMU

In 2012, four years after the financial crisis unfolded, the Commission issued its Communication on 'A Blueprint for a Deep and Genuine Economic and Monetary Union', where it identified the lasting effects of the financial crisis on the economic, social, and political stability of the EU.[251] The backlash of the 2008 and 2011 crises revealed that the weakness of the national economies and national labour markets had contagious effects across the entire EU.[252] This Communication pointed out that economic challenges and declining competitiveness called for intensified efforts to make progress in deepening the European Monetary Union (EMU).

The choice to address the crisis by focusing on advancing in the EMU was grounded on a specific growth-centred socioeconomic model. Deepening the EMU implied the enhancement of the European market economy, to consent businesses to thrive. This would also bring a substantial tax return which was believed to provide for well-functioning welfare systems, ultimately allowing a fair redistribution of wealth.[253]

Economic Goals of Europe 2020: A Decision Theoretic Approach to Wage Liability Regimes in Modern Europe', German Law Journal, 14(10), pp. 1981-2001, 2013; S. Clauwaert & I. Schömann, 'The Crisis and National Labour Law Reforms: A Mapping Exercise', Working Paper, 4, ETUI, Brussels, 2012.

251. European Commission, A Blueprint for a Deep and Genuine Economic and Monetary Union, COM(2012) 777 final, Brussels, 28 November 2012.
252. European Council, Report, Towards a Genuine Economic and Monetary Union ('The Four Presidents' Report'), in close collaboration with: José Manuel Barroso, President of the European Commission, Jean-Claude Juncker, President of the Eurogroup, Mario Draghi, President of the European Central Bank, Brussels, 5 December 2012.
253. M. Dawson, 'New Governance and the Displacement of Social Europe: The Case of the European Semester', European Constitutional Law Review, 14(1), pp. 191-209, 2018; C. Joerges & F. Roedl, 'The "Social Market Economy" as Europe's Social Model?', Working Paper,

Once determined that the priority was to reinforce the EMU, it was necessary to elaborate a programme to achieve that goal. In a 2012 Communication, the Commission thus called for a strategy to increase the EU's control on national economic and employment policies, with the precise objective to support growth-enhancing structural reforms.[254] The direction outlined in the 2012 Commission Communication was further developed in the 2012 Four Presidents' Report. There, the presidents of the European Council, the Commission, the Eurogroup and the European Central Bank (ECB) committed to the realisation of a stronger EMU based on a renewed convergence of national policies.[255] The Report stressed that the financial crisis had revealed serious weaknesses on different grounds, imposing action on four fronts: the establishment of a financial framework, the creation of a fiscal framework, the consolidation of EU economic policy integration, and stronger democratisation to improve the legitimacy and the accountability of EU policymaking.[256]

In 2015, the Five Presidents' Report further validated the direction defined in the 2012 Report and restated the commitment to strengthen the EMU through a multifaceted approach.[257] It confirmed initiatives in the financial, fiscal, economic, and political dimensions.[258] Compared to its 2012 predecessor, the Five Presidents' Report provided a more detailed strategy, as it presented a structured overview of the different initiatives to implement. The 2015 Report indicated that, in the context of the economic component of the agenda for a deeper EMU, the EU action should be based on a four-pillar strategy. These were the following:

European University Institute, Florence, 2004, where it is argued that EU socioeconomic model is coherent with the ordoliberal economic constitutional theory, that – in the view of the authors – might lead Europe to become a market without state, grounded on an economic constitution which poses constraints to political discretion and is persistently devoted to guarantee economic freedoms.

254. European Commission, A Blueprint for a Deep and Genuine Economic and Monetary Union, COM(2012) 777 final, Brussels, 28 November 2012.

255. European Council, Report, Towards a Genuine Economic and Monetary Union ('The Four Presidents' Report'), in close collaboration with: José Manuel Barroso, President of the European Commission, Jean-Claude Juncker, President of the Eurogroup, Mario Draghi, President of the European Central Bank, Brussels, 5 December 2012. The Four Presidents' Report set a rather ambitious timeline. The short-term plan was to improve the existing governance tools, with the effect of making national policies surveillance more effective and steering competitiveness. In the medium term (before 2017), the intention was to foster the EU integration in the taxation and employment fields. The long-term objective was identified with the establishment of a proper fiscal capacity and banking Union, allowing common issuance of public debt.

256. *Ibid.*, p. 3.

257. European Commission, Report, Completing Europe's Economic and Monetary Union ('The Five Presidents' Report'), In close cooperation with Donald Tusk (President of the European Council), Jeroen Dijsselbloem (President of the Eurogroup), Mario Draghi (President of the European Central Bank), and Martin Schulz (President of the European Parliament), Brussels, 22 June 2015.

258. *Ibid.* The Five Presidents' Report corrected the timeframe, while confirming the two-stage implementation process. Stage 1 (2015-2017) was conceived as dedicated to improving competitiveness, economic convergence and the completion of the fiscal Union. This was to be achieved on the base of the existing instruments. Stage 2 was deemed to focus on the completion of the EMU's economic and institutional architecture, through conferring binding legal nature to a set of benchmarks and convergence thresholds. The achievement of a genuine EMU was then foreseen for 2025.

(1) the creation of a Euro-system of competitiveness authorities;
(2) a strengthened implementation of the Macroeconomic Imbalance Procedure;
(3) a greater focus on employment and social performance; and
(4) a greater focus on stronger coordination of economic policies within a revamped European Semester.[259]

The inclusion of a social 'pillar' (pillar 3) is indicative of the holistic nature of the EU growth strategy.[260] Also, it is in that third pillar that the genesis of the future EPSR can be retraced. The policymaking process that led to the adoption of the EPSR is thus an expression of a political vision whereby labour law is perceived as a structural component of the EU growth-enhancing strategy.[261] These premises are in continuity with the prevalent policymaking approach, entailing the promotion of the economic underpinning of labour law over the emancipatory one.

2.6.2 *'Social Triple A' as an Economic Necessity*

The presence of social and employment dimensions in the 2015 Report reflected the same utilitarian approach towards social and labour policies that for decades had characterised the Commission's initiatives. The underlying narrative was that global

259. *Ibid.*, p. 7.

260. Besides the presence of a dedicated social pillar, it is interesting to note that the relevance of labour and social policies also emerges in the fiscal component of the EMU-deepening strategy. In that context, reinforcing the EU budgetary framework is deemed necessary to ensure sustainable and sound fiscal policymaking and to allow forms of fiscal solidarity across the EU in the direction of future common debt issuance. Quite interestingly from a labour and social policy perspective, the hypothesis of an EU unemployment insurance system was also advanced. Such system was presented as a possible way to increase budgetary solidarity within the EU: following the creation of a dedicated reserve, it would consent to link the transfer of national budgets to unemployment rates that, in turn, are indicative of a country's economic situation. *See also* European Council, The Four Presidents' Report, 2012, p. 11, which more precisely indicates that 'in this case, the level of contributions/benefits from/to the fiscal capacity would depend directly on labour market developments. In this scenario, the fiscal capacity would then work as a complement or partial substitute to national unemployment insurance system. Transfers could, for example, be limited to cyclical unemployment by covering only short-term unemployment'. The idea is to activate the unemployment related transfers only once the increase in short-term unemployment exceeds a certain threshold.

261. *See*, for instance, European Council, The Four Presidents' Report, 2012, p. 13: '[I]t is essential to complete the Single Market as it provides a powerful tool to promote growth. In addition, there is a need for a thorough assessment of the performance of labour and product markets in the euro area. [...] A well-functioning EMU requires efficient labour and product market'. Giubboni provides a very punctual analysis in S. Giubboni, 'The Rise and Fall of EU Labour Law', European Law Journal, 24(1), pp. 7-20, 2018. A similar stance is taken in C. Barnard, 'Internal Market v Labour Market: A Brief History' in M. de Vos (ed.), *European Union Internal Market and Labour Law: Friends or Foes?*, Intersentia, Cambridge, 2009, pp. 19-45. For a broader historical contextualisation of the function of social policy not only as a factor of protection but also as a way to promote growth *see* A. Neal, 'Comparative Labour Law and Industrial Relations: "A Major Discipline? – Who Cares?"' in R. Blanpain, C. Engels, M. Weiss & B. Aaron (eds), *Labour Law and Industrial Relations at the Turn of the Century: Liber Amicorum in Honour of Roger Blanpain*, Kluwer Law International, The Hague, 1998.

economic competition is mostly based on productivity rates and imposes an overreaching market rationale. This, in turn, demands highly inclusive and flexible labour markets as well as a well-trained and possibly cheap workforce.[262] A dynamic and adaptable workforce is an attractive factor for investments, allows firms to thrive, and leads to elevated employment rates. On the contrary, high levels of unemployment generally indicate that labour markets are embedded in regulatory rigidities (both regarding access to and exit from the labour market), creating an environment that is unfavourable to economic growth and productivity. While this link between employment protection standards, employment rates and economic growth has been challenged by empirical studies, it clearly influenced the inception of the EPSR.[263]

Labour standards were deemed to be essential as long as they can promote economic growth. By means of a 'social pillar', the EU rule-makers intended to adopt a policymaking compass to guide the adaptation of (national) labour and social policies.[264] As clearly expressed in the 2015 Report wording: 'Europe's ambition should be to earn a "social triple A". This is also an economic necessity. For EMU to succeed, labour markets and welfare systems need to function well and in a fair manner in all euro area Member States'.[265]

This narrative is not new. Differently from the past, however, now the EU intended to intervene in a more active manner in shaping national and EU labour and social policies. Looking more closely at the 2012 Communication and the 2012 and 2015 Reports, it is possible to identify two main justifications underpinning the renewed policymaking interest in social and labour standards. The first is to address in a consistent and more pervasive manner the normative barriers that prevent firms from being competitive on the market.[266] A specific example of this approach is the creation

262. European Commission, The Five Presidents' Report, 2015, p. 8: 'For EMU to succeed, labour markets and welfare systems need to function well and in a fair manner in all euro area Member States.'
263. A. Piasna & M.R. Myant (eds), *Myths of Employment Deregulation: How It Neither Creates Jobs Nor Reduces Labour Market Segmentation*, ETUI, Brussels, 2017. The authors conducted an empirical study which challenges the assumption that reduction of employment protection leads to job creation and decrease in labour market segmentation.
264. *See* the analysis of the social dimension of EU governance in M. Dawson, 'New Governance and the Displacement of Social Europe: The Case of the European Semester', European Constitutional Law Review, 14(1), pp. 191-209, 2018.
265. European Commission, The Five Presidents' Report, 2015, p. 8: 'For EMU to succeed, labour markets and welfare systems need to function well and in a fair manner in all euro area Member States.'
266. European Commission, Preparing for Next Steps on Better Economic Governance in the Euro Area, In close cooperation with Donald Tusk, Jeroen Dijsselbloem and Mario Draghi, 12 February 2015; P. Syrpis, *EU Intervention in Domestic Labour Law*, Oxford University Press, Oxford, 2007, pp. 13-49. Syrpis identifies an integrationalist rationale in the EU approach to labour law, whereby domestic labour provisions are taken down by the 'negative integration strategy' of the Court of Justice. Such approach has been explicitly endorsed by the European Commission, Completing the Internal Market, White Paper, COM(85) 310 final, Brussels, 14 June 1985. In particular, Syrpis argues that the negative integration technique is quite efficient in removing normative obstacle to economic freedoms, since targets those national (labour) measures which obstruct the functioning of the internal market.

of a European system of competitiveness boards, outlined in the Four and the Five Presidents' Reports. These national competitiveness authorities have the mandate to bolster productivity-driven reforms by advising national policymakers on labour market policies and wage-setting, with the specific goal to reduce labour rigidities.[267]

The second justification of the revamped EU strategy with regard to labour and social policies was connected with the promotion of deeper harmonisation of the national legal systems. On the one hand, this is important from an internal market perspective.[268] The coexistence of different regulatory regimes within the Union was perceived as an obstacle to economic cohesion and as one of the causes of (de)regulatory competition-based social standards.[269] On the other hand, convergence of labour standards is also a means to promote better working conditions, and it can be seen as a positive step for the re-emersion of the social dimension of EU labour policies.

It is worth noting that to implement the social policy competent of growth strategy outlined in the Four and Five President reports, the ideal way forward would be to adopt new EU legislation in the labour and social fields. However, the limited EU competences and the unanimity voting rule that apply to the Social Policy Title of the TFEU represented a barrier to a substantive expansion of the EU *acquis* in the area. Due to this bottleneck, the Commission's Communication and the Presidents' Reports turned to the European Semester to further develop the social and labour component of the EU economic and growth strategy. In 2015, it was thus decided that the cycle of

267. The instrument to improve the convergence in national competitiveness was identified in the creation of a system of competitiveness authorities (in the 2015 Five Presidents' Report) and was implemented through a Council of the European Union, Recommendation on the establishment of National Productivity Boards, 2016/C 349/01, Brussels, 20 September 2016. European Commission, The Five Presidents' Report, 2015, p. 8: indicated that '[Productivity Boards] would help to prevent economic divergence and would increase ownership of the necessary reforms at the national level. These [Productivity Boards] should be independent entities with a mandate to assess whether wages ae evolving in line with productivity and compare with developments in other Euro area countries and in the main comparable trading countries. [...] In the end, a competitive economy is one in which institutions and policies allow productive firms to thrive. In turn, the development of these firms supports the expansion of employment, investment and trade.' Similarly, the Council of the European Union, Recommendation on the establishment of National Productivity Boards, 2016/C 349/01, Brussels, 20 September 2016 refers to the objective of raising productivity as 'a multifaceted challenge which requires a set of well-balanced policies aimed at, in particular [...] reducing rigidities in the labour market'.
268. European Commission, Strengthening the Social Dimension of the Economic and Monetary Union, Communication, COM(2013) 690 final, Brussels, 2 October 2013, p. 13, where the Commission indicates that 'The recent changes to strengthen EU economic governance aim to reinforce the MEU, address some of the initial weaknesses of its design and make it more competitive and able to promote growth. In the Commission's view, developing the social dimension of EMU is an essential part of this process. [...] A well-functioning monetary union requires flexible markets and appropriate institutions to address the social situation and provide adequate safety nets.'
269. As an example, it is useful to refer to the European Commission, Memorandum on Directive on Transparent and Predictable Working Conditions, establishing EU rules on the extension of social and labour protection to casual workers and other forms of atypical workers, COM(2017) 797 final, Brussels, 21 December 2017. Among the reasons for the adoption of EU rules the Commission indicated that the fragmented regulatory framework was associated with unsustainable pressure for firms, as well as with untenable fiscal consequences for the Member States' public finance.

policy coordination and surveillance that takes place within the framework of the European Semester had to absorb more prominently social and labour policy objectives.[270] This led to the addition of a social inclusion objective among the employment guidelines.[271] At the same time, the Commission encouraged a more active participation of social policy actors (social partners) throughout the Semester process.[272]

All in all, the EU policymaking from 2012 to 2015 makes it rather clear that the EU social and employment agenda aimed at promoting the convergence of national policies and tackling labour market rigidities. It is in this period that the origins of the EPSR can be traced, as suggested by an explicit reference in the 2015 Report to a pillar ensuring 'greater focus on employment and social performance' as part of the EU strategy to complete the EMU. It was noted that the adoption of the Pillar can be interpreted as a positive sign for the revitalisation of the EU social dimension. At the same time, however, the EPSR was conceived in the context of the growth-enhancing agenda that was developed in order to create the right conditions for the deepening of the EMU.[273] Thus, despite more openness towards the pursuit of social justice values, there is a certain continuity in the approach to labour law.

270. Presidency of the Council of the European Union, European Semester 2015: Contribution to the European Council (25-26 June), 9304/15, Brussels, 10 June 2015.
271. For a deeper understanding on how the social policy guidelines are currently strongly tied to the economic targets that the European Semester aims to achieve, *see* P. Schoukens & J.B. Smets, 'Fighting Social Exclusion under EU Horizon 2020. Enhancing the Legal Enforceability of the Social Inclusion Recommendations?', European Journal of Social Security, 16(1), pp. 51-72, 2014, where the authors provide an assessment of the implementation, within the European Semester process, of the employment guideline n. 10 on social inclusion. It is argued that the social inclusion guideline is conceived as narrowly connected to rates of employment and the functioning of the labour market, which, in turn, have a strong impact on the prevention of macroeconomic unbalances.
272. European Commission, Strengthening the Social Dimension of the Economic and Monetary Union, Communication, COM(2013) 690 final, Brussels, 2 October 2013, p. 14: 'There is scope to strengthen the social dimension of EMU by better coordinating and monitoring employment and social policies and developments as part of the European Semester process, mobilising and targeting action and funds to better address social distress, removing the barriers to cross-border labour mobility within the EU and boosting the role of social dialogue.' Interestingly, in relation to the increased emphasis on social dialogue, in European Commission, New start for social dialogue – one year on, MEMO/16/823, Brussels, 16 March 2016, it is contended that social dialogue has a positive role on a country's economy. C. Welz, 'From Val Duchesse to Riga: How to Relaunch Social Dialogue?', Social Europe, 2015, https://socialeurope.eu/val-duchesse-riga-relaunch-social-dialogue. *See* European Commission, The Five Presidents' Report, 2015, p. 8: 'Employment and social concerns must feature highly in the European Semester'; European Commission, COM(2013) 690 final, 2013, p. 27: 'Coordination and surveillance of employment and social policies should be reinforced within the EMU governance, and convergence promoted in those areas. The current Broad Economic Policy Guidelines and Employment Guidelines could be reinforced by merging them into a single instrument.'
273. K. Lörcher & I. Schömann, 'The European Pillar of Social Rights: Critical Legal Analysis and Proposals', Report, 139, ETUI, Brussels, 2016.

3 THE EPSR: A PARADIGM SHIFT?

The proclamation of the EPSR brought a renewed emphasis on the social dimension of the Union. The Juncker Commission considered the EPSR one of the main achievements of its social agenda since it led to the establishment of the European Labour Authority (ELA), the revision of the Posting of Workers Directive, the adoption of the Directive on Work-Life Balance and the Directive on Transparent and Predictable Working Conditions.[274]

The Von der Leyen Commission confirmed the commitment to develop the EU social outlook further and to place the EPSR at the core of the social agenda.[275] This resulted in the drafting of progressive legislative proposals, such as a directive on minimum wages, a directive addressing the wage gap between men and women as well as one on the working conditions of platform workers.[276] It is therefore worth reflecting

274. Regulation (EU) 2019/1149 of the European Parliament and of the Council of 20 June 2019 establishing a European Labour Authority, amending Regulations (EC) No 883/2004 (EU) No 492/2011, and (EU) 2016/589 and repealing Decision (EU) 2016/344 (Text with relevance for the EEA and for Switzerland) PE/49/2019/REV/1 *OJ L 186, 11.7.2019, pp. 21-56;* Directive (EU) 2018/957 of the European Parliament and of the Council of 28 June 2018 amending Directive 96/71/EC concerning the posting of workers in the framework of the provision of services (Text with EEA relevance) PE/18/2018/REV/1 *OJ L 173, 9.7.2018, pp. 16-24*; Directive (EU) 2019/1158 of the European Parliament and of the Council of 20 June 2019 on work-life balance for parents and carers and repealing Council Directive 2010/18/EU PE/20/2019/REV/1 *OJ L 188, 12.7.2019, pp. 79-93*; Directive (EU) 2019/1152 of the European Parliament and of the Council of 20 June 2019 on transparent and predictable working conditions in the European Union PE/43/2019/REV/1 *OJ L 186, 11.7.2019, pp. 105-121*. The EPSR was presented as a very ambitious social initiative during different official events. For instance: European Commission, Speech by Thyssen, European Commissioner for Eurostat and Employment, Social Affairs, Skills and Labour Mobility, First outline of the European Pillar of Social Rights and reform of the Posting of Workers Directive, SPEECH/16/682, Brussels, 8 March 2016: 'If we want to avoid social fragmentation and social dumping in Europe, then Member States (MS) should agree on the EPSR as soon as possible.' Then, European Commission, European Pillar of Social Rights: Statement by President Juncker, Vice-President Dombrovskis and Commissioner Thyssen one year following its proclamation, STATEMENT/18/6390, Brussels, 13 November 2018: 'The European Pillar of Social Rights is designed to make a positive difference in the everyday life of all Europeans. […] The European Semester is now more social than ever, with the Pillar firmly integrated in the process to monitor social progress.' *See also* F. Hendrickx, 'The European Social Pillar: Labour Law Not Only Needs Rights', Global Workplace Law & Policy, 2017, http://global-workplace-law-and-policy.kluwerlawonline.com/2017/11/29/the-european-social-pillar-labour-law-not-only-needs-rights/.

275. Dombrovskis, Commissioner for 'An Economy that Works for People', and Nicolas Schmit, Commissioner for 'Jobs and Social Rights', indicated that the Commission will present an action plan for the implementation of the EPSR across the EU. In particular, Schmit made clear that its effort to strengthen Europe's social dimension will be based on the Pillar. Similarly, Dubravka Suica, Vice-President of the Commissioner and responsible for 'Democracy and Demography', announced that her work will be based on the principles laid down in the EPSR. For a deeper overview of the different Commissioners' programme: European Parliament, Report, Commitments made at the hearings of the Commissioners-designate Von der Leyen Commission 2019-2024, PE 629.837, Brussels, October 2020.

276. European Commission, Proposal for a Directive of the European Parliament and of the Council on Adequate Minimum Wages in the European Union, COM(2020) 682 final, Brussels, 28 October 2020; European Commission, Proposal for a Directive of the European Parliament and of the Council to Strengthen the Application of the Principle of Equal Pay for Equal Work or Work for Equal Value Between Men and Women Through Pay Transparency and Enforcement

on the extent to which the EPSR is leading to a recalibration of the EU rule-makers' approach to social and labour law issues.

3.1 Again a Social Agenda for Economic Growth?

Despite its market-embedded origins, when the idea of the EPSR was first put on the table, the emphasis was on the positive contribution that it would bring to the social dimension of the EU. This triggered hopes for a paradigm shift in the EU's approach to labour law.[277]

The EPSR was enthusiastically announced in September 2015 by the Commission President Juncker as part of the Commission's Social Package. It was introduced as an instrument pursuing the ambition to pair economic development with the improvement in living and working conditions.[278] After years of austerity and economic reforms merely aimed at overcoming the financial crisis, with the EPSR the Commission could now show its commitment to ensuring that economic growth and social progress go hand in hand. If those announcements were to become true, the Pillar could actually express the function whereby labour law adapts to the economic context while preserving its emancipatory dimension.[279]

However, when the 2016 Commission's Communication Launching a Consultation on the EPSR gave a more concrete shape to the initiative, it emerged that behind the rhetorical openness towards social aspirations, economic justifications were still central.[280] The Commission indeed launched the EPSR with the premise that: '[T]he best performing Member States in economic terms have developed more ambitious and efficient social policies, not just as a result of economic development, but *as a central part of their growth model*'[281] and that 'a stronger focus on employment and social performance [...] is not just a political or social imperative, it is also an *economic necessity*'[282] (emphasis added).

The approach of the 'four-pillar strategy' outlined in the Five Presidents' Report resonated loudly.[283] The economic and productivity rationale of the Pillar emerged as

Mechanisms, COM(2021) 93 final, Brussels, 4 March 2021; European Commission, Proposal for a Directive of the European Parliament and of the Council on Improving Working Conditions in Platform Work, COM(2021) 762 final, Brussels, 9 December 2021.

277. S. Garben, 'The European Pillar of Social Rights: An Assessment of Its Meaning and Significance', Cambridge Yearbook of European Legal Studies, 21, pp. 101-127, 2019; F. Hendrickx, 'The European Social Pillar: A First Evaluation', European Labour Law Journal, 9(1), pp. 3-6, 2018.
278. European Commission, Speech by M. Thyssen, European Commissioner for Eurostat and Employment, Social Affairs, Skills and Labour Mobility, First outline of the European Pillar of Social Rights and reform of the Posting of Workers Directive, SPEECH/16/682, Brussels, 8 March 2016.
279. This function of labour law was discussed in Chapter 1, section 2.2.3.
280. European Commission, Launching a consultation on a European Pillar of Social Rights, Communication, COM(2016) 127 final, Strasbourg, 8 March 2016.
281. *Ibid.*, p. 4.
282. *Ibid.*, pp. 4-5.
283. *Ibid.*; European Commission, Monitoring the implementation of the European Pillar of Social Rights, Communication, COM(2018) 130 final, Strasbourg, 13 March 2018.

rather strong.[284] The EPSR's contribution to EU policymaking was thus to be mainly measured in terms of labour market inclusivity and dynamics.[285]

3.2 Structure and Content of the EPSR

The EPSR was officially proclaimed at the European Council in Goteborg in November 2017. The document is articulated in 20 principles, structured around three chapters having the following main headings: Equal opportunities and access to the labour market, Fair working conditions, and Adequate and sustainable social protection.

These chapters are preceded by a preamble which revealed the ambiguous positioning of the EPSR with respect to the normative model underlying labour law. Quite eloquently, paragraphs 10 and 13 of the preamble respectively state that: 'Economic and social progress are intertwined, and the establishment of a European Pillar of Social Rights should be part of wider efforts to build a more inclusive and sustainable growth model *by improving Europe's competitiveness and making it a better place to invest*, create jobs and foster social cohesion' and 'A stronger focus on employment and social performance is particularly important to *increase resilience and deepen the Economic and Monetary Union*. For these reasons, the European Pillar of Social Rights is *notably conceived for the euro area* but is addressed to all Member States' (emphasis added).

The strong economic rationale of the Pillar also emerges from the content of its principles. The first chapter (on 'Equal opportunity and access to the labour market') draws a roadmap to improve the inclusiveness of labour markets. It addresses training and lifelong learning, gender equality, equal opportunities, and active support of employment. The accent is thus not placed on strengthening working conditions. The EPSR principles rather promote participation or, as Giubboni has recognised, 'access justice' into the labour market.[286] Here, the approach to labour law that had dominated in the previous decades is strongly present: the labour market is labour law's priority.

284. Z. Rasnača, 'Bridging the Gaps or Falling Short? The European Pillar of Social Rights and What It Can Bring to EU-Level Policymaking', Working Paper, ETUI, Brussels, 2017. This approach to the social dimension of EU integration also emerges from European Commission, Reflection Paper on the Social Dimension of Europe, Communication, COM(2017) 206 final, Brussels, 26 April 2017, p. 8: '[W]here convergence in economic performances over time is accompanied by convergence of social conditions, fears of social dumping diminish and support for the single market is nourished.' Similarly, on the occasion of the Rome Summit for the 60th anniversary of the EU, 25 March 2017, when EU leaders declared: '[W]e pledge to work towards a social Europe – a Union which, based on sustainable growth, promotes economic and social progress, as well as cohesion and convergence, while upholds the integrity of the internal market.'

285. K. Lörcher & I. Schömann, 'The European Pillar of Social Rights: Critical Legal Analysis and Proposals', Report, 139, ETUI, Brussels, 2016; S. Rainone, 'The European Pillar of Social Rights – Tell Me Where You Come from and I Will Tell You Who You Are', Zbornik Znanstvenih Razprav Letnik LXXX, Perspective on the European Pillar of Social Rights, pp. 133-178, 2020; F. Bonciu, 'The European Pillar of Social Rights: Too Little, Too Late?', Romanian Journal of European Affairs, 18(1), pp. 60-70, 2018.

286. S. Giubboni, 'Appunti E Disappunti Sul Pilastro Europeo Dei Diritti Sociali', Quaderni Costituzionali, 37(4), pp. 953-962, 2017. Access justice refers to the institutional effort to guarantee a fair and non-discriminatory access to the labour market, and implies measures aimed at enhancing vocational training, youth employment and gender equality.

The second chapter (on 'Fair working conditions') focuses on a wide range of matters that touch upon core labour standards. It contains principles on secure and adaptable employment, fair and adequate minimum wages, workers' information and consultation, social dialogue, and work-life balance. This chapter refers to crucial labour rights, reflecting the social and emancipatory spirit of labour law. Commentators have argued that the inclusion of Principle 6 on fair minimum wages indicates a (positive) change of approach towards wage policies: from wages as a cost factor, to wage-setting as an instrument to boost internal demand and social cohesion.[287] Moreover, Principle 6 recommends predictability and transparency in the definition of wages, while still leaving broad discretion to the Member States and not interfering with national industrial relation systems. It could, therefore, be read as a substantial step towards enhancing the social component of labour (or, at least, wage) policies.[288] However, it should also be noted that the Preamble of the EPSR includes a reference to the Rome Declaration of 27 March 2017, where it was stressed that linking wages to productivity is essential to sustain competitiveness and job creation.[289] This suggests that the concept of 'fair minimum wages' contained in Principle 6 still embodies labour market efficiency considerations.

Similar insights relate to Principle 8, dedicated to the promotion of social dialogue. It is undisputed that the support for the involvement and participation of social partners in the design and implementation of economic, employment and social policies bonds well with the betterment of working conditions. Strengthening workers' participation in the company management and supporting collective bargaining is crucial for uplifting the workers' bargaining position.[290] Yet, the link with economic objectives is, once again, present. The EPSR included a reference to the 'Reflection Paper on the Social Dimension of Europe', which suggests that the integration of social dialogue into economic strategies might lead to considerable constraints in the autonomy of unions and in the exercise of collective rights.[291] In the Reflection Paper, the Commission in fact presented the importance of valuing the involvement of social

287. T. Müller & T. Schulten, 'The European Social Pillar – Towards an EU Minimum Wage Policy?', Social Europe, 2017, https://socialeurope.eu/european-social-pillar-towards-eu-minimum-wage-policy.
288. European Commission, Reflection Paper on the Social Dimension of Europe, Communication, COM(2017) 206 final, Brussels, 26 April 2017: 'Integrating a social dimension within the EU economic agenda does not only support growth, but is also functional to social progress which, is believed, descends from economic growth. "Convergence of social standards is a key element of fair globalization. [...] There are several options for the social future of Europe [...] the political option chosen will have implication beyond the social field, stretching to the competitiveness of Europe, its capacity to harness and shape globalization".'
289. *Ibid.*
290. As discussed in Chapter 1, section 2.2.2.
291. This concern has more recently been confirmed by the Commission's approach to EU Social Dialogue, in relation to the decision of the European Commission to reject the EU social partners' request to give legislative implementation to a framework agreement that was stipulated in order to establish information and consultation rights in the public sector. *See* S. Rainone, 'After the "Hairdressing Agreement", the EPSU Case: Can the Commission Control the EU Social Dialogue?', Policy Brief, 15, ETUI, Brussels, 2020; judgment of 2 September 2021, *European Federation of Public Service Unions (EPSU) v. European Commission*, C-928/19, ECLI:EU:C:2021:656.

partners as a vehicle for facilitating the labour market adjustment process towards a more flexible economy: 'Countries in which social partners have been strongly involved in reforms of the labour market have shown lasting positive results as their involvement ensured the ownership of the reforms process by a wider range of stakeholders.'[292] A similar approach emerges from the Commission's Communication 'A New Start for Social Dialogue', in which social dialogue is addressed as part of the Union's economic strategy: 'Countries with a long tradition of social dialogue tend to have stronger, more stable economies and are often Europe's most competitive. Knowing the important role that *social dialogue plays and the positive benefits it has on a country's economy*, the challenge today is to enhance its role across all EU Member States'[293] (emphasis added).

More clearly embedded in the economic efficiency discourse is Principle 5 on Secure and adaptable employment. This principle states that 'the necessary flexibility for employers to adapt swiftly to changes in the economic context shall be ensured' and that 'entrepreneurship and self-employment shall be encouraged, occupational mobility shall be facilitated'. Principle 5 plainly indicates that labour standards must be responsive to the employers' economic needs and to the creation of a flexible and dynamic workforce.[294] It clearly promotes the idea of flexicurity and implies that employment protection rights should be framed within a normative context that encourages entrepreneurship.[295] It is quite interesting to notice that this principle, which reflects the employer's point of view and protects its interests, has been included in a policy instrument, the Pillar, whose announced intent is to reinforce the social dimension of the Union. This principle clearly has an economic underpinning and discourages the strengthening of employment protection, and might thus prevent future reforms aimed at reinforcing labour law's emancipatory rationale.

The third chapter of the EPSR is dedicated to 'Social protection and inclusion' and contains principles relating to social protection and social assistance policies. It addresses childcare, pension systems, unemployment benefits and minimum income, the inclusion of people with disability, healthcare, long-term care, housing, and access to essential services. It is undisputed that the full implementation of these principles would potentially lead to social progress. It is, however, important to make two observations. The first is that, here too, the wording of the principles places the accent

292. European Commission, COM(2017) 206 final, 2017, p. 12, under the heading 'What helps our societies and economies withstand a crisis'.
293. European Commission, Report, A new start for Social Dialogue, Brussels, August 2016.
294. Commission Staff Working Document Accompanying the Communication from the Commission on 'Establishing a European Pillar of Social Rights', SWD(2017) 210 final, Brussels, 26 April 2017; European Commission, Staff Working Document, Key Economic, Employment and Social Trends Behind a European Pillar of Social Rights, SWD(2016) 51 final, Strasbourg, 8 March 2016.
295. *Ibid.*, p. 32: 'The fundamentals on which the concept of "flexicurity" is based, namely flexible and reliable contractual arrangements, comprehensive lifelong learning strategies, active labour market policies and modern social security systems, are particularly pertinent in view of the aforementioned trends [...]. This offers workers the human capital they need to be secure and to be able to manage the adaptation challenges that will be increasingly required in the future world of work; and it offers employers the security that they will be able to find and retain the skills they need for growth and innovation.'

on aspects that are functional to the inclusiveness of labour markets and to sound public finances. As an example, the 'reintegration into the labour market' appears to be (among) the underlying objective(s) of Principle 13 on unemployment benefits,[296] Principle 14 on minimum income[297] and Principle 17 on the inclusion of people with disabilities.[298] Self-evidently, stressing the efficient functioning of labour markets and the economic sustainability of national welfare is quite at odds with the ontologically redistributive function of social protection systems.[299]

The second observation is that the centrality of social security systems (which, by the way, does not fall within the competencies of the Union) in the Pillar reflects a socioeconomic model that resembles the flexicurity paradigm. It indicates the proximity of the Union with the normative model whereby rule-makers should lower employment protection (as in Principle 5) and then reassign to social welfare policies the task of offsetting the social consequence of a more precarious labour market.[300] While this book is not the place to assess the appropriateness of this paradigm for achieving social progress, it is nevertheless important to stress that, in such a model, labour policies are distanced from social re-equilibration objectives, which are instead endowed upon social welfare systems. In this paradigm, the emancipatory component of labour law is therefore weakened.[301]

Overall, the Pillar is an instrument with an ambiguous normative approach. It introduced certain progressive elements that might constitute the premises for slowing down or even countering the marginalisation of the emancipatory component of labour law. It in fact confirmed a utilitarian view of labour rights with respect to the economic agenda, the objectives of full employment and labour market flexibility. At the same time, it should not be excluded that, if placed in a political context capable of enhancing its more social rationale, the Pillar could contribute to the socialisation of EU policy-making.[302]

---

296. 'The unemployed have the right to adequate activation support from public employment services to (re)integrated in the labour market and adequate unemployment benefits of reasonable duration, in line with their contribution and national eligibility rules. Such benefits shall not constitute a disincentive for a quick return to employment.'
297. 'Everyone lacking sufficient resources has the right to adequate minimum income benefits ensuring a life in dignity at all stages of life, and effective access to enabling goods and services. For those who can work, minimum income benefits should be combined with incentives to (re)integrate into the labour market.'
298. 'People with disabilities have the right to income support that ensures living in dignity, services that enable them to participate in the labour market and in society, and a work environment adapted to their needs.'
299. On the predominance of the economic rationale over the social objectives *see, inter alia*, S. Giubboni, 'Appunti E Disappunti Sul Pilastro Europeo Dei Diritti Sociali', Quaderni Costituzionali, 37(4), pp. 953-962, 2017.
300. As more extensively argued in S. Rainone, A. Aloisi, 'Time to Deliver? Assessing the Action Plan on the European Pillar of Social Rights', Policy Brief, ETUI, Brussels, 2021.
301. As discussed in Chapter 1, section 2.2.4.
302. S. Rainone, 'The European Pillar of Social Rights – Tell Me Where You Come from and I Will Tell You Who You Are', Zbornik Znanstvenih Razprav Letnik LXXX, Perspective on the European Pillar of Social Rights, pp. 133-178, 2020; F. Bonciu, 'The European Pillar of Social Rights: Too Little, Too Late?', Romanian Journal of European Affairs, 18(1), pp. 60-70, 2018; S. Garben, 'The European Pillar of Social Rights: Effectively Addressing Displacement?', European Constitutional Law Review, 14(1), pp. 210-230, 2018.

3.3 The Implementation of the EPSR

The EPSR has no direct enforceability and the main responsibility to implement lies with the Member States.[303] At the Union level, the EPSR predominantly finds actualisation within the European Semester and, limitedly to the competences established in the Treaties, through EU legislation.

3.3.1 Implementation Through the European Semester

Starting from the implementation through the European Semester, it is helpful to make a brief digression to explain how this governance mechanism actually works. Account will also be made of the adjustments that were introduced following its integration with the Next Generation EU (NGEU) strategy, which will be further discussed in section 4.2.[304]

The European Semester can, very simplistically, be described as a yearly process of national policy coordination, taking place in different stages. In the first phase, the national economic and employment situations are monitored and assessed by the Commission. The Commission's analysis takes the form of Country Reports that evaluate national progress in addressing the issues identified in the previous year. The Country Reports are formulated in consideration of specific economic and social priorities, which the Commission yearly defines in two instruments: the Annual Growth Survey (having an economic focus) and the Joint Employment Report (concerning employment policies).[305] Both these documents are drafted according to a broader set of integrated economic and employment guidelines, steering national policies coordination towards growth and competitiveness. This consents to connect the monitoring of national policies with the EMU-deepening agenda.

In the second phase, national governments define their reform programmes in accordance with the priorities identified in the Country Reports. In the National Reform Programmes, the Member States are expected to address the socioeconomic unbalances highlighted in the Country Reports and to define a strategy to strengthen labour markets and economic performances. These reform programmes are again evaluated by the Commission and the Council. This evaluation leads to the adoption of Country-Specific Recommendations (CSRs). In the third phase, the countries are supposed to digest the feedback formulated in the CSRs and correct their policies accordingly.

How does the Pillar fit into this framework? The connection between the Semester and the implementation of the EPSR is mainly obtained through the Social

303. European Commission, Delivering on the European Pillar of Social Rights – Commission adopts first concrete initiatives, IP/17/1006, Brussels, 26 April 2017.
304. B. Vanhercke & B. Verdun, 'From the European Semester to the Recovery and Resilience Facility – Some Social Actors Are (Not) Resurfacing', Working paper, 13, ETUI, Brussels, 2021; J. Creel, N. Leron & X. Ragot, 'Embedding the Recovery and Resilience Facility into the European Semester', Policy Brief, 14, ETUI, Brussels, 2021.
305. In 2020, the Annual Growth Survey was substituted by the Annual Sustainable Growth Strategy, *see* European Commission, Annual Sustainable Growth Strategy 2020, COM(2019) 605 final, Brussels, 17 December 2019.

Scoreboard.[306] The Social Scoreboard is a statistic-based instrument adopted in conjunction and in line with the EPSR, designed to benchmark social progress within the Union.[307] It contains a series of headline indicators that refer to the principles of the EPSR and are meant to track the performances of the Member States and to offer accessible data and figures on national social developments.[308] In line with the Principles of the EPSR, the Scoreboard's indicators predominantly focus on the functioning of the labour market. To give an example, the Scoreboard has a heading on 'Dynamic labour market and fair working conditions', which, on closer inspection, contains no criteria for assessing the fairness of working conditions. The benchmarking instead considers employment and unemployment rates, participation in activation or support to labour market policies and, lastly, the levels of household disposable income, which is the only indicator that tangibly concerns the quality of living conditions.[309]

The way in which the Social Scoreboard feeds into the European Semester is through its integration into the Commission's assessment of the Member States' economic and employment situation. For instance, its indicators are used for the analysis of national systems in the Joint Employment Report, which provides an overview of key employment and social developments in the Member States.[310] Similarly, the Commission considers the Scoreboard when drawing the picture of the Member States' progress and challenges in the country reports and in the CSRs.

The integration of the Social Scoreboard in the European Semester triggers ambivalent considerations. On the one hand, it can be argued that the Social Scoreboard is an important tool to 'socialise' the European Semester, which for too long focused on macroeconomic objectives.[311] On the other hand, the introduction of social and labour policy indicators predominantly focused on labour market inclusivity might have only mild effects on the development of policies for the improvement of working conditions.[312]

Besides the Social Scoreboard, the EPSR finds implementation within the Semester process also by serving as a compass for the periodical redefinition of the employment guidelines, which – together with the economic guidelines – inform the

---

306. European Commission, Staff Working Document, Social Scoreboard, SWD(2017) 200 final, Brussels, 26 April 2017.
307. European Commission, Monitoring the implementation of the European Pillar of Social Rights, Communication, COM(2018) 130 final, Strasbourg, 13 March 2018.
308. *Ibid.*
309. A revision of the Social Scoreboard is planned for the spring 2022, *see* p. 60. *See* the social scoreboard composite indicators, available on the Commission website: https://composite-indicators.jrc.ec.europa.eu/social-scoreboard/.
310. In particular, the headlines of the social scoreboard are also the headline indicators of the Joint Employment Report, where the performance of the Member States is analysed on the basis of the following criteria: the level of the indicators itself, and the progress made in respect to the previous year.
311. Z. Rasnača, 'Bridging the Gaps or Falling Short? The European Pillar of Social Rights and What It Can Bring to EU-Level Policymaking', Working Paper, ETUI, Brussels, 2017, pp. 26-30.
312. For an analysis of the potential of the EPSR within the European Semester framework *see, inter alia*, S. Garben, 'The European Pillar of Social Rights: Effectively Addressing Displacement?', European Constitutional Law Review, 14(1), pp. 210-230, 2018, p. 210.

whole cycle of national policy coordination. In 2017, the employment guidelines were indeed reformulated to be aligned with the principles of the EPSR. However, while one might have expected a stronger social outlook of said guidelines, the changes were minor and, counterintuitively, in the direction of an even more prominent focus on labour market efficiency.[313] With respect to the pre-Pillar period, Guideline 5 ('Boosting the demand for labour') and Guideline 8 ('Promoting equal opportunity for all, fostering social inclusion and combatting poverty') remained unchanged. The revision only concerned Guidelines 6, which from 'Enhancing labour supply, skills and competences' turned into 'Enhancing labour supply: access to employment, skills and competences' and Guidelines 7, which passed from 'Enhancing the functioning of labour markets' to 'Enhancing the functioning of labour markets and the effectiveness of social dialogue.' While the reference to social dialogue could be read as a positive acknowledgement of the social partners' role, it is important to note that it just relates to labour market reforms, and not fair labour standards setting.[314]

On account of these elements, the integration in the European Semester confirms the economic and labour market embedding of the Pillar principles. The contribution of the Pillar does not materialise in a proper refocusing of EU governance towards reforms that valorise the social and emancipatory underpinning of labour law.[315] The integration of the Pillar within the European Semester appears, in fact, to reinforce the centrality of labour market 'modernisation' within EU labour policies. This emerges from the CSRs addressed to the Member States in the 2018 and 2019 European Semester cycles, which took place once the EPSR was already adopted. As Clauwaert mentioned: 'While it is clear that the use of the Social Scoreboard has allowed the Commission to identify several critical situations in the broader social field in the Country Reports, this is not necessarily reflected in the proposed/adopted Commission/Council recommendations as had been hoped.'[316] A distinct discussion should be made of the 2020 CSRs, which were adopted in the midst of the COVID-19 pandemic and when macroeconomic surveillance was milder. This is further elaborated in section 4.2.

EU governance has been slightly adapted in the context of the EU recovery strategy following the COVID-19 emergency. As is further discussed in section 4 below, in order to cope with the economic and social crisis triggered by the pandemic, the EU has adopted an unprecedented financial facility to support national economies, as part of the NGEU strategy. In order to obtain financial support, Member States had to submit National Reform and Resilience Plans (NRRPs). The NRRPs had to meet certain

313. Commission proposal for Council Decision on guidelines for the employment policies of the Member States, COM(2017) 677 final 2017/0305 (NLE), Brussels, 22 November 2017.
314. *Ibid.* (para. 7): 'Reforms to the labour market, including the national wage-setting mechanisms, should follow national practices of social dialogues and allow the necessary opportunity for a broad consideration of socioeconomic issues, including improvements in competitiveness, job creation, life-long learning and training policies as well as real incomes.'
315. S. Clauwaert, 'The Country-Specific Recommendations (CSRs) in the Social Field: An Overview and Initial Comparison', ETUI, Brussels, 2019.
316. S. Clauwaert, 'The Country-Specific Recommendations (CSRs) in the Social Field: An Overview and Initial Comparison', ETUI, Brussels, 2018, p. 6.

preconditions, including that the national reforms would contribute to the implementation of the EPSR.[317] The monitoring of the enactment of these national plans and of the compliance with the Social Pillar has been entrusted to European governance and, in particular, to a (reformed) European Semester. This integration between the European Semester, Next Generation EU and EPSR was articulated in an Action Plan to implement the Pillar, which the Commission adopted in March 2021. In the same Action Plan, a new Social Scoreboard was also presented, enriched with new indicators on child poverty, disability employment gap, access to healthcare and long-term care, risk of poverty, and coverage of unemployment benefits.[318] These recent developments could result in a stronger commitment by national governments to implement the EPSR. However, some criticalities have already emerged. The first is the absence of corrective instruments supporting a proper actualisation of the Pillar's principles. Second, when assessing and approving the NRRPs, the Commission has considered compliance with the Pillar in a rather formalistic and superficial way.[319]

3.3.2 Implementation Through EU Law

The implementation of the EPSR is supposed to take place also through EU 'hard' law. Despite the limited competences of the EU in the areas covered by the Pillar, several legislative initiatives have emerged.

As has been mentioned already, the Directive (EU) 2019/1152 on transparent and predictable working conditions was adopted to address those working arrangements characterised by a very high degree of flexibility in relation to the time, the place or even the actual performance of the labour activity.[320] The directive reduced the employer's freedom in the determination of the working schedule. It prevented the most extreme cases of casualisation of work, introduced sanction mechanisms, and expanded rights for on-call workers.[321] Then, Directive (EU) 2019/1158 on work-life

317. Regulation (EU) 2021/241 of the European Parliament and of the Council of 12 February 2021 establishing the Recovery and Resilience Facility, *OJ L 57, 18.2.2021, pp. 17-75.*
318. S. Rainone & A. Aloisi, 'Time to Deliver? Assessing the Action Plan on the European Pillar of Social Rights', Policy Brief, ETUI, Brussels, 2021; M. Moschella, 'What Role for the European Semester in the Recovery Plan?', In-Depth Analysis, European Parliament Directorate General for Internal Policies, Brussels, 2020.
319. On the institutional context in which the RRF is placed, *see* B. Vanhercke & A. Verdun, 'The European Semester as Goldilocks: Macroeconomic Policy Coordination and the Recovery and Resilience Facility', Journal of Common Market Studies, 60(1), pp. 204-223, 2022.
320. Directive (EU) 2019/1152 of the European Parliament and of the Council of 20 June 2019 on transparent and predictable working conditions in the European Union, *OJ L 186, 11.7.2019, pp. 105-121.*
321. B. Bednarowicz, 'Delivering on the European Pillar of Social Rights: The New Directive on Transparent and Predictable Working Conditions in the European Union', Industrial Law Journal, 48(4), pp. 604-623, 2019. For instance, the directive on transparent and predictable working conditions introduces a maximum duration of the probationary period (Article 8), establishes that the employer cannot prohibit the workers from taking up employment with other employers (Article 9), prescribes a right of the worker to receive compensation in case the employer cancels a work assignment after a specified reasonable deadline (Article 10) and establishes a presumption of employment contract in presence of a minimum amount of paid hours (Article 11).

balance for parents and carers, which amended the previous EU rules on parental leave, paternity leave and carer's leave with the goal to promote a better coexistence between working life and a fairer redistribution of household obligations.[322] This resulted, for instance, in the establishment of the right to paid paternity leave.[323] Lastly, the Council adopted a Recommendation on access to social protection. It consists in a non-binding legislative measure that calls on the Member States to extend the scope of their social security systems to atypical workers. The idea behind the Recommendation was to limit the increasing divide in access to welfare and social safety nets between those who have a standard labour relationship and those who do not.[324]

These three measures represent an encouraging revitalisation of the legislative activity based on the Social Policy Title of the TFEU. However, on closer inspection, they only marginally address the quality of working conditions and do not remedy the precariousness that characterises atypical working relations.[325] With their minimalist regulatory approach, these legislative instruments valorise inclusivity in the labour market more than employment protection.[326] As a result, the emancipatory rationale of these initiatives is rather limited.[327]

It is worth mentioning that to foster legislative convergence on the issues covered by the Pillar, in 2019 the Commission proposed the activation of the passerelle clause provided in Article 48(7) TEU.[328] Passarelle clauses allow passing from a special legislative procedure (where the Council is the only legislator) to an ordinary legislative procedure (where the Council and the European Parliament are co-legislators), and

322. Directive (EU) 2019/1158 of the European Parliament and of the Council of 20 June 2019 on work-life balance for parents and carers and repealing Council Directive 2010/18/EU, *OJ L 188, 12.7.2019, p. 79-93*; K. Arbadjieva, 'Reshaping the Work-Life Balance Directive with COVID-19 Lessons in Mind', Working Paper, 1, ETUI, Brussels, 2022.
323. Article 4 confers the right to paternity leave of 10 working days.
324. Council Recommendation on Access to social protection for workers and the self-employed, adopted on 8 November 2019, *OJ C 387, 15.11.2019, pp. 1-8. See also* P. Schoukens, A. Barrio Fernandez & S. Montebovi, 'The EU Social Pillar: An Answer to the Challenge of the Social Protection of Platform Workers?', European Journal of Social Security, 20(3), pp. 219-241, 2018.
325. Insights on the shortcoming of the legislative measures implementing the EPSR can be found in S. Garben, 'The European Pillar of Social Rights: An Assessment of Its Meaning and Significance', Cambridge Yearbook of European Legal Studies, 21, pp. 101-127, 2019.
326. ETUC Resolution, Directive on Transparent and Predictable Working Conditions: A First Major Step Forward but Weaker than Expected, Brussels, 21 December 2017; D. Georgiou, 'The New EU Directive on Transparent and Predictable Working Conditions in the Context of New Forms of Employment', European Journal of Industrial Relations, First Online, 2022.
327. As discussed in Chapter 1, section 2.2.4.
328. European Commission, State of the Union 2018: Letter of intent to President Antonio Tajani and to Chancellor Sebastian Kurz, Strasbourg, 12 September 2018; European Commission, Infosheet on the Roadmap for the Future Commission's Initiative on 'More Efficient Law-making in Social Policy: Identification of Areas for an Enhanced Move to Qualified Majority', Brussels, 20 December 2018; European Commission, More efficient Decision-making in Social Policy: Identification of Areas for an Enhanced Move to Qualified Majority Voting, COM(2019) 186 final, Strasbourg, 16 April 2019.

from the unanimous voting rule within the Council to the qualified majority voting.[329] In the Commission's proposal, the passerelle clause would apply to employment matters,[330] and in particular to the two specific fields of non-discrimination and social protection of workers, currently subject to unanimity voting in the Council.[331] The idea was to ease the adoption of EU law in those areas to further develop the social dimension of the Union.

However, the usual reservations apply. First of all, the change of legislative procedure would concern social protection and equal treatment, and not employment protection. Second, even if this reform would facilitate legislation in the labour field, there is a high risk that the economic component would still be strong. A closer look at the Commission's justification for its initiative reveals a utilitarian approach, oriented at promoting EU growth, job creation and competitiveness. In relation to the procedural rules in the non-discrimination area, the Commission argued that: 'the lack of common EU rules to protect against discrimination in access to goods and services undermines the level playing field that is key for an effective and fair single market'.[332] Similarly, with reference to EU action in the field of access to social protection, the Commission stated that it is important to 'ensure that EU business makes the most of the changing world of work'.[333] Needless to say, these considerations place future labour policy initiatives within the EU economic strategy rather than into a genuinely social agenda.

Finally, it is important to mention that under the Von der Leyen Commission, the implementation of the Pillar has led to an interesting development.[334] The first consists of a proposal, followed by the adoption, of a directive on minimum wage, which

329. *Ibid*. European Commission, COM(2019) 186 final, 2019: the procedure to trigger a *passerelle* clause implies the adoption of a non-legislative initiative. Qualified majority voting means that the vote in favour must represent the 55% of the Member States and the 65% of the total EU population.
330. *Ibid*., p. 7, and European Trade Union Confederation, ETUC Submission on the European Commission Roadmap 'More Efficient Law-Making in Social Policy: Identification of Areas for an Enhanced Move to Qualified Majority Voting', Brussels, 19 January 2019. These documents identify three different possibly suitable options for *passerelle* clauses within the treaties. The first is enshrined Article 48(7) TEU, providing a general *passerelle* clause. The second is in Article 153(2) TFEU, last subparagraph, which contains a specific *passerelle* clause for social policy measures covered by Article 153(1)(d), (f) and (g) TFEU. In other words, this could cover measures on the protection of workers where their employment contract is terminated, on the representation and collective defence of workers' and employers' interests, and on conditions of employment for third-country nationals legally residing in the Union. It could not cover measures on non-discrimination, having their legal basis in Article 19 TFEU, and on social security and social protection of workers, with legal basis in Article 153(1)(c). The third option is found in Article 19(1) TFEU, which provides a specific *passerelle* clause applicable to measures on non-discrimination exclusively. Ultimately, the Commission opted for the general *passerelle* clause established in Article 48(7) TFEU.
331. Based on Article 153 TFEU, the other areas where either special legislative procedure or the unanimity voting rule within the Council are: protection of workers when employment contract is terminated; workers' and employers' representation and collective defence; conditions of employment of third-country nationals.
332. European Commission, COM(2019) 186 final, 2019, p. 10.
333. *Ibid*., p. 11.
334. European Commission, A Strong Social Europe for Just Transitions, Communication, COM(2020) 14 final, Brussels, 14 January 2020.

entered into force in October 2022 (Directive EU 2022/2041).[335] This directive requires Member States either to adopt an adequate minimum wage by law or to promote collective bargaining.[336] Then, the Commission advanced a proposal for a directive to close the gender pay gap and aimed at better enforcing the principle of equal pay between men and women.[337] This initiative was followed by a proposal for a directive concerning the working conditions of platform workers, which, if adopted, would introduce a presumption of employment.[338] Lastly, the right to collective bargaining of self-employed was addressed and expanded by the (non-binding) Commission's Guidelines on competition law and collective bargaining.[339]

These initiatives constitute a substantial step towards a paradigm shift in the way the Union approaches labour law, as they directly address the contractual and economic imbalance between businesses and workers.[340] EU labour law could thus return to the pursuit of social re-equilibration and rediscover its long-neglected emancipatory rationale. However, the road may be long and bumpy. For instance, the Action Plan for the implementation of the Pillar that the Commission presented in March 2021 showed that EU labour policies are still strongly oriented towards ensuring labour market flexibility and have a prominent economic rationale.[341] Besides the aforementioned legislative proposals, the Action Plan focused on strengthening the employability of workers in view of the ecological and digital transitions that the Union

335. European Commission, Proposal for a Directive of the European Parliament and of the Council on Adequate Minimum Wages in the European Union, COM(2020) 682 final, Brussels, 28 October 2020.
336. A. Aranguiz & S. Garben, 'Combating Income Inequality in the EU: A Legal Assessment of a Potential EU Minimum Wage Directive', European Law Review, 46(2), pp. 156-174, 2021; T. Müller, T. Schulten, 'The European Social Pillar – Towards An EU Minimum Wage Policy?', Social Europe, 2017, https://socialeurope.eu/european-social-pillar-towards-eu-minimum-wage-policy.
337. European Commission, Proposal for a Directive of the European Parliament and of the Council to Strengthen the Application of the Principle of Equal Pay for Equal Work or Work for Equal Value Between Men and Women Through Pay Transparency and Enforcement Mechanisms, COM(2021) 93 final, Brussels, 4 March 2021; K. Arbadjieva, 'Time to Close the Gender Pay Gap: The Need for an EU Directive on Pay Transparency', Policy Brief, 2, ETUI, Brussels, 2021.
338. European Commission, Proposal for a Directive of the European Parliament and of the Council on Improving Working Conditions in Platform Work, COM(2021) 762 final, Brussels, 9 December 2021; V. De Stefano & A. Aloisi, 'European Commission Takes the Lead in Regulating Platform Work', Social Europe, 2021, https://socialeurope.eu/european-commission-takes-the-lead-in-regulating-platform-work.
339. European Commission, Collective Bargaining Agreements for Self-Employed – Scope of Application of EU Competition Rules, Inception Impact Assessment, 6 January 2021; European Commission, Guidelines on the Application of EU Competition Law to Collective Agreements Regarding the Working Conditions of Solo Self-Employed Persons – Approval of the Content of a Draft for a Communication from the Commission, Annex, C(2021) 8838 final, Brussels, 9 December 2021; S. Rainone & N. Countouris, 'Collective Bargaining and Self-Employed Workers – The Need for a Paradigm Shift', Policy Brief, 11, ETUI, Brussels, 2021.
340. The protective function is particularly present in the initiative on minimum wage, in that on the gender pay gap and in the introduction of a presumption of employment for platform workers. Moreover, the proposal on minimum wage and the proposed guidelines on competition law reinforce the legitimacy of collective bargaining and, thus, also pursue the function of uplifting workers' bargaining power.
341. S. Rainone & A. Aloisi, 'Time to Deliver? Assessing the Action Plan on the European Pillar of Social Rights', Policy Brief, ETUI, Brussels, 2021.

has committed itself to.[342] Emphasis was placed on skills enhancement programmes and vocational training, while no proper consideration was given to how to address the increase in precariousness that will result from these transitions.[343]

Here too, therefore, the assessment is mixed. On the one hand, encouraging signs appeared leaving a window of opportunity for the emancipatory rationale of labour law. On the other hand, the Union has not (yet?) actually reversed the process that over the years had led to the weakening of workers' rights and of the emancipatory dimension of labour law.

4 THE EU RESPONSE TO COVID-19: A GAME CHANGER?

In Chapter 1, it was explained that, for labour law to regain its emancipatory nature, its original functions should be reinforced – namely the protective function, that of uplifting the workers' bargaining position, or the function of reconciling between economic and social interests.[344] Besides the EPSR, another opportunity for this to happen arose in the context of the Union's strategy to recover from the COVID-19 emergency.[345]

The pandemic changed the lives of millions of EU citizens and triggered an economic and social crisis, whose disruptive effects are yet to be fully comprehended. Since the enactment of the first lock-down measures, national governments – and especially those from the countries that were most hit by the virus – have been calling for a meaningful European response.[346] This quickly triggered two parallel and intertwined political debates, touching on two of the most sensitive issues regarding the future of the EU:

(i) How to (re)define the balance between economic (and fiscal) objectives and social values?
(ii) How much European integration is it desirable to achieve?

Regarding both issues, the elephant in the room was the generalised negative perception about the way in which the EU managed the 2011 Euro crisis.[347] Back then,

342. On the action plan, *see* L. Hochscheidt, 'Social Pillar Action Plan – Longer on Aspiration', Social Europe, 9.5.2021, https://socialeurope.eu/social-pillar-action-plan-longer-on-aspiration.
343. S. Fernandes & K. Kerneïs, 'The Porto Social Summit: Turning Principles into Actions', Notre Europe, Jacque Delors Institute, 3.5.2021, https://institutdelors.eu/en/publications/sommet-social-de-porto-passer-des-principes-a-laction/.
344. As discussed in Chapter 1, section 2.2.
345. M. Sandbu, 'Europe Has Rediscovered the Social Market Economy', Financial Times, 19.12.2021.
346. D. Ghailani et al., 'Social Protection of Non-standard Workers and the Self-Employed During the Pandemic', Report, 5, ETUI, Brussels, 2021.
347. *See, inter alia*: L. Rodgers, 'Theorising Labour Law in the State of Exception: Political and Judicial Responses to Crisis' in A. Blackham, M. Kullmann & A. Zbyszewska (eds), *Theorising Labour Law in a Changing World: Towards Inclusive Labour Law*, Bloomsbury Publishing, London, 2019, pp. 37-54; J. Jordan, V. Maccarrone & R. Erne, 'Towards a Socialization of the EU's New Economic Governance Regime? EU Labour Policy Interventions in Germany, Ireland, Italy and Romania (2009-2019)', British Journal of Industrial Relations, 59(1), pp. 191-213, 2021.

the countries with the highest debt and macroeconomic imbalances were pressured to 'lighten up' their national welfare and employment protection systems on the altar of economic and fiscal responsibility. The whole process was characterised by a moral hazard narrative and by a (political and economic) divide among 'low debt' and 'high debt' countries worryingly broadened.[348] The European Semester, the European Stability Mechanism (ESM) and the Troika had become for a wide portion of the EU population synonyms of austerity, neoliberalism, widening inequalities and generalised regression in working and living conditions.[349] The Euro crisis thus provoked an even more pronounced marginalisation of the emancipatory component of labour law across the Member States.[350]

In 2020, however, the threat of an economic crisis was approached differently.[351] Among the main preoccupations of the EU policymakers was to avoid exacerbating the social damage through further public spending cuts.[352] This more solidaristic attitude implied that, at least in the short term, the flexibilisation of employment protection systems was not on the agenda.

4.1 The Immediate Reaction to the COVID-19 Outbreak

As productive activities were put on hold to limit the spreading of the virus and as the ghost of the economic recession was approaching, the European Commission promptly supported the relief packages activated by national governments to assist national businesses and workers.[353]

In this context, a remarkable initiative was the Commission's decision to suspend the EU fiscal rules through the activation of the general escape clause of the Stability and Growth Pact (SGP).[354] This allowed Member States to temporarily derogate from

348. C. Degryse, 'The New European Economic Governance', Working Paper, 14, ETUI, Brussels, 2012.
349. F. Costamagna, 'National Social Spaces as Adjustment Variables in the EMU: A Critical Legal Appraisal', European Law Journal, 23(2), pp. 163-190, 2018.
350. A. Koukiadaki, 'The Economic Crisis and Collective Labour Rights in Europe', Revue Francaise des Affaires Sociales, 3, pp. 53-73, 2015.
351. Denmark, Austria, Sweden and The Netherlands, Non-Paper – EU Support for Efficient and Sustainable COVID-19 Recovery, Brussels, 26 May 2020.
352. European Commission, Coronavirus: The Commission mobilises all of its resources to protect lives and livelihoods, IP/20/582, Brussels, 2 April 2020; European Commission and European Council, A Roadmap for Recovery – Towards a More Resilient, Sustainable and Fair Europe, Brussels, 21 April 2021.

    'The shock of the pandemic is symmetric; it is important to avoid the recovery to become asymmetric. […] The EU's recovery plan must therefore be based on solidarity, cohesion and convergence.' And 'The European Union needs a Marshall-Plan type of investment effort to fuel the recovery and modernise the economy'.
353. S. Rainone, 'The European Response to the COVID-19 Crisis – Where Are We Going To?', Global Workplace Law & Policy, 4.6.2020, http://global-workplace-law-and-policy.kluwerlawonline.com.tilburguniversity.idm.oclc.org/2020/06/04/the-european-response-to-the-covid-19-crisis-where-are-we-going-to/.
354. A. Delivorias, 'The "General Escape Clause" Within the Stability and Growth Pact: Fiscal Flexibility for Severe Economic Shocks', Briefing, Think Tank European Parliament, Brussels,

the SGP fiscal rules whereby the state's deficit has to remain below 3% of gross domestic product (GDP) and national debts cannot be higher than 60% of GDP.[355] Member States could thus have more spending leeway, which they could use to provide social assistance and support for workers and businesses. The suspension of the budget rules had an immediate effect on the ability of the Member States to pursue social objectives, as emerged from the CSRs. In 2020, for the first time since the creation of the European Semester, the CSRs had a genuine social outlook.[356] In section 3.3.1 it was mentioned that, generally, the CSRs instructed Member States to increase the efficiency and financial sustainability of their public spending, to harmonise wages to the productivity levels and to reform pensions. In the 2020 cycle, instead, the recommendations promoted the setting up of income support mechanisms, social assistance and short-time work schemes.

A second notable initiative taken in the wake of the crisis consisted of the creation of a mechanism providing Support to mitigate Unemployment Risks in an Emergency (SURE). This instrument was conceived to provide a safety net for both employees and self-employed against the risk of loss of income and can be used to finance national short-term work schemes.[357] SURE was designed to ensure financial assistance to

27.3.2020; Council Regulation (EU) 2020/672 of 19 May 2020 on the establishment of a European instrument for temporary support to mitigate unemployment risks in an emergency (SURE) following the COVID-19 outbreak, ST/7917/2020/INIT, *OJ L 159, 20.5.2020, pp. 1-7.* In addition to that, also other measures were enacted with the objective to ensure the Member States a broader power of action, and to react with emergency actions and spending. First, EU state aid rules were made more flexible, thus widening the leeway for governments to provide support to undertakings in economic difficulty. Then, the ECB launched the PEEP package of EUR 750 billion, thus providing a monetary stimulus. The European Investment Bank set up a EUR 25 billion guarantee fund, thus substantially expanding the support to national companies. All resources still available in the EU budget have been channelled to support national governments and enterprises to limit the damages of the crisis. Access to existing EU Funds has been made more flexible. Finally, The Eurogroup meeting of 9 April 2020 reached consensus on establishing an Enhanced Conditions Credit Line of the ESM. This reformed ESM allowed Member States to access low-interests loan (up to 2% of their GDP) to face the direct and indirect healthcare costs. Especially in the Southern Member States, the ESM gained a very negative reputation, since it is perceived as a trigger for austerity measures, as it happened during the 2008 crisis. However, this time, access to ESM loans was subject to different rules, and there would not be any conditionality. Therefore, national governments could theoretically apply for loans without being subsequently required to undertake severe public spending reforms.

355. European Commission, Activation of the General Escape Clause of the Stability and Growth Pact, COM(2020) 123 final, Brussels, 20 March 2020.

356. S. Rainone, 'An Overview of the 2020-2021 Country-Specific Recommendations (CSRs) in the Social Field – The Impact of COVID-19', Background Analysis, 1, ETUI, Brussels, 2020.

357. European Commission, Proposal for a Council Regulation on the Establishment of a European Instrument for Temporary Support to Mitigate Unemployment Risk in an Emergency (SURE) Following the COVID-19 Outbreak, COM(2020) 139 final, Brussels, 2 April 2020. SURE was presented on the 1st of April as a quasi-immediate support consenting a quickly accessible relief for national finances. However, the process to enact the mechanism was slower than originally anticipated. The Council reached an agreement on the regulation at the end of May, but negotiations between the Commission and the Member States continued until Autumn 2020. Moreover, questions on the adequacy of the SURE programme have been raised. In particular, the main criticism concerned the duration of the loans (too short term for Italy and Spain) and the cost of the loans (not cheap enough for countries with solid public finances, like

Member States for up to EUR 100 billion; funds were provided in the form of loans low-interest rates from the European Commission to national governments.

With the SGP escape clause and SURE, the Union has shown unprecedented support for greater interventionism of national governments in the definition of social and labour policies.[358] Across the Member States, measures were implemented to safeguard employment levels through the creation of more encompassing short-term work schemes, financial support for businesses, different forms of support for the most vulnerable, direct income support for self-employed, tax relief, mortgage support, etc.[359] The social rationale of labour law was thus put back on the table.

While the suspension of the financial rules and SURE were conceived as short-term interventions, the road to the creation of an actual recovery strategy was longer and more tortuous. It took months of intense negotiations among the national governments to develop a common response.[360] Before the pandemic, Member States' usual reaction to economic downturns was to search for financing through borrowing on the financial markets, with the effect of increasing their sovereign debt. For countries with excessive debts (such as Italy, Greece or Spain, among others), this financing comes with quite a high price, in the form of high-interest payments. For those Member States, it is a vicious circle leading to a progressive augmentation of public debt which, in the long term, damages the state's ability to make the necessary public investments.

In addition to limiting domestic growth, high public debt leads to macroeconomic imbalances that can have repercussions on the growth of the entire Union and, in particular, negative effects on the Monetary Union and on the stability of the Euro.[361] This is why, since the Maastricht Treaty, the EU has adopted a governance system pressuring governments to reduce their debt and correct macroeconomic imbalances.[362] Part of this governance framework is the SGP with its budget rules. The reforms enacted by the Member States under the pressure of the EU fiscal framework often consisted of a reduction of domestic public spending and the easing of regulatory

Germany). *See* M. Beblavý, 'Protecting Employment in the Time of Coronavirus: What Is the EU's €100 Billion Going to Buy?', Policy Insights, 8, CEPS, Brussels, 2020.

358. S. Rainone, 'An Overview of the 2020-2021 Country-Specific Recommendations (CSRs) in the Social Field – The Impact of COVID-19', Background Analysis, 1, ETUI, Brussels, 2020.
359. M. Johnson & V. Pulignano, 'Editorial: Transforming Care Work Within an Era of Changing Priorities of Care Policy', Transfer, 27(3), pp. 275-278, 2021; *see also* the different contributions in S.S. Börner, 'Is the Coronoavirus Going to Reshape the European Welfare State?' in Friedrich Ebert Stiftung (ed.), *The Coronavirus Crisis and the Welfare State*, Social Europe Publishing, Berlin, 2021, pp. 20-27.
360. P. Bofinger, 'The "Frugal Four" Should Save the European Project', Social Europe, 4.5.2020, https://socialeurope.eu/the-frugal-four-should-save-the-european-project.
361. These are among the justifications for the economic governance system set up by the EU in the aftermath of the financial crisis of 2008; *see* European Commission, Reinforcing economic policy coordination, COM(2010) 250 final, Brussels, 12 May 2010.
362. A. Delivorias, 'Introduction to the Fiscal Framework of the EU: The Maastricht Treaty, the Treaty on Stability, Coordination and Governance, and the Stability and Growth Pact', Study, European Parliamentary Research Service, Brussels, 2021.

burdens that reduce firms' competitiveness, including taxation and labour standards.[363]

The 2011 Euro crisis aggravated the pressure on States' finances, which translated into weakened social protection systems, lower employment protections and efforts to dismantle national collective bargaining systems.[364] In countries with high public debt and where the social welfare systems were already broadly underfunded, the deregulatory push became even heavier. It is no coincidence that the countries most affected by the economic crisis are those that have experienced the most dramatic labour cost-cutting reforms.[365] It is also no coincidence that it was precisely those states whose social and labour policies had been most affected that, when the COVID-19 crisis blew, asked the EU for a genuinely solidaristic response; this time it had to be different.

4.2 The Next Generation EU

It is in this context that, during the 2020 April Eurogroup and European Council meetings, the creation of Eurobonds was strongly supported by a rather big group of governments, among which Italy, France, Spain and Portugal.[366] In this scenario, the European Commission would receive the mandate to borrow on the financial market on behalf of the Union, instead of letting the single Member States issue state bonds to finance the recovery. National governments could access to liquidity at a reduced cost since the interest rate of the communitarised debt would be substantially lower than the interest rate that applies to the borrowing of highly indebted countries.[367]

However, Eurobonds were harshly opposed by the so-called frugal Member States, who resisted any form of debt mutualisation. This coalition of 'frugal' countries was composed of The Netherlands, Denmark, Sweden and Austria. In their view, fiscal integration would encourage budgetary irresponsibility of the Southern Member States.[368] This political stalemate was eventually overcome by the adoption of a Franco-German position supporting the creation of an EU Recovery Fund financed

363. C. Degryse, 'The New European Economic Governance', Working Paper, 14, ETUI, Brussels, 2012.
364. An example for Italy is Article 8 Decreto Legge 138/2011, with which the Berlusconi government introduced the possibility for decentralised collective bargaining at the company level to derogate, also in a pejorative manner, to the working conditions established at the sectoral collective agreement or in national legislation refer to Berlusconi's law on the decentralisation of collective bargaining of 2011.
365. P. Pecinovsky, 'EU Economic Governance and the Right to Collective Bargaining: Part 2. From Imposed Restrictions of the Right by EU Member States Towards a Social Economic Governance', European Labour Law Journal, 10(1), pp. 43-68, 2019.
366. A. Boitani & R. Tamborini, 'Eurobonds and European Citizenship', Briefing, Friedrich Ebert Stiftung, 2020; M. Draghi, 'We Face a War Against Coronavirus and Must Mobilise Accordingly', Financial Times, 25.3.2020.
367. G. Porcaro et al., 'Post-Council Commentary', Podcast, Bruegel Think Tank, 24.4.2020.
368. P. Bofinger, 'The "Frugal Four" Should Save the European Project', Social Europe, 4.5.2020, https://socialeurope.eu/the-frugal-four-should-save-the-european-project.

through the EU budget.[369] To realise that, the German and French governments opened up to the possibility that it would exceptionally be the European Commission to borrow on the financial markets (basically, by issuing a sort of Eurobonds), and not the individual Member States. In their proposal, the resources that the Commission would collect from these bonds would then be redistributed among the countries in the form of grants.

The Franco-German proposal paved the way for the European Commission that, in May 2020, proposed an unprecedented recovery programme. The key innovations were twofold: an increase in the EU's own resources (namely the funds that the Member States may be asked to devolve to the Union and the ability of the Union to collect its own taxes),[370] and the possibility for the Commission to issue common debt to finance the recovery strategy.[371] The financial assistance could thus be provided to the Member States through grants and (differently from what was originally envisaged in the Franco-German proposal) also loans.[372]

The Commission's proposal was followed by months of intense negotiations within the European Council and the European Parliament, and an agreement was finally reached in December 2020, when the recovery package was officially launched under the name of NGEU.[373] The recovery plan that ended up being adopted was not too different from the original proposal of the Commission. Its biggest component was a 750 billion financial assistance mechanism, the Recovery and Resilience Facility (RRF). In order to be eligible for financial aid in the form of both grants and loans, Member States had to submit a National Recovery and Resilience Plan (NRRP) in which they indicate the investments and reforms that will be realised with the RRF funds. As anticipated in section 3.3.1, this meant that the 2021 European Semester cycle had to be drastically adapted and that in 2021, no CSRs were adopted.[374] The

369. French-German initiative for the European recovery from the coronavirus crisis, Paris, 18 May 2020.
370. European Commission, Proposal for a Council Decision on the System of Own Resources of the European Union, COM(2020) 445 final, Brussels, 28 May 2020 that led to the adoption of COUNCIL DECISION (EU, Euratom) 2020/2053 of 14 December 2020 on the system of own resources of the European Union and repealing Decision 2014/335/EU, Euratom.
371. European Commission, Proposal for a Council Regulation establishing a European Union Recovery Instrument to Support the Recovery in the Aftermath of the COVID-19 Pandemic, COM(2020) 441 final, Brussels, 28 May 2020, that led to Council Regulation (EU) 2020/2094 of 14 December 2020 establishing a European Union Recovery Instrument to support the recovery in the aftermath of the COVID-19 crisis.
372. Council Regulation (EU) 2020/2094 of 14 December 2020 establishing a European Union Recovery Instrument to support the recovery in the aftermath of the COVID-19 crisis, Article 2 establishing that EU financial support consists of up to EUR 312,500 million in 2018 prices for a programme financing recovery and economic and social resilience via support to reforms and investments as non-repayable support (grants) and up to EUR 360,000 million in 2018 prices in loans to Member States for a programme financing recovery and economic and social resilience via support to reforms and investments.
373. *Ibid.*, European Commission, Commission Welcomes Political Agreement on Recovery and Resilience Facility, Brussels, 18 December 2020.
374. As explained in this chapter, section 3.3.1.

NRRPs were to be prepared by the end of April 2021 and the Commission approved them in the following months.[375] The Commission's evaluation of the NRRPs focused primarily on the suitability of the national investment to support economic growth and enable the green and digital transition.[376] Besides that, the national governments were also required to indicate how the EU funds would implement the EPSR.[377]

Interestingly, these events and the launch of the Next Generation EU led the Union to take a rather progressive stance on the two politically sensitive issues mentioned above in section 4. With respect to the first issue ('How to (re)define the balance between economic and fiscal objectives and social values?'), the EU recovery strategy relieves, at least for the time being, the pressure that in the past had provoked the most highly indebted Member States to adopt radical public spending cuts and to lower labour costs. With an expansionist approach taking over the austerity narrative, it is thus possible to envisage a relaxation of the previously dominant fiscal standpoint on domestic labour policies. This relaxation is likely to be reduced, at least partially, once the escape clause of the SGP is lifted.[378] Still, the fiscal targets of the SGP may be subject to a substantial revision in the context of the forthcoming reform of the economic and fiscal governance of the Union.[379]

Regarding the second issue outlined in section 4 ('How much European integration is it desirable to achieve?'), the Union has embarked on a path of greater fiscal integration. This might be read as a step towards federalism - even if the EU institutions have repeatedly stressed that this is an exceptional solution that does not alter the nature of the Union.[380] The Union has now at its disposal powerful financial instruments of a communitarian nature that can be deployed to address the economic recovery. National governments are thus subject to less pressure to cut public spending and impose deregulatory labour reforms. Overall, this development might lead to greater regulatory autonomy for the national governments to challenge the, so far prevalent, economic (and labour-market-centric) approach to labour policies and to

375. C. Dias, K. Grigaitė & R. Segall, 'Recovery and Resilience Dialogue with the European Commission', In-Depth Analysis, Economic Governance Support Unit (EGOV), European Parliament, Brussels, 6.2021.
376. Recitals 10-12, 42, 48 and Article 3 of Regulation (EU) 2021/241 of the European Parliament and of the Council of 12 February 2021 establishing the Recovery and Resilience Facility *OJ L 57, 18.2.2021, pp. 17-75.*
377. *See* section 3.3.1. European Commission, Staff Working Document, Guidance to Member States on Recovery and Resilience Plans, Commission Staff Working Document, SWD(2021) 12 final, Brussels, 22 January 2021.
378. V. Dombrovskis, 'Budget Rules to Apply from 2023 to Avoid "Fiscal Risks"', Euroactive, 25.5.2021.
379. European Commission, The EU Economy after COVID-19: Implications for Economic Governance, COM(2021) 662 final, Strasbourg, 19 October 2021; European Commission, Economic Governance Review, COM(2020) 55 final, Brussels, 5 February 2020.
380. Articles 12 and 14 of Regulation establishing the Recovery and Resilience Facility: the Commission can grant loan to the Member States until 31 December 2023.

strengthen the emancipatory component of labour law.[381] Much, however, depends on how long the fiscal tolerance of the EU will last.[382]

5 CONCLUDING REMARKS

In this chapter, an attempt has been made to determine whether EU policymaking leans towards a specific normative model in relation to labour law. Section 2 outlined the evolution of the EU's approach from the adoption of the Treaty of Rome until the period prior to the promulgation of the EPSR. Section 3 discussed the Pillar, the context in which it emerged and its implications for EU labour law. Section 4 then focused on the EU response to the COVID-19 crisis. This chapter constitutes the first step to address the general research question of the research *(What role does the CJEU play in relation to the normative model underlying EU labour law?)*. The analysis of the approach of EU policymaking towards labour law is in fact functional to position the Court's case law into a normative context and to give a first definition of the Court's role.

This analysis has shown that, throughout the years, there has been an evolution in the dominant normative model of labour law in the Union. First, in its early stage, the European Community abided by a dual polity paradigm: internal market creation at the European level, and social and labour policies at the national level. This model was compatible with the social market economy theory developed by Muller Armack.[383] This first period was characterised by the absence of a particular normative model with respect to labour law, as national policymakers were left free to endow labour legislation with social justice values.

Then, there was a period of upward harmonisation, referred to as the 'Golden period' of labour law. During this time, the EC lawmakers promoted rules which clearly reflected both the protective function (e.g., the directive on acquired rights in the case of transfers of undertaking) and supported the employees' bargaining position (e.g.,

381. No reference to spending reviews and austerity measures can be so far found in the official documents providing for the RRF. A relaxation of the monitoring of public finances already had emerged during the 2020 European Semester Cycle, *see* S. Rainone, 'An Overview of the 2020-2021 Country-Specific Recommendations (CSRs) in the Social Field – The Impact of COVID-19', Background Analysis, 1, ETUI, Brussels, 2020.

382. An example of how the suspension of the SGP fiscal rules did not entail a complete abandonment of the monitoring of national public expenditure emerges from the in-depth review conducted by the Commission in the context of the Macroeconomic Imbalance procedure for Italy. European Commission, Staff Working Document, In-Depth Review for Italy, in accordance with Article 5 of Regulation (EU) No 1176/2011 on the Prevention and Correction of Macroeconomic Imbalances, SWD(2021) 407 final, Brussels, 2 June 2021.

'Policies such as the general dismissal ban ("blocco dei licenziamenti") tend to influence the composition but not the scale of the labour market adjustment. Italy is the only Member State that introduced a universal ban on layoffs at the beginning of the COVID-19 crisis. This measure has been prolonged until June 2021 for workers supported by STW schemes and until October 2021 for other categories of workers.' And 'a comparison with labour market developments in other Member States that did not introduce such a measure suggests that the dismissal ban was not particularly effective and proved redundant in view of the extended use of job retention schemes'.

383. Section 2.1.

the directive on information and consultation rights in the case of collective redundancies). It was said that those measures embody both emancipatory and economic components of labour law, in line with its three fundamental principles.[384]

This parenthesis of upward convergence did not last long, and labour law began to be approached more and more as a macroeconomic variable. The economic rationale of labour policies gained ground as they addressed the function of adapting labour legislation to the evolving economic environment. Throughout the years, the ability of labour law to pursue the protective function as well as the function of uplifting workers' bargaining power was thus severely diminished.

More pronounced deregulatory pressures on national labour legislation then emerged from the various governance processes launched by the Lisbon Agenda and by the Europe 2020 strategy, which led to the creation of the European Semester. With those, EU policymakers pursued the flexicurity agenda, which basically implied the full reorientation of labour policies onto the regulation of the labour market. This accelerated the erosion of the emancipatory rationale of labour law and thus advanced the departure from its original nature.

This transformation was only partially reversed by the adoption of the EPSR. It was noted that the EPSR was conceived as part of the strategy to deepen the EMU and this is reflected in the stronger emphasis on labour market inclusivity rather than on the actual working conditions. This does not detract from the fact that there are elements in the Pillar that, if decontextualised from the macroeconomic agenda in which they were originally included, could support a paradigm shift and revive the emancipatory function of labour law. Reference goes to Principle 6 on wages and Principle 8 on social dialogue, as well as those legislative initiatives on minimum wages, gender pay gap and platform workers that aim at giving implementation to the Pillar. Finally, a possible window of opportunity for the revaluation of labour law has also opened in the EU's reaction to the COVID-19 crisis. It is, however, too early to determine how the current lenient approach towards EU fiscal rules will unfold.[385]

In light of these insights, it seems now the time to address the first sub-research question (RQ1): *What (prevailing) normative model(s) is(are) underlying the approaches of EU institutional policymakers with respect to labour law?* From the analysis conducted in this chapter, it emerged that EU policymakers have contributed to the transformation of the original nature of labour law, by means of progressive marginalisation of its emancipatory function. This occurred from the 1980s onwards and accelerated in the mid-2000s when labour market flexibilisation became the dominant paradigm through which labour law was approached. In Chapter 1, section 2.2.4, it was discussed that when labour law is merely addressed in relation to the labour market functioning, its emancipatory component is substantially weakened. The adoption of the Pillar, its embedding into the more socially progressive agenda promoted by the Von der Leyen Commission, as well as the most recent policymaking connected to the NGEU, might, however, have marked a turning point and lead to a revival of the social and emancipatory rationale of EU labour law.

384. Section 2.2.
385. As discussed in section 4.2.

CHAPTER 3

The Court of Justice and Labour Law: A Case Study on the Transfer of Undertakings Directive

1 INTRODUCTION

Chapter 2 focused on identifying the prevailing normative model in EU policymaking with respect to labour law. It found that the EU approach has changed over the years, leading to a transformation in the function pursued by labour law. From the mid-1980s onwards, there has in fact been a progressive enhancement of the economic rationale. Only recently, with the adoption of the EPSR and the NGEU, there is more space for the re-valorisation of the emancipatory component.

The objective of this chapter is to discuss how the CJEU's case law has accompanied this transformative process. Has the Court strengthened, limited or even attempted to reverse the normative approach of EU rule-makers? Casting light on these issues allows us to address RQ2: *Is it possible to identify an underlying normative model in the case law of the CJEU with respect to labour law?*

The exploration that is outlined in this chapter consents also to give a first definition of the role of the Court with respect to labour law. It is worth recalling that, at this point of the book, the research is still collocated in the first layer of analysis (*see* Introduction, section 2) and that the case law of the Court is, in fact, addressed according to those evaluative paradigms typical of labour studies. It is through those lenses that this chapter outlines an analysis and assessment of the (eventual) normative inclination of the Court vis-à-vis the emancipatory dimension of labour law. The assumption that the Court has a policy-driven approach would be reinforced if such analysis reveals that the Court consistently valorises the economic rationale of the considered norms. Otherwise, the Court's (pro-employer) bias would emerge mitigated.

As for the structure and content of this chapter, the exploration of the normative model of labour law is conducted through a series of case studies on the case law on the EU directive on workers' rights in case of transfer of undertakings. In section 2, the directive on acquired rights in case of transfer of undertaking is presented and it is shown that its rules are the expression of a synthesis between the economic and the social dimension of labour law. In section 3, the reasons that make this directive an adequate subject for empirical legal analysis are discussed. In section 4, the methodology is explained, and in section 5 the case studies are presented. The focus is first on the Court's interpretation of the scope of application of the directive and, subsequently, of the rights conferred to workers (i.e., the right to continue the employment relationship with the transferee). Section 6 addresses RQ2 and provides a reflection on the Court's prevailing normative model in relation to the labour norms established in the directive. Section 6 concludes the chapter by proposing a first definition of the Court's role with respect to EU labour law.

2 DIRECTIVE 2001/23/EC ON ACQUIRED RIGHTS IN CASE OF TRANSFER OF UNDERTAKING

Directive 2001/23/EC on acquired rights in case of transfer of undertaking codifies the original Council Directive 77/187/EEC of 14 February 1977 and its subsequent amendments made by Directive 98/50/EC.[386] Directive 77/187/EEC was adopted as part of the 1974-1976 Social Action Programme, in a period where EC rule-makers actively pursued upward convergence of working conditions (Chapter 2, section 2.2).[387] This directive was in fact promulgated together with two other rather progressive instruments, a directive on information and consultation in case of collective redundancies and a directive to protect workers in the event of insolvency of the employer.[388]

The adoption of these provisions is all the more remarkable considering that, at the time they were introduced, the Treaty of Rome did not grant the European Community any legislative power in the area of employment and social policies. The legal basis for Directive 77/187/EC was in fact Article 100 TEEC (now Article 115

386. Council Directive 77/187/EEC of 14 February 1977 on the approximation of the laws of the Member States relating to the safeguarding of employees' rights in the event of transfers of undertakings, businesses or parts of businesses *OJ L 61, 5.3.1977, pp. 26-28*; Council Directive 98/50/EC of 29 June 1998 amending Directive 77/187/EEC on the approximation of the laws of the Member States relating to the safeguarding of employees' rights in the event of transfers of undertakings, businesses or parts of businesses *OJ L 201, 17.7.1998, p. 88-92;* Council Directive 2001/23/EC of 12 March 2001 on the approximation of the laws of the Member States relating to the safeguarding of employees' rights in the event of transfers of undertakings, businesses or parts of undertakings or businesses *Official Journal L 082, 22/03/2001 pp. 0016-0020.*

387. R. Blanpain, *Institutional Changes and European Social Policies after the Treaty of Amsterdam*, Kluwer Law International, The Hague, 1998, p. 11.

388. Council Directive 75/129/EEC of 17 February 1975 on the approximation of the laws of the Member States relating to collective redundancies *OJ L 48, 22.2.1975, pp. 29-30;* Council Directive 80/987/EEC of 20 October 1980 on the approximation of the laws of the Member States relating to the protection of employees in the event of the insolvency of their employer *OJ L 283, 28.10.1980, pp. 23-27.*

TFEU), consenting the Council to adopt directives with the aim of harmonising national legal systems where this was necessary to advance the expansion of the internal market.[389]

As can be deduced from its full title ('Directive on the approximation of the laws of the Member States relating to the safeguarding of employees' rights in the event of transfers of undertakings, businesses or parts of businesses'), Directive 77/187/EC introduced a floor of workers' rights in the event that their undertaking or part of the undertaking undergoes a business restructuring operation defined as a 'transfer'.[390] It is not a coincidence that one of the first legislative instruments adopted at the European level in the field of employment concerned transfer of undertakings. During the second half of the 1970s, Europe (as well as most of the Western world) was going through an economic recession, aggravated by the oil crisis,[391] which led to a considerable increase in business restructuring operations.[392] This risked provoking internal market distortion whereby business closures or transfers would take place in those countries with comparatively lower labour costs, thus enabling a social dumping spiral. To prevent this, the EC legislator decided to intervene by establishing a level playing field.[393]

Besides its internal market embedding, the directive also had a strong social rationale. This emerges from the preamble of Directive 77/187/EEC, where it was clearly expressed that the objective of the norm was to 'provide for the protection of employees in the event of a change of employer, in particular, to ensure that their rights are safeguarded'.[394]

389. Article 100 TEEC: 'The Council, acting by means of unanimous vote on a proposal of the Commission, shall issue directives for the approximation of such legislative and administrative provisions of the Member States as have a direct incident on the establishment or functioning of the Common Market.'
390. For early comments on Directive 77/187/EEC: J. Hunt, 'The Court of Justice as a Policy Actor: The Case of the Acquired Rights Directive', Legal Studies, 18(3), pp. 336-359, 1998; S. Hardy & R. Painter, 'Revising the Acquired Rights Directive', Industrial Law Journal, 25(2), pp. 160-168, 1996; J. Nazerali & K. Plumbley-Jones, 'New Acquired Rights Directive – A Step in the Dark?', European Business Law Review, 6(2), pp. 31-36, 1995.
391. I. Van Hiel, 'The Protection of Collectively Agreed Labour Conditions under the Transfer of Undertakings Directive' in J. de Bruyne, M. de Potter & I. Van Hiel (eds), *Policy Within and Through Law*, Maklu, Anterpen, 2015, pp. 283-294, p. 284.
392. Recital 1 of Directive 77/187/EEC: 'Whereas economic trends are bringing in their wake, at both national and Community level, changes in the structure of undertakings, through transfers of undertakings, businesses or parts of businesses to other employers as a result of legal transfers or mergers.'
393. Hence the choice to use Article 100 TEEC as legal basis. Recitals 3 and 4 of Directive 77/187/EEC: 'Whereas differences still remain in the Member states as regards the extent of the protection of employees in this respect and these differences should be reduced; whereas these differences can have a direct effect on the function of the Common Market.'
394. On the presence of a dual rationale – economic and social – *see* F. Valdés Dal-Ré, 'Transfers of Undertakings: An Experience of Clashes and Harmonies Between Community Law and National Legal Systems' in S. Sciarra (ed.), *Labour Law in the Courts: National Judges and the European Court of Justice*, Hart Publishing, Oxford, 2001, pp. 179-209, p. 183; D. Carvalho Martins, 'Transfer of an Economic Unit: Requirements, Effects and Recent CJEU Ruling', European Labour Law Journal, 9(1), pp. 24-49, 2018; E. Brameshuber, 'Balancing vs. Preservation of Rights under the Acquired Rights Directive', Industrial Law Journal, 45(3), pp. 443-454, 2016.

As to its regulatory content, Directive 77/187/EEC applied 'to the transfer of an undertaking, business or part of a business to another employer as a result of a legal transfer or merger'.[395] This implies that all transactions whereby a business (or part of a business) is transferred from one employer (the transferor) to another (the transferee) could potentially fall within this broad legal formula.[396] Then, the directive conferred three types of rights on workers. First, it stated that in the event of a transfer of a business, the employees had the right to continue without interruption or alteration of their employment relationship with the transferee.[397] It means that the terms and conditions of employment may not be detrimentally modified by the transferee. This is also the case when the employment relationship is regulated by collective agreements, whose terms have to be respected for a minimum period of one year. Second, neither the transferor nor the transferee may dismiss employees for reasons connected with the transfer. Only dismissals for economic, technical or organisational reasons are permitted.[398] Third, the directive requires both the transferor and the transferee to inform and consult the employees prior to the transfer.[399]

As mentioned, with the adoption of this directive, the Community legislator intended to achieve greater harmonisation of national rules by creating a floor of rights for workers. The aim was not, therefore, to regulate in detail the practice of transferring a business or a branch of a business. This explains why this directive has, in relation to certain aspects, left wide discretion to national legislators.[400] For example, Member States might decide that also the transferor remains liable in respect of obligations which arose prior to the transfer. The fact that the directive intended to impose only minimum standards of protection explains the 'more favourable clause' in Article 7 (now 8), according to which 'The directive shall not affect the right of Member States to apply or introduce law, regulations or administrative provisions which are more favourable to employees.'[401]

Directive 77/187/EEC was then amended in 1998 by Directive 98/50/EC.[402] The changes mainly concerned the scope of application as the concept of 'transfer of a

395. Article 1 Directive 77/187/EEC.
396. R.M. Beltzer, 'The Transfer of Undertakings and the Importance of Taking over Personnel: A Vicious Circle', International Journal of Comparative Labour Law and Industrial Relations, 23(1), pp. 139-155, 2007; G. Santoro-Passarelli, 'The Transfer of Undertakings: Striking a Balance Between Individual Workers' Rights and Business Needs', International Journal of Comparative Labour Law and Industrial Relations, 23(3), pp. 311-334, 2007.
397. Article 3(1) and 3(2) Directive 77/187/EEC, currently Article 3(1) and 3(3) Directive 2001/23/EC.
398. Article 4 Directive 77/187/EEC, currently Article 4 Directive 2001/23/EC.
399. Article 6 Directive 77/187/EEC, currently Article 7 Directive 2001/23/EC.
400. I. Van Hiel, 'The Protection of Collectively Agreed Labour Conditions under the Transfer of Undertakings Directive' in J. de Bruyne, M. de Potter & I. Van Hiel (eds), *Policy Within and Through Law*, Maklu, Anterpen, 2015, pp. 283-294.
401. Article 7 Directive 77/187/EEC, currently Article 8 Directive 2001/23/EC.
402. J. Nazerali, K. Plumbley-Jones, 'New Acquired Rights Directive – A Step in the Dark?', European Business Law Review, 6(2), pp. 31-36, 1995; J. Hunt, 'The Court of Justice as a Policy Actor: The Case of the Acquired Rights Directive', Legal Studies, 18(3), pp. 336-359, 1998, p. 17; S. O'Leary, *Employment law at the European Court of Justice: judicial structures, policies, and processes*, Hart Publishing, Oxford, 2002, p. 281; S. Hardy, R. Painter, 'Revising the Acquired Rights Directive', Industrial Law Journal, 25(2), pp. 160-168, 1996.

business' became narrower. The preamble of Directive 98/50/EC explained that an updating of Directive 77/187/EEC was necessary because 'considerations of legal security and transparency require that the legal concept of transfer be clarified in light of the case law of the Court of Justice'. This already speaks volumes about the significant impact that the case law of the Court has had on the definition of these rules.[403] Following this legislative amendment, workers were protected only if the transfer from the transferor to the transferee concerned an 'economic entity which retains its identity, meaning an organised grouping of resources which has the objective of pursuing an economic activity'.[404]

As is further discussed below, the effect of this reform was to limit the situations in which the directive would find application.[405] The amending directive also introduced the possibility for Member States to exclude the rules on continuation of employment following a transfer for those companies subject to 'bankruptcy proceedings or any analogous insolvency proceedings instituted with a view to the liquidation of assets'.[406] Clearly, this amendment also implied a narrowing of the scope compared to the original version of the legislation. However, this aspect is not further developed in the book; the case studies focus instead on the normative changes concerning the notion of 'transfer', as it is in relation to this notion that the case law of the Court has evolved the most. Finally, in 2001 the rules on acquired rights in the case of transfers were codified in Directive 2001/23/EC to consolidate the original text with the amendments introduced by Directive 98/50/EC.[407]

It is already interesting to note that the change in the scope of application of the directive following the 1998 reform is consistent with the evolution of the general approach of EC rule-makers with respect to labour law. In Chapter 2, it was indeed shown that EC policymaking had gradually become more receptive to the economic dimension of labour policies.[408] At the same time, the revisions in the provisions of the directive also bear the mark of the Court's case law, leading commentators to see in the Court a political actor supporting the Commission's deregulatory agenda.[409]

---

403. Recital 7 Directive 2001/23/EC, from which emerges that the 1977 directive was amended also 'in light of the impact of the internal market'.
404. Article 1(1)b Directive 98/50/EC.
405. Section 5.1.2 and Chapter 6, section 3.2.
406. Article 4a Directive 98/50/EC. The introduction of this possibility to derogate from the protective rules of the directive in case of bankruptcy codified the Court of Justice case law. *See* judgment of 7 February 1985, *Abels v. Bedrijfsvereniging voor de Metaalindustrie en de Electrotechnische Industrie*, C-135/83, ECLI:EU:C:1985:55; judgment of 25 July 1991, *Giuseppe d'Urso, Adriana Ventadori and others v. Ercole Marelli Elettromeccanica Generale SpA and others*, C-362/89, ECLI:EU:C:1991:326; judgment of 7 December 1995, *Luigi Spano and others v. Fiat Geotech SpA and Fiat Hitachi Excavators SpA*, C-472/93, ECLI:EU:C:1995:421; judgment of 12 November 1998, *Europièces SA v. Wilfried Sanders and Automotive Industries Holding Company SA*, C-399/96, ECLI:EU:C:1998:532.
407. European Commission, Proposal for a Council Directive on the Approximation of the Laws of the Member States Relating to the Safeguarding of Employees' Rights in the Event of Transfers of Undertakings, Businesses or Parts of Undertakings or Businesses (codified version), COM(2000) 259 final, Brussels, 2 May 2000.
408. *See* above, Chapter 2, section 5.
409. On the connection between the legal developments surrounding the Acquired Rights Directive and the emerging employment policy of the EU, as articulated by the political institutions, *see*

3 MARGIN OF GENERALISATION OF THE CASE STUDY

This section explains that the directive on acquired rights in case of transfer of undertakings constitutes an interesting legal instrument for empirical analysis in as much as it presents features that consent to a certain degree of generalisation in relation to the findings of the case studies.

3.1 The Court Can 'Choose' Between Different Functions

One of these features is that the directive embodies the three fundamental normative principles of labour law (as described in Chapter 1, section 2.1) and expresses both an emancipatory and an economic rationale.

First, the rule whereby the workers shall continue their employment relationship with the transferee has a clear protective function, as defined in Chapter 1, section 2.2.1.[410] This function informs the main rules of the directive and is, therefore, predominant. The directive prohibits employers from making detrimental changes to working conditions and also introduces a ban on dismissal. This substantially restricts the contractual freedom of the employer and, in particular, of the transferee.

Second, the directive also fulfils the function of uplifting workers' bargaining power, described in Chapter 1, section 2.2.2. It does so by ensuring that the terms and conditions laid down in the collective agreement which were applicable before the transfer remain applicable after the transfer.[411] The directive thus valorises collective bargaining as a means of mitigating the imbalance between the bargaining powers of the parties. Such an imbalance is particularly exacerbated in the context of business transfers, as in situations of business reorganisations workers are more vulnerable and precarious, and would be prepared to accept a deterioration in working conditions in order not to lose their jobs.[412]

Finally, the directive also expresses the labour law function of adapting workers' rights to the needs of businesses and of the economy, outlined in Chapter 1, section 2.2.3. Member States may in fact provide that the obligation of the transferee not to modify the working conditions of the transferred workers is limited in time.[413] It is, in

J. Hunt, 'The Court of Justice as a Policy Actor: The Case of the Acquired Rights Directive', Legal Studies, 18(3), pp. 336-359, 1998.

410. S. Giubboni, 'Freedom to Conduct a Business and EU Labour Law', European Constitutional Law Review, 14, pp. 172-190, 2018, on the 'the coessential protective and emancipating function' of the directive.

411. Article 3(3) Directive 2001/23/EC. *See* J. Prassl, 'Business Freedoms and Employment Rights in the European Union', Cambridge Yearbook of European Legal Studies, 17, pp. 189-209, 2015.

412. *See* Judgment of 25 July 1991, *Giuseppe d'Urso, Adriana Ventadori and others v. Ercole Marelli Elettromeccanica Generale SpA and others*, C-362/89, ECLI:EU:C:1991:326 (para. 11): 'The implementation of the rights conferred on employees by the Directive may not therefore be made subject to the consent of either the transferor or the transferee nor the consent of the employees' representatives or the employees themselves, with the sole reservation, as regards the workers themselves, that, following a decision freely taken by them, they are at liberty, after the transfer, not to continue the employment relationship with the new employer.'

413. Article 3(3) of Directive 2001/23/EC establishes that 'Following the transfer, the transferee shall continue to observe the terms and conditions agreed in any collective agreement on the

particular, significant to note that the Commission, already in its first legislative proposal of the directive, dating back to 1974, stated that the rule limiting the application of collective agreements to which the transferee is not a party (current Article 3.3) was designed to reconcile the interests of the employees and those of the transferee.[414] On the one hand, the interest of the employees is to continue their employment relationship under the same terms and conditions; on the other hand, the freedom of the transferee is not to be covered by a collective agreement unless with *erga omnes* effects (negative freedom of association). As the Commission itself noted 'it would be a breach of the right of free association to impose [without time limit] on the transferee against his will a collective agreement to which he is not already party'.[415] Moreover, in Article 4 the directive establishes that the prohibition on dismissal does not apply where there are organisational, technical and economic reasons. The compression of the employer's business freedom is therefore relative and by all means temporary.[416]

The presence of these three functions implies that the directive embodies all three of those fundamental principles of labour law described in Chapter 1, section 2.1: it addresses the uneven distribution of bargaining power among the parties (fundamental principle 1),[417] prevents labour from turning into a mere commodity (fundamental principle 2),[418] and is compatible with the market economy (fundamental principle 3).[419] It follows that the directive contains in a quite pronounced way both an emancipatory and an economic dimension. Its composite nature makes it a good testing ground for identifying whether the Court's reasoning leans towards a specific normative approach with respect to labour law.

For example, if it emerges that the Court gives a minimalist interpretation to the prohibition of dismissal or to the obligation of the transferee to respect the collective agreement applicable before the transfer, it could be inferred that the Court tends to marginalise the protective function, as well as that of supporting workers' bargaining power. This interpretation would indeed enhance the employer's position, with consequent compression of the emancipatory dimension of the directive.

---

same terms applicable to the transferor under that agreement, until the date of termination or expiry of the collective agreement or the entry into force or application of another collective agreement. *Member States may limit the period for observing such terms and conditions with the proviso that it shall not be less than one year*' (emphasis added).

414. European Commission, Proposal for a Directive of the Council on harmonisation of the legislation of Member States on the retention of the rights and advantages of employees in the case of mergers, takeovers and amalgamations, COM(74)351 Final/2, Brussels, 29 May 1974.
415. *Ibid.*, p. 6.
416. Articles 3(3) and 4(1) of the directive. *See* J. Prassl, 'Business Freedoms and Employment Rights in the European Union', Cambridge Yearbook of European Legal Studies, 17, pp. 189-209, 2015, where Prassl noted that 'The assertion that dynamic clauses would deny transferees necessary "room for manoeuvre" is, finally, difficult to sustain in the light of the Daddy's Dance Hall line of cases: the operation of the ARD does not mean that a transfer freezes employment conditions in all eternity.' And that 'As the Advocate General notes, "there is nothing to prevent [the parties] from renegotiating the clause in the contract that refers to the collective agreement".'
417. Section 2.1.1.
418. Section 2.1.2.
419. Section 2.1.3.

3.2 Normative Indeterminacy

The second reason for selecting the directive on transfer of undertaking is that its rules are characterised by a relatively high degree of regulatory vagueness and imprecision. This gives the Court ample room for manoeuvre to eventually express its normative preferences.[420]

More precisely drafted legislative instruments require the Court to rely more extensively on techniques of textual interpretation. In those cases, there would not be much material for a case study, as the Court's reasoning would be essentially uniform, constrained by the literal meaning of the rules. This is definitely not the case with the directive on acquired rights in case of transfer. Suffice it to recall, for example, that in its original version, the scope was simply defined by the rather vague concept of 'transfer of an undertaking to another employer as a result of a legal transfer'. Does this include the transfer of service contracts? How many assets and materials must be taken over for a transfer to occur? The text of the directive does not say. Similar considerations apply to the employment protection rules: what happens if the transferee decides to enter into a new collective agreement? Can workers, through their trade union representatives, waive some of the rights established by the directive? These are questions of crucial practical importance that are not addressed in the text of the directive. The Court can therefore range from interpretations that promote the emancipatory dimension to others that emphasise the economic one.

3.3 A Rich Body of Case Law

Another reason that makes the transfer directive an interesting field of exploration is that it entered into force in the late 1970s and a rich body of case law has developed since then. By the end of 2020, the Court had in fact delivered more than 70 judgments.

Moreover, the Court first ruled on the directive in 1983, meaning that the case law has spread over a period of almost 40 years now. This is a sufficiently long period of time for the case studies to identify eventual evolutions in the Court's approach towards labour law. It also consents to compare the Court's approach with the institutional policymaking and the evolution that was observed in Chapter 2.

420. A.C.L. Davies, A. Bogg & C. Costello, 'The Role of the Court of Justice in Labour Law' in A. Bogg, C. Costello & A.C.L. Davies (eds), *Research Handbook on EU Labour Law*, Edward Elgar Publishing, Cheltenham, 2016, pp. 114-149, where it is argued that 'While there has been much comment (particularly among UK scholars) on the Court's adoption of a purposive approach to interpretation, the drafting of most directives does not lend itself to a literal strategy. The ARD is a good illustration of this. [...] key terms were left undefined, leaving it to the Court to provide interpretative guidance', p. 135; S. O'Leary, *Employment Law at the European Court of Justice: Judicial Structures, Policies, and Processes*, Hart Publishing, Oxford, 2002: 'case law of the Court on the acquired rights directive casts ample light on the difficulties which inadequately drafted or highly compromising legislation can throw up', p. 5.

3.4 Debate on the Purposive Approach by the Court

Finally, an additional reason for focusing on the case law on the directive on transfer of undertakings is the existence of a rich academic debate on the Court's purposive approach while interpreting its provisions.[421]

It is possible to identify at least two moments when the Court's case law has attracted particular attention from commentators. The first moment coincided with a sudden change in case law in the mid-1990s in relation to the scope of application of the directive. At a certain moment the Court in fact opted for a narrower interpretation of the notion of 'transfer of a business'. As mentioned in section 2 above, this interpretation was subsequently incorporated into the text of the legislation, by means of amending directive 98/50/EC. Without unnecessarily anticipating the case studies, it is sufficient to mention that in 1994, the Court ruled that the directive applies even if the transferred business consisted exclusively of the work carried out by a single cleaner (*Schmidt*).[422] The year later, instead, the Court ruled that the directive applies only if the transfer concerns a 'stable economic entity' (*Strø Mølle Akustik*). Subsequently, in *Süzen* (1997), it further specified that this is only the case if the transferee takes over at least half of the material assets or of the personnel.[423]

Several commentators have interpreted this change of approach as a reflection of the Court's alignment with EU policymakers, and their efforts to relax employment standards. For instance, More observed that 'whilst employment protection was clearly the predominant aim of the Acquired Rights Directive as it emerged in the 1970s, the

421. Among the authors that have recognised a purposive approach in the Court's reasoning: J. Hunt, 'The Court of Justice as a Policy Actor: The Case of the Acquired Rights Directive', Legal Studies, 18(3), pp. 336-359, 1998; S. Hardy & R. Painter, 'Revising the Acquired Rights Directive', Industrial Law Journal, 25(2), pp. 160-168, 1996; J. Nazerali & K. Plumbley-Jones, 'New Acquired Rights Directive – A Step in the Dark?', European Business Law Review, 6(2), pp. 31-36, 1995; P. Davies, 'Transfers of Undertakings: Preliminary Remarks' in S. Sciarra (ed.), *Labour Law in the Courts: National Judges and the European Court of Justice*, Hart Publishing, Oxford, 2001, pp. 131-144; R.M. Beltzer, 'The Transfer of Undertakings and the Importance of Taking Over Personnel: A Vicious Circle', International Journal of Comparative Labour Law and Industrial Relations, 23(1), pp. 139-155, 2007; A.C.L. Davies, A. Bogg & C. Costello, 'The Role of the Court of Justice in Labour Law' in A. Bogg, C. Costello & A.C.L. Davies (eds), *Research Handbook on EU Labour Law*, Edward Elgar Publishing, Cheltenham, 2016, pp. 114-149; S. Giubboni, 'Freedom to Conduct a Business and EU Labour Law', European Constitutional Law Review, 14, pp. 172-190, 2018; J. Prassl, 'Freedom of Contract as a General Principle of EU Law? Transfers of Undertakings and the Protection of Employer Rights in EU Labour Law', Industrial Law Journal, 42(4), pp. 434-446, 2013; S. Weatherill, 'Use and Abuse of the EU's Charter of Fundamental Rights: On the Improper Veneration of "Freedom of Contract"', European Review of Contract Law, 10(1), pp. 167-182, 2014; M. Bartl & C. Leone, 'Minimum Harmonisation After Alemo-Herron: The Janus Face of the EU Fundamental Rights Review', European Constitutional Law Review, 11(1), pp. 140-154, 2015; J. McMullen, 'Leaving a Legacy: Recent Jurisprudence of the European Court on Transfer of Undertakings', Industrial Law Journal, 50(1), pp. 130-157, 2021.
422. Judgment of 14 April 1994, *Christel Schmidt v. Spar- und Leihkasse der früheren Ämter Bordesholm, Kiel und Cronshagen*, C-392/92, ECLI:EU:C:1994:134.
423. Judgment of 19 September 1995, *Ledernes Hovedorganisation, acting for Ole Rygaard v. Dansk Arbejdsgiverforening, acting for Strø Mølle Akustik A/S*, C-48/94, ECLI:EU:C:1995:290; judgment of 11 March 1997, *Ayse Süzen v. Zehnacker Gebäudereinigung GmbH Krankenhausservice*, C-13/95, ECLI:EU:C:1997:141.

Court has to tread a different path in attempting to adopt the application of the Directive to the changed, 'flexible', business environment of the 1990s'.[424] Similarly, Hunt identified a 'connection between the legal developments surrounding the Acquired Rights Directive to the emerging policy of the EU, as articulated by the political institutions' and feared the risk that the Court was sacrificing 'legal certainty at the altar of political pragmatism'.[425] And, according to Bourn, *Süzen* represented 'a substantial re-evaluation by the Court of the balance to be struck between the economic imperative to pursue the most cost-efficient forms of organisation and the need for the protection of workers' interests in a changing labour market'.[426]

It should be noted that the narrowing of the scope of application of the directive was not seen by all academic observers as an expression of an ideological bias of the Court. Beltzer, for instance, considered it a timely correction of an excessively broad and 'impractical' interpretation of the concept of transfer.[427] Similarly, Rubinstein welcomed the change of approach, which was in his view necessary in order to avoid that the directive would apply 'when I change the contractor who cut my lawn'.[428] Irrespective of the position taken, it is evident that this shift in the Court's reasoning instigated a rich academic debate and reinforced the perception of the Court as a policymaking actor.[429]

The second episode that led the Court to attract the attention of academic commentators coincided with the *Alemo-Herron* case, already discussed in Chapter 1.[430] In that judgment, the Court prevented transferred employees from claiming the application of a 'dynamic' contractual clause referring to a future collective agreement. The Court thus adopted a restrictive reading of the obligation of the transferee to apply in full the contractual terms and conditions in force before the transfer. Instead, the Court favoured an extensive interpretation of the transferee's freedom of contract, as it gave de facto direct effect to Article 16 CFREU.[431]

In *Alemo-Herron*, the Court distanced itself from its previous prevalent approach, characterised by a rather rigid and protective interpretation of the rights that the

424. G. More, 'The Acquired Rights Directive: Frustrating or Facilitating Labour Market Flexibility' in J. Shaw & G. More (eds), *New Legal Dynamics of European Union*, Clarendon Press, Oxford, 1995, pp. 129-147.
425. J. Hunt, 'The Court of Justice as a Policy Actor: The Case of the Acquired Rights Directive', Legal Studies, 18(3), pp. 336-359, 1998.
426. C. Bourn, 'When Does the Transfer of a Service Contract Constitute the Transfer of an Undertaking?', European Law Review, 23(1), pp. 59-64, 1998.
427. R.M. Beltzer, 'The Transfer of Undertakings and the Importance of Taking Over Personnel: A Vicious Circle', International Journal of Comparative Labour Law and Industrial Relations, 23(1), pp. 139-155, 2007.
428. C. Barnard, *EU Employment Law*, Oxford University Press, Oxford, 2012, p. 594, referring to Rubinstein [1994] ECR I-257.
429. J. Hunt, 'The Court of Justice as a Policy Actor: The Case of the Acquired Rights Directive', Legal Studies, 18(3), pp. 336-359, 1998; S. O'Leary, *Employment Law at the European Court of Justice: Judicial Structures, Policies, and Processes*, Hart Publishing, Oxford, 2002, p. 255.
430. Section 3.1.
431. J. Prassl, 'Freedom of Contract as a General Principle of EU Law? Transfers of Undertakings and the Protection of Employer Rights in EU Labour Law', Industrial Law Journal, 42(4), pp. 434-446, 2013.

directive confers to workers, and this too caused an intense academic debate.[432] Davies, Bogg, Costello, Weatherill, Bartl and Leone are among the scholars who read in *Alemo-Herron* an expression of the Court's normative preferences (their views were illustrated in Chapter 1, section 3.1).[433] In the same direction go Prassl's observations that the Court erred in its assessment of the underlying interests of the case, because 'the Acquired Rights Directive is not premised on an intended balance. On the contrary, it is explicitly worker protective, designed as a counter-weight to the impact of earlier market liberalizations'.[434] Equally critical was Giubboni, who stated that 'the ideological revision of the relationship between the internal market and labour law appears to be evident' and that *Alemo-Herron* 'now finalises the explicitly neoliberal restyling regarding the internal market doctrine initiated by the famous [Laval] quartet'.[435] The same concern was shared by Grussot, Pétursson and Pierce, who argued that 'the absence of taking into consideration the social dimension [by the Court] is blatant and problematic'.[436]

Fewer scholars raised milder voices. Martins observed that the Court has the arduous task of interpreting the provisions of the directive both in view of the underlying objectives of the directive and in view of the institutional context in which it is inserted, including the fundamental rights of the CFREU (among which is the freedom to conduct a business).[437] In light of the complexity of the legal interests to be weighed, Martins therefore considered that, in *Alemo-Herron*, the Court 'found a spot in the middle of the bridge' and struck an acceptable balance.[438] Similarly, Brameshuber suggested that 'although it is not derived explicitly from the directive itself, the balancing approach is not as far-fetched an idea as suggested by Prassl among others'.[439] In support of this view, Brameshuber noted that among the objectives of the directive is also that of 'facilitating the restructuring of enterprises with a view of making them more competitive and effective' and that the directive is based on the Union's competences concerning the harmonisation of the internal market, and not on the social policy chapter of the Treaty'.[440]

Overall, the fact that, over the years, commentators have perceived the Court as a purposive actor (either in one direction or in the other) makes the directive a good

432. S. O'Leary, *Employment Law at the European Court of Justice: Judicial Structures, Policies, and Processes*, Hart Publishing, Oxford, 2002, p. 250; *see* section 3.1.
433. *See supra* n. 131.
434. J. Prassl, 'Freedom of Contract as a General Principle of EU Law? Transfers of Undertakings and the Protection of Employer Rights in EU Labour Law', Industrial Law Journal, 42(4), pp. 434-446, 2013.
435. S. Giubboni, 'Freedom to Conduct a Business and EU Labour Law', European Constitutional Law Review, 14, pp. 172-190, 2018.
436. X. Groussot, T.G. Pétursson & J. Pierce, 'Weak Right, Strong Court – The Freedom to Conduct Business and the EU Charter of Fundamental Rights', Legal Research Paper Series, Lund University, Lund, 2014.
437. D. Carvalho Martins, 'Transfer of an Economic Unit: Requirements, Effects and Recent CJEU Ruling', European Labour Law Journal, 9(1), pp. 24-49, 2018.
438. *Ibid.*
439. E. Brameshuber, 'Balancing vs. Preservation of Rights under the Acquired Rights Directive', Industrial Law Journal, 45(3), pp. 443-454, 2016.
440. *Ibid.*

testing ground for case studies intending to explore the Court's role vis-à-vis EU labour law.

4 CASE STUDY'S STRUCTURE AND METHODOLOGY

This chapter aims to identify the underlying normative model in the case law with respect to labour law. The case studies that are presented in the next section focus on the Court's approach to the different functions enshrined in the directive (as seen in section 3.1 above) and thus to its emancipatory component. More precisely, the case studies address three different aspects of the directive: the scope of application, the rights conferred to workers concerning the continuation of their employment relationship after the transfer, and the purpose that the Court attributes to the norms. The insights emerging from the empirical analysis inform the first definition of the role of the Court with respect to labour law.

The first case studies (section 5.1) concern the scope of the directive. Understanding how the Court has interpreted the scope contributes, albeit indirectly, to outlining its approach to the social rationale of the directive. Indeed, the broader the scope of the norms, the more workers can claim the rights stipulated therein. As anticipated in section 2, the directive articulates its scope of application in two different concepts, each requiring a separate case study.[441] The first, in section 5.1.1, focuses on the notion of 'legal transfer'. The second, in section 5.1.2, addresses the concept of 'transfer of a business'. In both cases, the Court's reasonings are mapped on the basis of their implications for the coverage of the directive. The broader the interpretation of the two notions identifying the scope of application, the more the emancipatory rationale of the directive can find expression.

Section 5.2 turns to a case study on the rights that the directive confers to workers. In particular, the case study focuses on the employees' right to continue, under the same conditions, the employment relationship and not to be dismissed for reasoning connected to the transfer. This is not the only right that the directive establishes. However, it is in relation to this norm that the Court has developed the largest body of case law.[442] In this case study, the correlation between the Court's reasoning and its approach to the emancipatory component of the directive is quite direct. If it turns out that the rulings are characterised by a broad interpretation of the workers' rights, then the Court emphasises the social component of the directive. If, on the other hand, it emerges that these rights are interpreted narrowly, then it may be assumed that the Court is sensitive to the interests of the employer and valorises the economic underpinning of the directive. Similarly to the case study on the scope of application, here the analysis consists of a cartography of the Court's reasonings,

441. Since Council Directive 98/50/EC of 29 June 1998 amending Directive 77/187/EEC on the approximation of the laws of the Member States relating to the safeguarding of employees' rights in the event of transfers of undertakings, businesses or parts of businesses *OJ L 201, 17.7.1998, pp. 88-92.*

442. For instance, information and consultation rights were not included in the analysis, due to lack of relevant case law, while the provisions related to insolvent business were not included due to the fact that the Court's approach did not change much over time.

which are mapped on the basis of the approach towards the emancipatory rationale of the directive.

Finally, in section 6, the last case study concerns the Court's interpretation of the purpose of the directive. In its judgments, the Court usually justifies its reasoning by reference to the objective pursued by the analysed rules. This reference to the objective of the law is more argumentative than substantive since it is the interpretation given to the scope of application and to the workers' rights that ultimately affects the emancipatory effect of the directive. Therefore, the case study on the purpose of the directive has not been included in the main empirical analysis conducted in this chapter but is rather presented to contextualise the insights that emerge from it.

Before turning to the actual case studies, it is also necessary to provide some methodological indications. The case studies were conducted following an analysis of all the judgments of the Court on Directive 77/187/EEC and, later, Directive 2001/23/EC. These are 72 judgments, from 1983 to mid-2022.[443] To these 72 judgments, filters were then applied. As mentioned, only those judgments that dealt with one of the following aspects were included in the case studies: the scope of application (47), the right to continue the employment relationship and the prohibition of dismissal (30), and where the Court expressed a view on the purpose of the directive (62). Most of these judgments concern a plurality of issues and, for this reason, the same judgment may appear in more than one case study.

It was also mentioned that the case studies map the judgments on the basis of their proximity, or rather distance, to the emancipatory dimension of the directive. The criteria used to classify the Court's reasonings are both linked to direct and easily measurable aspects (e.g., whether the definition of 'legal transfer' is narrow or broad) but also to more indirect aspects which relate to the 'social versus economic' tension underpinning the norms (e.g., if the Court gives a broad interpretation to the freedom to conduct a business).

This mapping took place in several steps. The first step consisted in reading the cases and in classifying them in consideration of the aspects dealt with ('scope of application' – divided into 'legal transfer' and 'transfer of a business', 'workers' rights', and 'purpose'). A first database of judgments was thus created. The second step was to identify key reasonings that are then used to classify the case law. These key reasoning were selected in relation to their ability to reveal the Court's approach towards the emancipatory rationale of the directive. An example of recurrent reasoning that has been used in the case study is the Court's statement that 'the protection provided by the directive is a matter of public policy and is independent of the will of the parties'. Or, where the Court established that 'it is necessary that the transferred entity maintains its identity', or when it ruled that even 'a concession by a public body can result in a legal transfer'.

The third step of the methodology was to categorise these reasonings according to what they expressed in relation to the emancipatory component of the directive. For

443. Data extracted from Eur-lex database: https://eur-lex.europa.eu/legal-content/EN/ALL/?uri=CELEX:31977L0187 and https://eur-lex.europa.eu/legal-content/EN/ALL/?uri=CELEX:32001L0023 (links last checked on 28 February 2022).

instance, in relation to workers' rights, the reasoning in which the Court stated that 'the protection provided by the directive is a matter of public policy' has been considered among those that reinforce the protective function (and the emancipatory rationale) of the directive. As for the notion of 'transfer of a business', the selected reasonings to requirements that according to the Court have to be present in order for the directive to apply. These requirements thus have the effect of limiting the scope of application. In fact, the higher their number, the narrower the scope of application of the directive, and the less valorised its emancipatory effect. An example is the already mentioned reasoning whereby 'it is necessary that the transferred entity maintains its identity'. On the contrary, it was noted that when addressing the concept of 'legal transfer' the Court generally adopted the opposite approach, as it has throughout time identified a series of circumstances that have the effect of broadening the scope of such concept. The reasoning whereby 'a concession by a public body can result in a legal transfer' is a good example. In this case, the more and the broader the circumstances, the more the Court allows the directive to exercise its emancipatory function.

Lastly, the fourth step of the methodology was to give a visual representation of the case studies, to bring out eventual changes in the jurisprudence in a more immediate and accessible way.

5 THE CASE STUDIES

5.1 The Scope of Application

The case studies on the scope of application show how, over the years, the Court has changed its interpretation regarding the nature of business operations in which the workers are covered by the directive.[444] As already mentioned, the wider the scope, the greater the number of workers who will be able to benefit from the rights established in the directive. It follows that a broad interpretation of the scope of application enhances the protective and emancipatory function that is intrinsic to the directive.

Before moving to the case study, it is important to recall once again that the scope of application is defined by two elements that emerge from the wording of the directive. These elements were already present in Directive 77/187/EEC, but they were made even more evident following the legislative amendment by Directive 98/50/EC.

444. Several authors have written about the (evolution in the) Court's interpretation of the scope of application of the transfer of undertakings directives. *See*, *inter alia*: J. Nazerali & K. Plumbley-Jones, 'New Acquired Rights Directive – A Step in the Dark?', European Business Law Review, 6(2), pp. 31-36, 1995; A. Lo Faro, 'Judicial Developments of EC Social Policy and Intra-community Institutional Dialogues: How to Define a "Legal Transfer"' in S. Sciarra (ed.), *Labour Law in the Courts: National Judges and the European Court of Justice*, Hart Publishing, Oxford, 2001, pp. 210-228; J. McMullen, 'Some Problems and Themes in the Application in Member States of Directive 2001/23/EC on Transfer of Undertakings', The International Journal of Comparative Labour Law and Industrial Relations, 23(3), pp. 335-374, 2007; R.M. Beltzer, 'The Transfer of Undertakings and the Importance of Taking Over Personnel: A Vicious Circle', International Journal of Comparative Labour Law and Industrial Relations, 23(1), pp. 139-155, 2007; J. McMullen, 'Leaving a Legacy: Recent Jurisprudence of the European Court on Transfer of Undertakings', Industrial Law Journal, 50(1), pp. 130-157, 2021.

The original definition of the scope of the directive was as follows (emphasis added):

> **Box 1: Scope of Application**
>
> **Directive 77/187/EEC**
>
> *Article 1*
> 1. This Directive shall apply to the *transfer of an undertaking, business or part of a business to another employer* as a *result of a legal transfer* or merger.

The directive thus applies if there are two cumulative circumstances.[445] The first line of Article 1 referred to a 'transfer of an undertaking, business or part of a business to another employer'. The second part of the sentence instead mentioned that such transfer shall take place 'as a result of a legal transfer or merger'.

The Court has profusely ruled on both elements. First, section 5.1.1 concerns the case law concerning the concept of 'legal transfer' (since there is no judgment concerning the concept of 'merger'), which is the first precondition for the application of the directive. Then, section 5.1.2 turns to the case law on the concept of 'transfer of a business'. Table 1 and Table 2 are intended to highlight the developments in the Court's approach to the function of labour law.

It is especially in relation to the second element of the definition ('transfer of a business') that the Court's approach has varied the most. As mentioned, this change in the interpretation of the scope was transposed into the text of the directive which, in its current version, reads as follows (emphasis added):[446]

445. In the case law, the Court of Justice at times refers to three circumstances: the transfer, the business, and the contractual relation (*see* Judgment of 24 January 2002, *Temco Service Industries SA v. Samir Imzilyen and Others*, C-51/00, ECLI:EU:C:2002:48). However, with regard to this book, it was decided to limit the analysis to only the first two elements.

446. J. Hunt, 'The Court of Justice as a Policy Actor: The Case of the Acquired Rights Directive', Legal Studies, 18(3), pp. 336-359, 1998; J. Nazerali & K. Plumbley-Jones, 'New Acquired Rights Directive – A Step in the Dark?', European Business Law Review, 6(2), pp. 31-36, 1995; S. Hardy & R. Painter, 'Revising the Acquired Rights Directive', Industrial Law Journal, 25(2), pp. 160-168, 1996.

Box 2: Scope of Application

Directive 2001/23/EC

Article 1

1. (a) This Directive shall apply to any *transfer of an undertaking, business, or part of an undertaking or business to another employer* as a result of a *legal transfer* or merger.
   (b) Subject to subparagraph (a) and the following provisions of this Article, there is a *transfer* within the meaning of this Directive where there is a *transfer of an economic entity which retains its identity, meaning an organised grouping of resources which has the objective of pursuing an economic activity*, whether or not that activity is central or ancillary.

As already discussed in section 2, this legislative amendment has narrowed the scope of application of the directive.[447] Article 1 now requires that, for a transfer to another employer to take place, there must be an 'economic entity which retains its identity', and specifies that this only occurs in relation to an 'organised grouping of resources which has the objective of pursuing an economic activity'. This change in the wording of Article 1(1)b was intended to align the scope of the directive with the EU case law, and this fact alone is already an indication of the impact of the Court in defining the normative implications of the directive.[448]

Finally, it is also worth mentioning that the scope of the directive is not merely defined by these two elements. Article 1(1)(c) explicitly excludes administrative reorganisations of public administrative authorities. Moreover, Article 5 gives Member States the possibility to exclude transfers taking place in the context of bankruptcy proceedings or analogous insolvency proceedings, provided that certain conditions are met. However, these aspects are not included in the case studies. The case law on transfer of undertakings in the context of public administration is rather scarce,[449]

447. As discussed in section 2 of this chapter. *See also* A. Lo Faro, 'Judicial Developments of EC Social Policy and Intra-community Institutional Dialogues: How to Define a "Legal Transfer"' in S. Sciarra (ed.), *Labour Law in the Courts: National Judges and the European Court of Justice*, Hart Publishing, Oxford, 2001, pp. 210-228.

448. As discussed in section 2 of this chapter.

449. Judgments where the Court addressed transfer operations in the context of public administration: Judgment of 15 October 1996, *Annette Henke v. Gemeinde Schierke and Verwaltungsgemeinschaft Brocken*, C-298/94, ECLI:EU:C:1996:382 (where the Court ruled that the reorganisation of structures of public administration or transfer of administrative functions between public administration authorities do not constitute a transfer. Other cases that have touched on the public nature of the transferor or the transferee have been included in the context of the case studies on the scope of application of the directive. These are the following: judgment of 26 September 2000, *Didier Mayeur v. Association Promotion de l'information messine (APIM)*, C-175/99, ECLI:EU:C:2000:505; judgment of 11 November 2004, *Johanna Maria Delahaye, née Delahaye v. Ministre de la Fonction publique et de la Réforme administrative*, C-425/02, ECLI:EU:C:2004:706; judgment of 29 July 2010, *Federación de Servicios Públicos de la UGT*

while that on insolvency proceedings is quite technical. Moreover, in both cases, the Court's reasoning did not evolve significantly over time.[450]

5.1.1 Legal Transfer

At the time of writing, the concept of 'legal transfer' has been interpreted by the CJEU in 35 judgments. In 27 of these, the Court gave the same general and consistent definition of this notion and ruled that a legal transfer occurs when:

Box 3: Legal Transfer

A. There is change in the natural or legal person who is responsible for carrying on the business and who, by virtue of that fact incurs the obligation of an employer vis-à-vis the employees of the undertaking, regardless of whether or not the ownership of the undertaking is transferred.

The judgments that include this definition are shown in row A in Table 1.

This formula is broad and reflects a flexible reading of the scope of the directive. It potentially covers a wide range of transactions between the transferor and the transferee irrespective of the type of contractual arrangement entered into.

(UGT-FSP) v. Ayuntamiento de La Línea de la Concepción, María del Rosario Vecino Uribe and Ministerio Fiscal, C-151/09, ECLI:EU:C:2010:452; judgment of 20 January 2011, *CLECE SA v. María Socorro Martín Valor and Ayuntamiento de Cobisa*, C-463/09, ECLI:EU:C:2011:24; judgment of 26 November 2015, *Administrador de Infraestructuras Ferroviarias (ADIF) v. Luis Aira Pascual and Others*, C-509/14, ECLI:EU:C:2015:781; judgment of 20 July 2017, *Luís Manuel Piscarreta Ricardo v. Portimão Urbis EM SA and Others*, C-416/16, ECLI:EU:C:2017:574; judgment of 13 June 2019, *Cátia Correia Moreira v. Município de Portimão*, C-317/18, ECLI:EU:C:2019:499 (where the Court held that a transfer from a legal person governed by private law to a legal person governed by public law in principle falls within the scope of the directive) and judgment of 14 September 2000, *Renato Collino and Luisella Chiappero v. Telecom Italia SpA*, C-343/98, ECLI:EU:C:2000:441 (where the Court found that a transfer of a business before managed by a public body to a private company in principle falls within the scope of the directive).

450. Besides the case law referred to in footnote n. 405, the issue of transfer of insolvent businesses has been addressed in the following judgments: judgment of 7 February 1985, *Knud Wendelboe and others v. L.J. Music ApS, in liquidation*, C-19/83, ECLI:EU:C:1985:54; judgment of 7 February 1985, *Industriebond FNV and Federatie Nederlandse Vakbeweging (FNV) v. The Netherlands State*, C-179/83, ECLI:EU:C:1985:57; judgment of 11 July 1985, *Foreningen af Arbejdsledere i Danmark v. A/S Danmols Inventar, in liquidation*, C-105/84, ECLI:EU:C:1985:331; judgment of 7 March 1996, *Albert Merckx and Patrick Neuhuys v. Ford Motors Company Belgium SA*, C-171/94, Joined Cases C-171/94 and C-172/94, ECLI:EU:C:1996:87; judgment of 12 March 1998, *Jules Dethier Équipement SA v. Jules Dassy and Sovam SPRL*, C-319/94, ECLI:EU:C:1998:99; judgment of 22 June 2017, *Federatie Nederlandse Vakvereniging and Others v. Smallsteps BV*, C-126/16, ECLI:EU:C:2017:489; judgment of 16 May 2019, *Christa Plessers v. PREFACO NV and Belgische Staat*, C-509/17, ECLI:EU:C:2019:424; judgment of 9 September 2020, *EM v. TMD Friction GmbH and FL v. TMD Friction EsCo GmbH*, C-674/18, ECLI:EU:C:2020:682.

In 26 judgments, the Court identified further specific circumstances which enrich the definition of the concept of 'legal transfer'. These are marked with the letters B to M in Box 4 below and in Table 1. In those rulings, the Court established that the presence of one of the following circumstances does not prevent a business operation from falling within the notion of 'legal transfer':[451]

Box 4: Legal Transfer

B. The transferred workers are not in an employment relationship with the transferor but are just seconded in its premises.
C. The operation occurs among two companies belonging to the same group.
D. The transfer occurs in two-stage.
E. The overall operation occurred without written agreements.
F. There are no contractual relations between the transferor and the transferee.
G. The transferor still exercises extensive overriding powers of the transferee.
H. The transfer is the result of a unilateral declaration of an administrative or judicial body.
I. The transfer is the result of a concession by a public body.
J. The transfer is the result of a service provision awarded by a public body by means of public procurement.
K. The transferor and the transferee have a 'no profit' status.
L. The transferee is governed by public law.
M. The transfer occurs between a public body and a private company.

451. With regard to the elements corresponding to the letters K, L, M, it is important to note that these could also be considered related to the concept of 'business' instead of that of legal transfer. However, they have been included in this first case study because the Court consistently considered these elements in the part of the reasoning concerning the existence or non-existence of a legal transfer.

Table 1 Case Study on the Scope of Application: Concept of 'Legal Transfer'

	1	2	3	4	5	6	7	8	9	10	11	12	13	14	15	16	17	18	19	20	21	22	23	24	25	26	27	28	29	30	31	32	33	34	35
A	■	■	■	■	■	■	■	■	■	■	■	■	■	■		■	■		■		■	■				■		■	■	■	■	■	■	■	
B																									■										
C														■														■							
D		■		■	■						■		■			■																			
E																							■												
F					■				■		■		■				■	■														■		■	
G																												■							
H			■		■																										■				
I															■																				
J													■			■																			
K							■																								■				
L										■							■			■				■		■	■			■	■				■
M															■																				
	C-287/86 *Ny Mølle Kro*	C-324/86 *Daddy's Dance Hall*	C-144/87 *Berg*	C-101/87 *Bork International*	C-29/91 *Redmond Stichting*	C-209/91 *Rask*	C-382/92 *Com v. UK*	C-392/92 *Schmidt*	C-172/94 *Merckx*	C-298/94 *Henke*	C-13/95 *Süzen*	C-127/96 *Hernández Vidal*	C-173/96 *Hidalgo*	C-243/98 *Allen*	C-343/98 *Collino*	C-172/99 *Liikenne*	C-175/99 *Mayeur*	C-51/00 *Temco*	C-340/01 *Abler*	425/02 *Boor*	C-478/03 *Celtec*	C-232/04 *Securicor*	C-458/05 *Jouini*	151/09 *UGT*	C-242/09 *Albron*	C-463/09 *Clece*	C-108/10 *Scattolon*	C-458/12 *Amatori*	C-160/14 *Ferreira da Silva*	C-509/14 *Adif*	C-416/16 *Piscarreta*	C-200/16 *Securitas*	C-472/16 *Colino Siguenza*	C-60/17 *Somoza*	C-317/18 *Moreira*

Source: Author's own elaboration.

(A) There is change in the natural or legal person who is responsible for carrying on the business and who, by virtue of that fact incurs the obligation of an employer vis-à-vis the employees of the undertaking, regardless whether or not the ownership of the undertaking is transferred; **(B)** The transferred workers are not in an employment relationship with the transferor, but are just seconded in its premises; **(C)** The operation occurs among two companies belonging to the same group; **(D)** The transfer occurs in two-stage; **(E)** The overall operation occurred without written agreements; **(F)** There are no contractual relations between the transferor and the transferee; **(G)** The transferor still exercises extensive overriding powers of the transferee; **(H)** The transfer is the result of a unilateral declaration of an administrative or judicial body; **(I)** The transfer is the result of a concession by a public body; **(J)** The transfer is the result of a service provision awarded by a public body by means of public procurement; **(K)** The transferor and the transferee have a 'no profit' status; **(L)** The transferee is governed by public law; **(M)** The transfer occurs between a public body and a private company.

Each of these reasonings contributed to broadening the scope of application of the directive. On a closer look, the reasonings in Box 4 already provide two insights. The first is that the Court has a flexible understanding of the commercial operations through which a 'legal transfer' can take place. These include non-contractual and intra-corporate group transactions, as indicated by the letters B to G in Box 4.[452] The second insight is that the notion of 'legal transfer' covers not only operations that are governed by civil and company law but also administrative and public law. This emerges from the rulings indicated by the letters H to M in Box 4.

Looking at Table 1 and starting with the reasonings from letters B to G, it emerges that since the *Daddy's Dance Hall* (1998) judgment, the Court has accepted that the directive applies to operations that take place in two or more stages (D).[453] The *Daddy's Dance Hall* case concerned the situation where an employer was the lessee of a restaurant bar and dismissed all workers as a consequence of the termination of the lease. The lease was then taken over by another lessee, who opposed the application of the directive and the re-employment of the workers of the first lessee. According to the Court, however, it must be accepted that the directive 'is applicable in the event that this operation is carried out in two stages, where the undertaking is first transferred from the original lessee to the owner and the latter then transfers it to the new lessee'.[454]

In the *Sophie Redmond Stichting* judgment (1992), and later in other cases, the Court held that there is a 'legal transfer' even where the commercial transaction takes place without there being any contractual relationship between the transferor and the transferee (F).[455] There, in particular, the Court ruled that the directive applies when 'a municipality [...] finances through subsidies the activities of a foundation [...] decides to discontinue the subsidies, and thus causes the fundation to cease its activities and transfer them to another foundation carrying on the same activities'. As a corollary to

452. *See, inter alia*: A. Lo Faro, 'Judicial Developments of EC Social Policy and Intra-community Institutional Dialogues: How to Define a "Legal Transfer"' in S. Sciarra (ed.), *Labour Law in the Courts: National Judges and the European Court of Justice*, Hart Publishing, Oxford, 2001, pp. 210-228 and G. Santoro-Passarelli, 'The Transfer of Undertakings: Striking a Balance Between Individual Workers' Rights and Business Needs', International Journal of Comparative Labour Law and Industrial Relations, 23(3), pp. 311-334, 2007.

453. Judgment of 15 June 1988, *P. Bork International A/S, in liquidation v. Foreningen af Arbejdsledere I Danmark, acting on behalf of Birger E. Petersen, and Jens E. Olsen and others v. Junckers Industrier A/S*, C-101/87, ECLI:EU:C:1988:308; judgment of 19 May 1992, *Dr. Sophie Redmond Stichting v. Hendrikus Bartol and others*, C-29/91, ECLI:EU:C:1992:220; judgment of 11 March 1997, *Ayse Süzen v. Zehnacker Gebäudereinigung GmbH Krankenhausservice*, C-13/95, ECLI:EU:C:1997:141; judgment of 10 December 1998, *Francisca Sánchez Hidalgo and Others v. Asociación de Servicios Aser and Sociedad Cooperativa Minerva*, C-173/96, Joined Cases C-173/96 and C-247/96, ECLI:EU:C:1998:595; judgment of 25 January 2001, *Oy Liikenne Ab v. Pekka Liskojärvi and Pentti Juntunen*, C-172/99, ECLI:EU:C:2001:59.

454. Judgment of 10 February 1988, *Foreningen af Arbejdsledere i Danmark v. Daddy's Dance Hall A/S*, C-324/86, ECLI:EU:C:1988:72 (para. 8).

455. Judgment of 19 May 1992, *Dr. Sophie Redmond Stichting v. Hendrikus Bartol and others*, C-29/91, ECLI:EU:C:1992:220 (para. 14).

this ruling, in *Jouini* (2007) the Court stated that it is not even necessary for there to be a written agreement of any kind between the transferor and transferee (E).[456]

The scope of the directive was significantly expanded also by the *Albron* judgment (2010). In *Albron*, the Court applied the directive also to workers who were not contractually employees of the transferor, but who had been de facto working for him (B).[457] More precisely, following a secondment, a group of workers were assigned to company A even though they had an employment relationship with company B, which was part of the same group as company A. The business conducted by company A was then transferred to company C, outside the corporate group. At this point, the workers claimed that this operation consisted of a transfer of a business that had occurred between company A (as the transferor) and company C (as the transferee). Both companies A and C contested the application of the directive, on the basis of the fact that the transferred workers did not have a contractual relationship with company A (the transferor). Nevertheless, the Court ruled that a 'legal transfer' had occurred since there was a change in the legal person 'who is responsible for the economic activity [...] and who in that capacity establishes working relations as employer with the staff of the entity in some cases despite the absence of contractual relations with those employees'.[458] Basically, the Court found that the directive could apply even if the transferor was the 'non-contractual employer' of the transferred employees.[459]

The expansive and, in turn, protective effect of the Court's reasoning is evident. On the other hand, it is interesting to note that the broad interpretation that the Court gave to the notion of 'legal transfer' allowed the directive to be potentially misused by companies, to circumvent the application of other employment protection legislation. This emerges from the *Allen* and *Amatori* judgments, where the Court ruled that the directive could apply even to transactions taking place within the same group of companies (C).[460] In *Amatori*, the Court also held that there is a legal transfer when the 'transferor continues to exercise extensive overriding powers over the transferee' (G).[461] These judgments could be relied on by employers to displace and then lay off part of the workforce without having to incur the legal and economic consequences that follow collective redundancies. This could be the case, for example, when a company sets up an ad hoc branch to which it transfers the workers. This branch could then be transferred to another purposively created corporate entity, that after some time is forced into liquidation. From the analysis of the judgments, however, it does not appear that the Court had ever considered the risks that its broad interpretation of the

456. Judgment of 13 September 2007, *Mohamed Jouini and Others v. Princess Personal Service GmbH (PPS)*, C-458/05, ECLI:EU:C:2007:512 (para. 25).
457. Judgment of 21 October 2010, *Albron Catering BV v. FNV Bondgenoten and John Roest*, C-242/09, ECLI:EU:C:2010:625 (para. 29, 30).
458. C-242/09, *Albron Catering* (para. 28).
459. S. De Groof, 'The Scope of the Transfer of Undertaking Directive Further Enlarged Through the Heineken-Case', European Labour Law Journal, 1(4), pp. 508-512, 2010.
460. Judgment of 2 December 1999, *G. C. Allen and Others v. Amalgamated Construction Co. Ltd*, C-234/98, ECLI:EU:C:1999:594 (paras 17, 20); judgment of 6 March 2014, *Lorenzo Amatori and Others v. Telecom Italia SpA and Telecom Italia Information Technology Srl*, C-458/12, ECLI:EU:C:2014:124 (para. 49).
461. C-458/12, *Amatori* (para. 52).

scope of application of the directive could bring. The only exception is the recent *Ellinika* judgment, which is discussed in section 5.1.2 below as it does not pertain specifically to the concept of 'legal transfer'.[462] With its expansive interpretation of the notion of 'legal transfer' the Court's intention thus seems to have been first and foremost to bring a wide range of transactions within the scope of the directive, presumably to extend the coverage of its protection, and not to create opportunities for abuse.

The second group of rulings on 'legal transfer', concern the legal nature of the business transaction and of the actors involved (letters H to M in Box 4 and Table 1). Here too, the Court's interpretation has been consistently broad and flexible. In the judgments of *Berg*, *Sophie Redmond Stichting* and *Piscarreta*, the Court ruled that the directive applies even if the transfer of a business is the result of a unilateral act issued by a public body or a judicial body (H).[463] Similarly, in *Collino*, the 'legal transfer' resulted from a concession by a public body (I),[464] and in *Hidalgo* and *Liikenne* from a change in service provision awarded by a public body by means of public procurement (J).[465] The Court accepted that the transferor and transferee can have a 'not-for-profit' status (K), or can both (L) or just one of them (M) be governed by public law, without precluding the application of the directive.[466]

---

462. Judgment of 13 June 2019, *Ellinika Nafpigeia AE v. Panagiotis Anagnostopoulos and Others*, C-664/17, ECLI:EU:C:2019:496.
463. Judgment of 5 May 1988, *Harry Berg and Johannes Theodorus Maria Busschers v. Ivo Martin Besselsen*, C-144/87, ECLI:EU:C:1988:236 (para. 19); judgment of 19 May 1992, *Dr. Sophie Redmond Stichting v. Hendrikus Bartol and others*, C-29/91, ECLI:EU:C:1992:220 (para. 21); judgment of 20 July 2017, *Luís Manuel Piscarreta Ricardo v. Portimão Urbis EM SA and Others*, C-416/16, ECLI:EU:C:2017:574 (para. 32).
464. Judgment of 14 September 2000, *Renato Collino and Luisella Chiappero v. Telecom Italia SpA*, C-343/98, ECLI:EU:C:2000:441 (para. 32).
465. Judgment of 10 December 1998, *Francisca Sánchez Hidalgo and Others v. Asociación de Servicios Aser and Sociedad Cooperativa Minerva*, C-173/96, Joined Cases C-173/96 and C-247/96, ECLI:EU:C:1998:595 (para. 24); judgment of 25 January 2001, *Oy Liikenne Ab v. Pekka Liskojärvi and Pentti Juntunen*, C-172/99, ECLI:EU:C:2001:59 (para. 19).
466. On 'no profit' status: Judgment of 8 June 1994, *Commission of the European Communities v. United Kingdom of Great Britain and Northern Ireland*, C-382/92, ECLI:EU:C:1994:233 (para. 46); judgment of 20 July 2017, *Luís Manuel Piscarreta Ricardo v. Portimão Urbis EM SA and Others*, C-416/16, ECLI:EU:C:2017:574 (para. 34). On the situation where the transferor or the transferee are public bodies: judgment of 15 October 1996, *Annette Henke v. Gemeinde Schierke and Verwaltungsgemeinschaft Brocken*, C-298/94, ECLI:EU:C:1996:382 (para. 14); judgment of 26 September 2000, *Didier Mayeur v. Association Promotion de l'information messine (APIM)*, C-175/99, ECLI:EU:C:2000:505 (paras 28, 35); judgment of 11 November 2004, *Johanna Maria Delahaye, née Boor v. Ministre de la Fonction publique et de la Réforme administrative*, C-425/02, ECLI:EU:C:2004:706 (paras 30, 32); judgment of 29 July 2010, *Federación de Servicios Públicos de la UGT (UGT-FSP) v. Ayuntamiento de La Línea de la Concepción, María del Rosario Vecino Uribe and Ministerio Fiscal*, C-151/09, ECLI:EU:C:2010:452 (paras 23, 24); judgment of 20 January 2011, *CLECE SA v. María Socorro Martín Valor and Ayuntamiento de Cobisa*, C-463/09, ECLI:EU:C:2011:24 (para. 26); judgment of 6 September 2011, *Ivana Scattolon v. Ministero dell'Istruzione, dell'Università e della Ricerca*, C-108/10, ECLI: EU:C:2011:542 (para. 44); judgment of 26 November 2015, *Administrador de Infraestructuras Ferroviarias (ADIF) v. Luis Aira Pascual and Others*, C-509/14, ECLI:EU:C:2015:781 (para. 24); C-416/16, *Piscarreta* (para. 32); judgment of 13 June 2019, *Cátia Correia Moreira v. Município de Portimão*, C-317/18, ECLI:EU:C:2019:499 (paras 54, 55); judgment of 14 September 2000, *Renato Collino and Luisella Chiappero v. Telecom Italia SpA*, C-343/98, ECLI:EU:C:2000:441 (para. 33).

Table 1 shows that the 'expansive' tendency of the Court towards the concept of 'legal transfer' did not change significantly over time. There were no particular developments in the case law and the Court has never retracted or contradicted itself. On this point, therefore, the EU case law reflects (or at least does not oppose) the protective function inherent in the directive.

However, it is worth recalling that the Court's broad interpretation of the concept of 'legal transfer' is not sufficient on its own to define the scope of the directive. It must be combined with the notion of 'transfer of a business'. The Court's broad interpretation of the notion of 'legal transfer' thus only has the effect of bringing a wide range of commercial transactions within the *potential* coverage of the directive. In other words, it prevents national legislators from *a priori* excluding specific categories of business operations from the scope of application of the directive. In this, the Court has shown to be consistent with the legal basis of the directive, Article 100 TEEC (now Article 115 TFEU), designed to promote harmonisation in the internal market.[467]

5.1.2 Transfer of a Business

The concept of 'transfer of a business' has so far been addressed 35 times by the CJEU. As mentioned in section 5.1, this concept is meant to restrict the scope of the directive to those operations which, in addition to being a 'legal transfer', relate to the transfer of an activity identified as 'business'.

Differently from what was noted in relation to the notion of 'legal transfer', where the case law had an 'inclusive effect', here the approach of the Court could be defined as 'exclusive'. Throughout the years, the Court has, in fact, gradually added conditions to the original definition in Directive 77/187/EEC, making it narrower. Basically, the reasonings from A to M in Boxes 5 and 6 below provide a list of conditions that are necessary for a 'transfer of a business' to materialise. On closer inspection, it is not always clear that the aim of the Court was to establish requirements to restrict the scope of the directive. Some of the reasonings are alternatives to each other, while others can be considered cumulatively and can be present in the same judgment. It is in any case important to note that the more conditions there are, the less frequently workers can claim the rights conferred by the directive. It follows that the proliferation of the different specifications to the concept of 'transfer of a business' is symptomatic of a marginalisation of the emancipatory effect of the directive.

The conditions that the Court has, in time, identified in relation to the notion of 'transfer of a business' are essentially of two types. The first type concerns the characteristics that the transferred business entity must possess *before* the transfer (Box 5). The second type relates to the characteristics that the transferred entity must possess *after* the transfer (Box 6).

467. E. Brameshuber, 'Balancing vs. Preservation of Rights under the Acquired Rights Directive', Industrial Law Journal, 45(3), pp. 443-454, 2016; D. Carvalho Martins, 'Transfer of an Economic Unit: Requirements, Effects and Recent CJEU Ruling', European Labour Law Journal, 9(1), pp. 24-49, 2018.

The conditions that have to be present *before* the transfer are indicated in rows A to E of Table 2 and in Box 5 below:

Box 5: Transfer of a Business

Before the transfer, the business entity shall possess the following characteristics:

A. Being a stable economic entity, whose activity is not limited to performing only one specific works contract.
B. Being sufficiently autonomous and structured, or having a sufficient degree of functional autonomy or independence.
C. It comprises an organized group of persons and assets facilitating the exercise of an economic activity pursuing a specific objective.
D. When labour-intensive (where the contribution of assets is minimal with respect to manpower) a business is constituted by a group of workers engaged on a permanent or stable basis.
E. When labour-intensive, it is necessary that the transfer concerns workers who are specifically and permanently assigned to the transferred entity.

The characteristics that the transferred entity shall instead have *after* the transfer are identified in rows F to M in Table 2 and in Box 6 below:

Box 6: Transfer of a Business

After the transfer, the business entity shall possess the following characteristics:

F. The transferred entity has maintained its identity.
G. Fulfilment of the *Spijkers* criteria.
H. The transferee has taken over a body of material assets enabling the activities that were performed before the transfer.
I. The type of undertaking is a particularly important element to look at. If the nature of the business is asset-based, the identity is maintained if the majority of material assets are taken over; if the nature of the business is labour-intensive, the identity is maintained if the majority of the personnel is taken over.
J. The transferred entity is not reduced to the activity entrusted to it. The mere fact that the service provided is similar before and after the transfer is not conclusive.
K. The transfer of operating methods, including financing system, managerial staff, operational resources and applicable rules is determinant.
L. The retention of a functional link of interdependence and complementarity between the transferred assets and personnel is determinant.

M. The transferred unit cannot be dependent upon the economic choices, unilaterally made by the transferor.

Differently from the case study on the notion of 'legal transfer', Table 2 shows a significant jurisprudential development.

Table 2 Case Study on the Scope of Application: Concept of 'Transfer of a Business'

	1	2	3	4	5	6	7	8	9	10	11	12	13	14	15	16	17	18	19	20	21	22	23	24	25	26	27	28	29	30	31	32	33	34	35
A								■		■	■	■	■	■		■	■		■	■		■			■	■							■	■	
B											■	■								■					■	■								■	
C										■	■	■	■	■		■	■		■	■	■	■	■			■		■	■			■	■	■	■
D										■		■	■			■	■			■		■		■	■							■			
E											■	■	■			■				■	■	■	■												
F	■	■	■	■	■	■	■	■	■	■	■	■	■	■	■	■	■	■	■	■	■	■	■	■	■	■	■	■	■	■	■	■	■	■	■
G	■	■		■	■	■	■	■	■	■	■	■	■	■	■	■	■	■	■			■		■			■	■	■	■	■	■	■		■
H								■														■													
I										■	■	■	■	■		■	■		■					■	■		■	■	■	■	■	■	■		
J										■	■	■	■	■	■									■						■		■		■	■
K										■	■	■	■	■	■									■						■				■	■
L																					■						■			■					
M																																		■	
	C-24/85 *Spijkers*	C-287/86 *Ny Mølle Kro*	C-324/86 *Daddy's Dance Hall*	C-101/87 *Bork International*	C-29/91 *Redmond Stichting*	C-209/91 *Rask*	C-392/92 *Schmidt*	C-48/94 *Strø Mølle Akustik*	C-172/94 *Merckx*	C-13/95 *Süzen*	C-127/96 *Hernandez Vidal*	C-173/96 *Hidalgo*	C-234/98 *Allen*	C-172/99 *Liikenne*	C-175/99 *Didier Mayeur*	C-51/00 *Temco*	C-340/01 *Abler*	C-478/03 *Celtec*	C-232/04 *Securicor*	C-458/05 *Jouini*	C-466/07 *Klarenberg*	C-151/09 *UGT*	C-242/09 *Albron*	C-463/09 *Clece*	C-108/10 *Scattolon*	C-458/12 *Amatori*	C-160/14 *Ferreira Da Silva*	C-509/14 *Adif*	C-200/16 *Securitas*	C-416/16 *Piscarreta*	C-472/16 *Colino Sigüenza*	C-60/17 *Somoza*	C-194/18 *Dodič*	C-644/17 *Ellinika Nafpigeia*	C-298/18 *OSL Bus*

Source: Author's own elaboration.

Before the Transfer: **(A)** Being a stable economic entity, whose activity is not limited to performing only one specific works contract; **(B)** Being sufficiently autonomous and structured, or having a sufficient degree of functional autonomy or independence; **(C)** It comprises an organised group of persons and assets facilitating the exercise of an economic activity pursuing a specific objective; **(D)** When labour-intensive (where the contribution of assets is minimal with respect to manpower), a business is constituted by a group of workers engaged on a permanent or stable basis; **(E)** When labour-intensive, it is necessary that the transfer concerns workers who are specifically and permanently assigned to the transferred entity.

After the Transfer: **(F)** The transferred entity has maintained its identity; **(G)** Fulfilment of the Spijkers criteria; **(H)** The transferee has taken over a body of material assets enabling the activities that were performed before the transfer; **(I)** The type of undertaking is a particularly important element to look at. If the nature of the business is asset-based, the identity is maintained if the majority of material assets are taken over; if the nature of the business is labour-intensive, the identity is maintained if the majority of the personnel is taken over; **(J)** The transferred entity is not reduced to the activity entrusted to it. The mere fact that the service provided is similar before and after the transfer is not conclusive; **(K)** The transfer of operating methods, including financing system, managerial staff, operational resources and applicable rules is determinant; **(L)** The retention of a functional link of interdependence and complementarity between the transferred assets and personnel is determinant; **(M)** The transferred unit cannot be dependent upon the economic choices, unilaterally made by the transferor.

Table 2 suggests that the case law of the Court can be divided into three timeframes. The first period ranges from the *Spijkers* judgment (1986) to *Schmidt* (1994) included. There, the Court referred to only two requirements - and always the same ones - to qualify the definition of 'transfer of a business'. These requirements only apply to the situation *after* the transfer and consist of the fact that the transferred entity shall maintain its identity (F) and that the so-called *Spijkers* factors (G) have to be met. The *Spijkers* factors were defined in the *Spijkers* judgment, where the Court stated that, in order to determine whether an entity had been transferred, 'it is necessary to consider all the facts characterising the transaction in question, including

i) the type of undertaking or business,
ii) whether or not the business's tangible assets, such as buildings and movable property, are transferred,
iii) the value of its intangible assets at the time of the transfer,
iv) whether or not the majority of its employees are taken over by the new employer,
v) whether or not customers are transferred,
vi) the degree of similarity between the activities carried on before,
vii) and after the transfer and the period, if any, for which those activities were suspended'.[468]

The Court emphasised that these seven criteria were not to be considered either cumulatively or peremptorily: 'all those circumstances are merely single factors in the overall assessment which must be made and cannot therefore be considered in isolation'.[469]

In this early period, the Court's approach is thus characterised by a flexible and wide-ranging understanding of the circumstances that integrate a transfer of a business.[470] For example, in the *Sophie Redmond Stichting* case (1992), the Court held that the directive applies even if no material asset or movable had been transferred.[471] Similarly, in *Schmidt* (1994) the directive was found to apply in a situation where the transferred business consisted merely of a cleaning activity performed by a single employee.[472] Moreover, according to the *Merckx* judgment (1996), it did not even seem

468. Judgment of 18 March 1986, *Jozef Maria Antonius Spijkers v. Gebroeders Benedik Abattoir CV and Alfred Benedik en Zonen BV*, C-24/85, ECLI:EU:C:1986:127 (para. 13).
469. *Ibid.*
470. *Inter alia, see*: R.M. Beltzer, 'The Transfer of Undertakings and the Importance of Taking over Personnel: A Vicious Circle', International Journal of Comparative Labour Law and Industrial Relations, 23(1), pp. 139-155, 2007.
471. Judgment of 19 May 1992, *Dr. Sophie Redmond Stichting v. Hendrikus Bartol and others*, C-29/91, ECLI:EU:C:1992:220 (para. 29): 'As regards the movables, the fact that they were not transferred does not seem in itself to prevent the directive from applying, and it is for the national court to appraise their importance by incorporating them in the overall assessment which has to be made.'
472. Judgment of 14 April 1994, *Christel Schmidt v. Spar- und Leihkasse der früheren Ämter Bordesholm, Kiel und Cronshagen*, C-392/92, ECLI:EU:C:1994:134 (para. 16): 'The arguments of the Government of the Federal Republic of Germany and of the United Kingdom based on the absence of any transfer of tangible assets cannot be accepted either. The fact that in its case law the Court includes the transfer of such assets among the various factors to be taken into account

to matter to the Court that, following the transfer, the business had changed its name and the activity was carried on in a different establishment, with different facilities, and with less than half of the original workers.[473]

Within a short time, however, this relaxed attitude towards the scope of the directive visibly evolved into a far more selective approach. The case law between *Strø Mølle Akustik* (1995) and *Klarenberg* (2009) marks a period in which the Court began to introduce a number of requirements that the transferred entity must meet, both before and after the transfer. More of the specifications listed in Boxes 5 and 6 and in Table 2 began to appear. In the *Strø Mølle Akustik* decision, the Court departed from its previous reasoning and ruled that the business is transferred only if the transferee takes over a body of material assets enabling it to pursue the activities that were performed before the transfer (H).[474] The Court also established that, prior to the transfer operation, the business must constitute a stable economic entity, whose activity is not limited to performing only one specific works contract (A).[475] By adding these conditions, the Court evidently sought to prevent the mere change of service contract from falling within the scope of the directive. A transfer of an undertaking or part of it could take place only if the transferor acquired a stable, tangible and preferable asset-based enterprise. As mentioned in section 3.4 above, from a labour law's doctrinal perspective this evolution in the jurisprudential approach was broadly perceived as the expression of a normative inclination of the Court.[476]

The characteristics that the transferred business has to possess before and after the transfer were further elaborated in the *Süzen* judgment (1997), which the Court would then consistently quote in its subsequent case law.[477] There, the Court specified

by a national court to enable it, when assessing a complex transaction as a whole, to decide whether an undertaking has in fact been transferred does not support the conclusion that the absence of these factors precludes the existence of a transfer. The safeguarding of employees' rights, which constitutes the subject matter of the directive, as is clear from its actual title, cannot depend exclusively on consideration of a factor which the Court has in any event already held not to be decisive on its own (judgment in Case 24/85 *Spijkers v. Benedik* [1986] ECR 1119 (para. 12)).'

473. Judgment of 7 March 1996, *Albert Merckx and Patrick Neuhuys v. Ford Motors Company Belgium SA*, C-171/94, Joined Cases C-171/94 and C-172/94, ECLI:EU:C:1996:87 (paras 21 and 25).
474. Judgment of 19 September 1995, *Ledernes Hovedorganisation, acting for Ole Rygaard v. Dansk Arbejdsgiverforening, acting for Strø Mølle Akustik A/S*, C-48/94, ECLI:EU:C:1995:290 (para. 21).
475. C-48/94, *Strø Mølle Akustik* (para. 20).
476. Section 3.4. *See also* J. Nazerali, K. Plumbley-Jones, 'New Acquired Rights Directive – A Step in the Dark?', European Business Law Review, 6(2), pp. 31-36, 1995; P. Davies, 'Transfers of Undertakings: Preliminary Remarks' in S. Sciarra (ed.), *Labour Law in the Courts: National Judges and the European Court of Justice*, Hart Publishing, Oxford, 2001, pp. 131-144; S. Hardy & R. Painter, 'Revising the Acquired Rights Directive', Industrial Law Journal, 25(2), pp. 160-168, 1996.
477. Judgment of 11 March 1997, *Ayse Süzen v. Zehnacker Gebäudereinigung GmbH Krankenhausservice*, C-13/95, ECLI:EU:C:1997:141. On the impact of the Süzen case, *see, inter alia*, J. McMullen, 'An Analysis of the Transfer of Undertakings (Protection of Employment) Regulation 2006', Industrial Law Journal, 35(2), pp. 113-139, 2006; S. Laulom, 'The European Court of Justice in the Dialogue on Transfers of Undertakings: A Fallible Interlocutor?' in S. Sciarra (ed.), *Labour Law in the Courts: National Judges and the European Court of Justice*, Hart Publishing, Oxford, 2001, pp. 145-178.

that an economic entity exists only if it involves an organised group of persons and assets facilitating the exercise of an economic activity pursuing a specific objective (C). Moreover, in labour-intensive sectors (meaning those sectors where the contribution of assets is minimal with respect to manpower, as in the case of cleaning services) there has to be a group of workers engaged on a permanent or stable basis (E).[478]

In addition, from *Süzen* onwards, the Court reduced the scope of the *Spijkers* factors, by establishing that, in order to identify whether the business had maintained its identity, some of those factors are more important than others.[479] The Court, in fact, ruled that 'the mere fact that the service provided by the old and the new awardees of a contract is similar does not [...] support the conclusion that an economic entity has been transferred. An entity cannot be reduced to the activity entrusted to it' (J).[480] It then stated that, among the factors listed in *Spijkers*, the type of undertaking is a particularly important element to look at. If the business is asset-based, the identity is maintained only if the majority of material assets are taken over; if the nature of the business is labour-intensive, the identity is instead only maintained if the majority of the personnel is taken over (I).[481]

This new paradigm has been repeatedly taken up by the Court and has led to the consolidation of the rule that the directive only applies if the transferee acquires at least 50% of the assets or personnel, depending on the nature of the business.[482] This understanding of the notion of 'transfer of a business' has the effect of narrowing what appeared to be a much broader interpretation of the directive that the Court had adopted in *Schmidt*. It suffices to recall that in *Schmidt* the Court ruled that cleaning services could be the object of a 'transfer of business' even if the service was carried out by only one worker and with basically no assets.[483] It must be specified, however, that from a purely formal point of view, the *Süzen* ruling thus does not stand in open contradiction to the precedent in *Schmidt*. In the dispute at issue in *Schmidt*, the employer had autonomously extended the employment contract to the cleaner, and therefore, technically, the transferee had taken over the entirety of the workforce (one worker was the entire workforce).[484] However, the fact remains that, in emphasising the numerical requirement of at least 50% of the employees and by explicitly specifying that a transfer of an activity alone does not fall within the scope of the directive, the Court showed sensitivity to the arguments of the employers. It is highly doubtful whether, following decisions such as *Strø Mølle Akustik* and *Süzen*, the Court would

478. C-13/95, *Süzen* (paras 13 and 21).
479. R.M. Beltzer, 'The Transfer of Undertakings and the Importance of Taking Over Personnel: A Vicious Circle', International Journal of Comparative Labour Law and Industrial Relations, 23(1), pp. 139-155, 2007, p. 143.
480. C-13/95, *Süzen* (para. 15).
481. *Ibid.* (para. 14).
482. C. Barnard, *EU Employment Law*, Oxford University Press, Oxford, 2012, p. 597.
483. J. Hunt, 'The Court of Justice as a Policy Actor: The Case of the Acquired Rights Directive', Legal Studies, 18(3), pp. 336-359, 1998.
484. C-392/92, *Schmidt* (para. 15).

still find a transfer of a business in the circumstances that characterised the *Schmidt* case (namely, the transfer of a service provided by only one employee).[485]

Furthermore, this evolution in the case law entailed difficulties of interpretation as to the nature of the business and, in particular, to the distinction between 'asset-based' and 'labour-intensive'.[486] In some cases, the distinction is quite intuitive. This is the case in *Liikenne* (2000), where the Court found that a bus transport company was to be regarded as 'asset-based' because of the predominant contribution of the material assets (the buses).[487] However, in other cases, it was less simple. An example is the *Abler* case (2003), concerning the transfer of a catering service in a hospital. There, the Court found that the economic activity was asset-based, even if one could argue that the preparation and the provision of food and beverage have a prevalence of manpower.[488] Another example is the *Ferreira* case (2015), where the Court held that an air transport company was asset-intensive.[489] While the essentiality of the tangible assets (the aircraft) for the performance of the business activity (the transport of passengers) cannot be denied, it is worth considering that operating those aircraft requires highly qualified and trained pilots. Determining if the contribution of material assets trumps that of human labour is in this case less straightforward. A more recent case where the distinction between labour-intensive and asset-intensive businesses was rather blurred is *Securitas* (2017). The proceeding concerned a private security service, where the transferred workers had continued to use the same radio equipment that they had received from the transferor before the transfer. The transferee had only provided the staff with new uniforms. The question referred to by the national court was whether this situation consisted of a transfer of a business within the meaning of the directive. The CJEU acknowledged the uncertain nature of the

485. As mentioned in section 3.4, the more restrictive interpretation of the Court has been welcomed by some observers, as it was deemed necessary to prevent the directive from being applied too broadly.
486. Z. Even, 'Distinction Asset-Intensive/Labour Intensive Not Decisive; All Spijkers Criteria Relevant', European Employment Law Cases, 6, pp. 6-10, 2014; Even noted that 'the difference between asset-intensive companies and labour-intensive companies is not black and white. There are many shaeds of grey that can cause the other criteria put forward in the *Spijkers* case to take precedence.' It might be for this reason, Even observed, that the Dutch Supreme Court, as well as other jurisdictions (Austria, Germany, Ireland, UK). *See also* R.M. Beltzer, 'The Transfer of Undertakings and the Importance of Taking Over Personnel: A Vicious Circle', International Journal of Comparative Labour Law and Industrial Relations, 23(1), pp. 139-155, p. 145, 2007. Beltzer noted that 'one cleaning company, for instance, might operate on a market where most of the cleaning is done using simple tools, such as a bucket and mop, whereas another might use advanced machines for cleaning swimming pools. In the latter case the personnel are less likely to be deemed the main production factor'.
487. Judgment of 25 January 2001, *Oy Liikenne Ab v. Pekka Liskojärvi and Pentti Juntunen*, C-172/99, ECLI:EU:C:2001:59 (para. 39).
488. Judgment of 20 November 2003, *Carlito Abler and Others v. Sodexho MM Catering Gesellschaft mbH*, C-340/01, ECLI:EU:C:2003:629 (para. 36).
489. Judgment of 9 September 2015, *João Filipe Ferreira da Silva e Brito and Others v. Estado português*, C-160/14, ECLI:EU:C:2015:565 (para. 29).

activity in question and preferred not to express its view, leaving the issue open for the national judge.[490]

Another innovation brought along by *Süzen* was that the Court started looking also at whether the transfer had affected the operating methods of the company, including financing system, managerial staff, operational resources and applicable rules (K).[491] The scope of application was further restricted by the requirements introduced in the *Hernandez Vidal* judgment (1998).[492] There, the Court indicated that, prior to the transfer, the business entity must be sufficiently structured and autonomous (B).[493] In the same judgment, the Court also specified that, when dealing with labour-intensive activities, the directive applies only to workers who are specifically and permanently assigned to the transferred entity (E).[494]

Table 2 shows that the Court has been consolidating this restrictive approach more or less until the *Securicor* judgment (2005).[495] By doing that, the Court has substantially constrained the protective effect of the directive, especially if one considers the earlier case law. It is interesting to note that this change in the Court's approach has presumably been appreciated by national governments. As was mentioned in section 2, the 1998 Amending Council Directive explicitly mentioned that the intent of the reform was to align the scope of the directive with the Court's case law. The echo of the Court's reasoning is also quite clear when looking at the reformed wording chosen by the EU legislator: 'transfer of an economic entity which retains its identity, meaning an organised grouping of resources which has the objective of pursuing an economic activity'.[496]

From Table 2, it is also possible to identify a third period in the Court's jurisprudence. If from *Strø Mølle Akustik* to *Securicor* the judgments have firmly and consistently introduced a new (and narrower) interpretative paradigm, from *Securicor* (2005) onwards the Court's reasoning has been characterised by a certain margin of uncertainty and, at times, disarray and lack of coherence. In general, the Court maintained its restrictive approach to the scope of the directive. However, some of the specifications introduced in the previous years have become less recurrent.[497]

490. Judgment of 19 October 2017, *Securitas – Serviços e Tecnologia de Segurança SA v. ICTS Portugal – Consultadoria de Aviação Comercial SA and Others*, C-200/16, ECLI:EU:C:2017:780 (para. 33).
491. C-13/95, *Süzen* (para. 18).
492. Judgment of 10 December 1998, *Francisco Hernández Vidal SA v. Prudencia Gómez Pérez, María Gómez Pérez and Contratas y Limpiezas SL*, C-127/96, Joined Cases C-127/96, C-229/96 and C-74/97, ECLI:EU:C:1998:594.
493. C-127/96, *Hernández Vidal* (para. 27).
494. *Ibid.* (paras 27 and 32).
495. Judgment of 15 December 2005, *Nurten Güney-Görres v. Securicor Aviation (Germany) Ltd and Kötter Aviation Security GmbH & Co. KG*, C-232/04, Joined Cases C-232/04 and C-233/04, ECLI:EU:C:2005:778.
496. *See* P. Davies, 'Transfers of Undertakings: Preliminary Remarks' in S. Sciarra (ed.), *Labour Law in the Courts: National Judges and the European Court of Justice*, Hart Publishing, Oxford, 2001, pp. 131-144.
497. S. Rainone, 'Labour Rights in the Making of the EU and in the CJEU Case Law: A Case Study on the Transfer of Undertakings Directive', European Labour Law Journal, 9(3), pp. 299-325, 2018.

In particular, there is less insistence on the requirements that the business must fulfil after the transfer (I, J and K), and this leaves room for slightly more interpretative flexibility. At the same time, there appears to be some confusion about the conditions that need to be present for the business to be transferred. A significant example is the *Jouini* judgment (2007), where the Court seemed to contradict itself, first indicating that the transferred entity must be an *organised* group of assets and persons and then saying that it is not actually necessary for such a group to have an *organisational* structure since what really matters is that there is an *operational* grouping of assets and workers.[498] Similarly, in *Scattolon* (2011), the Court ruled that the transferred entity must not only present a certain level of autonomy but must also be independent, while not clarifying the difference between autonomy and independence.[499] It is almost as if the inconsistencies resulting from the multitude of previously established criteria have now been exposed.

Moreover, from Table 2 it appears that, since the 2010s, the Court has been less insistent on the requirements that labour-intensive businesses must meet. This is reflected in the scarcer presence of criteria D and E across the case law. A further softening of the requirements set out in previous years emerged also from the recent *OSL Bus* ruling (2020), where the Court overcame the strict separation between asset- and labour-intensive businesses.[500] This proceeding concerned the transfer of a road transport company and presented various similarities with the previous *Liikenne* case. In *Liikenne*, it is worth recalling, the Court applied the '*Süzen* doctrine' and ruled that the directive could not apply because the transferee did not acquire the majority of buses from the transferor. In *OSL Bus*, however, the Court departed from this approach and stated that 'it should, however, be noted that, since in paragraph 39 of the judgment of 25 January 2001, Liikenne, the Court was careful to point out that the fact that the tangible assets used for operating the bus routes were not transferred from the old to the new contractor constitutes a circumstance to be taken into account, it cannot be inferred from that point that the takeover of the buses must be regarded in the abstract as the sole determining factor of whether an undertaking whose activity consists in the public transport of passengers by bus has been transferred'.[501] The Court thus returned to a more flexible interpretation of the *Spiijkers* criteria and reduced the emphasis on the type of business to determine whether a business was transferred.

However, it should also be noted that, in this 'ambivalent' period, Table 2 also shows the emergence of two new conditions in the Court's case law (L and M). For the first time, in the *Klarenberg* case (2009) the Court referred to the maintenance of a functional link of interdependence and complementarity between the transferred

498. Judgment of 13 September 2007, *Mohamed Jouini and Others v. Princess Personal Service GmbH (PPS)*, C-458/05, ECLI:EU:C:2007:512 (para. 18).
499. Judgment of 6 September 2011, *Ivana Scattolon v. Ministero dell'Istruzione, dell'Università e della Ricerca*, C-108/10, ECLI:EU:C:2011:542 (para. 51).
500. Judgment of 27 February 2020, *Reiner Grafe and Jürgen Pohle v. Südbrandenburger Nahverkehrs GmbH and OSL Bus GmbH*, C-298/18, ECLI:EU:C:2020:121.
501. C-298/18, *OSL Bus* (para. 39).

assets and personnel.[502] Such link was, in the Court's view, a determinant to establish whether a transfer had occurred. The implications of this ruling may be restrictive: it could indeed be sufficient for the transferee not to maintain such a link among the transferred assets and personnel in his company to escape the application of the directive. The other condition (M) emerged in *Ellinika* (2019) where the Court established that the transferred unit cannot be dependent upon economic choices unilaterally made by the transferor.[503] This ruling may also be read as having an exclusionary effect, leaving outside the coverage of the directive those businesses that are in a situation of economic dependency vis-à-vis the transferee.

However, it is worth noting that with both rulings the Court might also have intended to address the risk of companies misusing the directive.[504] In relation to *Klarenberg*, the relevance of the 'functional link' between the assets and workers after the transfer may indeed lead to the application of the directive also in those cases where the transferee has purposively dispersed the assets and workers composing the transferred business in different departments in order to escape from the application of the directive. In those cases, the transferred entity appears not to have retained its identity, but if a functional link among the transferred productive factors is still present, then such identity is actually presumed to exist, and the directive applies. In *Ellenika*, instead, the Court actually addressed the risk of abuses connected with transfer operations concerning an economically-dependent business. In particular, it refers to the risk that a company orchestrates a transfer of one of its branches to a complicit transferee lacking real autonomy, with the intention to then make this new company insolvent and have it declared bankrupt. In this way, the application of the legal framework regulating collective redundancies (including severance payment, information and consultation rights) is avoided.

In any case, it is unclear whether the ambivalent case law in this third period relates to an actual evolution in the Court's approach to the emancipatory function of the directive. The increased flexibility of interpretation may also derive from the growing complexity and diversity of corporate restructuring throughout the years.[505]

All in all, from this case study emerges that the Court's interpretation of the notion of 'transfer of a business' has changed significantly over time. Until the mid-1990s, the Court had embraced a rather expansive interpretation of the situations that fall within the scope of the directive. Since the *Strø Mølle Akustik* and *Süzen*

502. Judgment of 12 February 2009, *Dietmar Klarenberg v. Ferrotron Technologies GmbH*, C-466/07, ECLI:EU:C:2009:85 (para. 47).

503. Judgment of 13 June 2019, *Ellinika Nafpigeia AE v. Panagiotis Anagnostopoulos and Others*, C-664/17, ECLI:EU:C:2019:496 (para. 69); *see* a commentary in J. McMullen, 'Leaving a Legacy: Recent Jurisprudence of the European Court on Transfer of Undertakings', Industrial Law Journal, 50(1), pp. 130-157, 2021.

504. C-664/17, *Ellinika Nafpigeia* (para. 49): 'As is apparent from paragraph 31 of the present judgment, the referring court seems nevertheless to have doubts as to whether, in the case before it, the transfer involves abuse by the transferor, the transferee or both those persons jointly, in order to conceal their true intention of facilitating the liquidation of the entity transferred without having to assume the financial consequences.'

505. S. Rainone, 'Labour Rights in the Making of the EU and in the CJEU Case Law: A Case Study on the Transfer of Undertakings Directive', European Labour Law Journal, 9(3), pp. 299-325, 2018.

judgments, however, the Court has considerably narrowed the scope. The case law started to refer to a number of criteria which, if not fulfilled, would exclude the existence of a transfer. Then, over the last 15 years the Court has fluctuated between rigidity and flexibility, a sign that its approach may evolve.

But, how can a restrictive reading of the notion of 'transfer of a business' be reconciled with the more inclusive approach that the Court has consistently taken vis-à-vis the notion of 'legal transfer'? With its broad interpretation of the concept of 'legal transfer', the Court expanded the range of situations *potentially* falling within the scope of the directive.[506] The more restrictive reading of the notion of 'transfer of a business' then was used by the Court as a sort of filer to identify those business operations to which the directive *actually* applies. In doing so, the Court reduced the coverage of the rights established in the directive, with the effect of limiting their protective and emancipatory effect.

5.2 Workers' Rights

The case study on the workers' rights established in the directive enters now the core of the exploration of the Court's approach towards the emancipatory rationale of labour norms.[507] The analysis that follows focuses on the most significant rights established in the directive. These are laid down in Article 3(1) (first sentence), Article 3(3), Article 4(1), 4(2) and Article 8. These provisions have undergone only marginal changes compared to the original version of Directive 77/187/EEC.[508] Due to a lack of relevant case law, Article 7 on information and consultation rights to the transferor's and transferee's workers has not been included in the analysis.[509]

Box 7: Workers' Rights

Article 3(1)

The transferor's rights and obligations arising from a contract of employment or from an employment relationship existing on the date of a transfer shall, by reason of such transfer, be transferred to the transferee.

Article 3(3)

Following the transfer, the transferee shall continue to observe the terms and conditions agreed in any collective agreement on the same terms applicable to

506. As discussed in section 5.1.2.
507. The protective function was discussed in Chapter 1, section 2.2.1.
508. Article 8 of Directive 2001/23/EC corresponds to Article 7 of Directive 77/187/EEC.
509. Equivalent rights were established in Articles 5 and 6 of Directive 77/187/EEC. The only two cases on which the Court of Justice ruled on aspects connected to information and consultation rights of workers' representatives are: judgment of 8 June 1994, *Commission of the European Communities v. United Kingdom of Great Britain and Northern Ireland*, C-382/92, ECLI:EU:C:1994:233 and judgment of 29 July 2010, *Federación de Servicios Públicos de la UGT (UGT-FSP) v. Ayuntamiento de La Línea de la Concepción, María del Rosario Vecino Uribe and Ministerio Fiscal*, C-151/09, ECLI:EU:C:2010:452.

the transferor under that agreement, until the date of termination or expiry of the collective agreement or the entry into force or application of another collective agreement.

Member States may limit the period for observing such terms and conditions with the proviso that it shall not be less than one year.

Article 4(1)

The transfer of the undertaking, business or part of the undertaking or business shall not in itself constitute grounds for dismissal by the transferor or the transferee. This provision shall not stand in the way of dismissals that may take place for economic, technical or organisational reasons entailing changes in the workforce.

Article 4(2)

If the contract of employment or the employment relationship is terminated because the transfer involves a substantial change in working conditions to the detriment of the employee, the employer shall be regarded as having been responsible for termination of the contract of employment or of the employment relationship.

Article 8

This Directive shall not affect the right of Member States to apply or introduce laws, regulations or administrative provisions which are more favourable to employees or to promote or permit collective agreements or agreements between social partners more favourable to employees.

It was mentioned that the rights conferred by the directive have the effect of compressing the contractual freedom and the freedom to conduct the business of the transferee.[510] This reflects a prominent protective function. The case study aims to show how the Court has engaged with such function: whether it accepts, or even reinforces it or, instead, nuances it. But that is not all; the directive also expresses the functions of uplifting workers' bargaining power and of adapting workers' rights to the need of the businesses. The way the Court interprets the effectiveness of collective agreements in force before the transfer vis-à-vis the transferee is indicative of its valorisation of one function over the other. Finally, if the Court appears to favour the preservation of the transferee's interests over a strict interpretation of workers' rights, this is an indication that the emancipatory rationale of the rules is being weakened by judicial interpretation.

The picture that emerges is thus rather eloquent with respect to the way in which the Court has approached the relationship between the emancipatory and economic rationale of the directive. And this is even more than in the previous case studies. While section 5.1 concerned the scope of the rights established in the directive, the case study

510. As discussed in section 3.1.

presented in this section reveals the actual intensity that the Court attaches to those rights.

The analysis of the case law showed that the Court's approach is essentially of two types. On the one hand, there are reasonings in which the rights down in the directive are interpreted in a strict manner, without derogations. These are indicated in rows A to E of Box 8 below and in Table 3. With these reasonings, the Court valorised the emancipatory rationale of the norms.

Box 8: Reasonings That Enhance the Emancipatory Rationale of the Directive

A. The protection provided by the directive is a matter of public policy and is independent of the will of the parties (transferor, transferee, employees).

B. The transfer of the employment relationships and of the related rights is an automatic consequence of the transfer and does not require further agreements or stipulations.

C. It is not allowed for the transferred workers or their representatives to waive or alter the rights that the directive confers them (unless national law allows the employment relationship to be altered in a manner unfavourable to employees in situations other than the transfer *and* provided that the transfer itself may never constitute the reason for the alteration).

D. The transferee cannot unilaterally alter the terms and conditions of the employment relationship, not even in a non-substantial manner (a corollary of reasoning C, and the same exception applies).

E. With respect to the transferred workers, the transferee is bound to observe the collective agreement that was in force with the transferor. This implies that the transferee is not allowed to impose the application of another collective agreement unless the conditions of Article 3(3) are fulfilled.

On the other hand, there are reasonings where the Court showed significant sensitivity to the economic interests of the transferee. In these cases, identified with the letters F to J below of Box 9 and in Table 3, the Court reduced the emancipatory reach of the directive. Workers' rights are read in a flexible manner, and the minimum standards of protection risk becoming also the maximum standards.

Box 9: Reasonings That Weaken the Emancipatory Rationale of the Directive

F. From the date of the transfer, the transferee is free to apply to the transferred workers a collective agreement which is different from that in force with the transferor.

G. With respect to the employment conditions of the transferred workers, the transferee must be in the position to make the adjustments and changes necessary to carry out his business operations.

H. The transferee must be able to assert his interests effectively in a contractual process to which it is a party and to negotiate the aspects determining changes in the working conditions of its employees with a view to his future economic activity (as an expression of his freedom of contract).
I. The transferee can apply pejorative terms and conditions of employment to the transferred workers, the only legal consequence being that he will be held responsible for the eventual termination of the contract, as established in Article 4(2).
J. If the transferred employee decided to terminate the employment contract because of substantial alteration in the working conditions, the employee has no right to receive the financial compensation on which he/she could rely in case of unlawful termination.

Clearly, the reasonings in Box 8 predominantly reflect the emancipatory rationale of the rules under consideration. Those in Box 9, instead, emphasise their economic dimension. Before analysing the findings presented in Table 4, it is also worth noting that in certain judgments the Court has displayed a 'bipolar' attitude. The same judgment can indeed address more than one interpretative issue concerning workers' rights. In some cases, the Court resolved certain legal questions by recurring to one of the reasonings in Box 8 (reflecting a protective approach) and others with reasonings in Box 9 (reflecting a more economic approach). Of the 30 judgments represented in the table, four have this 'double soul'.[511]

511. Judgment of 9 March 2006, *Hans Werhof v. Freeway Traffic Systems GmbH & Co. KG*, C-499/04, ECLI:EU:C:2006:168; judgment of 27 November 2008, *Mirja Juuri v. Fazer Amica Oy*, C-396/07, ECLI:EU:C:2008:656; judgment of 6 September 2011, *Ivana Scattolon v. Ministero dell'Istruzione, dell'Università e della Ricerca*, C-108/10, ECLI:EU:C:2011:542; judgment of 6 April 2017, *Unionen v. Almega Tjänsteförbunden and ISS Facility Services AB*, C-336/15, ECLI:EU:C:2017:276.

Table 3 Case Study on Workers' Rights

	1	2	3	4	5	6	7	8	9	10	11	12	13	14	15	16	17	18	19	20	21	22	23	24	25	26	27	28	29	30
A	■		■	■				■	■	■			■	■	■	■			■				■							■
B		■		■		■				■			■		■	■										■	■	■		
C	■			■	■		■	■			■		■	■	■					■				■						
D					■	■	■		■		■	■						■		■				■						
E																	■							■						
F																				■		■								
G																■				■	■	■		■	■				■	
H																					■				■					
I																	■												■	
J																	■													
	C-324/86 *Daddy's Dance Hall*	C-144/87 *Berg*	C-101/87 *Bork*	C-362/89 *D'Urso*	C-209/91 *Rask*	C-139/91 *Katsikas*	C-392/92 *Schmidt*	C-472/93 *Spano*	C-171/94 *Merckx*	C-305/94 *Rotsart*	C-343/98 *Collino and Chiappero*	C-175/99 *Didier Mayeur*	C-51/00 *Temco*	C-4/01 *Martin*	C-478/03 *Celtec*	C-499/04 *Werhof*	C-396/07 *Juuri*	C-466/07 *Klarenberg*	C-561/07 *Com v. Italy*	C-108/10 *Scattolon*	C-426/11 *Alemo-Herron*	C-328/13 *Österreichischer Gewerks.*	C-688/13 *Gimnasio*	C-336/15 *Unionen*	C-680/15 *Asklepios*	C-60/17 *Somoza*	C-509/17 *Plessers*	C-317/18 *Moreira*	C-344/18 *ISS*	C-674/18 *TMD Friction*

Source: Author's own elaboration.

Emancipatory Rationale Is Enhanced: **(A)** The protection provided by the directive is a matter of public policy and is independent of the will of the parties (transferor, transferee, employees); **(B)** The transfer of the employment relationships and of the related rights is an automatic consequence of the transfer and does not require further agreements or stipulations; **(C)** It is not allowed for the transferred workers or their representatives to waive or alter their rights that the directive confers them (unless national law allows the employment relationship to be altered in a manner unfavourable to employees in situations other than the transfer *and* provided that the transfer itself may never constitute the reason for the alteration); **(D)** The transferee cannot unilaterally alter the terms and conditions of the employment relationship, not even in a non-substantial manner (a corollary of reasoning C); **(E)** With respect to the transferred workers, the transferee is bound to observe the collective agreement that was in force with the transferor. This implies that the transferee is not allowed to impose the application of another collective agreement unless the conditions of Article 3(3) are fulfilled.

Emancipatory Rationale Is Weakened: **(F)** From the date of the transfer, the transferee is free to apply to the transferred workers a collective agreement which is different from that in force with the transferor; **(G)** With respect to the employment conditions of the transferred workers, the transferee must be in the position to make the adjustments and changes necessary to carry out his business operations; **(H)** The transferee must be able to assert his interests effectively in a contractual process to which it is a party and to negotiate the aspects determining changes in the working conditions of its employees with a view to his future economic activity (as an expression of his freedom of contract); **(I)** The transferee can apply pejorative terms and conditions of employment to the transferred workers, the only legal consequence being that he will be held responsible for the eventual termination of the contract, as established in Article 4(2); **(J)** If the transferred employee decided to terminate the employment contract because of substantial alteration in the working conditions, the employee has no right to receive the financial compensation on which he/she could rely in case of unlawful termination

The graphical representation in Table 3 clearly shows that, during the first decade and a half of judicial activity, the Court has been coherently adopting reasonings that valorised the emancipatory component of the directive. However, from the mid-2000s onwards, and more precisely, from the *Werhof* ruling (2006), something changed, and the Court appeared more open to considering the interests of the employer.[512]

Proceeding with chronological order, in *Daddy's Dance Hall* (1988) – and then in several of the subsequent cases – the Court interpreted the workers' rights established in the directive as a matter of public policy. This meant that the rights were read as mandatory, independently from the will of the parties (A).[513] *Daddy's Dance Hall* also established that the mandatory nature of the rights did not bind only the employer. Not even the workers and the unions representing them could validly consent to an alteration of the employment relation leading to a worsening of the working conditions (C): 'employee cannot waive the rights conferred on him by the mandatory provisions of Directive 77/187/EEC even if the disadvantages resulting from his waiver are offset by such benefits that, taking the matter as a whole, he is not placed in a worse position'.[514]

With the *Berg* case (1988), the Court also specified that the transfer of the employment relationship and the existing terms and conditions takes place automatically at the time of the transfer, even in the absence of any written agreement between the parties (B).[515] The directive's legal consequences are, thus, not conditional on the consent of the employees concerned.[516] Furthermore, with the *Rask* case (1991), the Court further strengthened the principle of the mandatory nature of the protection conferred to workers. In *Rask*, the Court ruled that the transferee is in fact prevented from introducing *non-substantial* alterations to the employment relationship if the transfer is the reason for such changes (D). The Court, more precisely, held that 'Article 3 of the Directive is to be interpreted as meaning that, upon a transfer, the terms and conditions of the contract of employment or employment relationship relating to wages, in particular those relating to the date of payment and the composition of wages, cannot be altered even if the total amount of the wages remains the same.'[517]

With these rulings, the Court established substantial limitations to the freedom of contract of the employer. Its interpretative approach is thus entirely in line with the emancipatory rationale of the directive. Most significantly, in the *D'Urso* case (1991), the Court stated that 'curtailing the freedom to carry on business [...] is inherent in the very purpose of the directive'.[518] However, from the mid-2000s, and especially since

512. Judgment of 9 March 2006, *Hans Werhof v. Freeway Traffic Systems GmbH & Co. KG*, C-499/04, ECLI:EU:C:2006:168.
513. Judgment of 10 February 1988, *Foreningen af Arbejdsledere i Danmark v. Daddy's Dance Hall A/S*, C-324/86, ECLI:EU:C:1988:72 (para. 14).
514. C-324/86, *Daddy's Dance Hall* (paras 15 and 18).
515. Judgment of 5 May 1988, *Harry Berg and Johannes Theodorus Maria Busschers v. Ivo Martin Besselsen*, C-144/87, ECLI:EU:C:1988:236 (para. 11).
516. *Ibid.*
517. Judgment of 12 November 1992, *Anne Watson Rask and Kirsten Christensen v. Iss Kantineservice A/S*, C-209/91, ECLI:EU:C:1992:436 (para. 31).
518. Judgment of 25 July 1991, *Giuseppe d'Urso, Adriana Ventadori and others v. Ercole Marelli Elettromeccanica Generale SpA and others*, C-362/89, ECLI:EU:C:1991:326 (para. 15).

the *Werhof* judgment (2007), the Court began to show greater sensitivity towards the transferee's interests, and the judicial reasoning started to change.[519] *Werhof* concerned an issue similar to the one that the Court would later address in the *Alemo-Herron* case (2013), discussed in Chapter 1, section 3.1. For the first time, the Court referred to the necessity to preserve the transferee's ability to make the adjustments and the changes that are necessary to carry out his business operations (G).[520]

Werhof related to the obligation of the transferee to observe the collective agreement that would have been applicable to the workers if the transfer had not occurred. Before the transfer, the workers were covered by the collective agreement on the iron and steel, metal and electrical industry. This agreement was not applied by the transferee to his own workers but, pursuant to Article 3(3), he had to observe said collective agreement in relation to the transferred workers. Then, when the social partners renewed the collective agreement and stipulated a wage increase, the transferred workers demanded the transferee to increase their wages accordingly. To support their claim, the workers held that their individual contract of employment, whose provisions were still applicable after the transfer by effect of Article 3(1), made an explicit reference to collective agreements concluded in the relevant sector. They argued that this clause must necessarily be read in a 'dynamic' manner, to cover not only collective agreements existing at the time of the transfer but also those concluded after the transfer had taken place.[521] The transferee, on the other hand, held that the contractual clause referring to the collective agreement had to be interpreted 'statically' (as opposed to dynamically). The transferee thus sustained that he was obliged to observe only the collective agreement in force at the time of the transfer and not any other future agreements.[522] Otherwise, he observed, his own freedom of association, which includes also the right not to join an association or trade union, would have been violated.

The Court, confronted with this issue, referred to past case law and in principle confirmed the mandatory character of the rights laid down in Articles 3 and 4.[523] It then reflected on the relationship between the protective effect of the directive and the transferee's contractual freedom. The Court shared the employer's view that also the (negative) freedom of association was at stake. In fact, a dynamic interpretation of the contractual clause would imply that the transferee would have to apply future collective agreements without being a signatory of such an agreement nor a member of the associations that negotiated it.[524] The Court eventually ruled that 'the wording of

519. *See, inter alia*, A.C.L. Davies, A. Bogg & C. Costello, 'The Role of the Court of Justice in Labour Law' in A. Bogg, C. Costello & A.C.L. Davies (eds), *Research Handbook on EU Labour Law*, Edward Elgar Publishing, Cheltenham, 2016, pp. 114-149; S. Giubboni, 'Freedom to Conduct a Business and EU Labour Law', European Constitutional Law Review, 14, 2018 pp. 172-190; C. Wynn-Evans, 'TUPE, Collective Agreements and the Static-Dynamic Debate', Industrial Law Journal, 39(3), pp. 275-279, 2010.
520. Judgment of 9 March 2006, *Hans Werhof v. Freeway Traffic Systems GmbH & Co. KG*, C-499/04, ECLI:EU:C:2006:168 (para. 31).
521. C-499/04, *Werhof* (para. 18).
522. *Ibid.* (para. 19).
523. *Ibid.* (para. 26).
524. *Ibid.* (para. 34).

the directive does not in any way indicate that the Community legislature intended that the transferee be bound by collective agreement other than the one in force at the time of the transfer' and that 'the directive was not intended to protect mere expectations to rights and, therefore, hypothetical advantages flowing from future changes to the collective agreements'. The Court thus eventually did not align with the position of the workers and held that the directive did not require the contractual clause referring to the collective agreement to be read in a dynamic manner.[525]

The directive was thus interpreted as an instrument that, while aiming at providing certain guarantees for workers, did not allow the employer's interests to be disregarded either. This reading was reinforced in subsequent case law, in which the Court appeared more open to considering the transferee perspective. Both in *Alemo-Herron* (2013) and *Asklepios* (2017), presenting a similar issue, the Court again valorised the economic underpinning of the directive and stated that 'the transferee must be able to assert his interests effectively in a contractual process to which it is a party and to negotiate the aspects determining changes in the working conditions of its employees with a view to his future economic activity' (H).[526]

As was discussed in Chapter 1 section 3.1, *Alemo-Herron* concerned a transfer of business to a transferee that was not covered by any collective agreement. At the time of the transfer, however, the individual employment contract contained a dynamic clause referring to (present and future) collective agreements stipulated in the relevant sector.[527] It should be recalled that such 'incorporation' of collective agreements by means of a contractual clause was a widespread practice in the UK, where collective bargaining does not have *erga omnes* effect.[528] In dealing with this case, the Court went further than in *Werhof*. Despite that this time the contractual clause was actually formulated in a dynamic manner and that Article 8 of the directive allowed the national systems to provide stronger forms of protection than the minimum standards prescribed in the directive, the Court held that a dynamic reading of the clause would impair the transferee's freedom to conduct a business.[529] For this reason, the Court ruled that the directive required the clause to be read in a static manner.

On closer inspection, it is interesting to note that the Court's increased consideration for the economic interests of the employer does not necessarily result in a dismissal of the workers' judicial claim. Examples are the *Österreichischer Gewerkschaftsbund* (2014) and *Asklepios* (2017) rulings, which deal with legal questions that

525. *Ibid.* (para. 29).
526. Judgment of 18 July 2013, *Mark Alemo-Herron and Others v. Parkwood Leisure Ltd*, C-426/11, ECLI:EU:C:2013:521 (para. 33); judgment of 27 April 2017, *Asklepios Kliniken Langen-Seligenstadt GmbH v. Ivan Felja and Asklepios Dienstleistungsgesellschaft mbH v. Vittoria Graf*, C-680/15, ECLI:EU:C:2017:317 (para. 23).
527. The individual contract of employment of the transferred workers indicated that 'during your employment with [name of the employer], your terms and conditions of employment will be in accordance with the collective agreement negotiated from time to time by [name of the collective body]'.
528. J. Prassl, 'Freedom of Contract as a General Principle of EU Law? Transfers of Undertakings and the Protection of Employer Rights in EU Labour Law', Industrial Law Journal, 42(4), pp. 434-446, 2013.
529. Judgment of 18 July 2013, *Mark Alemo-Herron and Others v. Parkwood Leisure Ltd*, C-426/11, ECLI:EU:C:2013:521 (paras 33-35).

are similar to those addressed in *Alemo-Herron*.[530] In both cases, the Court referred to *Alemo-Herron* and held that the directive should not be interpreted as to excessively constrain the rights of the transferee. However, in the end, the Court found a normative solution which ensured that the employees' claim could be upheld.[531] In *Österreichischer Gewerkschaftsbund*, the interpretative question posed to the Court concerned a national rule providing that the legal effects of a collective agreement continue until the social partners conclude a new agreement. The transferee claimed that this rule infringed his freedom of contract[532] and in addressing this point the Court followed the same argumentative approach already adopted in *Werhof* and *Alemo-Herron*: the interests of the workers and those of the employer need to be balanced out. Differently from those judgments, however, this time the Court did not uphold the position of the transferee and ruled that 'the rule maintaining the effects of a collective agreement, such as that at issue in the main proceedings, has limited effects, since it maintains only the legal effects of a collective agreement on the employment relationship directly subject to it before its rescission or a new individual agreement is concluded with the employees concerned. In those circumstances, it does not appear that such a rule hinders the transferee's ability to make the adjustments and changes necessary to carry on its operations'.[533]

A similar outcome was reached in *Asklepios*, which concerned the same situation that the Court had previously analysed in *Alemo-Herron*. The issue was whether the transferee was obliged to observe a clause in the individual employment contract referring to a collective agreement. *Asklepios* had also common aspects with the *Werhof* case, as they both originated from a German court and both related to a contractual clause that was formulated in a static manner. Interestingly, however, soon after *Werhof*, the German jurisprudence had changed its approach towards the legal effect of incorporating clauses and now provided that even static clauses should be read dynamically.[534] In addressing the issue, the CJEU formally adhered to the reasoning adopted in *Alemo-Herron*, but eventually reached a more nuanced solution. It ruled that 'while it follows from the case law of the ECJ referred to above [meaning *Werhof*], that Article 3 of Directive 2001/23/EC must be interpreted as meaning that it

530. Judgment of 27 April 2017, *Asklepios Kliniken Langen-Seligenstadt GmbH v. Ivan Felja and Asklepios Dienstleistungsgesellschaft mbH v. Vittoria Graf*, C-680/15, ECLI:EU:C:2017:317; judgment of 11 September 2014, *Österreichischer Gewerkschaftsbund v. Wirtschaftskammer Österreich – Fachverband Autobus-, Luftfahrt- und Schifffahrtsunternehmungen*, C-328/13, ECLI:EU:C:2014:2197.
531. *See, inter alia*, E. Brameshuber, 'Balancing vs. Preservation of Rights under the Acquired Rights Directive', Industrial Law Journal, 45(3), pp. 443-454, 2016.
532. Opinion of Advocate General Cruz Villalon of 3 June 2014, *Österreichischer Gewerkschaftsbund v. Wirtschaftskammer Österreich – Fachverband Autobus-, Luftfahrt- und Schifffahrtsunternehmungen*, C-328/13, ECLI:EU:C:2014:2197 (para. 30).
533. Judgment of 11 September 2014, *Österreichischer Gewerkschaftsbund v. Wirtschaftskammer Österreich – Fachverband Autobus-, Luftfahrt- und Schifffahrtsunternehmungen*, C-328/13, ECLI:EU:C:2014:2197 (para. 30).
534. This aspect is further explored in Chapter 6, section 4.3.3.

does not require a "static" clause to be treated as "dynamic" [...] the directive and Article 3 thereof should not be read as intended to prevent a dynamic clause from producing its effects'.[535] The Court justified the divergence from the solution reached in *Alemo-Herron* by arguing that its interpretation still ensured the preservation of the freedom to conduct a business of the employer since 'the national legislation at issue in the main proceedings provides for the possibility, after the transfer, for the transferee to adjust the working conditions existing at the date of the transfer, either consensually or unilaterally'.[536] It is interesting to note that with this decision the Court rejected the conclusion of Advocate General Bot, who had suggested the same approach as in *Alemo-Herron*.[537] According to Bot, in fact, Article 3 of the directive (and more precisely, Article 3.3) already struck a compromise between the interests of the transferee and that of the employees. This led him to argue that a more expansive reading of the applicability of collective agreements in force before the transfer would result in an excessive compression of the economic freedom of the employer.

Therefore, and despite the adoption of rhetorical arguments receptive to the economic interests of the transferee, *Österreichischer Gewerkschaftsbund* and *Asklepios* ultimately did not fully jeopardise the emancipatory potential of the directive. However, such potential was certainly not valorised as it was in the earlier case law.[538] In *Österreichischer Gewerkschaftsbund* and *Asklepios*, the Court embarked on a sort of balancing exercise between workers' rights and the transferee's freedom of contract. In those two judgments, the final assessment resulted in favour of the workers, but it is undeniable that this might not be the case in the future. In previous rulings, when the Court tended to give a more rigid interpretation of the protective function of the directive, as well as to the effectiveness of collective agreements in force before the transfer vis-à-vis the transferee, this balancing exercise between workers' rights and economic interest would have been inconceivable. The mandatory nature of workers' rights was the undisputed rule.[539]

Questions of interpretation concerning the effects of the static or dynamic clauses on the application of future collective agreements are not the only aspects where Table 3 shows more opening towards the interests of the transferee.[540] The Court has also accepted the possibility for the transferee not to apply the collective agreement in force at the time of the transfer to the transferred workers. In *Scattolon* (2011) and, more indirectly, in *Österreichischer Gewerkschaftsbund* (2014), the Court interpreted Article

535. C-680/15, *Asklepios* (paras 19 and 20).
536. *Ibid.* (para. 24).
537. Opinion of Advocate General Bot of 19 January 2017, *Asklepios Kliniken Langen-Seligenstadt GmbH v. Ivan Felja and Asklepios Dienstleistungsgesellschaft mbH v. Vittoria Graf*, C-680/15, ECLI:EU:C:2017:30 (para. 15).
538. On the normative consequences of an expansive approach towards the freedom of contract, *see* E. Gill-Pedro, 'Freedom to Conduct Business in EU Law: Freedom from Interference or Freedom from Domination?', European Journal of Legal Studies, 9(2), pp. 103-134, 2017 and X. Groussot, T.G. Pétursson & J. Pierce, 'Weak Right, Strong Court – The Freedom to Conduct Business and the EU Charter of Fundamental Rights', Legal Research Paper Series, 1, Lund University, Lund, 2014.
539. *See* Table 3.
540. *Ibid.*

3(3) of the directive as in principle allowing the transferee to apply to the transferred workers the collective agreement already in place in his business, even if different from the agreement that was applicable with the transferor (F).[541] However, the Court was not consistent on this point. In the *Juuri* (2008) and *Unionen* (2017) judgments, the Court in fact seemed to deny the possibility for the transferee to apply his own collective agreement to the transferred workers if, at the moment of the transfer, they were already covered by another agreement (E).[542] This confusion might be, in part, justified by an unclear wording in the text of the directive. Article 3(3) establishes that the transferee must observe the collective agreement in force with the transferor 'until the date of termination or expiry of the collective agreement or the entry into force or application of another agreement'. This norm is quite vague and is open to different interpretations. It is thus not clear whether 'application of another agreement' could also refer to the collective agreement already in force to the transferee, or whether it only refers to the situation whereby the collective agreement that was in force before the transfer ceases to produce legal effects because it reached its expiration or was substituted by its original signatories.

Table 3 also shows an evolution in the case law regarding the interpretation of Article 4(2), establishing that 'If the contract of employment or the employment relationship is terminated because the transfer involves a substantial change in working conditions to the detriment of the employee, the employer shall be regarded as having been responsible for termination of the contract of employment or of the employment relationship.' As mentioned, in its earlier case law, the Court had held that *no* pejorative contractual changes could be made by the transferee by reason of the transfer. The prevalent view was that 'the rules of the directive, in particular those concerning the protection of workers against dismissals, must be considered to be mandatory so that it is not possible to derogate from them in a manner unfavourable to employee'.[543] In the *Daddy's Dance Hall* judgment, the Court had also established that

541. Judgment of 6 September 2011, *Ivana Scattolon v. Ministero dell'Istruzione, dell'Università e della Ricerca*, C-108/10, ECLI:EU:C:2011:542 (para. 74), where the Court ruled that 'the rule in the first subparagraph of Article 3(2) of Directive 77/187, according to which "the transferee shall continue to observe the terms and conditions agreed in any collective agreement on the same terms applicable to the transferor under that agreement, until the date of … application of another collective agreement" must be interpreted as meaning that it is lawful for the transferee to apply, from the date of the transfer, the working conditions laid down by the collective agreement in force with him, including those concerning remuneration'. Moreover, in C-328/13, *Österreichischer Gewerkschaftsbund* (para. 33) the Court ruled that 'with regard to the terms and conditions agreed by the transferee's collective agreement […] it is not apparent from the file before the Court that those terms and conditions can apply to the transferred employees under the rule maintaining the effects of that collective agreement'. This implies that the sole obstacle for the transferee to apply the rule of his collective agreement was the fact that, under the Austrian system, the collective agreement in force with the transferor continued to exercise its effect after it was rescinded. It thus seems that, in absence of this specific rule, the transferee has the possibility to apply his collective agreement to the transferred workers from the moment of the transfer. On this point, *see also* paras 10 and 11 of the case.

542. Judgment of 27 November 2008, *Mirja Juuri v. Fazer Amica Oy*, C-396/07, ECLI:EU:C:2008:656 (paras 32-34); judgment of 6 April 2017, *Unionen v. Almega Tjänsteförbunden and ISS Facility Services AB*, C-336/15, ECLI:EU:C:2017:276 (para. 28).

543. C-324/86, *Daddy's Dance Hall* (para. 14).

workers' rights cannot be restricted even if with the employees' consent, and even if, taking the matter as a whole, the employees are not placed in a worse position than before the transfer. Only alterations that are not correlated to the transfer were deemed permissible.[544] This implied that the reference to 'substantial change in the working conditions' in Article 4(2) was read as relating (and allowing) solely those changes in working conditions that are unavoidable, such as when a transfer occurs from a public sector company to a private sector company. In this case, the overall regulatory regime changes regardless of the will of the parties, as it passes from public law to civil law.[545] Article 4(2) was initially interpreted as addressing those marginal and inevitable circumstances in which the workers were subject to a regime variation after the transfer. It was not, instead, read as consenting the transferee to modify, in its own interest, the terms and conditions of the employment relationship.

This view, however, changed over time. In *Juuri* (2008) and, more recently, in *ISS* (2020), the Court read Article 4(2) as allowing the transferee to alter the terms and conditions of employment in a manner that is detrimental to the employees (I).[546] The *ISS* judgment is particularly significant in this regard: the transferor was a cleaning company that managed three lots and transferred its activity not to one transferee, but to two. One transferee took over one lot, while the other transferee took over the other two. The question that was submitted to the Court was how to apply the directive and, in particular, ensure the continuation of the employment relationship of the workers in line with Article 3. The Court analysed two options, which had been put forward by the referring judge. The first was to transform the employment relationship, originally full-time, into two part-time employment relationships, one with each transferee in proportion to the task performed by the workers. This solution would entail an important change in the employment relationship with a clear deterioration in working conditions. The second option was that the workers continued the relationship with the transferee who had taken over the establishment where the workers were principally employed. In this way, the protection afforded to the employees by the directive would be applied in full. For the Court, however, this second option 'has the effect of disregarding the interests of the transferee, to whom there are transferred the rights and

544. C-324/86, *Daddy's Dance Hall* (para. 15).

545. Judgment of 26 September 2000, *Didier Mayeur v. Association Promotion de l'information messine (APIM)*, C-175/99, ECLI:EU:C:2000:505 (para. 56), where those changes were deemed to be a consequence of the difference in the legal nature between the transferor and the transferee. Nonetheless, the Court held that since a substantial change in working conditions had arisen directly from the transfer, should the transferred workers decide to terminate their contract of employment, such termination would be regarded as resulting from the action of the employer.

546. C-396/07, *Juuri* (para. 30), 'where the Court also held that the in the event where the transferred employee decides to terminate the employment relationship following a pejorative change in his working conditions after the transfer, Member States are not required to guarantee the employee a right to financial compensation, for which the transferee employer is liable, in accordance with the same conditions as the right upon which an employee can rely where the contract of employment or the employment relationship is unlawfully terminated by his employer'; judgment of 26 March 2020, *ISS Facility Services NV v. Sonia Govaerts and Atalian NV, formerly Euroclean NV*, C-344/18, ECLI:EU:C:2020:239 (paras 36-38).

obligations arising from a full-time employment contract although the worker concerned is to perform his or her tasks with that transferee only part-time'.[547] The Court therefore preferred the first option, with the part-time contracts. The fact that the workers are placed in a worse situation than before the transfer was not seen as problematic since would the employees not be content with their new contractual arrangements, they could rely on Article 4(2). This provision 'states that if the contract of employment is terminated because the transfer involves a substantial change in working conditions to the detriment of the employee, the employer is to be regarded as having been responsible for termination' (I).[548]

As argued by McMullen, this solution is rather absurd and is a significant departure from the position taken by the Court in its earlier case law.[549] The emphasis on the preservation of the contractual freedom of the employer runs counter to previous reasonings on the mandatory nature of the rights conferred by the directive. This is further aggravated by the fact that, in the *Juuri* judgment, the Court had already emptied the protective scope of Article 4(2). In *Juuri*, the Court had in fact ruled that when a worker terminates the employment contract because of substantial alterations in the working conditions, he cannot claim the financial compensation that applies in case of unlawful termination by the employer (J).[550]

To conclude, the case study reveals a pronounced evolution in the way the Court has interpreted the intensity of the protection that the directive confers on workers. Throughout time, the Court has changed its approach towards the emancipatory rationale of the directive. Until the *Werhof* judgment, the Court had maintained a rather rigid interpretation of workers' rights. From that judgment onwards, the Court has instead shown an increased sensitivity to the economic interests of the transferee. At times, this approach has led to an actual worsening of the workers' conditions (*Alemo-Herron, ISS*). In other cases, instead, the Court tried to strike a balance in order not to (fully) dismiss the workers' claims (*Österreichischer Gewerkschaftsbund, Asklepios*).

Overall, the Court seems to have opted for an interpretation of the directive that aims at reconciling the economic and social interests involved in situations of transfer of undertaking. As was explained in Chapter 1, this approach does not necessarily coincide with a full rejection of the emancipatory rationale of the directive.[551] Nevertheless, it is important to stress that the emancipatory dimension becomes more marginalised every time the Court adapts workers' rights to the employer's business interests.

547. C-344/18, *ISS Facility Services* (para. 31).
548. *Ibid.* (para. 36).
549. J. McMullen, 'Leaving a Legacy: Recent Jurisprudence of the European Court on Transfer of Undertakings', Industrial Law Journal, 50(1), pp. 130-157, 2021, according to whom 'ISS Facility Services illustrates the absurd results that can occur when the Court strives to maintain a balance between employer and employee interests at the expense of a single, employee-oriented approach.'
550. C-396/07, *Juuri* (para. 30).
551. *See* section 2.2.3.

6 THE COURT'S APPROACH TO LABOUR LAW

Overall, the case studies on the scope of application and on the rights conferred by the directive have shown that the Court has, over time, moved away from its initial emphasis on the emancipatory rationale. Instead, it has given greater weight to the interests of the employer. First, the notion of 'transfer of a business' has been considerably narrowed. Then, a similar trend was observed in relation to workers' rights, where business concerns gradually appeared in the Court's reasoning.

At the same time, however, the case studies have shown that the Court did not go so far as to actually reject this emancipatory component of the directive as one might infer from an anecdotal analysis of the most academically debated cases, such as *Alemo-Herron*. The case law analysis rather suggests that the Court is disposed to safeguard workers' rights as long as they can coexist with the economic freedoms of the employer. The current prevalent approach of the Court appears to be that of reconciling the social and economic underpinning of the directive. The effort to balance the social and economic dimensions led to a quite ambivalent and unpredictable case law. At times, this has resulted in a dismissal of the workers' quest for protection while, on other occasions, the Court has ruled in their advantage.

This ambiguity in the Court's approach also emerges clearly from the last case study presented in this chapter, concerning the Court's interpretation of the purpose of the directive (Tables 4 and 5). Boxes 10 to 13 present the different reasonings with which, throughout its whole case law, the Court has addressed the purpose of the directive. In total, a number of 15 reasonings have been identified and they can be divided into four groups.

Letters A to F relate to the valorisation of the emancipatory rationale of the directive:

Box 10: Valorisation of the Emancipatory Rationale of the Directive

A. The objective of the directive is to promote upward convergence regarding workers' rights.
B. The directive is intended to ensure that restructuring does not adversely affect the workers.
C. The objective is to preserve workers against potentially unfavourable consequences related to the change of the employer.
D. The directive wants to ensure that the employment relationship continues unchanged with the transferee so that the employees are not placed in a less favourable position solely as a result of the transfer.
E. The directive aims at ensuring the continuity of the employment relationship.
F. The objective is to safeguard the employees in the event of transfers of undertaking.

Reasonings G and H define the limits of the emancipatory rationale:

Box 11: Limits Are Drawn to the Emancipatory Rationale of the Directive

G. The directive is not aimed at protecting mere expectations or hypothetical advantages of the transferred workers.
H. The objective is not to extend employees' rights.

With the reasonings in letters I to L, the Court recalls that the function of the directive is also to advance the EU internal market:

Box 12: The Directive's Function Is Also to Facilitate the Expansion of the Internal Market

I. The directive is read in light of both Article 100 TEEC (currently 115 TFEU) and 117 TEEC (currently 151 TFEU).
J. The directive aims at ensuring comparable protection for workers' rights within the EU and at harmonizing the costs which those protective rules entail for European undertakings.
K. The directive aims at reducing the differences between national legislation on protection of employees by means of approximation without complete harmonization.
L. The directive aims at allowing the completion of the internal market.

Finally, letters M to O place the accent on the economic interests of the employer and emphasise the economic dimension of the directive:

Box 13: The Directive Shall Also Consider the Employers' Economic Interests

M. In interpreting the objective of the directive, the interests of the transferee cannot be disregarded.
N. The directive seeks to ensure a fair balance between the interests of the employees and those of the transferee.
O. The directive explicitly considers also the employers' freedom of contract and freedom to conduct a business.

Tables 4 and 5 below show that, although the considerations in Box 13 have made frequent appearances in recent years, the Court has never gone so far as to reject the social underpinning of the directive.

Table 4 Case Study on the Purpose of the Directive: Until 2003

	1	2	3	4	5	6	7	8	9	10	11	12	13	14	15	16	17	18	19	20	21	22	23	24	25	26	27	28	29	30	31
1	A B	D	D	D	D	D	D E	D	D	D	B D F	F	F	D F		F	E	F	C	C D F	E	E	E	D F	D E F	D F	E	E	E	F	F
2																															
3	I														J																
4																															
	C-135/83 *Abels*	C-19/83 *Knud*	C-179/83 *Industriebond*	C-105/84 *iDenmark*	C-235/84 *Com v. Italy*	C-237/84 *Com v. Belgium*	C-24/85 *Spijkers*	C-287/86 *Ny Mølle Kro*	C-324/86 *Daddy Dance Hall*	C-101/87 *Bork International*	C-362/89 *D'Urso*	C-29/91 *Redmond Stichting*	C-209/91 *Rask*	C-132/91 *Katsikas*	C-382/92 *Com v. UK*	C-392/92 *Schmidt*	C-48/94 *Strø Mølle Akustik*	C-172/94 *Merckx*	C-298/94 *Henke*	C-305/94 *Rotsart de Hertaing*	C-13/95 *Süzen*	C-127/96 *Hernández Vidal*	C-173/96 *Hidalgo*	C-399/96 *Europièces*	C-234/98 *Allen*	C-343/98 *Collino and Ch.*	C-172/99 *Liikenne*	C-175/99 *Didier Mayeur*	C-51/00 *Temco*	C-164/00 *Beckmann*	C-4/01 *Martin*

Source: Author's own elaboration.

Table 5 Case Study on the Purpose of the Directive: Until Mid-2022

	32	33	34	35	36	37	38	39	40	41	42	43	44	45	46	47
1		E	D F	E F	D F	E F	F	D F	E F	C D E F	D F	F	D F	F	D F	D F
2					G											
3				I L												
4													O	N O		N
	C-145/01 *Com v. Italy*	C-340/01 *Abler*	C-478/03 *Celtec*	C-232/04 *Securicor*	C-499/04 *Werhof*	C-458/05 *Jouini*	C-313/07 *Kirtuna*	C-396/07 *Juuri*	C-466/07 *Klarenberg*	C-151/09 *UGT-FSP*	C-386/09 *Briot*	C-463/09 *CLECE*	C-108/10 *Scattolon*	C-426/11 *Alemo-Herron*	C-458/12 *Amatori*	C-328/13 *Öst. Gewerksc.*

	48	49	50	51	52	53	54	55		56	57	58	59	60	61	62
1	F	E	E	D F	F	F	F	E F	D E	F	F	D	D F	E	D	D
2					G								H		H	
3																K
4				N	N O										N M	N
	C-688/13 *Gimnasio*	C-160/14 *Ferreira Da S.*	C-509 /14 *Adif*	C-336/15 *Unionen*	C-680/15 *Asklepios*	C-126/16 *Smallsteps*	C-416/16 *Piscarreta*	C-200/16 *Securitas*	C-472/16 *Colino Sig.*	C-60/17 *Somoza*	C-194/18 *Dodič*	C-509/17 *Plessers*	C317/18 *Correia Moreira*	C-664/17 *Ellinika Nafp.*	C-344/18 *ISS Facility S.*	C-674/18 *TMD Friction*

Source: Author's own elaboration.

Row 1 – Valorisation of Emancipatory Rationale of the Directive: **(A)** The objective of the directive is to promote upward convergence regarding workers' rights; **(B)** The directive is intended to ensure that restructuring does not adversely affect the workers; **(C)** The objective is to preserve workers against potentially unfavourable consequences related to the change of the employer; **(D)** The directive wants to ensure that the employment relationship continues unchanged with the transferee so that the employees are not placed in a less favourable position solely as a result of the transfer; **(E)** The directive aims at ensuring the continuity of the employment relationship; **(F)** The objective is to safeguard the employees in the event of transfers of undertaking. **Row 2 – Limits Are Drawn to the Emancipatory Rationale of the Directive**: **(G)** The directive is not aimed at protecting mere expectations or hypothetical advantages of the transferred workers; **(H)** The objective is not to extend employees' rights. **Row 3 – The Directive's Function Is Also to Facilitate the Expansion of the Internal Market**: **(I)** The directive is read in light of Article 100 TEEC and 117 TEEC; **(J)** The directive aims at ensuring comparable protection for workers' rights within the EU and at harmonising the costs which those protective rules entail for European undertakings; **(K)** The directive aims at reducing the differences between national legislation on protection of employees by means of approximation without complete harmonisation; **(L)**

The directive aims at allowing the completion of the internal market. **Row 4 – The Directive Shall Also Consider the Employers' Economic Interests**: **(M)** In interpreting the objective of the directive, the interests of the transferee cannot be disregarded; **(N)** The directive seeks to ensure a fair balance between the interests of the employees and those of the transferee; **(O)** The directive explicitly considers the employers' freedom of contract and freedom to conduct a business.

This last case study on the purpose of the directive complements those on the scope of application and on workers' rights. Together, they consent to finally address RQ2 (*Is it possible to identify an underlying normative model in the case law of the CJEU with respect to labour law?*). The empirical analysis conducted in this chapter showed that in its early jurisprudence, the Court displayed a full adherence to the emancipatory rationale of the directive. Then the Court's approach changed and became more responsive to the economic interests of the employer, but this did not lead to a complete sidelining of the emancipatory dimension.

It thus appears that since the two past decades, the Court has approached the directive in accordance with the normative model according to which labour law should seek to reconcile economic and social progress. When this model was first discussed in Chapter 1, section 2.2.3, it was explained that the pursuit of this paradigm does not imply, per se, the abandonment of the social objectives of labour law. The emancipatory component is present as long as the CJEU, overall, recognises that the directive is concerned with the improvement of working conditions. However, it was also noted that when labour law is predominantly appraised in light of economic considerations, the emancipatory dimension retreats in favour of the economic one. This has happened in a couple of judgments, such as *Strø Mølle Akustik*, *Süzen*, *Alemo-Herron*, and *ISS*. The Court has thus entered into a slippery slope, especially if it continues to rely on balancing exercises between workers' rights and the economic interest of the transferee.

7 CONCLUDING CONSIDERATIONS: A FIRST DEFINITION OF THE ROLE OF THE COURT

The case studies outlined in this chapter allowed the unveiling of the predominant normative approach of the Court towards the directive on transfer of undertakings. This concluding section frames the results of the case studies within a broader reflection on the role of the Court in defining the normative model of labour law within the EU. To this end, the evolution of the Court's reasoning is compared with the normative paradigm that had emerged from the analysis of the Union's institutional policymaking, carried out in Chapter 2.

From the case studies it emerges that the Court's approach towards the directive has developed in a manner that is overall compatible with what was observed in Chapter 2. While exploring institutional rule-making, it was noted that, there too, the approach towards labour law had changed. After a parenthesis valorising the social rationale, there has been a sharpening of the economic dimension in the 1990s and even more so during the Euro crisis. Only more recently, signs of rehabilitation of the emancipatory function have appeared. The development of the Court's approach towards the directive is rather similar.

However, it is important to note that the case studies did not reveal such a radical compression of the emancipatory component as in EU policymaking, with the exception of a few pronouncements. In Chapter 2 it was discussed that for a rather long time, the EU rule-makers' main normative model consisted of turning labour law into labour market regulation, in a way that does not consent to the emancipatory dimension to find expression.[552] Instead, the case studies have shown that the Court has over time favoured an interpretation of labour law which is mainly functional to reconcile economic and social progress and that, in this approach, the emancipatory component can still find expression.[553]

Of course, it would arguably be unthinkable to expect the case law to evolve as radically as EU policymaking. Indeed, even if the Court disposes of a rather wide interpretative leeway, the directive sets incontrovertible minimum standards and to disregard those would require an interpretation *contra legem*. Still, it is worth noting that rulings such as *Süzen*, *Alemo-Herron* and *ISS* demonstrate that even a legal instrument that is as ontologically 'workers-oriented' as Directive 2001/23/EC can be substantially weakened and lose its emancipatory effect. Not for nothing have these judgments been read by several academic commentators as an expression of the Court's ideological proximity to neoliberal thinking. The fact that the more business-oriented view has not fully prevailed in the case law thus does not mean that the Court cannot or will not in the future adopt a more unconcerned attitude towards the emancipatory dimension of the directive.

It is also interesting to note that the Court's restrictive approach to the scope, on the one hand, and that to workers' rights, on the other, emerged asynchronously. When the *Strø Mølle Akustik* and *Süzen* rulings narrowed the concept of 'transfer of a business', the Court was still consistent in its expansive interpretation of workers' rights (Table 3). Similarly, Tables 4 and 5 show that in those years, the Court still applied a purely socially oriented interpretation of the purpose of the directive. Curiously, it is precisely when the Court started to adopt a less stringent interpretation of the notion of 'transfer of a business' that it also began to read workers' rights in a more flexible and employer-oriented manner. This ambivalence is difficult to reconcile with the promotion of a specific and coherent deregulatory agenda by the Court. This, too, suggests that the consistency between the Court's normative approach and that of institutional policymaking is not full.

How, then, can the role of the Court be drawn with respect to the predominant normative model of labour law within the EU? The lack of complete homogeneity between the case law and the policymaking leads to exclude that the Court has played the role of leading actor in the marginalisation of the emancipatory rationale of labour law. At the same time, it cannot be ruled out that the Court might have a certain co-responsibility, as it has placed an increasing emphasis on the economic freedoms of the employer. Also, there was a clear convergence between the Court and the EU policymakers in relation to the choice to narrow the scope of application of the directive. It is therefore plausible that the role that was assumed by the CJEU is to *not oppose* the normative model emerging from institutional policymaking. The Court seems inclined to perform this role without distorting the emancipatory effects of labour norms. Still, it has also shown to be ready to adjust the protective effect of the labour norms when deemed necessary.

552. This normative model was presented in the Introduction, section 2.2.4.
553. This normative model was presented in the Introduction, section 2.2.3.

In the introduction of the book, it was explained that the research is embedded in two dogmatic premises. The first prepared the ground for the exploration on the normative foundations of labour law. It was explained that the emancipatory dimension of labour law is at risk when the economic rationale of labour norms is overemphasised. The second coincides with the assumption that EU case law expresses the normative preferences of the Court. In this view, the Court approaches labour law in a purposive manner and contributes to sideline its emancipatory dimension. How does the role of the Court that emerges from the case studies relate to these premises? On the one hand, it helps to clarify the normative model that the Court adheres to and to assess the transformative pressure the Court exerts with respect to the function of labour law. It has in fact been found that the Court does not appear to aggravate, but rather not oppose, the pressure exerted by political policymaking actors. Furthermore, this definition of the Court's role weakens (although does not refute) the perception of the Court as a policy actor with a preference for the economic dimension of labour norms. The case studies suggest that this perception should be nuanced since in only a few judgments the Court has displayed a deliberate preference for a business-oriented interpretation of the directive. In the vast majority of the cases, the Court has not abandoned the emancipatory rationale. Instead, it has embedded it in a more market-related discourse and set some boundaries in order to ensure the safeguarding of the employers' economic interests.

In fact, and as was anticipated in the introduction to the book, the definition of the role of the Court that emerges from this chapter has limitations.[554] The first limitation is not remediable in the context of this book and consists of the fact that it is based on the analysis of only one legislative instrument. The second limitation is that the case studies discussed in this chapter refer to a circumscribed epistemological framework as they were part of the first analytical layer of this research.[555] The case law was analysed with the view of identifying the Court's normative inclination. This framework does not consent to discern the factors that have underpinned the evolution of the case law and the progressive marginalisation of the economic rationale. It thus also does not allow to pin the evolution of the judicial reasonings to an ideological or normative preference of the Court.

Did the Court actually intend to align with the EU policymakers' approach to the normative model of labour law (as suggested by the definition of the Court's role above)? Is there even a real nexus between EU policymaking and the reasoning of the Court, or the partial convergence is a coincidence? Are there other dynamics that have underpinned the evolution of the case law? In the latter case, the jurisprudential evolution might be linked to further and more complex judicial lawmaking circumstances, which go beyond the normatively driven exercise of weighing the (economic and social) interests underlying labour law. For example, the Court's pronouncements may have been informed by the way in which the national referring courts formulate their reference questions. Or, they might be influenced by the national context,

554. *See* Introduction, section 4.4.
555. *See* Introduction, section 2.

whether political, normative or jurisprudential, in which the Court's rulings are received.

The potential relevance of these alternative judicial lawmaking logics is explored in the next chapters, which address what in the introduction was defined as the 'second analytical layer' of the research.[556] Chapters 4 and 5 propose an alternative theoretical framework, unrelated to labour law. There, different theories on judicial decision-making logics are presented. Chapter 6, then, turns to a second set of case studies in which those theories are 'tested'. That analysis ultimately consents to deepen the understanding of the Court's role with respect to labour law and to enrich the definition provided in this chapter, which was purely grounded in the analytical lenses of the labour law doctrine.

556. The second analytical layer of the book was presented in the Introduction, section 3.

CHAPTER 4

The Court of Justice as a Judicial Policymaker

1 INTRODUCTION

The book now turns to the second analytical layer of this research. This chapter moves away from the labour law doctrinal perspective and begins to explore the various theories of judicial lawmaking. It is through these theories that an attempt is made to answer RQ3: 'What are the logics that determine the Court's approach with respect to labour law, taking into account judicial lawmaking theories?'. Ultimately, the intention is to broaden the understanding of the role that the CJEU plays with respect to the predominant normative model underlying EU labour law.

This chapter describes those judicial lawmaking theories which attribute to the Court the role of a quasi-political and autonomous actor in the definition of the normative framework of the EU. These theories are then complemented by others outlined in Chapter 5 and suggesting that the Court is not driven by a policy agenda, but instead formulates its reasoning in consideration of a series of elements deriving from the national context.

In engaging with judicial lawmaking theories that portray the Court as a policymaking actor, the book enriches the epistemological framework that is used to appraise the Court's role towards the normative components underpinning labour norms. In fact, the theories that are described in this chapter not only provide convincing arguments on how the Court managed to take on a sort of policymaking role but also give helpful guidance for identifying various elements that, when present in the judicial reasoning, are symptomatic of a purposive approach of the Court.

1.1 Judicial Activism and EU Policymaking

As already noted before in this research,[557] it is indisputable that the CJEU's case law has contributed to the evolution of the European Community from an organisation of international law to a semi-federal entity. The doctrines of direct effect, the primacy of EU law, the principle of conforming interpretation, and the principle of state liability, to name a few, are crucial milestones for the legal and constitutional development of the EU that are the result of the Court's interpretative creativity.[558]

Besides supporting the constitutional maturation of the European Community, the Court's case law influenced the definition of specific policy areas, thus encroaching on the division of competences between the Community and the Member States. The establishment of the principle of mutual recognition in the context of the free circulation of goods,[559] the conferral of direct effect of the principle of non-discrimination,[560] and the policy ramification of the concept of EU citizenship,[561] are

---

557. *See* Introduction, section 3.
558. T. Hartley, 'Federalism, Courts and Legal Systems: The Emerging Constitution of the European Community', The American Journal of Comparative Law, 34(2), pp. 229-247, 1986, where the author observed that the European Community has been evolving towards a semi-federal system, and that the Court of Justice has played a fundamental role in this trajectory. For an overview of the contribution of the Court of Justice to the evolution that led the European Economic Community to transform in the more holistic EU, *see*, *inter alia*, J.H.H. Weiler, 'The Transformation of Europe', The Yale Law Journal, 100(8), pp. 2403-2483, 1991 and T. Horsley, *The Court of Justice of the European Union as and Institutional Actor: Judicial Lawmaking and Its Limits*, Cambridge University Press, New York, 2018, p. 3.
559. Episodes of usurpation of the lawmaking authority occurred in relation to the judicial establishment of the principles of market access and of mutual recognition in the context of the free movement of goods. *See* P. Syrpis, *EU Intervention in Domestic Labour Law*, Oxford University Press, Oxford, 2007, p. 23 and M.P. Maduro, *We the Court: The European Court of Justice and the European Economic Constitution: A Critical Reading of Article 30 of the EC Treaty*, Hart Publishing, Oxford, 1998, pp. 61-102, among others. In particular, Maduro, observed that the *Cassis de Dijon* case law market a phase in which the Court and the market become more important in the push for integration and harmonisation, and in changing the institutional balance of the European economic constitution. In this period, the Court became directly involved in deciding the degree of regulation of the common market.
560. Reference goes to judgment of 8 April 1976, *Gabrielle Defrenne v. Société anonyme belge de navigation aérienne Sabena*, C-43/75, ECLI:EU:C:1976:56 on non-discrimination on the ground of gender, as well as to judgment of 22 November 2005, *Werner Mangold v. Rüdiger Helm*, C-144/04, ECLI:EU:C:2005:709 and Judgment of 19 January 2010, *Seda Kücükdeveci gegen Swedex GmbH & Co. KG.*, C-555/07, ECLI:EU:C:2010:21 on non-discrimination on the ground of age. For an in-depth commentary on the Court's case law: O. Pollicino, *Discriminazione sulla Base del Sesso e Trattamento Preferenziale nel Diritto Comunitario*, Giuffrè, Milano, 2005.
561. According to Horsley, in T. Horsley, *The Court of Justice of the European Union as and Institutional Actor: Judicial Lawmaking and Its Limits*, 2018, the case law on EU citizenship rights is 'ripe with illustrations of the Court's use of directly effective EU norms as tools to recast discrete legislative choices to match its own institutional references as direct policymakers', p. 172. The judicial policymaking in this field is particularly striking, since the EU normative framework on the EU citizenship is clear in setting the divisions between the EU and national competences. Particularly significant are the *Baumbast*, the *Collins*,and the *Zambrano* case. In in *Baumbast* (judgment of 17 September 2002, *Baumbast and R v. Secretary of State for the Home Department*, C-413/99, ECLI:EU:C:2002:493), the Court had ruled that Member States could not deny residence rights to EU citizens on the ground that they did not have a medical insurance. In a similar vein, in *Collins* (judgment of 23 March 2004, *Brian Francis Collins v. Secretary of State for Work and Pensions*, C-138/02, ECLI:EU:C:2004:172) the Court showed its

just some of the many significant examples of the judicialisation of EU policymaking.[562] On top of these examples, the central role of case law in defining labour rights in case of transfer of undertakings was extensively discussed in Chapter 3.

The influence of the case law in policymaking can be ascribed to the phenomenon of judicial activism, referring to the ability and willingness of the judiciary to defy or support the other political powers in a given legal system.[563] From this angle, the Court can thus be considered a political actor, purposively going beyond the limits of proper judicial review to engage with policymaking.[564] According to this narrative, the Court is capable to go after specific policy outcomes and even to take the place of the legislative rule-makers in case of political deadlocks.

---

dissatisfaction vis-à-vis the scope of EU citizenship rights established by the EU Treaty and ruled that that EU citizenship allowed access to non-contributory social security payment if these are designed to facilitate access to national labour market. This conclusion is not supported by the EU primary law, which merely consented the national of a Member State to remain in the territory of another Member State as a job seeker. Moreover, and most notably, in *Zambrano* (judgment of 8 March 2011, *Gerardo Ruiz Zambrano v. Office national de l'emploi (ONEm)*, C-34/09, ECLI:EU:C:2011:124) the Court decoupled the EU citizenship rights from a logic of transnational mobility, where instead the treaty had clearly embedded it. The Court considered that EU citizenship consented the right to reside in EU territory a third-country national, father of a EU citizen, if the refusal of the residence right would prevent the genuine and effective enjoyment of the rights of the daughter as a EU citizen. *See also, inter alia*, M. Dawson, 'The Political Face of Judicial Activism: Europe's Law-Politics Imbalance' in B. de Witte, B. Muir & E. Dawson (eds), *Judicial Activism at the European Court of Justice*, Edward Elgar Publishing, Cheltenham, 2013, pp. 11-32.

562. U. Sadl, 'National Court and the Effectiveness of EU Law' in B. de Witte, J.A. Mayoral & U. Jaremba (eds), *National Court and EU Law: New Issues, Theories and Methods*, Edward Elgar Publishing, Cheltenham, 2006, pp. 68-105, where political power is intended in the meaning suggested by Max Weber: 'the chance that someone, in a social or political relationship manages to advance his own will against resistance, regardless on the ground on which his chance rests'. *See also* judgment of 21 June 1974, *Jean Reyners v. Belgian State*, C-2/74, ECLI:EU:C:1974:68, where the Court set aside a Belgian rule forbidding foreign lawyers to entry the Belgian Bar even if in possession of the necessary qualifications for admittance. The Court ruled on the ground of Article 52 EEC (now Article 49 TFEU) on the prohibition of discrimination based on nationality, even if the Treaty explicitly stated that restrictions on the freedom of establishment of nationals of a Member State in the territory of another Member State shall be abolished by progressive stages in the course of the transitional period. Since the transitional period had passed, the Court did not hesitate to give direct effect to Article 52 EEC, despite the fact that nowhere was it established that the inactivity of the legislative institutions would give policymaking authority to the Court. On this regard, *see* T. Horsley, *The Court of Justice of the European Union as and Institutional Actor: Judicial Lawmaking and Its Limits*, 2018, p. 159.
563. The concept of activism is juxtaposed to that of judicial passivism or judicial restraint, that indicates minimalism, caution and conserving approach to legal meaning. T. Ćapeta, 'Ideology and Legal Reasoning at the European Court of Justice' in E. Perisin & S. Rodin (eds), *The Transformation or Reconstitution of Europe: The Critical Legal Studies Perspective on the Role of the Courts in the European Union*, Hart Publishing, Oxford, 2018, pp. 89-120, citing previous judge P. Pescatore.
564. The activist role of the Court raised not only academic interest, but also institutional concern, especially from the Member States. In the context of the Intergovernmental Conference preceding the Amsterdam Treaty, the UK proposed (without success) to introduce a protocol to contain the Court's policymaking: 'when faced with more than one possible interpretation of provisions of Community law, the Court shall, unless there is a clear contrary intention, prefer the interpretation which least contains the freedom of the Member States'. *See* T. Horsley, *The Court of Justice of the European Union as and Institutional Actor: Judicial Lawmaking and Its Limits*, 2018, p. 233.

This perception of the Court as an activist institution, responsible for the progressive 'judicialisation' of EU policymaking, has widely emerged in the work of EU scholars. Some have expressed concern for the Court's encroachment in the lawmaking realm and have argued for erecting institutional boundaries to judicial activism. Most notably, Rasmussen strongly condemned the Court for exceeding the limits of its political mandate.[565] According to Rasmussen, the Court disposes of its interpretative function in an arbitrary and thus illegitimate manner, undermining the neutrality and fairness of its rulings.[566] By doing so, the Court jeopardises its authority, as well as the entire institutional balance of the EU and its democratic legitimisation.[567]

Although in a more guarded tone, also former EU Judge Mancini expressed reservations about the judicial activism of the Court, especially in view of the enhanced rule-making capacity of the political institutions of the Union.[568] Similarly, Horsley noted that the Court's lively interpretative creativity risks damaging its institutional legitimacy.[569] By exceeding the limits of its jurisdiction, the Court violates primary EU law and, according to Horsley, it would be appropriate to set up institutional control

565. H. Rasmussen, *On Law and Policy in the European Court of Justice: A Comparative Study in Judicial Policymaking*, Martinus Nijhoff/Dr W. Junk, Dordrecht, 1986, as commented by H. Schepel, 'Reconstructing Constitutionalization: Law and Politics in the European Court of Justice', Oxford Journal of Legal Studies, 20(3), pp. 457-468, 2000 where, quite provocatively, Schepel labelled Rasmussen 'a conflictualist', and noted that in his analysis of the Court of Justice's activism, he mainly saw struggle and actors while one could have instead sought equilibrium and system.
566. *Ibid.*; A.-M. Burley & W. Mattli, 'Europe Before the Court: A Political Theory of Legal Integration', International Organization, 47(1), pp. 41-76, 1993.
567. Accordingly, as Shapiro noted 'The endless debate over judicial self-restraint is largely a debate about what actions by courts risk undermining the myth of neutrality and independence', in M. Shapiro, 'The European Court of Justice: Of Institutions and Democracy', Israel Law Review, 32(1), pp. 3-50, 1998.
568. G.F. Mancini, 'The Making of A Constitution for Europe', Common Market Law Review, 26(4), pp. 595-614, 1989: 'Some observers argue [...] that the time has come for the Court to reconsider its philosophy. When democracy advances and politics asserts its claims, judges are bound to take a pace back. The reason for their being in the van has waned, and if they insist on remaining there, they risk to become so embroiled in the passions of the day as to imperil their most precious resource, their independence.'
569. The criticalities of the EU judicial lawmaking are clearly explained by Horsley: 'The absence of a comprehensive and rigorous Treaty-based critique of EU judicial activity in the scholarship is striking for two reasons. First, the Treaty framework provides no basis whatsoever to justify differentiating between the Court and the Union's administrative and political institutions with regard to compliance with its demands. The Court is formally designated an institution of the Union under Article 13 TEU. As such, long with the Union's political institutions, it is irrefutably subject to compliance with the EU Treaties. [...] Secondly, and more strikingly still, existing criticism of the Court and its role in EU integration raises concerns that the EU Treaty framework directly addresses.' In particular, the principal interlocutors (Member States, national courts and EU scholar) voice concerns that the Court of Justice often plays fast and loose with the basis character of the EU legal order as a system of limited, attributed competences (*see* Article 5(2) TEU). As Sharpf summarises 'While the Court's contribution to European integration is widely considered beneficial in politically correct discourse, its impact on the constitutional balance of the multilevel European polity does raise serious problems. Similarly, the Court is also routinely criticised for undermining democratic processes at both Union and national level through its approach to the judicial review of EU and Member State measures.' T. Horsley, *The Court of Justice of the European Union as and Institutional Actor: Judicial Lawmaking and Its Limits*, 2018, pp. 7, 8.

and monitoring systems to avoid such excesses.[570] De Witte, Muir and Dawson also agree with these observations and point to the desirability of a regulatory intervention that would promote transparency in the Court's decision-making process.[571]

However, besides leading to articulate criticism, the Court's judicial activism has led several scholars to become intrigued by the phenomenon of judicial contamination of EU politics. As a result, a body of literature began to focus on the Court's decision-making and on the dynamics that caused the judicialisation of EU policymaking.

1.2 Structure and Goals

This chapter focuses on the doctrines that address the Court as a policymaking institution and, in particular, on two theoretical declinations. In section 1, the Court is described through the lenses of the neofunctionalist theories and is depicted as able to express political and ideological inclinations in its rulings. According to neofunctionalism, the Court has succeeded in achieving an impactful role in EU policymaking because of its intuition to involve individuals (as plaintiffs) and national courts in its judicial activity. The Court is thus presented as able to stimulate litigation in selected policy areas and to use its interpretative authority to steer policymaking evolution.

Section 2 instead engages with the integrationalist narrative, which suggests that the Court is first and foremost driven by the objective of promoting greater integration within the EU. The Court is presented as the trustee of the integrationalist vocation of the Treaties. The integrationalist inclination often places the Court in a sort of informal partnership with the EU Commission. Both neofunctionalism and integrationalism perceive the Court as a purposive policymaker aimed at strengthening the EU legal system.[572] The main difference is that neofunctionalism gives a more strategic connotation to the Court, which is represented as capable of promoting complex dynamics, including the involvement of private individuals and national judiciaries.[573] Integrationalism instead considers the Court's decision-making as more linearly oriented at

570. *Ibid.* In particular, Horsley argued that the Court should reconsider its understanding of three fundamental constitutional issues: the formal status of Union law and the conditions under which it applies within Member States; the locus of political authority within the EU legal order; the objectives, values and limits governing European integration.
571. E. Muir, M. Dawson & B. de Witte, 'Introduction: The European Court of Justice as a Political Actor' in B. de Witte, B. Muir & E. Dawson (eds), *Judicial Activism at the European Court of Justice*, Edward Elgar Publishing, Cheltenham, 2013, pp. 1-11.
572. Stone Sweet, Mattli, Slaughter and Alter, among others, have contributed to the neofunctionalst theory and also share the view that the Court has an integrationalist vocation. *See*, A. Stone Sweet, *The Judicial Construction of Europe*, Oxford University Press, New York, 2004, p. 16; W. Mattli, A.-M. Slaughter, 'Revisiting the European Court of Justice', International Organization, 52(1), pp. 177-209, 1998; K. Alter, 'The European Court's Political Power: The Emergence of an Authoritative International Court in the European Union' in K. Alter (ed.), *The European Court's Political Power – Selected Essays*, Oxford University Press, Oxford, 2009, pp. 92-109. As it is shown in section 2.1.1 below, the functionalist account sees the Court's expansionary interpretation of economic freedom and, thus, of the internal market, as instrumental to incentivise private business actors to rely on EC law in order to see their economic interests satisfied.
573. *See* section 2.1.

deepening EU integration in order to implement the overarching rationale of the Treaties.

The aim of this chapter, as well of Chapter 5, is not to identify the most intriguing and compelling doctrine. The analysis of these doctrines is instead functional to elaborate interpretive lenses, alternative to those pertaining to the labour law scholarship, to evaluate the Court's approach to the directive on transfer of undertakings.

2 POLITICAL INCLINATION AND NEOFUNCTIONALIST THEORY

The Court's contribution to the evolution of the EU legal order can be read as the corollary of its self-attributed role as a policymaker.[574] According to this narrative, the Court has gradually emerged in the EC (and then EU) rule-making arena by developing normative positions in the same way as legislative and political institutions would do.[575] The Court has thus managed to impose its view on the EU legal order and specific EU policies, sometimes going beyond the competences conferred by the Treaty. And it is precisely as a result of the Court's political vision that the European Community has been transformed from a body of international law into a sui generis legislative system capable of substantially limiting the sovereignty of the Member States.[576]

This narrative is based on two assumptions. The first is that the Court acts with the mindset of a political rule-maker. The second assumption has been developed by the neofunctionalist theory and consists of the Court's strategic ability to transfer its political preferences into actual policymaking.

As for the first assumption, several prominent scholars, among which Horsley, Alter, Stone Sweet, Brunell, and Capeta, interpreted the Court's judicial activism as a manifestation of its political ambitions, in which also an ideological component plays a role.[577] This is hardly unrealistic since, as Wilkund explains, judicial adjudication is

574. *See, inter alia*, T. Horsley, *The Court of Justice of the European Union as and Institutional Actor: Judicial Lawmaking and Its Limits*, 2018, p. 156; J.H.H. Weiler, 'Federalism Without Constitutionalism: Europe's Sonderweg' in K. Nicolaïdis & R. Howse (eds), *The Federal Vision: Legitimacy and Levels of Governance in the United States and the European Union*, Oxford University Press, Oxford, 2001; E. Muir, M. Dawson & B. de Witte, 'Introduction: The European Court of Justice as a Political Actor' in B. de Witte, B. Muir & E. Dawson (eds), *Judicial Activism at the European Court of Justice*, Edward Elgar Publishing, Cheltenham, 2013, pp. 1-11.

575. T. Horsley, *The Court of Justice of the European Union as and Institutional Actor: Judicial Lawmaking and Its Limits*, 2018, p. 152; M. Höreth, 'The Least Dangerous Branch of European Governance? The European Court of Justice under the Checks and Balances Doctrine' in B. de Witte, B. Muir & E. Dawson (eds), *Judicial Activism at the European Court of Justice*, Edward Elgar Publishing, Cheltenham, 2013, pp. 32-56.

576. *Ibid.*; S. Bardutzky & E. Gahey, 'The Subjects and Objects of EU Law: Exploring a Research Platform' in S. Bardutzky & E. Fahey (eds), *Framing the Subjects and Objects of Contemporary EU Law*, Edward Elgar Publishing, Cheltenham, 2017, pp. 1-30.

577. *Ibid.*; T. Ćapeta, 'Ideology and Legal Reasoning at the European Court of Justice' in E. Perisin & S. Rodin (eds), *The Transformation or Reconstitution of Europe: The Critical Legal Studies Perspective on the Role of the Courts in the European Union*, Hart Publishing, Oxford, 2018, pp. 89-120; K.J. Alter, 'Who Are the "Masters of the Treaty"? European Governments and the European Court of Justice', International Organization, 52(1), pp. 121-147, 1998; A. Stone Sweet & T. Brunell, 'Constructing a Supranational Constitution' in *The Judicial Construction of Europe*, Oxford University Press, New York, 2004.

per se political, especially when it relates to the EU legal system. In absence of clear meta rules on interpretation, the decision-making of the Court is characterised by a high degree of discretion, which allows the judges' ideological preferences to slip in.[578] The Court's room for manoeuvre lies not only in deciding which rule to apply but, as Capeta suggests, also in choosing the interpretive approach with which to address that rule.[579] This opens the possibility that the Court's legal reasoning is purposively constructed with the aim of achieving a specific legal decision and a specific policy-making effect. In particular, Capeta and Kennedy observed that ideology and subjectivity can enter into the Court's legal reasoning through judicial techniques such as the proportionality assessment, which give the judge's assessments more structure and argumentative force.[580]

It is nevertheless important to note that the EU judges have consistently refuted the allegation of being driven by ideological motives and non-normative paradigms.[581] Still, according to Burley and Mattli, such denial is quite meaningless since admitting the contrary would undermine the Court's legitimacy and reputation.[582]

The second assumption, namely that the Court adopted a strategic approach aimed at influencing EU policymaking, is central to the neofunctionalist theory. Neofunctionalism was initially elaborated by Haas, a political scientist who dedicated his work to the study of supranational integration.[583] It was subsequently developed by other scholars, among which Mattli, Stone Sweet and Slaughter, and has found quite widespread support in academic literature.[584] The neofunctionalist theory is rather elaborate and requires a larger part of this section to illustrate its principles.

2.1 The Two Postulates of Neofunctionalism

Neofunctionalism rests on two postulates. The first is that, since the origins of the European Community, the Court has sought to involve individuals and national courts in the judicial construction of the European legal system. Initially, this coincided with

578. O. Wiklund, 'Taking the World View of the European Judge Seriously' in O. Wiklund (ed.), *Judicial Discretion in European Perspective*, Norstedts Juridik, Stockholm, 2003, pp. 29-47, where the author reflects on the repercussion that the political nature of adjudication causes on the neutrality of the judicial activity.
579. T. Ćapeta, 'Ideology and Legal Reasoning at the European Court of Justice' in E. Perisin & S. Rodin (eds), *The Transformation or Reconstitution of Europe: The Critical Legal Studies Perspective on the Role of the Courts in the European Union*, Hart Publishing, Oxford, 2018, pp. 89-120.
580. *Ibid.*; D. Kennedy, 'Proportionality and "Deference" in Contemporary Constitutional Thought', Harvard Public Law Working Paper, 179, 2016.
581. S. Rodin, 'The Subject and Object in the Interpretation of EU Law' in S. Bardutzky & E. Fahey (eds), *Framing the Subjects and Objects of Contemporary EU Law*, Edward Elgar Publishing, Cheltenham, 2017, pp. 31-44.
582. A.M. Burley & W. Mattli, 'Europe Before the Court: A Political Theory of Legal Integration', International Organization, 47(1), pp. 41-76, 1993.
583. P.C. Schmitter, 'Ernst B. Haas and the Legacy of Neofunctionalism', Journal of European Public Policy, 12(2), pp. 255-272, 2006.
584. *Inter alia*, W. Mattli & A.-M. Slaughter, 'Revisiting the European Court of Justice', International Organization, 52(1), pp. 177-209, 1998; A. Stone Sweet, *The Judicial Construction of Europe*, Oxford University Press, New York, 2004.

the creation of a common economic space (section 2.1.1). The second postulate is that the Court has also played an essential role in shaping EU legal systems beyond the single market by expanding policymaking in non-economic areas (section 2.1.2).[585]

2.1.1 Enforcing EU Law Through Individuals and National Courts

The first postulate essentially indicates that the Court had the intuition that non-institutional actors, such as individuals in their capacity as litigants, could play a fundamental role in the evolution of EC law. The Court thus embarked on a process of involving individuals, and especially individuals acting as commercial operators and representing an economic interest, in the judicial elaboration of EC law through rulings that satisfied their claims and aspirations. By enhancing the economic opportunities of (prospective) litigants, the Court stimulated their participation in the development of case law and thus made them active subjects of EC policymaking.[586]

According to neofunctionalists, this process started when the Court realised the potential to make EC law directly relevant and, therefore, directly applicable to individuals and not just to Member States. Once that was achieved, individuals would have the possibility to invoke EC law in domestic courts, leading to an increase in EC law-based litigation. The idea was that EC law would enter national courtrooms through the claims of business actors, interested in taking advantage of the economic freedoms established in EC law so as to expand their market prospects. Such litigation would, in turn, lead to the progressive dismantling of those national rules which hindered the full realisation of the internal market. Basically, according to this narrative, the Court found a way to exploit the economic relevance of its rulings for business actors in order to promote the development of the EC regulatory framework, starting from the internal market. At the same time, the Court realised that providing a greater incentive to base domestic litigation on EC law would also strengthen its own role and authority in intervening and shaping national and EU legal systems.[587]

Neofunctionalists contend that the 'alliance' between the Court and non-institutional business actors was achieved in different stages. First, the Court enhanced the normative force of EC law vis-à-vis national legal systems. This occurred with the landmark judgments *Costa v. Enel* and *Van Gend en Loos*. In *Costa v. Enel*, the Court

585. W. Mattli & A.-M. Slaughter, 'Revisiting the European Court of Justice', International Organization, 52(1), pp. 177-209, 1998 where they note that Stone and Caporaso 'develop an analytical framework that is generally congruent with neofunctionalist priorities' and that 'Central to their study is the proposition that the constitutionalization of the Treaty of Rome relies on the initiative of self-interested private actors and the supporting response by supranational institutions', p. 182.

586. S. Bardutzky & E. Fahey, 'The Subjects and Objects of EU Law: Exploring a Research Platform' in S. Bardutzky & E. Fahey (eds), *Framing the Subjects and Objects of Contemporary EU Law*, Edward Elgar Publishing, Cheltenham, 2017, pp. 1-30; J.H.H. Weiler, 'Van Gend En Loos: The Individual as Subject and Object and the Dilemma of European Legitimacy', International Journal of Constitutional Law, 12(1), pp. 94-103, 2014.

587. A. Stone Sweet, *The Judicial Construction of Europe*, Oxford University Press, New York, 2004, p. 110.

gave EC law precedence over national rules.[588] Then, in *Van Gend en Loos*, it established that certain norms of EC law had direct effect and could be invoked in disputes between private individuals or against government bodies.[589] In so doing, the Court took EC law out of the realm of international law and intervened in the definition of its relationship with national regulatory systems.[590] The implications were by no means just theoretical. Individuals now could directly rely on Community law to invoke the disapplication of national law that obstructed their fundamental economic freedoms.

The innovative contribution of the *Van Gend en Loos* and *Costa v. Enel* judgments, however, goes beyond the doctrines of the primacy of EC law and its direct effect. Weiler noted that the real game changer was that those doctrines were established in a legal system which consented individuals to submit, via national courts, references for a preliminary ruling directly to the CJEU.[591] By means of the preliminary ruling mechanism, national courts and, indirectly, private litigants are given the possibility of referring questions of interpretation of Community law to the CJEU. Following *Van Gend en Loos* and *Costa v. Enel*, it became clear that, if the Court found an incompatibility between national and Community law, national law had to be reformed.[592] Preliminary rulings to the CJEU thus began to be conceived as a way to achieve decentralised enforcement of EC law. The CJEU thus gradually became a point of reference for those business actors who saw EC law, and especially the economic freedoms, as a means to broaden their commercial horizons.[593]

588. Judgment of 15 July 1964, *Flaminio Costa v. E.N.E.L.*, C-6/64, ECLI:EU:C:1964:66, p. 594.
589. Judgment of 5 February 1963, *NV Algemene Transport- en Expeditie Onderneming van Gend & Loos v. Netherlands Inland Revenue Administration*, C-26/62, ECLI:EU:C:1963:1, p. 12. *See, inter alia*, J.H.H. Weiler, 'Van Gend En Loos: The Individual as Subject and Object and the Dilemma of European Legitimacy', 2014.
590. *Ibid*. Among others, O. Wiklund, 'Taking the World View of the European Judge Seriously' in O. Wiklund (ed.), *Judicial Discretion in European Perspective*, Norstedts Juridik, Stockholm, 2003, pp. 29-47; A. Stone Sweet & M. McCown, 'Discretion and Precedent in European Law' in O. Wiklund (ed.), *Judicial Discretion in European Perspective*, Norstedts Juridik, Stockholm, 2003, p. 84.
591. J.H.H. Weiler, 'Van Gend En Loos: The Individual as Subject and Object and the Dilemma of European Legitimacy', International Journal of Constitutional Law, 12(1), pp. 94-103, 2014.
592. C-6/64, *Costa v. Enel*: 'The executive force of Community law cannot vary from one State to another in deference to subsequent domestic laws, without jeopardising the attainment of the objectives of the Treaty' and 'The precedence of Community law is confirmed by Article 189, whereby a regulation "shall be binding" and "directly applicable in all Member States". This provision, which is subject to no reservation, would be quite meaningless if a State could unilaterally nullify its effects by means of a legislative measure which could prevail over Community law'; C-26/62, *Van Gend en Loos*: 'The conclusion to be drawn from this is that the Community constitutes a new legal order of international law for the benefit of which the states have limited their sovereign rights, albeit within limited fields, and the subjects of which comprise not only Member States but also their nationals. Independently of the legislation of Member States, Community law therefore not only imposes obligations on individuals but is also intended to confer upon them rights which become part of their legal heritage. These rights arise not only where they are expressly granted by the Treaty, but also by reason of obligations which the Treaty imposes in a clearly defined way upon individuals as well as upon the Member States and upon the institutions of the Community.'
593. S. Bardutzky & E. Fahey, 'The Subjects and Objects of EU Law: Exploring a Research Platform' in S. Bardutzky & E. Fahey (eds), *Framing the Subjects and Objects of Contemporary EU Law*, Edward Elgar Publishing, Cheltenham, 2017, pp. 1-30, p. 5; D. Kukovec, 'Subject-Object

Costa v. Enel and *Van Gend en Loos* were just the beginning of the path with which the Court consolidated and further strengthened the EC legal framework. In the *Simmenthal* judgment, the Court ruled that national courts are obliged to disapply national law when it conflicts with EC law, without waiting for a ruling of the national Constitutional Court, or any national higher judicial authority, on the matter.[594] Subsequently, in *Francovich* as well as in *Brasserie du Pecheur - Factortame*, the Court ruled that individuals could claim damages from the state for failure to implement EU law.[595] In *Kobler* and *Traghetti del Mediterraneo*, the Court went further and applied the same principle in case of failure to implement EU law by national courts and tribunals of last instance.[596]

As the CJEU gave EC law the necessary attributes to produce a disruptive effect on national legal systems, the expansionary potential of EC case law on the exercise of the economic freedoms conferred by the Treaties began to become clear to business actors.[597] The *Dassonville* and *Cassis de Dijon* judgments are among the best-known and most significant examples of judicial contribution to the expansion of the internal market.[598] In *Dassonville*, the Court in essence ruled that EC law in principle precluded all national legislation that restricted intra-Community trade.[599] More specifically, it established that those national measures which are capable of hindering, directly or indirectly, actually or potentially, access to the market must be justified by the Member State with reference to a legitimate objective. Until then, the dominant interpretation

---

Dialectics and Social Change' in S. Bardutzky & E. Fahey (eds), *Framing the Subjects and Objects of Contemporary EU Law*, Edward Elgar Publishing, Cheltenham, 2017, pp. 45-63.

594. Judgment of 9 March 1978, *Amministrazione delle Finanze dello Stato v. Simmenthal SpA*, C-106/77, ECLI:EU:C:1978:49 (paras 17 and 21): 'It follows from the foregoing that every national court must, in a case within its jurisdiction, apply Community law in its entirety and protect rights which the latter confers on individuals and must accordingly set aside any provision of national law which may conflict with it, whether prior or subsequent to the Community rule.'
595. Judgment of 19 November 1991, *Andrea Francovich and Danila Bonifaci and others v. Italian Republic*, C-6/90, ECLI:EU:C:1991:428 (para. 37). Judgment of 5 March 1996, *Brasserie du Pêcheur SA v. Bundesrepublik Deutschland and The Queen v. Secretary of State for Transport, ex parte: Factortame Ltd and others*, C-46/93, ECLI:EU:C:1996:79 (para. 20): '[...] the full effectiveness of Community law would be impaired if individuals were unable to obtain redress when their rights were infringed by a breach of Community law'.
596. Judgment of 30 September 2003, *Gerhard Köbler v. Republik Österreich*, C-224/01, ECLI: EU:C:2003:513 (para. 59); judgment of 13 June 2006, *Traghetti del Mediterraneo SpA v. Repubblica italiana*, C-173/03, ECLI:EU:C:2006:391 (para. 36). *See also* M. Cartabia, 'Europe and Rights: Taking Dialogue Seriously', European Constitutional Law Review, 5, pp. 5-31, 2009.
597. M.P. Maduro, *We the Court: The European Court of Justice and the European Economic Constitution: A Critical Reading of Article 30 of the EC Treaty*, Hart Publishing, Oxford, 1998, p. 79.
598. Judgment of 11 July 1974, *Procureur du Roi v. Benoît and Gustave Dassonville*, C-8/74, ECLI:EU:C:1974:82; judgment of 20 February 1979, *Rewe-Zentral AG v. Bundesmonopolverwaltung für Branntwein*, C-120/78, ECLI:EU:C:1979:42; A. Stone Sweet, T. Brunell, 'Constructing a Supranational Constitution', The American Political Science Review, 92(1), pp. 63-81, 1998; K. Lenaerts, 'Interlocking Legal Orders in the European Union and Comparative Law', International and Comparative Law Quarterly, 52, 2003, pp. 873-906, 1998.
599. Judgment of 11 July 1974, *Procureur du Roi v. Benoît and Gustave Dassonville*, C-8/74, ECLI:EU:C:1974:82 (para. 12); C. Barnard & S. Deakin, 'Market Access and Regulatory Competition', Jean Monnet Working Paper 9/01, 2001.

was that EC law only prohibited measures that discriminated against goods produced in other countries. As Syrpis noted, the effect of *Dassonville* was to impose a more pervasive impact on the freedom of movement of goods by widening the scrutiny of the Court vis-à-vis national measures and accelerating the creation of a single market.[600]

This expansive thrust towards fundamental economic freedoms was further strengthened by the *Cassis de Dijon* ruling.[601] There, the Court established the principle of mutual recognition, whereby products legally traded in one Member State can also be traded in another Member State, with only a few exceptions grounded on public interest. *Cassis de Dijon* thus provided traders with an additional tool to challenge and progressively dismantle protectionist national legislations, and to expand the scope of the single market.[602] This caused a significant increase in the number of legal disputes based on Community law, whereby business actors claimed the enforcement of EC law. *Cassis de Dijon* thus triggered a deregulatory trend that resulted in the decay of national regulatory barriers to infra-Community trade. In practice, a vicious circle was set up. The more the Court accommodated the demands of economic actors by giving direct effect to fundamental economic freedoms against national legislation, the more these actors would promote judicial proceedings seeking to enforce EC law.[603]

Individuals, national courts and the CJEU thus became the protagonists of the judicial expansion of the European economic space. This phenomenon did not only take place in relation to the free movement of goods but concerned economic freedoms in general. At the same time, the effects of this case law were felt in various areas of national law, including labour law. In this regard, the deregulatory results (also referred to as 'negative integration') of the *Viking* and *Laval* judgments have been addressed extensively by labour scholars.[604] Suffice to recall that in these judgments the Court ruled that the scope of economic freedoms can go as far as limiting the exercise of collective labour rights and the right to strike.[605] More recently, business

600. P. Syrpis, *EU Intervention in Domestic Labour Law*, Oxford University Press, Oxford, 2007, p. 23.
601. Judgment of 20 February 1979, *Rewe-Zentral AG v. Bundesmonopolverwaltung für Branntwein*, C-120/78, ECLI:EU:C:1979:42 (also known as *Cassis de Dijon*) (para. 14).
602. M.P. Maduro, *We the Court: The European Court of Justice and the European Economic Constitution: A Critical Reading of Article 30 of the EC Treaty*, Hart Publishing, Oxford, 1998, p. 61: 'With Cassis de Dijon, the Dassonville doctrine was given new life and Article 30 began its progressive extension which allows it to catch any State measure capable of interfering with the market in respect of the trade in goods [...].' *See also* K.A. Armstrong, 'Mutual Recognition' in C. Barnard & J. Scott (eds), *The Law of the Single European Market: Unpacking the Premises*, Hart Publishing, Oxford, 2002, pp. 225-269.
603. A. Stone Sweet, *The Judicial Construction of Europe*, Oxford University Press, New York, 2004, pp. 45-109.
604. Judgment of 11 December 2007, *International Transport Workers' Federation and Finnish Seamen's Union v. Viking Line ABP and OÜ Viking Line Eesti*, C-438/05, ECLI:EU:C:2007:772; judgment of 18 December 2007, *Laval un Partneri Ltd v. Svenska Byggnadsarbetareförbundet, Svenska Byggnadsarbetareförbundets avdelning 1, Byggettan and Svenska Elektrikerförbundet*, C-341/05, ECLI:EU:C:2007:809.
605. *See, inter alia*, C. Barnard, 'The Calm after the Storm: Time to Reflect on EU (Labour) Law Scholarship Following the Decisions in Viking and Laval' in A. Bogg, C. Costello & A.C.L. Davies (eds), *Research Handbook on EU Labour Law*, Edward Elgar Publishing, Cheltenham, 2016, pp. 337-362; S. Deakin, 'The Lisbon Treaty, the Viking and Laval Judgments and the Financial Crisis: In Search of New Foundations for Europe's "Social Market Economy"' in

operators might have capitalised on the Court's expansive interpretation of the freedom to conduct a business (established in Article 16 CFREU). As explained in Chapter 1 section 3 and in Chapter 3 section 5.2,[606] Article 16 CFREU was indeed at the centre of a series of judgments (among which *Alemo-Herron* and *Aget Iraklis*) where the Court upheld employers' claims against national employment protection legislation.[607]

2.1.2 Development of Non-internal Market-Related Policies

In addition to its role in the formation of the internal market, the case law of the Court has undoubtedly contributed to the expansion of the Union's competences in other regulatory areas. This brings us to the second postulate of the neofunctionalist theory, according to which the Court's judicial creation of the internal market has produced a spillover effect into non-market policy fields.[608] In these areas, the Court has transferred the same dynamics of involvement of individuals and national courts that had led to the formation of the internal market.[609]

A significant example of neofunctionalist logic applied to a non-directly economic domain is the case law on the principle of non-discrimination. Despite the limited normative instruments originally provided by EC law, the Court managed to develop a

N. Bruun, K. Lörcher & I. Schömann (eds), *The Lisbon Treaty and Social Europe*, Hart Publishing, Oxford and Portland, Oregon, 2012, pp. 19-43: 'the decisions in Viking and Laval involve a rejection of the compromise stuck at the time of the Rome Treaty between economic integration and string labour law institutions at the national level', p. 24.

606. *Inter alia*: S. Giubboni, 'Freedom to Conduct a Business and EU Labour Law', European Constitutional Law Review, 14, pp. 172-190, 2018; E. Gill-Pedro, 'Freedom to Conduct Business in EU Law: Freedom from Interference or Freedom from Domination?', European Journal of Legal Studies, 9(2), pp. 103-134, 2017; X. Groussot, T.G. Pétursson & J. Pierce, 'Weak Right, Strong Court – The Freedom to Conduct Business and the EU Charter of Fundamental Rights', Legal Research Paper Series, 1, Lund University, Lund, 2014; S. Weatherill, 'Use and Abuse of the EU's Charter of Fundamental Rights: on the Improper Veneration of "Freedom of Contract"', European Review of Contract Law, 10(1), pp. 167-182, 2014.

607. Judgment of 9 March 2006, *Hans Werhof v. Freeway Traffic Systems GmbH & Co. KG*, C-499/04, ECLI:EU:C:2006:168; judgment of 18 July 2013, *Mark Alemo-Herron and Others v. Parkwood Leisure Ltd*, C-426/11, ECLI:EU:C:2013:521; judgment of 27 April 2017, *Asklepios Kliniken Langen-Seligenstadt GmbH v. Ivan Felja and Asklepios Dienstleistungsgesellschaft mbH v. Vittoria Graf*, C-680/15, ECLI:EU:C:2017:317; judgment of 11 September 2014, *Österreichischer Gewerkschaftsbund v. Wirtschaftskammer Österreich – Fachverband Autobus-, Luftfahrt- und Schifffahrtsunternehmungen*, C-328/13, ECLI:EU:C:2014:2197; judgment of 26 March 2020, *ISS Facility Services NV v. Sonia Govaerts and Atalian NV, formerly Euroclean NV*, C-344/18, ECLI:EU:C:2020:239; judgment of 26 March 2020, *ISS Facility Services NV v. Sonia Govaerts and Atalian NV, formerly Euroclean NV*, C-344/18, ECLI:EU:C:2020:239. Other cases in which the employer has relied on Article 16 can be found in the field of non-discrimination: Judgment of 14 March 2017, *Samira Achbita and Centrum voor gelijkheid van kansen en voor racismebestrijding v. G4S Secure Solutions NV*, C-157/15, ECLI:EU:C:2017:203 and, indirectly, judgment of 14 March 2017, *Asma Bougnaoui and Association de défense des droits de l'homme (ADDH) v. Micropole SA*, C-188/15, ECLI:EU:C:2017:204.

608. A. Stone Sweet, *The Judicial Construction of Europe*, Oxford University Press, New York, 2004, p. 16.

609. O. Pollicino, *Allargamento dell'Europa a est e rapporto tra Corti costituzionali e Corti europee*, Giuffrè, Milano, 2010, p. 60.

considerable *acquis* on equal treatment in the employment context.[610] It all started with the *Defrenne II* judgment, in which the Court gave direct effect to Article 119 TEEC (now 157 TFEU), establishing the principle of equal pay for men and women. With this ruling, the Court stated that the plaintiff, a Belgian female flight attendant, was entitled to challenge a pension pay system which treated her unfavourably on the grounds that she was a woman.[611] A few years later, in the *Ruckdeschel* judgment, the Court further reinforced the normative force of the principle of non-discrimination, stating that it is to be regarded as 'a specific enunciation of a general principle of equity which is one of the fundamental principles of EC law'.[612]

Thereafter, EU law and the case law of the Court took on an increasingly central role in the strategic litigation of the promoters of the right to equality, as Stone Sweet illustrates very clearly in his book 'Judicial construction of Europe'.[613] The moment of greatest jurisprudential ferment is between the late 1970s to the 1990s, but even in more recent times, the Court has shown a newfound judicial activism in this area.[614] Suffice it to mention that in 2008, in the *Mangold* judgment, the Court ruled that the principle of non-discrimination on the ground of age was to be considered a general principle of EU law and therefore had to be given direct horizontal effect (hence also in the context of a dispute between individuals and not only in disputes between individuals and the state).[615] This ruling raised criticism from (some) academic observers, who believed the Court stretched too much the EU legal framework to the detriment of national legal autonomy.[616] What is certain is that, in line with the

610. A. Stone Sweet, *The Judicial Construction of Europe*, Oxford University Press, New York, 2004, pp. 147-199; O. Pollicino, *Discriminazione sulla Base del Sesso e Trattamento Preferenziale nel Diritto Comunitario*, Giuffrè, Milano, 2005.
611. Judgment of 8 April 1976, *Gabrielle Defrenne v. Société anonyme belge de navigation aérienne Sabena*, C-43/75, ECLI:EU:C:1976:56. *See also* R.R. Geyer, *Exploring European Social Policy*, Polity Press, Cambridge, 2000, p. 109.
612. Judgment of 19 October 1977, *Albert Ruckdeschel & Co. and Hansa-Lagerhaus Ströh & Co. v. Hauptzollamt Hamburg-St. Annen; Diamalt AG v. Hauptzollamt Itzehoe*, C-117/76, ECLI: EU:C:1977:160 (para. 7).
613. A. Stone Sweet, *The Judicial Construction of Europe*, Oxford University Press, New York, 2004, p. 157.
614. N.A. Papadopoulos, 'Criticizing the Horizontal Direct Effect of the EU General Principle of Equality', Human Rights Law Review, 4, pp. 437-447, 2011; T. Ćapeta, 'Ideology and Legal Reasoning at the European Court of Justice' in E. Perisin & S. Rodin (eds), *The Transformation or Reconstitution of Europe: The Critical Legal Studies Perspective on the Role of the Courts in the European Union*, Hart Publishing, Oxford, 2018, pp. 89-120; E. Muir, M. Dawson & B. de Witte, 'Introduction: The European Court of Justice as a Political Actor' in B. de Witte, B. Muir & E. Dawson (eds), *Judicial Activism at the European Court of Justice*, Edward Elgar Publishing, Cheltenham, 2013, pp. 1-11; M. Dawson, 'The Political Face of Judicial Activism: Europe's Law-Politics Imbalance' in B. de Witte, B. Muir & E. Dawson (eds), *Judicial Activism at the European Court of Justice*, Edward Elgar Publishing, Cheltenham, 2013, pp. 11-32.
615. Judgment of 22 November 2005, *Werner Mangold v. Rüdiger Helm*, C-144/04, ECLI: EU:C:2005:709 (para. 75).
616. F. Fontanelli, 'All's Well That Ends Honeywell', Diritticomparati.it, 2010, https://www.diritticomparati.it/alls-well-that-ends-honeywell/. What attracted most criticism and accusations of activism was that the Court of Justice stated that individuals had the possibility of claiming respect for this principle even with reference to events that had taken place before the entry into force in the national context of the legislation implementing EU directive on equal treatment in the context of employment policies.

neofunctionalist theory, the *Mangold* case stimulated subsequent legal proceedings brought by workers who claimed that they had been subjected to unequal treatment and, ultimately, this resulted in the consolidation of the Court's expansive approach to age discrimination.[617]

The case law on the principle of non-discrimination eventually led EU lawmakers to adopt a set of legislative instruments consolidating the Court's reasoning. This body of legislation on equal treatment constituted one of the first and most important examples of the expansion of the European Community's competences beyond the internal market.[618] At the same time, the case law on the principle of non-discrimination brought social significance to the rulings of the CJEU. The actors and the active 'subjects' of EU law thus evolved: they are not just business operators, but also workers.[619]

2.2 The Relevance of a Collaborative Relationship with National Courts

According to the neofunctionalist doctrine, it is also thanks to the key role played by national courts that the Court has succeeded in giving a strong normative impact to its case law.[620] As already mentioned, the engagement of national courts with the CJEU is

617. Judgment of 19 January 2010, *Seda Kücükdeveci gegen Swedex GmbH & Co. KG.*, C-555/07, ECLI:EU:C:2010:2; judgment of 19 April 2016, *Dansk Industri (DI), acting on behalf of Ajos A/S v. Estate of Karsten Eigil Rasmussen*, C-441/14, ECLI:EU:C:2016:278. *See also* E. Bribosia, A. Navasartian, L. Fromant & I. Rorive, 'e-Nact Handbook, Module 2: The Charter's Social and Non-discrimination Provisions in the Employment Field', E-learning National Active Charter Training, EUI, 2018.
618. In the 1970s, the Council adopted, with unanimity rules, the first wave of directives on the principle of non-discrimination between men and women: Directive 75/117/EC on equal pay, Directive 76/207 on equal treatment, and Directive 79/7/EC on social security. These provisions were then repealed by other directives which expanded the personal and material scope of the principle, and eventually led to the current rich normative framework: Directive 2000/43/EC on the principle of equal treatment between persons irrespective of racial or ethnic origins, Directive 2000/78/EC on equal treatment in the field of employment and occupation, Directive 2004/113/EC on equal treatment between men and women in the access to and supply of goods and services, Directive 2006/54/EC on equal opportunities and equal treatment of men and women in matters of employment, and Directive 2010/41/EU on equal treatment between men and women engaged in an activity in a self-employed capacity. At the level of primary law, the Treaty of Amsterdam complemented Article 119 TEEC (now Article 157 TFEU) with Article 13 TEC (now 19 TEU), which is a horizontal norm allowing the EU to promote regulatory interventions to protect a wide range of categories.
619. The message is the one that the Court enunciated in *Defrenne II* (judgment of 8 April 1976, *Gabrielle Defrenne v. Société anonyme belge de navigation aérienne Sabena*, C-43/75, ECLI: EU:C:1976:56): EC law is intended to ensure social progress and seek the constant improvement of the living and working conditions (para. 10).
620. A. Stone Sweet & T. Brunell, 'Constructing a Supranational Constitution', The American Political Science Review, 92(1), 1998, pp. 63-81, 2011; W. Mattli & A.-M. Slaughter, 'Constructing the European Community Legal System from the Ground Up: The Role of Individual Litigants and National Courts', 56 European University Institute, Florence, 1996 and W. Mattli & A.M. Slaughter, 'The Role of National Courts in the Process of European Integration' in A.M. Slaughter, A. Stone Sweet & J. Weiler (eds), *The European Court and National Court – Doctrine and Jurisprudence: Legal Change in Its Social Context*, Hart Publishing, Oxford, 1998, pp. 253-276. Mattli and Slaughter explain that crucial to this strategy has been the intuition of the Court of Justice to forge alliance with national lower-level courts. This occurred by means of

enabled by the preliminary reference mechanism (originally established in Article 177 TCEE and now in Article 267 TFEU). Through this mechanism, the CJEU receives questions of interpretation of EU law that emerge from national judicial proceedings that present a connection with EU law.[621]

As argued by Weiler, the CJEU 'needs' the national courts. First, being consulted by national courts consent to create a connection with the individuals, who can then also become co-protagonists of judicial policymaking. Moreover, the Court 'needs' a national court to ensure the proper implementation and enforcement of EU law. With preliminary rulings, the Court can indeed rule, albeit indirectly, on the conformity of national law with EU law.[622]

For their part, national courts also have a significant interest in referring questions to the Court.[623] By submitting a preliminary question to the CJEU, national judges seek the assistance of a hierarchically superior judicial authority, whose interpretation of EU law could be helpful to reach a solution in the pending dispute. Furthermore, referring a preliminary ruling to the Court is a way for national courts to carve out a more prominent role for themselves within the domestic judicial scene. Indeed, the preliminary ruling mechanism promoted the decentralised control of the legality of domestic legislation with respect to EU law. This had important repercussions on the national judiciaries since it offered district judges the possibility to perform an assessment that was previously exclusively conducted by Supreme Courts.[624]

It is also important to note that, originally, the instrument of the preliminary reference was introduced in the Treaty of Rome as a minor procedural mechanism. The Treaty's constituents conceived it merely as a vehicle to promote conformity in the interpretation and implementation of EC law. The founding fathers and constituents had instead identified the action for annulment (now Article 263 TFEU) as the main judicial remedy.[625] The CJEU was thus supposed to deal mainly with proceedings brought by the European Commission or by the governments of the Member States in the event of failure to implement Community law, or in the event of an infringement of

the preliminary ruling procedure, which appealed to national judges since allowed them to create a direct dialogue with the Court of Justice and strengthen their position within the domestic judiciary system.

621. J. Pertek, *La Pratique du Renvoi Préjudiciel en Droit Communautaire*, Litec, Paris, 2001, p. 16.
622. J.H.H. Weiler, 'Van Gend En Loos: The Individual as Subject and Object and the Dilemma of European Legitimacy', International Journal of Constitutional Law, 12(1), pp. 94-103, 2014.
623. K. Lenaerts, 'Interpretation and the Court of Justice: A Basis for Comparative Reflection', The International Lawyer, 41(4), pp. 1011-1032, 2007; K.J. Alter, 'Who Are the "Masters of the Treaty"? European Governments and the European Court of Justice', International Organization, 52(1), pp. 121-147, 1998, where the author further elaborates on the role of national courts, and places their relationship with the Court of Justice at the core of the (judicial) integration of the EU legal system.
624. *Ibid.*
625. Article 263 TFEU establishes that 'the Court of Justice of the European Union shall review the legality of legislative acts, of acts of the Council, of the Commission and of the European Central Bank [...] of the European Parliament and of the European Council intended to produce legal effects vis-à-vis third parties. [...] It shall for this purpose have jurisdiction in actions brought by a Member State, the European Parliament, the Council or the Commission on grounds of lack of competence, infringement of an essential procedural requirement, infringement of the Treaties or of any rule of law relating to their application, or misuse of powers'.

the Treaties by the Community institutions themselves.[626] This reflected the fact that the European Community was created in accordance with an intergovernmentalist model, in which the highest political and regulatory authority resided with the Member States.[627]

Things have turned out differently. Preliminary rulings have become by far the most widespread judicial instrument.[628] This, according to neofunctionalist views, is owed to an intuition of the CJEU which succeeded in transforming the preliminary reference mechanism into a bridge between the European and national dimensions. Article 177 TEEC (now Article 267 TFEU) was turned into a sort of Trojan horse to stimulate the development of Community law from within.[629] This transformation proved essential for the Court to realise its strategy of self-empowerment, which, as seen, is based on the involvement of non-institutional national actors.

The emergence of the preliminary ruling as a procedural instrument supporting the (alleged) neofunctionalist nature of the Court took place gradually. First, the Court attributed to EC law those characteristics which turned it into a sui generis legal system, capable of having a significant impact on national legislation. This occurred through the doctrines of primacy and direct effect established in the *Van Gend en Loos*, *Costa Enel* and *Simmenthal* judgments, discussed above.[630] Subsequently, the Court strengthened the scope and effectiveness of the preliminary ruling mechanism itself. With the *Traghetti del Mediterraneo* and *Kobler* rulings, the Court established the possibility of sanctioning the refusal by a court of last instance to refer a preliminary question to the CJEU. Then, the Court adopted a rather extensive interpretation of the subject matter of the questions that may be referred to by national courts.[631]

Finally, it is important to note that the crucial role of national courts in EU judicial policymaking is recognised not only by the neofunctionalist doctrine. There is also another branch of scholarship which has particularly focused on the relationship

626. J.H.H. Weiler, 'The Transformation of Europe', The Yale Law Journal, 100(8), pp. 2403-2483, 1991.
627. K.J. Alter, 'Who Are the "Masters of the Treaty"? European Governments and the European Court of Justice', 1998, where the Court's doctrinal precedents are described as building blocks which allowed the Court's judgments as well as the European integration process that descended from those judgments to emancipate from the initially envisaged intergovernmental character. The author explains that even when Member States disagreed with the Court's judicial activism, they were institutionally unable to reverse the most crucial doctrines, such as the doctrines of direct effect and supremacy of EU law – which led to an intense and decentralised judicial review on the compatibility of national law with EU law.
628. Over 753 cases brought before the Court of Justice in 2020, 556 were preliminary ruling proceedings. *See* Court of Justice of the European Union, The Year in Review – Annual Report 2020, p. 56.
629. U. Sadl, 'Does the Court of Justice Make Law in Small Steps? (Circumstantial) Evidence from the Free Movement of Persons Jurisprudence', Paper presented at the EUI Faculty Seminar, EUI, 2020.
630. Section 2.1.1.
631. J. Pertek, *La Pratique du Renvoi Préjudiciel en Droit Communautaire*, Litec, Paris, 2001, pp. 50-58.

between national courts and the CJEU, framing it in the concept of 'trans-judicial dialogue'.[632] This theory is further explored in Chapter 5, section 4.

2.3 Limits of the Neofunctionalist Theory

According to the neofunctionalist narrative, the Court has made strategic use of its judicial creativity, managing to trigger dynamics that have strongly contributed to the maturation of the EU legal system. The Court is thus presented as a policymaker, whose ambition goes beyond mere judicial activity but also covers the political and normative sphere.[633] It was indeed explained that, from a neofunctionalist perspective, the main underlying logics of EU case law are the development of specific EU policy areas and the strengthening of the Court's jurisdictional authority. As fascinating and convincing as this theory might be, it also has weaker aspects. In particular, there are three main objections that can be directed at it.

The first objection is that, while there is no doubt that in some areas of law the judgments have stimulated EU policymaking, this consideration alone does not prove that the Court exerts sufficient influence to steer the policymaking of the other political institutions of the Union.[634]

The response that neofunctionalists Stone Sweet and Caporaso gave to this initial observation is that the Court has succeeded in establishing itself in the arena of EU policymaking by virtue of the fact that its rulings have long-term resonance in the EU legal system. In order to correct the normative implications of the Court's reasoning, the political institutions have to comply with the pace of legislative procedures. These procedures are complex and involve different institutional players in which different political forces are represented.[635] It follows that the lawmaking process is lengthy, and the final regulatory outcome would most likely be the result of a political compromise. It hardly would differ from the normative solution established in the case law.[636]

632. National jurisprudence can either validate the dynamism of the Union and of the Court of Justice or can impose external limits, to which the jurisprudence of the Court of Justice will be confronted. G. Martinico, 'Judging in the Multilevel Legal Order: Exploring the Techniques of "Hidden Dialogue"', King's Law Journal, 21, pp. 257-281, 2010; M. Cartabia, 'Europe and Rights: Taking Dialogue Seriously', European Constitutional Law Review, 5, pp. 5-31, 2009. More extensive reference to literature on trans-judicial dialogue that is presented in Chapter 5, section 4 below.

633. K. Lenaerts, 'Interlocking Legal Orders in the European Union and Comparative Law', International and Comparative Law Quarterly, 52, pp. 873-906, 2003.

634. *Ibid.*; M. Shapiro, 'The European Court of Justice: Of Institutions and Democracy', Israel Law Review, 32(1), pp. 3-50, 1998.

635. A. Stone Sweet & J.A. Caporaso, 'From Free Trade to Supranational Polity: The European Court and Integration' in W. Sandholtz & A. Stone Sweet (eds), *European Integration and Supranational Governance*, Oxford University Press, Oxford, 1998, pp. 93-133.

636. As a recent example, *see* the scope of application of Directive (EU) 2019/1152 of the European Parliament and of the Council of 20 June 2019 on transparent and predictable working conditions in the European Union PE/43/2019/REV/1 *OJ L 186, 11.7.2019, pp. 105-121* and of Directive (EU) 2019/1158 of the European Parliament and of the Council of 20 June 2019 on work-life balance for parents and carers and repealing Council Directive 2010/18/EU PE/20/2019/REV/1 *OJ L 188, 12.7.2019, pp. 79-93,* defined as follows: 'This Directive lays down minimum rights that apply to every worker in the Union who has an employment

These neofunctionalist arguments are however further challenged by Conant, who argues that only in particular circumstances, and very rarely, the Court's judgments exert an actual influence on EU policymaking. For a judicial (policymaking) solution to have a normative impact, a concurrent mobilisation of both institutional and private actors is necessary. In other words, there needs to be social ferment and the formulation of clear demands by civil society.[637] Conant also noted how social mobilisation, though necessary, is often not sufficient.[638] In fact, there is always the possibility that even in the presence of clear social support, other EU political institutions will react in a timely manner and succeed in containing, through legislation, the policymaking of the Court. This consists of the erection of institutional barriers to prevent the Court's judgments from finding effective political traction.[639]

According to Conant, an emblematic example is the reaction of the European Commission and national governments to the *Dassonville* and *Cassis de Dijon* judgments. As mentioned, neofunctionalists consider these rulings and their broadening effect on the single market as a demonstration of the success of the Court's political and regulatory strategy. Conant, instead, suggested looking at how the activism of the Court has been received at the institutional level. The progressive judicial deregulation had caused a growing concern among Member States, who saw the risk of losing control over the European integration process.[640] Driven by this common concern, national governments therefore decided to curb the normative consequences of the *Cassis de Dijon* jurisprudence. This led to an agreement to expand the EC competences subject to qualified majority voting instead of unanimity, including those on the functioning of the internal market.[641] These voting rules were negotiated during the intergovernmental conference in preparation for the SEA and were subsequently introduced in the Treaty. In doing so, institutional actors (and first and foremost national governments) regained the reins of the regulatory function for a long time

contract or employment relationship as defined by the law, collective agreements or practice in force in each Member State *with consideration to the case law of the Court of Justice.*' (emphasis added).

637. A. Stone Sweet, *The Judicial Construction of Europe*, Oxford University Press, New York, 2004, p. 148.
638. L.J. Conant, *Justice Contained: Law and Politics in the European Union*, Cornell University Press, Ithaca, New York, 2018, p. 23.
639. W. Mattli & A.-M. Slaughter, 'Revisiting the European Court of Justice', International Organization, 52(1), pp. 177-209, 1998, p. 13.
640. L.J. Conant, *Justice Contained: Law and Politics in the European Union*, Cornell University Press, Ithaca, New York, 2018, p. 12.
641. *See* Article 13 of the SEA introducing Article 8a: 'The Community shall adopt measures with the aim of progressively establishing the internal market over a period expiring on 31 December 1992 […]. The internal market shall comprise an area without internal frontiers in which the free movement of goods, persons, services and capitals is ensured in accordance with the provisions of this Treaty.' *See also* Article 18 SEA introducing Article 100: 'By way of derogation from article 100 and save where otherwise provided in this Treaty, the following provisions shall apply for the achievement of the objectives set out in Article 8a. The Council shall, acting by a qualified majority on a proposal from the Commission in cooperation with the European Parliament and after consulting the Economic and Social Committee, adopt the measures for the approximation of the provisions laid down by law, regulation or administrative action in Member States which have as their objective the establishment and functioning of the internal market.'

blocked by unanimity voting and recovered the lawmaking space that the Court had in the meantime attributed to itself.[642]

The second critical observation that can be advanced to the neofunctionalist theory is that it does not have solid empirical support. As has been described in section 2.1.1, the key point of the neofunctionalist narrative is that the Court's judgments have raised the interests of individual actors, who have turned to EU law and to the Court to reinforce their judicial actions and claims. Basically, neofunctionalists suggest that more and more litigants saw in the EU case law a strategic avenue to satisfy their (mostly economic) interests and demands. This assumption should therefore be reflected in a clear tendency on the part of the Court to deliver judgments which accommodate the legal demands of economic actors and promote the enlargement of the internal market and the dismantling of internal regulatory barriers.[643] However, studies conducted by Stone Sweet and McCrown show that, in the area of the free movement of goods, the Court supported the arguments of business operators only in slightly more than 50% of cases. It is somewhat doubtful that this figure, although it can perhaps be considered promising for the purposes of litigation strategies on the part of traders, indicates the existence of an actual agenda on the part of the Court.[644]

The third critical observation which might be directed at neofunctionalism is that it focuses only on the policymaker ambition of the Court and does not give adequate attention to the role of other institutional actors. Alternative theoretical models on the CJEU's decision-making, including some that are presented in Chapter 5, place the Court's rulings in a more scattered and multidimensional context, in which several actors intervene in defining judicial reasoning. Those actors can be the governments of the Member States, the European Commission, the national judicial authorities or the national legislators. To give an example, in section 2.2 it was mentioned that the neofunctionalist theory acknowledges the role of national courts, but not more than as a channel to consent the Court to exercise its interpretative function. Other scholars, among whom Weiler, have instead noted that, in the EU multi-systemic context, national courts have a more complex function than simply providing the Court with opportunities to address salient issues.[645] As is discussed in Chapter 5, national judges have ample room for manoeuvre in formulating the preliminary questions addressed to

642. L.J. Conant, *Justice Contained: Law and Politics in the European Union*, Cornell University Press, Ithaca, New York, 2018, p. 13. As Conant explained 'Member States regained control over the European regulatory process by specifying the degree of standardization and mutual recognition they could tolerate. Throughout the policy process, justice was contained. Initially justice was confined to the individual disputes that arose before the ECJ. Ultimately, justice was contained by its limited application to partially harmonized standards.'

643. K. Alter, 'Explaining National Court Acceptance of European Court Jurisprudence: A Critical Evaluation of Theories of Legal Integration' in A.M. Slaughter, A. Stone Sweet & J. Weiler (eds), *The European Court and National Court – Doctrine and Jurisprudence: Legal Change in Its Social Context*, Hart Publishing, Oxford, 1998, pp. 227-252.

644. W. Mattli & A.-M. Slaughter, 'Revisiting the European Court of Justice', International Organization, 52(1), pp. 177-209, 1998.

645. J.H.H. Weiler, 'Federalism Without Constitutionalism: Europe's Sonderweg' in K. Nicolaïdis & R. Howse (eds), *The Federal Vision: Legitimacy and Levels of Governance in the United States and the European Union*, Oxford University Press, Oxford, 2001.

the Court. Moreover, especially the judges of the higher courts have succeeded in establishing a rather sophisticated dialectical relationship with the Court.

The role of national institutions and legal systems appears neglected too. There is in fact a whole theory (intergovernmentalism – which is also discussed in Chapter 5, section 2) that contends that the Court is inclined to adopt reasoning that reflects the preferences of Member States. At the same time, various academics, including EU constitutional scholars such as Maduro, Pollicino and Cartabia, argue that it would be inaccurate to describe the Court's decision-making without considering the weight of national legal traditions.[646]

Finally, it is worth noting that neofunctionalist theory is not the only one portraying the CJEU as a policymaker capable of having a propulsive role in the normative evolution of the European Community. There is also the integrationalist narrative, to which the next section devotes an extended reflection.

3 THE COURT OF JUSTICE AS THE TRUSTEE OF EU INTEGRATION: THE INTEGRATIONALIST THEORY

In the previous section, it has been illustrated that the neofunctionalist theory portrays the Court as a strategic actor, capable of advancing specific policy areas and, at the same time, its interpretative authority and influence in the European context. It is important to note, however, that this judicial activism might also be explained through an integrationalist perspective.

According to the integrationalist narrative, the *ethos* of the Court is, essentially, to promote the process of European integration, with a tendency towards federalism.[647] After all, greater economic, legal and political convergence is the main objective underlying the Treaties and is the *raison d'etre* of the Union.[648]

646. O. Pollicino, 'Corte di giustizia e giudici nazionali: il moto "ascendente", ovverosia l'incidenza delle "tradizioni costituzionali comuni" nella tutela apprestata ai diritti dalla Corte dell'Unione', 1, Consulta Online, 2015; M. Poiares Maduro, 'Three Claims of Constitutional Pluralism' in M. Avbelj & J. Komárek (eds), *Constitutional Pluralism in the European Union and Beyond*, Hart Publishing, London, 2012, pp. 67-84; M. Cartabia, 'Europe as a Space of Constitutional Interdependence: New Questions about the Preliminary Ruling', German Law Journal, 16(6), pp. 1791-1796, 2015.
647. W. Mattli & A.-M. Slaughter, 'Revisiting the European Court of Justice', International Organization, 52(1), pp. 177-209, 1998; J. Bengoetxea, 'The Scope for Discretion, Coherence and Citizenship' in O. Wiklund (ed.), *Judicial Discretion in European Perspective*, Norstedts Juridik, Stockholm, 2003, pp. 48-74; A. Stone Sweet, *The Judicial Construction of Europe*, Oxford University Press, New York, 2004, p. 120; J.H.H. Weiler, 'Federalism Without Constitutionalism: Europe's Sonderweg' in K. Nicolaïdis & R. Howse (eds), *The Federal Vision: Legitimacy and Levels of Governance in the United States and the European Union*, Oxford University Press, Oxford, 2001.
648. T. Ćapeta, 'Ideology and Legal Reasoning at the European Court of Justice' in E. Perisin & S. Rodin (eds), *The Transformation or Reconstitution of Europe: The Critical Legal Studies Perspective on the Role of the Courts in the European Union*, Hart Publishing, Oxford, 2018, pp. 89-120, where the author suggests that the integrationalist rationale of the EU legal system appears evident already in Article 1 TEU, which refers to the endeavour to create an ever close Union.

3.1 The Court as the Guardian of the Treaties

Similar to the neofunctionalist narrative, the integrationalist theory argues that the Court's reasoning is driven by objectives that go beyond the neutral activity of interpretation and involve normative considerations. Contrary to neofunctionalism, however, the policy effects of the judgments are not a manifestation of the Court's rule-making ambitions. They are, instead, an expression of the integrationalist rationale that permeates the EU legal system.[649] This integrationalist *ethos* should thus not be perceived as a political stance or an ideological preference, but rather as a reflection of the function that the Court has been called upon to play. The EEC founding fathers created a complex and delicate multi-level system, in which institutional conflicts are easily provoked. The CJEU was then set up with the mandate to promote the respect of the Treaties and to ensure the correct exercise of the competences and powers conferred on the various institutional actors.[650]

The fact that the Court has been endowed with an intrinsically integrationalist mandate does not prevent the Court from being perceived as 'too' activist by national governments or other European institutions. Borrowing Shapiro's metaphor, the Court may be seen as the 'junkyard dog' of the EU. It was sought by the founding Treaties in order to provide the European legal system with a shield against possible future recalcitrance or negligence on the part of the political actors involved. Still, it might lead to undesired behaviours and consequences. After all, as Shapiro put it: 'The junkyard dog is a fierce dog kept confined during business hours and set loose to roam the junk yard all night attacking any and all interlopers. As to the owner of the junk yard who, for some reason, enters at midnight and comes to canine grief, there is a saying: "If you buy a junk yard dog ...".'[651]

The belief that the Court is driven by an integrationalist vocation is particularly widespread among EU scholars.[652] There are, however, different views as to how the integrationalist ethos of the Treaty finds its way into the Court's reasoning. For

649. J.H.H. Weiler, 'The Transformation of Europe', The Yale Law Journal, 100(8), pp. 2403-2483, p. 2474, 1991.
650. T. Horsley, *The Court of Justice of the European Union as and Institutional Actor: Judicial Lawmaking and Its Limits*, Cambridge University Press, New York, 2018, p. 150. Horsley notes that 'The Court of Justice did not see its institutional role as defined under the Treaty framework, namely as an agent to the Member States as Treaty principals. Instead, the Court can be seen to have assumed the role of "trustee" within the EU legal order.'
651. M. Shapiro, 'The European Court of Justice: Of Institutions and Democracy', Israel Law Review, 32(1), pp. 3-50, 1998. In particular, Shapiro wrote that 'Upon closer examination, this great constitutionalising feat of the ECJ is not such an extreme act of judicial independence as it might appear. The signatories did want the treaty to be supreme in the sense of imposing judicially enforceable obligations on their fellow states. [...] In a treaty basically concerned with economic activities of states with large private economic sectors, formal supremacy without direct effect would have been very unsatisfactory to the members themselves. [...] Undoubtedly, the Member States had not clearly worked out in their own minds exactly the constitutionalizing that occurred but [...] that is what they got.'
652. P. Eeckhout, 'The European Court of Justice and the Legislature', Yearbook of European Law, 18(1), pp. 1-28, p. 15, 1998; A.C.L. Davies, A. Bogg & C. Costello, 'The Role of the Court of Justice in Labour Law' in A. Bogg, C. Costello & A.C.L. Davies (eds), *Research Handbook on EU Labour Law*, Edward Elgar Publishing, Cheltenham, 2016, pp. 114-149; J. Prassl, 'The

example, Everling contended that the integrationalist nature derives from the pragmatism with which the Court approaches its interpretative activity. While ruling, the Court would simply tend to adhere as closely as possible to the objectives of the Treaty, in which the integrationalist rationale is, as mentioned, strongly present.[653] Previous Judge Mancini had thus referred to integrationalism as part of the 'genetic code transmitted to the Court by the founding fathers'.[654] Along these lines, Conway argued that integrationalism results in large part from the reliance on teleological interpretive techniques that lead the Court to approach EU law in a systemic, quasi-constitutional manner. This leads the Court to generalise the integrationalist thrust of the Treaties and inoculate it in a widespread manner throughout its rulings.[655] Wilkund shares this view suggesting that the Court tends to interpret EU law according to what Dworking called 'the method of coherence'. This implies that the Court interprets EU law to make it the best possible implementation of the overarching goals of the Treaties, including, of course, promoting European integration.[656]

Cichowski and Stein have noted, instead, that the Court generally confirms the legal arguments formulated by the legal services of the European Commission, which regularly submits observations on pending cases. As is discussed in more detail in section 3.3, the Commission is the political institution of the Union with the most 'European' and integrationalist vocation. Cichowski and Stein thus suggested that the Court might turn to the opinion of the Commission to reinforce its integrationalist approach.[657]

Finally, the Court's integrationalist attitude might also be the result of a lack of proper institutional representation of the Member States' interests within the EU judiciary. The CJEU is in fact an exception with respect to the EU institutional architecture which generally ensures that national interests find adequate expression through intergovernmental methods of governance. In the legislative branch, Member States can assert their prerogatives in the Council. There are even intergovernmental practices that apply to rule-making procedures within the Commission, for instance for the adoption of implementing and delegated acts (the so-called comitology).[658] However, this is not the case in the Court decision-making process. The Treaties have

---

Interaction of EU Law and National Law: Between Myth and Reality' in A. Bogg, C. Costello & A.C.L. Davies (eds), *Research Handbook on EU Labour Law*, Edward Elgar Publishing, Cheltenham, 2016, pp. 42-63.

653. U. Everling, 'The Court of Justice as a Decisionmaking Authority', Michigan Law Review, 82, pp. 1294-1310, 1984.

654. G.F. Mancini & D.T. Keeling, 'Democracy and the European Court of Justice', The Modern Law Review, 57(2), pp. 175-190, 1994.

655. G. Conway, *The Limits of Legal Reasoning and the European Court of Justice*, Cambridge University Press, Cambridge, 2012; Conway suggests that the Court has the tendency to rely on a teleological type of interpretation that aims at 'a high, systemic level of generality', p. 27.

656. S. Strömholm, 'Introductory Address' in O. Wiklund (ed.), *Judicial Discretion in European Perspective*, Norstedts Juridik, Stockholm, 2003, pp. 1-10.

657. R.A. Cichowski, *The European Court and Civil Society: Litigation, Mobilization and Governance; Themes in European Governance*, Cambridge University Press, Cambridge, 2007, p. 44; E. Stein, 'Lawyers, Judges, and the Making of a Transnational Constitution', The American Journal of International Law, 75(1), pp. 1-27, 1981.

658. L. Raffini, *La Democrazia in Mutamento. Dallo Stato-nazione all'Europa*, Firenze University Press, Firenze, 2010.

carefully shielded the Court from the direct influence of the Member States, and this allegedly results in a greater integrationalist inclination compared to the other EU institutions.[659]

While there may be different views on how the integrationalist rationale enters into the Court's reasoning, there is a general consensus in relation to its manifestation and normative implications. This is described in the next section.

3.2 Integrationalism in the Court of Justice's Reasoning

The Court's integrationalist orientation is expressed essentially in two ways. The first way is through an expansive judicial reading of the sui generis nature of the EU legal system, which has brought EU law away from the realm of international law and closer to that of a federal system.[660] The second coincides with the Court's inclination to interpret the competences of the Union in a broad manner.[661]

3.2.1 The Creation of a Sui Generis Legal System

Starting from the first of these expressions of judicial integrationalism, the Court tends to interpret the adoption of EU Treaties as an act by which the Member States consciously limited their sovereignty. This leads the Court to conceive the relationship between EU law and domestic law through a monist approach. In international law, monism indicates that supranational law (and thus also EU law) has constitutional value and is therefore directly applicable within the national legal system.[662]

The quasi-federal sense of the Court for the European Community emerged from the very beginning, with the jurisprudential definition of the principles of primacy (*Costa Enel*)[663] and direct effect of EC law (*Van Gend en Loos*).[664] The principle of direct effect was subsequently reinforced by the Court in the *Simmenthal* case where, as

659. The EU judges do not represent their country of origins when exercising their mandate and the only possibility for national governments to interact with the Court is via their legal services through the submission of amicus brief while the case is pending. Article 19 TEU and Article 253 TFEU.

660. *Inter alia*, T. Hartley, 'Federalism, Courts and Legal Systems: The Emerging Constitution of the European Community', The American Journal of Comparative Law, 34(2), pp. 229-247, 1986; J.H.H. Weiler, 'Van Gend En Loos: The Individual as Subject and Object and the Dilemma of European Legitimacy', International Journal of Constitutional Law, 12(1), pp. 94-103, 2014; S. Bardutzky & E. Fahey, 'The Subjects and Objects of EU Law: Exploring a Research Platform' in S. Bardutzky & E. Fahey (eds), *Framing the Subjects and Objects of Contemporary EU Law*, Edward Elgar Publishing, Cheltenham, 2017, pp. 1-30.

661. T. Horsley, *The Court of Justice of the European Union as and Institutional Actor: Judicial Lawmaking and Its Limits*, Cambridge University Press, New York, 2018, p. 172; S. Garben, 'Competence Creep Revisited', Journal of Common Market Studies, 57(2), pp. 205-222, 2017.

662. G.F. Mancini, 'The Making of a Constitution for Europe', Common Market Law Review, 26(4), pp. 595-614, 1989.

663. Judgment of 15 July 1964, *Flaminio Costa v. E.N.E.L.*, C-6/64, ECLI:EU:C:1964:66; *see supra* n. 552.

664. Judgment of 5 February 1963, *NV Algemene Transport- en Expeditie Onderneming van Gend & Loos v. Netherlands Inland Revenue Administration*, C-26/62, ECLI:EU:C:1963:1; *see supra* n. 552.

already mentioned, it was established that national courts are required to disapply rules of domestic law which conflict with EC law.[665] For those rules of EU law which do not enjoy direct effect, the Court has instead resorted to the duty of conforming interpretation. This principle establishes that, in the absence of adequate legislative implementation of EU law, the national court is obliged to interpret domestic rules in a manner which complies with EU law.[666] In addition, the Court has also ruled that Member States are liable for non-contractual liability in the event of their failure to implement EU law.[667]

The maturation of the EU legal system has also taken place through the judicial recognition of a whole body of fundamental rights, the respect of which the Court has assumed the task of guaranteeing.[668] In this regard, the Court has directly contributed to provide the European Community with a more solid constitutional framework. The Court's rulings establishing that the European Community has the responsibility and obligation to respect fundamental rights have indeed activated the political institutions and triggered an evolution in the EC legal system.[669] The first step in that direction was the joint declaration of 1977 in which the European Parliament, the Council and the Commission established that the EC legal system recognised the 'general principles of law and in particular the fundamental rights, principles and rights on which the constitutional law of the Member States is based'.[670] Later, this commitment was

665. Section 2.1.1. Judgment of 9 March 1978, *Amministrazione delle Finanze dello Stato v. Simmenthal SpA*, C-106/77, ECLI:EU:C:1978:49 (para. 17).
666. Judgment of 13 November 1990, *Marleasing SA v. La Comercial Internacional de Alimentacion SA*, C-106/89, ECLI:EU:C:1990:395 (para. 13).
667. Judgment of 19 November 1991, *Andrea Francovich and Danila Bonifaci and others v. Italian Republic*, C-6/90, ECLI:EU:C:1991:428 (para. 37); judgment of 13 June 2006, *Traghetti del Mediterraneo SpA v. Repubblica italiana*, C-173/03, ECLI:EU:C:2006:391 (para. 36); judgment of 30 September 2003, *Gerhard Köbler v. Republik Österreich*, C-224/01, ECLI:EU:C:2003:513 (para. 59).
668. E. Muir, 'The Court of Justice: A Fundamental Rights Institution among Others' in B. de Witte, B. Muir & E. Dawson (eds), *Judicial Activism at the European Court of Justice*, Edward Elgar Publishing, Cheltenham, 2013, pp. 76-102. In judgment of 17 December 1970, *Internationale Handelsgesellschaft mbH v. Einfuhr- und Vorratsstelle für Getreide und Futtermittel*, C-11/70, ECLI:EU:C:1970:114 (para. 4) the Court ruled that fundamental rights forms an integral part of the general principles of law protected by the Court of Justice. In judgment of 14 May 1974 *J. Nold, Kohlen- und Baustoffgroßhandlung v. Ruhrkohle Aktiengesellschaft*, C-4/73, ECLI: EU:C:1974:51 the Court ruled that it cannot uphold measures that are incompatible with fundamental rights as recognised in the constitutional traditions common to the Member States (para. 13). Judgment of 13 July 1989, *Hubert Wachauf v. Bundesamt für Ernährung und Forstwirtschaft*, C-5/88, ECLI:EU:C:1989:321 (para. 19) establishes that the Court can assess the respect of fundamental rights when a Member States acts in implementation of EU law. In Judgment of 18 June 1991, *Elliniki Radiophonia Tiléorassi AE (ERT) and Panellinia Omospondia Syllogon Prossopikou v. Dimotiki Etairia Pliroforissis and Sotirios Kouvelas and Nicolaos Avdellas and others*, C-260/89, ECLI:EU:C:1991:254 (para. 43) where the Court ruled that it can assess the respect of fundamental rights when the national legislation is an exception to one of the fundamental freedoms of the internal market.
669. E. Muir, 'The Court of Justice: A Fundamental Rights Institution among Others' in B. de Witte, B. Muir & E. Dawson (eds), *Judicial Activism at the European Court of Justice*, Edward Elgar Publishing, Cheltenham, 2013, pp. 76-102.
670. Joint Declaration by the European Parliament, the Council and the Commission Concerning the Protection of Fundamental Rights and the European Convention for the Protection of Human Rights and Fundamental Freedoms, *Official Journal C 103, 27/04/1977 pp. 0001-0002.*

reiterated in further EC legal instruments and primary law. An example is Article F of the Maastricht Treaty, where respect for fundamental rights is also anchored in the recognition of the ECHR and the common constitutional traditions of the Member States, echoing the case law of the Court. The greatest step forward in the constitutional direction, however, was the promulgation (in 2000) and the attribution of binding effect (in 2008) to the CFREU.[671]

The CJEU has thus sought to give EU law a de facto constitutional value in national legal systems. In doing so, it promoted the monist conception of the relationship between EU law and national law and ultimately contributed to strengthening the legal basis of the European integration process.[672]

3.2.2 Widening the EU Competences

The second manifestation of the Court's integrationalist vocation is the tendency to interpret the Union's competences in an extensive manner.[673] The more policy areas are subject to EU law, the greater the regulatory convergence between the Member States and, thus, the greater the integrationalist drive. Numerous examples can be given, the most significant perhaps being those concerning fundamental economic freedoms (and especially the freedom of movement of goods) and the principle of non-discrimination.

---

671. A. Jacobs, 'The Future of the Charter on Fundamental Rights of the European Union' in F. Dorssemont, K. Lörcher, S. Clauwaert & M. Schmitt (eds), *The Charter of Fundamental Rights of the European Union and the Employment Relation*, Hart Publishing, London, 2019, pp. 39-53.
672. A. Stone Sweet, *The Judicial Construction of Europe*, Oxford University Press, New York, 2004, p. 82.
673. G. Conway, *The Limits of Legal Reasoning and the European Court of Justice*, Cambridge University Press, Cambridge, 2012, p. 199; J.J.H.H. Weiler, 'The Transformation of Europe', The Yale Law Journal, 100(8), pp. 2403-2483, 1991. Weiler noted that the Court of Justice case law contributed to the expansion of the EU competence through four techniques: extension, absorption, incorporation and expansion. According to Weiler, 'extension is the mutation in the area of autonomous Community jurisdiction' and the most remarkable example is the creation of a nucleus of EU fundamental rights. Absorption occurs, often unintentionally, when the Community legislative authorities, in exercising substantive legislative powers bestowed on the Community, impinge on areas of Member State jurisdiction outside the Community's explicit competences. A striking example is the *Casagrande* case (judgment of 3 July 1974, *Donato Casagrande v. Landeshauptstadt München*, C-9/74, ECLI:EU:C:1974:74), where the Court ruled that 'to the extent that national measures, even in areas over which the Community has no competence [in this case, education policy], conflict with the Community rule, these national measures will be absorbed and subsumed by the Community measure'. Incorporation is a term which Weiler borrowed from the constitutional history of the United States and denotes the process by which the federal Bill of Rights, initially perceived as applying to measures of the federal government alone, was extended to state action through the Fourteenth Amendment. Finally, Weiler identified 'expansion' as 'the most radical form of jurisdictional mutation. Whereas absorption concerned Community legislation in a field in which the Community had clear original jurisdiction, [...] expansion refers to the case in which the original legislation of the Community "breaks" jurisdictional limits. A significant example is the implied powers doctrine, having "the facto consequence of permitting the Community to legislate and act in a manner not derived from clear grants of power in the Treaty itself"'.

3.2.2.1 The Deepening of the Internal Market via Negative Integration

As Weiler noted, the area in which the Court's integrationalist vocation has become most evident is the construction of the single market and the advancement of economic integration.[674] As repeatedly mentioned, the fundamental objective of the European Community was the creation of a single market.[675] This implies that when the Court interpreted Treaties' provisions, especially in the earlier stage of the EC, the integrationalist rationale was very much linked with, and virtually indistinguishable from, the economic rationale. Fostering EU integration by means of market expansion was also fully in line with mainstream neoliberal theories that for long have dominated the EU economic narrative and to which the Court is undoubtedly exposed.[676]

The most significant example of judicial expansion of EC competences in the field of the internal market is provided by the *Dassonville* and *Cassis de Dijon* judgments, already extensively discussed in section 2.1.1 on neofunctionalism. The relevance of these judgments from an integrationalist perspective derives from their impact in promoting (market) integration going beyond the plain normative content of EC law. It should indeed be considered that, originally, the EEC Treaty rules on freedom of movement of goods had a rather narrow scope. The Treaty of Rome merely prohibited Member States from imposing import and export restrictions when those constituted means of arbitrary discrimination.[677] In *Dassonville*, the Court sensibly expanded this prohibition, by also adding the interdiction of measures restricting access to the internal market, regardless of their discriminatory effect. The Court thus introduced a scrutiny based on the market access approach which implied that 'all trading rules enacted by the Member States which are capable of hindering, directly or indirectly, actually or potentially, intra-Community trade are to be considered as measures having an effect equivalent to qualitative restrictions'.[678] The integrationalist drive further increased with *Cassis de Dijon*, where the Court established the principle of mutual recognition. As explained in section 2.1.1, this principle created the presumption that if a good could be sold and distributed in one Member State, then it could also be marketed in the other Member States.[679]

In the previous section, it was already explained how *Dassonville* and *Cassis de Dijon* opened a wave of judicial deregulation of national rules on cross-border trade. What is important to emphasise here is that this deregulation boosted negative

674. Weiler, *ibid.*
675. P. Syrpis, *EU Intervention in Domestic Labour Law*, Oxford University Press, Oxford, 2007, pp. 72-75.
676. C. Kaupa, 'Maybe Not Activist Enough? On the Court's Alleged Neoliberal Bias in Its Recent Labor Cases' in B. de Witte, B. Muir & E. Dawson (eds), *Judicial Activism at the European Court of Justice*, Edward Elgar Publishing, Cheltenham, 2013, pp. 56-75.
677. *See* Articles 30, 34, 35, 36 TEEC, now respectively Articles 36, 40, 41 and 42 TFEU.
678. Judgment of 11 July 1974, *Procureur du Roi v. Benoît and Gustave Dassonville*, C-8/74, ECLI:EU:C:1974:82 (para. 5); C. Barnard & S. Deakin, 'Market Access and Regulatory Competition', Jean Monnet Working Paper 9/01, 2001.
679. The Court allows trade prohibitions only if they are justified on the basis of mandatory requirements based on public health, security and other grounds specified in Article 36 TEEC (now Article 42 TFEU). Judgment of 20 February 1979, *Rewe-Zentral AG v. Bundesmonopolverwaltung für Branntwein*, C-120/78, ECLI:EU:C:1979:42 (para. 15).

integration (as opposed to integration by means of legislation) which gave a strong impetus to the expansion of the internal market.[680] The judicial construction of the internal market also occurred in the absence of any official incentive from the EU political institutions. On the contrary, it took place during a particularly difficult period for European integration, which had been going on since 1965, when the so-called *crise de la chaise vide* began.[681] This expression refers to the political obstructionism caused by the French government, which decided to boycott European Council meetings. This behaviour was a manifestation of the disappointment of the French government for the lack of convergence of the other EEC Member States on the French preferences regarding the definition of the common agricultural market.[682]

The crisis officially ended with the Luxembourg Compromise (1966) by which the French government obtained to reinforce the intergovernmental logic of EC lawmaking.[683] Among other things, the Compromise reduced the Commission's autonomy vis-à-vis national governments in proposing legislative initiatives and gave each Member State a de facto veto power for matters of important national interest. Admittedly, the agreement also envisaged the enlargement of EEC competences subject to qualified majority voting, but the presence of the veto power made this change more cosmetic than substantive. The result was that the EEC decision-making came to a substantial halt, preventing the advancement of the integration process and the completion of the single market by legislative means.[684]

It was only through the case law of the Court and judgments such as *Dassonville* and *Cassis de Dijon* that the conditions were created for the deepening of the internal market and for reopening a political debate on the future of European integration.[685] The wave of negative judicial integration and its deregulatory effects on the national legal framework convinced the governments of the Member States that the time had come to resume negotiations and amend the EEC Treaty. It was indeed in their common interest to avoid that the process of European integration proceeded exclusively by judicial intervention, over which the political institutions had no control.

It was thus in the framework of the Intergovernmental Conference that led to the ratification of the SEA (1987) that the national delegations agreed to extend the scope of EC competences subject to the qualified majority rule, including in the area of the internal market. As Conant explained, this finally allowed a resumption of rule-making

680. S. Weatherill, 'The Common Market: Mission Accomplished?' in V. Heiskanen & K. Kulovesi (eds), *Function and Future of European Law*, Helsinki University Press, Helsinki, 1999, pp. 33-57.
681. Réunion du Conseil des ministres de l'Agriculture (Bruxelles, 30 juin 1965), where France, represented by Edgard Pisani, Minister for Agriculture, and Valéry Giscard d'Estaing, Minister for the Economy and Finance, noted its disagreement with the delegations of the other five Member States of the European Communities on the method of financing the Common Agricultural Policy.
682. *Ibid.*
683. Note on the proceedings of the extraordinary meeting of the Council held on 17 and 18 January 1966 in Luxembourg, Strasbourg, 20 January 1966.
684. *Ibid.*
685. J. Bengoetxea, 'The Scope for Discretion, Coherence and Citizenship' in O. Wiklund (ed.), *Judicial Discretion in European Perspective*, Norstedts Juridik, Stockholm, 2003, pp. 48-74.

by the political institutions, which regained the ground that had in the meantime handed over to the judiciary.

Although the SEA unblocked the work of the European political and lawmaking institutions, the integrationalist thrust of the CJEU did not end with that episode. A significant example of judicially driven deregulation involving the economic fundamental freedoms occurred in the second half of the 2000s. As recalled while illustrating the neofunctionalist theory, this period saw a series of judgments (the infamous 'Laval Quartet') that strongly affected national labour law and social security systems.[686] With those rulings, the Court gave a rather far-reaching interpretation of the freedom of establishment and the freedom to provide services, which overrode the national industrial relations systems.[687]

This renewed emphasis on economic freedoms might also be reconducted to the integrationalist rationale of the CJEU. As Cartabia suggested, a revival of judicial activism during the mid-2000s might be attributable to another episode of political crisis that had occurred in the European system shortly before those rulings.[688] This coincides with the failed attempt to promulgate the Treaty establishing a Constitution for Europe, which in 2005 risked causing a halt to the process of European integration.[689] The Court's integrationalist drive of those years could thus be read as an attempt to avoid that the failure to realise the political design of a constitution would plunge the EU back into an identity crisis. By giving a boost to the internal market, the Court reaffirmed the relevance and impact of EU law, thus banishing the spectre of political deadlock and immobility.

3.2.2.2 The Expansive Approach to the Principle of Non-discrimination

As anticipated in section 3.2.2, the expansion of the single market was not the only policy effect of the Court's integrationalist approach. In fact, it has already been described how the CJEU gave rise to a rich case law on the principle of non-discrimination, with which it took the first steps towards the expansion of the EEC's competence in the field of social policies. Here too, the same judgments that in section 2.1.2 were read from a neofunctionalist perspective can now be placed into an integrationalist narrative.

686. S. Evju, 'The Right to Collective Action under the European Social Charter', European Labour Law Journal, 2(3), pp. 196-224, 2011.
687. F. Dorssemont, 'The Right to Take Collective Action v Fundamental Economic Freedoms in the Aftermath of Laval and Viking. Foes Are Forever!' in M. de Vos (ed.), *European Union Internal Market and Labour Law: Friends or Foes?*, Intersentia, Cambridge, 2009, pp. 45-105; J. Prassl, "The Interaction of EU Law and National Law: Between Myth and Reality' in A. Bogg, C. Costello & A.C.L. Davies (eds), *Research Handbook on EU Labour Law*, Edward Elgar Publishing, Cheltenham, 2016, pp. 42-63.
688. M. Cartabia, 'Europe and Rights: Taking Dialogue Seriously', European Constitutional Law Review, 5, pp. 5-31, 2009.
689. A. Jacobs, 'The Janus Head of the European Union: The Social Market Economy Versus Ultraliberal Policies' in J. Wouters, L. Verhey & P. Kiiver (eds), *European Constitutionalism Beyond Lisbon*, Intersentia, 2009.

An important example concerns the expansive interpretation of the concept of 'equal pay' in Article 119 TEEC (hereinafter referred to with its current numbering: 'Article 157 TFEU'). This expansive interpretation took place in gradual steps. At first, in the *Defrenne I* judgment (1971), the Court adopted a rather narrow reading of the scope of the notion of 'pay'. It only included social security schemes or benefits that constitute a direct or indirect payment to the worker. Retirement pension schemes that are directly governed by legislation without any element of agreement within the undertaking were thus excluded. The reason was that in those cases 'the part due from the employers in the financing of such schemes does not constitute a direct or indirect payment to the worker'.[690] Then, in *Defrenne II* (1976), with a historical ruling, the Court gave direct effect to the principle of equal pay and ruled that it applies 'not only to the action of public authorities, but also extends to all agreements which are intended to regulate paid labour collectively, as well as to contracts between individuals'.[691]

Subsequently, in the *Bilka* judgment, the Court modified its position regarding the applicability of the principle of equal pay to pension schemes. It accepted that this principle also covers pension schemes that are established by the employer with the effect of supplementing the social benefits paid under national legislation.[692] According to the Court, benefits paid to employees under such schemes are to be referred to the employment relationship and thus relate to the notion of 'pay'.[693] A further step was then made in the *Barber* decision (1990), where the Court loosened its interpretation of 'pay' to encompass virtually all occupational pensions and occupational social security benefits.[694] In *Barber*, the Court ruled that Article 157 TFEU applies also to pension schemes that are not set up and administered by the employer, but by an external legal person (in this case a trustee) to whom the setup and administration of the scheme were contracted out. The evolution of case law is remarkable. While in *Defrenne I* the Court brought within the concept of 'equal pay' only the pension schemes that have been stipulated by the employer, the *Barber* case established that 'even if the contributions paid to those schemes and the benefits which they provide are in part a substitute for those of the general statutory scheme, that fact cannot preclude the application of Article [157 TFEU]'.[695]

Meanwhile, the Court had also broadened the reading of 'equal pay' to include practically all the benefits inherent in the employment relationship.[696] In the *Kowalska*

690. Judgment of 25 May 1971, *Gabrielle Defrenne v. Belgian State*, C-80/70, ECLI:EU:C:1971:55 (paras 7 and 8).
691. Judgment of 8 April 1976, *Gabrielle Defrenne v. Société anonyme belge de navigation aérienne Sabena*, C-43/75, ECLI:EU:C:1976:56 (para. 39).
692. A. Stone Sweet, *The Judicial Construction of Europe*, Oxford University Press, New York, 2004, p. 157; S. O'Leary, *Employment Law at the European Court of Justice: Judicial Structures, Policies, and Processes*, Hart Publishing, Oxford, 2002, p. 147.
693. Judgment of 13 May 1986, *Bilka – Kaufhaus GmbH v. Karin Weber von Hartz*, C-170/84, ECLI:EU:C:1986:204 (paras 20-22).
694. Judgment of 17 May 1990, *Douglas Harvey Barber v. Guardian Royal Exchange Assurance Group*, C-262/88, ECLI:EU:C:1990:209.
695. *Ibid.* (para. 27).
696. A. Stone Sweet, *The Judicial Construction of Europe*, Oxford University Press, New York, 2004, p. 157.

judgment, for instance, the Court established that Article 157 TFEU is infringed when national legislation requires employers to pay severance grants on termination of the employment relationship only to the full-time workers. The exclusion of part-time workers constitutes discrimination based on gender since a considerably lower percentage of men than women work part-time.[697] The Court also observed that severance payments are to be considered a form of deferred pay to which the worker is entitled by reason of his employment, and which therefore falls within the scope of the prohibition of discrimination under Article 157 TFEU.[698]

Subsequently, the Court began to expand the scope of the principle of gender equality also beyond the (already broadly conceived) concept of pay. In the judgments *Dekker* and *Webb*, for example, the Court established the prohibition of discrimination in relation to pregnancy and maternity leave.[699] Within the scope of that principle, the Court also subsumed discriminatory conducts directed at transgender persons.[700] Most notably, in *P v. S*, the Court ruled that unequal treatment related to gender reassignment is a discrimination based on the sex of the person concerned. This follows from the fact that treating someone differently because they have had gender reassignment is equivalent to discriminating against them in relation to individuals of the sex that they had before the operation.[701]

Similar to what occurred in the context of the internal market, the jurisprudential ferment on the principle of non-discrimination provoked a substantial regulatory impact, promoting greater integration between the legal systems of the Member States.[702] Although the major jurisprudential developments occurred in the 1990s, here too there was an integrationalist momentum during the second half of the 2000s. Mention can be made of the *Mangold* case (2005) and the subsequent *Kücükdeveci* judgment (2010), this time concerning age-based discrimination. In those cases, the Court gave the principle of non-discrimination on the basis of age the value of a general principle of EU law having horizontal direct effect, with disruptive impact on national labour policies.[703] As for the case law that in the 2000s further expanded the internal market (the Laval Quartet), also this episode of judicial activism might be read as the

697. Judgment of 27 June 1990, *Maria Kowalska v. Freie und Hansestadt Hamburg*, C-33/89, ECLI:EU:C:1990:265 (para. 16).
698. *Ibid.* (para. 10). Similar considerations were made with regard to sick pay in the judgment of 13 July 1989, *Ingrid Rinner-Kühn v. FWW Spezial-Gebäudereinigung GmbH & Co. KG*, C-171/88, ECLI:EU:C:1989:328.
699. Judgment of 8 November 1989, *Elisabeth Johanna Pacifica Dekker v. Stichting Vormingscentrum voor Jong Volwassenen (VJV-Centrum) Plus*, C-177/88, ECLI:EU:C:1990:383; judgment of 14 July 1994, *Carole Louise Webb v. EMO Air Cargo (UK) Ltd*, C-32/93, ECLI:EU:C:1994:300.
700. O. Pollicino, *Discriminazione sulla Base del Sesso e Trattamento Preferenziale nel Diritto Comunitario*, Giuffrè, Milano, 2005.
701. Judgment of 30 April 1996, *P v. S and Cornwall County Council*, C-13/94, ECLI:EU:C:1996:170 (para. 21).
702. As discussed in section 2.1.2.
703. Judgment of 22 November 2005, *Werner Mangold v. Rüdiger Helm*, C-144/04, ECLI:EU:C:2005:709; judgment of 19 January 2010, *Seda Kücükdeveci gegen Swedex GmbH & Co. KG.*, C-555/07, ECLI:EU:C:2010:21. *Inter alia*, D. Wyatt, 'Horizontal Effect of Fundamental Freedoms and the Right to Equality after Viking and Mangold, and the Implications for Community Competence', Legal Research Paper series, published in Croatian Yearbook of European Law & Policy, Oxford, 2008.

Court's reaction to the failed promulgation of the Treaty establishing a Constitution for Europe. Recalling what has been mentioned in section 3.2.2.1, it could have been an attempt by the Court to prevent the legal system of the Union from being affected by the political stalemate.[704]

3.3 Informal Partnership with the European Commission

While introducing the integrationalist theories, it was said that the integrationalist rationale of the Court's rulings can be interpreted as a reflection of the socioeconomic and political objectives established by the Treaties.[705] This would place the CJEU in a communion of intentions with the European Commission, which is indeed the European institution that best embodies the Union's interests and has the task of advancing European integration.[706]

Interestingly, the convergence between the two institutions can, to a certain extent, be measured. The Commission systematically intervenes in proceedings before the Court with legal opinions where it provides recommendations on how the points of law raised should be decided. In a manner analogous to the amicus briefs submitted by the national governments (that are discussed in Chapter 5, section 2.3), these written observations do not constrain the Court. They do, however, offer a viewpoint of an institution that is driven by an integrationalist ethos and for this reason they may be of particular interest to the Court.

Several scholars have investigated the degree of convergence between the Court's judgments and the legal observations issued by the Commission's legal services.[707] In 1996, Kilroy conducted a study on the case law in the area of free movement of goods and found that 'in 99 over 114 cases where the Commission intervened, the Court sided with the Commission. The Commission "predicted" the CJEU in 86% of the times'.[708] This finding was confirmed by Stone Sweet and

704. M. Cartabia, 'Europe and Rights: Taking Dialogue Seriously', European Constitutional Law Review, 5, pp. 5-31, 2009; B. Vesterdorf, 'A Constitutional Court for the EU?', International Journal of Constitutional Law, 4(4), pp. 607-617, 2006. Vesterdorf's contribution is from October 2006 and is well placed to capture the perception of the Court's case law in the aftermath of the failed ratification of the Treaty establishing a Constitution for Europe.
705. As also discussed in section 2.1.2.
706. C. Barnard, 'EU Employment Law and the European Social Model: The Past, the Present and the Future', Current Legal Problems, 67, pp. 199-237, 2014.
707. Article 98 Rules of Procedure of the Court of Justice, listing the actors that are entitled to participate in preliminary ruling proceedings and Article 23 of the Statute of the Court of Justice. Pursuant to Article 23 of the Statute of the CJEU: 'In the cases governed by Article 267 TFEU, the decision of the court or tribunal of a Member State which suspends its proceedings and refers a case to the Court of Justice shall be notified to the Court by the court or tribunal concerned. The decision shall then be notified by the Registrar of the Court to the parties, to the Member States and to the Commission [...]. Within two months of this notification, the parties, the Member States, the Commission and, where appropriate, the institution, body, office or agency which adopted the act the validity to interpretation of which is in dispute, shall be entitled submit statements of case or written observations to the Court.'
708. B. Kilroy, *Member State Control or Judicial Independence? The Integrative Role of the European Court of Justice, 1958-1994*, University of California, Los Angeles, 1996.

McCrown, who conducted similar research, again focusing on the free movement of goods, and found an incidence higher than 80%.[709]

Stone Sweet and McCrown also delved into the areas of social policy and gender equality and observed that, in those areas, the convergence was even higher, at around 90%.[710] The Court's decisions in social policies were also analysed by Cichowski, who summarised her research in a study published in 2007. The results indicate that the legal arguments put forward by the Commission feed into the Court's reasoning 84% of the time (202 out of 240 cases analysed).[711] An interesting study was also conducted by Stein, who analysed a pool of 11 landmark rulings that had a particularly decisive effect on the constitutional maturation of the EC. Among these rulings, only in one (*Walrave*)[712] the Court adopted a reasoning that departed from the legal arguments outlined by the European Commission.[713]

These studies suggest the existence of a sort of informal partnership between the Court and the European Commission, which might be rooted in their shared commitment to European integration.[714] This informal partnership might have arisen due to a series of reciprocal advantages. From the point of view of the Court, accommodating the positions proposed by the Commission's legal services can be quite useful. First, the Commission's legal observations can help the Court to identify the best reasoning in

709. A. Stone Sweet & M. McCown, 'Discretion and Precedent in European Law' in O. Wiklund (ed.), *Judicial Discretion in European Perspective*, Norstedts Juridik, Stockholm, 2003, pp. 84.
710. *Ibid.*
711. R.A. Cichowski, *The European Court and Civil Society: Litigation, Mobilization and Governance; Themes in European Governance*, Cambridge University Press, Cambridge, 2007, p. 87: 'The Commission's success rate is approximately 84%: 202 out of 240 observations are successful at predicting the final ECJ decision [...] As the ECJ acts to protect its legitimacy and uphold EU interests, it is not surprising that the Commission's position was much more likely to predict the final outcome of the case.'
712. Judgment of 12 December 1974, *B.N.O. Walrave and L.J.N. Koch v. Association Union cycliste internationale, Koninklijke Nederlandsche Wielren Unie and Federación Española Ciclismo*, C-36/74, ECLI:EU:C:1974:140.
713. E. Stein, 'Lawyers, Judges, and the Making of a Transnational Constitution', The American Journal of International Law, 75(1), pp. 1-27, 1981. Stein analysed 11 landmark judgments from the origins of the Court of Justice activity until the 1980s: *Van Gend en Loos, Costa v. Enel, Simmenthal, Internationale Handelsgesellschaft, Lutticke, Reyners, Walrave, Defrenne II, Franz-Grad, Van Duyn, ERTA*. Stein observed that only in *Defrenne II* the Court ventured beyond the Commission lead, when it ruled that treaty provisions on gender equality had direct effect on private law relationship among individuals. Moreover, in the *Van Gend en Loos* case, the Court seemed to have taken a more restrictive stance with respect to the strongly integrationalist position of the Commission that suggested the Court to clearly state the supremacy of EC law on national law. However, the Court promulgated the principle of supremacy of EC law not even a year later, in the *Costa v. Enel* case.
714. M.P. Maduro, *We the Court: The European Court of Justice and the European Economic Constitution: A Critical Reading of Article 30 of the EC Treaty*, Hart Publishing, Oxford, 1998, p. 10. Maduro suggested that the Court was guided by the Commission in the direction of more legal integration, and that this led to an alliance between the Court and the Commission and in the creation of an habit of obedience. Moreover, as reported in J. Bengoetxea, 'The Scope for Discretion, Coherence and Citizenship' in O. Wiklund (ed.), *Judicial Discretion in European Perspective*, Norstedts Juridik, Stockholm, 2003, pp. 48-74, judges Koopmans and Mancini argued that the Commission has, in the past, shown the propension to rely on the Court to consolidate EU integration in areas in which it had already been established and to foster EU policy making in other areas not yet reached by legislation.

view of advancing the interests of the Union and strengthening the integration process, as this is generally also the Commission's intention. Then, in conforming to the Commission's legal opinion, the Court can be almost certain to promote European integration in a manner that complements and does not conflict with, the Commission's political and policymaking strategy.[715] Judgments that follow the Commission's positions might have also a greater prospect of being implemented at the national level, because of the political pressure that may be associated with it.[716] Finally, as Pescatore, a former CJEU judge, pointed out, the Court tends to rely on the Commission's arguments partly because its legal services have a reputation for producing high-quality legal analysis.[717]

For its part, the Commission also derives considerable benefits from intervening in judicial proceedings before the Court. As observed by former Advocate General Maduro, the Commission has found in the Court a valuable ally in advancing European integration, especially on economic policies.[718] Moreover, the Court's judgments have proven particularly helpful in strengthening the enforceability of EU law, as they help to create a 'habit of obedience' towards the European legal system.[719] It has also been noted that the Commission often approaches the Court's judicial activity in a utilitarian manner. Indeed, it is not unusual for the Commission to initiate a judicial action before the Court (e.g., action for failure to fulfil obligations or for annulment) and then use its standing as a plaintiff to advance an integrationalist agenda.[720]

A significant example of the informal partnership between the Court and the European Commission can be found in the - by now familiar - *Cassis de Dijon* judgment, especially if considering the policy initiatives adopted by the Commission in the aftermath of the judgment.[721] First, in establishing the principle of mutual recognition, the Court obtained a result that was de facto equivalent to that proposed by the Commission's legal services in their legal opinion of the case.[722] As mentioned,

715. E. Stein, 'Lawyers, Judges, and the Making of a Transnational Constitution', The American Journal of International Law, 75(1), pp. 1-27, 1981.
716. P. Pescatore, 'Le recours, dans la jurisprudence de la Cour de justice des Communautés européennes, à des normes déduites de la comparaison des droits des Etats membres', Revue internationale de droit comparé, 32(2), 1980, pp. 337-359, 1981.
717. *Ibid.*
718. M.P. Maduro, *We the Court: The European Court of Justice and the European Economic Constitution: A Critical Reading of Article 30 of the EC Treaty*, Hart Publishing, Oxford, 1998, p. 10; similarly, G.F. Mancini, 'The Making of a Constitution for Europe', Common Market Law Review, 26(4), pp. 595-614, 1989: 'As the executive-political branch of the Community, the Commission may not have always lived up to those expectations, but as "watchdog of the Treaty", that is both as the prosecutor of Member State infractions and as amicus curiae in cases referred by the national courts, it has undoubtedly played a positive role. In other words, the Commission had led the Court - particularly by assuaging the concern some of the judges may gave felt regarding the acceptability of their rulings - on the path towards further integration and increased Community power.'
719. *Ibid.*
720. F. Snyder, 'The Effectiveness of European Community Law: Institutions, Processes, Tools and Techniques', The Modern Law Review, 56(1), pp. 19-54, 1993.
721. M.P. Maduro, *We the Court: The European Court of Justice and the European Economic Constitution: A Critical Reading of Article 30 of the EC Treaty*, 1998, p. 10.
722. The Commission proposed to answer the preliminary question as follows: 'The fixing of a minimum wine-spirit content for potable spirits, which is applicable to domestic products and

this assonance is far from unusual. But even more telling is that, without delay, the Commission capitalised on the integrationalist momentum created by the judgment. In 1979, the Commission adopted the 'Cassis de Dijon' Communication, addressed to national governments, the European Parliament and the Council, in which it acknowledged the implications of the mutual recognition doctrine for the internal market and urged national governments to adapt their importation and exportation policies.[723] Contextually, the Commission announced actions against national commercial practices that did not comply with the Court's case law and drafted a series of guidelines to help Member States readjust their trading practices.[724]

The centrality of the mutual recognition policies for the Commission's integration strategy also emerged from the 1985 White Paper 'Completing the Internal Market'.[725] There, the Commission stated that 'the general thrust of the Commission's approach [...] will be to move away from the concept of harmonisation towards that of mutual recognition and equivalence'.[726] The Commission thus basically announced its decision to take advantage of the deregulatory trend initiated by the Court's case law, implying that negative integration was officially preferred to regulatory convergence. As mentioned, this approach allowed market integration to proceed despite the stalemate caused by the still strong intergovernmental structure of the EC legislative process.[727]

Finally, it is interesting to note that the informal alliance between the CJEU and the European Commission can be read, from the Court's point of view, as an expression of what Staudt, Epstein, Wiedenbeck, Lindstädt and Vander Wielen call the 'partnership judicial regime'.[728] This regime identifies the attitude of a court that 'should not eliminate its role in the [political] decision-making process, but neither should it

imported products without distinction, may be justified in the interests of consumer protection and fair competition between producers of potable spirit. However, such rules are excessive and therefore constitute a prohibited measure having an effect equivalent to quantitative restriction on imports where their consequence is that, notwithstanding a suitable indication, typical products from other Member States, manufactured according to a particular process and characterized traditionally by an alcohol content which is lower than the limit fixed may not be put into circulation in the Member State concerned or may be put into circulation there only if they conform to reasonable requirements.' *See* C-120/78, *Cassis de Dijon*, p. 659.

723. Communication from the Commission concerning the consequences of the judgment given by the Court of Justice on 20 February 1979 in case 120/78 ('Cassis de Dijon') *Official Journal C 256, 03/10/1980 pp. 0002-0003.*

724. *Ibid.*: 'The Commission will therefore have to tackle a whole body of commercial rules which lay down that products manufactures and marketed in one Member States must fulfil technical or qualitative conditions in order to be admitted to the market of another and specifically in all cases where the trade barriers occasioned by such rules are inadmissible according to the very strict criteria set out by the Court. [...] The Commission is confident that this approach will secure great freedom of trade for the Community's manufacturers, so strengthening the industrial base of the Community, while meeting the expectations of consumers.'

725. European Commission, Completing the Internal Market, White Paper, COM(85) 310 final, Brussels, 14 June 1985.

726. *Ibid.* (para. 13).

727. On the empty chair crisis, *see* section 3.2.2.1.

728. N. Staudt et al., 'Judging Statutes: Interpretive Regimes', Loyola of Los Angeles Law Review, 38, pp. 1909-1970, 2005. The authors indicate that the partnership regime is characterised by a court that pays attention to changed political and institutional circumstances, current public values, and a court that can adapt anachronistic or outdated norms.

elevate its own preferences above all others'. This description nicely depicts the attitude with which, according to integrationalist theory, the Court exercises its judicial activism. The partnership regime in fact recognises that the Court has carved out an influential role for itself in EU policymaking. At the same time, it also highlights that the Court exercises this role only in view of the realisation of the integrationalist nature of the Treaties and in complementarity with the other Communitarian institution par excellence, the European Commission.

3.4 Weak Aspects of the Integrationalist Theory

Just like neofunctionalism, the integrationalist theory has been subject to criticism. The fact that the case law of the Court has played a crucial role in the process of European integration is almost undisputed. What has been contested, however, is whether deepening European integration was the actual intention behind the reasonings of the Court.

According to Lenaerts, President of the CJEU at the time of writing, the Court's activism is not so much a symptom of its integrationalist vocation as an expression of what EU judges have deemed necessary to ensure the continuity and resilience of the European legal order.[729] The judgments that have been most criticised for their boldness were thus adopted to protect EU law from national recalcitrance and protectionism.[730] In other words, according to Lenaerts, the Court's focus on ensuring the survival of the legal system should not be mistaken for an integrationalist (and political) strategy. In relation to *Cassis de Dijon*, Lenaerts suggested that the Court's main objective was to break the political deadlock that was slowing down the implementation of the Treaties. The incrementally expansive effect that the judgment and the principle of mutual recognition had on the internal market therefore was a consequence, and not the objective, of the Court's reasoning. The same consideration applies to the rulings on direct effect, primacy of EU law, non-contractual liability of the state, as well as to those on fundamental rights since they were aimed at reinforcing the EC legal framework.[731]

Another critical observation, although diametrically opposed to the one advanced by Lenaerts, is raised by Horsley, who identified a contradictory aspect in the integrationalist narrative. Horsley noted that if integrationalism explains the Court's activism in situations of political impasses, it does not justify judicial policymaking in

729. K. Lenaerts, 'Some Thoughts about the Interaction Between Judges and Politicians', University of Chicago Legal Forum, 1, 1992, pp. 93-1331.
730. *Ibid.* In Lenaerts's view, the Court of Justice has shown a particular sensitivity for facilitating political processes. According to this account, the Court is perceived as the protector of the rule of law and of the democratic process, when the political actors are unable to do adequately pursue such process. The Court of Justice, thus, acquires features that are similar to those of a constitutional court.
731. C-26/62, *Van Gend en Loos*; C-6/64, *Costa v. Enel*; C-46/93, *Brasserie du Pecheur*; C-6/90, *Frankovich;* judgment of 12 November 1969, *Erich Stauder v. City of Ulm – Sozialamt*, C-29/69, ECLI:EU:C:1969:57; C-11/70, *Internationale Handelsgesellschaft;* C-43/75, *Defrenne II.*

periods when the EU legislative institutions had regained control of their functions.[732] Instead, there are numerous examples of judicial activism which prima facie appears politically 'unnecessary'. These include the case law that has given rise to a body of employment-related rights in relation to the principle of non-discrimination. For instance, the two judgments *Mangold* and *Kücükdeveci*, already mentioned in section 3.2.2.2, came at a time when the European legislator had already shown that it was able to take the necessary legislative initiatives without incurring substantial political blockage.[733] In sections 3.2.2.1 and 3.2.2.2, it was mentioned that Cartabia suggested that the 2000s judicial activism might be a reaction of the Court to the failed ratification of the Treaty establishing a Constitution for Europe, in order to avoid a political stalemate. However, even if these assumptions would be true, they don't make the Court's activism 'necessary' for the future of European integration.[734] The Court has thus gone beyond what was actually required if its underpinning logic is *just* an integrationalist ethos. It might instead indicate that the Court is a more ambitious political player.

This seems corroborated by the general perception among lawyers that some of these 'integrationalist' rulings actually are an expression of the Court's ideological proximity with EU (neoliberal) policymaking. In the Laval Quartet, for instance, the Court's reasoning was mostly read as influenced by the position of those economic and institutional actors who were pushing for more space for competition on wages in the enlarged EU.[735]

Weiler, moreover, noted that if the Court's intention was to foster European integration, then it is not clear why the Court would choose reasonings that have the effect of provoking resistance from national policymakers.[736] The judicial activism of the Court has in fact generally not been received well by national governments. At times, this has led them to assume a rather defensive stance and to create institutional barriers to European integration.[737] Among other examples, Weiler pointed to the creation of COREPER (Committee of permanent representatives from the national governments) and the institutionalisation of the European Council, both bodies with a strong intergovernmental character and functional to constrain the integrationalist

732. T. Horsley, *The Court of Justice of the European Union as and Institutional Actor: Judicial Lawmaking and Its Limits*, Cambridge University Press, New York, 2018, p. 167.
733. C-144/04, *Mangold;* C-555/07, *Kücükdeveci*, where the Court ruled that the principle of non-discrimination on the ground of age was to be considered a general principle of EU law and therefore had to be given direct horizontal effect.
734. M. Cartabia, 'Europe and Rights: Taking Dialogue Seriously', European Constitutional Law Review, 5, pp. 5-31, 2009.
735. The fierce opposition from the Member States against these judgments is further discussed in Chapter 5 section 2.5. C. Barnard, 'The Calm after the Storm: Time to Reflect on EU (Labour) Law Scholarship Following the Decisions in Viking and Laval' in A. Bogg, C. Costello & A.C.L. Davies (eds), *Research Handbook on EU Labour Law*, Edward Elgar Publishing, Cheltenham, 2016, pp. 337-362.
736. A.-M. Burley & W. Mattli, 'Europe Before the Court: A Political Theory of Legal Integration', International Organization, 47(1), pp. 41-76, 1993.
737. J.H.H. Weiler, 'The Community System: the Dual Character of Supranationalism', Yearbook of European Law, 1(1), pp. 267-306, 1981.

thrust of the Court.[738] This suggests that if the Court's objective had been to actually advance the process of European integration, its rulings would have probably taken greater care not to antagonise national sensibilities, thus reducing the risk of intergovernmental bottlenecks.[739]

All in all, the different nature of the criticisms that have been advanced against the integrationalist theories is already an eloquent illustration of the difficulty that observers have when attempting to discern the Court's decision-making logics. It is in fact interesting to note that the discussed objections stem from two contrasting dogmatic perspectives. It was said that Lenaerts suggested that an integrationalist vocation is not attributable to the CJEU since the Court aims at guaranteeing what is strictly necessary for the survival of the legal system established by the Treaties, nothing more. At the same time, Horsley and Weiler argued that the Court's activism can be so disruptive that it goes beyond a mere integrationalist rationale. It instead better reflects a quasi-political ambition on the part of the Court, perhaps closer to that described by neofunctionalist theories.

A further critical remark that can be made about the integrationalist theory concerns the supposed informal partnership between the Court and the European Commission. On closer inspection, it should not be excluded that the similarity between their legal positions is not dictated by the common integrationalist vocation but, rather, by an attitude of obedience, or even loyalty, on the part of the Court towards the Commission. If this were the case, the approach that characterises the Court's decision-making would no longer be an expression of the 'partnership judicial regime' identified by Staudt, Epstein, Wiedenbeck, Lindstädt and Vander Wielen.[740] Instead, the Court's modus operandi would fall under another regime described by the same authors, namely the 'executive judicial regime'. The consideration that the Court gives to the Commission's legal opinions may in fact be a manifestation of the Court's inclination to follow (or 'obey') the preferences of the Commission, regardless of the normative rationale underpinning those positions.

Finally, it is worth mentioning that there is also a weakness that the integrationalist theory shares with the neofunctionalist theory. Just like neofunctionalism, integrationalism overlooks the possibility that the Court's reasoning may be influenced by factors that are external to the legal and institutional system of the EU. Both theories don't consider the pressure that might derive from Member State governments, constitutional traditions or national jurisprudence. This observation prompted scholars

738. *Ibid.*, and J.H.H. Weiler, 'The Transformation of Europe', The Yale Law Journal, 100(8), pp. 2403-2483, 1991; A.-M. Burley & W. Mattli, 'Europe Before the Court: A Political Theory of Legal Integration', 1993. *See also* G.F. Mancini, 'The Making of a Constitution for Europe', Common Market Law Review, 26(4), pp. 595-614, 1989 where the author, in relation to the COREPER, observed that 'The permanent representatives are ambassadors and the subcommittees are composed of national officials. While a minister may occasionally be expected to deal with a given problem in a supranational spirit, it would be naïve to expect an ambassador or a national bureaucrat, whatever his leanings, to assist wilfully in the process of the wasting away of Member State power, thereby blighting his own career.'
739. J.H.H. Weiler, 'The Community System: the Dual Character of Supranationalism', 1981.
740. N. Staudt et al., 'Judging Statutes: Interpretive Regimes', Loyola of Los Angeles Law Review, 38, pp. 1909-1970, 2005.

such as Ovádek to provide a more nuanced account of the Court's integrationalism. In a recent empirical study designed to explore 'how pro-integration is the European Court of Justice',[741] Ovádek noted that while the case study showed a pro-supranational (or integrationalist) inclination, it rejects the narrative that the Court is completely free to act, as there are intergovernmental dynamics that should not be overlooked.

4 CONCLUDING REMARKS

This chapter was dedicated to two theories that attribute to the CJEU the role of a (quasi) policymaker, able to define in quasi-autonomy the Union's legal order.

Section 2 concerned the neofunctionalist theory, according to which the Court aims at realising its own ambition to develop specific policy areas and to increase the penetration of EU law within the national context. At the same time, neofunctionalists argue that the Court uses its case law to enhance its own judicial authority. To achieve these objectives, the Court is deemed to have used skilful strategies to engage individuals (and especially economic operators) as potential litigants and as potential initiators of EU law-based litigation before national courts. It was also held that the Court has exploited the opportunities presented by the preliminary ruling mechanism to involve national courts, which are the essential link between domestic systems and EU judicial rule-making.

Section 3 then turned to the integrationalist theory. According to the integrationalist narrative, the Court obeys a less strategic and complex logic, although is similarly driven by the policymaking objective of creating a tighter EU. The fundamental rationale of the judicial interpretation is the promotion of EU integration and this prompted the Court to defranchise EC law from the logics of international law and led the Court to give an expansive reading of the EC and EU. Ultimately, this approach has resulted in the Court acting as the trustee of the Treaties and creating an informal alliance with the European Commission.

How do these theories help to answer RQ3 (*What are the logics that determine the Court's approach with respect to labour law, taking into account judicial lawmaking theories*)? First of all, it should be considered that both neofunctionalist and integrationalist theories assume that EU case law is the manifestation of the Court's normative inclinations. Transposing the theoretical discussion into the context of labour law, the Court's approach towards a specific normative position – be it the enhancement of the protective function of the economic rationale – can be read as the expression of a strategy to valorise a specific normative position. However, it is important to note that the Court's normative inclination needs to be placed in a broader strategic design. This could be of integrationalist nature, to provoke a regulatory spillover, or to increase its jurisprudential authority (as suggested by neofunctionalist theories). Indeed, under

741. M. Ovádek, 'Supranationalism, Constrained? Locating the Court of Justice on the EU Integration Dimension', European Union Politics, 22(1), pp. 46-69, 2021.

both neofunctionalist and integrationalist perspectives, the Court's normative preferences do not relate to individual cases, but rather to a wider policymaking strategy. This is to be kept in mind when linking these theories to the case studies presented in Chapter 3 which showed that the Court departed from the valorisation of the protective function to adopt a more economic-oriented reading of the transfer of undertakings directive. Through the lenses of the judicial lawmaking theories here analysed, this evolution might indicate that the Court has found that was more functional for the pursuit of its objectives (be they integrationalist or neofunctional) to first adopt a more rigid approach to workers' rights and then move towards a more flexible reading.

It should also be recalled that the consideration of the different theories on the Court's decision-making dynamics is ultimately functional to the conduct of a second empirical study on the same directive on transfer of undertakings, in Chapter 6. It is then worth noting that for both the neofunctionalist and integrationalist theories it is possible to identify certain symptomatic indicators to look for in the case law (which are further discussed in Chapter 6, when presenting the second case study on Directive 2001/23/EC). Starting with neofunctionalism, it was noted that this theory contends that the Court has established dynamics of quasi-complicity with individuals in their capacity as litigants. For example, the Court actively stimulates the interest of economic operators and traders so that they would progressively rely on EU case law to broaden their commercial horizons and eventually deepen the EU internal market. This suggests that a helpful indicator for testing the validity of the neofunctionalist theory may be the degree of convergence between the Court's judgments and the claims brought by the litigants before the national court. It is in fact presumed that a neofunctionalist Court would be inclined to go along with the claims of the litigant in order to stimulate others to start similar cases.

Regarding the integrationalist theory, instead, it was illustrated that the integrationalist vocation is likely to lead the Court to adopt positions similar to those proposed by the Commission in its legal opinions. Hence, to identify whether the Court responds to integrationalist logic, it might be helpful to observe the affinity between the Court's reasoning and the arguments put forward by the Commission's legal services.

As anticipated in the introduction to this chapter, the neofunctionalist and integrationalist theories do not exhaust the judicial lawmaking logics that are tested in the case studies in Chapter 6. Chapter 5 discusses a second series of theories which, instead of depicting the Court as a purposive policymaker, define it as subject to the influence of national normative and judicial context(s).

CHAPTER 5

The Relevance of the National Context in the Reasoning of the Court

1 INTRODUCTION

This chapter continues the exploration of the judicial lawmaking theories of the CJEU, still within the second analytical layer of the research. The theories presented in this chapter thus complement neofunctionalism and integrationalism with a view of addressing RQ3 (*What are the logics that determine the Court's approach with respect to labour law, taking into account judicial lawmaking theories?*).

Differently from the theories discussed in Chapter 4, here the Court is not portrayed as a purposive policymaker. While not denying the contribution of EU case law to the maturation of the EU legal order, this second group of theories suggests that the Court's reasonings tend to accommodate the various claims and concerns (political, normative, constitutional, jurisprudential) that emanate from the national level. The Court is therefore seen as unable to intervene effectively in EU policymaking *unless* the political context allows it to do so. And, when that occurs, the Court's reasoning reflects the legal solutions that emerge from the national framework.

Like Chapter 4, this chapter contributes to broadening the epistemological framework required to properly examine the dynamics underlying the formation of the Court's reasoning. Section 1 introduces the intergovernmentalist theories, according to which EU case law reflects the preferences of the (most influential) national governments. Section 2 focuses on the views of those EU lawyers and constitutionalists who contend that national judicial systems and legal traditions play an important role in determining the Court's reasoning. The underlying principle is that for the Court's judgments to exert the desired normative impact, they must be accepted and properly implemented in the national legal systems. This implies that the Court must be careful to adopt legal reasonings that fit smoothly into the legal context of the Member States. Particular attention is paid to two different models that have, over time, been attributed to the Court: the majoritarian and the pluralist approach. When following a majoritarian approach, the Court tends to encapsulate in its judgments the normative solution that emerges as prevailing in the legislative landscape of the Member States. The pluralist approach, on the other hand, requires the Court to be more cautious not to override the national legal framework and to leave sufficient discretion to the domestic legislature. Section 3 then discusses the trans-judicial dialogue and shows how the dynamics between the CJEU and national judges can be decisive for the evolution of the case law.

Differently from neofunctionalism and integrationalism, the theories examined in this chapter open up the possibility that the Court's approach to labour law may be influenced by dynamics of national origin that are unrelated to the Court's normative preferences. It should be noted that in no way do these theories intend to challenge the independence of the Court and its judges vis-à-vis the Member States.[742] The underlying idea is rather that this independence does not prevent the Court from being influenced by national institutional actors.

To conclude these introductory remarks, it should also be noted that the theories covered in this chapter are not entirely at odds with those discussed in Chapter 4. Certainly, the main message here is that it would be inaccurate to portray the Court as a purposive policymaker, as this would fail to take into account a whole range of dynamics emanating from the national context. However, the presence of 'interferences' from the domestic level does not per se preclude the Court from having its own normative preferences. In other words, the theories may have, at least in part, a cumulative relevance.

742. T. Ćapeta, 'Ideology and Legal Reasoning at the European Court of Justice' in E. Perisin & S. Rodin (eds), *The Transformation or Reconstitution of Europe: The Critical Legal Studies Perspective on the Role of the Courts in the European Union*, Hart Publishing, Oxford, 2018, pp. 89-120. Article 253 TFEU establishes that: 'The Judges and Advocates-General of the Court of Justice shall be chosen from persons whose independence is beyond doubt and who possess the qualifications required for appointment to the highest judicial offices in their respective countries or who are jurisconsults of recognised competence; they shall be appointed by common accord of the governments of the Member States for a term of six years, after consultation of the panel provided for in Article 255', and Article 255: 'A panel shall be set up in order to give an opinion on candidates' suitability to perform the duties of Judge and Advocate-General of the Court of Justice and the General Court before the governments of the Member States make the appointments referred to in Article 253 and 254. The panel shall comprise seven persons chosen from among former members of the Court of Justice and the General Court, members of national supreme courts and lawyers of recognised competence, one of whom shall be proposed by the European Parliament. The Council shall adopt a decision establishing the panel's operating rules and a decision appointing its members. It shall act on the initiative of the President of the Court of Justice.'

2 INTERGOVERNMENTALISM

Intergovernmentalist theories contend that the CJEU generally formulates its reasonings in consideration of the preferences of national governments. They also suggest that certain Member States are more effective than others in influencing EU case law.[743]

This narrative has a historical underpinning, and is linked to the fact that, at the time of the Treaty of Rome, the original role that the signatory Member States assigned to the Court was limited to three main tasks:[744]

- watching that the Council of Ministers and the Commission do not exceed their powers;
- mitigating the normative uncertainty of EU law;
- deciding, as a neutral institution, on the Commission's and Member States' claims about the infringements of the EEC Treaties' obligations.

The Court's main function was thus to preserve the inter-institutional balance between the different lawmaking bodies of the Community. There was no hint or suspicion that the Court could actually engage in policymaking in the way that it would later do, and there was no doubt that national governments were the 'masters of the Treaties'.[745]

It was only later that the Court began to play a more central position in defining the Community's legal order. This was largely linked to the increasingly widespread use of the preliminary ruling mechanism (initially established in Article 177 TEEC, now 267 TFEU), which proved crucial in ensuring a more consistent interpretation and implementation of EU law in the Member States.[746] While a large group of scholars (such as neofunctionalists or integrationalists) argue that the Court's case law has over the years abandoned its initial intergovernmentalist approach in favour of a more communitarian orientation, intergovernmentalists disagree. According to the proponents of this theory, the growing importance of the Court's jurisprudence in EU policymaking has not significantly altered the original institutional balance. In particular, they argue that the decisive role of national governments has not substantially diminished and that the CJEU remains committed to ensuring that the Union does not exceed the powers conferred on it by the Member States in the Treaties.[747]

743. *Inter alia, see* G. Garrett, R.D. Kelemen & H. Schulz, 'The European Court of Justice, National Governments, and Legal Integration in the European Union', International Organization, 2(1), pp. 149-176, 1998.
744. K.J. Alter, 'Who Are the "Masters of the Treaty"? European Governments and the European Court of Justice', International Organization, 52(1), pp. 121-147, 1998.
745. *Ibid.*
746. It is sufficient to note that in 2020 the Court of Justice ruled on 556 references for a preliminary ruling and on 37 direct actions, while in 1961 it ruled on 24 direct action and just one reference for a preliminary ruling. *See* Court of Justice of the European Union, Annual Report 2020 – Judicial Activity, Luxembourg, 2021.
747. K.J. Alter, 'Who Are the "Masters of the Treaty"? European Governments and the European Court of Justice', 1998.

2.1 The Realist and the Neorational Variants

Looking more closely at the intergovernmentalist theory, it is possible to identify two main schools of thought: the realist and the neorational doctrines. The realist view is quite radical. It portrays the Member States as having ultimate control over EU policymaking, including the judicial decisions of the CJEU. Realists argue that the Court plays a rather subordinate role to the Member States and that judicial creativity and discretion have played a negligible role in the development of EU law.[748]

For example, Scheingold described the Court as a mere validator of political decisions and contented that EU case law resulted in only minor and indirect policy effects.[749] In a similar vein, Moravcisk argued that the EU integration process is a synthesis of different national interests, which takes place mainly in the meetings of the European Council, where all national governments are represented.[750] Institutions with a more transnational and communitarian nature (such as the European Commission and the CJEU itself), instead, have no real possibility of intervening in the definition of European policies, unless their priorities coincide with the interests of national governments.[751]

The neorational theory shares the realists' view that the Court's reasoning tends to reflect the preferences of the Member States, but adopts a more nuanced perspective. According to Garrett and Weingast, two of the main proponents of neorationalism, accommodating the needs of the Member States is not necessarily the Court's only priority. The dominant rationale of the Court's case law is instead to ensure respect for EU law and to advance the integration process.[752] There is therefore an assonance with integrationalist theories. Neorationalists in fact do not reject the possibility that the Court may adopt judgments that significantly affect the immediate interests of national governments, provided that this is necessary for the proper implementation of the Treaties.[753] However, and this is the main difference with the theories outlined in Chapter 4, Garrett and Weingast contended that what is often perceived as the Court's integrationalist vocation is instead an intrinsic manifestation of Member States' sovereignty. They suggested that even the most 'activist' rulings of the Court assist the Member States to find a point of convergence in their political negotiations and to move

748. A.-M. Burley & W. Mattli, 'Europe Before the Court: A Political Theory of Legal Integration', International Organization, 47(1), pp. 41-76, 1993.
749. S. Scheingold, 'The Law in Political Integration: The Evolution and Integrative Implications of Regional Legal Processes in the European Community', Occasional Paper in International Affairs, 27, Harvard University Centre for International Affairs, 1971.
750. A. Moravcsik, 'Liberal Intergovernmentalism and Integration: A Rejoinder', Journal of Common Market Studies, 33(4), 1995, pp. 611-628, 1993.
751. A. Stone Sweet, *The Judicial Construction of Europe*, Oxford University Press, New York, 2004, p. 16. The author notes that more recently Moravcsik turned to a softer version of intergovernmentalism, closer to neorationalism.
752. G. Garrett, 'The Politics of Legal Integration in the European Union', International Organization, 49(1), pp. 171-181, 1995; G. Garrett & B.R. Weingast, 'Ideas, Interests and Institutions: Constructing the EC Internal Market' in *The Role of Ideas in Foreign Policy*, Cornell University Press, 1993, pp. 173-206.
753. A.-M. Burley & W. Mattli, 'Europe Before the Court: A Political Theory of Legal Integration', 1993.

forward with EU policymaking. The Court's rulings often provide a pretext for activating a political process in which the dominant political proposal will ultimately be the one that finds the most space in the intergovernmental logic that governs the Council and, ultimately, EU rule-making.[754] Thus, although the Court's activism may sometimes appear inconvenient for national governments, it is, in fact, a valuable tool to prevent heads of state from getting embroiled in exhausting and potentially stalling political discussions.[755]

2.2 Member States' Interests in the Court's Reasoning

Among the various scholars who have contributed to the elaboration of the intergovernmental theory (in both its realist and neorational declinations), Garrett has perhaps been one of the most prolific. And, not coincidentally, he is also one of the most prominent critics of neofunctionalism and integrationalism, arguing that these theories overlook the influence of national governments on the Court's reasoning.[756] In a study with Kelemen and Schmitz, Garrett showed that the Court's legal arguments tend to reflect the interests of national governments, whether they are explicitly stated or simply inferred or anticipated by EU judges.[757] More specifically, the authors found that the convergence between the Court's reasoning and the preferences of the national governments is all the more evident in relation to legal issues that are particularly sensitive for the Member States, such as those relating to economic freedoms or to the constitutional order.[758] Moreover, they noted that the legal position of the national governments is more likely to influence the legal reasoning when the Court does not have a strong judicial precedent to rely upon.

Garrett, Kelemen and Schultz's argument is corroborated by Pollack's theory of a principal-agent relationship between the Member States and the Court. According to this narrative, the Court is empowered to deliberate autonomously but, at the same time, the Court is also bound to meet the expectations and political interests of the Member States. Indeed, it was the Member States who originally entrusted the Court with the task of ensuring that the Union acted within, and not beyond, the competences conferred on it by the EU Treaties.[759]

Intergovernmentalism does not necessarily imply a complete assonance between the preferences of the Member States and the policy effects of the Court's judgments.

754. K.J. Alter, 'Who Are the "Masters of the Treaty"? European Governments and the European Court of Justice', 1998.
755. G. Garrett, 'International Cooperation and Institutional Choice: The European Community's Internal Market', International Organization, 46(2), pp. 533-560, 1992.
756. *Ibid.*, G. Garrett, 'The Politics of Legal Integration in the European Union', International Organization, 49(1), pp. 171-181, 1995.
757. G. Garrett, R.D. Kelemen & H. Schulz, 'The European Court of Justice, National Governments, and Legal Integration in the European Union', International Organization, 2(1), pp. 149-176, 1998.
758. *Ibid.*
759. M.A. Pollack, 'Principal-Agent Analysis and International Delegation: Red Herrings, Theoretical Clarifications and Empirical Disputes', Bruges Political Research Paper, 2, College of Europe, Bruges, 2007.

However, its proponents contend that the Court takes into account the interest of the Member States even in those judgments that at prima facie can be regarded as examples of judicial activism. But how is, then, the situation to be interpreted where the question submitted to the Court involves the conflicting interests of several Member States? In that case, whatever conclusion the Court reaches, at least one of the national positions will be undermined. Garrett observed that, in such scenarios, the Court tends to side with the most politically influential states - which he identified as Germany and France, especially in relation to legal issues concerning the functioning of the single market.[760]

Garrett used the example of *Cassis de Dijon* to support his arguments. This is quite interesting for two main reasons. The first is that this judgment had already been taken as example by proponents of neofunctionalist and integrationalist theories to support their different views. The second reason is that, in *Cassis de Dijon*, the Court went against the position of the German authorities.[761] The judgment, in fact, clashed with the decision of the German Federal Administrative Tribunal, which had confirmed the ban on importing the beverage Cassis de Dijon into Germany. It also clashed with the submission of the German government, which had intervened in the proceedings before the Court with arguments in favour of the existing domestic legislation. Still, according to Garrett, the fact that the judgment did not reflect the legal position of the German Federal Administrative Court and the German government does not mean that the Court did not pursue the best interests of the German state. The Court's expansive interpretation of economic freedoms indeed had the effect of liberalising trade between Member States and, ultimately, served well their economic interests.[762] Garrett also noted that Germany was the Member State that benefited the most economically from

760. G. Garrett, 'International Cooperation and Institutional Choice: The European Community's Internal Market', International Organization, 46(2), pp. 533-560, 1992. There, Garrett argued that the primacy of the German and French positions is rooted in the policy choices, that then led to the SEA Treaty (1985) and that had to be adopted in the aftermath of the economic crisis that troubled European and global economic at the end of the 1970s. While all the Member States (12 at the time) convened on the need to boost European competitiveness, there was no agreement on how to reach that objective. Through an extreme simplification, there was a clash between different forms of capitalism. The UK was in favour of total liberalisation and deregulation, Germany and France opted for a selective and controlled approach to internal market integration and the Southern states and Ireland argued for an interventionist internal market and by significant compensatory development assistance. The solution was the outcome of complex negotiations among national representatives and therefore has a strong intergovernmental character. Nevertheless, the position of German and France, that stood in the 'middle' was then transposed in the SEA and thus since then informed EU economic integration.
761. G. Garrett, 'The Politics of Legal Integration in the European Union', International Organization, 49(1), pp. 171-181, p. 174, 1995: 'Thus, even on a generous interpretation, the potential costs of the Cassis decision for the German government were not large. But this does not mean that there were no incentives for the government to fight hard in the ECJ, particularly if the government anticipated that it would eventually lose the case' and 'It would obviously be better for the German government to have the court - rather than the government-further the free trade cause (lest the government be accused of bullying).'
762. A.-M. Burley & W. Mattli, 'Europe Before the Court: A Political Theory of Legal Integration', 1993; W. Phelan, *In Place of Inter-State Retaliation: The European Union's Rejection of WTO-Style Trade Sanctions and Trade Remedies*, Oxford University Press, Oxford, 2015, p. 42.

the principle of mutual recognition established in *Cassis de Dijon* and from the broadening effect on the internal market: 'Germany is the most competitive economy in Europe. As a result, national economic performance would benefit greatly from the removal of further barriers to trade across the continent.'[763]

2.3 Amicus Briefs

A very important tool for Member States to convey to the Court their normative preferences in relation to questions of interpretation is the so-called amicus briefs. Like the Commission's legal opinions, national governments are allowed to intervene in proceedings before the Court and to express legal considerations about the possible resolution of the dispute.[764] Amicus briefs are thus certainly one of the best vectors of national interests, as they allow the Court to be directly exposed to the constellation of political and normative interests that underlie the proceeding. Through amicus briefs, national governments reveal their policy position and may even threaten not to comply with the judgment if the Court does not take into account the legal arguments they suggest.[765] The courtroom can thus be turned into an alternative and unofficial policymaking arena.

Influencing EU law through the judiciary is a rather attractive solution for national governments since, compared to traditional lawmaking, it allows them to avoid long and potentially unsatisfactory political negotiations.[766] Moreover, if a Member State succeeds in directing the Court's reasoning, it is quite difficult to reverse the policy outcome reached in the case law. It is of course always possible to change the effect of a judgment through legislative intervention, but this requires a concerted

763. G. Garrett, 'The Politics of Legal Integration in the European Union', International Organization, 49(1), pp. 171-181, 1995.
764. Article 98 Rules of Procedure of the Court of Justice, listing the actors that are entitled to participate in preliminary ruling proceedings and Article 23 of Statute of the Court. Pursuant to Article 23 of the Statute of the Court, 'In the cases governed by Article 267 TFEU, the decision of the court or tribunal of a Member State which suspends its proceedings and refers a case to the Court of Justice shall be notified to the Court by the court or tribunal concerned. The decision shall then be notified by the Registrar of the Court to the parties, to the Member States and to the Commission [...]. Within two months of this notification [...] the Member states [...] shall be entitled to submit statements of case or written observation to the Court.'
765. For a deeper analysis of the possible Member States' reactions to EU case law from the point of view of the Court of Justice: G. Garrett, R.D. Kelemen & H. Schulz, 'The European Court of Justice, National Governments, and Legal Integration in the European Union', International Organization, 2(1), pp. 149-176, 1998.
766. The fact that national governments submit observation to the Court in order to advance their policy preferences is also supported by S.A. Nyikos, 'The European Court of Justice and National Courts: Strategic Interaction Within the EU Judicial Process', University of Virginia, 2000. The author conducted a study on 579 CJEU decisions and notes that governments' observations are likely to disagree with the preemptive opinions eventually formulated by the referring national judge. Through the amicus briefs, the national government provides counterarguments and tries to reduce the impact of alternative legal solutions. *See* p. 30: '[...] when the national court sends a preliminary opinion and the Member State sends written observation, the Member State government is most likely to disagree with the court's interpretation (69.6%)'.

effort on the part of national governments, which can only be achieved quickly in the case of particularly controversial rulings.

This contributes to explaining the tendency of certain national governments to submit legal opinions even in proceedings that do not directly concern their own legal system. A perfect example is the UK government, which has produced a very high number of amicus briefs both in proceedings concerning domestic legislation and in proceedings concerning the legislation of other Member States.[767] In this regard, it is interesting to look at the results of a study conducted by Cichowski on the Court's judgments in the social and labour policy field from 1976 to 2003. Cichowski collected data on Member States submitting legal observations in situations where that state's legislation was not directly at issue (either because national legislation was not subject to scrutiny by the Court in infringement proceedings or because the reference for a preliminary ruling originated in another country). The study found that the UK government had presented amicus briefs in almost half of the cases (44% of the preliminary rulings submitted by UK courts).[768] Most interestingly, from the study it emerged that the UK legal services, in their amicus briefs, sought to steer the reasoning of the CJEU towards more regressive positions, in line with the political views of the UK government at the time in the Council.

While judicial proceedings before the Court can become an avenue for national governments to advance their own normative and political agenda, not all governments demonstrate the same propensity to interact with the Court. In the time frame considered by the study, Cichowski found a wide variability. The UK had the most 'active' legal services with 136 amicus briefs presented, while the Luxembourgian government only intervened in two proceedings.[769] To explain the different approaches of the Member States, Dederke and Naurin identified two factors that appear to increase the likelihood of amicus brief submission by a national government.[770] First, there is the salience of the case, meaning the anticipated relevance of the policy implications for the national legal system and the national economy, as well as for the evolution of the EU integration. As remarked by Bierrernan and Wissel (who for years worked as officers in the EU litigation teams of the Dutch government), the salience of the case can also be measured in terms of its financial repercussions for the government.[771]

The second factor, according to Dederke and Naurin, is the size of the country, both in terms of territory and population. The bigger the Member State, the more resources it can convey to its legal services in Luxembourg.[772] Similarly, the likelihood

767. *Ibid.*
768. R.A. Cichowski, *The European Court and Civil Society: Litigation, Mobilization and Governance – Themes in European Governance*, Cambridge University Press, Cambridge, 2007, pp. 86-87.
769. *Ibid.*, p. 86.
770. J. Dederke & D. Naurin, 'Friends of the Court? Why EU Governments File Observations Before the Court of Justice', European Journal of Political Research, 57, pp. 867-882, 2018.
771. M. Bulterman & C. Wissels, 'Strategies Developed By – And Between – National Governments to Interact with the ECJ' in B. de Witte, B. Muir & E. Dawson (eds), *Judicial Activism at the European Court of Justice*, Edward Elgar Publishing, Cheltenham, 2013, pp. 264-278.
772. J. Dederke & D. Naurin, 'Friends of the Court? Why EU Governments File Observations Before the Court of Justice', 2018.

that the judges of a given state make a reference to the Court is generally proportional to the amount of national proceedings that are instituted before the national judiciary. This, too, often depends on the population and on the size of a country. The larger and more populated a country is, the more courts there are, and the more legislation is generated. Dederke and Naurin supported their argument with an empirical study carried over the reference period 1997-2007, which showed that most amicus briefs come from some of the largest or most populated countries in the EU, at least before its eastern enlargement (the UK, Germany, France, Italy and the Netherlands respectively).[773]

2.4 The Ability of National Governments to Redirect the Court's Jurisprudence

According to the intergovernmental perspective, the Court's consideration for the Member States' preferences is linked to the awareness that the effectiveness of EU judgments depends largely on their acceptance at the national level. When the Court's rulings are particularly at odds with the domestic legal order, there is a risk that they will not be properly implemented or even ignored.[774] Even more radically, if the Court's rulings clash with the direct preferences of national governments, the latter may decide to take institutional action to counteract the undesirable jurisprudential effects.[775] This can be done by initiating EU legislation, or by amending existing laws in order to neutralise the most critical aspects of the Court's pronouncements. More peremptorily, judicial 'restraint' can also lead to a reform of the EU Treaties.

It is precisely to avoid this kind of recalcitrance that, according to the intergovernmental narrative, the Court prefers not to collide with Member States' preferences. Admittedly, if the Court did actually have similar concerns, they would not be merely conjectural, as there are significant precedents. A remarkable example of the ability of national governments to 'rebel' against the Court's activism can be found in the

773. *Ibid.* Poland was excluded from the Dederke and Naurin's analysis since the country only joined the EU in 2006. The study also shows that Malta, Bulgaria, Slovenia and Luxembourg, which are among the smallest Member States, are the countries that presented the lowest number of amicus briefs. However, it should be noted that both Cichowski's and Dederke and Naurin's studies provide only a partial picture of the national governments' rate of participation into the Court's proceedings, since they don't consider that certain Member States have acceded/entered into the EU at a later stage. They also did not explore whether there is a possible connection between the high number of amicus briefs originating from UK, Germany, France, Italy and the Netherlands and the fact that five over these six countries are also the founding Member States of the European Communities.

774. W. Mattli & A.-M. Slaughter, 'Revisiting the European Court of Justice', International Organization, 52(1), pp. 177-209, 1998, with reference to Garrett's work.

775. G. Garrett, R.D. Kelemen & H. Schulz, 'The European Court of Justice, National Governments, and Legal Integration in the European Union', 1998. *See also* A. Stone Sweet, *The Judicial Construction of Europe*, Oxford University Press, New York, 2004, p. 16, where the author suggests that spill-over effect depends on the extent to which national governments are willing to endorse the policy outcome of the Court's case law. Or, L.J. Conant, *Justice Contained: Law and Politics in the European Union*, Cornell University Press, Ithaca, New York, 2018, pp. 50-95, where the author noticed that the policy effect of the Court of Justice's case law can be constrained.

political response that followed the *Barber* judgment. The Member States' reaction was so intense that eventually led to the ratification of the so-called Barber Protocol, as an annex to the Maastricht Treaty.[776] As already mentioned in Chapter 4, section 3.2.2.2, with the *Barber* judgment the Court considerably broadened the scope of the principle of equal pay for men and women established in Article 119 TEEC (now 157 TFEU). In this decision, the Court ruled that the concept of 'pay' was to be understood as including pension payments even when the pension fund is not set up and administered by the employer but by a third party, which was a common structure covering a significant portion of pension schemes.[777] The Court also ruled that 'the application of the principle of equal pay must be ensured in respect of each element of remuneration and not only on the basis of a comprehensive assessment of the consideration paid to workers'.[778]

This judgment was particularly controversial because it required the adaptation of the pension systems in several Member States, with considerable financial consequences. It was of little value that the Court limited the temporal effect of its judgment to only employment relationships established after the judgment, with the exception of 'workers who before the date of the judgments had initiated legal proceedings or raised an equivalent claim'.[779] Fearing that the *Barber* case was a prelude to even more interventionist case law in the field of social security and pension systems, Member States decided not to take any further risks. They seized the opportunity offered by the intergovernmental negotiations that preceded the adoption of the Maastricht Treaty and signed a protocol (hence called the 'Barber Protocol') on the interpretation of Article 119 TEEC. With a wording stricter than that of the Court, national governments reiterated that the *Barber* judgment has effect only in relation to future employment relationships. The objective was clearly to contain once and for all the regulatory implications and financial repercussions of the Court's case law on non-discrimination and social security systems.[780]

776. Protocol concerning Article 119 of the Treaty establishing the European Community: "For the purposes of Art. [141] of this Treaty, benefits under occupational social security schemes shall not be considered as remuneration if and in so far as they are attributable to periods of employment prior to May 17, 1990 [the date of the ECJ's ruling in Barber], except in the case of workers [...] who have before that date initiated legal proceedings or raised an equivalent claim under the applicable national law." *See also* T. Horsley, *The Court of Justice of the European Union as and Institutional Actor: Judicial Lawmaking and Its Limits*, Cambridge University Press, New York, 2018, p. 233, where the author noted that the Member States insert Protocols to the Treaties to intervene and limit the scope of the Court of Justice policy making.
777. Judgment of 17 May 1990, *Douglas Harvey Barber v. Guardian Royal Exchange Assurance Group*, C-262/88, ECLI:EU:C:1990:209.
778. C-262/88, *Barber* (para. 35). M. Höreth, 'The Least Dangerous Branch of European Governance? The European Court of Justice under the Checks and Balances Doctrine' in B. de Witte, B. Muir & E. Dawson (eds), *Judicial Activism at the European Court of Justice*, Edward Elgar Publishing, Cheltenham, 2013, pp. 32-56; G. Conway, *The Limits of Legal Reasoning and the European Court of Justice*, Cambridge University Press, Cambridge, 2012, p. 97.
779. C-262/88, *Barber* (para. 45).
780. T. Horsley, *The Court of Justice of the European Union as and Institutional Actor: Judicial Lawmaking and Its Limits*, Cambridge University Press, New York, 2018, p. 231, where the author referred to the Barber protocol as an example of Member State interventions to recast judicial policy choices. Horsley identified further examples in the Treaties reforms occurring as

An analysis of the Court's subsequent case law indicates that the Member States' initiative had the desired effect. The *Barber* case was in fact the last judgment in which the Court adopted a particularly broad interpretation of the concept of 'equal pay'.[781] It would take more than a decade for the Court to show again signs of judicial activism regarding the principle of non-discrimination in the employment relation context.[782]

2.5 Weaknesses of the Intergovernmental Theory

The intergovernmental theory has provoked intense academic debate. Several scholars, including Stone Sweet and Alter, have expressed doubts about the ability of national governments to influence the Court's legal reasoning. According to Stone Sweet, the major weakness of Garrett's theory is the biased perspective on the Court's decision-making, as it focuses exclusively on the role of national governments, with the result that other potentially relevant dynamics are overlooked.[783] Moreover, Alter observed that, while it is true that the Court was originally constituted to oversee that the European Community did not go beyond its competences, over time its reasonings moved away from intergovernmental logics.[784] This has been possible because the judicial activity of the Court and the policymaking of political institutions are characterised by radically different time frames. National governments derive their authority from their electoral mandate and tend to follow the pace of politics, which imposes a relatively short-term agenda. This is not the case for the CJEU, whose legitimacy is instead linked to the impact and effectiveness of its case law. As Alter noted, the judicial construction of Europe is made up of small steps, but their effects reverberate and evolve over time.[785]

The Court's advantage over institutional rule-making is that the policy impact of case law is generally incremental and therefore not immediately perceptible. As national governments tend to focus only on the immediate policy implications, only clearly disruptive judgments catch the policymakers' attention and trigger their

response to the case law on capital movement and on positive action in relation to non-discrimination on the ground of gender.

781. A. Stone Sweet, *The Judicial Construction of Europe*, Oxford University Press, New York, 2004, p. 170.
782. O. Pollicino, *Discriminazione sulla Base del Sesso e Trattamento Preferenziale nel Diritto Comunitario*, Giuffrè, Milano, 2005.
783. A. Stone Sweet, *The Judicial Construction of Europe*, 2004, p. 17. The author's position is opposite to intergovernmentalism: Member States' preferences have no relevant weight for the Court of Justice. Instead, the Court tends to expand the effectiveness of EU law and the scope of supranational governance.
784. K.J. Alter, 'Who Are the "Masters of the Treaty"? European Governments and the European Court of Justice', International Organization, 52(1), pp. 121-147, 1998.
785. *Ibid.* The Court's doctrinal precedents are described as building blocks which allowed the Court's judgments as well as the European integration process that descended from those judgments to emancipate from the initially envisaged intergovernmental character. The author explains that even when Member States disagreed with the Court's judicial activism, they were institutionally unable to reverse the most crucial doctrines, such as the doctrines of direct effect and supremacy of EU law – which led to an intense and decentralised judicial review on the compatibility of national law with EU law.

eventual opposition.[786] As mentioned in Chapter 4, section 2.3, these different time-frames of action and reaction have enabled the Court to introduce and consolidate key principles that have ultimately shaped EU integration. Suffice to recall the principles of direct effect, primacy of EC law, disapplication of non-coherent national law, non-contractual liability for failure to implement EU law, and so on.

Moreover, Alter noted that one of the greatest 'oversight' of national governments was to allow the Court to expend the reach of the preliminary reference mechanism. In doing so, they also indirectly permitted the Court to interfere in national and EU legal systems. Preliminary rulings have, in fact, been crucial for the strengthening of the Court's legitimacy as a supranational court, as noted in Chapter 4, section 2.2.[787] At the same time, through a broad interpretation of the admissibility of references for preliminary rulings, the Court promoted a decentralised judicial review of the national legislation as to its compatibility with EU law.[788] National lower (or district) judges were in fact given the opportunity to assess whether national law respected EU law. In case of uncertainty, the Court's case law empowered them to bypass the national superior courts and to directly refer a preliminary question to the CJEU. By establishing this dialogical relationship with national judges, the CJEU has undoubtedly weakened the relevance of intergovernmental dynamics. The fact that the Court has, over the years, continued to expand the scope of the preliminary ruling mechanism is therefore in stark contrast to the intergovernmental narrative. If national governments are able to influence the decision-making of the CJEU so significantly, then it is not clear why they would have deliberately consented to the emergence of potentially disruptive trans-judicial dynamics.[789] It is more likely that national governments were unaware of, or did not have the means to counteract the process of judicial empowerment resulting from the expansion of the reach of the preliminary ruling mechanism through the case law of the Court of Justice.

As Horsley pointed out, another notable episode in which the Court has shown itself to be unconcerned with the regulatory preferences of national governments is the Court Opinion 2/13 on the draft agreement on the EU accession to the European Court of Human Rights (ECHR).[790] The draft agreement in question was negotiated by the Commission on a mandate from the Member States and was intended to implement Article 6(2) TEU, establishing that 'The Union shall accede to the European Convention for the Protection of Human Rights and Fundamental Freedoms. Such accession shall not affect the Union's competences as defined in the Treaties.' It is important to bear in

786. K. Alter, 'The European Court's Political Power: The Emergence of an Authoritative International Court in the European Union' in K. Alter (ed.), *The European Court's Political Power – Selected Essays*, Oxford University Press, Oxford, 2009, pp. 92-109.
787. J. Pertek, *La Pratique du Renvoi Préjudiciel en Droit Communautaire*, Litec, Paris, 2001, p. 21.
788. *Ibid.*
789. C-6/64, *Costa v. Enel*; C-26/62, *Van Gend en Loos*. In doing so, the Court has been careful not to (excessively) encroach on sensitive aspects of the national systems, and refrained from adopting reasonings that could cause immediate set-back in the integration process.
790. Judgment of 18 December 2014, *Opinion pursuant to Article 218(11) TFEU – Draft international agreement – Accession of the European Union to the European Convention for the Protection of Human Rights and Fundamental Freedoms – Compatibility of the draft agreement with the EU and FEU Treaties*, C-2/13, ECLI:EU:C:2014:48.

mind that the national delegations negotiating the Lisbon Treaty decided to introduce Article 6 TEU in light of the Court's previous Opinion 2/94.[791] In that earlier opinion, the Court had in fact stated that the EU could not accede to the ECHR until the Treaties provided an adequate legal basis. It was therefore quite surprising that, although the Lisbon Treaty now provided a clear legal basis, and despite the fact that national governments had specifically taken steps to negotiate an accession agreement, in Opinion 2/13, the Court still found that the agreement was incompatible with the EU Treaty.[792] As Horsely observed: 'the Full Court was absolutely clear in its decision that whatever the Member States has/have agreed as constituent authorities, the terms of the EU's accession to the ECHR must fully respect the integrity of its particular normative view'.[793]

Another weakness of intergovernmental theory is the scant empirical support.[794] Burley and Mattli raised this objection, particularly in relation to the *Cassis de Dijon* case, which Garrett had included among the intergovernmentalism examples. Burley and Mattli argued that the fact that the Court reached a conclusion that was substantially different from that proposed by the German government was a clear indication of the lack of intergovernmentalist logic in the Court's reasoning.[795] In their view, it would be rather bold to interpret any beneficial effects that the principle of mutual recognition might have had for the German economy as a validation of the intergovernmental thesis. This would mean attributing to the Court a strategic and predictive thinking that is not within its competence or capacity. Furthermore, Burley and Mattli observed that the *Cassis de Dijon* ruling found widespread opposition among the various national governments. It indeed took some time before national governments accepted the principle of mutual recognition. This seems to indicate that the economic

791. Judgment of 28 March 1996, *Accession by the Community to the European Convention for the Protection of Human Rights and Fundamental Freedoms*, C-2/94, ECLI:EU:C:1996:140.
792. A. Jacobs, 'The Janus Head of the European Union: The Social Market Economy Versus Ultraliberal Policies' in J. Wouters, L. Verhey & P. Kiiver (eds), *European Constitutionalism Beyond Lisbon*, Intersentia, Cambridge, 2009.
793. T. Horsley, *The Court of Justice of the European Union as and Institutional Actor: Judicial Lawmaking and Its Limits*, 2018, pp. 145-147, where the author observed that: 'The Full Court was absolutely clear in its decision that, whatever Member States has agreed as constituent authorities, the terms of the EU's accession to the ECHR must fully respect the integrity of its particular normative view.'
794. A.-M. Burley & W. Mattli, 'Europe Before the Court: A Political Theory of Legal Integration', 1993.
795. C-120/78, *Cassis de Dijon* (paras 10 and 12). *Ibid.*, where Burley and Mattli advance this objection, in G. Garrett, 'The Politics of Legal Integration in the European Union', International Organization, 49(1), pp. 171-181, 1995 Garrett explained that the position of the German government in the *Cassis de Dijon* case did not reflect the actual position of Germany vis-à-vis exportation of goods and the mutual recognition principle. Garrett indeed argued that Germany's opposition to the principle in the *Cassis de Dijon* case was part of a sophisticated political strategy that led the Council to adopt a stance which was, finally, in line with Germany's interests. According to Garrett, by showing discontent in the aftermath of the *Cassis de Dijon* decision, the consent of the German government to the mutual recognition principle was perceived as a concession, while ultimately such principle is/was ultimately beneficial for German economy.

liberalisation that followed *Cassis de Dijon* took place in spite of – and not as a result of – the preferences of national governments on this issue.[796]

Hatzopoulos also criticised the intergovernmentalist tenet that the Court would tend to favour the most influential state in the event of a clash between national interests. This, Hatzopoulous noted, seems inconsistent with the fact that only a few of the thousands of judgments handed down by the Court have been criticised for preferring one Member State over another.[797] Poor empirical evidence emerges also from the analysis conducted by Nyikos and Cichowski. Their studies show no inclination on the part of the Court to go along with the legal arguments put forward by national governments in their amicus briefs. Nyikos analysed a selection of 579 cases and concluded that the Member States are quite ineffective in persuading the Court. More precisely, the author observed that 'of those actors that have the ability through written and oral observation to influence the CJEU, Member States have empirically had the least effect upon the ECJ's decisional calculus'.[798] Cichowski focused on the case law in the field of social and labour policies between 1971 and 2003 and reached similar conclusions. Her research suggests that the probability of national governments successfully preempting the Court's decision is between 40% and 70%.[799] Cichowski also indicated that 'the Commission's observations predict ECJ rulings far better than do observations filed by Member State governments' and that this 'bring[s] into question claims that the ECJ decisions are systematically influenced by the policy positions of the Member States'.[800] It was actually observed that, almost ironically, the higher the number of national governments submitting amicus briefs, the less likely is that the Court finds a national rule compliant with EU law.[801] These results apply regardless of the financial implications that the Court's judgments have on the finances of the state. Cichowski found that, even in the most 'financially important' cases, the Court disregarded the legal arguments proposed by the national governments in 57% of the cases.[802] However, it is interesting to note that empirical studies do not lead to unequivocal results. In an already mentioned study from 2021, Ovádek sought to

796. A.-M. Burley & W. Mattli, 'Europe Before the Court: A Political Theory of Legal Integration', International Organization, 47(1), pp. 41-76, 1993.
797. V. Hatzopoulos, 'Actively Talking to Each Other: The Court and the Political Institutions' in B. de Witte, B. Muir & E. Dawson (eds), *Judicial Activism at the European Court of Justice*, Edward Elgar Publishing, Cheltenham, 2013, pp. 102-141.
798. S.A. Nyikos, 'The European Court of Justice and National Courts: Strategic Interaction within the EU Judicial Process', University of Virginia, 2000, p. 34. The empirical study revealed that the 'ECJ agreed with the Commission across areas of law 72.4%, the national court 57.4% and the Member State government of the country in which the case originated 44.1% of the time.'
799. R.A. Cichowski, *The European Court and Civil Society: Litigation, Mobilization and Governance; Themes in European Governance*, Cambridge University Press, Cambridge, 2007, pp. 85-88.
800. *Ibid.* (Table 3.4 p. 86).
801. A. Stone Sweet, *The Judicial Construction of Europe*, 2004, pp. 187, 188: 'In cases where four or more Member States participate in the argument stage of the proceedings, the Court has found for the plaintiff 60 per cent of the time; in cases where only one Member State intervenes, the Court does so only 52 per cent of the time.'
802. R.A. Cichowski, *The European Court and Civil Society: Litigation, Mobilization and Governance; Themes in European Governance*, 2007, pp. 88, 89.

reveal the Court's institutional preferences and created a dataset of judgments concerning inter-institutional disputes (hence, no preliminary rulings were considered). The data showed that the Court is not immune to intergovernmental dynamics, as it is 'sensitive to the number of Member States signalling their stance on a case through interventions'.[803]

To conclude, intergovernmental theory has found support but also (fierce) criticism. The next section illustrates alternative theories developed by legal scholars that share with intergovernmentalism the view that the Court is influenced by the national context. The focus, however, this time is not placed on the political preferences of the national governments but on the legal practices emerging from the national regulatory context.[804]

3 THE RELEVANCE OF NATIONAL LEGAL SYSTEMS IN THE COURT'S REASONING

The national context can influence the Court's reasoning even without direct pressure from national governments. Legal scholars such as Maduro, Weiler, Cartabia, Walker, Pollicino, Lenaerts and Martinico, among others, have observed that the Court tends to be influenced by the legal and constitutional systems of the Member States.[805] The coexistence, within the EU, of a multiplicity of divergent national systems and the frequent risk of constitutional conflicts, made the Court aware and attentive to national normative sensitivities. According to this perspective, the Court generally refrains from adopting rulings that are likely to encounter significant resistance at the national level. It rather opts for legal arguments that conform, at least in part, with the characteristics of national legal systems and can therefore be easily assimilated into the national regulatory context.[806]

803. M. Ovádek, 'Supranationalism, Constrained? Locating the Court of Justice on the EU Integration Dimension', European Union Politics, 22(1), pp. 46-69, 2021.

804. O. Pollicino, 'Corte di giustizia e giudici nazionali: il moto "ascendente", ovverosia l'incidenza delle "tradizioni costituzionali comuni" nella tutela apprestata ai diritti dalla Corte dell'Unione', 1, Consulta Online, 2015; M. Poiares Maduro, 'Contrapunctual Law: Europe's Constitutional Pluralism in Action' in N. Walker (ed.), *Sovereignty in Transition*, Hart Publishing, Portland, 2003, pp. 501-537; B. Guastaferro, 'Beyond the Exceptionalism of Constitutional Conflicts: The Ordinary Functions of the Identity Clause', Yearbook of European Law, 31(1), pp. 263-318, 2012.

805. *Ibid. See also, inter alia*: N. Walker, 'The Idea of Constitutional Pluralism', The Modern Law Review, 65(3), pp. 317-359, 2002; J.H.H. Weiler, 'The Community System: The Dual Character of Supranationalism', Yearbook of European Law, 1(1), pp. 267-306, 1981; J. H. H. Weiler, 'Prologue: Global and Pluarlist Constitutionalism – Some Doubts' in Gròinne de Burca & J.H.J. Weiler (eds), *The Worlds of European Constitutionialism*, Cambridge University Press, Cambridge, 2012, pp. 8-19; K. Lenaerts, 'Interpretation and the Court of Justice: A Basis for Comparative Reflection', The International Lawyer, 41(4), pp. 1011-1032, 2007.

806. N. Walker, 'Late Sovereignty in the European Union' in N. Walker (ed.), *Sovereignty in Transition*, Hart Publishing, Portland, 2003, pp. 3-32; M. Kumm & V. Ferreres Comella, 'The Primacy Clause of the Constitutional Treaty and the Future of Constitutional Conflict in the European Union', International Journal of Constitutional Law, 3(2-3), pp. 473-492, 2005; N. Walker, 'The Idea of Constitutional Pluralism', The Modern Law Review, 65(3), pp. 317-359, 2002; M. Poiares Maduro, 'Interpreting European Law: Judicial Adjudication in a Context of

3.1 The Common Constitutional Traditions of the Member States

The perception of the Court as sensitive to the various (potentially conflicting) national legal traditions also implies that the Court adopts a pacifying and harmonising approach. According to this view, the Court is indeed portrayed as careful to ensure the coexistence of an expansive EU legal system with its multi-jurisdictional and multi-constitutional framework.[807] This irenic attitude finds its origins in the Court's awareness of the importance of obtaining a degree of tolerance on the part of the national regulatory authorities. Without a positive relationship with the national normative context, the Court's legitimacy and interpretative authority within the Union may in fact be jeopardised.[808]

According to this line of thought, to achieve the necessary acquiescence and openness on the part of national legal systems, the Court began to display a certain reverence towards the fundamental and constitutional principles of the various national legal systems.[809] Initially, this found expression in the valorisation of the 'constitutional traditions common to the Member States' which became one of the main sources of inspiration for the Court.[810] References to the constitutional traditions were often embedded in comparative reasoning, to guide the Court's interpretation of EC law.[811] This approach allowed the Court to strengthen the acceptance of its rulings

Constitutional Pluralism', European Journal of Legal Studies, 1(2), pp. 1-21, 2008; S. Sankari, 'Constitutional Pluralism and Judicial Adjudication: On Legal Reasoning, Minimalism and Silence by the Court of Justice' in G. Davies & M. Avbelj (eds), *Research Handbook on Legal Pluralism and EU Law*, Edward Elgar Publishing, Cheltenham, 2018, pp. 309-322.

807. K. Lenaerts, 'Interlocking Legal Orders in the European Union and Comparative Law', International and Comparative Law Quarterly, 52, pp. 873-906, 2003: '[...] The European Union, which centrally rests on the Community legal order, has its own variant of "E pluribus unum", that is a set of interlocking legal orders showing mutual respect for each other based on equivalent levels of judicial protection of the rule of law.'
808. O. Pollicino, *Allargamento dell'Europa a est e rapporto tra Corti costituzionali e Corti europee*, Giuffrè, Milano, 2010, p. 60; J.H.H. Weiler, 'Federalism Without Constitutionalism: Europe's Sonderweg' in K. Nicolaïdis & R. Howse (eds), *The Federal Vision: Legitimacy and Levels of Governance in the United States and the European Union*, Oxford University Press, Oxford, 2001, p. 68: 'Constitutional actors in the Member State accept the European constitutional discipline not because as a matter of legal doctrine, as is the case in the federal state [...]. They accept it as an autonomous voluntary act, endlessly renewed on each occasion, of subordination, in the discrete areas governed by Europe to a norm which is the aggregate expression of other wills, other political identities, other political communities. [...] When acceptance and subordination is voluntary, and repeatedly so, it constitutes an act of true liberty and emancipation from collective self-arrogance and constitutional fetishism: a high expression of Constitutional Tolerance.'
809. O. Pollicino, *Discriminazione sulla Base del Sesso e Trattamento Preferenziale nel Diritto Comunitario*, Giuffrè, Milano, 2005, p. 14.
810. K. Lenaerts, 'Interlocking Legal Orders in the European Union and Comparative Law', 2003.
811. O. Pollicino, *Allargamento dell'Europa a est e rapporto tra Corti costituzionali e Corti europee*, Giuffrè, Milano, 2010, p. 56; A. Stone Sweet & T. Brunell, 'Constructing a Supranational Constitution', The American Political Science Review, 92(1), pp. 63-81, 1998; O. Pollicino, 'Corte di giustizia e giudici nazionali: il moto "ascendente", ovverosia l'incidenza delle "tradizioni costituzionali comuni" nella tutela apprestata ai diritti dalla Corte dell'Unione', 1, Consulta Online, 2015; K. Lenaerts, 'Some Thoughts about the Interaction Between Judges and Politicians', University of Chicago Legal Forum, 1, pp. 93-1331, 1992; G. Martinico, 'The "Polemical" Spirit of European Constitutional Law: On the Importance of Conflicts in EU Law',

within the Member States while, step by step, expanding the EU legal system.[812] As Pollicino noted, the legal traditions of the Member States had become one of the main sources of inspiration for the Court's case law.

A clear example of the Court's consideration for the national constitutional traditions can be found in the EU case law on fundamental rights.[813] It all began with the *Stauder* judgment, in which the Court established that it had the jurisdiction to rule on the respect of fundamental rights on the grounds that they are part of the general principles of law of the Member States.[814] With this argument, the Court bypassed the limited competences conferred by the Treaty of Rome, where no mention of fundamental rights was made. Later, in the *Internationale Handelsgesellschaft*, the Court further specified that its approach to fundamental rights drew from the constitutional traditions common to the Member States.[815] It is also interesting to note that in *Internationale Handelsgesellschaft* the Court had, for the first time, affirmed that Community law had primacy over the constitutional law of the Member States. The reference to the 'common constitutional traditions of the Member States' could thus have been a way, for the Court, to moderate its interpretative boldness and increase the acceptance of the primacy principle at the national level.[816]

On the one hand, the Court sought the expansion of European integration beyond the competences of the Treaty. On the other hand, the Court softened its ruling with references to the national constitutional orders. The reference to constitutional traditions of the Member States gradually became a stable characteristic of the Court's

German Law Journal, 16(6), pp. 1343-1374, 2015; M. Cartabia, 'Europe and Rights: Taking Dialogue Seriously', European Constitutional Law Review, 5, pp. 5-31, 2009.

812. U. Sadl, 'Does the Court of Justice Make Law in Small Steps? (Circumstantial) Evidence from the Free Movement of Persons Jurisprudence', Paper presented at the EUI Faculty Seminar, EUI, 2020.

813. P. Pescatore, 'Le recours, dans la jurisprudence de la Cour de justice des Communautés européennes, à des normes déduites de la comparaison des droits des Etats membres', Revue internationale de droit comparé, 32(2), pp. 337-359, 1980; G. Conway, *The Limits of Legal Reasoning and the European Court of Justice*, Cambridge University Press, Cambridge, 2012, p. 29.

814. Judgment of 12 November 1969, *Erich Stauder v. City of Ulm – Sozialamt*, C-29/69, ECLI: EU:C:1969:57, p. 422: 'The protection guaranteed by fundamental rights is, as regards Community law, assured by various provisions in the Treaty, such as Article 7 and 40(3); this is written law supplemented in its turn by unwritten Community law, derived from the general principles of law in force in Member States.' It is interesting to note that a reference to the law of the Member States has the effect to partially compensate the boldness that the Court shown in the previous paragraph, where it stated that Community law could only be assessed with reference to the general principles of EC law: 'The question put to the Court concerns the compatibility of the contested measure with the general principles of Community law in force. This is in fact the only law with which it could be concerned because Community institutions are subject only to that law and the Court of Justice can only examine regulations adopted by those institutions in light of that law.'

815. C-11/70, *Internationale Handelsgesellschaft* (para. 4): '[...] respect for fundamental rights forms an integral part of the general principles of law protected by the Court of Justice. The protection of such rights, whilst inspired by the constitutional traditions common to the Member States, must be ensure within the framework of the structure and objective of the Community'.

816. *Inter alia*, O. Pollicino, *Allargamento dell'Europa a est e rapporto tra Corti costituzionali e Corti europee*, 2010, pp. 55-56.

fundamental rights jurisprudence.[817] The influence of the national constitutional context on the Court is particularly evident in *Nold*.[818] There, the Court established that 'In safeguarding these [fundamental rights], the Court is bound to draw inspiration from the constitutional traditions common to the Member States, and it cannot therefore uphold measures which are incompatible with fundamental rights recognised and protected by the constitutions of those states.'[819] Similarly, in *Hauer*, the Court compared different national constitutional frameworks to inform its interpretation of the right to property and the freedom to conduct a business.[820]

The hermeneutical approach based on the common constitutional traditions was overall received positively by national rule-makers and, following the ratification of the Maastricht Treaty, it was formalised in Article 6 TEU.[821] As noted by Lenaerts, by using the common national constitutional traditions as a source of argumentative inspiration, the Court allowed national normative frameworks to contaminate its reasoning and, in turn, the entire EU legal system.[822] However, several legal scholars, among which Pollicino, Cartabia and Maduro, noticed that this interpretative approach had over time become unsustainable for the Court.[823] One reason was that the first wave of EEC enlargement following the accession of new Member States made the comparative technique more difficult to implement. This aggravated the difficulties that the Court was experiencing in reconciling the different national legal traditions, particularly in relation to those judgments concerning market freedoms. There, the situation was in fact often characterised by a clash between the interests of an exporting Member State

817. P. Pescatore, 'Le recours, dans la jurisprudence de la Cour de justice des Communautés européennes, à des normes déduites de la comparaison des droits des Etats membres', Revue internationale de droit comparé, 32(2), pp. 337-359, 1980; A. Stone Sweet, *The Judicial Construction of Europe*, 2004, p. 88.
818. Judgment of 14 May 1974, *J. Nold, Kohlen- und Baustoffgroßhandlung v. Ruhrkohle Aktiengesellschaft*, C-4/73, ECLI:EU:C1974:51.
819. *Ibid.* (para. 13). *See also* G.F. Mancini, 'The Making of a Constitution for Europe', Common Market Law Review, 26(4), pp. 595-614, p. 610, 1989.
820. Judgment of 13 December 1979, *Liselotte Hauer v. Land Rheinland-Pfalz*, C-44/79, ECLI: EU:C:1979:290 (para. 20): '[...] it is necessary to consider also the indications provide by the consider also the indications provided by the constitutional rules and practices of the nine Member States'.
821. Article 6(3) TEU: 'Fundamental rights, as guaranteed by the European Convention for the Protection of Human Rights and Fundamental Freedoms and as they result from the constitutional traditions common to the Member States, shall constitute general principles of the Unions' law.' Among the multiple instances, *see* Judgment of 15 May 1986, *Marguerite Johnston v. Chief Constable of the Royal Ulster Constabulary*, C-222/84, ECLI:EU:C:1986:206. The case concerns a provision of UK procedural law establishing that, in certain cases, the acts of the political authorities can be exempted from a judicial scrutiny on the respect of the principle of non-discrimination. The Court referred to the constitutional traditions common to the Member States and ruled that EC law prevented the derogation to the principle of non-discrimination established in the UK provision. More recently, in judgment of 8 September 2015, *Criminal proceedings against Ivo Taricco and Others*, C-105/14, ECLI:EU:C:2015:555.
822. K. Lenaerts, 'Interlocking Legal Orders in the European Union and Comparative Law', International and Comparative Law Quarterly, 52, pp. 873-906, 2003.
823. M. Poiares Maduro, 'Interpreting European Law: Judicial Adjudication in a Context of Constitutional Pluralism', European Journal of Legal Studies, 1(2), pp. 1-21, 2008; O. Pollicino, 'Corte di giustizia e giudici nazionali: il moto "ascendente", ovverosia l'incidenza delle "tradizioni costituzionali comuni" nella tutela apprestata ai diritti dalla Corte dell'Unione', 2015; M. Cartabia, 'Europe and Rights: Taking Dialogue Seriously', 2009.

and those of an importing Member State. It thus appeared more complex to contain the deterioration of the trust and tolerance of national judicial and constitutional authorities, which had meanwhile found expression in German and Italian constitutional jurisprudence.[824] It suffices to mention that in the *Solange I* and *Granital* rulings (that are further discussed in sections 4.4.1.1, 4.4.1.2, and 4.4.1.3), the German and Italian constitutional judges set a number of limits to the expansive force of EU law on national systems.[825]

The emergence of these dynamics led the Court to adjust its approach and to replace the mere (and sometimes just cosmetic) reference to common constitutional traditions with greater self-restraint and complacency towards the national regulatory frameworks.[826] From an analysis of the academic literature, it emerges that there are two distinct judicial strategies that the Court has employed to recover the lost margin of constitutional openness. These are the majoritarian (section 3.2) and the pluralistic approaches (section 3.3).

3.2 The Majoritarian Approach

The majoritarian approach characterises those rulings where the Court's reasoning complies with the legal solutions that are already present, or that are similar to the solutions that are already present, in the majority of the Member States.[827]

Several scholars have suggested that, in an attempt to mitigate the growing distrust of national judiciaries towards EU judicial activism, the Court may have begun to adjust its reasoning to the national regulatory context.[828] This found expression in the tendency to opt for reasonings that reflect the prevailing legal practice across the Member States.[829] At the same time, however, the Court had not fully given up the judicial creativity that had characterised its rulings from the outset. As Maduro and Pollicino suggested, the Court's predominant legal reasoning until the 2000s could thus be described as 'majoritarian activism'.[830]

824. *Ibid.* and O. Pollicino, *Allargamento dell'Europa a est e rapporto tra Corti costituzionali e Corti europee*, 2010, pp. 275-280.
825. Judgment of the German Constitutional Court of 29 May 1974, *Solange I*, 2 BvL, 52/71; judgment of the Italian Constitutional Court of 8 June 1985, n. 169, *Granital.*
826. O. Pollicino, *Allargamento dell'Europa a est e rapporto tra Corti costituzionali e Corti europee*, 2010, p. 61.
827. O. Pollicino, *Discriminazione sulla Base del Sesso e Trattamento Preferenziale nel Diritto Comunitario*, 2005, p. 246.
828. On the Member States' reaction to bold Court of Justice's policy making, *see* J.H.H. Weiler, 'The Transformation of Europe', The Yale Law Journal, 100(8), pp. 2403-2483, 1991 and O. Pollicino, *Allargamento dell'Europa a est e rapporto tra Corti costituzionali e Corti europee*, Giuffrè, Milano, 2010, pp. 56-59.
829. M.P. Maduro, *We the Court: The European Court of Justice and the European Economic Constitution: A Critical Reading of Article 30 of the EC Treaty*, Hart Publishing, Oxford, 1998, p. 61.
830. *Ibid.* and O. Pollicino, *Allargamento dell'Europa a est e rapporto tra Corti costituzionali e Corti europee*, 2010, pp. 56-59.

Lenaerts identified four different manifestations of the majoritarian matrix with which the Court can engage with national legislative frameworks.[831] If a legal concept is common to all the Member States, the Court has an easy choice as it has no option but to read EU law in a manner compatible with that legal concept.[832] When there is no complete uniformity but strong convergence among national provisions, the Court tends to opt for the solution which is shared by the majority of the Member States.[833] If, instead, there is no sufficient convergence between the national legislations, the Court would normally identify the dominant priorities stemming from the national orders and 'import' them into its reasoning.[834] Finally, in the event of a total lack of homogeneity between the national practices, the Court would refrain from imposing a communitarian solution, as that would not find sufficient support at the domestic level.[835] Lenaerts, however, warned that even if these four paradigms can often be

831. K. Lenaerts, 'Interlocking Legal Orders in the European Union and Comparative Law', 2003.
832. *Ibid.* Lenaerts refers to judgment of 17 December 1970, *Einfuhr- und Vorratsstelle für Getreide und Futtermittel v. Köster and Berodt & Co*, C-25/70, ECLI:EU:C:1970:115; judgment of 6 March 2001, *Roderick Dunnett and Others v. European Investment Bank*, T-192/99, ECLI: EU:T:2001:72; judgment of 26 June 2001, *The Queen v. Secretary of State for Trade and Industry, ex parte Broadcasting, Entertainment, Cinematographic and Theatre Union (BECTU)*, C-173/99, ECLI:EU:C:2001:356; *see also* opinion of Advocate General Tizzano of 8 February 2001, *The Queen v. Secretary of State for Trade and Industry, ex parte Broadcasting, Entertainment, Cinematographic and Theatre Union (BECTU)*, C-173/99, ECLI:EU:C:2001:356, which stressed that in the Preamble of the CFREU there is a reference to the valuable contribution of the comparative law method as source of inspiration for interpreting fundamental rights.
833. *Ibid.*, C-222/84, *Johnston*. In M.P. Maduro, *We the Court: The European Court of Justice and the European Economic Constitution: A Critical Reading of Article 30 of the EC Treaty*, 1998, p. 73. Maduro noticed that also several judgments in the freedom of movement of goods respond to this logic. Among those: C-120/78, *Cassis de Dijon* (German law contains stricter minimum requirements in relation to the alcohol content of various spirits; para. 12); judgment of 26 June 1980, *Criminal proceedings against Herbert Gilli and Paul Andres*, C-788/79, ECLI: EU:C:1980:171; judgment of 16 December 1980, *Criminal proceedings against Anton Adriaan Fietje*, C-27/80, ECLI:EU:C:1980:293; judgment of 17 March 1983, *Criminal proceedings against De Kikvorsch Groothandel-Import-Export BV*, C-94/82, ECLI:EU:C:1983:85; judgment of 13 March 1984, *Criminal proceedings against Karl Prantl*, C-16/83, ECLI:EU:C:1984:101; judgment of 4 December 1986, *Commission of the European Communities v. Federal Republic of Germany*, C-179/85, ECLI:EU:C:1986:466; judgment of 12 March 1987, *Commission of the European Communities v. Hellenic Republic*, C-176/84, ECLI:EU:C:1987:125; judgment of 12 March 1987, *Commission of the European Communities v. Federal Republic of Germany*, C-178/84, ECLI: EU:C:1987:126; judgment of 14 July 1988, *3 Glocken GmbH and Gertraud Kritzinger v. USL Centro-Sud and Provincia autonoma di Bolzano*, C-407/85, ECLI:EU:C:1988:401; judgment of 14 July 1988, *Criminal proceedings against Zoni*, C-90/86, ECLI:EU:C:1988:403; judgment of 7 March 1990, *GB-INNO-BM v. Confédération du commerce luxembourgeois*, C-362/88, ECLI: EU:C:1990:102; judgment of 18 May 1993, *Schutzverband gegen Unwesen in der Wirtschaft e.V. v. Yves Rocher GmbH*, C-126/91, ECLI:EU:C:1993:191.
834. Judgment of 2 December 1971, *Aktien-Zuckerfabrik Schöppenstedt v. Council of the European Communities*, C-5/71, ECLI:EU:C:1971:116; C-6/90, *Frankovich*; C-46/93, *Brasserie du Pecheur*; judgment of 17 September 1997, *Dorsch Consult Ingenieurgesellschaft mbH v. Bundesbaugesellschaft Berlin mbH*, C-54/96, ECLI:EU:C:1997:413.
835. Judgment of 17 February 1998, *Lisa Jacqueline Grant v. South-West Trains Ltd*, C-249/96, ECLI:EU:C:1998:63; judgment of 17 April 1986, *State of the Netherlands v. Ann Florence Reed*, C-59/85, ECLI:EU:C:1986:157. In M.P. Maduro, *We the Court: The European Court of Justice and the European Economic Constitution: A Critical Reading of Article 30 of the EC Treaty*, 1998, p. 73, it was suggested that also the following cases responded to this logic: Judgment of 8 November 1979, *Firma Denkavit Futtermittel GmbH v. Minister für Ernähung, Landwirtschaft und Forsten des Landes Nordrhein-Westfalen*, C-251/78, ECLI:EU:C:1979:252; judgment of 5

found in the Court's reasoning, there are no hard and fast rules. There are, for instance, cases where, regardless of the level of convergence between national rules, the Court prefers a legal solution reflecting a specific national practice because it considers it to be the most suitable for the EU legal order.[836]

3.2.1 Examples of the Majoritarian Approach

The Court's majoritarian activism has been first identified and explored by Maduro in the area of market integration and, more precisely, in the case law on the free movement of goods. In his book 'We, the Court', Maduro explained that 'The increased scope of free movement rules, supported by formal reasoning, was tempered with a majoritarian (in a European scale) review of State regulations. This also permitted the Court to avoid entering into complex policy judgments (which could be open to criticism) regarding conflicting values in the application of those rules. It was another form of securing legitimacy while promoting market integration. Formal reasoning was the legal authority behind the Court's expansion of the scope of Community law rules and of market integration; the majoritarian approach was the policy authority behind the outcome of the Court's decisions.'[837]

According to Maduro, a significant example of the majoritarian approach can be found in the judgment *Commission v. Italy*. This case concerned an Italian legislation which was in apparent conflict with the freedom of movement of goods.[838] This Italian law required that only wine-based products can be sold as 'vinegar', with the effect of excluding from the Italian market all those products that are distributed as 'vinegar' in other Member States without being wine-based. In Maduro's view, the Court reached a majoritarian solution as it considered the different legal approaches in the various Member States and then found that the notion of 'vinegar' that was in force in Italy was comparatively narrower than those that are found in other Member States. On the base of that, the Court decided that the Italian legislation was not compatible with EU rules on the free movement of goods.[839]

February 1981, *Officier van justitie v. Koninklijke Kaasfabriek Eyssen BV*, C-53/80, ECLI:EU:C:1981:35; judgment of 11 May 1989, *Commission of the European Communities v. Federal Republic of Germany*, C-76/86, ECLI:EU:C:1989:184.

836. K. Lenaerts, 'Interlocking Legal Orders in the European Union and Comparative Law', 2003; C-11/70, *Internationale Handelsgesellschaft*; judgment of 21 September 1983, *Deutsche Milchkontor GmbH and others v. Federal Republic of Germany*, C-215/82, ECLI:EU:C:1983:233.

837. M.P. Maduro, *We the Court: The European Court of Justice and the European Economic Constitution: A Critical Reading of Article 30 of the EC Treaty*, 1998, p. 25.

838. Judgment of 9 December 1981, *Commission of the European Communities v. Italian Republic*, C-193/80, ECLI:EU:C:1981:298.

839. *Ibid.* (para. 22): 'The argument based on the protection of public health used by the Italian government as justification for its national legislation is not acceptable because it has no justification in the case of vinegars of agricultural origin which it is not denied contain no harmful substances and are normally consumed in other Member States and which must therefore be regarded as harmless to health.'

Another expression of the Court's majoritarian logics is its reasoning in the *Keck* judgment.[840] *Keck* concerned a French law prohibiting the practice of resale at a loss, consisting in selling a good at a price that is lower than its purchase price. Although this rule was in principle a restriction of the fundamental freedom of movement of goods, the Court found it compatible with EU law. The *Keck* judgment has been much discussed in legal doctrine because the Court had departed from its previous expansive approach to the internal market, based on the *Dassonville* and *Cassis de Dijon* onwards.[841] On closer inspection, however, an analysis of the judicial lawmaking logics shows that there is no actual contradiction. According to Maduro, the case law of the Court on free movement of goods is generally underpinned by a majoritarian rationale. From the judicial reasoning in *Keck*, for instance, it is clear that the Court could not identify a dominant regulatory solution from the national legal landscape. 'Saving' the national rule, even when not fully compliant with a market-expanding logic, appeared to be a logical choice from a majoritarian perspective.[842]

Looking beyond the free circulation of goods but remaining in the area of the internal market, Pollicino suggested that the majoritarian approach also emerged from the reasoning in the *Schindler* judgment.[843] There too, the Court ruled in favour of a national law that had a restrictive effect on the EU economic freedoms. More precisely, it was about a UK law limiting the advertising and the distribution of tickets for large-scale lotteries and, thus, limiting the freedom of foreign operators to provide services in other Member States. Interestingly, the Court grounded this exception on explicit majoritarian considerations and argued that 'it is not possible to disregard the moral, religious and cultural aspects of lotteries [...] in all Member States. The general tendency of the Member States is to restrict, or even prohibit, the practice of gambling and to prevent it from being a source of private profit'.[844]

Pollicino also identified a majoritarian approach in the Court's case law on fundamental rights and, in particular, on the principle of non-discrimination on the ground of gender,[845] noting that the majoritarian appreciation of national legal

840. Judgment of 24 November 1993, *Criminal proceedings against Bernard Keck and Daniel Mithouard*, C-267/91, ECLI:EU:C:1993:905.

841. C-267/91, *Keck* (para. 17). M.P. Maduro, *We the Court: The European Court of Justice and the European Economic Constitution: A Critical Reading of Article 30 of the EC Treaty*, 1998, p. 78; O. Pollicino, *Discriminazione sulla Base del Sesso e Trattamento Preferenziale nel Diritto Comunitario*, 2005, pp. 17 and 226; O. Pollicino, *Allargamento dell'Europa a est e rapporto tra Corti costituzionali e Corti europee*, 2010, p. 60. In particular, Pollicino suggested that the Court chose a clearer self-restrain approach in the interpretation of the economic freedoms since institutional actors at the national level appeared more and more reluctant to accept the excessive economic deregulation caused by the judicial policymaking of the Court.

842. C-267/91, *Keck*. The absence of a dominant solution is highlighted both in para. 8 of the judgment and in para. 6 of the Advocate General opinion.

843. Judgment of 24 March 1994, *Her Majesty's Customs and Excise v. Gerhart Schindler and Jörg Schindler*, C-275/92, ECLI:EU:C:1994:119. *See* O. Pollicino, *Allargamento dell'Europa a est e rapporto tra Corti costituzionali e Corti europee*, 2010, pp. 141, 145.

844. C-275/92, *Schindler* (para. 60). The UK provisions had the effect to prohibit the importation of material intended to enable UK nationals to participate in lotteries organised in other Member States, and therefore established a barrier to the freedom to provide services.

845. O. Pollicino, *Discriminazione sulla Base del Sesso e Trattamento Preferenziale nel Diritto Comunitario*, 2005, p. 17.

solutions might even have for some time kept the Court from adopting more progressive rulings.[846] An example is the *Grant* case, where the Court established that Directive 76/207/EC prohibiting discrimination on the ground of gender could not apply in cases of discrimination on the ground of sexual orientation. The Court based this conclusion on the fact that 'in the present state of the law within the Community, stable relationships between two persons of the same sex are not regarded as equivalent to marriage or stable relationship outside marriage between persons of opposite sex'.[847] This suggests that, in order to comply with the prevailing legal trend among the Member States, the Court decided not to make a jurisprudential 'leap', but to sit on the conservative side.

Interestingly, the *Grant* judgment was a step back from the earlier *P v. S* case where the Court, with a rather bold decision, held that the same Directive 76/207/EC prohibited discrimination against transsexuals.[848] Pollicino suggested that the Court's greater attention to the national context in *Grant*, compared to *P v. S* could be read as an attempt to realign the policy impact of its judgments to the more widespread legal practice in the Member States.[849] Moreover, it cannot be excluded that the Court also wanted to spare potentially high financial consequences for the national governments. In both *Grant* and *P v. S*, the legal issue at stake in fact had links with the allocation of social welfare rights, and it may be that the Court considered that giving homosexuals the same (and more generous) social security treatment as heterosexuals would have a significant impact on the public finances of Member States. The more relaxed approach in *P v. S* could be explained by the assumption that the Court considered the financial impact of equal treatment for transgender people to be more sustainable than in the case of homosexuals, given their relatively small number.[850]

Again in relation to the non-discrimination principle, other expressions of the majoritarian approach can be found in the *Abrahamson* and *Kalanke* judgments, both

846. There are exceptions. For instance, opinion of Advocate General La Pergola of 26 October 1999, *Tanja Kreil v. Bundesrepublik Deutschland*, C-285/98, ECLI:EU:C:1999:525, where in footnote 49 the Advocate General noted that the German protection of women is peculiar and not compatible with principle of non-discrimination and should be withdrawn. The German law in question was a constitutional provisions (Article 12 Grundgesetz) forbidding the access of women to role in the army which implied the use of weapons. *See also* M. Cartabia, 'Europe and Rights: Taking Dialogue Seriously', 2009.
847. Judgment of 17 February 1998, *Lisa Jacqueline Grant v. South-West Trains Ltd*, C-249/96, ECLI:EU:C:1998:63 (para. 35).
848. Judgment of 30 April 1996, *P v. S and Cornwall County Council*, C-13/94, ECLI:EU:C:1996:170; the Court's approach vis-à-vis the application of the principle of non-discrimination to transgender persons was further confirmed by the judgment of 7 January 2004, *K.B. v. National Health Service Pensions Agency and Secretary of State for Health*, C-117/01, ECLI:EU:C:2004:7 and Judgment of 27 April 2006, *Sarah Margaret Richards v. Secretary of State for Work and Pensions*, C-423/04, ECLI:EU:C:2006:256.
849. O. Pollicino, *Discriminazione sulla Base del Sesso e Trattamento Preferenziale nel Diritto Comunitario*, 2005, pp. 234-240.
850. *Ibid.* Opinion of Advocate General Tesauro of 14 December 1995, *P v. S and Cornwall County Council*, C-13/94, ECLI:EU:C:1995:444 (para. 9), where A.G. Tesauro considered that transsexuals constituted a rather limited number of person (one man over 30,000 and one woman on 100,000) while the number of homosexual in Europe was quantified to be around 35 million people.

on 'positive actions'.[851] In those decisions, the Court ruled that national measures aimed at promoting female employment through so-called reverse discrimination (e.g., reserving a minimum quota or adopting a more female-friendly attitude) violate the EU principle of non-discrimination on the ground of gender. This might be linked to the fact that positive actions were still quite rare in the European context at the time and therefore difficult to sustain from a majoritarian perspective.

3.2.2 Implications of the Majoritarian Approach for the Court's Policymaking

The majoritarian activism paradigm assumes that the Court's reasoning is influenced by the prevailing legal practices of the Member States. This has a series of corollaries.

First, it implies that the policy effects of EU judgments derive less from the normative preferences of the Court than from the established regulatory landscape of the Member States. This implies that the judicial elevation of market integration as the controlling rationale of EU case law should not be read as an expression of the neoliberal inclination of the Court, as neofunctionalists or integrationalists suggest. Instead, market expansion can be understood as the result of the Court's efforts to interpret the fundamental freedoms of the Treaty in a manner that is compatible with the national context where the judgment needs to be implemented. As Maduro observed, 'there is no "laissez-faire" policy guiding the decisions of the Court; rather, cases have been decided from a majoritarian point of view, taking the European Union as the relevant political community'.[852]

Similar observations apply to the Court's approach to the principle of non-discrimination and to its reluctance to give an extensive interpretation to Directive 72/96/EC. There too, the Court's reasoning may have been based less on the Court's ideological preferences and more on considerations relating to the national legal context.[853] This seems to be confirmed by the fact that a few years later, when the legislative scene in the Member States had moved in a more progressive direction, the Court reversed the *Grant* ruling. In the *Maruko* decision, the Court in fact ruled that EU law on non-discrimination prohibits national rules that do not recognise the same survival benefits regime for married couples and for (homosexual) couples in a civil partnership.[854]

851. Judgment of 6 July 2000, *Katarina Abrahamsson and Leif Anderson v. Elisabet Fogelqvist*, C-407/98, ECLI:EU:C:2000:367; judgment of 17 October 1995, *Eckhard Kalanke v. Freie Hansestadt Bremen*, C-450/93, ECLI:EU:C:1995:322. *See* O. Pollicino, *Discriminazione sulla Base del Sesso e Trattamento Preferenziale nel Diritto Comunitario*, 2005, p. 245.

852. M.P. Maduro, *We the Court: The European Court of Justice and the European Economic Constitution: A Critical Reading of Article 30 of the EC Treaty*, 1998, p. 24.

853. O. Pollicino, *Discriminazione sulla Base del Sesso e Trattamento Preferenziale nel Diritto Comunitario*, 2005, p. 245.

854. Judgment of 1 April 2008, *Tadao Maruko v. Versorgungsanstalt der deutschen Bühnen*, C-267/06, ECLI:EU:C:2008:179.

A further implication of majoritarian activism is that this decision-making approach inevitably leads to favouring the most common legal practices over 'minoritarian' legal traditions.[855] This means that legal solutions that are not in line with the prevailing regulatory landscape are less likely to be reflected in the case law. The under-representation of non-majoritarian legal traditions might then raise further serious problems from the point of view of respect for democratic principles and institutional balance.[856]

3.2.3 The Critical Aspects of the Majoritarian Theory

The theory of majoritarian activism helps to rationalise the Court's decision-making and attributes a conciliative attitude to the Court's reasoning. Nevertheless, the analysis of EU jurisprudence reveals inconsistencies which undermine the accuracy of this theory.

While several examples have been brought to demonstrate the majoritarian inclination of EU case law, there does not seem to be sufficient evidence to prove that this is in fact the predominant decision-making logic of the Court. There are multiple judgments where the Court has proposed a communitarian approach resulting from the judicial creativity of the Court against a dominant national normative solution. This is the case, for instance, in *Rottman*, on the rights deriving from EU citizenship, where the Court deviated from the solution emerging from the domestic context.[857] Reference may also be made to the *Francovich* judgment in which it was established that if Member States do not fulfil their obligation to implement European law, they can be held liable for non-contractual damages suffered by the plaintiffs.[858] On the one hand, it could certainly be argued that the principle of state's liability was the exasperated outcome of the chronic neglect of EU law implementation duties by certain Member States. For example, *Francovich* concerned a delay of seven years by the Italian State in implementing Directive 90/987/EC on protection against insolvency of the employer.[859] On the other hand, the judgment sparked discussions in the academic world and was considered by some as too intrusive into the national legal orders.[860] Harlow,

855. *Ibid.* (para. 11).
856. The example of the case law on positive action to counteract discrimination on the base of gender in the employment area is quite revealing, where the more 'progressive' legislations enacted in the land of Bremen (Germany) (C-450/93, *Kalanke*) and in Sweden (C-407/98, *Abrahamsson*) were set aside by the ruling of the Court. O. Pollicino, *Discriminazione sulla Base del Sesso e Trattamento Preferenziale nel Diritto Comunitario*, 2005, pp. 95-101, where the author noted that, at the time, legislative provisions on 'positive actions' were present only in an handful of Member States.
857. Judgment of 2 March 2010, *Janko Rottman v. Freistaat Bayern*, C-135/08, ECLI:EU:C:2010:104.
858. C-6/90, *Frankovich*.
859. Council Directive 80/987/EEC of 20 October 1980 on the approximation of the laws of the Member States relating to the protection of employees in the event of the insolvency of their employer *OJ L 283, 28.10.1980, pp. 23-27.*
860. P. Craig, 'Francovich, Remedies and the Scope of Damages Liability', Law Quarterly Review, 109, pp. 595-621, 1993; M. Ross, 'Beyond Francovich', The Modern Law Review, 56(1), pp. 55-73, 1993.

for example, described the Court as 'selfish' for imposing the principle of supranational liability on national systems.[861]

Judicial activism is thus difficult to reconcile with the majoritarian narrative. In this regard, Schutze observed that the theory of 'majoritarian activism' is a legal construction having the sole effect of concealing the boldness of the Court's policy-making, its neoliberal spirit, and its deliberate encroachment on the national constitutional traditions.[862] According to Schutze, when the Court refers to the national legal context it always does so with respect to a few Member States. Basically, the Court only refers to national legal traditions in order to lend greater legitimacy to its reasoning, based on a pretentious use of comparative techniques, when in fact the intention is to promote the economic integration of the Union.

Finally, it is worth noting that even Pollicino and Maduro, which are among the scholars who have contributed the most to the development of the majoritarian theory, have admitted that since the early 2000s, the majoritarian character of the Court's decision-making has weakened. They both identified a shift in the interpretative approach towards a more marked judicial pluralism, which is discussed in the next section.[863] Instead of resorting to the solution prevailing in the majority of the Member States, the Court thus seems to have turned in favour of a greater sensitivity to the legal and constitutional specificities of each national system.

3.3 The Pluralistic Approach

Around the 2000s, EU law scholars increasingly discussed the emergence of a pluralist approach in the Court's reasoning. Indeed, there was a common perception that the Court's reasoning was becoming more open and deferential towards the legal solutions of the individual Member States.[864]

---

861. C. Harlow, 'Francovich and the Problem of the Disobedient State', European Law Journal, 2, pp. 199-225, 1996.
862. R. Schutze, 'Judicial Majoritarianism Revisited: "We, the Other Court"?', European Law Review, 43(2), pp. 269-280, 2018, where the author contended that '[...] the European Court of Justice hardly ever expressly engages in the type of "state-counting" that Maduro suggests. Indeed: having looked at all Article 34 cases myself, the Court hardly ever engages in any significant comparative law exercise'.
863. Pollicino however noted that there are exceptions to this trend. O. Pollicino, 'Corte di giustizia e giudici nazionali: il moto "ascendente", ovverosia l'incidenza delle "tradizioni costituzionali comuni" nella tutela apprestata ai diritti dalla Corte dell'Unione', 1, Consulta Online, 2015, p. 14. The author referred to Judgment of 14 September 2010, *Akzo Nobel Chemicals Ltd and Akcros Chemicals Ltd v. European Commission*, C-550/07, ECLI:EU:C:2010:512 where, in relation to the confidentiality of communications with lawyers who work within the undertaking or the group of undertakings, the Court observed that '[...] no predominant trend towards protection under legal professional privilege of communications within a company or group with in-house lawyers may be discerned in the legal systems of the 27 Member States of the Union'.
864. J. Gerards, 'Pluarlism, Deference and the Margin of Appreciation Doctrine', European Law Journal, 17(1), pp. 80-120, 2011; G. Martinico, 'Judging in the Multilevel Legal Order: Exploring the Techniques of "Hidden Dialogue"', King's Law Journal, 21, pp. 257-281, 2010; M. Poiares Maduro, 'Three Claims of Constitutional Pluralism' in M. Avbelj and J. Komárek (eds), *Constitutional Pluralism in the European Union and Beyond*, Hart Publishing, London, 2012,

3.3.1 The Heterarchical Understanding of the EU Legal Order

According to the pluralistic logic, the Court pays attention to the national normative context and avoids imposing a specific EU legal solution, especially when the judicial proceeding concerns a sensitive policy area or a sensitive aspect of the national constitutional order.[865] In those situations, the Court tends to refrain from declaring that a national provision is in conflict with EU law, all the more so when that national provision embodies constitutional values.[866]

As Horsley observed, 'Through the pluralist lens, the Court's proclamations concerning the formal status of EU law are placed alongside Member States' conceptions of the EU legal order in a new, heterarchical, not hierarchical relationship.'[867] As in the majoritarian logic, here too there is a conciliatory or irenic intent of the Court, which seeks to combine its own judicial policymaking with the respect for the constitutional prerogatives of the Member States. Only, instead of using the majoritarian view as the underpinning logic for its reasoning, the Court now pays attention to the preservation of national legal identities.[868]

3.3.2 The Origins of the Pluralist Approach

The origins of the pluralist approach can be traced back to a concatenation of events, linked to the transformation - both legal and political - of the European order.

Pollicino, Martinico and Weiler, among others, have noted that the progressive enlargement of the EU to include new Member States has led to greater diversification in legal traditions and cultural orientations.[869] This has prompted the Court to adapt its reasoning to the increasing constitutional diversity of the European order.[870] In a community of six Member States, it was relatively easy to identify common features in

pp. 67-84; K. Jaklic, *Constitutional Pluralism in the EU*, Oxford University Press, Oxford, 2014; S. Sankari, 'Constitutional Pluralism and Judicial Adjudication: On Legal Reasoning, Minimalism and Silence by the Court of Justice' in G. Davies & M. Avbelj (eds), *Research Handbook on Legal Pluralism and EU Law*, Edward Elgar Publishing, Cheltenham, 2018, pp. 309-322; O. Pollicino, *Allargamento dell'Europa a est e rapporto tra Corti costituzionali e Corti europee*, 2010, p. 144; among others.

865. G. Martinico, 'The "Polemical" Spirit of European Constitutional Law: On the Importance of Conflicts in EU Law', 2015; J. Gerards, 'Pluarlism, Deference and the Margin of Appreciation Doctrine', 2011.
866. J.H.H. Weiler, 'Prologue: Global and Pluarlist Constitutionalism - Some Doubts' in Gròinne de Burca & J.H.J. Weiler (eds), *The Worlds of European Constitutionialism*, Cambridge University Press, Cambridge, 2012, pp. 8-19.
867. T. Horsley, *The Court of Justice of the European Union as and Institutional Actor: Judicial Lawmaking and Its Limits*, 2018, p. 129. Horsley extensively refers to the work of Jaklic, who mapped the different conceptualisations of pluralism that legal scholars have, in time, elaborated in relation to the EU constitutional model.
868. B. Guastaferro, 'Beyond the Exceptionalism of Constitutional Conflicts: The Ordinary Functions of the Identity Clause', 2012; G. Martinico, 'The "Polemical" Spirit of European Constitutional Law: On the Importance of Conflicts in EU Law', 2015.
869. J.H.H. Weiler, 'The Transformation of Europe', The Yale Law Journal, 100(8), pp. 2403-2483, p. 2456, 1991.
870. G. Martinico, 'The "Polemical" Spirit of European Constitutional Law: On the Importance of Conflicts in EU Law', 2015.

national legal traditions and to formulate legal reasoning that somehow 'spoke' to most of these traditions. Over time and following successive accessions, this exercise had become increasingly complex. This was particularly the case after 2004-2007, when the accessions concerned countries that until 15 years earlier had been satellite states or even part of the USSR and whose democratic transition was in fact just beginning.[871]

Another factor often associated by legal scholars with the emergence of the pluralist approach is the progressive weakening of the constitutional tolerance exhibited by national judiciaries. Maduro and Pollicino observed that, around the time of the ratification of the Maastricht Treaty, certain national Supreme Courts began to show signs of closing themselves off from the European order.[872] While the impact of trans-judicial dynamics on the decision-making of the Court is discussed in section 4, it is nonetheless already interesting to note that the pluralist approach might have been the reaction of the Court to contain such expressions of discontent.[873]

Finally, this shift in the direction of pluralism might also be explained in light of the reforms that the Maastricht Treaty brought to EU primary law.[874] As pointed out by Maduro, Article F(1) of the Maastricht Treaty established that the Union is bound to consider the national identities of the Member States.[875] That provision was then incorporated into the Lisbon Treaty, and Article 4(2) TEU now provides that 'The Union shall respect the equality of the Member States before the Treaties as well as their *national identities* inherent to their fundamental structure, political and constitutional, inclusive of regional and local self-governments [...]' (emphasis added).

Academic scholars have elaborated two different views as to how Article 4(2) TEU led to a more pluralistic inclination in the Court's reasoning.[876] Some scholars, among whom Pollicino, von Bogdandy, Schill, Cartabia, Van Gestel and de Poorter suggested that Article 4(2) TEU codified in the primary law of the Union the rule that

871. O. Pollicino, *Allargamento dell'Europa a est e rapporto tra Corti costituzionali e Corti europee*, 2010, p. 137. At the moment of writing, Poland and Hungary seem to be in a regressive phase.
872. M. Poiares Maduro, 'Three Claims of Constitutional Pluralism' in M. Avbelj & J. Komárek (eds), *Constitutional Pluralism in the European Union and Beyond*, Hart Publishing, London, 2012, pp. 67-84; Horsley, *The Court of Justice of the European Union as and Institutional Actor: Judicial Lawmaking and Its Limits*, 2018, p. 244.
873. X. Groussot, 'Constitutional Dialogues, Pluralism and Conflicting Identities' in M. Avbelj & J. Komárek (eds), *Constitutional Pluralism in the European Union and Beyond*, Hart Publishing, London, 2012, pp. 319-342.
874. J.H.H. Weiler, 'Prologue: Global and Pluarlist Constitutionalism – Some Doubts' in Gròinne de Burca & J.H.J. Weiler (eds), *The Worlds of European Constitutionialism*, Cambridge University Press, Cambridge, 2012, pp. 8-19.
875. *See* opinion of Advocate General Maduro of 8 October 2008, *Michaniki AE v. Ethniko Symvoulio Radiotileorasis and Ypourgos Epikrateias*, C-213/07, ECLI:EU:C:2008:544, further discussed in Chapter 5, section 3.3.3.
876. For an in-depth discussion on the potential of Article 4(2) TEU: B. Guastaferro, 'Beyond the Exceptionalism of Constitutional Conflicts: The Ordinary Functions of the Identity Clause', 2012; L. Azoulai, 'The Court of Justice and the Social Market Economy: The Emergence of an Ideal and the Conditions for its Realization', 2008; O. Pollicino, *Allargamento dell'Europa a est e rapporto tra Corti costituzionali e Corti europee*, 2010, p. 176, where the author noted that in relation to the area of freedom, security and justice, the pluralistic approach is also supported by Article 67(1) TEU, establishing that 'the Union shall constitute an area of freedom, security and justice with respect for fundamental rights and the different legal systems and traditions of the Member States'.

the Court should respect national constitutional identities. According to this interpretation of Article 4(2) TEU, in the event of incompatibility between EU and national law, if the national rule relates to a value of a constitutional nature, the Court must seek to safeguard it, at the cost of limiting the primacy of EU law.[877]

Other scholars, on the other hand, perceived Article 4(2) TEU as more inherent to the question of the division of competences between Member States and the EU, and not so much as a rule to resolve possible conflicts of a constitutional nature. Guastaferro, in particular, contended that Article 4(2) TEU was not intended to circumscribe the primacy of EU law, but 'was conceived as an instrument to undermine the creeping encroachment of EU powers upon sensitive areas related to national identity and sovereignty'.[878] A similar view was shared by Lenaerts, who stated that 'the role of Article 4(2) TEU is twofold. As a competence rule, it imposes limits on EU regulations, even in cases where such regulations would otherwise be permissible. As an interpretative rule, it provides guidance for the CJEU and the Member States' courts on how to interpret the relationship between the EU and Member States' law'.[879] This view was also confirmed by Bonelli, who noted that this second reading of the pluralist scope of Article 4(2) TEU has so far found greater support in the case law of the Court.[880]

---

877. Pollicino, *Ibid.*, pp. 176-177; M. Cartabia, '"Unita nella diversità": il rapporto tra la Costituzione europea e le costituzioni nazionali' in F. Donati & G. Morbidelli (eds), *Una costituzione per l'Unione europea*, Giappichelli, Torino, 2006; A. von Bogdandy & S. Schill, 'Overcoming Absolute Primacy: Respect for National Identity under the Lisbon Treaty', Common Market Law Review, 48, pp. 1417-1454, 2011. In a similar direction, also M. Kumm & V. Ferreres Comella, 'The Primacy Clause of the Constitutional Treaty and the Future of Constitutional Conflict in the European Union', International Journal of Constitutional Law, 3(2-3), pp. 473-492, 2005; R. Van Gestel & J. De Poorter, *In the Court We Trust: Cooperation, Coordination and Collaboration Between the ECJ and Supreme Administrative Courts*, Cambridge University Press, Cambridge, 2019, p. 17: 'Although the exact scope and meaning of the identity clause is still developing, at least one thing is certain, namely: the CJEU cannot unilaterally decide what the national identity of its Member States entails. That would run against the very idea by the Treaty [...] that national identity deserves protection against interference by EU institutions.' Or, T. Konstadinides, 'Constitutional Identity as a Shield and as a Sword: The European Legal Order Within the Framework of National Constitutional Settlement', Cambridge Yearbook of European Legal Studies, 13, pp. 195-218, 2011. Interestingly, also Martinico, in G. Martinico, 'The "Polemical" Spirit of European Constitutional Law: On the Importance of Conflicts in EU Law', 2015, contended that Article 4(2) TEU reflects the intention to regulate constitutional conflicts, but it actually ends up having the opposite effect: 'this provision [Article 4(2) TEU] has been described as the codification of a new concept of primacy and as a basis for a more cooperative phase among courts. I think this clause represents the apex of a broader process, but at the same time I do not perceive this process (of partial convergence) as one of a progressive route towards pacification in the relationship between constitutional poles'.
878. B. Guastaferro, 'Beyond the Exceptionalism of Constitutional Conflicts: The Ordinary Functions of the Identity Clause', 2012: 'Asserting that it would be the Treaty itself, by requiring the EU to respect the national identities, to implicitly empower national courts to set aside EU provisions encroaching upon Member States' constitutional identities, would mean attaching to the identity clause a meaning which is substantially inconsistent with EU law.'
879. K. Lenaerts, 'Discovering the Law of the EU: The European Court of Justice and the Comparative Law Method', 2018.
880. M. Bonelli, 'The Taricco Saga and the Consolidation of Judicial Dialogue in the European Union. CJEU, C-105/14 Ivo Taricco and others, ECLI:EU:C:2015:555; and C-42/17 M.A.S., M.B., ECLI:EU:C:2017:936 Italian Constitutional Court, Order no. 24/2017', Maastricht Journal of European and Comparative Law, 25(3), pp. 357-373, 2018.

3.3.3 *Constitutional Pluralism in the Court of Justice's Case Law*

It is a shared view among scholars that the pluralist approach is particularly suitable for the advancement of the constitutional maturity of the EU legal system. The departure from the majoritarian logics in fact enabled the Court to steer the definition of the constitutional order in a more heterarchical and multifocal direction. The lack of normative homogeneity that characterises the different national systems could thus become a source of constitutional enrichment.[881]

The Court's pluralist vocation led various scholars, including Weiler, Penice, Martinico, Cartabia, Gerards, Jaklic, Maduro and Pollicino, to focus on the pluralist constitutional model that was emerging from the EU case law.[882] It is particularly interesting to turn once again to the work of Maduro, who developed his pluralist theory during the period in which he held the post of Advocate General at the CJEU. His thinking may therefore be quite revealing of the Court's lawmaking logics since he had the actual opportunity to propose his theoretical approach directly to the Court through his AG opinions.[883] In Maduro's view, the Court should conceive the relationship between EU and national legal orders according to what he called the 'principles of contrapunctual law'. This term is borrowed from musical vocabulary: 'Counterpoint is the musical method of harmonising different melodies that are not in a hierarchical

881. I. Pernice, 'Multilevel Constitutionalism and the Treaty of Amsterdam: European Constitution-Making Revisited?', 1999; O. Pollicino, *Allargamento dell'Europa a est e rapporto tra Corti costituzionali e Corti europee*, 2010, pp. 176-179.

882. In O. Pollicino, *Discriminazione sulla Base del Sesso e Trattamento Preferenziale nel Diritto Comunitario*, 2005, Pollicino anchored his analysis of the Court case law to a majoritarian understanding of EU judicial policymaking. In O. Pollicino, *Allargamento dell'Europa a est e rapporto tra Corti costituzionali e Corti europee*, 2010 and in O. Pollicino, 'Corte di giustizia e giudici nazionali: il moto "ascendente", ovverosia l'incidenza delle "tradizioni costituzionali comuni" nella tutela apprestata ai diritti dalla Corte dell'Unione', 2015, the author identified an evolution in the Court's decision-making approach. Even more evident is the transformation in of Maduro's perception of the Court's interpretative attitude. In M.P. Maduro, *We the Court: The European Court of Justice and the European Economic Constitution: A Critical Reading of Article 30 of the EC Treaty*, 1998, Maduro had identified the majoritarian activism as the main rationale in EU case law, at last concerning the free circulation of goods. His subsequent work instead reflects a clear pluralistic perception of the Court's policymaking. *See* M. Poiares Maduro, 'Three Claims of Constitutional Pluralism', 2012, where Maduro declared that the seminal article by Mac Cornich 'Beyond the sovereign State' and the Maastricht treaty judgment from the German Federal Constitutional Tribunal were important elements in his own path towards constitutional pluralism. Maduro, in fact, explained that 'my initial interest in the ideas that led to constitutional pluralism was not so much determined by the risks of constitutional conflicts, but more by an inquiry into the character of the European Constitution itself'. *See also* I. Pernice, 'Multilevel Constitutionalism and the Treaty of Amsterdam: European Constitution-Making Revisited?', Common Market Law Review, 36, pp. 703-750, 1999; M. Cartabia, 'Europe and Rights: Taking Dialogue Seriously', 2009; G. Martinico, 'Judging in the Multilevel Legal Order: Exploring the Techniques of "Hidden Dialogue"', 2010; J. Weiler, 'Europe: The Case Against the Case of Statehood', European Law Journal, 4(1), pp. 43-62, 1998; N. Walker, 'The Idea of Constitutional Pluralism', The Modern Law Review, 65(3), pp. 317-359, 2002.

883. M. Poiares Maduro, 'Three Claims of Constitutional Pluralism', 2012; M. Poiares Maduro, 'Contrapunctual Law: Europe's Constitutional Pluralism in Action', 2003.

relationship inter se.'[884] Translating this concept into judicial lawmaking logics means that even if the underlying rationale (and the premises) of the EU and national legal orders may be different, they must also be somewhat compatible with each other.

Within the EU there are multiple claims of constitutional primacy (from the national Supreme Courts on the one hand and from the CJEU on the other), and this requires the Court to elaborate a paradigm for their harmonious coexistence. It is therefore important for the Court to accept this heterogeneity and to allow national constitutional orders to contribute to the development of the Union's legal system.[885] In case of conflict between national and EU legal orders, Maduro recommended that 'EU law adapts itself to the national constitutional claims by giving national courts a higher discretion on those areas.' His interpretation of the pluralist approach seems thus to show more proximity with the second of the two above-mentioned readings of Article 4(2) TEU. The contrapunctual law theory also attaches great importance to the role of dialogue between national and European courts. This aspect is, however, further elaborated in section 4, specifically dedicated to trans-judicial dialogue.

Interestingly, Maduro had the opportunity to put his theory into practice in his capacity as Advocate General when he wrote the opinion in the *Michaniki* case.[886] *Michaniki* originated from a preliminary ruling submitted by the Greek Council of State, concerning the compatibility of a Greek constitutional provision with EU secondary legislation. More precisely, the CJEU was asked to assess whether Article 24 of Directive 93/37/EC, on the conditions for participation in public procurement contracts, precluded a norm of the Greek Constitution establishing that media companies are excluded from participation in public procurements. Advocate General Maduro formulated an opinion based on the principles of his pluralist understanding of the relationship between the EU and national law.

First, the opinion referred to Article F(1) of the Maastricht Treaty, which required the Union to respect the national identities of the Member States. Maduro stated that 'the national identity concerned clearly includes the constitutional identity of the Member States'[887] and that 'the preservation of national constitutional identity can also enable a Member State to develop, within certain limits, its own definition of a legitimate interest capable of justifying [...] a restriction of the obligations imposed by Community law'.[888] This legitimate interest can thus 'be relied upon by a Member State to justify its assessment of constitutional measures. [...] It is, nevertheless, necessary to point out that that respect owed to the constitutional identity of the Member States cannot be understood as an absolute obligation to defer to all national constitutional

884. M. Poiares Maduro, 'Contrapunctual Law: Europe's Constitutional Pluralism in Action', 2003, p. 523.
885. *Ibid.*
886. Judgment of 16 December 2008, *Michaniki AE v. Ethniko Symvoulio Radiotileorasis and Ypourgos Epikrateias*, C-213/07, ECLI:EU:C:2008:731. *See* comments O. Pollicino, *Allargamento dell'Europa a est e rapporto tra Corti costituzionali e Corti europee*, 2010, p. 146 and B. Guastaferro, 'Beyond the Exceptionalism of Constitutional Conflicts: The Ordinary Functions of the Identity Clause', 2012.
887. Opinion of Advocate General Maduro of 8 October 2008, *Michaniki AE v. Ethniko Symvoulio Radiotileorasis and Ypourgos Epikrateias*, C-213/07, ECLI:EU:C:2008:544 (para. 31).
888. *Ibid.* (paras 32 and 33).

rules. [...] Just as Community law takes the national constitutional identity of the Member States into consideration, national constitutional law must be adapted to the requirements of the Community legal order. In the present case, the national constitutional rules can be taken into consideration to the extent that they fall within the discretion available to the Member States in order to ensure the observance of the principle of equal treatment required by the directive. The exercise of that discretion must, however, remain within the limits fixed by the principle and by the directive itself'.[889] Furthermore, Maduro suggested that the Court should assess whether the Greek measure respects those conditions by applying a proportionality test.[890] Ultimately, the Court did not place as much emphasis on national constitutional identities as the Advocate General's opinion, although the judgment eventually reached the same conclusions.

It should be noted that the model of contrapunctual law defined by Maduro is just one among the possible expressions of judicial pluralism. Examples of pluralism can in fact be found well before the Court's pronouncement in the *Michaniki* case. Pollicino, for instance, suggested that the pluralist turn of the Court took place with the *Omega* case.[891] This proceeding originated from an order of the German police preventing the opening of a 'laserdrome'. A laserdrome is a playground where customers are provided with laser guns with which they can simulate fights and shoot each other. The order of the German police established that this type of activity constituted an affront to human dignity because it simulated acts of murder and violence, which are contrary to the fundamental values of German society.[892]

The issue eventually reached the CJEU, which was asked whether the decision of the police to shut down the laserdrome constituted an infringement of the economic freedom set by the EU Treaty. The Court adopted a pluralist approach and found that the order of the police was justified as it expressed national constitutional principles. More precisely, the Court stated that 'It is not indispensable in that regard for a restrictive measure issued by the authority of a Member State to correspond to a conception shared by all Member States as regards the precise way in which the fundamental right or legitimate interest in question is to be protected.'[893] Quite interestingly, in an attempt to conceal the change of approach from the (previously more widespread) majoritarian logic, in *Omega* the Court undertook a manipulative interpretation of its earlier *Schindler* judgment (already mentioned in section 3.2.1 as

889. *Ibid.* (para. 33).
890. Ultimately, the opinion of A.G. Maduro suggested that the Greek Constitutional law went too far, since the provisions prescribed a general incompatibility whose scope exceeded what is necessary to observe the principle of equal treatment and therefore to ensure effective competition in the sector.
891. O. Pollicino, *Allargamento dell'Europa a est e rapporto tra Corti costituzionali e Corti europee*, 2010, p. 141 and O. Pollicino, 'Corte di giustizia e giudici nazionali: il moto "ascendente", ovverosia l'incidenza delle "tradizioni costituzionali comuni" nella tutela apprestata ai diritti dalla Corte dell'Unione', 2015, with reference to judgment of 14 October 2004, *Omega Spielhallen- und Automatenaufstellungs-GmbH v. Oberbürgermeisterin der Bundesstadt Bonn*, C-36/02, ECLI:EU:C:2004:614.
892. C-36/02, *Omega* (para. 7).
893. *Ibid.* (para. 37).

an example of majoritarian logic): 'Although, in paragraph 60 of Schindler, the Court referred to moral, religious or cultural considerations which lead all Member States to make the organisation of lotteries and other games with money subject to restrictions, it was not its intention, by mentioning that common conception, to formulate a general criterion for assessing the proportionality of any national measure which restricts the exercise of an economic activity.'[894]

Azoulai, Pollicino, Martinico and Guastaferro, among others, also noticed that the Court often resorted to the pluralist approach in cases concerning a potential conflict between a national measure and the EU economic freedoms. Examples can be found in *Dynamic Medien, Azores, Say Wittgenstein* and *Gambelli,* where the Court showed particular flexibility towards national rules, after recognising them as an expression of the national constitutional identity.[895]

Pluralistic reasonings present a number of characteristics that could be adopted as 'indicators' for the case studies in Chapter 6. The first is that the Court generally identifies a particular national norm as reflecting a national constitutional value. While this is a clear sign of a pluralistic approach, it is not always present. There are also decisions, particularly in the field of fundamental rights, in which the Court has adopted a pluralistic approach without explicitly referring to the constitutional identity of the Member State.[896] An example is the *Schmidberger* judgment, which concerned a potential conflict between the free movement of goods and the fundamental rights of freedom of expression and freedom of association. The question was whether the decision of the (Austrian) national authorities to allow a demonstration by environmental protesters, which eventually led to a complete blockage of traffic on the Brenner motorway, infringed on the free movement of goods. The Court decided that there was no such infringement. After referring to Article F(1) of the Maastricht Treaty (the precursor of Article 4(2) TEU), the Court ruled that 'taking account of the Member States' wide margin of discretion [...] the competent national authorities were entitled to consider that an outright ban on the demonstration would have constituted unacceptable interference with the fundamental rights of the demonstrators to gather and express peacefully their opinion in public'.[897]

894. *Ibid.*

895. L. Azoulai, 'The Court of Justice and the Social Market Economy: The Emergence of an Ideal and the Conditions for Its Realization', Common Market Law Review, 45, pp. 1335-1356, 2008; B. Guastaferro, 'Beyond the Exceptionalism of Constitutional Conflicts: The Ordinary Functions of the Identity Clause', 2012 and G. Martinico, 'Judging in the Multilevel Legal Order: Exploring the Techniques of "Hidden Dialogue"', 2010. Judgment of 14 February 2008, *Dynamic Medien Vertriebs GmbH v. Avides Media AG*, C-244/06, ECLI:EU:C:2008:85 and Judgment of 22 December 2010, *Ilonka Sayn-Wittgenstein v. Landeshauptmann von Wien*, C-208/09, ECLI:EU:C:2010:806; judgment of 6 September 2006, *Portuguese Republic v. Commission of the European Communities*, C-88/03, ECLI:EU:C:2006:511; judgment of 6 November 2003, *Criminal proceedings against Piergiorgio Gambelli and Others*, C-243/01, ECLI:EU:C:2003:597.

896. Judgment of 12 June 2003, *Eugen Schmidberger, Internationale Transporte und Planzüge v. Republik Österreich*, C-112/00, ECLI:EU:C:2003:333 (para. 71). The Court does not specifically refer to the constitutional values of Austria, but more generally draws inspiration from 'the constitutional traditions common to the Member States and from the guidelines supplied by international treaties for the protection of human rights on which the Member States have collaborated or to which they are signatories'.

897. C-112/00, *Schmidberger* (para. 89).

A further indicator of the pluralist approach is that the Court recognises a wide margin of discretion for the national legislature. It should be noted, however, that the Court sometimes grants this discretion only nominally, applying a proportionality test to determine whether the national legislature has made an acceptable use of such discretion. In fact, proportionality tests are, by nature, not objective, as they might convey a purposive reasoning, concealed behind an apparently technical and neutral exercise.[898]

Finally, the pluralistic approach is generally characterised by the conferral of a rather wide margin of appreciation to the national courts. This is the case even when the Court identifies the proportionality test as the most appropriate interpretative tool for resolving the legal issue, but it does not 'run' it, leaving it to the national judge. In those cases, the Court formulates interpretative guidelines and, in doing so, recognises that it is for the referring judge to determine whether the national norm in question complies with EU law.[899]

A more recent example where all three indicators can be found is the *Wabe* judgment of July 2021, where the CJEU decided on two joint cases referred by German courts.[900] The issue concerned the possible discriminatory nature of the employer's policy of prohibiting the wearing of religious symbols in the workplace. In both cases, these policies led to the dismissal of female employees wearing the Islamic veil. In its previous rulings *Achbita* and *Bougnaoui*, the Court ruled that these policies may be justified in consideration of the employer's freedom to conduct a business (Article 16 CFREU), provided that they are appropriate, necessary and applied in a consistent and systematic manner. One of the questions put to the CJEU in *Wabe* concerned the relationship between those precedents and the jurisprudence of the German constitutional court, which had instead given a more restrictive interpretation of the employer's ability to impose discriminatory treatment.[901] There was therefore a potential conflict between two different fundamental rights, which are protected differently at the EU and national levels. On the one hand, the freedom to conduct a business, to which the Court has historically given a rather extensive reading, and on the other hand, the principle of non-discrimination on religious grounds which is interpreted broadly in the German legal system. In addressing this issue, the CJEU chose a clearly pluralist paradigm. First, it specified that 'the directive [...] leaves a margin of discretion to the Member States, taking into account the diversity of their approaches as regard the place accorded to religion and beliefs within their respective systems'.[902] Then, it stated that

898. On the proportionality test, *see* J. Gerards, 'Pluralism, Deference and the Margin of Appreciation Doctrine', European Law Journal, 17(1), pp. 80-120, 2011.
899. *Ibid.*; L. Azoulai, 'The Court of Justice and the Social Market Economy: The Emergence of an Ideal and the Conditions for Its Realization', 2008; G. Martinico, 'The "Polemical" Spirit of European Constitutional Law: On the Importance of Conflicts in EU Law', 2015; B. Guastaferro, 'Beyond the Exceptionalism of Constitutional Conflicts: The Ordinary Functions of the Identity Clause', 2012.
900. Judgment of 15 July 2021, *IX v. WABE eV and MH Müller Handels GmbH v. MJ*, C-804/18, Joined Cases C-804/18 and C-341/19, ECLI:EU:C:2021:594.
901. C-804/18, *WABE* (para. 34(2)b).
902. *Ibid.* (para. 86).

it is for the national legal systems and their courts to weigh up the possible legitimate aims which may be invoked to justify unequal treatment.[903]

In this way, the Court showed to give proper consideration to German constitutional values without, at the same time, renouncing its own precedents and its inclination towards a broad interpretation of the economic prerogatives of the employer. It is also interesting to note that the Court adapted the Union's value structure to the German system without undermining the integrity of the Union's legal order. Indeed, while the Court granted to national legislators a rather wide discretion to balance the different rights and interests at stake,[904] it recalled that 'the margin of discretion [...] afforded to the Member States in the absence of a consensus at EU level must, however, go hand in hand with supervision, by the EU judicature, consisting in determining whether the measures taken at national level were justified in principle and proportionate'.[905] This safeguard clause shows that the pluralist model of judicial interpretation is susceptible to being applied in a more or less stringent manner. As will be seen in the following section, this implies that a formally pluralist argumentation does not always correspond to an effective enhancement of national constitutional values, but may be an argumentative expedient to reinforce the legitimacy of the policy implications of the rulings.

3.3.4 But How Pluralistic Is the Court Really?

Pluralist theories have sparked a wide academic interest. Nevertheless, like with the other judicial lawmaking dynamics, there are some aspects that are not particularly convincing.

First, as was also observed with regard to the majoritarian approach, an analysis of the Court's case law of the last 20 years shows that there are many significant exceptions.[906] *Kreil, Filipiak, Maruko, Mangold, Kücükdeveci, Ruffel, Laval, Viking, Alemo-Herron, Aget Iraklis* and *Melloni* are only some of the best-known examples of judgments in which the Court has been criticised for having ruled that national norms embodying constitutionally protected values are not compatible with EU law.[907] In

903. *Ibid.* (para. 87).
904. *Ibid.* (para. 88).
905. *Ibid.* (para. 86).
906. Among others, A. Arnull, 'Judicial Activism and the European Court of Justice: How Should Academics Respond?' in B. de Witte, B. Muir & E. Dawson (eds), *Judicial Activism at the European Court of Justice*, Edward Elgar Publishing, Cheltenham, 2013, pp. 211-233.
907. Judgment of 11 January 2000, *Tanja Kreil v. Bundesrepublik Deutschland*, C-285/98, ECLI: EU:C:2000:2; judgment of 19 November 2009, *Krzysztof Filipiak v. Dyrektor Izby Skarbowej w Poznaniu*, C-314/08, ECLI:EU:C:2009:719; judgment of 1 April 2008, *Tadao Maruko v. Versorgungsanstalt der deutschen Bühnen*, C-267/06, ECLI:EU:C:2008:179; C-144/04, *Mangold*; C-555/07, *Kücükdeveci*; judgment of 3 April 2008, *Dirk Rüffert v. Land Niedersachsen*, C-346/06, ECLI:EU:C:2008:189; C-438/05, *Viking*; C-426/11, *Alemo-Herron*; *C-201/15, AGET Iraklis*; judgment of 26 February 2013, *Stefano Melloni v. Ministerio Fiscal*, C-399/11, ECLI: EU:C:2013:107.

those cases, the Court adopted an expansive interpretation of the Union's competences, quite the opposite of judicial restraint.[908] Moreover, Maduro himself, in his Advocate General's opinion in the *Viking* case, proposed an approach that does not seem much compatible with the pluralist paradigm. This suggests that it may not be so easy to transpose the 'contrapunctual law', as well as other paradigms of constitutional pluralism, into the actual legal reasoning of the Court.

The *Viking* case concerned a conflict between the freedom of establishment under Article 43 TEC (now 49 TFEU) and the right to strike, constitutionally protected by the national (Finnish) legal system. At first, AG Maduro stated that the two opposing rights were to be considered equal, both pertaining to the normative category of fundamental rights.[909] But then, and despite these premises, the pluralistic approach was not reflected in the substance of the argumentation. In the remainder of the opinion, Maduro assessed the validity of the exercise of the right to strike on the basis of the degree of interference with the functioning of the internal market.[910] More than a pluralistic approach, the legal argumentation - which was then largely transposed into the Court's judgment - adhered to a clear market rationale.[911] Indeed, Maduro's argument seemed to lean towards economic liberalism in that it placed economic freedoms at a higher level than the national constitutional principle establishing the right to strike.[912]

This gap between the pluralist rhetoric, on the one hand, and the essentially EU-centred and integrationalist argumentation, on the other hand, was also noted and addressed by Advocate General Trstenjak, in a legal opinion for a later case. In her

908. *Inter alia*, N. Bruun & J. Malmberg, 'Lex Laval: Collective Actions and Posted Work in Sweden' in R. Blanpain, F. Hendrickx (eds), *Labour Law Between Change and Tradition: Liber Amicorum Antoine Jacobs*, Kluwer Law International, Alphen aan den Rijn, 2011; S. Deakin, 'The Lisbon Treaty, the Viking and Laval Judgments and the Financial Crisis: In Search of New Foundations for Europe's "Social Market Economy"' in N. Bruun, K. Lörcher & I. Schömann (eds), *The Lisbon Treaty and Social Europe*, Hart Publishing, Oxford and Portland, Oregon, 2012, pp. 19-43, where Deakin argued that the Laval case: '[...] radically altered the nature of the relationship between social policy and internal market by asserting that national labour rules were liable, in and of themselves, to distort competition, and as such had to be justified by reference to a strict test of proportionality'.

909. Opinion of Advocate General Maduro of 23 May 2007, *International Transport Workers' Federation and Finnish Seamen's Union v. Viking Line ABP and OÜ Viking Line Eesti*, C-438/05, ECLI:EU:C:2007:292 (para. 15).

910. *Ibid.* (para. 60): 'the key question [...] is to what ends collective action may be used and how far it may go' and (para. 62) 'Collective action that has the effect of partitioning the labour market and that impedes the hiring of seafarers from certain Member States in order to protect the jobs of seafarers in other Member State would strike at the heart of the principle of non-discrimination on which the common market is founded.'

911. *Ibid.* (para. 59): 'workers throughout Europe must accept the recurring negative consequences tare inherent to the common market's creation of increasing prosperity, in exchange for which society must commit itself to the general improvement of their living and working conditions, and to the provision of economic support to those workers who, as a consequence of market forces, come into difficulties'.

912. *Ibid.* (para. 25): '[...] the Court has consistently recognized the public interests relating to social policy may justify certain restrictions on freedom of movement, as long as these restrictions do not go beyond what is necessary. The Court has never accepted, however, that such restrictions would fall outside the scope of the provisions on freedom of movement altogether'.

opinion in *Commission v. Germany*,[913] Trstenjak commented on the Court's reasoning in the earlier *Viking* and *Laval* cases and noted that those judgments 'suggests, in fact, the existence of a hierarchical relationship between fundamental [economic] freedoms and fundamental rights in which [constitutionally protected] fundamental rights are subordinated to fundamental freedoms and, consequently, may restrict fundamental freedoms only with the assistance of a written or unwritten ground of justification'.[914] In order to correct this imbalance between economic integration and constitutional values, Trstenjak suggested resorting to genuine proportionality tests, where values and principles embodied in the conflicting norms are actually treated as equivalent.[915]

The gap between the 'theory' and the 'practice' of the pluralist approach is again present in the case law that followed the entry into force of the Lisbon Treaty and the CFREU. The revision of the Treaty and the conferring of binding force on the CFREU have indeed had the effect of reinforcing the process of constitutional maturation of the EU legal system and this seems to have led to greater boldness on the part of the Court.[916] This is evidenced by the fact that, since the late 2000s, the Court has refrained from referring to national constitutions or international treaties when ruling on potential conflicts between fundamental principles of the EU and national law. Instead, it has shown a tendency to rely on normative instruments that are part of EU primary law, such as the EU Treaties and the CFREU.

This approach can also be seen in the case law on social and labour law, such as the *Kücükdeveci*, *Ajos*, *Dominguez*, *Alemo-Herron* and *Aget Iraklis* judgments.[917] In these rulings, the Court did not examine the national provisions in issue in light of the national constitutional and legal systems, but addressed the question of interpretation exclusively through the lens of the EU legal framework. This type of reasoning is hardly compatible with a pluralist judicial lawmaking logic. Considering that these rulings were handed down in the mid-to-late 2000s, they may instead represent an attempt by

913. Opinion of Advocate General Trstenjak of 14 April 2010, *European Commission v. Federal Republic of Germany*, C-271/08, ECLI:EU:C:2010:183.

914. *Ibid.* (paras 183 and 184): 'Such an analytical approach suggests, in fact, the existence of a hierarchical relationship between fundamental freedoms and fundamental rights in which fundamental rights are subordinated to fundamental freedoms and, consequently, may restrict fundamental freedoms only with the assistance of a written or unwritten ground of justification.'

915. *Ibid.*; *see also* V. Trstenjak, 'National Sovereignty and the Principle of Primacy in EU Law and Their Importance for the Member States', Beijing Law Review, 4(2), pp. 71-76, 2013.

916. *See* G. Di Federico, 'Fundamental Rights in the EU: Legal Pluarlism and Multi-Level Protection After the Lisbon Treaty' in *The EU Charter of Fundamental Rights: From Declaration to Binding Instrument*, Springer, Dordrecht, 2011, pp. 15-55. On the Court's reference to the CFREU to strengthen the enforcement of the general principles of EU law, *see* Z. Rasnača, 'Procedure: Litigating Before EU Courts in the Light of the Charter' in F. Dorssemont, K. Lörcher, S. Clauwaert & M. Schmitt (eds), *The Charter of Fundamental Rights of the European Union and the Employment Relation*, Hart Publishing, London, 2019, pp. 163-188.

917. C-555/07, *Kücükdeveci*; judgment of 19 April 2016, *Dansk Industri (DI), acting on behalf of Ajos A/S v. Estate of Karsten Eigil Rasmussen*, C-441/14, ECLI:EU:C:2016:278; judgment of 24 January 2012, *Maribel Dominguez v. Centre informatique du Centre Ouest Atlantique and Préfet de la région Centre*, C-282/10, ECLI:EU:C:2012:33; C-426/11, *Alemo-Herron*; C-441/14, *Ajos*.

the Court to prevent the failed ratification of the Constitution for Europe from hampering European integration, as discussed in section 3.2.2.2.[918]

Finally, it should be borne in mind that there are elements that suggest that the Court's willingness to adopt a pluralist approach is linked to the attitude of national courts. In particular, it may be related to the degree of tolerance towards EU judgments that emerges from the national (constitutional) jurisprudence. Indeed, the Court's judicial restraint appears to be greater when domestic case law indicates that national courts are not open to supranational judicial policymaking. On the contrary, in times of (at least apparent) greater relaxation towards the EU case law, the Court seems to indulge in more judicial activism.[919] This fluctuating attitude makes it difficult to identify the prevailing decision-making approach of the Court. In fact, the Court is rather 'agile' in adapting its reasoning to the impression of openness or rather closure emerging from the national context and, in particular, from the national Supreme Courts. Trans-judicial dialogue is further discussed in the next section, but it is already interesting to refer to the *Taricco* saga, which is indicative of the Court's potentially opportunistic attitude towards constitutional pluralism.[920]

Taricco I concerned a conflict between Italian criminal procedural law and EU law, where the Court found that the Italian statute of limitations for tax and financial crimes was incompatible with EU secondary legislation. The Court, therefore, instructed the Italian courts to disregard the statute of limitations not only with respect to future legal disputes but also with respect to pending tax proceedings. In so ruling, the CJEU went against the case law of the Italian Constitutional Court, which had previously ruled that the principle of non-retroactivity (whereby changes in legal norms and practices should apply only to future situations) also covered tax crimes and, therefore, also the statute of limitations.[921] Moreover, according to the Constitutional Court, the principle of non-retroactivity was to be regarded as a manifestation of the constitutional principle of legality. With this judgment, the CJEU had thus essentially ruled that EU secondary legislation could trump the constitutionally protected principle of legality.

In order to prevent this judgment from having disruptive effects on the domestic legal system, the Italian Constitutional Court decided to refer a preliminary ruling question to the CJEU, asking to clarify the implications of its judgment. The Italian Constitutional Court's referral could be seen as an invitation to the CJEU to reconsider its earlier decision and to take better account of the national legal framework. In the judgment that followed (*Taricco II*), the Court showed that it had taken the Italian

918. M. Cartabia, 'Europe and Rights: Taking Dialogue Seriously', 2009, pp. 4, 21.
919. J.H.H. Weiler, 'Van Gend En Loos: The Individual as Subject and Object and the Dilemma of European Legitimacy', International Journal of Constitutional Law, 12(1), pp. 94-103, 2014; J.H.H. Weiler, 'The Transformation of Europe', The Yale Law Journal, 100(8), pp. 2403-2483, 1991.
920. Judgment of 5 December 2017, *Criminal proceedings against M.A.S. and M.B.*, C-42/17, ECLI:EU:C:2017:936; M. Bonelli, 'The Taricco Saga and the Consolidation of Judicial Dialogue in the European Union. CJEU, C-105/14 Ivo Taricco and others, ECLI:EU:C:2015:555; and C-42/17 M.A.S., M.B., ECLI:EU:C:2017:936 Italian Constitutional Court, Order no. 24/2017', Maastricht Journal of European and Comparative Law, 25(3), pp. 357-373, 2018.
921. *Ibid.*, p. 364.

court's request seriously and modified its reasoning. The Court, in fact, retraced its steps and ruled that Italian courts were not obliged to apply the *Taricco I* judgment if this would result in a breach of the constitutional principle of legality.[922]

The *Taricco II* judgment can certainly be regarded as a decision characterised by a pluralist logic. At the same time, however, it confirms that the pluralist approach can be used by the Court in response to pressures from national constitutional courts. Thus, rather than reflecting its genuine ethos, the CJEU seems to resort to a pluralist paradigm for utilitarian reasons, namely to strengthen the legitimacy and acceptance of its rulings.

4 TRANS-JUDICIAL DIALOGUE

When looking at the normative implications of the EU case law, there is little doubt that national courts have played a crucial role as the CJEU's main interlocutors. As mentioned, the dialectical interaction between the CJEU and national courts can be described as a 'trans-judicial dialogue'.[923]

This dialogue can take an indirect form when the national court refers to the case law of the CJEU in domestic proceedings.[924] Depending on the national court's approach to EU case law, an attitude of openness or, on the contrary, of closure towards the Court's jurisprudence may emerge. The dialogue between courts can also take a more direct form, and this occurs through the procedural instrument of the

922. In particular, with reference to Article 325 TFEU and Directive 2006/112 on the common system of value added tax. *See* judgment of 8 September 2015, *Criminal proceedings against Ivo Taricco and Others*, C-105/14, ECLI:EU:C:2015:555 (para. 58).
923. S. Sciarra, 'Integration Through the Court: Article 177 as a Pre-Federal Device' in S. Sciarra (ed.), *Labour Law in the Courts: National Judges and the European Court of Justice*, Hart Publishing, Oxford, 2001, pp. 1-24, p. 21; S. O'Leary, *Employment Law at the European Court of Justice: Judicial Structures, Policies, and Processes*, Hart Publishing, Oxford, 2002, pp. 63, 67-69; A. Rosas, 'The European Court of Justice in Context: Forms and Patterns of Judicial Dialogue', European Journal of Legal Studies, 1(2), 2007; A. Dyevre, 'Domestic Judicial Defiance and the Authority of International Legal Regimes', European Journal of Law and Economics, 44, pp. 453-458, 2017; R. Van Gestel & J. De Poorter, *In the Court We Trust: Cooperation, Coordination and Collaboration Between the ECJ and Supreme Administrative Courts*, Cambridge University Press, Cambridge, 2019, p. 71, where the authors noted that different meanings have, in time, been attached to the concept of 'judicial dialogue': 'judicial dialogue as a concept has been used in a sort of counterfactual to explain interaction between the CJEU and national courts in terms of power games instead of harmonious communicative interactions'. What they found from interviewing national and EU judges is that while 'a judicial dialogue presupposes a two-way communication style that goes beyond the current Q&A procedure, most CJEU judges see their relationship with the referring courts as a form of cooperation rather than a form of dialogue'.
924. G. Martinico, 'Judging in the Multilevel Legal Order: Exploring the Techniques of "Hidden Dialogue"', 2010; T. Tridimas, 'The ECJ and the National Courts: Dialogue, Cooperation, and Instability' in D. Chalmers & A. Arnull (eds), *The Oxford Handbook of European Union Law*, Oxford University Press, Oxford, 2015, pp. 1-30; R. Van Gestel & J. De Poorter, *In the Court We Trust: Cooperation, Coordination and Collaboration Between the ECJ and Supreme Administrative Courts*, 2019, where the authors identified three types of dialogue: before, during and after the Court decides on a question of interpretation.

preliminary reference (Article 267 TFEU).[925] As already mentioned in Chapter 4, section 2.2, the Treaty of Rome conferred on the CJEU the exclusive jurisdiction to interpret EU law. This means that, when in doubt about the interpretation of EU law, national courts should refrain from consulting the national Supreme Courts and instead refer a preliminary question directly to the CJEU, whose interpretation has an *erga omnes* effect in all Member States.[926]

Pertek has keenly observed that by centralising the 'authentic interpretation' jurisdiction of EU law in the hands of the Court, the Treaties have endowed to the national lower courts the role of 'courts éuropéennes de droit commun'.[927] With respect to the possibility of directly submitting a request for interpretation to the CJEU, national lower judges are in fact placed on an equal footing with higher and Supreme Courts. As discussed below, this proved difficult to reconcile with the domestic intra-courts dynamics, traditionally characterised by a hierarchical structure in which the higher courts shape the relationship between supranational and domestic law.

4.1 The Trans-judicial Dialogue as an Instrument of Contamination Between European and National Legal Systems

The preliminary ruling mechanism frames the dialogical interaction between national courts and the CJEU as a mostly voluntary cooperation, since the coercive and hierarchical component is only marginal.[928] Most of the time, a request for a preliminary ruling in fact originates from a spontaneous choice of the national court.[929] Tridimas accordingly defined the trans-judicial dialogue as a form of cooperative supranationalism, which takes shape in a relationship that is 'dialectical, full of circumspection and deference, albeit occasionally tense, and based on an incomplete and somewhat unstable political bargaining'.[930]

From the CJEU's perspective, national courts can be a valuable ally, as it is through them that preliminary rulings are issued and then implemented. Whenever a national court makes a reference for a preliminary ruling, the Court is given the opportunity to express, with *erga omnes* effect, how national (as well as EU) authorities should interpret and enforce EU law. As discussed while presenting neofunctionalism in Chapter 4 (section 2.2), the increased popularity of the preliminary ruling procedure among national judges has had a boosting effect on the legitimacy and authority of the

925. For one of the first complete overviews of the functioning and effect of preliminary ruling into the EU legal order, J. Pertek, *La Pratique du Renvoi Préjudiciel en Droit Communautaire*, Litec, Paris, 2001.
926. *Ibid.*, p. 13.
927. *Ibid.*, p. 27.
928. G. Martinico, 'Judging in the Multilevel Legal Order: Exploring the Techniques of "Hidden Dialogue"', 2010; T. Tridimas, 'The ECJ and the National Courts: Dialogue, Cooperation, and Instability', 2015; T. Pavone & R.D. Kelemen, 'The Evolving Judicial Politics of European Integration: The European Court of Justice and National Courts Revisited', European Law Journal, pp. 1-22, 2019.
929. S. Sciarra, 'Integration Through the Court: Article 177 as a Pre-Federal Device', 2001.
930. T. Tridimas, 'The ECJ and the National Courts: Dialogue, Cooperation, and Instability', 2015.

CJEU.[931] And this explains the (successful) efforts of the CJEU to turn Article 267 TFEU into much more than a mere technical instrument for resolving doubts about the interpretation of EU law.[932] Also from the point of view of the national courts, interacting with the CJEU has considerable advantages. As Nyikos observed, through the preliminary ruling mechanism national courts can have an additional judicial avenue to validate or pursue a particular legal solution that is struggling to emerge in the national context. This is particularly the case where the national legal doctrine relies heavily on the jurisprudential interpretation of the national Supreme Courts.[933] Second, a reference to the CJEU may lend greater authority to the decision by which the national referring court defines the legal dispute.[934] Third, and more obviously, a reference for a preliminary ruling has the effect of facilitating the national court's task of interpretation, which is partly delegated to the CJEU.[935] Finally, and perhaps most interestingly in the context of this book, references for a preliminary ruling enable national courts to interact with the CJEU and thus to participate, albeit indirectly, in a formative moment of EU policymaking. All the 'historic' judgments of the Court originated from a reference for a preliminary ruling, meaning that were the result of the initiative of a national judge who decided to bring a question of interpretation to the CJEU. In identifying and addressing such questions, national courts have thus substantially contributed to EU judicial policymaking and have become true subjects of EU law.[936] In other words, and quoting Sciarra: 'the EU treaties placed national courts at the centre of an unborn and yet unpredictable institutional equilibrium'.[937]

931. J.H.H. Weiler, 'The Transformation of Europe', 1991; G.F. Mancini, 'The Making of a Constitution for Europe', 1989; S. Bardutzky & E. Fahey, 'The Subjects and Objects of EU Law: Exploring a Research Platform' in S. Bardutzky & E. Fahey (eds), *Framing the Subjects and Objects of Contemporary EU Law*, Edward Elgar Publishing, Cheltenham, 2017, pp. 1-30.
932. Very significant examples are the judgments C-6/64, *Costa v. Enel* and *C-26/62, Van Gend en Loos*, regarding direct effect and the principle of primacy of EU law. Or C-106/77, *Simmenthal* with which the Court of Justice has established that national courts are obliged to disapply domestic law when it obstructs the implementation of European legislation. All these milestones were the result of a dialectical process with national courts, which had the initiative to refer these fundamental questions on inter-ordinal relations to the Court of Justice.
933. S.A. Nyikos, 'Strategic Interaction among Courts Within the Preliminary Reference Process – Stage 1: National Court Preemptive Opinions', European Journal of Political Research, 45, pp. 527-550, 2006.
934. K. Alter, 'Explaining National Court Acceptance of European Court Jurisprudence: A Critical Evaluation of Theories of Legal Integration' in A.M. Slaughter, A. Stone Sweet & J. Weiler (eds), *The European Court and National Court – Doctrine and Jurisprudence: Legal Change in Its Social Context*, Hart Publishing, Oxford, 1998, pp. 227-252.
935. T. Tridimas, 'The ECJ and the National Courts: Dialogue, Cooperation, and Instability', 2015.
936. M. Cartabia, 'Europe and Rights: Taking Dialogue Seriously', 2009: 'although following the wording of Article 234 TCE [currently 267 TFEU] the preliminary ruling is conceived as a duty and an obligation for the supreme courts, it is, in fact, above all, a great opportunity for them. It is short-sighted to refuse the preliminary rulings for fear of losing freedom, sovereignty and independence. The bright side of the moon is that the preliminary ruling is a great change for national judges to take part in the building up of the European constitution'. *See also* M. Claes, 'Luxembourg, Here We Come? Constitutional Courts and the Preliminary Reference Procedure', German Law Journal, 16(6), pp. 1331-1342, 2015.
937. S. Sciarra, 'Integration Through the Court: Article 177 as a Pre-Federal Device', 2001, p. 4.

4.2 The Preliminary Ruling Procedure

It was mentioned that the main instrument that national courts have for establishing a direct interaction with the CJEU is the preliminary ruling procedure, established in Article 267 TFEU.[938] This mechanism was already there in the Treaty of Rome (in Article 177 TCEE) and has been subject to only marginal changes since then.[939] This provision allows a national court to refer a question directly to the CJEU if it considers that there is doubt as to the interpretation or validity of a rule of EU law. This book only deals with questions of interpretation and not with questions of validity, which are also more marginal from a quantitative point of view.

Article 267 TFEU mentions two different types of possible interaction between the referring national court and the CJEU: one is entirely voluntary while the other has an element of imposition. The trans-judicial dialogue of a voluntary nature is the most frequent. The Treaty indeed gives all judicial authorities (unless they are courts of last resort) the *possibility* to refer a question to the Court for a preliminary ruling. The interaction is instead imposed when the national court is a court of last resort, meaning a court 'against whose decisions there is no judicial remedy under national law'. In this case, the national judges are *obliged* to make a preliminary reference to the CJEU if they have doubts about the interpretation of EU law. The reason for this constraint is to ensure that the CJEU, and not the national Supreme Courts, has the ultimate authority on the interpretation (and validity) of EU law. By giving the Court the final say on the interpretation of EU law, the Treaties sought to avoid the proliferation of different regulatory regimes across the Member States.[940]

It has been said that the preliminary ruling mechanism gives national courts the possibility to intervene in the formation of EU judicial policymaking.[941] However, in Chapter 4, section 2.2, it was also noted that the involvement of national courts took time to develop. The preliminary ruling procedure had in fact a slow start before becoming a widespread instrument: as Nyikos and Mancini observed, it took three years from the entry into force of the Rome Treaty before the Court received the first request for a preliminary ruling.[942] From there it was a gradual crescendo and the preliminary ruling became the most widely used judicial instrument of EU law.[943]

938. S. O'Leary, *Employment Law at the European Court of Justice: Judicial Structures, Policies, and Processes*, 2002, p. 67.
939. With regard to the discipline of Article 267, the Treaty of Lisbon revised the existing rule only to establish a faster procedure in case the trial pending before the referring court concerns a person in detention. In this sense, the Rules of Procedure have also been amended in January 2008 to provide for an urgent preliminary ruling procedure which may be used in the case of disputes concerning persons in detention, but also parental authority and custody of minors.
940. J. Pertek, *La Pratique du Renvoi Préjudiciel en Droit Communautaire*, Litec, Paris, 2001, p. 18.
941. O. Pollicino, *Allargamento dell'Europa a est e rapporto tra Corti costituzionali e Corti europee*, 2010, p. 43; J.H.H. Weiler, 'The Transformation of Europe', 1991.
942. This first request for a preliminary ruling was made by the Gerechtshof of The Hague (The Netherlands). *See* S.A. Nyikos, 'The European Court of Justice and National Courts: Strategic Interaction Within the EU Judicial Process', University of Virginia, 2000, p. 3; G.F. Mancini, 'The Making of a Constitution for Europe', 1989, p. 605.
943. Just in relation to the most recent years: in 2015 the Court received 436 requests, 470 in 2016, 533 in 2017, 568 in 2018, 641 in 2019, 556 in 2020 and 567 in 2021.

While in 1961 the Court had received only one request, in 1970 the applications became 32; 99 in 1980; 151 in 1990; 224 in 2000; 385 in 2010; and 567 in 2021.[944]

4.2.1 *The Establishment of the Dialogical Relationship and the 'Hidden Dialogue'*

Given its importance for the enforcement of EU law, the Court has over the years adopted a broad interpretation of the admissibility of the references for preliminary rulings. For example, the Court has defined the notion of 'court or tribunal', which refers to the body from which the preliminary ruling request may legitimately originate, more broadly than is usually the case in national procedural law.[945] Indeed, this concept has been interpreted by the Court to cover a wide range of adjudicating institutions and authorities, even if they are not strictly speaking part of the judicial context.[946]

At the same time, the Court has also given a broad interpretation of the conditions under which the national court may (or, if of last resort, must) refer a preliminary question to the Court, stating that, in principle, this may occur in all cases of uncertainty as to the interpretation of EU law. There are only three exceptions in which the CJEU *can* refrain from issuing a ruling, and where the national court is exempted from making a reference. The first exception was defined in the *Da Costa* judgment. There the Court ruled that preliminary references are not necessary when concerning a legal issue that is materially identical to one that has already been ruled upon by the Court.[947] The second and third exceptions were subsequently identified in the *Cilfit* case. One is the situation where the interpretation of EU law can be easily deduced from

944. In total, since its inception, the court has received 12,481 requests for preliminary rulings, compared to 92,000 direct actions. *See* Court of Justice of the European Union, Annual Report 2021 – Judicial Activity, Luxembourg, 2022.
945. Judgment of 30 June 1966, *G. Vaassen-Göbbels (a widow) v. Management of the Beambtenfonds voor het Mijnbedrijf*, C-61/65, ECLI:EU:C:1966:39 and judgment of 16 October 1997, *Maria Antonella Garofalo and Others v. Ministero della Sanità and Unità sanitaria locale (USL) n° 58 di Palermo*, Joined Cases C-69/96 to C-79/96, ECLI:EU:C:1997:492, where the Court of Justice set out the criteria for establishing whether a body of a Member State can be considered as a 'court or tribunal' within the meaning of Article 267 TFEU. These criteria are the following: the legal origin of the body, its permanent character, the binding nature of its decisions, the presence of adversarial proceedings, the application of rules of law and its independence. For a deeper analysis: D.P. Domenicucci, 'Il Ruolo del Giudice Nazionale e il Procedimento Pregiudiziale', Seminario per Magistrati: Il Diritto dell'UE in Materia di Parità di Genere, ERA – Accademia di diritto Europeo, 2012. The Court has often been referred to by professional bodies and, on these occasions, has been in favour of giving them the status of jurisdiction, at least with regard to applications for membership of the professional body or disciplinary measures. *See also* judgment of 30 November 1995, *Reinhard Gebhard v. Consiglio dell'Ordine degli Avvocati e Procuratori di Milano*, C-55/94, ECLI:EU:C:1995:411, where the Court recognised the Council of the Order of Advocates and Procurators of Milano (The Milan Bar Council) as a judicial body entitled to make references for a preliminary ruling under Article 267 TFEU.
946. J. Pertek, *La Pratique du Renvoi Préjudiciel en Droit Communautaire*, Litec, Paris, 2001, p. 50.
947. Judgment of 27 March 1963, *Da Costa en Schaake NV, Jacob Meijer NV, Hoechst-Holland NV v. Netherlands Inland Revenue Administration*, C-28/62, ECLI:EU:C:1963:6.

the case law of the Court. The other is when the correct application of the EU rule in question is so obvious as to leave no scope for any reasonable doubt.[948]

Besides giving a broad interpretation of the range of questions that can be referred to through the preliminary ruling procedure, with the *Kobler* and *Traghetti del Mediterraneo* cases the Court has further strengthened the relevance of such a mechanism by essentially turning it into a sort of judicial remedy.[949] In these judgments, the Court in fact ruled that if a court of last instance improperly evades its obligation to make a reference for a preliminary ruling, and if a party is financially damaged by such refusal, he or she is entitled to claim compensation from the Member State in which the court is located.[950]

Having clarified when it is possible (or necessary) to make a reference for a preliminary ruling, it is also important to note that ultimately it is up to the national courts whether to actually make use of it. National courts in fact have a wide margin of discretion in identifying potential interpretative doubts and in formulating the reference to the CJEU.[951] Once the existence of an interpretative doubt has been 'diagnosed', the domestic court has the possibility to decide whether to solve it on its own or to refer it to the Court (although this possibility is substantially limited in the case of courts of last instance). The way in which the national judge deals with this first assessment is already quite revealing of its approach towards the CJEU and trans-judicial dialogue. So much so that scholars such as Cartabia, Martinico, Tridimas, van Gestel and de Poorter have resorted to the notion of 'hidden dialogue'.[952] For example, an attitude of closure can be identified when, in the face of an obvious interpretative doubt, the national judge prefers to deal with it himself rather than refer it to the CJEU.

948. *Ibid.*; judgment of 6 October 1982, *Srl CILFIT and Lanificio di Gavardo SpA v. Ministry of Health*, C-283/81, ECLI:EU:C:1982:335. For different analysis: F. Pani, 'L'obbligo (flessibile) di rinvio pregiudiziale e i possibili fattori di un suo irrigidimento. Riflessioni in margine alla sentenza Association France Nature Environnement', European Papers, 2(1), pp. 383-391, 2017. The same exceptions were later incorporated into the Rules of Procedure of the Court, in Article 104.
949. C-224/01, *Kobler*; *C-173/03, Traghetti del Mediterraneo*. *See also* M. Cartabia, 'Europe and Rights: Taking Dialogue Seriously', 2009, p. 32.
950. In C-224/01, *Kobler* (para. 59), the Court ruled that the principle that Member States are obliged to make good damage caused to individuals by infringements of Community law for which they are responsible is also applicable where the alleged infringement stems from a decision of a court adjudicating at last instance where the rule of Community law infringed is intended to confer rights on individuals, the breach is sufficiently serious and there is a direct causal link between that breach and the loss or damage sustained by the injured parties. In C-173/03, *Traghetti del Mediterraneo* (para. 42), the Court reiterated the reasoning of the previous *Kobler* judgment and also stated that EU law also precludes national legislation which limits such liability solely to case of intentional fault and serious misconduct on the part of the court, if such a limitation were to lead to exclusion of the liability of the Member State concerned in other cases where a manifest infringement of the applicable law was committed.
951. In R. Van Gestel & J. De Poorter, *In the Court We Trust: Cooperation, Coordination and Collaboration Between the ECJ and Supreme Administrative Courts*, 2019, p. 4.
952. T. Tridimas, 'The ECJ and the National Courts: Dialogue, Cooperation, and Instability' in D. Chalmers & A. Arnull (eds), *The Oxford Handbook of European Union Law*, Oxford University Press, Oxford, 2015, pp. 1-30; G. Martinico, 'The "Polemical" Spirit of European Constitutional Law: On the Importance of Conflicts in EU Law', 2015.

A manifestation of trans-judicial coldness, even if not ostentatious and indirect, can have an impact on the reasoning of the Court, especially when widespread across the Member States' judiciary. As was seen in section 3.3.4 on pluralism, the Court has shown a tendency to modulate its judicial activism on the basis of its perception of the (closed or open) attitude of the domestic judicial authorities towards its rulings.

4.2.2 *Superior and Lower Courts: A Different Kind of Dialogue*

Looking at the overall activity of the CJEU, an analysis of the requests for preliminary rulings received over the years shows that higher courts make proportionally less use of Article 267 TFEU than lower courts. The case of Germany is quite illustrative: Germany is indeed the Member State from which most preliminary ruling requests originate, but the Federal Constitutional Court has, so far, made only two references for a preliminary ruling.[953] A similar situation can be found in Italy, where the Constitutional Court has made only four requests, or in France, Spain and Poland, where the constitutional courts have made just one request.[954]

How to explain the different attitudes between superior and lower courts? Martinico, Cartabia and Tridimas interpreted the reticence of higher courts to rely on Article 267 TFEU as an attempt to resist the (perceived) erosion of their role as guardians of the domestic constitutional and legal order.[955] This might be especially the case in countries in which the relationship between domestic and supranational sources of law respond to a dualist model, as opposed to the monist paradigm earlier described in Chapter 4, section 3.2.1. According to the dualistic model, supranational law and domestic law are two separate legal orders in which supranational sources acquire legal effect only when transposed by the domestic legal order.[956] It is therefore understandable that in such systems constitutional courts can have a tense relationship with the CJEU. From their perspective, recognising in full the CJEU's judicial and

953. For an overview of the German court approach to preliminary ruling, *see* J. Kokott, 'Report on Germany' in A.M. Slaughter, A. Stone Sweet & J. Weiler (eds), *The European Court and National Court – Doctrine and Jurisprudence: Legal Change in Its Social Context*, Hart Publishing, Oxford, 1998, pp. 77-133.
954. For an overview, *see* M. Cartabia, 'The Italian Constitutional Court and the Relationship Between the Italian Legal System and the European Union' in A.M. Slaughter, A. Stone Sweet & J. Weiler (eds), *The European Court and National Court – Doctrine and Jurisprudence: Legal Change in Its Social Context*, Hart Publishing, Oxford, 1998, pp. 133-144; P. Ruggeri Laderchi, 'Report on Italy' in A.M. Slaughter, A. Stone Sweet & J. Weiler (eds), *The European Court and National Court – Doctrine and Jurisprudence: Legal Change in Its Social Context*, Hart Publishing, Oxford, 1998, pp. 147-169; V. Barsotti et al., *Italian Constitutional Justice in Global Context*, Oxford University Press, Oxford, 2016, pp. 205-226.
955. G. Martinico, 'The "Polemical" Spirit of European Constitutional Law: On the Importance of Conflicts in EU Law', 2015; T. Tridimas, 'The ECJ and the National Courts: Dialogue, Cooperation, and Instability', 2015; M. Cartabia, 'Europe and Rights: Taking Dialogue Seriously', 2009.
956. A. Stone Sweet, *The Judicial Construction of Europe*, Oxford University Press, New York, 2004, p. 82.

interpretative authority would imply a limitation of national sovereignty and of their own autonomy.[957]

In recent years, however, there has been a gradual opening towards the Court, even in dualist systems. Pavone and Tridimas interpreted this more dialogical attitude as an attempt by the national superior courts to prevent trans-judicial dialogue from becoming an exclusive prerogative of the lower courts.[958] As mentioned, lower courts in fact have historically shown a much greater propensity to engage in dialogue with the CJEU, as illustrated by Alter and Dyevre among others.[959]

According to a theory originally developed by Alter, the openness of lower courts to engage in dialogue with the CJEU can be explained in light of domestic inter-court competition and judicial empowerment dynamics.[960] Lower courts may in fact rely on the preliminary ruling procedure to obtain greater interpretative autonomy from the higher courts[961] and to introduce into the domestic legal order reasoning that differs from, and therefore challenges, that of the Supreme Courts, thus defying the rigid hierarchy between courts.[962]

This dynamic has been particularly accentuated following the *Simmenthal* judgment, in which the CJEU held that national courts (regardless of their jurisdictional hierarchy) are obliged to disapply rules of domestic law that conflict with EU law.[963] The CJEU thus granted to lower judges the de facto possibility to control the conformity of national law with EU law, which was until then a prerogative of the Supreme Courts. National lower court saw this as an opportunity to reaffirm their role in ensuring the compliance of national norms vis-à-vis the EU legal order, and gradually increased their use of the preliminary ruling mechanism. This, in turn, had the effect to bring EU law

957. R. Van Gestel & J. De Poorter, *In the Court We Trust: Cooperation, Coordination and Collaboration Between the ECJ and Supreme Administrative Courts*, 2019, p. 41. It took until 1977 for the first constitutional court (of Belgium) to refer a question to the Court of Justice.
958. T. Pavone & R.D. Kelemen, 'The Evolving Judicial Politics of European Integration: The European Court of Justice and National Courts Revisited', 2019; T. Tridimas, 'The ECJ and the National Courts: Dialogue, Cooperation, and Instability', 2015; E. Bribosia et al., 'e-Nact Handbook, Module 2: The Charter's Social and Non-discrimination Provisions in the Employment Field', E-learning National Active Charter Training, EUI, 2018.
959. K. Alter, 'Explaining National Court Acceptance of European Court Jurisprudence: A Critical Evaluation of Theories of Legal Integration' in A.M. Slaughter, A. Stone Sweet & J. Weiler (eds), *The European Court and National Court – Doctrine and Jurisprudence: Legal Change in Its Social Context*, Hart Publishing, Oxford, 1998, pp. 227-252; A. Dyevre, 'Domestic Judicial Defiance and the Authority of International Legal Regimes', European Journal Law and Economics, 44, pp. 453-481, 2017.
960. *Ibid.*, K. Alter, 'Explaining National Court Acceptance of European Court Jurisprudence: A Critical Evaluation of Theories of Legal Integration' in A.M. Slaughter, A. Stone Sweet & J. Weiler (eds), *The European Court and National Court – Doctrine and Jurisprudence: Legal Change in Its Social Context*, Hart Publishing, Oxford, 1998, pp. 227-252. Alter's intuition was further developed by other authors. *Inter alia, see*: S. Sciarra, 'Integration through the Court: Article 177 as a Pre-Federal Device', 2001, p. 6; T. Horsley, *The Court of Justice of the European Union as and Institutional Actor: Judicial Lawmaking and Its Limits*, 2018, p. 228; P. Ruggeri Laderchi, 'Report on Italy', 1998.
961. K. Alter, 'Explaining National Court Acceptance of European Court Jurisprudence: A Critical Evaluation of Theories of Legal Integration', 1998.
962. S. Sciarra, 'Integration Through the Court: Article 177 as a Pre-Federal Device', 2001, p. 6.
963. C-106/77, *Simmenthal* (para. 17).

more and more into domestic proceedings and to reinforce the interpretative authority of the CJEU.[964]

Interestingly, in a recent study, Dyevre, Glavina and Atanasova found that since the 2000s the traditional division between higher and lower courts has become narrower, with an increase in references for preliminary rulings from appellate and higher courts.[965] This trend has been explained on account of the division of labour and resources within national judicial hierarchy.[966] In particular, Glavina suggested that the ever-increasing volume of cases pending before first-instance judges is discouraging them from referring questions to the CJEU.[967] Still, on closer inspection, the recent growth in preliminary ruling requests originating from higher jurisdictions hardly involves courts that are in a situation of imposed cooperation with the CJEU, thus suggesting that those courts may still be rather reticent to embrace the judicial dialogue dynamics.[968]

4.2.3 Establishing the Dialogue and 'Preemptive Opinions' of National Courts

Whether it is a higher or a lower court, the national judge must follow certain formats and standards when formulating a request for a preliminary ruling to the CJEU. The request must be well reasoned and provide the factual and regulatory framework in which the dispute is set.[969] In addition, the national judge may briefly state its views on

964. M. Cartabia, 'Europe and Rights: Taking Dialogue Seriously', 2009. There are, however, exceptions: J. Krommendijk, 'The Highest Dutch Courts and the Preliminary Ruling Procedure: Critically Obedient Interlocutors of the Court of Justice', European Law Journal, 2019, pp. 1-22, in relation to the Dutch judiciary which, according to the author, does not display the intention to influence the CJEU's rule-making.
965. A. Dyevre, M. Glavina & A. Atanasova, 'Who Refers Most? Institutional Incentives and Judicial Participation in the Preliminary Ruling System', Journal of European Public Policy, 27(6), pp. 912-930, 2019.
966. A. Dyevre, M. Glavina & A. Atanasova, 'Who Refers Most? Institutional Incentives and Judicial Participation in the Preliminary Ruling System', 2019.
967. M. Glavina, 'Judicial Hierarchy in the Preliminary Ruling Procedure: Exploring the Relationship Between the First and the Second Instance Courts', European Papers, 5(2), pp. 799-823, 2020.
968. Still, there are exceptions. To date, the constitutional court of Belgium has made 44 references, the court of cassation has made 100 and the council of state 101. Taken together, these referrals amount to around 40% of all referrals made by national courts. Although they do not reach these proportions, the Dutch and Hungarian higher courts have also frequently used the instrument of the preliminary reference. For precise data: Court of Justice of the European Union, Annual Report 2020 – Judicial Activity, Luxembourg, 2021. For pertinent literature, *see* A. Dyevre, 'Domestic Judicial Defiance and the Authority of International Legal Regimes', European Journal of Law and Economics, 44, pp. 453-481, 2017 and U. Sadl, 'National Court and the Effectiveness of EU Law' in B. de Witte, J.A. Mayoral & U. Jaremba (eds), *National Court and EU Law: New Issues, Theories and Methods*, Edward Elgar Publishing, Cheltenham, 2006, pp. 68-105.
969. Court of Justice of the European Union, Recommendations to national courts and tribunals, in relation to the initiation of preliminary ruling proceedings, 2016/C 439/01, 25 November 2016. *See also* judgment of 26 January 1993, *Telemarsicabruzzo SpA and Others v. Circostel, Ministero delle Poste e Telecomunicazioni and Ministero della Difesa*, C-320/90, Joined Cases C-320/90, C-321/90 and C-322/90, ECLI:EU:C:1993:26 (para. 2).

the resolution of the interpretative question.[970] Nyikos observed that when availing of this possibility, the referring judge de facto offers a 'preemptive opinion', whose function is to influence the Court's reasoning.[971] In such cases, it cannot be excluded that the reference for a preliminary ruling conceals the intention of the referring judge to intervene in the judicial policymaking of the CJEU. Behind the referral, there might be thus an attempt to influence the predominant interpretation of national or EU law.

Nyikos conducted a study on the referral for preliminary rulings submitted to the CJEU from 1961 to 1995. The analysis showed that national courts submitted preemptive opinions in 41.3% of cases. An even higher value (48%) emerged from the research conducted by van Gestel and de Poorter, who focused on preliminary requests submitted by supreme administrative courts.[972] Niykos identified three factors whose presence is linked to a greater likelihood that the national judge expresses an opinion on the solution to the interpretative question. The first is that the national courts that most often formulate preemptive opinions are also those that make frequent use of the preliminary ruling mechanism.[973] The second factor is the participation of the national government as a litigant in the main proceedings. When the national government is a party in the dispute the referring judge tends to submit its own view in relation to the interpretative issue object of the referral to the CJEU. Third, lower courts appear to be more inclined than higher courts to formulate preemptive opinions.[974]

970. The referring court has to provide this information in the case of urgent preliminary ruling procedures – *see* Article 104b(1) of the Rules of Procedure of the Court. For other preliminary ruling proceedings, the legal basis for the preemptive opinions is also Rule 17 in Court of Justice of the EU, Recommendations to national courts and tribunals, in relation to the initiation of preliminary ruling proceedings, 2016/C 439/01, 25 November 2016: 'In its request for a preliminary ruling, the referring court or tribunal must provide precise references for the national provisions applicable to the facts of the dispute in the main proceedings, and accurately identify the provisions of EU law whose interpretation is sought or whose validity is challenged. The request should include, if need be, a brief summary of the relevant arguments of the parties to the main proceedings. It is helpful to bear in mind in that context that it is only the request for a preliminary ruling that will be translated, not any annexes to that request.'

971. S.A. Nyikos, 'The European Court of Justice and National Courts: Strategic Interaction Within the EU Judicial Process', 2000. The author referred to the example of the judgment of 10 April 1984, *Sabine von Colson and Elisabeth Kamann v. Land Nordrhein-Westfalen*, C-14/83, ECLI:EU:C:1984:153, where the national court (Hamburg) clearly expressed its view on the resolution of the interpretative question to the Court of Justice. R. Van Gestel & J. De Poorter, *In the Court We Trust: Cooperation, Coordination and Collaboration Between the ECJ and Supreme Administrative Courts*, 2019, pp. 200-230, where the authors instead of 'preemptive opinion' use the term 'provisional answer', to be understood as 'offering the right answer, offering a number of alternative answer and offering general answer with an additional assessment of their potential consequences for the national legal order'.

972. The ratio of preemptive opinions submitted by supreme administrative courts versus lower administrative courts until 2019: Germany 8/7; France 13/1; UK 4/3; The Netherlands 13/6; Belgium 8/1; Austria 18/13; Denmark 3/0; Spain 9/3; Czech Republic 11/9; Poland 11/3. *See* R. Van Gestel & J. De Poorter, *In the Court We Trust: Cooperation, Coordination and Collaboration Between the ECJ and Supreme Administrative Courts*, 2019, p. 76.

973. S.A. Nyikos, 'The European Court of Justice and National Courts: Strategic Interaction within the EU Judicial Process', 2000, p. 27, where the author noted that repeat plyers submit preemptive opinions around 44% of the times and first-time courts only 30.6%.

974. S.A. Nyikos, 'Strategic Interaction among Courts Within the Preliminary Reference Process – Stage 1: National Court Preemptive Opinions', European Journal of Political Research, 45, pp.

Nyikos's study also gave interesting insights into the impact of the referring courts' preemptive opinions on the CJEU's reasoning, as it showed that the Court ruled in line with the reasoning suggested by the national court 57.4% of the time.[975] Interestingly, most of these cases concerned areas of EU law on which the Court had not previously ruled and therefore could not rely on its own judicial precedent.[976]

The potential influence of preemptive opinions on EU case law opens up potentially problematic questions concerning the institutional balance within the EU legal order. National courts which make more frequent use of preliminary rulings and more often submit a preemptive opinion might indeed have a greater impact on the reasoning of the Court than those national courts which are not as active. This implies that the EU case law may reflect more the legal views of the judiciary in countries with a long tradition of judicial dialogue with the CJEU (such as Germany, Italy, France, Spain, the UK, Poland, Belgium, the Netherlands), and less the judicial traditions of countries where judges are less involved in trans-judicial dynamics.[977]

It is also worth noting that preemptive opinions constitute important dialectical elements from the point of view of trans-judicial dialogue, as through them national judges can show deference, exhibit scepticism or even hostility towards the CJEU.[978] In fact, and as previously discussed, the attitude of national courts might have a great impact on the degree of judicial activism exhibited by the Court in its rulings.[979] It follows that if the elements provided by the referring judge in the preemptive opinion are indicative of the openness, or rather the closure, of the national judiciary to a particular line of argument, they may steer the approach of the CJEU accordingly.

4.3 The Limits of the Court's Discretion

When the Court receives a reference for a preliminary ruling with questions of interpretation, it has the opportunity to rule on the meaning of EU law with *erga omnes* effect. While the Court disposes of a fairly wide margin of appreciation in elaborating its legal reasoning, there are limits to its interpretative creativity. Some of these limits are endogenous to the legal system of the Union, while others arise from the multilevel and multinational context in which the trans-judicial dialogue is embedded.

527-550, 2006, where she observed that lower court submitted preemptive opinion 48% of the cases, while appeal court 28.6% and last instance court 47.1%.

975. R. Van Gestel & J. De Poorter, *In the Court We Trust: Cooperation, Coordination and Collaboration Between the ECJ and Supreme Administrative Courts*, 2019, p. 97, where the authors indicate that even when the case law shows that the Court does not directly engages with the provisional answers of the referring court 'this does not imply that the CJEU is ignoring the signals it receives from the referring national court'.
976. S.A. Nyikos, 'The European Court of Justice and National Courts: Strategic Interaction Within the EU Judicial Process', 2000, p. 34.
977. Court of Justice of the European Union, Annual Report 2020 – Judicial Activity, Luxembourg, 2021: until the end of 2020, the number of references per country was the following: Germany, 2.780; Italy, 1.627; The Netherlands, 1.094; France, 1.073; Belgium, 955; Spain, 621; The UK, 672.
978. R. Van Gestel & J. De Poorter, *In the Court We Trust: Cooperation, Coordination and Collaboration Between the ECJ and Supreme Administrative Courts*, 2019.
979. As discussed in section 4.2.1 above.

4.3.1 *Limits from Within the EU Legal System*

First, the CJEU does not have jurisdiction to rule on all areas of law that fall within the regulatory competence of the Union.[980] Although the Treaty of Lisbon extended the range of the matters which can be reviewed by the Court, there are still exceptions. These include police operations for the maintenance of public order and EU acts adopted in the field of common foreign and security policy.[981] These are limitations of competence which have no particular impact on the trans-judicial dynamics and are therefore not further discussed in the book.

For the exploration of judicial lawmaking, it is instead more important to note that the Court has to respect certain constraints while addressing the preliminary questions submitted by the national judge. The Court must limit itself to interpreting EU law and cannot comment on the merits of the case or the validity of a rule of national law.[982] Also, the ruling has to remain within the scope of what is necessary to provide the referring court with sufficient elements to apply EU law correctly.

In this regard, Tridimas distinguished two types of rulings that the Court can issue.[983] The first type is 'guidance cases', in which the Court leads the national court on how to resolve the interpretative issue concerning EU law, but does not settle the dispute. The second type is 'deference cases'. Here the Court simply clarifies the interpretation of EU law and leaves ample discretion to the national court as to the resolution of the legal issue central to the dispute. This type of ruling may indicate a pluralist approach by the Court as they provide ample space for national legal

980. The 1992 Maastricht Treaty introduced the so-called pillar structure, whereby the competences of the CJEU differed depending on the policy area. At the time, the Court's jurisdiction was essentially confined to the 'Community Pillar'. The reforms introduced by the Treaty of Amsterdam broadened the Court's jurisdiction, with a partial inclusion of policies on the control of supplies, asylum, immigration and judicial cooperation in civil matters.
981. However, the Court may now review the legality of restrictive measures taken by the EU against natural or legal persons (Article 257 TFEU) and may rule on the compatibility with the treaties of international agreements concluded under the Common Foreign and Security Policy. In these areas, however, restrictions remained because, under Article 68 TEC, only superior national courts, whose decisions are not subject to internal appeal, could make a reference to the CJEU. Furthermore, rules concerning the maintenance of law and order and the safeguarding of internal security were excluded from the jurisdiction of the Court. As regards judicial cooperation in criminal matters, Article 35 TEU allowed access to the preliminary ruling mechanism only to courts which had made a declaration of acceptance of the court's jurisdiction. Furthermore, the control could not concern the validity and proportionality of police operations, nor, again, measures relating to public security. The entry into force of the Lisbon Treaty led to an important strengthening of judicial review in the Union. The Court has extended its ability to give preliminary rulings on rules relating to the Area of Freedom, Security and Justice. In particular, the limitations provided for in Article 68 TEC and Article 35 TEU have been removed.
982. *See also* judgment of 1 December 1998, *Criminal proceedings against André Ambry*, C-410/96, ECLI:EU:C:1998:578 (para. 19): 'it must be borne in mind that the Court has no jurisdiction, in the context of the application of article 177 of the Treaty [the predecessor of Article 267 TFEU], to decide whether national rules are compatible with Community law, although it may provide the court with the interpretation of all relevant aspects of Community law in order to enable that court to assess the compatibility of the rules with the Community measures in question'.
983. T. Tridimas, 'The ECJ and the National Courts: Dialogue, Cooperation, and Instability', 2015.

solutions. However, sometimes the Court oversteps its boundaries and issues 'outcome cases', where it tells the national court how the main proceedings should be resolved and considerably reduce the national court's margin of discretion.[984] From the perspective of trans-judicial dialogue, they may be rather useful for the referring judge, who is dispensed from having to extrapolate a practical solution from the Court's reasoning. However, they also run the risk of being perceived as inappropriate interference in the judicial lawmaking of national courts.[985]

4.3.2 Dialectical Limits

There are also limits to the Court's decision-making that do not relate to the rules of procedure of the CJEU. Rather, these limits derive from the normative and judicial context in which the Court exercises its interpretative activity inasmuch as trans-judicial dialogue dynamics may indeed significantly condition the reasoning of the CJEU.

First, it should be considered that the CJEU is entitled to rule on the preliminary request solely on the basis of the legal and factual elements provided by the national courts in its submission.[986] The way in which these elements are presented by the referring court thus has a substantial impact on the Court's appreciation of the legal issue.[987]

Then, and more importantly, the Court's reasoning might be influenced by the legal and judicial traditions that in each Member State govern the relationship with EU law and, in particular, the recognition (or not) of the judicial authority of the CJEU in

984. R. Van Gestel & J. De Poorter, *In the Court We Trust: Cooperation, Coordination and Collaboration Between the ECJ and Supreme Administrative Courts*, 2019, pp. 85-87, where the authors referred to this category as the 'ready-made answer', where the Court provides an answer to the referring court that offers a ready-made solution for the decision in the case the national court needs to decide The authors analysed a pool of cases where the referring courts are administrative judges and found that in 47% of cases the Court realised a 'ready-made answer'.
985. G. Biagioni, 'Norme processuali e principio di effettività: ulteriori sviluppi nella giurisprudenza comunitaria', Il diritto dell'Unione Europea, 9(1), pp. 201-212, 2004. A significant example of an 'outcome case' is the judgment of 27 February 2003, *Santex SpA v. Unità Socio Sanitaria Locale n. 42 di Pavia, and Sca Mölnlycke SpA, Artsana SpA and Fater SpA*, C-327/00, ECLI:EU:C:2003:109, concerning the compatibility of a national measure with the principle of effectiveness, in which the Court makes assessments that unequivocally lead to the resolution of the main proceedings. Similarly, in judgment of 14 December 1995, *Peterbroeck, Van Campenhout & Cie SCS v. Belgian State*, C-312/93, ECLI:EU:C:1995:437, the Court held that a time limit provided for in Belgian procedural law was not appropriate on the basis of procedural circumstances 'such as those at issue in the main proceedings'.
986. S. Sciarra, 'Integration Through the Court: Article 177 as a Pre-Federal Device' in S. Sciarra (ed.), *Labour Law in the Courts: National Judges and the European Court of Justice*, Hart Publishing, Oxford, 2001, pp. 1-24.
987. S.A. Nyikos, 'Strategic Interaction among Courts Within the Preliminary Reference Process – Stage 1: National Court Preemptive Opinions', 2006 and A. Dyevre, N. Lampach & M. Glavina, 'Chilling or Learning? The Effect of Negative Feedback on Interjudicial Cooperation in Nonhierarchical Referral Regimes', Journal of Law and Courts, 10(1), pp. 87-112, 2022, where the authors observed that the Court of Justice at time provides negative feedback to referring judges in case of poor-quality references.

the domestic legal system. These legal and judicial doctrines are generally referred to as 'counter-limits', and they represent the national constitutional court's reactions to the encroaching competences of the EU, and to the restriction of national sovereignty that results from it.[988] Since the Treaty of Rome, the establishment of the EC legal order has imposed legal and jurisdictional limitations on national authorities and, in some cases, this has been met with resistance. Counter-limits are in fact most frequently found in the case law of those Member States that adopt a dualist conception of the relationship between domestic and supranational law. As already mentioned, in the dualist approach supranational law (in this case EU law) becomes binding as a result of a voluntary limitation of the national legal system, which abdicates a portion of its sovereignty. However far-reaching this limitation may be, it can never be regarded as absolute.[989]

Counter-limits are thus an expression of a defensive attitude on the part of national (supreme) courts, aimed at protecting the Member State's sphere of constitutional autonomy.[990] From the point of view of trans-judicial dialogue, they signal to the CJEU that activist ruling might be perceived as a violation of national constitutional autonomy. Would a Court's judgment be found to infringe the residual sovereignty of the Member States, national Supreme Courts reserve the prerogative to declare such judgment as inapplicable within the national legal system. In this case, the trans-judicial cooperation would be jeopardised, as well as the perceived legitimacy of the Court's authority.[991]

There are two types of counter-limits. The first consists in those principles and values enshrined in national law that pertain to the identity of the state,[992] while the second relates to the concept of '*kompetenz-kompetenz*'. This principle refers to the

988. V. Barsotti et al., *Italian Constitutional Justice in Global Context*, Oxford University Press, Oxford, 2016, p. 214; B. De Witte, 'Sovereignty and European Integration: The Weight of Legal Tradition' in A.M. Slaughter, A. Stone Sweet & J. Weiler (eds), *The European Court and National Court – Doctrine and Jurisprudence: Legal Change in Its Social Context*, Hart Publishing, Oxford, 1998, pp. 277-305.
989. O. Pollicino, 'Corte di giustizia e giudici nazionali: il moto "ascendente", ovverosia l'incidenza delle "tradizioni costituzionali comuni" nella tutela apprestata ai diritti dalla Corte dell'Unione', 2015.
990. *Ibid.*; A. Dyevre, 'European Integration and National Courts – A Strategic Analysis of Judicial Behaviour', SSRN, available at https://bit.ly/3LJXEkV, 2009, pp. 1-52; T. Horsley, *The Court of Justice of the European Union as and Institutional Actor: Judicial Lawmaking and Its Limits*, 2018, pp. 214, 226; V. Trstenjak, 'National Sovereignty and the Principle of Primacy in EU Law and Their Importance for the Member States', Beijing Law Review, 4(2), pp. 71-76, 2013; A. Tizzano, 'Ancora sui rapporti tra Corti europee: principi comunitari e c.d. controlimiti costituzionali', Il diritto dell'Unione Europea, 12(3), pp. 734-744, 2007.
991. T. Tridimas, 'The ECJ and the National Courts: Dialogue, Cooperation, and Instability', 2015; T. Horsley, *The Court of Justice of the European Union as and Institutional Actor: Judicial Lawmaking and Its Limits*, 2018, p. 236; S. Douglas-Scott, 'Subjects and Objects of EU Human Rights Law' in S. Bardutzky & E. Fahey (eds), *Framing the Subjects and Objects of Contemporary EU Law*, Edward Elgar Publishing, Cheltenham, 2017, pp. 105-123.
992. M. Cartabia, 'The Italian Constitutional Court and the Relationship Between the Italian Legal System and the European Union', 1998, p. 214; B. De Witte, 'Sovereignty and European Integration: The Weight of Legal Tradition', 1998; A. Stone Sweet, *The Judicial Construction of Europe*, Oxford University Press, New York, 2004, p. 201.

prerogative of national courts to assess whether a legal act emanating from the EU – and thus also the Court's judgments – has encroached on national competences.[993]

Counter-limits of both kinds have contributed greatly to the development of EU trans-judicial dialogue and it is logical to assume that they have also influenced the lawmaking of the CJEU. Prominent scholars such as Mancini, De Witte, Martinico, Pollicino, Tridimas and Sciarra have suggested that EU case law can be seen as a series of attempts by the Court to impose its monist understanding of EU law and to overcome the national counter-limits.[994] It is precisely because of the potential dialectical significance of the counter-limits that the remainder of this section explores in more detail their possible weight in the Court's decision-making.

4.4 The Counter-Limits

Counter-limits emerged in Italy and in Germany in the 1970s, where (supreme) national courts established that fundamental principles pertaining to the national constitutional order are inviolable and shall not be cast aside by EC law. These counter-limits are discussed in section 4.4.1. Only in a later stage of EU integration, the German Constitutional Court held that national courts also retained the faculty to control that the CJEU does not interpret EU law in a way that goes beyond the Union's competences. The *kompetenz-kompetenz* principle is illustrated in section 4.4.2. Subsequently, section 4.4.3 describes how these doctrines have spread in other legal systems.

4.4.1 The Inviolable Constitutional Principles of the National Legal System

4.4.1.1 Italy

The counter-limits first emerged as a response of the Italian Constitutional Court to the CJEU's case law on the direct effect of EC law. It may be helpful to recall that in *Costa v. Enel*, the CJEU had established that (some) Treaty provisions could be directly invoked by individuals in legal disputes before national courts.[995] In *Simmenthal*, the Court further reinforced this principle and ruled that, when confronted with a conflict between national and EC law, national courts had to disapply national law without

993. O. Pollicino, *Allargamento dell'Europa a est e rapporto tra Corti costituzionali e Corti europee*, 2010, p. 373; T. Horsley, *The Court of Justice of the European Union as and Institutional Actor: Judicial Lawmaking and Its Limits*, 2018, p. 228; A. Dyevre, 'European Integration and National Courts – A Strategic Analysis of Judicial Behaviour', SSRN, available at https://bit.ly/3LJXEkV, 2009, pp. 1-52; J. Kokott, 'Report on Germany', 1998.
994. G.F. Mancini, 'The Making of a Constitution for Europe', Common Market Law Review, 26(4), pp. 595-614, 1989; B. De Witte, 'Sovereignty and European Integration: The Weight of Legal Tradition', 1998; O. Pollicino, 'Corte di giustizia e giudici nazionali: il moto "ascendente", ovverosia l'incidenza delle "tradizioni costituzionali comuni" nella tutela apprestata ai diritti dalla Corte dell'Unione', 2015; S. Sciarra, 'Integration Through the Court: Article 177 as a Pre-Federal Device', 2001.
995. C-6/64, *Costa v. Enel*.

having to first refer a question to the national constitutional court.[996] For Italian courts, these principles meant deviating from the domestic constitutional principle that '*lex posteriori derogat priori*', whereby if a national law was adopted after an instrument of EC law, the latter would decay. It also meant a departure from the centralised system of constitutionality review, exclusively endowed to the Constitutional Court.[997]

It therefore took more than ten years before Italian constitutional jurisprudence could accept the primacy of EU law. This openness, however, was not unconditional. First, the Italian Constitutional Court kept on claiming to be the only jurisdictional authority with the competence to declare the invalidity of national law, even in case of clear conflict with national law. This will change only with the *Granital* ruling, which is discussed in section 4.4.1.3 below. Moreover, the Constitutional Court identified normative safeguards to limit the pervasiveness of EC law in the national legal system. In 1973, with the *Frontini* judgment, the Italian Constitutional Court defined for the first time the counter-limits,[998] by establishing that the limitations of sovereignty deriving from EC law cannot 'grant the institutions of the EEC the unacceptable power to violate the fundamental principles of our constitutional order or the inalienable rights of the human person'.[999] In *Frontini*, the Constitutional Court essentially ruled that there is a core of inviolable values and principles that belong to the constitutional identity of the Italian state and that cannot be affected by present or future EC law.

4.4.1.2 Germany

The Italian Constitutional Court was not alone in setting limits for the CJEU. A similar jurisprudential approach was developed by the German Federal Constitutional Court.[1000] In the German context, counter-limits appeared as a reaction to the judicial activism that the CJEU had shown in *Internationale Handelsgesellschaft*.[1001] In that judgment, the Court had established the primacy of EC law over German constitutional law by ruling that 'the validity of a Community measure or its effects within a Member State cannot be affected by allegations that it runs counter to either fundamental rights

996. C-106/77, *Simmenthal* (para. 17).
997. P. Ruggeri Laderchi, 'Report on Italy' in A.M. Slaughter, A. Stone Sweet & J. Weiler (eds), *The European Court and National Court – Doctrine and Jurisprudence: Legal Change in Its Social Context*, Hart Publishing, Oxford, 1998, pp. 147-169.
998. *Ibid.* and, *inter alia*, A. Dyevre, 'European Integration and National Courts – A Strategic Analysis of Judicial Behaviour', SSRN, 2009; G. Repetto, 'Pouring New Wine into New Bottles? The Preliminary Reference to the CJEU by the Italian Constitutional Court', German Law Journal, 16(6), pp. 1449-1470, 2015; V. Barsotti et al., *Italian Constitutional Justice in Global Context*, Oxford University Press, Oxford, 2016, p. 214.
999. 27 December 1973 no. 183, *Frontini v. Ministero delle Finanze* [1974] RDI 154.
1000. E.J. Lohse, 'The German Constitutional Court and Preliminary References – Still a Match Not Made in Heaven?', German Law Journal, 16(6), pp. 1491-1508, 2015; J. Kokott, 'Report on Germany' in A.M. Slaughter, A. Stone Sweet & J. Weiler (eds), *The European Court and National Court – Doctrine and Jurisprudence: Legal Change in Its Social Context*, Hart Publishing, Oxford, 1998, pp. 77-133.
1001. Judgment of 17 December 1970, *Internationale Handelsgesellschaft mbH v. Einfuhr- und Vorratsstelle für Getreide und Futtermittel*, C-11/70, ECLI:EU:C:1970:114.

as formulated by the constitution of that State or the principles of a national constitutional structure'.[1002]

This superiority of EC law over national constitutional law was firmly rejected by the German Constitutional Tribunal with the *Solange I* decision (1974). In *Solange I*, the German judge clearly stated that the primacy of Community law was to be rejected 'as long as' (in German '*Solange*') the EC legal system would develop sufficient guarantees for the protection of fundamental rights.[1003] Until then, the Federal Constitutional Court retained the prerogative to review the conformity of EU law with the German constitution.

It is worth noting that in both Germany and Italy, counter-limits have emerged as a response to the case law of the CJEU on the primacy of EC law over national rules on (constitutional) fundamental rights. Interestingly, the resistance displayed by the national constitutional court seems to have provoked a counterreaction on the part of the CJEU. Rather than backtracking, the Court actually addressed the concerns of the national courts regarding the protection of constitutional values and began to expand its jurisprudence on the protection of fundamental rights.[1004] Significant examples in this sense are the judgments *Nold*, *Hauer*, *Defrenne* and *Wachauf*, already discussed in Chapters 4 and 5 (section 3.1) of this book.[1005]

4.4.1.3 The Court's Reactions and National Counteractions

The expansion of EU case law into the matter of fundamental rights can hence be seen as a dialectical reaction to the emersion of the counter-limits. It is one of the most prominent examples of normative implications of the trans-judicial dialogue among national and EU courts. As well summarised by Stone Sweet, 'one hugely important, but wholly unintended consequence of the CJEU elaboration of the supremacy doctrine has been the progressive construction of a charter of rights for the EC. [...] The move, however, was not voluntary. An incipient rebellion against supremacy, led by national courts, drove the process'.[1006]

The Court's greater sensitivity towards fundamental rights eventually succeeded to soften the positions of national constitutional courts. A first indication can be found

1002. *Ibid.* (para. 3).
1003. 29 May 1974, *Solange I*, 37 BVerfGE 271.
1004. *Inter alia*, *see*: E. Muir, 'The Court of Justice: A Fundamental Rights Institution among Others' in B. de Witte, B. Muir & E. Dawson (eds), *Judicial Activism at the European Court of Justice*, Edward Elgar Publishing, Cheltenham, 2013, pp. 76-102; O. Pollicino, 'Corte di giustizia e giudici nazionali: il moto "ascendente", ovverosia l'incidenza delle "tradizioni costituzionali comuni" nella tutela apprestata ai diritti dalla Corte dell'Unione', 2015.
1005. Judgment of 14 May 1974, *J. Nold, Kohlen- und Baustoffgroßhandlung v. Ruhrkohle Aktiengesellschaft*, C-4/73, ECLI:EU:C:1974:51; judgment of 8 October 1996, *Anke Heuer v. Bundesrepublik Deutschland*, C-189/94, Joined Cases C-178/94, C-179/94, C-188/94, C-189/94 and C-190/94, ECLI:EU:C:1996:375; judgment of 8 April 1976, *Gabrielle Defrenne v. Société anonyme belge de navigation aérienne Sabena*, C-43/75, ECLI:EU:C:1976:56; judgment of 13 July 1989, *Hubert Wachauf v. Bundesamt für Ernährung und Forstwirtschaft*, C-5/88, ECLI:EU:C:1989:321.
1006. A. Stone Sweet, *The Judicial Construction of Europe*, Oxford University Press, New York, 2004, p. 201.

in German constitutional jurisprudence, in the *Meanwhile* ruling (1981). In that judgment, the German constitutional tribunal stated that the EC case law on fundamental rights was being closely monitored and, depending on future developments, the position established in *Solange I* may be soon overcome.[1007]

Signs of distension were also observed in Italian jurisprudence. Ten years after *Simmenthal*, with the *Granital* judgment (1984), the Italian Constitutional Court finally accepted that lower courts could perform a decentralised review of national legislation with respect to the EC law.[1008] It is worth noting, however, that this openness did not mark an abandonment of the counter-limit doctrine. In the same ruling, the Italian Constitutional Court in fact confirmed that domestic law implementing the EC Treaty could still be subject to constitutional review and assessed with respect to the fundamental principles enshrined in the Italian constitution.[1009]

Nevertheless, these encouraging signs might have motivated the CJEU to further expand its fundamental rights jurisdiction and embark on a path of constitutional maturation.[1010] And that seemed to work well. The German Federal Constitutional Court eventually decided that the time was ripe to recognise the principles of the primacy and direct effect of EC law. This came about in 1986 with the *Solange II* judgment, where the German constitutional judge announced that it would refrain from exercising constitutional review over EC law *as long as* the EC provided the same level of protection of fundamental rights as guaranteed in the domestic constitutional order.[1011]

This gradual acceptance of the Court's jurisdictional authority by national constitutional judges is indicative of the Court's ability to constructively interpret the signals and warnings emerging from domestic case law. The Court in fact engaged with the counter-limits and incorporated into its jurisprudence the very object of the reservations and objections of the national constitutional courts, namely the protection of fundamental rights.[1012] Pollicino referred to this strategy as the 'progressive communitarisation of the counter-limits'.[1013]

1007. Mittlerweile, 36 NJW 1258 (1983). In this ruling, the German Constitutional Tribunal established that the protection of fundamental rights set in the EC does not need to be exactly the same as that established in the German constitution. *See also* J. Kokott, 'Report on Germany', 1998.
1008. 8 June 1984 no. 170, *Granital. See also* M. Cartabia, 'The Italian Constitutional Court and the Relationship Between the Italian Legal System and the European Union' in A.M. Slaughter, A. Stone Sweet & J. Weiler (eds), *The European Court and National Court – Doctrine and Jurisprudence: Legal Change in Its Social Context*, Hart Publishing, Oxford, 1998, pp. 133-144.
1009. *Ibid.*
1010. O. Pollicino, 'Corte di giustizia e giudici nazionali: il moto "ascendente", ovverosia l'incidenza delle "tradizioni costituzionali comuni" nella tutela apprestata ai diritti dalla Corte dell'Unione', 2015.
1011. 22 October 1986, *Solange II*, 73 BVerfGE 339.
1012. A. Stone Sweet, *The Judicial Construction of Europe*, 2004, p. 115; J.H.H. Weiler, 'The Transformation of Europe', 1991.
1013. O. Pollicino, *Allargamento dell'Europa a est e rapporto tra Corti costituzionali e Corti europee*, Giuffrè, Milano, 2010, pp. 334-436.

4.4.1.4 *The Normalisation of the Counter-Limits*

Despite the progress of the CJEU in constructively engaging with the defensive reactions of German and Italian constitutional judges, the counter-limits doctrine was not neutralised. National constitutional courts continued from time to time to resort to counter-limits to preserve a sphere of internal sovereignty which, in their view, needed to be protected from external encroachment.[1014]

As for the Italian legal system, the *Fragd* and *Federfarma* are significant examples. In *Fragd* (1989), the Constitutional Court reiterated its authority to 'assess the conformity of EC law with the fundamental principles of the Italian Constitution, including fundamental rights'.[1015] In *Federfarma* (2005), the Higher Administrative Court (Consiglio di Stato) refused to submit a preliminary reference to the CJEU concerning a potential incompatibility of a domestic rule with EU law. This refusal was justified on the grounds that only the Constitutional Court could assess the validity of national legislation, which was a regressive argument since it evoked the pre-*Granital* doctrine.[1016] A more recent example is the *Taricco II* case (already discussed in section 3.3.4). There, in its preliminary request to the CJEU, the Italian Constitutional Court held that the previous *Taricco I* judgment was irreconcilable with the principles of legality and non-retroactivity of criminal law. According to the Italian constitutional judge, these principles are an expression of the constitutional identity of the Italian state and, for this reason, it asked the CJEU to adjust its previous *Taricco I* decision.[1017]

In German jurisprudence too, the doctrine of the inviolability of fundamental constitutional principles never completely disappeared. In the *Maastricht Urteil* judgment (1993), the Federal Constitutional Court even broadened the grounds on which it

1014. E.J. Lohse, 'The German Constitutional Court and Preliminary References – Still a Match Not Made in Heaven?', German Law Journal, 16(6), pp. 1491-1508, 2015.

1015. 13 April 1989 no. 168, *Fragd* [1990] I Foro It. 1855, where the Italian constitutional court applied the counter-limits doctrine and held that it could control the conformity of EC law with the fundamental principles of the Italian constitution, especially fundamental rights. *See* P. Ruggeri Laderchi, 'Report on Italy' in A.M. Slaughter, A. Stone Sweet & J. Weiler (eds), *The European Court and National Court – Doctrine and Jurisprudence: Legal Change in Its Social Context*, Hart Publishing, Oxford, 1998, pp. 147-169.

1016. In *Federfarma*, the Council of State refused to make a preliminary reference to the CJEU concerning the conformity with European law of legislation implementing an EU provision concerning the fundamental right to health. The Council of State argued that 'it is not possible to refer to the Court of Luxembourg a question for a preliminary ruling, the answer to which cannot be taken into account because it is absorbed by the decision of the Italian Court in the area of the protection of fundamental rights'. Although counter-limits remain part of national constitutional jurisprudence, it is interesting to note that in 2008 the Italian constitutional court demonstrated a willingness to engage in dialogue with the CJEU by making a preliminary reference for the first time (cc 103/2008). *See* in D.U. Galetta, 'The European Union in the Constitutional Framework of the Member States: The Italian Case' in R. Arnold (ed.), *Limitations of National Sovereignty Through European Integration*, Springer, Dordrecht, 2016, pp. 87-99.

1017. C-105/14, *Taricco I*; M. Bonelli, 'The Taricco Saga and the Consolidation of Judicial Dialogue in the European Union: CJEU, C-105/14 Ivo Taricco and others, ECLI:EU:C:2015:555; and C-42/17 M.A.S., M.B., ECLI:EU:C:2017:936 Italian Constitutional Court, Order no. 24/2017', 2018.

reserved the faculty to assess the compatibility of EU law with the German constitutional order. In addition to the fundamental rights and legal principles of the Basic Law, the German Constitutional Court included the principles of democracy and national sovereignty.[1018] Subsequently, in the *Lissabon Urteil* (2009) the Constitutional Court further added the principles and values that embody the 'national identity', which it defined with a detailed list of criteria.[1019] In the same ruling, the German Constitutional judge announced that, in case of interference with these principles by the CJEU or other EU institutions, EU law would be declared inapplicable in the domestic legal system.

Finally, it should be noted that the concept of 'inviolable constitutional principles' has so far only been used as a formal warning. National constitutional courts have never gone so far as to effectively deploy it against a ruling of the CJEU.

4.4.2 Kompetenz-Kompetenz

In the *Maastricht* ruling, besides reiterating the inviolability of the fundamental principles of the national constitutional system, the German Constitutional Court established a second set of counter-limits. These related to the *kompetenz-kompetenz* doctrine, according to which only national judges (and, therefore, not the CJEU) have the jurisdiction to control that EU acts – including the judgments of the CJEU – do not infringe the repartition of competences between the EU and the Member States.[1020] In the *Maastricht Urteil*, it was ruled that EU law applies in the German legal system only by virtue of a voluntary limitation of sovereignty by the national lawmaking authorities. It is therefore the task of the Federal Constitutional Court, as the protector of the national constitutional order, to ensure that the acts of the EU do not further reduce national sovereignty. When an EU act is found to have been adopted outside the competences conferred to the EU, the national constitutional judge retains the power to

1018. 12 October 1993, *Maastricht*, 20EuGRZ 429, 33 ILM 388 (1994). *See* E.J. Lohse, 'The German Constitutional Court and Preliminary References – Still a Match not Made in Heaven?', German Law Journal, 16(6), pp. 1491-1508, 2015 and J. Kokott, 'Report on Germany', 1998.

1019. Interestingly, the Constitutional Tribunal included among the factors determining constitutional identity, the freedom of the German parliament to decide on the annual state budget. *See also* judgment of the German Federal Constitutional Court of 30 June 2009, *Lissabon*, 2 be 2/08. G. Martinico, 'The "Polemical" Spirit of European Constitutional Law: On the Importance of Conflicts in EU Law', 2015.

1020. A. Dyevre, 'European Integration and National Courts – A Strategic Analysis of Judicial Behaviour', SSRN, available at https://bit.ly/3LJXEkV, 2009, pp. 1-52; O. Pollicino, *Allargamento dell'Europa a est e rapporto tra Corti costituzionali e Corti europee*, 2010, p. 373. It should be noted that the *kompetenz-kompetenz* question has never been openly addressed by Italian jurisprudence, but Cartabia suggests that, were this question to arise, the constitutional court would reserve this competence exclusively for itself. M. Cartabia, 'The Italian Constitutional Court and the Relationship Between the Italian Legal System and the European Union' in A.M. Slaughter, A. Stone Sweet & J. Weiler (eds), *The European Court and National Court – Doctrine and Jurisprudence: Legal Change in Its Social Context*, Hart Publishing, Oxford, 1998, pp. 133-144.

declare that such act was adopted '*ultra vires*'. By doing so, the act is prevented from producing legal effects within the national legal system.[1021]

As Kokott and De Witte observed, the elaboration of the *kompetenz-kompetenz* doctrine by the German Constitutional Tribunal can be interpreted as an invitation to the CJEU to be more cautious in its judicial lawmaking.[1022] When the *Maastricht Urteil* was pronounced (1993), EU case law had already shown its expansionary potential in relation to the European internal market (*see* the *Dassonville* and *Cassis de Dijon* jurisprudence). The entry into force of the Maastricht Treaty codified this expansion and strengthened the constitutional and political maturity of the Union. The German Constitutional Court might have been alarmed by the incremental competence creep resulting from the EU case law and the new Treaty and resorted to these additional counter-limits to safeguard the integrity of the national legal order.

It is important to note that, in formulating its *kompetenz-kompetenz* doctrine, the German court departed from a fundamental principle established in EU case law. The *Foto Frost* judgment (1987) had in fact established that only the CJEU had the authority to declare the invalidity of an EU legal act.[1023] This contradiction with EU case law did not seem to deter the German Constitutional Court, which reaffirmed the *kompetenz-kompetenz* principle in several subsequent judgments, most notably in the *Bananenmarket* ruling and in the *Lissabon Urteil.*[1024]

A more recent example of the *kompetenz-kompetenz* doctrine is the judicial saga concerning the state bond-purchasing programme by the ECB.[1025] In Germany, a heated debate had developed on whether the purchase of national bonds was actually within the ECB's competences.[1026] Said programme was first brought to the attention of the German Constitutional Court in the *Gauwaier* case (2014), mostly known as the *OMT* case. In the course of the proceeding, the German judge decided to suspend the case and submit a reference for a preliminary ruling to the CJEU. In its preliminary ruling request, the Constitutional Tribunal asked the Court to verify the potential incompatibility between the ECB's bond-purchasing programme and the EU Treaties. In its reference to the Court, the German Constitutional Tribunal did not conceal the

1021. A. Stone Sweet, 'Constitutional Dialogues in the European Community' in A.M. Slaughter, A. Stone Sweet & J. Weiler (eds), *The European Court and National Court – Doctrine and Jurisprudence: Legal Change in Its Social Context*, Hart Publishing, Oxford, 1998, pp. 305-331.

1022. 12 October 1993, *Maastricht*, 20EuGRZ 429, 33 ILM 388 (1994). '[...] if standards of competences were interpreted in this way, such interpretation would not have binding effect in Germany'. *See* J. Kokott, 'Report on Germany', 1998 and B. De Witte, 'Sovereignty and European Integration: The Weight of Legal Tradition', 1998.

1023. Judgment of 22 October 1987, *Foto-Frost v. Hauptzollamt Lübeck-Ost*, C-314/85, ECLI: EU:C:1987:452; A. Stone Sweet, *The Judicial Construction of Europe*, Oxford University Press, New York, 2004, p. 202.

1024. Judgment of the German Federal Constitutional Tribunal, 7 June 2000, *Bananenmarket c. Verfahren*, 2 BvL 1/97; judgment of the German Federal Constitutional Tribunal, 30 June 2009, *Lissabon*, 2 BvE 2/08.

1025. Judgment of the German Federal Constitutional Tribunal, 14 January 2014, *Outright Monetary Transaction (OMT)*, BVerfGE 134, 366; 2 BvR 2728/13; judgment of the German Federal Constitutional Tribunal, 5 May 2020, *Weiss*, 2 BvR 859/15, 2 BvR 1651/15; 2 BvR 2006&15; 2 BvR 980/16.

1026. *See* R. Van Gestel & J. De Poorter, *In the Court We Trust: Cooperation, Coordination and Collaboration Between the ECJ and Supreme Administrative Courts*, 2019, p. 63.

doubts about the legality of the financial programme. As Tridimas observed that request for a preliminary ruling 'more than a genuine request for guidance, [...] was an invitation to repent'.[1027] The CJEU, however, found no grounds for unlawfulness in the ECB's programme and concluded that the ECB had acted within its competence in the field of monetary policy.[1028]

The answer of the CJEU did not seem to convince the German constitutional judges. A few years after the *OMT* judgment, in the *Weiss* case (2020), another bond-purchasing programme of the ECB raised similar legal concerns that were once again brought before the German Constitutional Tribunal.[1029] This time, the Constitutional Tribunal was asked by the applicants to examine the (in)validity of the act by which the German government and Parliament had agreed to another government bond-purchasing programme of the ECB (the so-called Public Sector Purchase Programme (PSPP)). According to the applicants that brought the case before the Constitutional Tribunal, the PSPP entailed an expansion of the Union's competences that went beyond what was stipulated in the Treaties and, therefore, implied an unlawful curtailment of national sovereignty. Moreover, it was contended that with its state bond-purchasing programmes, the ECB had caused an acceleration of the financial integration of the Union without the Treaty providing a legal basis for this.[1030]

It must also be stressed that this dispute took place in a context in which the ECB's actions were strongly criticised in the German public debate. The most critical voices were raised among the conservatives and the Bundesbank, which had long been vocal against the ECB's intervention in national debts through the purchase of national bonds and against greater European fiscal integration. Their dissent was mainly rooted in the view that by purchasing government bonds, the ECB contravened the prohibition of direct aid to national economies, established in Article 123 TFEU as well as in Council Regulation 3603/92/EC. Ultimately, the fear was that these policies would end up endangering the soundness of EU finances.[1031]

1027. Already that first preliminary was characterised by aggressive tones referring to the possibility of not implementing EU acts adopted in violation of EU competences. M. Claes, 'Luxembourg, Here We Come? Constitutional Courts and the Preliminary Reference Procedure', German Law Journal, 16(6), pp. 1331-1342, 2015, where the author observed that 'the German Bundensvfassungericht also made reference to the position of several of its European counterparts [...] as if wanting to present itself to the Court has "the leader of the pack", as representing other constitutional and higher courts that do not accept the absolute primacy of EU law and final authority of the Court'. Tridimas noted that 'more than a genuine request for guidance, it was an invitation to repent', in T. Tridimas, 'The ECJ and the National Courts: Dialogue, Cooperation, and Instability' in D. Chalmers & A. Arnull (eds), *The Oxford Handbook of European Union Law*, Oxford University Press, Oxford, 2015, pp. 1-30.

1028. E.J. Lohse, 'The German Constitutional Court and Preliminary References – Still a Match Not Made in Heaven?', 2015.

1029. Judgment of the German Federal Constitutional Tribunal, 5 May 2020, *Weiss*, 2 BvR 859/15, 2 BvR 1651/15; 2 BvR 2006&15; 2 BvR 980/16.

1030. *Ibid.* (para. 33).

1031. Commission Regulation (EEC) No 3603/92 of 14 December 1992 amending Regulations (EEC) No 1356/92 and (EEC) No 1910/92 on a special intervention measure. Article 123 TFEU prohibits the ECB or national central banks (NCBs) from purchasing public debt instruments on the primary markets. Moreover, secondary market purchase of public debt instruments – although allowed, in principle, under the monetary financing prohibition – must not be used to circumvent the objectives of the prohibition on monetary financing. *See* European Central

Addressed with the same legal issue for a second time, the German Constitutional Tribunal again decided to refer the matter to the CJEU by submitting another preliminary reference. Although in its reference the German Constitutional Tribunal chose a more cautious tone than in the *OMT* case, the message was clear. The German judge plainly stated that if the CJEU were to conclude that the PSPP had been launched beyond ECB competences, any legal act connected to that programme will be considered *ultra vires* in the domestic legal system. In particular, the German court recalled that *ultra vires* acts are incompatible with the principle of democracy, protected by the German Basic Law and part of the constitutional identity of the German State.[1032]

While ruling on the case, the CJEU remained consistent with the precedent set in the *OMT* judgment. The Court thus confirmed that the ECB's bond-purchasing programme did not raise any issues with regard to the Union's competences. The instruments that were adopted by the ECB were indeed found to be proportionate to the pursuit of the Union's policy objectives.[1033] This ruling was not well received by the referring judge. The German Federal Constitutional Tribunal did not hide its strong discontent in relation to the Court's decision and decided to resort for the first time to the *kompetenz-komptenz* doctrine. The constitutional judges thus declared that the *Weiss* ruling was adopted *ultra vires* and had no effect on the national legal system. More precisely, the German Constitutional Court established that 'in its judgment of 11 December 2018, the CJEU held that the Decision of the ECB Governing Council on the PSPP and its subsequent amendments were still within the ambit of the ECB's competences. This view manifestly fails to give consideration to the importance and scope of the principle of proportionality [...] which also applies to the division of competences, and is no longer tenable from a methodological perspective given that it completely disregards the actual effects of the PSPP. Therefore, the judgment of the CJEU of 11 December 2018 manifestly exceeds the mandate conferred upon it in Article 19(1) second sentence TEU, resulting in a structurally significant shift in the order of competences to the detriment of the Member States. To this extent, the Court of Justice's judgment itself constitutes an ultra vires act and thus had no binding effect'.[1034]

In the aftermath of the judgment of the German Constitutional Court, the CJEU published a lapidary press release recalling that 'the Court of Justice alone [...] has

Bank, Report, Monthly Bulletin October, Frankfurt, 2012. *See also* T. Capeta, 'The Weiss/PSPP Case and the Future of Constitutional Pluralism in the EU', SSRN Electronic Journal, 2020.

1032. Judgment of 11 December 2018, *Proceedings brought by Heinrich Weiss and Others*, C-493/17, ECLI:EU:C:2018:1000 (paras 14 and 15).

1033. *See* A.A.M. Mooij, 'The Weiss Judgment: The Court's Further Clarification of the ECB's Legal Framework Case C-493/17 Weiss and Others, EU:C:2018:1000', Maastricht Journal of European and Comparative Law, 26(3), pp. 449-465, 2019.

1034. Judgment of the German Federal Constitutional Tribunal, 5 May 2020, *Weiss*, 2 BvR 859/15, 2 BvR 1651/15; 2 BvR 2006/15; 2 BvR 980/16 (para. 119). The Constitutional Court eventually demanded the German legislation to apply a stricter scrutiny to the power transferred to the ECB and to revise its mandate would that scrutiny show a structural alteration in the competences conferred to the EU. This also implies that it is up to the ECB's governing Council to demonstrate that the actions taken to implement the government bond-purchasing programme are in accordance with the principle of proportionality and did not go beyond the competences of the ECB.

jurisdiction to rule that an act of an EU institution is contrary to EU law'.[1035] It will be interesting to observe whether the severe German reaction will have an effect on future CJEU's rulings on ECB's bond-purchasing programmes. In the meantime, the analysis of Steinbeis in his Verfassungsblog editorial on the *Weiss* case is quite on spot: 'it is not a conflict, but an elaborate business between two courts who negotiate with each other at eye level where the respective competences and control powers being an end'.[1036] In other words, this episode is part of an intense trans-judicial dialogue with potentially substantial impact on both EU and national case law.

4.4.3 *The Spread of Counter-Limits in National Constitutional Jurisprudence*

It was mentioned that counter-limits, whether they take the form of inviolable constitutional principles of national law or of the *kompetenz-kompetenz* doctrine, can be conceived as a shield that constitutional judges have erected to protect domestic legal systems from the activist incursions of the CJEU.[1037]

While initially limited to Italian and German jurisprudence, counter-limits have gradually spread across Europe.[1038] They first appeared in those Member States that

1035. Court of Justice of the European Union, Press Release Following the Judgment of the German Constitutional Court of 5 May 2020, 58/20, Luxembourg, 8 May 2020.
1036. M. Steinbeis, 'We Super-Europeans', VerfBlog, 9 May 2020, https://verfassungsblog.de/we-super-europeans/.
1037. As discussed in section 4.4.2 above.
1038. In principle, both the Netherlands and Belgium constitute an exception, as they are characterised by a monist conception of the relationship between domestic law and supranational sources. The monist tradition generally implies that national courts have no problem recognising the primacy of European law over domestic law. In particular, Dutch courts have always been very compliant and loyal to the CJEU, even when not satisfied with the latter's rulings. *See, inter alia*, M. Claes, 'Luxembourg, Here We Come? Constitutional Courts and the Preliminary Reference Procedure', German Law Journal, 16(6), pp. 1331-1342, 2015. A similar approach had for long prevailed in Belgium. The Belgian Constitutional Court was the first to make a preliminary reference to the CJEU, and EU case law has always been accepted in the national system. With 27 May 1971, *Fromagerie Franco-Suisse Le Ski v. Etat Belge* [1971] I Pas. 896, [1971] JT 471, la Cour de Cassation consecrated the monist model, later confirmed in the *Orfinger* judgment (C.E., *Orfinger*, 5 novembre 1996, n. 62.921, in *JT*, 1997, p. 254), which attributes constitutional value to European law. *See also* H. Bribosia, 'Report on Belgium' in A.M. Slaughter, A. Stone Sweet & J. Weiler (eds), *The European Court and National Court – Doctrine and Jurisprudence: Legal Change in Its Social Context*, Hart Publishing, Oxford, 1998, pp. 1-40. Even within this generally relaxed attitude, in Case no. 62/2016 of 28 April 2016, B8.7 the Belgian Constitutional Court did refer to national relation in relation to EU law. *See* R. Van Gestel & J. De Poorter, *In the Court We Trust: Cooperation, Coordination and Collaboration Between the ECJ and Supreme Administrative Courts*, 2019, p. 43. The Belgian Constitutional Court, in particular, ruled that the constitutional protection of fundamental rights, established in Article 34 of the Constitution, could trump EU Treaties. More precisely, the Court held that 'In no case does Article 34 of the Constitution permit that the national identity included in the political and constitutional basic structures or the core values of the protection awarded by the constitution to legal subjects can be eroded in a discriminatory manner.' Constitutional resistance has also been raised in France. It is worth recalling the Conseil Constitutionnel judgment 2006-540, in which the doctrine of the counter-limits entered into French jurisprudence. On that occasion, it was established that the French constitutional judge has the power to check that the internal transposition of European

have been part of the EU for a longer period and have been directly exposed to the progressive expansion of the normative and policymaking implications of the Court's case law. Forms of opposition to the activism of the CJEU however emerged also in those Member States that joined the EU only more recently, in the 2004-2007 enlargement. It is worth recalling that most of these states were, until relatively recently, satellites of, or even part of, the USSR, making their transition to a democratic and free market-based state rather abrupt. As Sarduski wrote, during this 'westward' transition, the national constitutional courts took over the role of guardian of the new legal order and of the newfound sovereignty.[1039] Pollicino noted that they also claimed a crucial role in defining (and in protecting) the boundaries of national sovereignty in

law is in accordance with the national rules which are 'inherent to the constitutional identity of France'. In the *Arcelor* decision (287110/2007), the Conseil d'État went so far as to uphold the supremacy of the entire constitution over European law. The Conseil d'État also defined a series of criteria to identify when the normative parameter for determining the legitimacy of a domestic act transposing EU law is EU law or the French constitution. The French courts have never openly addressed the *kompetenz-kompetenz* issue, but there are reasons to suspect that the Conseil Constitutionnel would claim such competence. *See* J. Plotner, 'Report on France' in A.M. Slaughter, A. Stone Sweet & J. Weiler (eds), *The European Court and National Court – Doctrine and Jurisprudence: Legal Change in Its Social Context*, Hart Publishing, Oxford, 1998, pp. 41-76 and F.-X. Millet & N. Perlo, 'The First Preliminary Reference of the French Constitutional Court to the CJEU: Revolution de Palais or Revolution in French Constitutional Law?', German Law Journal, 16(6), pp. 1471-1490, 2015. The traditional trans-judicial closure seems to be weakening following the CJEU's *Melki Abdeli* case (judgment of 22 June 2010, *Aziz Melki and Sélim Abdeli*, C-188/10, Joined Cases C-188/10 and C-189/10, ECLI:EU:C:2010:363), in which the Court demonstrated a flexible and conciliatory approach to French constitutional prerogatives by finding that the French rule whereby the Constitutional Court may receive complaints regarding the compatibility of national law with EU law is in line with the EU Treaties. As far as Spanish constitutional jurisprudence is concerned, there are no particular clashes with the Court of Justice, although there has been a recent move towards the theory of counter-limits. In the *Melloni* judgment (judgment of 26 February 2013, *Stefano Melloni v. Ministerio Fiscal*, C-399/11, ECLI:EU:C:2013:107), the Court of Justice ruled that the national court did not have the power to decide not to apply a decision of European law (European Arrest Warrant), even if there was a conflict with the Spanish Constitution, if the decision was found to be compatible with primary EU law (specifically, Article 53 CFREU). The Spanish Constitutional Court eventually reached a decision compatible with that of the Court of Justice in *Melloni*. However, the Spanish judge based the validity of the European Arrest Warrant not on EU law, as suggested by the Court of Justice, but on the Spanish constitutional order. Furthermore, it declared that there were constitutional limits to the recognition of the superiority of European law over domestic law, in that it could not allow domestic constitutional standards to be compromised by the application of European law and the CFREU (*see* M. Rodríguez-Izquierdo Serrano, 'The Spanish Constitutional Court and Fundamental Rights Adjudication after the First Preliminary Reference', German Law Journal, 16(6), pp. 1509-1528, 2015). Less clear is the position of the UK courts with respect to trans-judicial dialogue (A. Fusco, 'The Supreme Court of the United Kingdom and Preliminary References to the European Court of Justice: An Opencast Constitutional Lab', German Law Journal, 16(6), pp. 1529-1542, 2015). Craig noted that acts of rebellion will rarely emerge from the English courts. Nevertheless, Craig suggested that if the *kompetez-kompetenz* issue had been addressed, the British constitutional courts would have taken conservative positions aimed at protecting the sovereignty of the British system over the European one. *See* P.P. Craig, 'Report on the United Kingdom' in A.M. Slaughter, A. Stone Sweet & J. Weiler (eds), *The European Court and National Court: Doctrine and Jurisprudence – Legal Change in Its Social Context*, Hart Publishing, Oxford, 1998, pp. 195-224.

1039. W. Sadurski, '"Solange, Chapter 3": Constitutional Courts in Central Europe – Democracy – European Union', European Law Journal, 14(1), pp. 1-35, 2008.

relation to the EU legal order.[1040] The national constitutional courts thus emerged as particularly influential in defining the normative framework and the guiding principles on which the rules of society were to be refunded. In order to exercise this role, these courts had themselves adopted forms of judicial activism and had acted as quasi-political actors, at times even entering into conflict with legislative and governmental institutions.[1041]

It is therefore not surprising that the constitutional courts of the Central Eastern European countries have generally been quite reluctant to grant the CJEU full jurisdictional authority to intervene in matters of constitutional relevance.[1042] The counter-limits doctrine thus found fertile ground. Indeed, the general mistrust of Eastern European constitutional judges towards the CJEU was expressed in a tendency to 'play *Solange*' and to adopt a restrictive interpretation of the Union's competences.[1043]

Counter-limits have emerged most prominently in Czech and Polish jurisprudence. Even before accession to the EU, the Czech Constitutional Court held that it would retain the power to control that EU acts (including the CJEU's judgments) complied with the constitutional principles of the Czech Republic. More precisely, the

1040. O. Pollicino, 'Dall'Est una Lezione sui Rapporti tra Diritto Costituzionale e Diritto Comunitario', Il diritto dell'Unione Europea, 11(4), pp. 819-852, 2006.

1041. *Ibid.*; O. Pollicino, *Allargamento dell'Europa a est e rapporto tra Corti costituzionali e Corti europee*, Giuffrè, Milano, 2010, p. 280.

1042. M. Vatsov, 'European Integration Through Preliminary Rulings? The Case of the Bulgarian Constitutional Court', German Law Journal, 16(6), pp. 1591-1622, 2015, where the author, in describing the attitude of the Bulgarian courts towards the EU order, found the presence of counter-limits in as much as the Constitutional Court persists in considering only the national constitutional order, and not EU law, as the relevant parameter of legitimacy for assessing national measures of transposition of EU law (rulings: 1/2014; 3/2002; 1/2008; 3/2004). The question of kompetenz-kompetenz has not been addressed so far, but Vatsov suggests that, if questioned on this issue, the constitutional court would claim that competence. According to V. Viţă, 'The Romanian Constitutional Court and the Principle of Primacy: To Refer or Not to Refer?', German Law Journal, 16(6), pp. 1623-1662, 2015, similar considerations can be applied to Romania, where the national higher courts show a general sense of unease with the principle of primacy and the use of preliminary rulings (*see* Data Retention case 1258/2009). The doctrine of counter-limits, although not explicitly articulated, can be identified in case C-80/2014, where the Constitutional Court adopted a '*Solange II*' approach. In Hungary, in the *Lisbo*' decision (32/2008. 8-3-3008 [HUN-2006-3-005]; 283), the Constitutional Court attributed to itself the kompetenz-kompetenz regarding the enlargement of the EU competences resulting from the entry into force of the Lisbon Treaty (a similar stance was already expressed in ruling 17/2004, 25-5-2004 [HUN-2004-2-005]:280). Furthermore, F. Gárdos-Orosz, 'Preliminary Reference and the Hungarian Constitutional Court: A Context of Non-reference', German Law Journal, 16(6), pp. 1569-1590, 2015 reported that, on that occasion, the rule of law, the democratic principle and the popular democracy have been identified by the Constitutional law as counter-limits. Finally, it is interesting to note that the Baltic Republic are, among the more 'recent' Member States, in an atypical position, characterised by a more positive attitude towards EU integration. There, the positive attitude towards the authority of the Court of Justice and the rather frequent use of the preliminary ruling instrument indicated a widespread effort, among the judiciary, to develop the national legal order in line with EU law. *See* O. Pollicino, *Allargamento dell'Europa a est e rapporto tra Corti costituzionali e Corti europee*, 2010, pp. 308-316; D. Piqani, 'Constitutional Courts in Central and Eastern Europe and Their Attitude Towards European Integration', European Journal of Legal Studies, 1(2), pp. 1-22, 2007.

1043. W. Sadurski, '"Solange, Chapter 3": Constitutional Courts in Central Europe – Democracy – European Union', European Law Journal, 14(1), pp. 1-35, 2008.

constitutional judge claimed the competence to verify that EU case law did not alter the requisites and foundations of democracy.[1044] Later, in the *Sugar quota* decision, with a tone that was reminiscent of the approach of its German counterpart in the *Solange II* judgment, the Czech Constitutional Court stated that even after the accession to the EU it would retain the role of ultimate guarantor of national constitutional traditions and values.[1045] In a subsequent judgment concerning the domestic act ratifying the Lisbon Treaty, the Czech court further strengthened its defensive approach, by expanding the scope of the inviolable constitutional principles, to include a broadly defined concept of 'sovereignty'.[1046]

The culmination of the dialogical closure was reached with the *Holubec* ruling (2012) where, for the first time in the history of the Union, the Czech Constitutional Court gave practical application to the doctrine of *kompetenz-kompetenz*.[1047] This case concerned a dispute over social security benefits and, in deciding on the legal issue, the constitutional judge was confronted with an earlier EU judgment, the *Landtová* judgment, which was potentially relevant to the proceeding. In *Landtová*, the CJEU had found the Czech pension system to be in breach of the EU principle of non-discrimination, in as much as it excluded persons without Czech nationality from claiming in the Czech territory contributions they had previously paid to the Slovak social security fund.[1048] This rule entailed that persons of Slovak nationality, legally resident in Czechia, could not exercise their pension rights. Despite finding Czech legislation contrary to EU law, Pollicino and Bobek noted that the CJEU was cautious

1044. Judgment of 25 June 2002, file No. Pl. ÚS 36/01. *See* O. Pollicino, *Allargamento dell'Europa a est e rapporto tra Corti costituzionali e Corti europee*, 2010, p. 295 and J. Přibáň, 'The Semantics of Constitutional Sovereignty in Post-sovereign "new" Europe: A Case Study of the Czech Constitutional Court's Jurisprudence', International Journal of Constitutional Law, 13(1), pp. 180-199, 2015.

1045. Judgment of the Czech Constitutional Court, 8 March 2006, Pl. US 80/04 [CZE-2006-1-002]. D. Piqani, 'Constitutional Courts in Central and Eastern Europe and their Attitude Towards European Integration', European Journal of Legal Studies, 1(2), pp. 1-22, 2007 and Z. Kühn, 'The Czech Republic: From a Euro-Friendly Approach of the Constitutional Court to Proclaiming a Court of Justice Judgment Ultra Vires' in A. Albi, S. Bardutzky (ed.), *National Constitutions in European and Global Governance Democracy, Rights, the Rule of Law*, Springer, Dordrecht, 2019, pp. 795-833.

1046. Judgment of the Czech Constitutional Court, 26 November 2008, PI US 19/08, where it was essentially stated that the transfer of power of national bodies to the EU cannot go so far as to frustrate the essence of the Czech Republic as sovereign and democratic state governed by the rule of law.

1047. The *Holubec* case was ruled eight years before the *Weiss* judgment of the German Constitutional Tribunal discussed above in section 4.4.2. Judgment of the Czech Constitutional Court, 31 January 2012, Pl. US 5/12. *See also* M. Bobek, 'Landtová, Holubec, and the Problem of an Uncooperative Court: Implications for the Preliminary Rulings Procedure', European Constitutional Law Review, 10, pp. 54-89, 2014 and Z. Kühn, 'The Czech Republic: From a Euro-Friendly Approach of the Constitutional Court to Proclaiming a Court of Justice Judgment Ultra Vires', 2019.

1048. Judgment of 22 June 2011, *Marie Landtová v. Česká správa socialního zabezpečení*, C-399/09, ECLI:EU:C:2011:415. *See, inter alia*, G. Martinico, 'The "Polemical" Spirit of European Constitutional Law: On the Importance of Conflicts in EU Law', 2015; M. Bobek, 'Landtová, Holubec, and the Problem of an Uncooperative Court: Implications for the Preliminary Rulings Procedure', 2014.

to minimise the incompatibility and not to interfere with national constitutional aspects.[1049]

This notwithstanding, in the *Holubec* case the Czech Constitutional Court declared that the EU *Landtová* judgment did not have any legal relevance and could not be applied in the domestic legal system because, in pronouncing it, the CJEU had acted *ultra vires*. The Constitutional Court further argued that the CJEU had failed to take into account the historical and political context of the Czech social security system, linked to the complex separation of the Czech and Slovak Republics.[1050]

The doctrine of counter-limits also found its way into Polish constitutional jurisprudence.[1051] As Piqani noted, the Constitutional Court had claimed the *kompetenz-kompetenz* already in a judicial proceeding on the Treaty of Accession of Poland to the EU, where the Polish judge resorted to a rhetoric infused with sovranist overtones.[1052] This ruling was followed by a period of greater trans-judicial openness but then the defensive attitude eventually reappeared.[1053] A significant example is the ruling where the Polish Constitutional Court was asked to assess the constitutionality of the act of ratification of the Lisbon Treaty.[1054] There, the Polish Court reiterated the inviolability of the principles pertaining to constitutional identity and reaffirmed the *kompetenz-kompetenz* doctrine. But, if the Lisbon Treaty ruling already reflected trans-judicial coldness, the final burst occurred in October 2021. That is when the Polish Constitutional Court essentially declared that the EU Treaties, as well as the

1049. O. Pollicino, 'Qualcosa è Cambiato? La Recente Giurisprudenza delle Corti Costituzionali dell'Est vis à vis il Processo di Integrazione Europea', Diritticomparati.it, 15.11.2012, https://www.diritticomparati.it/qualcosa-e-cambiato-la-recente-giurisprudenza-delle-corti-costituzionali-dellest-vis-a-vis-il-proces/?print-posts=print and Bobek (*ibid.*). Both authors explain that the strong reaction of the Czech constitutional judge can be understood as the result of an internal conflict between different organs of the national judiciary and, in particular, between the Constitutional Court and the Supreme Administrative Court.

1050. *See also* J. Přibáň, 'The Semantics of Constitutional Sovereignty in Post-sovereign "New" Europe: A Case Study of the Czech Constitutional Court's Jurisprudence, 2015.

1051. D. Piqani, 'Constitutional Courts in Central and Eastern Europe and Their Attitude Towards European Integration', 2007.

1052. Judgment of the Polish Constitutional Court, 11 May 2005, K 18/04 [POL-2005-1-006]. It is interesting to note that a rather rigid approach to trans-judicial dialogue is also taken by the Court of Justice. Rigid tones emerge from the Court of Justice's side, in judgment of 19 November 2009, *Krzysztof Filipiak v. Dyrektor Izby Skarbowej w Poznaniu*, C-314/08, ECLI:EU:C:2009:719, where the Court of Justice required the Polish referring court to disapply a domestic provision on social security as conflicting with EU law, despite the fact that the same provision would shortly thereafter lose its effectiveness as a result of a ruling by the Polish Constitutional Court.

1053. As noted in O. Pollicino, *Allargamento dell'Europa a est e rapporto tra Corti costituzionali e Corti europee*, 2010 and S. Sileoni, 'La Corte Costituzionale Polacca, il Mandato d'Arresto Europeo e la Sentenza sul Trattato di Adesione all'UE', Quaderni Costituzionali, 4, pp. 894-896, 2005. Reference goes, for instance, to the judgment of the Polish Constitutional Court, 27 April 2005, P L 1/05 on the European Arrest Warrant, where the constitutional judge found the national legislation transposing EU framework decision on the arrest warrant to be unconstitutional, but it deferred the legal effects of the declaration of unconstitutionality so that the extradition object of the decision could be, in the meanwhile, executed.

1054. Judgment of the Polish Constitutional Court, 24 November 2010, K 32/09 on the Lisbon Treaty.

CJEU's judgments interpreting them, are *ultra vires*.[1055] One could not think of a stronger implementation of the counter-limits.

The October 2021 ruling was a reaction to an EU judgment of July 2021, in which the CJEU found that a recent governmental reform of the Polish judicial system was in breach of EU law. In particular, the CJEU ruled that the creation of a disciplinary chamber with the power to lift the judges' immunity was incompatible with the principle of independence of judges because it would expose them to political interference.[1056] Most notably, according to the CJEU, this reform of the Polish judicial system was contrary to Article 47 CFREU, establishing the right to an effective remedy and to a fair trial, and Article 19(1) TEU, 'requiring the Member States to provide guarantees that national courts and tribunal meet requirements capable of guaranteeing effective judicial protection, including those relating to the independence and impartiality of these bodies'.[1057]

The Polish Government reacted very coldly to the CJEU's decision and gave no reassurances about its willingness to intervene and change the judicial system in accordance with the CJEU's ruling.[1058] The Polish government's lack of action prompted the European Commission to ask the CJEU to impose fines on the Polish state for failing to comply with the Court's ruling of July 2021.[1059] At this point, the Polish government turned to the Polish Constitutional Court, with a question of (un)constitutionality of said ruling of the CJEU. The Polish Constitutional Court then sided with the government and found that the Court's interpretation of the EU Treaties as well as the EU Treaties themselves were to be considered incompatible with the Polish Constitution as they infringed national sovereignty.[1060] Essentially, the CJEU found the Polish judicial reform in breach of the rule of law and the response of the Polish Constitutional Court was to declare that the principles of EU law on which the CJEU had based its ruling are unconstitutional.[1061] As a reaction to the Constitutional Court's ruling, the European Commission promptly issued a statement reiterating that 'the EU

1055. Judgment of the Polish Constitutional Court, 7 October 2021, K 3/21.
1056. Judgment of 15 July 2021, *European Commission v. Republic of Poland*, C-791/19, ECLI:EU:C:2021:596. *See also* European Commission, Press Release: Rule of Law: European Commission refers Poland to the European Court of Justice to Protect Independence of Polish Judges and Asks for Interim Measures, Brussels, 31 March 2021.
1057. C-791/19, *Commission v. Poland (Régime disciplinaire des juges)* (para. 47).
1058. D.S. Shekhaway, 'Rule of Law Crisis Deepens in Poland: Fresh Attack on the EU', A Path for Europe, 22.11.2021, https://pathforeurope.eu/rule-of-law-crisis-deepens-in-poland-fresh-attack-on-the-eu/.
1059. European Commission, Press Release: Independence of Polish Judges: Commission Asks European Court of Justice for Financial Penalties Against Poland on the Activity of the Disciplinary Chamber, Brussels, 7 September 2021.
1060. In particular, according to the Constitutional Tribunal, the Court of Justice's reading of the Treaties implied that the Union's institutions [including the Court of Justice] act outside the scope of the competences conferred upon them by the Republic of Poland in the Treaties; the Constitution is not the supreme law of the Republic of Poland and does not have precedence as of its binding force and application; the Republic of Poland cannot function as a democratic and sovereign state' and that therefore, the EU Treaties must be considered incompatible with Articles 8 and 10(1) of the Polish Constitution. Judgment of the Polish Constitutional Court, 7 October 2021, K 3/21 (para. 1).
1061. S. Biernat & E. Łętowska, 'This Was Not Just Another Ultra Vires Judgment!', Verfassungsblog, 27.10.2021, https://verfassungsblog.de/this-was-not-just-another-ultra-vires-judgment/.

law has primacy over national law', including 'constitutional provisions'.[1062] It remains to be seen how this serious conflict will evolve, both judicially and politically.

This digression on the emergence of counter-limits across the Member States' judiciary showed that the CJEU can encounter considerable resistance, especially when its rulings are perceived as too 'intrusive' or activist. The next section discusses how the Court has been able to engage with manifestation of trans-judicial closure by adapting its reasonings and addressing the concerns expressed by national courts.

4.5 Trans-judicial Dialogue in Action

In sections 4.4.1 and 4.4.2, it was explained that the emergence of counter-limits can be interpreted as a reaction of national supreme and constitutional courts to the CJEU's expansive interpretation of EU law. It was also discussed that the CJEU has responded to counter-limits by providing greater guarantees with respect to fundamental rights and national constitutional principles. These trans-judicial dynamics can be interpreted as a prime example of judicial (constitutional) dialogue.

In this section, the scope of the investigation is narrowed to a series of examples regarding judicial proceedings which touch on the notion of 'general principles of EU law'. These examples allow to identify in a more tangible way the implications of the trans-judicial dialogue on EU case law. It is shown that the outburst of judicial activism by the CJEU (section 4.5.1) was followed by a defensive reaction on the part of the national courts (section 4.5.2) and that this reaction led the CJEU to use greater caution in the elaboration of its reasoning (section 4.5.3). For the sake of completeness, it should be noted that, in parallel with these examples, the Court has also delivered judgments which, prima facie, are inconsistent with a dialectical trans-judicial attitude. These exceptions should be reported, as they illustrate the difficulties of placing the Court's reasoning within a clear judicial lawmaking framework (as will be discussed in section 4.5.4).

4.5.1 The Judicial Activism of the Court of Justice

As already mentioned in the course of the book,[1063] the CJEU provoked a heated academic debate when it delivered the *Mangold* judgment (2006).[1064] The *Mangold*

1062. European Commission, Press Release: European Commission Reaffirms the Primacy of EU Law, Brussels, 7 October 2021. *See also*, 'Polish Constitutional Court Declares EU Treaties Ultra Vires in Poland', EULawLive, 7.10.2021, https://eulawlive.com/polish-constitutional-court-declares-eu-treaties-ultra-vires-in-poland/.

1063. *See* Chapter 4, sections 2.1.2 and 3.2.2.2.

1064. Especially regarding C-144/04, *Mangold*, harsh criticism was formulated by Roman Herzog (the former president of the German Federal Constitutional Tribunal), and by Luder Gerken (director of Center of European Policy): R. Herezog & L. Gerken, 'Stop the European Court of Justice', EuObserver, 10.9.2008, https://euobserver.com/opinion/26714. *See also* comments in T. Ćapeta, 'Ideology and Legal Reasoning at the European Court of Justice' in E. Perisin & S. Rodin (eds), *The Transformation or Reconstitution of Europe: The Critical Legal Studies Perspective on the Role of the Courts in the European Union*, Hart Publishing, Oxford, 2018, pp. 89-120. In O. Pollicino, 'Corte di giustizia e giudici nazionali: il moto "ascendente", ovverosia l'incidenza delle "tradizioni costituzionali comuni" nella tutela apprestata ai diritti dalla Corte

case concerned a reform of German labour law that allowed employers to make more flexible use of fixed-term contracts for workers over 52 years of age. In particular, this reform established that once workers turned 52, it was no longer necessary for the employer to provide justification for stipulating fixed-term contracts.[1065] When addressed with a preliminary ruling on the compatibility of the German reform with EU law, the Court identified an incongruence with Directive 2000/78/EC setting a general framework for equal treatment in the area of employment. The directive in fact includes age among the forbidden grounds of discrimination. However, Directive 2000/78/EC was not directly applicable in this case as the dispute arose when the period left to the national governments for the implementation was not yet over. Nevertheless, the Court ruled that the principle of equal treatment on grounds of age must be considered a general principle of the EU as it 'is found [...] in various international instruments and in the constitutional traditions common to the Member States'.[1066] By including equal treatment on the ground of age among the general principles of EU law, the Court claimed the competence to assess the compliance of the German reform on fixed-term contracts, and eventually found it discriminatory and in breach of EU law. Going even further, the Court stated that the prohibition of age discrimination had to be regarded as a principle having direct horizontal effect, meaning that it could also be invoked in a dispute between private individuals. The only condition for the direct effect to apply was that the national legal proceeding must fall within the scope of EU law, which was the case here.

It was the first time that a Court judgment had given direct horizontal effect to a principle of EU law that was not (yet) expressed in applicable secondary legislation (since the period to implement Directive 2000/78/EC was not over).[1067] The impact of this ruling was potentially disruptive for national legal systems, as the Court gave to individuals a subjective right to claim before a national court the enforcement of a principle of EU law over national legal provisions.

A similar legal reasoning was reiterated by the CJEU a couple of years later in *Kücükdeveci* (2010), again concerning German legislation.[1068] This time the dispute concerned a national legislation which did not include in the computation of the notice period for dismissal the period of employment completed by the employees before reaching the age of 25. As in *Mangold*, the CJEU ruled that the general principle of EU law prohibiting all discrimination on the ground of age precluded the national rule in question. It also reaffirmed that the prohibition of discrimination had direct effect and

dell'Unione', 1, Consulta Online, 2015, the author defined the reasoning of the Court as an 'example of creative interpretation on the verge of manipulation'.

1065. Judgment of 22 November 2005, *Werner Mangold v. Rüdiger Helm*, C-144/04, ECLI: EU:C:2005:709 (paras 17, 18).

1066. *Ibid.* (para. 74).

1067. *Inter alia*, D. Wyatt, 'Horizontal Effect of Fundamental Freedoms and the Right to Equality after Viking and Mangold, and the Implications for Community Competence', Legal Research Paper series, published in Croatian Yearbook of European Law & Policy, Oxford, 2008; E. Muir, 'Enhancing the Effects of Community Law on National Employment Policies: The Mangold Case', European Law Review, 36(1), pp. 879-891, 2006.

1068. Judgment of 19 January 2010, *Seda Kücükdeveci gegen Swedex GmbH & Co. KG.*, C-555/07, ECLI:EU:C:2010:21.

could be invoked in a dispute between private individuals.[1069] The *Mangold* and *Kücükdeveci* judgments were later echoed in *Ajos – Dansk Industry* (2016), a case brought to the CJEU through a reference for a preliminary ruling from the Danish Supreme Court. The proceeding concerned a Danish law excluding old-age pension recipients from the right to receive redundancy pay in case of dismissal. Here too, the EU judges found a violation of the general principle of non-discrimination on grounds of age, again ascribed among the rights having direct effect.[1070]

The creative and expansive approach of the CJEU with regard to the concept of 'general principles of EU law' that characterises the *Mangold, Kücükdeveci* and *Ajos* judgments can be considered an expression of judicial activism, and this mainly for two reasons. The first is that the Court's legal reasoning is only apparently based on legal doctrine. In reality, it conceals a rather arbitrary exercise of judicial discretion. For instance, the Court stated that the principle of non-discrimination on grounds of age is widely recognised in the constitutional traditions of the Member States and in instruments of international law. However, Herzog and Gerken observed that this line of argument is an artifice. There is no common legal culture and no shared constitutional tradition with regard to the principle of non-discrimination on grounds of age.[1071] Quite eloquently, Herzog and Gerken argued that 'this general principle of community law was a fabrication. In only two of the then 25 Member States, namely Finland and Portugal, is there any reference to a ban on age discrimination, and in not one international treaty is there any mention at all of there being such a ban, contrary to the terse allegation of the CJEU. [...] To put it bluntly, with this construction which the CJEU more or less pulled out of the hat, they [the CJEU judges] were acting not as part of the judicial power but as the legislature'.[1072]

The second indication of judicial activism is that in all these judgments the Court adopted an 'outcome' ruling, with encroaching effects on national labour policies. It is indeed worth recalling that employment and social security matters are particularly sensitive issues for the Member States as they are at the heart of their socioeconomic model, and broadly fall outside the Union's competences.[1073] In finding that domestic legislation was incompatible with the general principle of EU law, the Court required national institutions to intervene in the regulation of domestic labour market, with

1069. *Ibid.* (para. 27). To support the thesis of horizontal direct effect, the Court of Justice also referred to Article 21 CFR, which had recently acquired the status of a binding legal norm (para. 21).

1070. Judgment of 19 April 2016, *Dansk Industri (DI), acting on behalf of Ajos A/S v. Estate of Karsten Eigil Rasmussen*, C-441/14, ECLI:EU:C:2016:278 (para. 27).

1071. *See, inter alia*, G. Martinico, 'The "Polemical" Spirit of European Constitutional Law: On the Importance of Conflicts in EU Law', German Law Journal, 16(6), pp. 1343-1374, 2015; V. Papa, 'The Dark Side of Fundamental Rights Adjudication? The Court, the Charter and the Asymmetric Interpretation of Fundamental Rights in the AMS Case and Beyond', European Labour Law Journal, 6(3), pp. 190-214, 2015; M. Dawson, 'The Political Face of Judicial Activism: Europe's Law-Politics Imbalance' in B. de Witte, B. Muir & E. Dawson (eds), *Judicial Activism at the European Court of Justice*, Edward Elgar Publishing, Cheltenham, 2013, pp. 11-32.

1072. R. Herezog & L. Gerken, 'Stop the European Court of Justice', EuObserver, 10.9.2008, https://euobserver.com/opinion/26714.

1073. *Ibid.*

potentially high financial repercussions.[1074] The CJEU thus substantially interfered in the policymaking of Member States, and it is plausible that this interference was not easily accepted by the national regulatory and judicial authorities.

4.5.2 *The Reaction of National Courts*

The *Mangold*, *Kücükdeveci* and *Ajos* judgments provoked not only a lively academic debate[1075] but also reactions from national courts. From a trans-judicial dialogue perspective, these reactions can be read as a defensive response to the judicial activism of the CJEU.

The first court to make its voice heard was the German Federal Constitutional Court, in the *Honeywell* judgment.[1076] In *Honeywell*, the dispute concerned the same domestic legislation and the same legal issue that had previously been addressed by the CJEU in the *Mangold* case. It related to a worker who had passed the age of 52 and who challenged the invalidity of a fixed-term contract that had been concluded without adequate justification. In support of his claim, the worker referred to the *Mangold* judgment where, as was previously described, the CJEU found that the legislation in question was defined as discriminatory and contrary to EU law. The proceeding eventually reached the German Federal Labour Tribunal, which decided to raise an objection of constitutionality and to submit to the Federal Constitutional Tribunal a question concerning the implications of the *Mangold* judgment into the internal legal order. In its referral, the Federal Labour Court clearly indicated that in its view the Mangold judgment was an *ultra vires* act by which the CJEU had pushed EU law out of its boundaries, encroaching upon the German Basic Law.[1077]

The Constitutional Court at first confirmed to have competence to assess the validity of EU acts (among which the CJEU's case law) – and their compliance with the principle of attribution of competences, in line with the *kompetenz-kompetenz* doctrine.[1078] Already in doing so, the Constitutional Tribunal contradicted the *Foto-Frost* principle, according to which only the CJEU detains such a prerogative.[1079] Then, the constitutional judge provided guidance on the conditions under which a CJEU's judgment can be declared *ultra vires*. It stressed that such a decision should not be adopted lightly, but had to be taken with caution in order not to undermine the unity

1074. C. de la Porte & P. Emmenegger, 'The Court of Justice of the European Union and Fixed-Term Workers: Still Fixed, but at Least Equal', Working Paper, 1, ETUI, Brussels, 2016.

1075. *Inter alia*: *ibid.*; D. Wyatt, 'Horizontal Effect of Fundamental Freedoms and the Right to Equality after Viking and Mangold, and the Implications for Community Competence', 2008; E. Muir, 'Enhancing the Effects of Community Law on National Employment Policies: The Mangold Case', 2006.

1076. Judgment of the German Constitutional Court, 6 July 2010, BvR 2661/06, *Honeywell*. *See also* E.M. Payandeh, 'Constitutional Review of EU Law after Honeywell: Contextualising the Relationship Between the German Constitutional Court and the EU Court of Justice', Common Market Law Review, 48(1), pp. 9-38, 2011.

1077. Judgment of the German Constitutional Court, 6 July 2010, BvR 2661/06, *Honeywell* (paras 34-39).

1078. *Ibid.* (para. 45).

1079. *See* section 4.4.2. C-314/85, *Foto Frost*.

and coherence of EU law.[1080] In case of doubts, it was important to give the CJEU the opportunity to clarify, by means of a preliminary reference, the exact scope of the contested act.[1081] Furthermore, the constitutional judge stated that to be *ultra vires*, the act must entail a 'structurally significant shift in the structure of competences between Member States and a supranational organisation'.[1082] And it was precisely for these reasons that the German Constitutional Court ultimately found that the infringement of the division of competences between the EU and the Member States in the *Mangold* case was not significant enough for an *ultra vires* declaration.

The German Constitutional Court exhibited a rather defensive attitude but still showed to be open to dialogue with the CJEU. This is a nuanced expression of trans-judicial tension, not as explicit as that resulting from the Czech Constitutional Court in the *Landtová* judgment or from the Polish Constitutional Tribunal in its decision on the judiciary system. The message to the CJEU was nevertheless clear: the relationship between the European and national legal systems had to be conceived according to a dualist model, in continuity with what the German Constitutional Tribunal had previously affirmed in its judgments on the Maastricht and Lisbon Treaties.[1083] The German constitutional judges essentially warned that, even if there was no violation of national sovereignty this time, they would remain vigilant and would continue to ensure that the Court does not overstep its competences. From the point of view of trans-judicial dialogue, this was an intimation to be more cautious in its future reasoning.[1084]

The German constitutional judge was not alone in responding to the CJEU's 'invention' concerning the doctrine of direct effect of the general principles of EU law. In 2016, it was the turn of the Danish Supreme Court, which ruled on the *Ajos* case. The *Ajos* case had, in fact, originated from a preliminary reference by the Danish Supreme Court which then had the task to implement the CJEU's ruling in the domestic proceeding.[1085] Unlike the German Constitutional Tribunal, the Danish constitutional judge decided not to dwell on sophisticated doctrinal arguments on the counter-limits. Instead, it rejected the *Ajos* judgment in its entirety.[1086] First, it was found that since the

1080. Judgment of the German Constitutional Court, 6 July 2010, BvR 2661/06, *Honeywell* (with special reference to paras 61, 105 and 114).
1081. Interestingly, the Federal Constitutional Court remained consistent with this doctrine when, years later, in C-493/17, *Weiss*, it decided to make a preliminary reference to the Court of Justice to allow the Court to clarify (and correct) the Outright Monetary Transaction judgment (C-62/14, *Gauwaier – OMT*).
1082. Judgment of the German Constitutional Court, 6 July 2010, BvR 2661/06, *Honeywell* (paras 102 and 103).
1083. E.J. Lohse, 'The German Constitutional Court and Preliminary References – Still a Match Not Made in Heaven?', German Law Journal, 16(6), 2015, pp. 1491-1508, 2011.
1084. E.M. Payandeh, 'Constitutional Review of EU Law after Honeywell: Contextualising the Relationship Between the German Constitutional Court and the EU Court of Justice', 2011; T. Tridimas, 'The ECJ and the National Courts: Dialogue, Cooperation, and Instability' in D. Chalmers & A. Arnull (eds), *The Oxford Handbook of European Union Law*, Oxford University Press, Oxford, 2015, pp. 1-30; F. Fontanelli, 'All's Well That Ends Honeywell', Diritticomparati.it, 2010, https://www.diritticomparati.it/alls-well-that-ends-honeywell/.
1085. O. Terkelsen, 'The Danish Ajos Case and the Danish Approach to International Law', European Public Law, 24(2), pp. 183-193, 2018.
1086. Judgment of the Danish Supreme Court, 6 December 2016, 15/2014.

Ajos decision established that the Danish legislation was in breach of the EU principle of non-discrimination on grounds of age, there was no scope for interpreting domestic law in accordance with the Court's judgment. However, contrary to the CJEU's instructions, the Supreme Court decided that it would not disapply the domestic (discriminatory) legislation. The Danish judge justified its decision by arguing that the Danish Accession Act (the legal act by which Denmark became a Member State of the EU) did not explicitly indicate that the 'general principles of EU law' were to be considered hierarchically superior to domestic law.[1087] This ruling can be considered an indirect expression of the *kompetenz-kompetenz* doctrine, even if in a more indirect manner than its German equivalent.[1088]

From the perspective of trans-judicial dialogue, both *Honeywell* and *Ajos* are clear attempts by national courts to curb the CJEU's broad interpretation of the domestic legal implications of the general principles of EU law. The Danish and German supreme judges in fact found that the Court's judicial activism conflicted with their understanding of national sovereignty and expressed their opposition to this sort of attempt of the Court to overstretch its jurisdiction.

4.5.3 *The Effects of Trans-judicial Dialogue on the Court of Justice's Reasoning*

This section concerns the potential impact that the judgments of the German and Danish constitutional courts have had on the EU case law on general principles of EU law. For the sake of consistency, the focus remains on case law in the field of employment, albeit in areas other than that of non-discrimination on grounds of age.

Since the German Federal Constitutional Court handed down the *Honeywell* judgment in 2010, the CJEU has been involved in at least three other proceedings dealing with general principles of EU law in an employment-related area: *Dominguez* (2012), on the right of workers to receive annual paid leave; *AMS* (2014) on the right to information and consultation of workers; and *Egenberger* (2018), on the principle of non-discrimination on grounds of religious belief. In all these cases there are elements that indicate that the CJEU has acknowledged and engaged with the defensive position of the Danish and German constitutional judges. The Court has indeed displayed more caution in applying its doctrine on the direct effect of general principles of EU law, limiting its impact on the national legal systems.

Proceeding in chronological order, in the *Dominguez* case, the CJEU received a preliminary question from the French Court of Cassation.[1089] The question concerned

1087. *See also* H. Krunke & S. Klinge, 'The Danish Ajos Case: The Missing Case from Maastricht and Lisbon', European Papers, 3(1), pp. 157-182, 2018.
1088. The Supreme Court ruled that the question whether a rule of EU law can be given direct effect in Danish law, as required under EU law, turns first and foremost on the law on accession by which Denmark accessed to the EU. *See* unofficial translation of judgment of the Danish Supreme Court, 6 December 2016, 15/2014, p. 14, available here https://domstol.dk/media/2udgvvvb/judgment-15-2014.pdf.
1089. Judgment of 24 January 2012, *Maribel Dominguez v. Centre informatique du Centre Ouest Atlantique and Préfet de la région Centre*, C-282/10, ECLI:EU:C:2012:33.

the possibility of enforcing, in a dispute between private individuals (and therefore in a 'horizontal' situation), the EU fundamental principle whereby every worker is entitled to paid annual leave. This right is established in Article 31 CFREU and in Article 7(1) of the Working Time Directive.[1090] The Court found that in the French system, this principle was clearly violated since only workers who had been employed for at least one month could benefit from the right to paid leave. Having established the incompatibility between French law and the fundamental EU principle, the Court did not, however, go so far as to require the referring court to cast aside the national provision, as it had previously done in *Mangold*, *Kücükdeveci* and *Ajos*. The Court instead opted for a more restrictive approach, as it did not recognise direct enforceability (or direct effect) to the right to annual leave in a dispute between private individuals.[1091]

It is interesting to note that the Court reached this conclusion even if the legal question in *Dominguez* was rather similar to those raised in *Mangold, Kücükdeveci* and *Ajos*. On closer inspection, the self-restraint approach of the Court may have been influenced by Advocate General Trstenjak. The AG opinion advised the Court against applying the '*Mangold* and *Kücükdeveci* doctrine' even though, in theory, there were conditions for giving direct horizontal effect to the general legal principle in question. Perhaps alerted by the German Federal Constitutional Court's ruling, AG Trstenjak warned that, before extending this effect to other areas of law, the Court should carefully consider the normative and financial repercussions of its reasoning.[1092] In particular, the Advocate General indicated that it was 'necessary to avoid encasing social standards in cement without any regard for economic and social reality'. The *Dominguez* judgment can thus be read as an effort by the Court to restrict its own doctrine of horizontal direct effect.[1093]

Turning now to the *AMS* ruling, here too the Court renounced extending the *Mangold* doctrine on the general principles of EU law, even if the context appeared rather similar.[1094] The preliminary reference originated again from the French Cour de Cassation and concerned the EU's fundamental right to information and consultation for workers – laid down in both Article 27 CFREU and Directive 2002/14/EC. The question of interpretation submitted to the Court was whether such fundamental right

1090. Directive 2003/88/EC of the European Parliament and of the Council of 4 November 2003 concerning certain aspects of the organisation of working time *Official Journal L 299, 18/11/2003 pp. 0009-0019;* Article 31(2) CFREU: 'Every worker has the right to limitation of maximum working hours, to daily and weekly rest period and to an annual period of leave.'

1091. C-282/10, *Dominguez* (para. 32).

1092. V. Papa, 'The Dark Side of Fundamental Rights Adjudication? The Court, the Charter and the Asymmetric Interpretation of Fundamental Rights in the AMS Case and Beyond', European Labour Law Journal, 6(3), pp. 190-214, 2015. *See also* opinion of Advocate General Trstenjak of 8 September 2011, *Maribel Dominguez v. Centre informatique du Centre Ouest Atlantique and Préfet de la région Centre*, C-282/10, ECLI:EU:C:2011:559 (paras 146-159).

1093. Opinion of Advocate General Trstenjak of 8 September 2011, *Maribel Dominguez v. Centre informatique du Centre Ouest Atlantique and Préfet de la région Centre*, C-282/10, ECLI: EU:C:2011:559 (para. 158). *See also* D. Leczykiewicz, 'Horizontal Effect of Fundamental Rights: In Search of Social Justice or Private Autonomy in EU Law?', Oxford Legal Studies Research Paper, 38, University of Oxford, Oxford, 2013.

1094. Judgment of 15 January 2014, *Association de médiation sociale v. Union locale des syndicats CGT and Others*, C-176/12, ECLI:EU:C:2014:2.

could have a direct effect on the domestic proceeding, involving a dispute between private individuals. In other words, whether the principle could have horizontal direct effect and be invoked by the litigants. The issue arose because French legislation unduly excluded certain categories of workers from assessing the quantitative threshold that, if met, determines the application of Directive 2002/14/EC.[1095] The CJEU found that the French legislation was clearly in breach of the directive. It also established that the right of workers to information and consultation is a fundamental principle of EU law, which is potentially capable of direct effect in the national context.[1096] However, the Court ruled out the possibility that the relevant provision of Directive 2002/14/EC, namely that on the determination of the threshold, could have a horizontal direct effect.[1097]

The Court's legal justification for this conclusion is rather obscure. The argument of the Court was that the provision of Directive 2002/14/EC defining the scope of the right to information and consultation was not an actual expression of the general principle of EU law as enunciated in Article 27 CFREU. This reasoning is quite odd since it is hard to believe that the provision of Directive 2002/14/EC defining the scope of the rights to information and consultation does not constitute an actual expression of those rights.[1098] The attribution of information and consultation rights is clearly what Article 27 CFREU is about: 'Workers or their representatives must, at the appropriate levels, be guaranteed information and consultation in good time in the cases and under the conditions provided for by Community law and national laws and practices.'

The Court thus ruled that an infringement of directive 2002/14/EC could not be regarded as a breach of the general principle of information and consultation rights and,[1099] for this reason, the doctrine of *Mangold* and *Kücükdeveci* could not be replicated.[1100] The Court concluded that there was no ground for asking the referring court to disapply domestic legislation in horizontal situations, even if that legislation was contrary to EU law.[1101] As in *Dominguez*, the *AMS* judgment suggests that the Court was more cautious not to interfere in nationally sensitive policy areas.[1102]

The same self-restraint attitude can be observed in the more recent *Egenberger* judgment, on the principle of non-discrimination with respect to religious belief.[1103] In this case, the request for a preliminary ruling was submitted by the German Federal Labour Tribunal, which asked the CJEU to clarify two legal issues. The first was whether German legislation allowing religious organisations to recruit their workers in

1095. V. Papa, 'The Dark Side of Fundamental Rights Adjudication? The Court, the Charter and the Asymmetric Interpretation of Fundamental Rights in the AMS Case and Beyond', 2015.
1096. C-176/12, *AMS* (para. 27).
1097. *Ibid.* (paras 41 and 46).
1098. S. Rainone, 'Enforcing EU Information and Consultation Rights' in Z. Rasnača, A. Koukiadaki, N. Bruun & K. Lorcher (eds), *Effective Enforcement of EU Labour Law*, Hart, Portland, 2022.
1099. C-176/12, *AMS* (para. 46).
1100. *Ibid.* (para. 47).
1101. *Ibid.* (para. 36).
1102. V. Papa, 'The Dark Side of Fundamental Rights Adjudication? The Court, the Charter and the Asymmetric Interpretation of Fundamental Rights in the AMS Case and Beyond', 2015.
1103. Judgment of 17 April 2018, *Vera Egenberger v. Evangelisches Werk für Diakonie und Entwicklung e.V.*, C-414/16, ECLI:EU:C:2018:257.

consideration of their religion was in breach of Directive 2000/78/EC establishing a general prohibition of discrimination. Secondly, in the event of such incompatibility between the German law and the directive, the referring judge asked whether national courts were obliged to disapply national legislation also in disputes between private individuals, thus raising the issue of horizontal direct effect.

On the first point, the CJEU found that the German legislation had a discriminatory effect, which is generally prohibited by Directive 2000/78/EC. However, the Court also noted that, under the same directive, violations of the principle of non-discrimination on grounds of religious belief must be assessed in light of the principle of proportionality.[1104] It then ruled that it was for the referring judge to conduct the proportionality test and to balance the principle of non-discrimination with the right of autonomy of churches and similar organisations.[1105] With what can be considered as a 'guidance' judgment,[1106] the Court then considered the situation where the national court was to determine that the German legislation did not pass the proportionality test and was therefore in breach of Directive 2000/78/EC. In such a case, the CJEU ruled that this incompatibility should be remedied by the national referring judge through the effort of interpreting national law in a manner consistent with the directive. Should this not prove possible, the Court recalled that the prohibition of all discrimination on grounds of religion or beliefs is a general principle of EU law. This entails that it has an overriding force, capable of having direct effect on disputes between private individuals.[1107] Only as a last remedy, therefore the national court would be required to disapply contrary provision of national law.[1108]

Although the reasoning of the CJEU is consistent with the *Mangold* doctrine, the tone of the legal argumentation is substantially different. The *Egenberger* judgment is in fact characterised by greater caution in outlining the implications of the horizontal direct effect on the general principle in question. First of all, the CJEU preferred not to express a conclusive opinion on the violation of the principle of non-discrimination by the national legislation. By delegating the implementation of the proportionality test, the Court recognised wide discretion to the referring judge in determining how EU law should find application in the national legal system.[1109] Moreover, the Court had been clear in presenting the disapplication of national legislation as a remedy of last resort; this solution was in fact to be considered only after the domestic judge had failed in

1104. Council Directive 2000/78/EC of 27 November 2000 establishing a general framework for equal treatment in employment and occupation, *Official Journal L 303, 02/12/2000 pp. 0016-0022*, Article 2(2).
1105. C-414/16, *Egenberger* (para. 59).
1106. T. Tridimas, 'The ECJ and the National Courts: Dialogue, Cooperation, and Instability', 2015; R. Van Gestel & J. De Poorter, *In the Court We Trust: Cooperation, Coordination and Collaboration Between the ECJ and Supreme Administrative Courts*, 2019, pp. 85-87.
1107. C-414/16, *Egenberger* (paras 76 and 77).
1108. *Ibid.* (para. 79).
1109. *Ibid.* (para. 68); *see also* E. Frantziou, 'Mangold Recast? The ECJ's Flirtation with Drittwirkung in Egenberger', European Law Blog, 24.4.2018, https://europeanlawblog.eu/2020/06/23/the-commissions-proposal-for-a-european-minimum-wage-another-ultra-vires-challenge-for-the-eu/.

interpreting national law in a manner consistent with EU law.[1110] Also, in this case, the CJEU displayed judicial restraint. Like in the other examples, also *Egenberger* can thus be read as a dialectical reaction to the warnings received from the German and Danish constitutional tribunal in previous proceedings.

4.5.4 *Case Law Challenging the Trans-judicial Dialogue Narrative*

Dominguez, *AMS* and *Egenberger* bring some robustness to the thesis that trans-judicial dialogue has a substantial impact on EU case law. However, it would be improper not to mention that, in the same years, the CJEU also issued judgments which, at least at a first glance, suggest the opposite. Reference goes to EU case law in which the Court has not hesitated to give (de facto) direct horizontal effect to the principle of freedom to conduct a business, enshrined in Article 16 CFREU. *Alemo-Herron (2012)*, *Achbita* (2016) and *Bougnaoui* (2016) are examples of rulings where the Court did not show any sign of the judicial restraint approach that was identified in the case law discussed in the previous section.[1111]

The *Alemo-Herron* ruling has already been extensively discussed in this book.[1112] In Chapter 1, section 3.1 and Chapter 3, section 5.2, it was mentioned that the CJEU instructed the referring judge to disregard established national legal practices in order to ensure that the employer could exercise its freedom to conduct a business.[1113] As for the *Achbita* and *Bougnaoui* judgments, they relate to a potential breach of Directive 2000/78/EC by a Belgian (in the case of *Achbita*) and French (in the case of *Bougnaoui*) employment practice. More precisely, both cases concerned the employer's decision to dismiss a female employee following her decision to wear the Islamic veil at the workplace. The dismissed workers claimed that the employer's decision constituted a violation of the prohibition of discrimination on the grounds of religious beliefs, established in Directive 2000/78/EC. In *Achbita*, the Court examined the legal issue in light of the freedom to conduct a business and essentially held that Article 16 CFREU gave the employer a wide margin of manoeuvre in managing its business. This, according to the CJEU, could justify differences in treatment such as that at issue.[1114] This reasoning was then confirmed in *Bougnaoui*.[1115]

1110. C-414/16, *Egenberger* (para. 73): 'a national court cannot validly consider that it is impossible for it to interpret a provision of national law in conformity with EU law merely because that provision has consistently being interpreted in a manner that is incompatible with EU law'.
1111. C-426/11, *Alemo-Herron*; C-157/15, *Achbita*; C-188/15, *Bougnaoui*.
1112. Mostly in Chapter 1, section 3.1 and Chapter 3, section 5.2.
1113. *See, inter alia*: J. Prassl, 'Freedom of Contract as a General Principle of EU Law? Transfers of Undertakings and the Protection of Employer Rights in EU Labour Law', Industrial Law Journal, 42(4), pp. 434-446, 2013; E. Gill-Pedro, 'Freedom to Conduct Business in EU Law: Freedom from Interference or Freedom from Domination?', European Journal of Legal Studies, 9(2), pp. 103-134, 2017; X. Groussot, T.G. Pétursson & J. Pierce, 'Weak Right, Strong Court – The Freedom to Conduct Business and the EU Charter of Fundamental Rights', Legal Research Paper Series, 1, Lund University, Lund, 2014.
1114. C-157/15, *Achbita* (para. 38). *See also* J.R. Marín Aís, 'Freedom of Religion in the Workplace v. Freedom to Conduct a Business, the Islamic Veil Before the Court of Justice: Ms. Samira Achbita Case', European Papers, 26.4.2018.
1115. C-188/15, *Bougnaoui* (para. 33).

These cases are examples of judicial activism, where the Court gave Article 16 CFREU a much wider scope than it would prima facie appear from the EU legal order. By establishing that in relations between private individuals, the employer may legitimately rely on the fundamental principle of freedom to conduct a business, the Court indirectly gave direct horizontal effect to Article 16 CFREU. In doing this, the Court contradicted the *Dominguez*, *AMS* and *Egenberger* judgments, instead characterised by judicial restraint towards the horizontal direct effect of EU principles of EU law.

It should be noted that this different interpretative approach with respect to the freedom to conduct a business inevitably casts shadows on the narrative whereby trans-judicial dialogue dynamics substantially impact the Court's reasoning. However, it is equally important to note that, at least with respect to the aforementioned rulings, these shadows can be partially contextualised. First of all, it should be considered that *Alemo-Herron*, *Achbita* and *Bougnaoui* were in all likelihood approached by the Court as cases dealing with the conflict between the emancipatory function of labour law, on the one hand, and the employer's economic freedoms (and in particular the freedom to conduct a business), on the other. In other words, it might not have even occurred to the Court that the legal questions at issue were also inherent to the relationship between the EU legal order and national law. The main focus of the Court was to provide 'adequate' room for the freedom to conduct a business of the employer, and the fact that Article 16 CFREU was given direct applicability might have been 'just' a side effect.[1116] This possibility is supported by the fact that neither the referring court in the preliminary rulings nor the CJEU in the judgments explicitly mentioned the doctrine of 'direct effect', or the impact that general principles of EU law should have in domestic systems.

Second, the expansive interpretation of the reach of Article 16 CFREU on national law has to some extent been mitigated in the more recent *Wabe* judgment, where the Court ruled on two joint cases originating from German courts.[1117] As already mentioned in section 3.3.3, in *Wabe* the Court was asked to rule on a question very similar to those already dealt with in *Achbita* and *Bougnaoui*, concerning whether a policy of neutrality of the employer was discriminatory with respect to women wearing the Islamic veil. The Court had also to establish whether the freedom to conduct a business laid down in Article 16 CFREU prevents national constitutional jurisprudence from developing a stricter prohibition of discrimination than that elaborated by the CJEU. The German constitutional court had in fact ruled that the ban on religious clothing may be justified only on the basis of a sufficiently specific risk, such as a threatened economic disadvantage of the employer. The EU case law was instead more relaxed on the matter. In addressing the issue, the CJEU formally confirmed its reasoning in *Achbita* and *Bougnaoui* and stated that neutrality policies of the employer may include

1116. For instance, in C-188/15, *Bougnaoui*, the Court does not explicitly refer to Article 16 CFREU. In none of the cases discussed in this section, the Court directly discussed the direct effect of the CFREU, probably connected to the fact that this issue was not expressly addressed by the referring judges in their request for preliminary ruling.

1117. Judgment of 15 July 2021, *IX v. WABE eV and MH Müller Handels GmbH v. MJ*, C-804/18, Joined Cases C-804/18 and C-341/19, ECLI:EU:C:2021:594.

a ban on religious symbols.[1118] On a closer inspection, however, in *Wabe* the Court restricted the direct effect of Article 16 CFREU in two ways. First, by specifying that the freedom to conduct a business can legitimise neutrality policies only if the absence of those policies would expose the employer to adverse consequences of significant scale and severity, which is for the national judge to assess.[1119] Then, the Court found that, in any case, under the margin of discretion granted by Directive 2000/78/EC, Member States can establish stricter prohibitions to discriminatory treatments and that, therefore, the German constitutional jurisprudence could apply to the dispute at hand.

The implications of Article 16 on national employment provisions emerge as mitigated by *Wabe*, and it should not be excluded that this is the result of the Court's efforts to modulate its reasoning in light of national case law. Indeed, it is only in *Alemo-Herron* that the attribution of direct effect to Article 16 CFREU actually led to the rejection of a consolidated national legal practice.[1120] In *Achbita* and *Bougnaoui*, the Court did not identify any incompatibility between EU and national legislation and therefore did not interfere in the regulatory choices of the domestic legislator.

In conclusion, although the mentioned case law on Article 16 CFREU raises questions as to the actual impact of the trans-judicial dialogue on the Court's reasoning, they do not rule out the possibility of the trans-judicial dialogue having an impact on EU case law.

5 CONCLUDING REMARKS

This chapter has discussed several theories that present the judicial lawmaking of the Court as closely intertwined with the national context.

In section 2 the intergovernmental thesis was explored, according to which Court's judgments reflect the preferences of national governments or at least the most influential among them. Section 3 then dealt with the possibility that the CJEU is largely inspired by national legal practices and traditions. There, two possible approaches were identified. One is the majoritarian logic, according to which the Court's legal reasoning reflects the legal solution that prevails across the Member States. The second is the pluralist approach, whereby the Court tends to leave room for the normative discretion of national legislators. Finally, section 4 turned to the trans-judicial dynamics and their potential to influence the Court's decision-making. The trans-judicial

1118. E. Howard, 'Headscarves and the CJEU: Protecting Fundamental Rights or Pandering to Prejudice', Maastricht Journal of European and Comparative Law, 28(5), pp. 648-666, 2021.
1119. C-804/18, *WABE* (paras 67 and 70), where the Court added this additional specification to the reasoning outlined in the *Achbita* and *Bougnaoui* precedents, and which is curiously phrased in a similar manner to the condition outlined in the German constitutional jurisprudence (*see* para. 34(2)b).
1120. C-426/11, *Alemo-Herron* (para. 37): 'Having regard to all the foregoing, the answer to the three questions referred is that Article 3 of Directive 2001/23 must be interpreted as precluding a Member State from providing, in the event of a transfer of an undertaking, that dynamic clauses referring to collective agreements negotiated and adopted after the date of transfer are enforceable against the transferee, where that transferee does not have the possibility of participating in the negotiation process of such collective agreements concluded after the date of the transfer.'

dialogue emerged as a plausible interpretative lens to observe the development of EU case law, especially in the area of fundamental rights and general principles of EU law.

It is now time to reflect on these theories in relation to RQ3 (*What are the logics that determine the Court's approach with respect to labour law, taking into account judicial lawmaking theories?*). The theories analysed in this chapter suggest that the Court is subject to a number of concerns and pressures of national origin. They thus imply that it would be incorrect to consider EU case law uniquely as an expression of the Court's own preferences in relation to the legal issues at stake.

These reflections can be transposed into the case law on labour law. They suggest that the weight that the judicial reasonings give to the social and economic dimension of labour norms might be the result of a series of factors which do not pertain, per se, to the Court's normative assessment of the conflicting interests at stake. Such factors include the preferences of national governments, the efforts to accommodate the coexistence of national and EU legal systems, and trans-judicial logics. These considerations provide new analytical lenses for looking at the results emerging from the case studies conducted in Chapter 3, which showed that the case law of the Court had moved towards an appreciation of the economic rationale of the analysed labour norms. Indeed, the theories outlined in this chapter hint that the valorisation of the economic dimension might (also) be the result of a changing contextual framework, be it legal, jurisprudential or political, which has influenced the reasoning of the Court.

Similar to what was noted with respect to neofunctionalism and integrationalism, the exploration of the theories presented in this chapter served to provide an adequately rich theoretical framework in view of conducting a second empirical analysis on the directive on transfer of undertakings. Here too, it is possible to identify some indicators that might be used in the case studies in the next chapter to 'test' these theories. Starting from intergovernmentalism, it might be helpful to look at whether the Court takes up in its line of argumentation the position that national governments propose in their amicus briefs. In relation to the majoritarian and the pluralistic theories, consideration could be given to the margin of discretion that the Court recognises to the national legislator (which might be an indication of pluralism) and to whether the Court makes use of comparativist techniques (which would indicate a majority approach). The possible relevance of trans-judicial dynamics could instead emerge from the extent to which the preemptive opinions of the referring judge are reflected in the Court's argumentations.

It is worth stressing that already the plausibility of the judicial lawmaking theories described in this chapter undermines the perception that the Court acts as a purposive policymaker vis-à-vis labour norms. The theories illustrated in this chapter in fact contribute to portraying the Court as embedded in a highly complex context, where multiple factors meet and overlap. Its judicial and interpretative activity thus takes place at a sort of crossroads, where different instances, pressures and interests are channelled.

CHAPTER 6

What's Behind the Decision-Making of the Court of Justice? A Case Study on Directive 2001/23/EC

1 INTRODUCTION

This chapter constitutes the final and empirical step in the exploration of the second analytical layer of the research. It should be recalled that the objective of this book is to define the role of the CJEU in relation to the normative model underlying EU labour law. The judicial lawmaking doctrines illustrated in the previous two chapters have contributed to enriching the theoretical framework with which to address this issue. This framework is now 'put into practice' through a second set of case studies, with the intention of detecting the dynamics that might have influenced the reasoning of the Court. The insights emerging from these case studies ultimately consent to address RQ3: *What are the logics that determine the Court's approach with respect to labour law, taking into account judicial lawmaking theories?* By engaging with this question, the book ultimately intends to test the dogmatic assumption whereby the Court expresses a normative bias when interpreting labour norms, with the effect of further marginalising their emancipatory dimension. This assumption informed one of the premises of the research conducted in the book and is based on a rather widespread perception of the labour law doctrine. Embarking in an empirical exercise inevitably contributes to casting further light on the role of the CJEU in relation to the normativity of labour law.

A first definition of the role of the CJEU has already been drawn in Chapter 3, where the case law on transfer of undertakings was assessed in relation to the balancing between the economic and social dimensions.[1121] There, the analysis was

1121. The definition was outlined in Chapter 3, section 7.

fully embedded in the labour law doctrinal framework, with a main focus on the emancipatory rationale of the norms. From the case studies, it emerged that, in the past three decades, the Court shows quite a sensitivity to the economic freedom of the employer. It was concluded that the Court's interpretation of labour provisions overall reflects the intent to reconcile economic and social purposes.[1122] This suggested that the role of the Court with respect to the normative model of labour law is to not oppose the predominant approach that characterises institutional policymaking. The compression of the emancipatory effect that was observed in the case studies was in fact less radical than what occurred in EU policymaking. This thus led to exclude that the Court had played a dominant role in the progressive marginalisation of the emancipatory dimension of EU labour law. Still, the case studies presented in Chapter 3 do not provide specific insights on the origins of the Court's reasoning and could lead to the assumption that the greater openness towards business interests is an expression of the Court's normative inclination.

That whole exploration was situated in the first analytical layer of the research, pertaining to the labour law doctrine. The empirical analysis that is presented in this chapter instead engages with the second analytical lawyer, focused on the judicial lawmaking logics of the Court. Looking closer at the dynamics underlying the decision-making of the Court indeed consents to enrich the understanding of what lies behind the Court's reasoning. It thus allows contextualising in a broader framework the development of the case law towards a more economic-oriented approach.

Should it emerge from this series of case studies that the case law is the result of a variety of pressures stemming from the national context (as the theories outlined in Chapter 5 argue), the definition of the role of the Court that was suggested in Chapter 3 should be revised. In that case, the partial erosion of the emancipatory rationale should not be (solely) attributed to an attempt of the Court to not contradict the dominant normative approach of EU policymaking, as preliminarily suggested. Rather, it would be the result of a series of dynamics of national origins, be the dialectical exchange with national courts, the preferences of national governments, or the consideration for the legal traditions of the Member States. Accordingly, the Court's role with respect to labour law might thus be to convey and express a series of interests and logics which are, in themselves, external to the normativity of labour norms, which are interpreted in the proceedings.

If, however, the case studies reveal that the case law reflects the neofunctionalist or the integrationalist theories (discussed in Chapter 4), the perception of the Court as a policy actor would be reinforced. Nevertheless, it is worth recalling that according to these theories, the Court's approach to the analysed norms is not necessarily an expression of a preference vis-à-vis the normative implications of *those* norms at stake. The Court might instead be leaning towards a specific interpretation in order to achieve

1122. This corresponds to the function of labour law outlined in Chapter 1, section 2.2.3.

broader policy goals. It was in fact seen that, from a neofunctionalist perspective, the Court pursues the interpretative solution that increases the relevance of EU law for (prospective) litigants and, at the same time, enhances its own interpretative authority. Integrationalism instead suggests that the Court tends to adopt the reasoning that is most functional to the expansion of the Union's competences.

According to both the neofunctionalist and integrationalist narrative, the (partial) alignment of the case law with the normative position of EU institutional policymakers that was observed in Chapter 3 might not be accidental. Endowed with political thinking, the Court may consider that complying with the institutional rule-making approach is somewhat functional to the realisation of its own normative preferences. For instance, the Court might have been inclined to give a broad interpretation of Article 16 CFREU (on the freedom to conduct a business) in consideration of the fact that the interests of economic actors are since a long time at the centre of EU policymaking. With a significant prospect to find in EU law a valuable ally to expand their economic interest, these actors are more likely to rely on EU law and on the Court's judicial authority in domestic judicial arenas. Or, the Court might be inclined to align with the legal opinions that the European Commission presents in the proceedings because these generally express an integrationalist view. In both cases, the definition of the Court's role with respect to labour law that was formulated in Chapter 3 would also need to be partially revised. The Court's role would indeed be to pursue the normative model that best suits the realisation of its policymaking agenda.

Actually, only if none of the judicial lawmaking theories described in Chapters 4 and 5 is sufficiently reflected in the case studies, it should be concluded that the definition of the role of the Court emerging from the epistemological framework of the labour law discipline does not benefit from being complemented by the doctrinal lenses provided by the analysed judicial lawmaking theories.

As for the structure of this chapter, section 2 provides some guidance to the interpretation of the case studies, explaining their subject, structure and methodology. Section 3 concerns the case studies testing the neofunctionalist and integrationalist theories. Section 4 instead focuses on those theories contending that the Court is subject to a certain degree of pressure from the national context. These are intergovernmentalism, the majoritarian and pluralist theories as well as the trans-judicial dialogue narrative. The finding of the case studies illustrated in both sections 3 and 4 are complemented by an Annex,[1123] where precise references to the different judgments can be found. Finally, section 5 addresses RQ3 (*What are the logics that determine the Court's approach with respect to labour law, taking into account judicial lawmaking theories?*). To this end, further elements – not addressed in the theories outlined above – are also considered. Those are the degree of influence of the Advocate General's opinions and the possible relevance of the identity of the judge rapporteur in defining the Court's reasoning.

1123. The Annex is placed after Chapter 7.

2 OBJECTS, STRUCTURE AND METHODOLOGY OF THE CASE STUDY

2.1 Objects

Just like in Chapter 3, the case studies presented here are based on the Court's rulings on the directive on workers' rights in case of transfer of undertakings. The aim of this chapter is to bring to light the judicial lawmaking logic behind the Court's reasoning. In order to best identify the dynamics underpinning the case law, the chapter focuses not only on the general picture but also on those judgments that have marked an evolution in the Court's approach to the directive. Observing those 'evolutionary moments' in the case law can indeed be particularly revealing of the possible relevance of the judicial lawmaking dynamics described in Chapters 4 and 5. Were the case studies to reveal the prevalence of a particular lawmaking logic, then this logic could contribute to a better understanding of the Court's approach to labour law.

As has already emerged from Chapter 3, the Court's attitude towards the emancipatory component of the directive is characterised by two evolutionary moments.[1124] The first is when the Court began to narrow the scope of application of the directive by adopting a more restrictive interpretation of the concept of 'transfer of a business'. In this respect, it is interesting to explore what led the Court to move from its reasoning in *Schmidt* (1994), where it held that even the mere hiring of one cleaner constituted a transfer of an undertaking,[1125] to *Strø Mølle Akustik* (1995) and *Süzen* (1997). In *Strø Mølle Akustik*, the Court stated that the directive does not apply unless the transferee takes over tangible assets from the transferor.[1126] Then, in *Süzen*, the Court consolidated that more restrictive reasoning by developing a twofold principle: in labour-intensive sectors, the directive applies only if the transferee takes over most of the workforce; and in capital-intensive sectors, only if the transferee acquires most of the tangible assets.[1127]

The second evolutionary moment concerned the Court's approach to workers' rights. At first, these rights had been consistently interpreted as inviolable. The limitation of the employer's contractual freedom was deemed necessary in order to allow the directive to pursue its protective function.[1128] Moreover, the Court had adopted a strict interpretation of the effectiveness of collective agreements in force before the transfer vis-à-vis the transferee. Since the *Werhof* case, the Court has instead begun to give a more flexible reading to workers' rights and showed more sensitivity to the freedom to conduct a business of the transferee.[1129]

It is clear that the change in the jurisprudential approach has led to a weakening of the emancipatory effect of the directive, both as regards the interpretation of the

1124. Chapter 3, section 6.
1125. C-392/92, *Schmidt* (para. 16).
1126. C-48/94, *Strø Mølle Akustik* (para. 20).
1127. C-13/95, *Süzen* (paras 13 and 21).
1128. C-324/86, *Daddy's Dance Hall* (paras 15 and 18) and other judgments discussed in Chapter 3, section 5.2.
1129. C-499/04, *Werhof* (para. 31).

notion of 'transfer of a business' and as regards workers' rights. Precisely for this reason, an in-depth understanding of the judicial lawmaking logics could provide interesting insights into what led the Court to deviate from its original approach.

2.2 Structure

As mentioned, the case studies presented in this chapter are designed to test the theories discussed in Chapters 4 and 5. Each theory has been dedicated (at least) one case study and, to attempt to maintain a certain degree of expository coherence and clarity, the description of the findings emerging from each case study follows the same structure. First, a brief reference is made to the basic principles of the judicial lawmaking theory and its possible implications for the Court's jurisprudence on the directive on transfer of undertakings. Second, the case study identifies the indicator(s) which, on the basis of what emerged in Chapters 4 and 5, has(have) been selected for testing the various judicial lawmaking theories. Third, the focus goes on the above-mentioned evolutionary moments in the case law and, in relation to those, the salience of the judicial lawmaking theory is assessed. But before engaging in the actual case studies, the next subsection provides methodological indications.

2.3 Methodology

The case studies were elaborated to test whether the theories on judicial lawmaking discussed in Chapters 4 and 5 are reflected in the Court's case law on the transfer of undertaking directive. This empirical analysis has been developed in several steps. The first step was to identify a set of indicators that could reveal the eventual relevance of each of the judicial lawmaking theories in the Court's case law. These indicators were outlined across Chapters 4 and 5, but it might be helpful to recall them here as well.

For the neofunctionalist theory, the case study looks at the way the Court accommodates the litigants' claims. With regard to integrationalism, attention is paid to the convergence between the Court's reasoning and the position submitted by the legal services of the European Commission. Intergovernmentalism is tested by looking at the convergence between the Court's reasoning and the amicus briefs submitted by national governments. For the pluralist and majoritarian theories, it is observed whether the Court adopts a comparatist approach, whether it tends to validate national law or practices and whether it leaves a margin of discretion to the national court. Finally, the relevance of trans-judicial dynamics is assessed by looking at the convergence between the Court's judgments and the preemptive opinions of the referring courts, the margin of discretion that the Court leaves to supreme or constitutional courts and the Court's attitude towards national jurisprudence.

The second step that was taken in preparation for the case studies was to go through the Court's judgments on the directive on transfer of undertakings as well as the opinions of the Advocates General, with the aim of detecting the presence of said indicators, and a database was created. As already stated in the introduction of this research, the restricted access to documents concerning judicial proceedings constituted a limitation for this empirical exploration.[1130] Therefore, the scope of the analysis was kept as wide as possible. The presence of the relevant indicators has been explored also in relation to proceedings and questions of interpretation that were not taken into consideration in the case studies of Chapter 3. There, the analysis was limited to specific reasonings on the notion of 'legal transfer', 'transfer of a business' and on the workers' rights inherent to the continuation of the employment relationship. Although these three aspects continue to constitute the main focus of the case studies also in this chapter, the exploration has been enlarged to a broader pool of judgments, in order to increase the potential for generalisation of the insights that emerge from the analysis. This means that the analysis includes not only the judgments in which the CJEU formulated the reasoning considered in Chapter 3, but covers all the questions of interpretation submitted to the CJEU in those three areas (legal transfer, transfer of a business, and conferred rights).[1131] Moreover, for the specific case study on intergovernmentalism, the analysis was carried out on *all* rulings that the Court has ruled on the directive. This choice was made in consideration of the scarcity of data on the position of the national governments regarding the legal issues addressed in the reasonings. In many instances, in fact, the content of the amicus briefs is not reported in the final judgment nor in the AG opinion. Broadening the scope of analysis was thus in this case functional to collect as much data as possible.

It is also worth recalling what was already noted in relation to the case studies in Chapter 3, namely that a single judgment can cover several aspects.[1132] A significant example is the *Daddy's Dance Hall* judgment, where the Court ruled on the notion of 'legal transfer',[1133] the concept of 'transfer of a business',[1134] as well as on the rights conferred on workers.[1135] Furthermore, there may also be multiple questions of interpretation relating to the same aspect.[1136]

The third and final methodological step has been to compare the data collected in the different case studies in view to identify the relevance of the different judicial

1130. As discussed in the introduction, section 4.4.

1131. In the case studies carried out in Chapter 3, it was not necessary to focus on individual questions. There, the focus was on the presence of specific reasonings inherent to only a few articles of the directive, which were considered to be particularly revealing of the Court's approach to the emancipatory function of the directive. Now, in order to widen the empirical analysis, the case studies tested the judicial lawmaking logics for each of the questions on which the Court has ruled.

1132. Chapter 3, section 4

1133. C-324/86, *Daddy's Dance Hall* (paras 9 and 10).

1134. *Ibid.* (para. 10).

1135. *Ibid.* (para. 17).

1136. An example is judgment of 6 November 2003, *Serene Martin, Rohit Daby and Brian Willis v. South Bank University*, C-4/01, ECLI:EU:C:2003:594, where four legal issues relating to the workers' rights aspect were raised. These are the following: Q1: Are rights that are contingent upon the employee's dismissal, also contemplating early retirement – covered by Article 3?; Q2: when those benefits or rights derive from statutory instruments that give effect to a collective agreement applicable to the transferor, are they transferred pursuant to Article 3 or are those excluded as they fall within the exception of Article 3(3)?; Q3: Can the employee forego his rights and accept less beneficial rights after the transfer?; Q4: What happens if the employees accept less favourable rights?

lawmaking logics. For this purpose, a first series of graphic visualisations was elaborated.[1137] On the basis of those, further, more comprehensive and simplified graphs and tables have been then created. These 'visual aids' are found across the sections of the chapter, to bring to light the salience (or lack thereof) of the different lawmaking dynamics with respect to the evolutionary moments of the jurisprudence.

3 A PURPOSIVE APPROACH BEHIND LABOUR LAW ADJUDICATION

The theories presented in Chapter 4 were neofunctionalism and integrationalism. In both, the Court has the characteristics of a policymaker: it has a policy objective and it adopts a strategy to pursue it. As mentioned in the opening of this chapter, if these theories were to be confirmed, it would mean that the jurisprudential evolution in relation to the transfer of undertaking directive reflects a policy orientation of the Court. It would imply that the weakening of the social dimension observed in the case studies of Chapter 3 is not coincidental, but was intended by the Court. These theories, therefore, partly validate the concerns emerging from those labour law studies that identify in the Court the inclination to behave as a policy actor.[1138] The neofunctionalist and integrationalist logics, however, also contend that the Court's approach to the interpretative questions submitted to its assessment is not necessarily motivated by a normative preference on those specific issues and on the subjective interests underlying the proceeding. Rather, the Court's valorisation of a specific normative model of labour law should be conceived as part of a broader policymaking agenda.

3.1 Neofunctionalism

As explained in Chapter 4 section 2.1.1, the neofunctionalist theory suggests that the Court understood the importance that individuals, in their capacity as litigants, have for the development of the EU legal system. By introducing EU law into their judicial claims, litigants reinforce and expand the EU legal system. In turn, the increased relevance of EU law prompts a growing number of preliminary ruling requests for the Court, with the effect of strengthening its interpretative authority. According to neofunctionalism, the Court would thus tend to rule in favour of those litigants who are the most inclined to rely on EU law to pursue their interests. In other words, the Court's reasonings generally accommodate the normative position that is most likely to appeal to prospective litigants.

In section 2.1.2, it was seen that the jurisprudential development regarding the internal market during the 1980s and the principle of non-discrimination in the 1990s can be ascribed to the neofunctionalist logic. A neofunctionalist perspective can also be adopted for the case law on transfer of undertakings. Following this narrative, the

1137. See figures 15 to 42 in the Annex.
1138. This perception was discussed in Chapter 1, section 3 and Chapter 3, section 3.4.

marginalisation of the emancipatory component of the directive could be interpreted as an attempt of the Court to appeal to certain private actors and invite them to initiate further legal proceedings.

For example, in Chapter 3, it was noted that the Court had initially adopted a broad interpretation of the scope of application of the directive and that a prime example of this approach was the *Schmidt* judgment. There, the Court ruled that even the cleaning activity carried out by a single individual constituted an economic entity, with the effect that a transfer of undertaking took place even if only one cleaner was employed by another principal. This judgment was not well received by some observers, who called on the Court to pay more attention to the situation of (potential) transferees who feared the economic consequences of the broad interpretation of workers' rights that had so far prevailed in EU case law.[1139] Then, with the *Strø Mølle Akustik* and *Süzen* rulings, the Court changed its approach. It is possible that the Court decided to engage with the critics and to adapt its reasoning to give more consideration to the interests of employers. The narrowing of the scope of application in the *Strø Mølle Akustik* and *Süzen* might thus have been driven by an effort to encourage economic operators to further rely on EU law.[1140]

The same neofunctionalist logic can be applied to the Court's case law on workers' rights. In that respect, the more flexible reading that emerged from *Werhof* onward might have been intended to encourage employers to seek EU-based litigation with the aim of expanding their economic freedoms.[1141] It is actually difficult to speculate what the ultimate strategy of this approach might be. Perhaps, that of promoting a general sense of 'trust' on the part of business operators towards the Court and its interpretation of EU law. Accordingly, the emphasis on economic freedom might be accentuated in times of economic crises, when national governments tend to react in a discordant, uncoordinated manner and EU economic freedoms risk being hampered. It is just a speculation but, following this line of thought, the Court may have seen the directive on transfer of undertakings as (one of) the instrument(s) for reinforcing the growth model based on the deepening of the internal market, in assonance with the policies of EU policymakers.

As for the indicator through which the neofunctionalist theory is tested in the case study, the focus is on the satisfaction of the litigants' interests.

1139. Opinion of Advocate General Cosmas of 24 September 1998, *Francisco Hernández Vidal SA v. Prudencia Gómez Pérez, María Gómez Pérez and Contratas y Limpiezas SL*, C-127/96, Joined Cases C-127/96, C-229/96 and C-74/97, ECLI:EU:C:1998:426 (para. 73, footnote 36), where the AG noted that the judgment in C-392/92, *Schmidt* 'was not well received': *see, for example*, Jean Deprez: 'transfert d'entreprise. La notion de transfer d'entreprise au sense de la directive éuropéenne du 14.2.1977 et de l'article L 122-12 alinea 2 du code du travail: jurisprudence française et Communautaire', in RJS 5/95. *See also* Dr Manfred Zuleeg Ist der Standard des deutschen Arbeitsrechts durch europäische Rechtsprechung bedroht? Bemerkungen zum Urteil Christel Schmidt des Europäischen Gerichtshofs', in 'Das Arbeitsrecht der Gegenwart', pp. 41-54, and Dr Bernd Waas, 'Betriebsübergang durch "Funktionsnachfolge"?', in EuZW 17/94, pp. 528/532.

1140. This development was discussed in Chapter 3, section 5.1.2.

1141. C-499/04, *Werhof* was indeed followed by a series of references from a series of preliminary references where national applicants (employers) challenged the application of workers' protective rules on the ground of Article 16 CFREU. *See* Tables 4 and 5.

Figure 1 Satisfaction of Litigants' Interests: Total Questions Answered by the Court on Legal Transfer, Transfer of a Business and Workers' Rights (1983-March 2022)[1142]

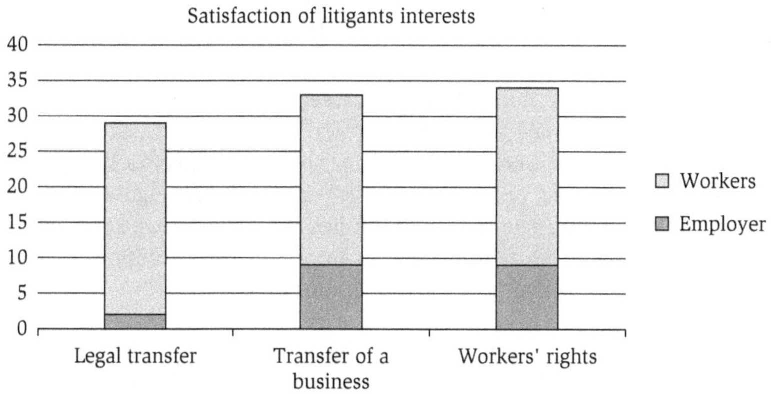

Author's own elaboration. *See* Figure 15 to Figure 17 in the Annex for more details.

The analysis of the case law revealed a very clear picture (*see* Figure 1). Considering all the questions addressed to the Court, the litigants whose interest is more often satisfied are the workers.

Figure 2 Satisfaction of Litigants' Interests Before and After Strø Mølle Akustik *(C-48/94) as Percentage of Total Questions on 'Transfer of a Business' (1983-March 2022)*[1143]

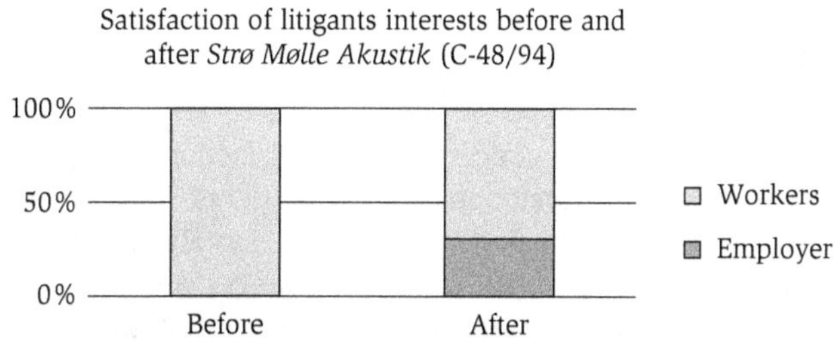

Author's own elaboration. The total number of questions considered before and after *Strø Mølle Akustik* is 7 and 33 (of which 8 is Not Applicable (NA)). *See* Figure 16 in the Annex for more details.

However, a closer look at the two main evolutionary moments in the Court's case law reveal a slightly different picture. Figure 2 concerns the Court's interpretation of the concept of 'transfer of a business' and unpacks the situation before and after the

1142. The figure does not include the 'not applicable' (NA) situations, meaning when the Court's judgment was not the outcome of a reference for a preliminary ruling but of a direct action of the Commission against a Member State.

1143. *See supra* n. 1028.

Strø Mølle Akustik judgment. It may be helpful to recall that *Strø Mølle Akustik* was the first judgment in which the Court departed from its very broad interpretation of the concept of 'transfer of a business'.[1144] Previously, the Court had consistently held that the directive could apply simply following a loose assessment of the presence of the *Spijkers* factors (*see* Chapter 3, section 5.1.2).[1145] In *Strø Mølle Akustik*, the Court instead stated that the transfer must concern a stable economic entity and that the transferee must take over a body of material assets enabling the pursuit of the same activities that were performed before the transfer. The *Strø Mølle Akustik* reasoning, which remained more or less unaltered until very recently, reflects a stronger sensitivity to the economic interests of the employer.[1146] Interestingly, Figure 2 suggests that the Court's case law might respond to the neofunctionalist narrative. Following the *Strø Mølle Akustik* case, the Court in fact began to accept legal solutions proposed by employers, while before it had only ruled in favour of workers.

Figure 3 Satisfaction of Litigants' Interests Before and After Werhof *(C-499/04) as Percentage of Total Questions on Workers' Rights (1983-March 2022)*[1147]

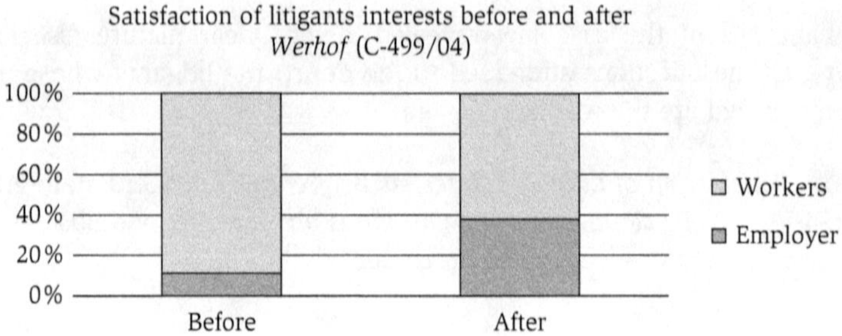

Author's own elaboration. The total number of questions before and after *Werhof* is 28 and 18 respectively. *See* Figure 17 in the Annex for more details.

Figure 3 shows similar data concerning the satisfaction of litigants' interests in relation to the questions of interpretation of workers' rights, this time before and after the *Werhof* case. In *Werhof*, for the first time, the Court established that the transferee must be allowed 'to make the adjustments and changes necessary to carry on his business operators'.[1148] As discussed in Chapter 3, section 5.2, this line of argumentation had the effect of constraining the emancipatory effect of the directive.[1149] Here too, Figure 3 indicates that in the judgments following *Werhof*, the Court ruled more often

1144. C-48/94, *Strø Mølle Akustik* (para. 20).
1145. In particular with reference to C-24/85, *Spijkers* (para. 13).
1146. As discussed in Chapter 3, section 5.1.2.
1147. *See supra* n. 1085.
1148. *See* Chapter 3, section 5.2. C-499/04, *Werhof* (para. 31).
1149. C-499/04, *Werhof* (para. 29).

than before in favour of the employers' legal claims.[1150] This trend too appears consistent with neofunctionalist judicial lawmaking.

At the same time, it is important not to look at the case study in a univocal direction. It is, indeed, reasonable to wonder whether the more frequent satisfaction of the employer's interests following the *Strø Mølle Akustik* and *Werhof* judgments is the consequence, rather than the cause, of the Court's interpretative change. Moreover, there are a number of elements that cast shadows on a neofunctionalist reading of the case law.

The first is that a neofunctionalist logic does not seem to be compatible with the actual distribution of the winning and losing parties with respect to questions of interpretation relating to the notion of 'transfer of a business'. Figure 16 in the Annex indicates that in only four of the judgments immediately following *Strø Mølle Akustik*, the Court endorsed the position of the employer.[1151] After that, in the nine following judgments, the Court interpreted the scope of the directive in a manner favourable to the worker.[1152] Figure 16 in the Annex shows that then there was a 'mixed' period with alternating reasonings, at times the satisfied litigant would be the worker[1153] and at

1150. C-108/10, *Scattolon* (para. 75); C-426/11, *Alemo-Herron* (para. 33); C-458/12, C-680/15, *Asklepios* (para. 23).

1151. Judgment of 7 March 1996, *Albert Merckx and Patrick Neuhuys v. Ford Motors Company Belgium SA*, C-171/94, Joined Cases C-171/94 and C-172/94, ECLI:EU:C:1996:87; judgment of 11 March 1997, *Ayse Süzen v. Zehnacker Gebäudereinigung GmbH Krankenhausservice*, C-13/95, ECLI:EU:C:1997:141; judgment of 10 December 1998, *Francisco Hernández Vidal SA v. Prudencia Gómez Pérez, María Gómez Pérez and Contratas y Limpiezas SL*, C-127/96, Joined Cases C-127/96, C-229/96 and C-74/97, ECLI:EU:C:1998:594; judgment of 10 December 1998, *Francisca Sánchez Hidalgo and Others v. Asociación de Servicios Aser and Sociedad Cooperativa Minerva*, C-173/96, Joined Cases C-173/96 and C-247/96, ECLI:EU:C:1998:595.

1152. Judgment of 2 December 1999, *G. C. Allen and Others v. Amalgamated Construction Co. Ltd*, C-234/98, ECLI:EU:C:1999:594; judgment of 25 January 2001, *Oy Liikenne Ab v. Pekka Liskojärvi and Pentti Juntunen*, C-172/99, ECLI:EU:C:2001:59; judgment of 26 September 2000, *Didier Mayeur v. Association Promotion de l'information messine (APIM)*, C-175/99, ECLI:EU:C:2000:505; judgment of 24 January 2002, *Temco Service Industries SA v. Samir Imzilyen and Others*, C-51/00, ECLI:EU:C:2002:48; judgment of 20 November 2003, *Carlito Abler and Others v. Sodexho MM Catering Gesellschaft mbH*, C-340/01, ECLI:EU:C:2003:629; judgment of 15 December 2005, *Nurten Güney-Görres v. Securicor Aviation (Germany) Ltd and Kötter Aviation Security GmbH & Co. KG*, C-232/04, Joined Cases C-232/04 and C-233/04, ECLI:EU:C:2005:778; judgment of 13 September 2007, *Mohamed Jouini and Others v. Princess Personal Service GmbH (PPS)*, C-458/05, ECLI:EU:C:2007:512; judgment of 12 February 2009, *Dietmar Klarenberg v. Ferrotron Technologies GmbH*, C-466/07, ECLI:EU:C:2009:85; judgment of 29 July 2010, *Federación de Servicios Públicos de la UGT (UGT-FSP) v. Ayuntamiento de La Línea de la Concepción, María del Rosario Vecino Uribe and Ministerio Fiscal*, C-151/09, ECLI:EU:C:2010:452.

1153. Judgment of 9 September 2015, *João Filipe Ferreira da Silva e Brito and Others v. Estado português*, C-160/14, ECLI:EU:C:2015:565; judgment of 26 November 2015, *Administrador de Infraestructuras Ferroviarias (ADIF) v. Luis Aira Pascual and Others*, C-509/14, ECLI: EU:C:2015:781; judgment of 20 July 2017, *Luís Manuel Piscarreta Ricardo v. Portimão Urbis EM SA and Others*, C-416/16, ECLI:EU:C:2017:574; judgment of 11 July 2018, *Ángel Somoza Hermo and Ilunión Seguridad SA v. Esabe Vigilancia SA and Fondo de Garantia Salarial (Fogasa)*, C-60/17, ECLI:EU:C:2018:559; judgment of 13 June 2019, *Ellinika Nafpigeia AE v. Panagiotis Anagnostopoulos and Others*, C-664/17, ECLI:EU:C:2019:496; judgment of 27 February 2020, *Reiner Grafe and Jürgen Pohle v. Südbrandenburger Nahverkehrs GmbH and OSL Bus GmbH*, C-298/18, ECLI:EU:C:2020:121.

times the employer.[1154] It seems, thus, that the more restrictive approach to the scope of application was not actually reflected in a consistent trend regarding a greater satisfaction of the position of the litigant playing the role of the employer.

The second unconvincing element with regard to the neofunctionalist narrative is that, when comparing Figure 16 and Figure 17 in the Annex, the picture is discordant. In the reference period where the Court adopted a narrower (and employers' friendly) interpretation of the notion of 'transfer of a business', the Court issued rulings interpreting workers' rights in a way that generally accommodated the workers' claims. If the Court had actually sought to attract a certain type of litigant in order to enhance the relevance of EU law (in this case the directive), what would be the point of adopting conflicting interpretations, from the point of view of the satisfaction of the parties' interests, in the same period of time?

Then, there is the fact that the neofunctionalist logic fails to explain the Court's approach to the efficacy, vis-à-vis the transferee, of those clauses that in an employment contract regulate the working conditions by means of reference (in a static or dynamics manner) to a collective agreement. These have been discussed in Chapter 3 section 5.2, in connection with the *Werhof*, *Alemo-Herron* and *Asklepios* cases. In *Werhof*, the Court stated that Article 3(3) of the directive did not require the transferee to comply with the wage increase established by a collective agreement that came into force after the time of the transfer.[1155] This interpretation might have stimulated the reference for a preliminary ruling in *Alemo-Herron*, which was also concluded in favour of the employer.[1156] However, the neofunctionalist logic does not seem to explain the *Österreichischer Gewerkschaftsbund* and *Asklepios* judgments, also concerning collective agreements that would have been applicable if the employees had continued to work for the transferor but that the transferee refused to observe.[1157] In those

1154. Judgment of 20 January 2011, *CLECE SA v. María Socorro Martín Valor and Ayuntamiento de Cobisa*, C-463/09, ECLI:EU:C:2011:24; judgment of 6 March 2014, *Lorenzo Amatori and Others v. Telecom Italia SpA and Telecom Italia Information Technology Srl*, C-458/12, ECLI:EU:C:2014:124; judgment of 7 August 2018, *Jorge Luís Colino Sigüenza v. Ayuntamiento de Valladolid and Others*, C-472/16, ECLI:EU:C:2018:646.

1155. C-499/04, *Werhof* (para. 36).

1156. C-426/11, *Alemo-Herron*, where the preliminary questions show that the Court's interpretation in *Werhof* was central in the interpretation of the legal issue at stake (paras 16, 17 and 19).

1157. In judgment of 11 September 2014, *Österreichischer Gewerkschaftsbund v. Wirtschaftskammer Österreich – Fachverband Autobus-, Luftfahrt- und Schifffahrtsunternehmungen*, C-328/13, ECLI:EU:C:2014:2197, the legal question concerned the continuation of legal effects of a collective agreement after its termination, in case of transfer. The Court found that such a continuation of legal effects is compatible with EU law since 'The rule maintaining the effects of a collective agreement, such as that at issue in the main proceedings, has limited effects, since it maintains only the legal effects of a collective agreement on the employment relationships directly subject to it before its rescission or a new individual agreement is concluded with the employees concerned. In those circumstances, it does not appear that such a rule hinders the transferee's ability to make the adjustments and changes necessary to carry on its operations' (para. 30). Judgment of 27 April 2017, *Asklepios Kliniken Langen-Seligenstadt GmbH v. Ivan Felja and Asklepios Dienstleistungsgesellschaft mbH v. Vittoria Graf*, C-680/15, ECLI:EU:C:2017:317 instead concerned a situation which was comparable to that in *Alemo-Herron*. The referring judge asked whether Article 3 of the directive precludes the applicability, after the transfer, of a contractual provision agreed between the workers and the transferor according to which the employment relationship is governed not only by the

proceedings, the employers' claim was based on the same restrictive approach that the Court had adopted in *Werhof* and *Alemo-Herron*. However, as was discussed in Chapter 3, section 5.2, the CJEU partially retraced its steps and eventually sided with the workers' position.

In conclusion, the case study shows elements that might be read as compatible with the neofunctionalist theory, but - also due to the rather complex and not very tangible nature of this theory - the results are overall not particularly convincing.

3.2 Integrationalism

Integrationalism has been described in Chapter 4 as the inclination of the CJEU to adopt reasonings that promote the EU integration process. The Court's activism would thus not be an expression of its own ideological agenda aimed at advancing specific policies in certain fields. Rather, it might be a reflection of the Court's role as guarantor of the Treaties and of their intrinsically integrationalist rationale.

In Chapter 4, section 3.2, it was also explained that the integrationalist rationale finds expression mainly in two ways. The first is the assertion of the autonomy of the Union's legal system vis-à-vis the Member States and the defranchising from the intergovernmental logic. The second is the Court's inclination to give a broad interpretation of the competences of the Union and the scope of application of EU law. This has often coincided with a loose understanding of economic freedoms, functional to pursue the completion of the internal market.[1158] It was also noted, in Chapter 4, section 3.3, that the integrationalist logic places the Court in a kind of informal partnership with the European Commission, which is the other EU institution with an inherently integrationalist ethos.[1159]

So, how would an integrationalist logic find expression in the Court's case law in relation to labour law? It is important to bear in mind that an integrationalist reasoning would reflect the model of integration that, at that particular historical moment, the Court intends to pursue. On the one hand, the primary objective of the Treaties is, or at least for a long time was, to establish a European economic area, and this implies that the Court may lean towards a restrictive reading of the emancipatory rationale of labour law, especially when conflicting with economic freedoms. On the other hand, it has been noted that an integrationalist logic might have also prompted the Court to

collective agreement in force on the date of the transfer, but also by further agreements supplementing it, modifying it or replacing it. Differently from what decided in *Alemo-Herron*, here the Court ruled that this legal practice was compatible with the directive, since 'the national legislation at issue in the main proceedings provides for the possibility, after the transfer, for the transferee to adjust the working conditions existing at the date of the transfer, either consensually or unilaterally' (para. 24).

1158. This was discussed in Chapter 4, section 3.2.2.

1159. Article 17(1) TEU can be considered one of the utmost expressions of the integrationalist mandate of the European Commission: 'The Commission shall promote the general interest of the Union and take appropriate initiatives to that end. It shall ensure the application of the Treaties, and of measures adopted by the institutions pursuant to them. It shall oversee the application of Union law under the control of the Court of Justice of the European Union.'

develop non-market related areas such as, for example, the principle of non-discrimination.[1160] Therefore, it cannot be excluded that, in certain periods of time, the model of integration that the Court intended to achieve involved upwards harmonisation of labour and social policies. In that context, it is plausible that the Court would lean towards an extensive interpretation of labour rights.

In order to identify the normative direction that is most compatible with the prevailing integrationalist thrust in a given historical period, it is helpful to look at the policies pursued by the European Commission, which were discussed in Chapter 2. And this is also why the case study on integrationalism looks at the degree of consistency between the Court's reasoning and the legal opinion provided by the Commission's legal services during the proceedings.

Before turning to the actual case study, it is worth noting that already the empirical analysis conducted in Chapter 3 had revealed several elements that reflect an integrationalist approach. First of all, from the outset, the Court adopted a decidedly expansive interpretation of the concept of 'legal transfer', thus conferring a broad scope to the directive, as discussed in Chapter 3, section 5.1.1. The Court has indeed brought within the concept of 'legal transfer' a very wide range of commercial transactions. These include, for example, business operations between companies belonging to the same corporate group,[1161] a public concession or public procurement,[1162] and operations taking place in several steps.[1163] With these reasonings, the Court contributed to expanding the reach of EU law, and this is certainly in line with an integrationalist logic.[1164]

This consideration applies even if, following the *Strø Mølle Akustik* decision, the Court began to give a narrower reading to the second component that determines the scope of the directive, namely the concept of 'transfer of a business'. The concept of 'legal transfer' is functional to identify the range of business transactions to which the

1160. As discussed in Chapter 4, section 3.2.2.1.

1161. Judgment of 2 December 1999, *G. C. Allen and Others v. Amalgamated Construction Co. Ltd*, C-234/98, ECLI:EU:C:1999:594; judgment of 6 March 2014, *Lorenzo Amatori and Others v. Telecom Italia SpA and Telecom Italia Information Technology Srl*, C-458/12, ECLI:EU:C:2014:124.

1162. Judgment of 14 September 2000, *Renato Collino and Luisella Chiappero v. Telecom Italia SpA*, C-343/98, ECLI:EU:C:2000:441 (public concession); judgment of 10 December 1998, *Francisca Sánchez Hidalgo and Others v. Asociación de Servicios Aser and Sociedad Cooperativa Minerva*, C-173/96, Joined Cases C-173/96 and C-247/96, ECLI:EU:C:1998:595 (public procurement); judgment of 25 January 2001, *Oy Liikenne Ab v. Pekka Liskojärvi and Pentti Juntunen*, C-172/99, ECLI:EU:C:2001:59 (public procurement).

1163. Judgment of 10 February 1988, *Foreningen af Arbejdsledere i Danmark v. Daddy's Dance Hall A/S*, C-324/86, ECLI:EU:C:1988:72; judgment of 15 June 1988, *P. Bork International A/S, in liquidation v. Foreningen af Arbejdsledere I Danmark, acting on behalf of Birger E. Petersen, and Jens E. Olsen and others v. Junckers Industrier A/S*, C-101/87, ECLI:EU:C:1988:308; judgment of 19 May 1992, *Dr. Sophie Redmond Stichting v. Hendrikus Bartol and others*, C-29/91, ECLI:EU:C:1992:220; judgment of 11 March 1997, *Ayse Süzen v. Zehnacker Gebäudereinigung GmbH Krankenhausservice*, C-13/95, ECLI:EU:C:1997:141; judgment of 10 December 1998, *Francisca Sánchez Hidalgo and Others v. Asociación de Servicios Aser and Sociedad Cooperativa Minerva*, C-173/96, Joined Cases C-173/96 and C-247/96, ECLI:EU:C:1998:595; judgment of 25 January 2001, *Oy Liikenne Ab v. Pekka Liskojärvi and Pentti Juntunen*, C-172/99, ECLI:EU:C:2001:59.

1164. This 'inclusive' approach of the Court is summarised in Table 1.

directive may apply. The notion of 'transfer of a business' instead relates to additional factual conditions that, when present in any of the business transactions covered by the concept of 'legal transfer', make the directive effectively applicable.[1165]

The integrationalist logic also emerges from the expansion of the economic rationale that has characterised the case law on workers' rights since the *Werhof* case, as discussed in Chapter 3, section 5.2.[1166] In fact, this shift in jurisprudence has given the transferee a wider margin of manoeuvre, based on a broad interpretation of Article 16 CFREU on the freedom to conduct a business. It is worth recalling that the CFREU was adopted in 2000 and became part of the primary law of the Union with the proclamation of the Lisbon Treaty in 2009. It could thus be that the broad reading of Article 16 CFREU can be interpreted as an expression of momentum of judicial activism with which the Court responded to the failed attempt to ratify the Treaty establishing a Constitution for Europe. This interpretation of the Court's activism in the second half of the 2000s was proposed by Cartabia, (as was discussed in Chapter 4, sections 3.2.2.1 and 3.2.2.2), and provides a narrative that may indeed explain the sudden relevance of Article 16 CFREU in the context of transfers of undertakings.[1167]

More tangible and more convincing indications of the plausibility of the integrationalist theory are offered by the actual case study. As Figure 4 indicates, the case law has, in fact, shown a significant convergence between the Court's reasoning and the positions that the legal services of the European Commission have presented during the proceedings. As noted in the methodological section, the submissions of the various parties intervening in the proceedings before the Court are not publicly available.[1168] The text of the judgments and the Advocate General's opinions provide only a partial picture of the Commission's legal positions. This means that in some cases, the Commission's position on the question referred to the Court could not be ascertained. Nevertheless, even with this limitation, it has been possible to identify the Commission's legal argumentations in relation to 66 questions of interpretation and in 55 of these they were ultimately confirmed in the Court's final reasoning.[1169]

1165. As discussed in Chapter 3, section 5.1.2.
1166. As discussed in Chapter 3, section 5.2.
1167. *See* M. Cartabia, 'Europe and Rights: Taking Dialogue Seriously', European Constitutional Law Review, 5, pp. 5-31, 2009. Cartabia argued that there is a connection between the activism of the Court of Justice and the manifestation of weakness of the political process of European integration, and one of these manifestations was the failed ratification of the Treaty establishing a constitution for Europe. According to Cartabia, the 'revived' activism of the Court found expression in the Court being more and more a 'fundamental rights' adjudicator: 'The Charter, put in the hands of the Court, is bringing about many benefits but also many risks, the most obvious one being that the European Court of Justice acting more and more often as a Court of rights is willy-nilly a potential element of centralisation and standardisation.'
1168. As discussed in the Introduction, section 4.4.
1169. Here all issues relating to the directive have been considered, not only the legal questions concerning the scope of application of the directive and those concerning the rights that the directive confers to workers.

Figure 4 Conformity Between the Reasoning of the Court and the Position of the Commission per Question Answered by the CJEU (1983-March 2022)

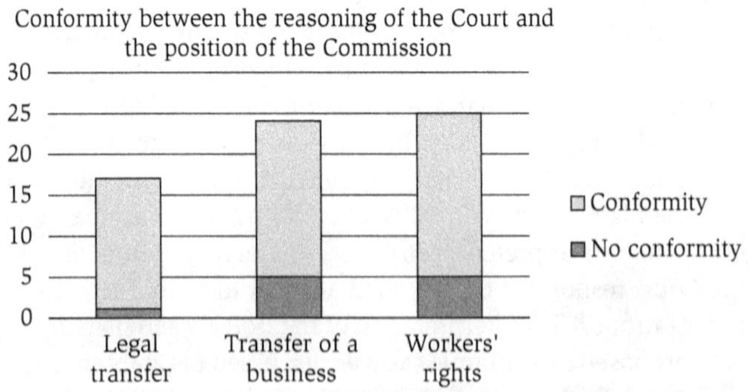

Author's own elaboration. *See* Figure 18, Figure 19 and Figure 20 in the Annex for more details.

Figure 4 shows that the available data concerning the definition of 'legal transfer' reveal a strong convergence between the Court and the Commission. The assonance is also clear in relation to the notion of 'transfer of a business' and workers' rights. For a more detailed reading of the case study, reference can also be made to the Annex, in particular to Figure 19 and Figure 20.

Beginning with the concept of 'transfer of a business', an aggregate reading of Figure 19 in the Annex with the case studies described in Chapter 3 (and especially Table 2) shows that the evolution of the case law reflects the position expressed by the legal services of the Commission.[1170] As shown in the case study explored in Chapter 3, the initial approach of the Court was to give a broad interpretation to the situations covered by the notion of 'transfer of a business'. Among the most significant examples of this lax attitude are the *Ny Mølle Kro* and *Daddy's Dance Hall* judgments, where the Court adopted a flexible reading of the criteria set out in the *Spijkers* case.[1171] As indicated in Figure 19 of the Annex, in those judgments, the Court followed the reasoning proposed by the Commission. Unfortunately, from the text of the judgment and from the AG opinion, it was not possible to reconstruct the Commission's legal

1170. Table 2.

1171. Judgment of 18 March 1986, *Jozef Maria Antonius Spijkers v. Gebroeders Benedik Abattoir CV and Alfred Benedik en Zonen BV*, C-24/85, ECLI:EU:C:1986:127, discussed in Chapter 3, section 5.1.2, p. 96. Judgment of 17 December 1987, *Landsorganisationen i Danmark for Tjenerforbundet i Danmark v. Ny Mølle Kro*, C-287/86, ECLI:EU:C:1987:573 (para. 18), where the Court retained sufficient that the business the operation is actually continued or resumed by the new employer, with the same or similar activities. In judgment of 10 February 1988, *Foreningen af Arbejdsledere i Danmark v. Daddy's Dance Hall A/S*, C-324/86, ECLI: EU:C:1988:72 (para. 10), the Court merely noted that the directive applies 'provided that the economic unit in question retains its identity; that is so in particular when, as in this case, the business is carried on without interruption by the new lessee with the same staff as were employed in the business before the transfer'. This reflects a rather broad and flexible approach towards the concept of 'transfer of a business' and leaves an interpretative margin of manoeuvre to the national referring judge.

opinion in the *Schmidt* case. This would have enriched the case study since that judgment represents the apex of the wide interpretative approach of the Court.[1172]

Then, the Court changed its reasoning in a restrictive sense. The *Strø Mølle Akustik* and *Süzen* judgments anchored the application of the directive to certain peremptory requirements that had previously been absent, such as the transfer of the majority of assets or personnel.[1173] Here too, the Court and the Commission's positions were aligned.[1174] The existence of an inter-institutional convergence between the Commission and the CJEU is also corroborated by the fact that the sudden interpretative shift in *Strø Mølle Akustik* was subsequently codified in a policymaking initiative of the Commission and, later, in legislation (Directive 98/50/EC). In Chapter 3 it was mentioned that the original Directive 77/187/EEC was modified by Directive 98/50/EC and that the amendments mainly concerned the scope of application.[1175] It was also recalled that the recitals of the amending directive explicitly referred to the fact that a legislative revision had become necessary in order to codify the Court's case law on the concept of 'transfer of a business'.[1176] This is reflected in the revised text of Article 1, which now indicates that the transfer must relate to an 'economic identity', meaning an 'organised grouping of resources which has the objective of pursuing an economic activity'. As it was also noted in Chapter 3, section 5.1.2, these are clear references to the Court's decisions in *Stro Molle* and *Süzen*, which were delivered three years and one year, respectively, before the legislative revision.[1177]

This episode prompted several commentators to characterise the Court as a political actor and to consider the jurisprudential change - as well as the legislative reform - as an expression of the policy preferences of the CJEU.[1178] But there is even

1172. Judgment of 14 April 1994, *Christel Schmidt v. Spar- und Leihkasse der früheren Ämter Bordesholm, Kiel und Cronshagen*, C-392/92, ECLI:EU:C:1994:134, the Court found that the directive applies even if the transfer operation concerned just one worker, performing cleaning services (para. 15). *See* Chapter 3, section 5.1.2.
1173. As discussed in Chapter 3, section 5.1.2. In judgment of 19 September 1995, *Ledernes Hovedorganisation, acting for Ole Rygaard v. Dansk Arbejdsgiverforening, acting for Strø Mølle Akustik A/S*, C-48/94, ECLI:EU:C:1995:290 (paras 20 and 21), the Court ruled that the directive does not apply unless there is transfer of a body of material assets enabling the activities that were performed before the transfer. It was also decided that the transferred business must constitute a stable economic entity, whose activity is not limited to performing only one specific works contract. In judgment of 11 March 1997, *Ayse Süzen v. Zehnacker Gebäudereinigung GmbH Krankenhausservice*, C-13/95, ECLI:EU:C:1997:141 (paras 13 and 21), the Court specified that the transferred entity must relate to an organised group of persons and assets facilitating the exercise of an economic activity pursuing a specific objective and that, depending on the type of sector (labour-intensive or capital-intensive) certain *Spijkers* criteria were more important than others (respectively, the transfer of the majority of the personnel, or the majority of material assets).
1174. *See* Figure 19.
1175. Chapter 3, section 2.
1176. *Ibid.*
1177. Chapter 3, section 5.1.2.
1178. As discussed Chapter 3, section 3.4. *Inter alia, see* G. More, 'The Acquired Rights Directive: Frustrating or Facilitating Labour Market Flexibility' in J. Shaw & G. More (eds), *New Legal Dynamics of European Union*, Clarendon Press, Oxford, 1995, pp. 129-147; J. Hunt, 'The Court of Justice as a Policy Actor: The Case of the Acquired Rights Directive', Legal Studies, 18(3), pp. 336-359, 1998; C. Bourn, 'When Does the Transfer of a Service Contract Constitute the Transfer of an Undertaking?', European Law Review, 23(1), pp. 59-64, 1998.

more to the story, showing that the relationship between policymaking and EU case law is more intertwined than it would seem at first glance. In 1994 – and thus before the Court pronounced *Strø Mølle Akustik* (1995) and narrowed the scope of application of the directive – the Commission had already made a proposal to amend Directive 77/187/EEC. This proposal was eventually withdrawn, as it did not obtain sufficient institutional and political support.[1179] Rather interestingly, it was in this 1994 proposal that, for the first time, the idea of reducing the scope of the directive on transfer of undertakings was introduced. The Commission's proposal indeed suggested adding to Article 1 of Directive 77/187/EEC the following wording: 'The transfer of an activity which is accompanied by the transfer of an economic entity which retains its identity shall be deemed to be a transfer within the meaning of the directive. *The transfer of only an activity of an undertaking, business or part of a business, whether or not it was previously carried out directly, does not in itself constitute a transfer within the meaning of the directive*' (emphasis added).

Clearly, the second part of the sentence (in italics) was meant to correct the implications of the *Schmidt* judgment, where the Court had found the directive to apply even in the situation where the object of the transfer consisted of the work carried out by a single cleaner.[1180] In light of this, the interpretative change that the Court inaugurated in *Strø Mølle Akustik* might be seen as the Court's attempt to align its case law to the policy position of the Commission. This is corroborated by the fact that from *Süzen* onwards the Court began to use expressions which are very similar to those of the 1994 proposal, such as that 'the transferred entity is not reduced to the activity entrusted to it. The mere fact that the service provided is similar before and after the transfer is not conclusive'.[1181] The possibility that it was the Commission that

1179. Proposal for a Council Directive on the approximation of the laws of the Member States relating to the safeguarding of employees' rights in the event of transfers of undertakings, businesses or parts of businesses/* COM/94/300 final – CNS 94/0203 */ *OJ C 274, 1.10.1994, pp. 10-15.*

1180. On this aborted proposal and the intention to contain the broad interpretative approach of the Commission, *see, inter alia,* A. Lo Faro, 'Judicial Developments of EC Social Policy and Intra-community Institutional Dialogues: How to Define a "Legal Transfer"' in S. Sciarra (ed.), *Labour Law in the Courts: National Judges and the European Court of Justice,* Hart Publishing, Oxford, 2001, pp. 210-228, p. 217.

1181. C-13/95, *Süzen* (para. 15). See also opinion of Advocate General Cosmas of 24 September 1998, *Francisco Hernández Vidal SA v. Prudencia Gómez Pérez, María Gómez Pérez and Contratas y Limpiezas SL,* C-127/96, Joined Cases C-127/96, C-229/96 and C-74/97, ECLI: EU:C:1998:426, footnote 17: 'It is interesting to note that, shortly after the judgment in *Schmidt* and as a result of the critical response it provoked, the Commission incorporated in its Proposal for a Directive (94/C 274/08) COM(94)300 final – 94/0203(CNS) (OJ 1994 C 274, p. 10) amending Directive 77/187 a provision (Article 1(1), second subparagraph) which reads: "The transfer of an activity which is accompanied by the transfer of an economic entity which retains its identity shall be deemed to be a transfer within the meaning of this Directive. The transfer of only an activity of an undertaking, business or part of a business, whether or not it was previously carried out directly, docs not in itself constitute a transfer within the meaning of the Directive." That proposal was strongly criticised, both by the Parliament (OJ 1997 C 33, p. 81), which adopted Amendment 4 deleting that subparagraph, and before that by the Committee of the Regions (OJ 1996 C 100, p. 25, point 1.1) and the Economic and Social Committee (OJ 1995 C 133, p. 13, points 1.2.3 and 1.3); it was not in the end incorporated in Directive 98/50'. On the same point, *see also* opinion of Advocate General Poiares Maduro of

influenced the Court's more restrictive interpretation is also supported by the fact that in *Strø Mølle Akustik* (where the Court introduced the requirement of transfer of tangible assets), the Advocate General made a direct reference to the Commission's 1994 proposal.[1182]

In relation to *Strø Mølle Akustik,* Bettiet and Belgrave wrote that 'both the Court and the Commission seemed to share the view that it should only be certain type of contracting out which should provide employment protection. These are the situations where there is a stable economic entity which is transferred, rather than where there is only an activity of an undertaking'.[1183] Their consideration appears correct, but with the specification that it may have been the Commission that first inspired the Court's reasoning and not the other way around, as might appear prima facie from the chronology of the Court's ruling and the actual adoption of the amending directive (1998).

Even if the 1994 proposal was never adopted, it left a legacy in the Court's case law.[1184] What does this episode mean in terms of judicial lawmaking logic? It surely is a convincing sign of a partnership between the Court and the Commission. On the one

16 June 2005, *Nurten Güney-Görres v. Securicor Aviation (Germany) Ltd and Kötter Aviation Security GmbH & Co. KG*, C-232/04, Joined Cases C-232/04 and C-233/04, ECLI-:EU:C:2005:395 (footnote 9).

1182. Opinion of Advocate General Cosmas of 10 May 1995, *Ledernes Hovedorganisation, acting for Ole Rygaard v. Dansk Arbejdsgiverforening, acting for Strø Mølle Akustik A/S*, C-48/94, ECLI:EU:C:1995:130 (para. 12). At first, the Advocate General provides a manipulative reading of the earlier *Spijkers* judgment, in stating that 'in the *Spijkers* judgment [...] the Court stated that [...] there cannot be a transfer [...] solely by virtue of the fact that the assets of that undertaking have been disposed of but that it is necessary to assess whether the business was disposed of as a going concern'. This is a manipulative reinterpretation since, as also noted by S. Laulom, 'The European Court of Justice in the Dialogue on Transfers of Undertakings: A Fallible Interlocutor?' in S. Sciarra (ed.), *Labour Law in the Courts: National Judges and the European Court of Justice*, Hart Publishing, Oxford, 2001, pp. 145-178, p. 154, in *Spijkers* 'the Court's approach consists not so much in defining the concept of the transfer of an undertaking, as in detailing the circumstances to be taken into consideration by the national courts in order to characterise a transfer situation'. Subsequently, the AG continued: 'Moreover, the Commission followed that decision it its proposal for a directive which it recently submitted to the Council in order to revise Directive 77/187/EEC.'

1183. J. Bennett & S.L. Belgrave, 'Taking Stock of Rygaard', Public Procurement Law Review, 1, pp. 16-25, 1996.

1184. *See also* opinion of Advocate General Cosmas of 24 September 1998, *Francisco Hernández Vidal SA v. Prudencia Gómez Pérez, María Gómez Pérez and Contratas y Limpiezas SL*, C-127/96, Joined Cases C-127/96, C-229/96 and C-74/97, ECLI:EU:C:1998:426 (footnote 17). Opinion of Advocate General Poiares Maduro of 16 June 2005, *Nurten Güney-Görres v. Securicor Aviation (Germany) Ltd and Kötter Aviation Security GmbH & Co. KG*, C-232/04, Joined Cases C-232/04 and C-233/04, ECLI:EU:C:2005:395 (footnote 9). *See also* A. Lo Faro, 'Judicial Developments of EC Social Policy and Intra-community Institutional Dialogues: How to Define a "Legal Transfer"' in S. Sciarra (ed.), *Labour Law in the Courts: National Judges and the European Court of Justice*, Hart Publishing, Oxford, 2001, pp. 210-228 and Economic and Social Committee, Opinion on the proposal for a Council Directive on the approximation of the laws of the Member States relating to the safeguarding of employees' rights in the event of transfers of undertakings, businesses or parts of businesses, 95/C 133/07, Brussels, 31 May 1995; European Parliament, Legislative resolution embodying Parliament's opinion on the proposal for a Council Directive on the approximation of the laws of the Member States relating to the safeguarding of employees' rights in the event of transfers of undertakings, businesses or parts of businesses, C4-0151/94 94/0203(CNS), Brussels, 3 February 1997.

hand, the Commission has undoubtedly drawn inspiration from the Court's rulings. Suffice it to mention that, in both the 1994 proposal and the amending Directive 98/50/EC, the Commission introduced the principle whereby the transferred business 'must maintain its identity', which was first elaborated in the *Spijkers* case.[1185] On the other hand, from *Strø Mølle Akustik* onwards the Court aligned its interpretative approach to the more restrictive position that the Commission presented in the 1994 proposal.

Moving now to the case study on workers' rights, it is worth recalling that, also here, the Court's reasoning led to a progressive marginalisation of the emancipatory function of the directive (as seen in Chapter 3, section 6). In *Werhof*, *Alemo-Herron*, *Österreichischer Gewerkschaftsbund*, *Asklepios,* and *ISS*, the Court placed an unprecedented emphasis on the freedom of contract of the transferee, thus sidelining the rights of the transferred workers.[1186] Using Figure 20 in the Annex as a point of reference, it is quite interesting to note that, even in those cases, the reasoning of the Court and the position of the Commission's judicial services converge.[1187]

If, in general, the case study suggests that the Court is moved by an integrationalist logic, it is worth mentioning that there are also less convincing elements. It is indeed not clear how the abrupt change of approach in relation to the scope of application between *Schmidt* and *Strø Mølle Akustik* contributed to the advancement of a genuine integrationalist logic. In the period of time between these two judgments (less than two years), there have been no significant changes either in the socioeconomic and political context or in the EU regulatory framework. In other words, there is no indication of what, from a strategic or policymaking point of view, suddenly led the Court to consider that a more restrictive reading of the concept of 'transfer of a business' was a suitable expression of the integrationalist rationale.

This could indicate that the change in interpretation may have been caused mainly by the Court's tendency to follow the legal opinions of the European Commission's legal services. If this were the case, the relationship between the Court and the Commission would not reflect a true communion of intentions and a partnership aimed at advancing a common integrationalist agenda. It would rather be a manifestation of a relation of dependency that sees the Court somewhat subordinated to the Commission. In this respect, reference can be made to the theory of Staudt, Epstein, Wiedenbeck, Lindstädt and Vander Wielen (discussed in Chapter 4, section 3.3), as they argued that when the judiciary shows deference vis-à-vis the governmental institutions, the prevalent judicial paradigm is not the 'partnership regime' but the so-called executive regime.[1188]

A second element that raises doubts about the integrationalist logic is that there are also cases in which the Court has adopted innovative reasoning breaking with its own precedents without aligning with the Commission's legal opinion. A recent and

1185. C-24/85, *Spijkers* (para. 11).
1186. C-499/04, *Werhof*; C-426/11, *Alemo-Herron*; C-328/13, *Österreichischer Gewerkschaftsbund*; C-680/15, *Asklepios*; C-344/18, *ISS Facility Services.*
1187. Figure 20.
1188. N. Staudt et al., 'Judging Statutes: Interpretive Regimes', Loyola of Los Angeles Law Review, 38, pp. 1909-1970, 2005.

significant example is the *OSL Bus* judgment on the concept of a 'transfer of a business'.[1189] It should be recalled that, in this case, the Court found that there had been a transfer between two companies providing bus passenger transport services, without the transferee having acquired the majority of the transferor's buses.[1190] This ruling was in contrast to the *Liikenne* precedent where, in relation to similar factual circumstances (transfer of a transport on-road business), the Court ruled that the directive could not apply in the absence of an acquisition of the majority of the buses.[1191] In *OSL Bus*, the Court thus overcame the rigid division between labour-intensive and capital-intensive business and, in doing so, it departed from the position of the European Commission, which had instead chosen a more restrictive approach, in line with the previous case law.

All in all, the picture is not entirely uniform, but the case study revealed interesting elements in support of the integrationalist theory. The analysis in fact suggests that the progressive jurisprudential marginalisation of the emancipatory function of the directive may well be, in some cases, a reflection of the integrationalist rationale of the Court or, at least, of its inclination to align with the positions of the European Commission.

4 INFLUENCES FROM THE NATIONAL CONTEXT

In this section, the theories explained and considered in Chapter 5 are tested against the case law on the directive. The focus is thus on intergovernmentalism, on the Court's consideration of national legal systems – either through a majoritarian or pluralistic logic – and on the possible relevance of trans-judicial dialogue.

The case studies explore whether the Court's reasoning reflects pressures of national origin expressed by national governments, emerging from domestic legal practices, and from the national judiciary. If such elements were to be found, then the progressive downsizing of the emancipatory function of the directive described in Chapter 3 should not be (fully) ascribed to the normative orientation or political strategy of the Court. Rather, it would be the result of the Court's tendency to accommodate preferences emerging from the national context. The normative effects of the case law may thus have more to do with the Court's efforts to maintain

1189. Judgment of 27 February 2020, *Reiner Grafe and Jürgen Pohle v. Südbrandenburger Nahverkehrs GmbH and OSL Bus GmbH*, C-298/18, ECLI:EU:C:2020:121, as discussed in Chapter 3, section 5.1.2.

1190. *Ibid.* (para. 40).

1191. Judgment of 25 January 2001, *Oy Liikenne Ab v. Pekka Liskojärvi and Pentti Juntunen*, C-172/99, ECLI:EU:C:2001:59 (para. 39) and C-298/18, *OSL Bus* (para. 39), where the Court explains the reason why the Liikenne doctrine should not apply in the situation at stake (see also discussion in Chapter 3, section 5.2of this book). It is worth recalling that the *Liikenne* case was an expression of the line of case law inaugurated by *Süzen*, according to which in capital-intensive sectors (such as passengers transport via bus) a transfer occurs only if there is a transfer of material assets, whereas in labour-intensive sectors a transfer occurs only if the transferee takes over the majority of the personnel.

harmonious transnational relations than with the actual political preferences of the Court.[1192]

4.1 Intergovernmentalism

In Chapter 5 it was explained that intergovernmental theories contend that the Court tends to formulate its reasoning taking into account the preferences of national governments. It was discussed that there are two different declinations of intergovernmentalism.[1193] One is the realist model, which mostly depicts the Court as a validator of Member States' choices. The other is the neorational theory, which recognises a greater margin of autonomy in the Court's reasoning. At the same time, also the neorational theory argues that EU case law ultimately tend to find solutions that benefit Member States, especially the most influential ones.

If the change in case law on the directive on the transfer of undertakings were to be read in an intergovernmental logic, this would mean that both the narrowing of the scope of application in the mid-1990s and the enhancement of the economic freedom of the employer starting with the *Werhof* case reflect the preferences of national governments. The partial convergence between the marginalisation of the emancipatory dimension observed both in the Court's judgments and in the Union's policymaking might thus be the result of the same intergovernmental logic that governs EU integration.[1194]

In both the neorationalist and realist variants, the indicator for identifying the presence of intergovernmental logic in the case study is the convergence between the positions expressed by national governments and the Court's reasoning. A convergence can be identified in a Court's change of interpretation following the explicit opposition of national governments to a particular jurisprudential approach. A similar situation was observed in Chapter 5, in relation to the *Barber* judgment and the adoption of the Barber Protocol annexed to the Maastricht Treaty.[1195] Another way in which this convergence between the Court and the preferences of the Member States could emerge is through the alignment between the Court's ruling and the amicus briefs submitted by national governments.[1196]

Turning now to the case study, it must first be noted that the empirical analysis concerning the intergovernmental theory has encountered important limitations.

1192. J. Hunt, 'The Court of Justice as a Policy Actor: The Case of the Acquired Rights Directive', Legal Studies, 18(3), pp. 336-359, 1998.
1193. *See* Chapter 4, section 2.1.
1194. The partial alignment between EU institutional lawmaking and the Court of Justice's approach to the transfer of undertakings directive was discussed in Chapter 3, section 7.
1195. Chapter 5, section 2.4.
1196. As discussed in Chapter 5, section 2.3.

Figure 5 Convergence Between the Court's Reasoning and the Amicus Briefs Submitted by National Governments Considering the Totality of the Questions Answered by the Court on the Directive (1983-March 2022)[1197]

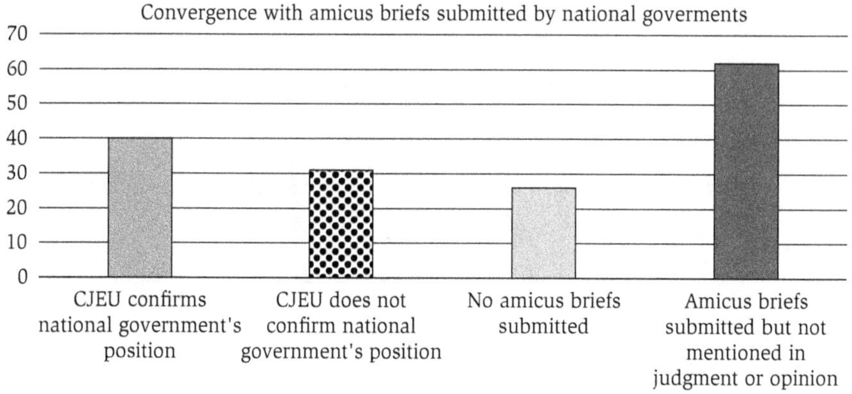

Author's own elaboration. *See* Table 7, Figure 21, Figure 22, and Figure 23 in the Annex for more details.

Figure 5, as well as Table 7 in the Annex, show that in around half of the cases, it was not possible to identify the position expressed by the national governments in relation to the question submitted to the Court.[1198] Even with this disclaimer, it is still interesting that, on the basis of the available data, the Court quite often decides the question of interpretation in line with at least one amicus brief.

1197. In 40 cases, the Court confirms the position of at least one the intervening national governments, while in 24 cases, the Court does not seem to follow any of the positions presented by national governments. *See* Annex, Table 7, p. 280. However, it could be that the Court tends to report in its reasoning more often the positions of national governments when accepting their legal arguments.

1198. Considering only the questions raised in the context of preliminary ruling procedures, the total number of questions analysed by the Court was 159, and in as many as 62 of these it was not possible to identify whether there was convergence or not between the position of the national governments and that of the Court of Justice.

Figure 6 Convergence Between the Court's Reasoning and Amicus Briefs, Considering the Totality of the Questions Answered by the Court on the Directive (1983-March 2022)

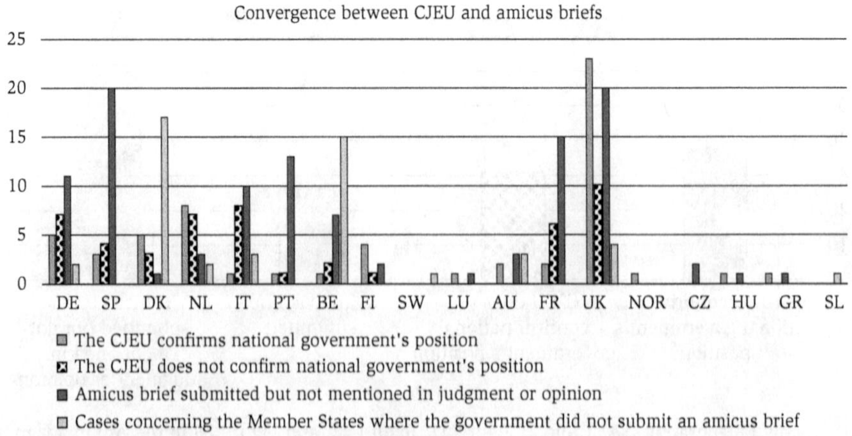

Author's own elaboration. *See* Table 7, Figure 21, Figure 22, and Figure 23 in the Annex for more details.

Figure 7 Convergence Between the Court's Reasoning and Amicus Briefs, Considering the Question Addressing Workers' Rights (1983-March 2022)

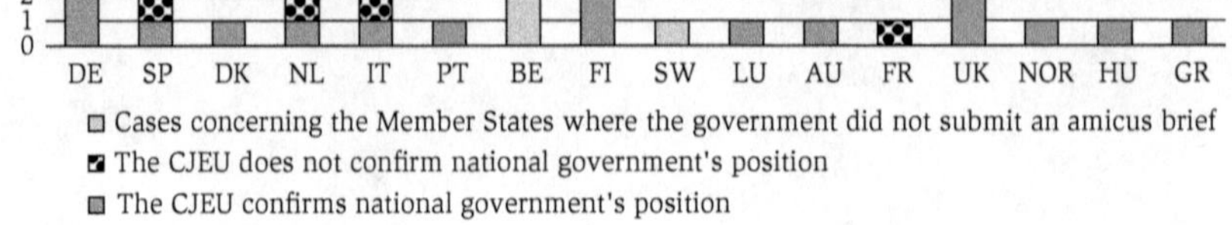

Author's own elaboration. *See* Table 7, Figure 21, Figure 22, and Figure 23 in the Annex for more details.

Figure 8 Convergence Between the Court's Reasoning and Amicus Briefs, Considering the Question Addressing the Notion of 'Transfer of a Business' (1983-March 2022)

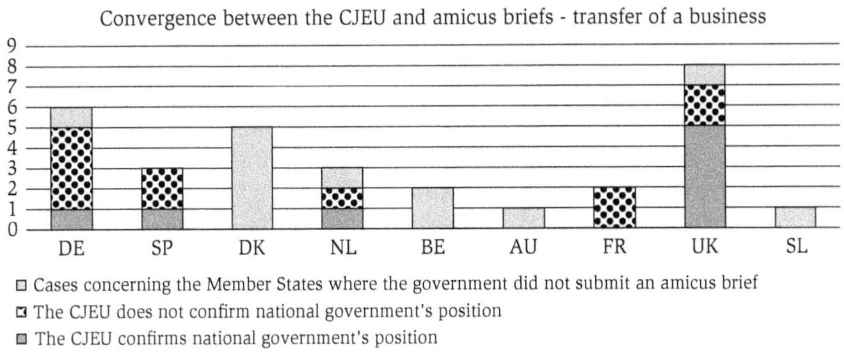

Author's own elaboration. *See* Table 7, Figure 21, Figure 22, and Figure 23 in the Annex for more details.

Although the collected data are not complete, interesting elements emerge from Figures 6, 7 and 8. From Figure 6 it appears that the Member States whose positions have most often been accepted by the Court are Germany, the Netherlands and the UK.[1199] These are also governments that are particularly active in submitting amicus briefs. Denmark and Belgium, however, are the two Member States whose governments appear the least interested in intervening in proceedings, even when these concern rules of national legal systems. It, therefore, seems that national governments have different perceptions regarding the likelihood of influencing the Court's reasoning.[1200]

Figures 7 and 8 break the level of convergence per government per area touched upon by the different questions of interpretation.[1201] It appears that Germany has been much more successful in the area of workers' rights, whereas the UK was quite influential (or able to predict) in relation to the Court's reasoning both regarding workers' rights and the concept of 'transfer of a business'.

Turning now to a closer look at the questions concerning the notion of 'transfer of a business', Figure 22 in the Annex indicates the impossibility to identify a clear, general trend, not least because of the paucity of data collected. This, prima facie,

1199. This confirms the trend noted by R.A. Cichowski, *The European Court and Civil Society: Litigation, Mobilization and Governance; Themes in European Governance*, Cambridge University Press, Cambridge, 2007, pp. 86-87, as reported in *See* Chapter 5, section 2.3, p. 160.

1200. J. Dederke & D. Naurin, 'Friends of the Court? Why EU Governments File Observations Before the Court of Justice', European Journal of Political Research, 57, pp. 867-882, 2018 noted that other factors might also play a role in the Court's assessment on whether to submit an amicus brief, such as, for example, the salience of the cases. *See* Chapter 5, section 2.3, p. 161.

1201. The UK submitted amicus briefs in 15 cases that did not deal with rules of the domestic legal system. This implies that the UK government expressed its legal position on 37 legal issues that had no direct domestic impact.

applies also when focusing on specific judgments. For instance, the Court ruled against the preferences of the national governments in *Schmidt*.[1202] It should be recalled that, there, the Court established that a transfer of a business could take place even when the transferee took over the employment contract of a single cleaner. Then, the case study offers no indications as to the amicus briefs submitted by national governments in the *Strø Mølle Akustik* case. This decision is particularly significant since there the Court departed from its previous broader interpretation and ruled that the directive applied only if the transferee takes over material assets from the transferor. The Court further elaborated the new, narrower approach in *Süzen*, where it was established that in case of labour-intensive business, the transfer occurs only if the transferee hires the majority of the personnel. In this case, the Court made explicit reference to the positions of national governments and aligned itself with the position proposed by the UK.[1203] All in all, it does not seem to be possible to assert that the sudden change in jurisprudence between *Schmidt* and *Strø Mølle Akustik* and *Süzen* is clearly the result of intergovernmental logic. Or, at least, this is not apparent from the amicus briefs.

On closer inspection, nevertheless, it is interesting to note that in both *Schmidt* and *Süzen*, the German government had advocated for restricting the scope of application of the directive only to situations where the transferee takes over material assets.[1204] The German government had also intervened in *Strø Mølle Akustik*, presumably with the same position. As mentioned, however, the German position is not explicitly revealed neither in the Court's judgment nor in the Advocate General's opinion. Still, the fact that the restrictive approach in *Strø Mølle Akustik* is aligned with the position that the German government had proposed in *Schmidt* indicates that the Court eventually began to consider the concerns arising from the national context.

Turning now to the case study on workers' rights, Figure 23 in the Annex shows that there is a certain degree of convergence between the governments' amicus briefs and the Court's reasoning. In particular, this convergence can be detected in relation to those rulings where the Court started placing the accent on the economic freedoms of the transferee. Reference is made to the *Werhof* and *Alemo-Herron* judgments, concerning the applicability of a collective agreement entered into force after the transfer. There, the Court de facto balanced out the emancipatory functions of the directive with the interest of the transferee to conduct its business.[1205] In both cases, the German and

1202. Judgment of 14 April 1994, *Christel Schmidt v. Spar- und Leihkasse der früheren Ämter Bordesholm, Kiel und Cronshagen*, C-392/92, ECLI:EU:C:1994:134 (para. 10).

1203. Judgment of 11 March 1997, *Ayse Süzen v. Zehnacker Gebäudereinigung GmbH Krankenhausservice*, C-13/95, ECLI:EU:C:1997:141 (para. 19).

1204. Judgment of 14 April 1994, *Christel Schmidt v. Spar- und Leihkasse der früheren Ämter Bordesholm, Kiel und Cronshagen*, C-392/92, ECLI:EU:C:1994:134 (para. 9); opinion of Advocate General La Pergola of 15 October 1996, *Ayse Süzen v. Zehnacker Gebäudereinigung GmbH Krankenhausservice*, C-13/95, ECLI:EU:C:1996:385 (para. 9). *See also* S. Laulom, 'The European Court of Justice in the Dialogue on Transfers of Undertakings: A Fallible Interlocutor?' in S. Sciarra (ed.), *Labour Law in the Courts: National Judges and the European Court of Justice*, Hart Publishing, Oxford, pp. 145-178, p. 159, 2001, on the fact that the *Schmidt* judgment had caused turbulent reaction in the German academic and legal context.

1205. As discussed in Chapter 3, section 5.2.

the UK governments had argued in favour of a more flexible interpretation of the workers' acquired rights and, eventually, the Court accommodated their request.[1206]

In conclusion, it is important to stress that this case study could only rely on incomplete data. However, the apparent relevance of amicus briefs in some of the most salient judgments suggests that intergovernmental logics might have played a significant role in the judicial lawmaking of the Court.

4.2 Influence of National Legal Traditions

In Chapter 5, it was noted that the national context can influence the case law of the Court even without direct pressure from national governments. It was discussed that there have been numerous occasions where the Court, in formulating its reasoning, paid particular attention to the legal and constitutional systems of the Member States.[1207] The consideration for national legal practices finds expression in the tendency of the Court to refrain from rulings that are likely to encounter resistance in the national context. As it was discussed in Chapter 5, section 3, judgments that are in accordance with national legal traditions have higher chances to be accepted and implemented.

According to this perspective, the Court's decision-making might be driven by the effort to ensure a smooth coexistence between the EU legal system and the multi-level constitutional framework. Should this logic apply to the case law on the directive on transfer of undertakings, it would mean that - similarly to what was said in relation to intergovernmentalism - the Court's approach to the emancipatory component of the law does not reflect (just) its own policy preferences. On the contrary, it might (also) be the expression of the Court's attempt to find a synthesis, a point of convergence with the national legal systems. In particular, if it were to be found that the Court is guided by majoritarian logic, then its reasonings would be a reflection of the legal solutions that are more widespread across the Member States. If, on the other hand, the Court were to follow a more pluralist approach, the case law would show a deferential attitude towards the national legal practices of the legal system in which the EU judgment is to be implemented.

Starting with the case study on the majoritarian approach, the indicator that was used is the Court's reliance on comparativist methodology and preference for the legal solution that is the greatest common denominator within the national legal systems. Interestingly, in *none* of the cases analysed was there any indication that the Court had opted for the legal solution that was the most widespread in the Member States. Moreover, there is no trace of comparative reasoning in the judgments nor in the

1206. M. Bartl & C. Leone, 'Minimum Harmonisation after Alemo-Herron: The Janus Face of the EU Fundamental Rights Review', European Constitutional Law Review, 11(1), pp. 140-154, 2015: 'It is not insignificant to note that the UK's (mainly) Conservative government has argued for the very same result finally reached by the ECJ.' The fact that the UK Government supported a static interpretation of the directive is also reported by Prassl in J. Prassl, 'Freedom of Contract as a General Principle of EU Law? Transfers of Undertakings and the Protection of Employer Rights in EU Labour Law', Industrial Law Journal, 42(4), pp. 434-446, p. 437, 2013.
1207. Chapter 4, section 3.

Advocate General's opinions. There is therefore no evidence that the majoritarian logic might have played a relevant role in the Court's interpretation of the directive.

Turning now to the pluralist narrative, the case study relied on two indicators to measure whether the Court considers the legal practices of the country from which the case originates. The first indicator is whether the Court has ruled that a national legal provision is not compatible with EU law. The second indicator concerns the margin of appreciation left to the referring court in deciding how to transpose the EU rules, as interpreted by the Court, into national context and in the judicial dispute.

Starting with the first indicator (the attitude towards national legislation), what emerges from the case study is of little significance. In fact, as can be seen from Figure 24 in the Annex, almost two-thirds of the questions approached by the Court did not even indirectly concern the compatibility of national legislation with EU law. Rather, the Court was asked to indicate how the directive should be applied to specific business operations.[1208] Looking at the data for the different subject areas depicted in Figure 25 and Figure 26 in the Annex, the only trend that emerges is that the Court ruled more often for the non-conformity between national and European law in the last 20 years than in the past. However, the scarcity of data does not give particular strength to this observation either.

Among the examples that suggest that the Court gave little consideration to the legal context of the Member States are the *Alemo-Herron* and the *Moreira* judgments. As for *Alemo-Herron*, it has already been stressed that this case consecrated the Court's departure from a protective understanding of the directive.[1209] In the ruling, there are no signs that the Court has reflected on the possible complications in the implementation of the ruling in the national legal context. The Court indeed found a UK legal tradition incompatible with the directive. The incorporation of dynamic contractual clauses referring to (future) collective agreements was in fact a legal practice common in the UK, having the objective of ensuring that transferred employees could continue to be covered by sectorial collective bargaining.[1210]

The second example suggesting that the pluralist narrative does not convincingly explain the case law on the directive is the more recent *Moreira* judgment.[1211] This case concerned a Portuguese law that, subsequent to transfers of businesses governed by public law, required the transferred workers to undergo a public selection procedure in order to continue their employment relationship with the transferee.[1212] This rule

1208. Considering all the questions decided by the Court in its rulings on Directive 2001/23/EC (and therefore not only those related to the aspects analysed in Chapter 3), in 118 cases the focus was not on national legislation but rather on the analysis of a commercial transaction and its possible framework under EU law. In the remaining 43 issues, 26 times the Court ruled against the compatibility of national legislation with the Directive, and only 17 times in favour (*see* Annex, Figure 24).

1209. As discussed in Chapter 1, section 3.1 and Chapter 3, section 5.2.

1210. As seen in Chapter 1, section 3.1 and Chapter 3, section 5.2, these contractual clauses ensure that the collective agreement applies to workers in absence of an *erga omnes* effect of collective agreement.

1211. Judgment of 13 June 2019, *Cátia Correia Moreira v. Município de Portimão*, C-317/18, ECLI:EU:C:2019:499.

1212. The scope of application of the directive was discussed in Chapter 3, section 5.1.

constituted a clear departure from the Court's case law on Article 3 of the directive. From *Berg* (1988) onwards, in fact, the Court had consistently ruled that the transfer of the employment relationship and of the related rights is an automatic consequence of the transfer.[1213] In an attempt to 'save' the national legal practice, the Portuguese referring judge appealed to the Court's pluralistic sensitivity and made a direct reference to Article 4(2) TEU, which - as was seen in Chapter 5, section 3.3.3 - establishes that the Union shall respect the national identities of the Member States.[1214] The Court, however, did not follow this interpretation and did not read Article 4(2) TEU as demanding the valorisation of national practices when conflicting with EU law. Instead, the Court ruled that: 'With regard to the national court's reference to Article 4(2) TEU, it should be observed that the provision stipulates that the Union must respect, *inter alia*, the national identities inherent in the fundamental structures, political and constitutional, of the Member States. In that regard, it should be pointed out that, in an area where the Member States have transferred competence to the Union, such as the matter of safeguarding employees' rights in the event of transfers of undertakings, that provision cannot be interpreted so as to deprive a worker of the protection granted to her by the Union law in force in that area.'[1215] Interestingly enough, the *Moreira* ruling helps to clarify the doctrinal debate on the meaning of Article 4(2) TEU mentioned in Chapter 5, section 3.3.3 and to reduce its pluralistic significance.[1216] The Court seems in fact to interpret Article 4(2) TEU as predominantly linked to the repartition of competences between the European and the Member States and not so much to the protection of national constitutional interests.[1217]

1213. Judgment of 5 May 1988, *Harry Berg and Johannes Theodorus Maria Busschers v. Ivo Martin Besselsen*, C-144/87, ECLI:EU:C:1988:236 (para. 11). *See* Table 3.
1214. C-317/18, *Correia Moreira* (para. 34): 'Does EU legislation, in particular Directive 2001/23, in conjunction with Article 4(2) TEU, preclude a national rule which, even in the case of a transfer falling within the scope of that directive, requires that workers in all cases undergo a public competitive selection procedure and become bound by a new relationship with the transferee where that transferee is a municipality?'
1215. *Ibid.* (paras 61 and 62).
1216. As discussed in Chapter 5, section 3.3.3.
1217. This interpretation of Article 4(2) TEU appears in line with the reading proposed by Guastaferro, Lenaerts and Bonelli. *See* the debate in Chapter 5, section 3.3.4 and relevant literature: B. Guastaferro, 'Beyond the Exceptionalism of Constitutional Conflicts: The Ordinary Functions of the Identity Clause', Yearbook of European Law, 31(1), pp. 263-318, 2012; K. Lenaerts, 'Discovering the Law of the EU: The European Court of Justice and the Comparative Law Method', 2018; M. Bonelli, 'The Taricco Saga and the Consolidation of Judicial Dialogue in the European Union. CJEU, C-105/14 Ivo Taricco and others, ECLI: EU:C:2015:555; and C-42/17 M.A.S., M.B., ECLI:EU:C:2017:936 Italian Constitutional Court, Order No. 24/2017', Maastricht Journal of European and Comparative Law, 25(3), pp. 357-373, 2018.

Figure 9 Margin of Discretion That the CJEU Leaves to the National Referring Judge per Question Considered by the Court (1983-March 2022)

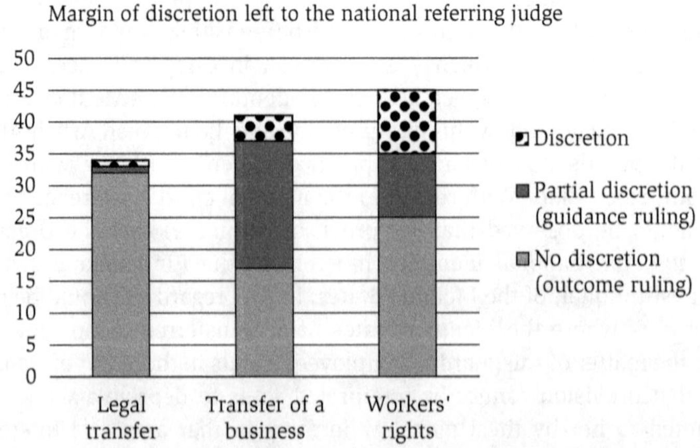

Author's own elaboration. *See* Figure 27, Figure 28, and Figure 29 in the Annex for more details.

Little evidence of a pluralistic logic also emerges from the case study on the margin of discretion that the Court leaves to the referring judges. Figure 9 shows that there is no clear predominance of one attitude over the other. As regards the concept of 'transfer of a business', the Court has often given 'outcome' or 'guideline' rulings, leaving relatively small discretion to the national judge.[1218] Figure 28 in the Annex reveals that this is also the case with respect to those judgments that have marked the evolutionary moment in relation to the scope of application (*Schmidt*, *Strø Mølle Akustik* and *Süzen*). In *Schmidt* and *Strø Mølle Akustik*, the Court left no interpretative discretion to the referring judge and in *Süzen* it issued a 'guidance ruling'.

Figure 29 in the Annex shows a similar situation with respect to the reasoning on workers' rights. Here, there is a slight predominance of cases in which the Court did not grant any margin of discretion to the referring court. 'Outcome' judgments were adopted in *Werhof* and *Alemo-Herron*, where the Court moved towards a more economic conception of the protections conferred by the directive. Even in those cases, therefore, the Court did not appear to be particularly concerned about ensuring that its 'new' reasoning could find an easy implementation in the national regulatory context.

All in all, the case studies discussed in this section illustrate that the judicial evolution observed in Chapter 3 cannot be satisfactorily explained in pluralistic terms.

1218. Outcome and guidance rulings were discussed in Chapter 5, section 4.3.2. T. Tridimas, 'The ECJ and the National Courts: Dialogue, Cooperation, and Instability' in D. Chalmers & A. Arnull (eds), *The Oxford Handbook of European Union Law*, Oxford University Press, Oxford, 2015, pp. 1-30; R. Van Gestel & J. De Poorter, *In the Court We Trust: Cooperation, Coordination and Collaboration Between the ECJ and Supreme Administrative Courts*, Cambridge University Press, Cambridge, 2019, pp. 85-87.

4.3 Trans-judicial Dialogue

The last of the judicial lawmaking dynamics presented in Chapter 5 concerns the trans-judicial dialectics.

In Chapter 5, section 4.2.2, it was explained that a distinction can be made between lower and higher national courts. With the lower courts, the Court has established a relationship of open dialogue, with rather frequent exchanges through the preliminary ruling mechanism. This is not the case with the national supreme or constitutional courts, which have displayed a more defensive attitude. Although Article 267 TFEU establishes that those courts are in a condition of 'imposed cooperation' with the CJEU in case of interpretative doubts on EU law, they are generally more reluctant to rely on the preliminary ruling mechanism.[1219] Their role as guarantors of the national legal order may thus have conditioned the trans-judicial dynamics with the CJEU.

Over the years, constitutional courts have developed the so-called counter-limits, which are judicial doctrines potentially limiting the domestic impact of EU case law. There are two types of counter-limits. The first type concerns the inviolability of those national rules and principles that pertain to the constitutional identity of the state.[1220] The other is the doctrine of *kompetenz-kompetenz*, whereby national courts retain the prerogative to determine when an EU act has been adopted outside the competence of the Union (and therefore is *ultra vires*).[1221] It was explained that in order to not clash with the counter-limits, the Court might tend not to adopt reasoning which could provoke defensive reactions from national higher judges.

Would the logic of trans-judicial dialogue underpin the case law on the directive on transfer of undertakings, then the marginalisation of the emancipatory function that was observed in Chapter 3 would be the result of a dialectical confrontation with national courts. The case study presented in this section is based on three indicators. The first is the level of convergence between the preemptive opinions expressed by national judges, especially supreme or constitutional judges, and the Court's reasoning. It is worth recalling that 'preemptive opinions' are direct or indirect indications that the national referring judge presents to the CJEU in view of influencing its reasoning.[1222] The second indicator consists of an adaptation of a criterion already used in the case study on the pluralist approach, namely the frequency with which the Court grants interpretative discretion to the national court. This time, however, the focus is on cases where the national judge is a supreme or constitutional court. As mentioned in Chapter 5, section 4.3.1, Tridimas explained that 'outcome' rulings can be seen as an expression of judicial activism and may therefore be received reluctantly, especially when the national referring court is a Supreme Court. The third indicator considered by

1219. As explained in Chapter 5, section 4.2, national courts of last resort (meaning courts against whose decisions there is no judicial remedy under national law) have the obligation to refer a preliminary ruling if an interpretative doubt on the meaning of EU law arises.
1220. As discussed in Chapter 5, section 4.4.1.
1221. As discussed in Chapter 5, section 4.4.2.
1222. Preemptive opinions were discussed in Chapter 5, section 4.2.3.

the case study is the way the Court interacts with national jurisprudence, whether it conforms or, instead, departs from national case law.

Overall, the case study reveals interesting elements that suggest a certain relevance of trans-judicial dynamics in relation to the case law on the directive on transfer of undertakings.

4.3.1 Preemptive Opinions

Figure 10 Convergence Between the Reasoning of the CJEU and the Preemptive Opinion Expressed by the Referring Judge per Each of the Questions Submitted (1983-March 2022)

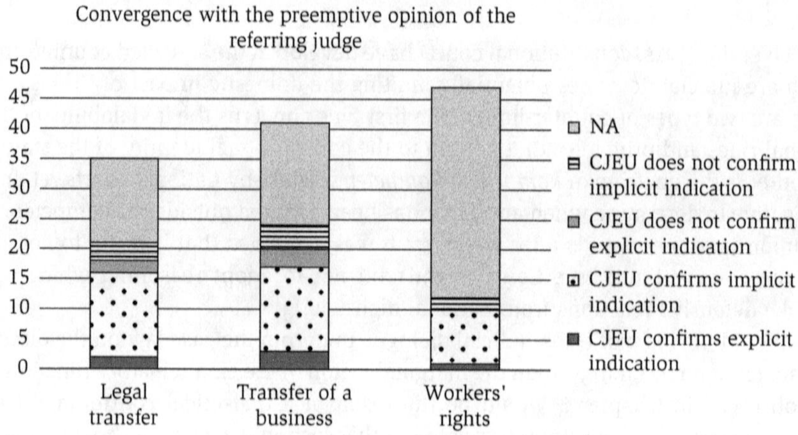

Author's own elaboration. *See* Figure 30, Figure 31, Figure 33, and Figure 35 in the Annex for more details.

Starting from the analysis of the preemptive opinions, Figure 10 shows that, despite the margin of indeterminacy that characterises the study, there are far more times in which the CJEU confirms the preemptive opinions than those in which it ignores them.[1223] It should be noted that not in all cases reported in the case study it was possible to identify an explicit suggestion by the national judges. Most of the time, the national judge formulated indirect indications pointing towards a preference for a certain interpretative solution.[1224]

1223. 'NA' (or 'non-applicable') refers to the legal questions where it was not possible to identify a preemptive opinion, neither in the Court's judgment or in the AG opinion.

1224. An example of implicit preemptive opinion can be found in judgment of 27 April 2017, *Asklepios Kliniken Langen-Seligenstadt GmbH v. Ivan Felja and Asklepios Dienstleistungsgesellschaft mbH v. Vittoria Graf*, C-680/15, ECLI:EU:C:2017:317, where the national referring judge implicitly supported a different outcome than in the *Alemo-Herron* case. The questions submitted in the request for a preliminary ruling provide the Court of Justice with manifold elements that may justify a departure from the *Alemo-Herron* judgment. *See* para. 14, where the German judge asks whether the *Alemo-Herron* doctrine applies 'also where neither the

Figure 11 Convergence Between the Court's Reasoning and the Preemptive Opinion Expressed by the Referring Judge when Supreme or Constitutional Courts, per Each of the Questions Submitted (1983-March 2022)

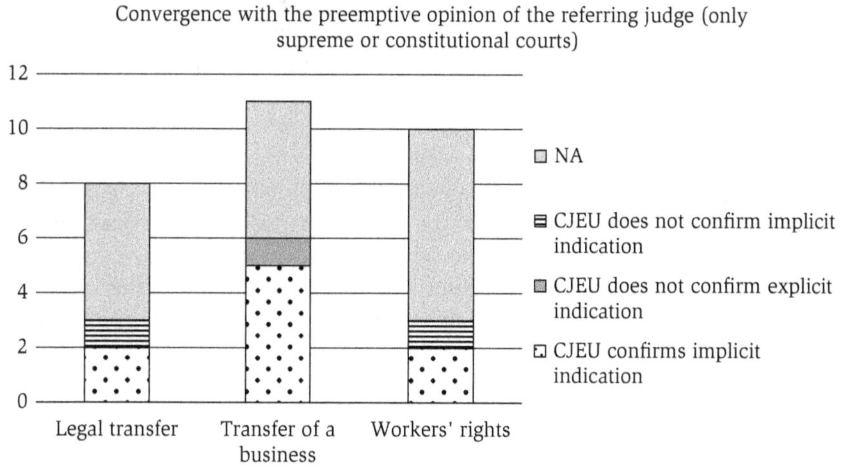

Author's own elaboration. *See* Figure 32, Figure 34, and Figure 36 in the Annex for more details.

Figure 11 confirms that the Court has the tendency to consider the preemptive opinions of national courts more often if the referring court is a supreme or constitutional court. However, this assonance is not full and fails to explain the evolution of the judicial approach in relation to the notion of 'transfer of a business' (*see also* Figure 33 and Figure 34 in the Annex). For example, in the *Strø Mølle Akustik* judgment, which marked the more restrictive reading of the scope of application, the CJEU did not attach relevance to the indications, albeit implicit, that were provided by the referring court.[1225] Moreover, and more recently, in the *Dodič* judgment, the Court disagreed with the interpretation proposed by the Slovenian Supreme Court, from which the

transferor nor the transferee is party to a collective agreement or is affiliated to such a party, that is, where, even prior to the transfer of the undertaking or business, the provisions in the collective agreement would not have been applicable to the employment relationship with the transferor in the absence of the term referring to them in the agreement made, in the exercise of freedom of contract, in the contract of employment?', or 'in so far as national law provides for both consensual and unilateral adjustments by the transferee?'.

1225. Judgment of 19 September 1995, *Ledernes Hovedorganisation, acting for Ole Rygaard v. Dansk Arbejdsgiverforening, acting for Strø Mølle Akustik A/S*, C-48/94, ECLI:EU:C:1995:290. The referring Danish judge asked the CJEU whether the directive applies when: 'An agreement is made between Contractor A and Contractor B under which some of Contractor A's workers are to continue working for Contractor B and Contractor B is to take over materials on the building site in order to complete the contracted work.' The question seems to assume that all circumstances (workers transferred and the transfer of material for the completion of the work in the building site) are relevant factor to consider, regardless of the amount of workers transferred and the value of the material assets, in light of the Spjkers criteria. However, the Court attached particular importance that the transfer merely related to two apprentices and

reference for a preliminary ruling originated.[1226] In the main dispute, the Slovenian Supreme Court was asked by one of the litigants to refer a preliminary question to the CJEU concerning the interpretation of the concept of 'transfer of a business' in the banking sector. However, the Supreme Court did not comply with this request. Instead, it conducted an autonomous assessment of the facts and found that the conditions for applying the directive were not met. It was the Slovenian Constitutional Court, to which the same case was subsequently referred, that instructed the Supreme Court to re-examine the case and to comply with the obligation to refer a request for a preliminary ruling under Article 267 TFEU.[1227] The *Dodič* case then eventually landed at the CJEU, which established that the situation at stake in the judicial proceeding could very well constitute a case of transfer of a business within the meaning of the directive. In reaching this conclusion, the CJEU departed from the position of the Slovenian Supreme Court, according to which the operation at stake could not fall within the scope of application of the directive. This dialogical interaction can be read as disharmonic, in that the CJEU does not engage with the interpretative preferences of the national Supreme Court.

Passing now to the case law on workers' rights (Figure 35 and Figure 36 in the Annex), it is interesting to note that the, by now (in)famous, *Alemi-Herron* case is among the judgments where the Court departed from the preemptive opinion of the national judge. The case originated from the UK Supreme Court (the House of Lords), which, in its request for a preliminary ruling, implicitly suggested approaching the matter differently from what the Court did in the *Werhof* case.[1228] As already discussed in Chapter 3, section 5.2, in the *Werhof* case, the employees had requested the transferee to benefit from the salary increase stipulated in the new version of the collective agreement, which entered into force after the transfer. The Court concluded that the directive could not be relied upon to give 'dynamic' effects to a contractual clause referring to a collective agreement when such clause only contained a 'static' reference. According to the Court, a dynamic reading of a static clause would have implied an infringement of the (negative) freedom of association of the transferee, since 'future collective agreements apply to a transferee who is not party to a collective agreement and [...] his fundamental right not to join an association could be affected'.[1229]

In *Alemo-Herron*, the reference for a preliminary ruling clearly illustrated the differences between the legal issue at stake and those raised in the *Werhof* case. First, the referring judge underlined that the clause in the individual employment contract incorporating the collective agreement was this time formulated in a dynamic manner

---

an employee, and that the materials assigned to complete the work could not be considered a 'body of assets enabling the activities of the transferor undertaking to be carried on in a stable way' (paras 21 to 23).

1226. Judgment of 8 May 2019, *Jadran Dodič v. Banka Koper and Alta Invest*, C-194/18, ECLI: EU:C:2019:385.

1227. C-194/18, *Dodič* (para. 24).

1228. Judgment of 18 July 2013, *Mark Alemo-Herron and Others v. Parkwood Leisure Ltd*, C-426/11, ECLI:EU:C:2013:521.

1229. Judgment of 9 March 2006, *Hans Werhof v. Freeway Traffic Systems GmbH & Co. KG*, C-499/04, ECLI:EU:C:2006:168.

in that it referred to *future* collective agreements. Also, unlike the German prevailing legal practice at the time of *Werhof*, the UK legal system allowed contractual terms to retain their dynamic nature after the transfer.[1230] Second, the referring judge specified that there was no contention by the employer that a dynamic reading of the employees' rights under national law breached his freedom of association established under Article 11 of the European Convention on Human Rights and Fundamental Freedoms. It should be stressed that this violation was instead found by the Court in the *Werhof* case.[1231] Notwithstanding these indications, the CJEU chose to replicate to a broad extent the approach of *Werhof* and found that the directive does not allow the UK legal practice on dynamic clauses in case of transfer of undertakings.

Another example of discrepancy between the preemptive opinions of the national judges and the Court's reasoning is the *Moreira* case, already discussed in section 4.2 above. *Moreira* concerned the compatibility with the directive of a Portuguese law establishing that the transferred employees had to be subject to public competition in order to maintain their employment relationship with the transferee. In consideration of the consolidated case law on the automaticity of the transfer of workers' acquired rights, the Court found the Portuguese legislation to be incompatible with the directive. In reaching this conclusion, the CJEU did not follow the clear preemptive opinion of the referring judge, who argued that the rules governing public competitions were part of the inviolable constitutional identity of the State.[1232] Ultimately, therefore, the Court did not address the Portuguese judge's reference to counter-limits and accepted the risk of a defensive reaction in the national judicial context.

In general, the case study shows that preemptive opinions may have a certain impact on the Court's reasoning. Nevertheless, there are significant exceptions, indicating that their influence should not be overemphasised.

1230. C-426/11, *Alemo-Herron*. In *Werhof*, the national normative setting consisted in a German law that adopts a static approach to the protection of employees after a transfer of an undertaking or business. It provided that collective agreed rules become part of the employment contract with the content only that they possess at the time when the business is transferred, and that they are not updated after the transfer (para. 17). By contrast, the question in *Alemo-Herron* is whether a Member State is prohibited from extending to employees, in the event of a transfer of an undertaking or business, 'dynamic' protection as a result of the application of domestic contract law, namely a protection by virtue of which the transferee may be bound not only by the collective agreements in force at the time of the transfer at issue, but also subsequent to that transfer (para. 18).

1231. *Ibid.* The referring national judge observed that, differently from *Werhof*, there is no contention by the employer that the standing of the employees' dynamic right under national law to collectively agreed terms and conditions would amount to breach of that employer's rights under Article 11 of the European Convention on Human Rights and Fundamental Freedoms (para. 19.3).

1232. C-317/18, *Correia Moreira* (para. 61).

4.3.2 *Margin of Appreciation*

Figure 12 Margin of Discretion That the CJEU Leaves to the National Referring Judge when Supreme or Constitutional Court, per Question Considered by the Court (1983-March 2022)

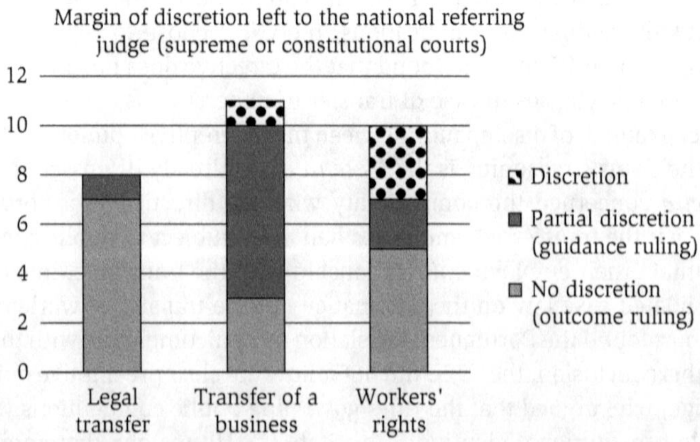

Author's own elaboration. *See* Figure 27, Figure 28, and Figure 29 in the Annex for more details.

Turning now to an analysis of the margin of appreciation left to the referring judge, a comparison between Figures 12 and 9 suggests that the Court's approach does not change significantly when dealing with a request from a supreme or constitutional court. When considering the whole case law of the Court, the empirical analysis does not show elements that are particularly meaningful from a trans-judicial perspective.

Looking more closely at the case law on workers' rights, Figure 29 and Figure 36 in the Annex offer an ambivalent picture. On the one hand, there is the *Dodič* case, where the Court was careful not to overly encroach upon the sensibilities of the referring court. It is true that, as noted in section 4.3.1, in *Dodič* the Court adopted a reasoning that was not in line with the interpretative approach of the referring court (the Slovenian Supreme Court). However, in defining the issue the Court was careful to give the national court considerable room for manoeuvre in deciding how to implement its interpretation of the directive in the national regulatory context: 'Ultimately, it is for the national court, which has sole jurisdiction to determine the facts in the case before it and to interpret the national legislation, to determine or not whether there was a transfer of a part of an undertaking.'[1233] On the other hand, this deferential attitude towards higher national courts is sometimes absent. A telling example is the *Alemo-Herron* case, where the Court decided the issue peremptorily, leaving no room for the House of Lords, which was the referring court.[1234]

1233. C-194/18, *Dodič* (para. 45).
1234. C-426/11, *Alemo-Herron* (para. 37): 'Having regard to all the foregoing, the answer to the three questions referred is that Article 3 of Directive 2001/23 must be interpreted as

The situation is slightly different when considering the case law on the concept of 'transfer of a business' (Figure 28 and Figure 34 in the Annex). Here, the Court adopted an imposing attitude in relatively fewer cases when the reference for a preliminary ruling originated from a Supreme Court. But again, there are significant exceptions. One of those is the *Abler* case, where the referring judge was the Austrian Supreme Court.[1235] The request for a preliminary ruling concerned a situation where one company succeeded another in running a hospital canteen and did not take over the staff, nor acquired any equipment from the transferor.[1236] The CJEU found that the catering activity was business intensive and the guiding principle, therefore, was that the directive applies if the transferee has taken over most of the assets. However, the Court also specified that it was not relevant that the transferee had not purchased such assets from the transferor because the mere transfer of the use of such assets was sufficient.[1237] The Court's answer can undoubtedly be considered an 'outcome' decision, as it leaves no margin of discretion to the Austrian court: 'The answer to the question of the referring court must therefore be that Article 1 of Directive 77/187 must be interpreted as applying to a situation in which a contracting authority which had awarded the contract for the management of the catering services in a hospital to one contractor terminates that contract and concludes a contract for the supply of the same services with a second contractor, where the second contractor uses substantial parts of the tangible assets previously used by the first contractor and subsequently made available to it by the contracting authority, even where the second contractor has expressed the intention not to take on the employees of the first contractor.'[1238]

Interestingly, from Figure 33 in the Annex, it may be noted that the Court's reasoning in *Abler* was in line with the implicit preemptive opinion of the national referring court. Thus, even if the margin of appreciation was virtually absent, the Court's reasoning could still be read in light of cooperative trans-judicial dynamics in so far as it did not take a position contrary to that of the national court.

precluding a Member State from providing, in the event of a transfer of an undertaking, that dynamic clauses referring to collective agreements negotiated and adopted after the date of transfer are enforceable against the transferee, where that transferee does not have the possibility of participating in the negotiation process of such collective agreements concluded after the date of the transfer.'

1235. Judgment of 20 November 2003, *Carlito Abler and Others v. Sodexho MM Catering Gesellschaft mbH*, C-340/01, ECLI:EU:C:2003:629.
1236. C-340/01, *Abler* (para. 19).
1237. *Ibid.* (para. 42).
1238. *Ibid.* (para. 43).

4.3.3 *The Court's Approach to National Jurisprudence*

Figure 13 The Court's Approach to National Jurisprudence per Question Submitted (1983-March 2022)

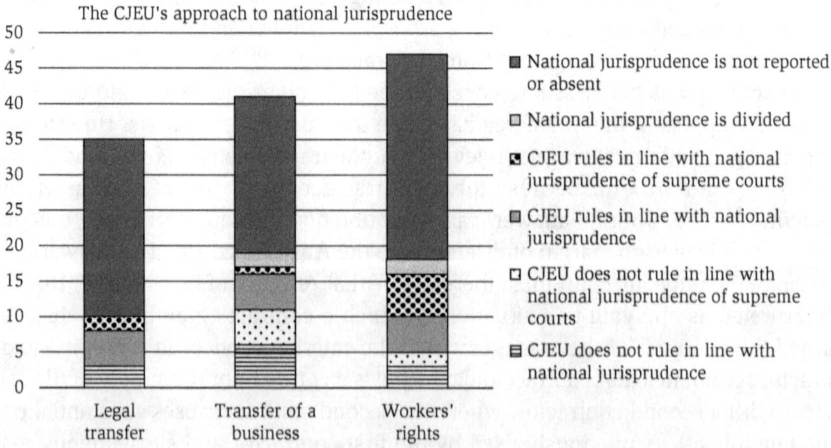

Author's own elaboration. *See* Figure 37, Figure 38, and Figure 39 for more details.

Turning to the case study on the Court's approach to national jurisprudence, Figure 13 shows an uneven picture of the different issues addressed in the case law. As regards the concept of 'transfer of a business', there seems to be no inclination of the Court to follow national case law, even when of a constitutional nature.[1239] On the other hand, the situation appears different when looking at the concept of legal transfer and the definition of workers' rights.

Considering the case law on workers' rights and, more specifically, the 'dynamic clauses saga' the focus goes once again to the *Werhof*, *Alemo-Herron* and *Asklepios* rulings. In relation to these judgments, the case study indicates that national case law may have played a significant role in the definition of the Court's reasoning. These cases should by now be familiar to the reader. In these rulings, the Court departed from a protective and emancipatory approach to show greater sensitivity towards the economic freedoms of the employer.[1240] In *Werhof*, the Court held that the transferred employees could not obtain from the transferee the application of the collective agreement which had entered into force after the transfer. It is worth noting that this

1239. On the lack of alignment between the CJEU and national jurisprudence from supreme and constitutional court, *see* S. Laulom, 'The European Court of Justice in the Dialogue on Transfers of Undertakings: A Fallible Interlocutor?' in S. Sciarra (ed.), *Labour Law in the Courts: National Judges and the European Court of Justice*, Hart Publishing, Oxford, 2001, pp. 145-178, p. 161, where the author explained that the *Schmidt* case had caused a sharp controversy within the judiciary in Germany as well as in other Member States, and that some national courts refused to follow such a broad interpretation of the concept of 'transfer of a business'.

1240. As was discussed in Chapter 3, section 5.2 onwards.

case concerned a situation where the individual employment contract of the transferred workers contained a *static* reference to a collective agreement, as it merely mentioned the agreement in force at the time of the transfer. In *Alemo-Herron*, the Court had further extended this reasoning to the situation where the contractual clause made a *dynamic* reference to also future agreements negotiated in the context of sectoral collective bargaining.[1241] Finally, in *Asklepios*, the Court softened its reasoning somewhat as it reached a different conclusion despite a very similar factual situation to that in *Alemo-Herron*. In particular, in *Asklepios*, the Court held that the employees could rely on the dynamic clause even after the transfer because in the case at hand the compression of the employer's freedom of contract was not excessive.[1242]

The case study shows that, in relation to these three judgments, the Court's reasoning can be explained, at least in part, through a trans-judicial dialogue perspective. First, the *Werhof* case originated from a German judge and the Court adopted a decision that was fully in line with German case law. At the time of the *Werhof* case, the German Federal Labour Court's main interpretative approach was in fact that, in the case of a transfer of a business, contractual clauses referring to collective bargaining should always be read *statically* after the transfer. More precisely, the German court had ruled that 'the collectively agreed rules become a constituent part of the contract of employment with the content that they possess at the time when the business is transferred and subsequent amendments are not relevant, because a right to benefit from the advantage of further dynamic development in negotiation cannot be inferred, since the protection granted to the rights of workers is static'.[1243] This reasoning was incorporated almost literally by the CJEU in its judgment.

Turning now to the *Alemo-Herron* case (originating from the House of Lords), it should be noted that the *Werhof* judgment had caused a division in UK jurisprudence.[1244] Before *Werhof*, national courts had consistently interpreted the directive on transfer of undertakings and its implementing regulation as being entirely compatible with the dynamic references to collective agreements, which would keep producing their effect after the transfer.[1245] This implied that it was not contentious that contractual terms that contained explicit references to future collective agreements retained their effectiveness vis-à-vis the transferee. But then, as noted by the Advocate General in his opinion, the *Werhof* decision had given rise 'to conflicting decisions in UK courts, some taking the view that the judgment prevents any dynamic clause

1241. C-426/11, *Alemo-Herron* (para. 10). The clause was the following: 'During your employment with [Lewisham], your terms and conditions of employment will be in accordance with collective agreements negotiated from time to time by the [NJC] ..., supplemented by agreements reached locally through [Lewisham]'s negotiating committees.'
1242. C-680/15, *Asklepios* (para. 24): 'In the present case it is clear from the decision to refer and, in particular, from the wording of the question referred, that the national legislation at issue in the main proceedings provides for the possibility, after the transfer, for the transferee to adjust the working conditions existing at the date of the transfer, either consensually or unilaterally.'
1243. Opinion of Advocate General Ruiz-Jarabo Colomer of 15 November 2005, *Hans Werhof v. Freeway Traffic Systems GmbH & Co. KG*, C-499/04, ECLI:EU:C:2005:686 (para. 35).
1244. Opinion of Advocate General Cruz Villalon of 19 February 2013, *Mark Alemo-Herron and Others v. Parkwood Leisure Ltd*, C-426/11, ECLI:EU:C:2013:82 (para. 2).
1245. *Ibid.* (para. 34).

referring to collective agreements from being transferred, while others consider that it relates to the very specific case of the German legislation, which limited the scope of such clauses'.[1246] Those UK judges who were in favour of the preservation of the dynamic clauses justified their argument by noting that the compression of the transferee's freedom of contract was not permanent. Their argument was that the dynamic clause referring to a future agreement is the result of a contract between the parties that could be amended at any time.[1247]

Ultimately, the CJEU found the UK practice on dynamic clauses to be incompatible with the directive read conjunctively with Article 16 CFREU on the freedom to conduct a business. It is plausible that the fact that UK jurisprudence was divided - and even more so in relation to an EU judgment - gave the Court greater interpretive audacity in formulating its reasoning.

Still, that was not the end of the story. It is interesting to note that the specific argument that some British judges had put forward when arguing for the preservation of the dynamic clauses, namely that the employer could at any time renegotiate the content of the workers' individual contracts, was then picked up by the CJEU a few years later in the *Asklepios* judgment.[1248] In *Asklepios*, the reference for a preliminary ruling came from the German Federal Labour Court. Basically, the German judge asked the CJEU to adjust the reasoning that was adopted in *Alemo-Herron* and *Werhof*. Since December 2005 - and thus just a couple of months before the Court delivered the *Werhof* judgment - the Federal Labour Court had indeed radically changed its approach to dynamic clauses in case of transfer of undertakings.

As noted by Rémy, the Federal Labour Court had operated a spectacular jurisprudential revirement. Departing from the prevailing jurisprudential position at the time of the referral to the CJEU in *Werhof*, the German court established that when a clause referring to a collective agreement is formulated in a dynamic way, the transferee should not read it statically but, instead, should maintain its literal, dynamic meaning.[1249] The preliminary reference to the CJEU in *Asklepios* was therefore aimed at removing any elements of conflict between this new domestic jurisprudence and the EU case law. The CJEU then proceeded accordingly and found that the directive could allow contractual clauses referring to collective bargaining to preserve their dynamic character even after the transfer. In doing so, the Court adjusted its own previous reasoning in both *Werhof* and *Alemo-Herron* and thus suggests that the national jurisprudential context could be determinant for the definition of judicial reasoning.

All in all, trans-judicial dynamics have proved to be quite relevant in shaping the Court's approach to the directive. The case studies in fact showed significant instances where the Court has been careful not to interfere with the normative preferences emerging from the national judicial context.

1246. *Ibid.* (para. 2).
1247. *Ibid.* (para. 37).
1248. C-680/15, *Asklepios*.
1249. P. Rémy, 'L'arrêt "Alemo-Herron" de la CJUE et la directive transfert: faut-il encore prendre au sérieux la Cour de justice?', Revue de droit du travail, 12, pp. 789-797, 2013.

5 CONCLUDING REMARKS ON THE JUDICIAL LAWMAKING LOGICS

5.1 The Prevailing Judicial Lawmaking Logics

In the previous sections, the case studies were presented and the compatibility of the different judicial lawmaking theories with the case law on the directive on transfer of undertakings was assessed. Some theories appeared more convincing than others.

The case studies found no indication of majoritarian activism and constitutional pluralism in the analysed jurisprudence. The neofunctionalist theory was instead neither refuted nor validated. In fact, the case study shows elements that could be read from a neofunctionalist perspective, such as that certain judgments, like *Strø Mølle Akustik* and *Werhof*, led to an increase in litigation where employers saw their claims satisfied.[1250] However, these were exceptions and, overall, the case study highlighted a number of inconsistencies.[1251]

The intergovernmentalist theory is instead more widely corroborated. However, it should be recalled that the results may have been distorted by the scarcity of the data collected. Still, it was noted that some national governments tend to propose amicus briefs rather frequently and that they might, after all, have succeeded in impacting the Court's reasoning.[1252] The interpretation of workers' rights in the *Werhof* and *Alemo-Herron* judgments is, for example, in line with the restrictive approach suggested by the legal services of the German and British governments.

Far stronger elements have emerged from the analysis of the indicators characterising integrationalism and trans-judicial dynamics. The case study carried out in section 3.2 found the presence of the typical characteristics of integrationalism in the Court's jurisprudence. The Court has consistently maintained a broad interpretation of the concept of 'legal transfer' and has been inclined to go along with the legal solutions proposed by the European Commission. Convergence with the Commission's legal position is also present in those judgments that marked the evolution towards a narrower understanding of the emancipatory function of the directive, such as in *Werhof* and *Alemo-Herron* on workers' rights, and in *Strø Mølle Akustik* and *Süzen* on the concept of 'transfer of a business'. Moreover, it was shown that the change of approach on the notion of 'transfer of a business' was probably inspired by a Commission's proposal for an amending directive (later withdrawn).[1253] However, it has also been noted that it is not possible to determine with certainty whether the inclination to follow the Commission's arguments is an expression of an actual integrationalist vocation of the Court. It may also result from the Court's tendency to follow the Commission's preferences, regardless of the policy implications. Lastly, the convergence between the Court and the Commission is not full. Suffice it to recall the divergence of views in the *OSL* case, where the Court departed from its well-established

1250. As showed in section 3.1 above.
1251. *Ibid.*
1252. Section 4.1.
1253. Section 3.2.

precedent (*Liikenne*) to adopt a more flexible interpretation of the scope of application of the directive.[1254]

Finally, the case studies conducted in section 4.3 revealed interesting elements of the potential relevance of trans-judicial dynamics. On the one hand, admittedly, the analysis of the preemptive opinions was not particularly enlightening (e.g., the Court accommodated the referring court's opinion in *Asklepios* but not in *Alemo-Herron*),[1255] and the same goes for the margin of discretion that the Court accorded to supreme or constitutional judges.[1256] On the other hand, the case study conducted in section 4.3.3 found that the Court tends not to conflict with the jurisprudence of national higher courts. When a reference for a preliminary ruling comes from a supreme or constitutional court, the Court in fact seems more reluctant to adopt 'outcome' decisions. A particularly significant example is that the Court showed a rather deferential attitude towards the preferences of the German Federal Labour Court in the *Werhof* and *Asklepios* cases. It was thus noted that the consideration for the national jurisprudence might have contributed to the Court's overall approach to the legal questions on dynamic clauses. Similarly, it was considered that in *Alemo-Herron* the Court may have opted for a bolder decision also in view of the fact that UK case law was divided on the issue.[1257]

Overall, the case studies draw a complex picture. Thus, the answer to RQ3 (*What are the logics that determine the Court's approach with respect to labour law, taking into account judicial lawmaking theories?*) cannot be univocal since the empirical analysis did not allow the identification of one predominant judicial lawmaking logic.

1254. Section 3.2.
1255. Section 4.3.1.
1256. Section 4.3.2.
1257. *Ibid.*

Table 6 Aggregated Findings for Key Cases

Case Number	*Case Name*	*Litigant Who Sees Its Interests Satisfied*	*Conformity Between Reasoning of the Court and the Position of the Commission*	*Convergence Between the Reasoning of the CJEU and the Position of the National Governments in the Amicus Briefs*	*CJEU's Approach to National Legislation*	*The Discretion That the CJEU Leaves to the Referring Judge*	*Convergence Between the Reasoning of the CJEU and the Preemptive Opinion or Nuanced Suggestion Expressed by the Referring Judge*	*Domestic Hierarchy of the Referring Court*	*The CJEU's Approach to National Jurisprudence*	*Convergence Between the Reasoning of the CJEU and the Opinion of the Advocate General*	*Judge Rapporteur*
C-392/92	*Schmidt*	Workers	NA	CJEU does not confirm national government's position	NA	No discretion	NA	District or appeal court	CJEU does not rule in line with national jurisprudence	Substantial differences	F. Grévisse
C-48/94	*Strø Mølle*	Employer	Same	NA	NA	No discretion	CJEU does not follow implicit indications	District or appeal court	NA	Some differences and similarities	J.C. Moitinho de Almeida
C-13/95	*Süzen*	Employer	Same	CJEU confirms national government's position	NA	Partial discretion (guideline ruling)	CJEU follows explicit indications	District or appeal court	NA	Some differences and similarities	J.P. Puissochet
C-499/04	*Werhof*	Employer	Same	CJEU confirms national government's position	NA	No discretion	NA	District or appeal court	CJEU rules in line with national jurisprudence of Supreme Courts	Some differences and similarities	J. Malenovský

Case Number	*Case Name*	*Litigant Who Sees Its Interests Satisfied*	*Conformity Between Reasoning of the Court and the Position of the Commission*	*Convergence Between the Reasoning of the CJEU and the Position of the National Governments in the Amicus Briefs*	*CJEU's Approach to National Legislation*	*The Discretion That the CJEU Leaves to the Referring Judge*	*Convergence Between the Reasoning of the CJEU and the Preemptive Opinion or Nuanced Suggestion Expressed by the Referring Judge*	*Domestic Hierarchy of the Referring Court*	*The CJEU's Approach to National Jurisprudence*	*Convergence Between the Reasoning of the CJEU and the Opinion of the Advocate General*	*Judge Rapporteur*
C-426/11	*Alemo-Herron*	Employer	Same	CJEU confirms national government's position	Rejects	No discretion	CJEU does not follow implicit indications	Supreme or constitutional court	National jurisprudence is divided	Substantial differences	J. Malenovský
C-680/15	*Asklepios*	Workers	NA	CJEU confirms national government's position	NA	Partial discretion (guideline ruling)	CJEU follows implicit indications	Supreme or constitutional court	CJEU rules in line with national jurisprudence of Supreme Courts	Some differences and similarities	J. Malenovský

Source: Author's own elaboration.

Table 6 summarises the case studies' insights in relation to the two main transformative moments in the Court's case law. By 'zooming' in on those proceedings, the intention is merely to pinpoint the main judicial lawmaking dynamics that might have played a role in the judicial evolution. The first three judgments (*Schmidt*, *Strø Mølle Akustik*, *Süzen*) concern the interpretative change on the concept of 'transfer of a business'. The Court had initially adopted a broad approach, which culminated in the *Schmidt* judgment. Subsequently, with *Strø Mølle Akustik* and *Süzen*, the Court opted for a significantly more restricted reading of the scope of application of the directive The three other judgments (*Werhof*, *Alemo-Herron*, *Asklepios*) concern the 'dynamic versus static' saga. In those cases, the Court departed from a protective approach towards workers' rights and gave more consideration to the transferee's economic interests.

Starting from the first group of rulings, Table 6 indicates that the most convincing theories of judicial lawmaking are the neofunctionalist and the integrationalist. It seems that an intergovernmental logic cannot be excluded either. In *Strø Mølle Akustik* and *Süzen*, the Court upheld the employer's position, and this could be read in neofunctionalist terms, as discussed in section 3.1. In both *Strø Mølle Akustik* and *Süzen*, the Court aligned itself with the Commission, and this could indicate that the Court is particularly receptive to the Commission's preferences. It suggests an integrationalist rationale underlying the reasonings. In *Süzen*, the Court took into account the preferences of those national governments which, as seen in section 4.1, were against an overly broad interpretation of the concept of 'transfer of a business'.

In light of that, the change of approach regarding the scope of application might be the result of several judicial lawmaking logics, consisting of the Court's attempt to: (i) strengthen European integration in conformity with the direction provided by the European Commission (integrationalism), (ii) reinforce its jurisdictional authority among employers (neofunctionalism), and (iii) be cautious not to contradict the preferences of national governments (intergovernmentalism).

Turning now to the second group of judgments (*Werhof*, *Alemo-Herron*, *Asklepios*), it is worth recalling that these rulings share an unprecedented consideration for the freedom to conduct the business of the transferee. At the same time, these cases also present interesting differences. In *Werhof* and *Alemo-Herron*, the Court ruled against the applicability of the so-called dynamic clauses, while in *Asklepios* the Court reached the opposite conclusion. Table 6 indicates that these variations could be explained by a multiplicity of factors that may have intervened to influence the Court's reasoning. In *Werhof*, the Court's reasoning was consistent with the position of the European Commission, the German government and the German Federal Labour Court. The *Alemo-Herron* ruling is in line with the Commission's and the UK government's position and arose from a divided national jurisprudential context. In *Asklepios*, the Court upheld the position of an amicus brief (although from the Norwegian government and not from the German government, which appears odd since the case originated from Germany),[1258] the preemptive indications of the referring court, and the prevailing national jurisprudence.

Interestingly, these three judgments present elements that are typical both of the integrationalist theory (discussed in Chapter 4 section 3), where the Court was depicted as a purposive policymaker, as well as of the theories presented in Chapter 5, where the possibility that EU judgments may be influenced by the national context was discussed. Intergovernmental traits are emerging from the convergence of the Court's reasoning with the amicus briefs of national governments. Moreover, the Court's effort to conform to the prevailing jurisprudence in the national context suggests the influence of trans-judicial dialogue dynamics.

Adding further complexity to the exploration of the prevailing judicial lawmaking logics, it is also interesting to note that the theories presented in Chapters 4 and 5 may not have exhausted the possible narratives. Indeed, there may be other relevant dynamics, such as the influence of the Advocate General's opinions, or the possible impact of the normative preferences and ideological orientation of the reporting judge. These factors have also been considered in the course of the empirical analysis and the results of the case studies can be found in Figure 14 below and in Figure 40 to Figure 42 and Table 8 and Table 9 in the Annex, and have been summarised in the last two columns of Table 7 above. The collocation of these case studies close to the concluding segment of this chapter reflects the residual consideration that the investigation conducted in this book gives to these judicial lawmaking dynamics. Eventual proximity with AG opinions, as well as the relevance of the ideological preferences of the judge rapporteur are in fact hardly compatible with the theories presented in Chapters 4 and 5, as they take the reasoning of the Courts out of any broader structural logic. On the contrary, the Court's case law would result characterised by a rather high level of arbitrariness which could not be attributed to the Court itself as a judicial authority but to the ideological inclinations of the individuals working in it (judge rapporteurs and Advocates General).

1258. Opinion of Advocate General Bot of 19 January 2017, *Asklepios Kliniken Langen-Seligenstadt GmbH v. Ivan Felja and Asklepios Dienstleistungsgesellschaft mbH v. Vittoria Graf*, C-680/15, ECLI:EU:C:2017:30 (para. 103).

Figure 14 Convergence Between the Court's Reasoning and the Opinion of the Advocate General per Question Considered by the Court (1983-March 2022)

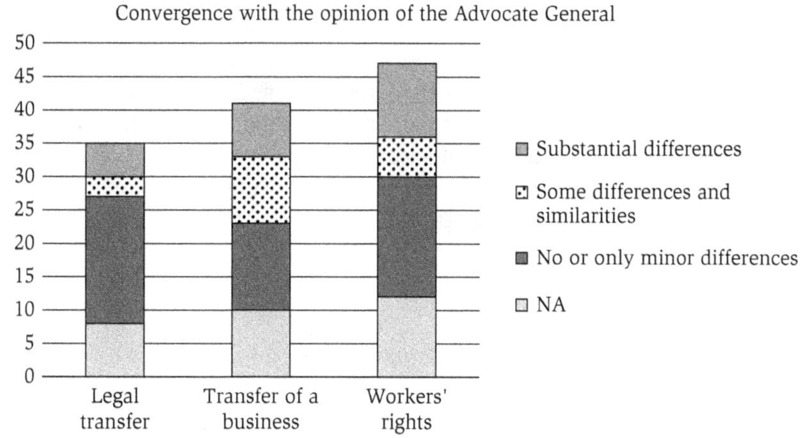

Author's own elaboration. *See* Figure 40, Figure 41 and Figure 42 for more details.

With regard to the case study on the opinions of the Advocate General, Figure 14 indicates no particular convergence. It should thus be excluded that the Court's approach to the directive is strongly influenced by the AG's opinions on the Court's reasoning. This holds true both when considering the whole case law on transfer of undertaking as well as the identified 'evolutionary moments'. No clear similarity can be discerned with regard to the interpretative change in the concept of 'transfer of a business' that occurred between the *Schmidt*, *Strø Mølle Akustik* and *Süzen* decisions. Nor is there any significant homogeneity between the Court and the Advocate General with regard to the increasing emphasis on contractual freedom in *Werhof* and *Alemo-Herron*.

More interesting elements can be found in relation to the judge rapporteur responsible for each judgment. From Table 8 and Table 9 in the Annex, it emerges that, over the years, the cases on transfer of undertakings have been assigned to a limited number of judges rapporteur who, therefore, may have developed a certain interpretative pattern. This could explain certain variations in the Court's jurisprudence. Looking at Table 6 and at the judgments on the concept of 'transfer of a business', the rapporteur judge in the *Strø Mølle Akustik* case is in fact different from the judge responsible for the *Schmidt* case. Then, Table 9 in the Annex indicates that until the mid-2000s, most of the cases were assigned to judge Puissochet. This could contribute to explaining the consistency with which the judgments in those years adopted a restrictive attitude to the scope of application. Subsequently, since the *Jouini* judgment, the judge rapporteur who has most frequently dealt with Directive 2001/23/EC has been Judge Malenovsky. Interestingly, his 'taking over' corresponded with the beginning of the more 'erratic' attitude towards the concept of 'transfer of a business' observed in Chapter 3 section 5.1.2. Moreover, it is significant to note that the first case on workers' rights that was assigned to Judge Malenovsky was precisely the *Werhof* judgment. This is quite significant since, it is worth recalling, *Werhof* inaugurated the trend of valorisation of the employer's contractual freedoms.

Malenovsky was also the judge rapporteur in *Alemo-Herron* and *Asklepios*. This may well be a coincidence. At the same time, the findings indicate the possibility that the change in the approach towards the emancipatory function of the directive *also* stemmed from the normative and ideological inclinations of the judge rapporteur. In that case, however, it is important to stress that these would be the preferences of the individual judge and not of the Court as an institution.

5.2 Concluding Remarks

In this chapter, a series of case studies have been proposed to 'test' the judicial lawmaking logics discussed in Chapters 4 and 5. This empirical analysis was situated in the second analytical layer in which the research conducted in this book has been articulated. If the case studies in Chapter 3 were fully embedded in the epistemological framework of the labour law discipline, the analysis conducted in this chapter looked at the Court through the lenses of judicial lawmaking studies. These two approaches complement each other in providing a fuller picture of the role of the Court vis-à-vis the normative model of labour law, whose contours will be drawn in the next, conclusive chapter.

This chapter has applied the judicial lawmaking theories described in Chapters 4 and 5 to the case law of the CJEU on transfer of undertakings, in an attempt to answer RQ3: *What are the logics that determine the Court's approach with respect to labour law, taking into account judicial lawmaking theories?*

The case studies conducted suggest that the Court's reasoning is influenced by a plurality of dynamics. It was not possible to identify a predominant narrative, but integrationalism, trans-judicial dialogue and (albeit to a lesser extent) intergovernmentalism were identified as the most plausible logics. The relevance of the ideological inclination of the judge rapporteur cannot be excluded either. Plausible neofunctional dynamics have been detected only with reference to the judicial evolution in the area of 'transfer of a business' that occurred after *Schmidt*.

Overall, the analysis revealed that the normative implications of the judgments can be traced back to a number of factors that are not necessarily related to the Court's preferences regarding the normative model of labour law. National judicial authorities, national governments and the European Commission have indeed emerged as potentially influential actors in shaping the Court's reasoning. Among the most convincing judicial lawmaking dynamics, only the integrationalist logic is compatible with the view that the Court's rulings reflect its normative preferences. Moreover, even then, the approach with respect to the emancipatory function of labour law would at most be a mediated expression of the Court's integrationalist ethos.

In conclusion, the empirical exploration carried out in this chapter indicates that the evolution of the case law on transfer of undertakings and the increased sensitivity to the interests of the employer should not be readily interpreted as a result of the normative inclination of the Court with respect to the function of labour law but should (also) be considered as the expression of a number of overlapping external dynamics.

Conclusion

1 INTRODUCTION

The main theme of this book was to seek an answer to the following central research question: What role does the CJEU play in relation to the normative model underlying EU labour law?

As discussed in Chapter 1, the interest in approaching this issue derives from two distinct premises that permeate EU labour law studies.[1259] The first is that labour law was originally conceived with social, emancipatory features. However, when labour law is seen foremost as a labour market instrument, it loses its emancipatory rationale and its ability to pursue the ideal of social justice it was originally intended to achieve. The second premise coincides with the dogmatic assumption that, by approaching labour law in a purposive manner, the CJEU contributes to the marginalisation of its emancipatory component. This assumption is grounded in a widespread perception in the labour law discipline and has been explored, and in a way challenged, throughout the book.

In shedding light on the Court's role with respect to the normative model of labour law, this book has engaged with both premises. On the one hand, it has assessed the Court's approach to the emancipatory dimension of labour law by looking at how it rules on the transfer of undertakings directive. Moreover, this book has also revealed the limitations of studies that consider the normative implications of the Court's case law exclusively through the lens of the labour law epistemological framework. When relying solely on the labour law doctrinal perspective, the rule-making activity of the Court risks being reduced to its positioning in the 'social versus economic' tension. It was instead shown that the Court's decision-making is populated by a range of dynamics that transcend the balancing of values underpinning the rules that the Court is asked to interpret. Enlarging the conceptual framework beyond the labour law

1259. Chapter 1, section 1.

discipline thus contributed to enriching the understanding of the role played by the Court in shaping the normative model of EU labour norms.

In view of better presenting the contribution of these epistemologically complementary explorations and of a multidisciplinary approach, the book has essentially developed two separate studies on the same set of judicial proceedings. Each segment of the research was situated in a different analytical layer. In the first part, the case law of the Court is appraised through the dogmatic lenses of labour law. This approach characterised Chapters 2 and 3 where RQ1 (*What (prevailing) normative model(s) is(are) underlying the approaches of EU institutional policy makers with respect to labour law?*) and RQ2 (*Is it possible to identify an underlying normative model in the case law of the Court of Justice with respect to labour law?*) were addressed. In the second part of the research, the Court's interpretative activity was not considered in light of its normative implications, but the focus was on the judicial lawmaking logics. Chapters 4 to 6 thus dealt with RQ3 (*What are the logics that determine the Court's approach with respect to labour law, taking into account judicial lawmaking theories?*).

Interestingly, the results emerging from both studies suggest that the assumption according to which the Court plays an active role in marginalising the emancipatory dimension of labour law should be nuanced. The transformative significance of the Court's case law emerges as rather mitigated, as well as the overall impact of the (eventual) normative preferences of the Court.

2 THE MAIN FINDINGS

The first part of the research was embedded in the labour law disciplinary framework and has been structured to provide a first (albeit eventually incomplete) definition of the role of the Court vis-à-vis the normative model of labour law. First of all, in Chapter 2, an attempt has been made to determine whether EU policymaking adopts a specific normative model in relation to labour law. This exploration has been functional to contextualise the case law within the predominant approach emerging from EU policymaking, in view of discerning eventual alignment and common traits. This analysis has shown that, throughout the years, there has been an evolution in the dominant normative paradigm of labour law in the Union. The first phase of European integration was characterised by the absence of a particular regulatory model with respect to labour law. Then, a period of upward harmonisation regarding social and labour standards can be identified. It was in those years that labour law instruments embodying both emancipatory and economic components of labour law were adopted, including Directive 77/187/EEC on transfer of undertakings. After that, however, labour law began to be addressed essentially as a macroeconomic variable. The ability of labour law to pursue the protective function as well as the function of uplifting workers' bargaining power was thus severely diminished. This occurred in the context of the flexicurity agenda and its promotion of labour law as essentially aimed at ensuring a well-functioning labour market.

It was, nevertheless, also noted that the way in which the Von der Leyen Commission has so far approached the implementation of the EPSR, as well as the recent initiatives taken in the context of the recovery strategy to overcome the COVID-19 crisis, may lead to a greater strengthening of the emancipatory component of labour law. Hence, all this led to answering RQ1 (*What (prevailing) normative model(s) is(are) underlying the approaches of EU institutional policymakers with respect to labour law?*) by noting that EU policymaking has been long dominated by a paradigm that conceives labour law as predominantly performing the function to regulate the labour market. Recently, however, a window of opportunity to avoid the full dissipation of the emancipatory dimension of labour law has emerged with the initiatives in the context of the EPSR and of the Next Generation EU.

In Chapter 3, a series of case studies on the directive on transfer of undertakings have been illustrated to discuss the Court's approach to the emancipatory rationale and to assess it in relation to the dominant approach emerging from EU policymaking. This, ultimately, would reveal to what extent the Court's reasoning exercises a deregulatory pressure on labour law when compared to the EU policymaking institutions. Chapter 3 aimed to answer RQ2 (*Is it possible to identify an underlying normative model in the case law of the Court of Justice with respect to labour law?*). It was observed that there has been an evolution in the Court's interpretation of the scope of the directive and the rights thereby conferred. Initially, the reasoning of the Court fully valorised the protective function of the directive and provided a strict reading of the effectiveness of the collective agreements that were in force before the transfer vis-à-vis the transferee, but then the Court started to show more sensitivity for the economic interests of the employers. Ultimately, the case studies suggested that the normative model pursued by the Court coincides with an understanding of labour law that seeks to reconcile economic and social progress.[1260] It thus emerged a certain degree of convergence emerged between the Court's approach and EU institutional policymaking. In both cases, there was a sharpening of the economic dimension in the 1990s and in the Euro crisis years and, only recently, signs of rehabilitation of the emancipatory function. However, it is important to note that in the Court's case law, there has not been such a radical compression of the emancipatory component as there has been in EU policymaking, with the exception of a few pronouncements (including the much-debated *Alemo-Herron* case).

Chapter 3 then concluded by proposing a first, tentative, definition of the role of the Court with respect to the normative function of labour law. This definition was embedded in the first analytical layer of the research and merely considered the case law in consideration of its labour law implications. The case studies led to reject the view that the Court has played the role of leading actor in the marginalisation of the emancipatory rationale of labour law. Rather, it appeared more plausible that the role that was assumed by the Court is to not oppose the normative model emerging from institutional policymaking. The Court tendentially performs this role without distorting the emancipatory effects of labour law norms. However, it has also shown to be ready to substantially reduce the scope and salience of workers' rights established in the

1260. As discussed in Chapter 3, section 6.

directive when the compression to the economic freedom of the employer is deemed excessive.

From the fourth chapter onwards, the book entered into the second part of the research and moved to the second analytical layer. The objective was to inquire whether the adoption of a different epistemological framework, namely that of judicial lawmaking, would enrich the understanding of the Court's approach towards labour law and its normative model. In this second part of the research, the aim was to address RQ3: *What are the logics that determine the Court's approach with respect to labour law, taking into account judicial lawmaking theories?* Chapters 4 and 5 have outlined the theoretical framework, by discussing possibly relevant judicial lawmaking theories, and Chapter 6 has 'tested' them with a series of case studies, again performed on the directive on transfer of undertakings. Chapter 4 concerned two judicial lawmaking theories which attribute to the Court the role of a quasi-political and autonomous actor in EU policymaking: neofunctionalism and integrationalism. According to the neofunctionalist theory, the Court aims at realising its own political ambitions. It develops specific policy areas in order to make the EU legal system more pervasive and compelling within the national context. At the same time, neofunctionalists argue that the Court uses its case law to enhance its judicial authority. To achieve these objectives, the Court has sought to engage individuals (and especially economic actors) as potential litigants and thus potential initiators of EU law-based litigation before national courts. The integrationalist perspective instead perceives the Court as performing the role of trustee of the Treaties' and, therefore, as directing its interpretative activity towards an expansive reading of EU law. From this perspective, Court's reasonings aim at strengthening and expanding the competences of the Union, primarily in relation to the European economic area, but not only. It has been seen, for instance, that an integrationalist rationale can be found also in the case law on non-discrimination. According to the proponents of integrationalism, the Court is also in a sort of informal partnership with the European Commission, which is the other European institution with an inherently integrationalist vocation.

It was explained that if the neofunctionalist or integrationalist logics were to be confirmed by the case studies, the characterisation of the Court as a policy actor would be reinforced. But, not necessarily as a policy actor in terms of the specific balancing of values underlying labour standards. The Court's inclination for a specific normative model of labour law could instead be read as functional to realise its (broader) political objectives (be them integrationalist, to provoke a regulatory spillover, or to increase its jurisprudential authority, as suggested by neofunctionalist theories).

In Chapter 5, other theories on judicial lawmaking of the CJEU were discussed. This time the Court was not presented as an autonomous policy actor, but as strongly influenced by the national context. According to the intergovernmental theory, the Court's judgments reflect the preferences of national governments, or at least of the most influential among them. The majoritarian theory, instead, assumes that the Court's judgments reflect the legal solutions that tend to prevail in the Member States. Then, the pluralist theory contends that the Court is careful not to encroach upon the legal traditions of the countries from which the preliminary rulings originate. Finally, the trans-judicial dialogue narrative considers the possibility that the Court's reasonings respond to dialectical dynamics with national courts. It has been said that if these theories were to find validation from the case studies, EU case law should not (just) be seen as an expression of the Court's preferences in relation to the normative issue at stake. Instead, the case law would also reflect a series of factors which are external to the normative implications of the proceedings. These factors relate to the national legal context, judicial dynamics or intergovernmental logics.

Chapter 6 concluded the second analytical layer of the research with a second set of case studies. An empirical analysis was again conducted on the case law on the directive on transfer of undertakings, this time in order to test the various theories of judicial lawmaking. The empirical analysis relied on a number of indicators, each related to a different theory. For neofunctionalism, the case study looked at how the Court accommodated the litigants' claims. For integrationalism, the focus was on the level of convergence between the Court's reasoning and the position submitted by the legal services of the European Commission during the proceedings. The indicator for the intergovernmentalist theory was the convergence between the Court's reasoning and the amicus briefs submitted by national governments. For the pluralist and majoritarian theories, it was observed whether the Court adopted a comparatist approach, whether it tended to validate national law or practices and whether it left a margin of discretion to the national court. With regard to trans-judicial dialogue, the indicators were multiple, consisting of the convergence between the Court's judgments and the preemptive opinions of the referring courts, the margin of discretion that the Court leaves to supreme or constitutional courts, and the Court's attitude towards national jurisprudence.

In light of the case studies, RQ3 (*What are the logics that determine the Court's approach with respect to labour law, taking into account judicial lawmaking theories?*) was finally answered. The case studies revealed that, although it is not possible to identify a clearly dominant judicial lawmaking logic, the Court's reasoning reflects characteristics that especially corroborate integrationalist and intergovernmentalist influences, as well as the impact of trans-judicial dialogue with national courts. This, on the one hand, implies that the Court's rulings reflect a range of pressures stemming from national institutional actors (be they Member States governments or judicial authorities). This finding emerged particularly in connection with the enhancement of the economic freedoms of the employer in the *Werhof*, *Alemo-Herron* and *Asklepios* judgments. In addition, the case studies showed that the Court has the inclination to follow the legal position proposed by the legal services of the European Commission. With regard to this, it must however be stressed that this attitude is not necessarily an expression of an integrationalist logic but may also simply indicate a subservient attitude of the Court with respect to the Commission. The judicial lawmaking theories proved helpful to enrich the understanding of what could lay behind the Court's reasoning touching upon the rationale of labour law. Observing the Court's case law only through the lenses of the labour law discipline thus does not provide a complete picture, as it does not capture all the interests and dynamics that influence the interpretative activity of the Court.

Mindful of the insights emerging from this enriched epistemological framework, the research conducted in this book has now reached the maturity to address the main and overarching research question, namely: *What role does the Court of Justice play in relation to the normative model underlying EU labour law?*

It is worth recalling that, through an analysis exclusively conducted through the dogmatic lenses of the labour law doctrine in Chapter 3, it was argued that the role assumed by the Court was to not oppose the normative model emerging from institutional policymaking.[1261] The findings provided by the exploration of the additional analytical layer on judicial lawmaking instead indicate that the answer to the central research question should be more articulated. This research has shown that the Court's decision-making appears influenced by a logic of synthesis with respect to the normative claims made by multiple actors, institutional or otherwise, involved in the proceedings. The definition of the Court's role with respect to the normative model of labour law must therefore take this multidimensional context into account. Framing this role merely in terms of policymaking orientations and normative bias seems reductionist since it assumes that the judgments would only embody the Court's normative preferences. The role of the Court with respect to the normative model of labour law seems to be rather that of giving expression, in a not necessarily consistent manner, to the various concerns, requests and expectations that populate the *institutional, strategic, human,* and *trans-judicial* context in which the case law is adopted.

Concerns and pressures coming from the *institutional* context are addressed by the Court by means of its cooperative attitude towards the Commission and towards the positions of national governments. The *strategic* dimension comes to the fore in relation to the possibility that the Court's informal alliance with the Commission underlies an integrationalist rationale, aiming at expanding and strengthening the EU legal system. The *human* aspect relates to the possible impact of the ideological preferences of the judge rapporteur. Finally, there is the *trans-judicial* element in that the Court is also cautious not to undermine the collaborative relationship with national courts.

In conclusion, this book has demonstrated the importance of broadening the doctrinal and analytical lenses through which the Court's approach to labour law is assessed. The exploration of judicial lawmaking logics has, in fact, enriched the understanding of the Court's role in relation to the emancipatory function of labour law, nuancing its characterisation as a purposive normative actor. This becomes clear when comparing the two different definitions of the Court's role with respect to labour norms. The definition that emerges from the first part of the research reflects the limitations of labour law's theoretical framework, with the risk of too quickly associating the policy implications of judgments with the normative inclination of the Court. The definition of the Court's role that stems from the second part of the book is instead enriched by the epistemological contribution of judicial lawmaking theories and reflects a more complex reality. This conclusion leads to a recommendation for future studies on EU labour law, which is to adopt greater caution in assessing the Court's approach to labour law norms. In particular, this research suggests the importance of distinguishing the normative impact of judgments from the normative bias of the CJEU

1261. As discussed in Chapter 3, section 7.

and engaging with judicial lawmaking theories when formulating reflections on the role of the Court vis-à-vis the normative model of labour law.

3 RESHAPING THE PERCEPTION OF THE COURT OF JUSTICE IN RELATION TO LABOUR LAW

The analysis conducted allows to revisit and to some extent correct the two justifying premises of the research, with the effect of reshaping the perception of the CJEU vis-à-vis the normative role of labour law.

The first premise concerned the transformation of labour law in case of substantial erosion of its emancipatory component. The initial part of the research showed that the Court's approach to the directive on transfer of undertakings did not aggravate the weakening of the emancipatory dimension of those norms. Indeed, the case study conducted in Chapter 3 showed that the valorisation of the economic rationale of the analysed directive did not go so far as to systemically undermine its protective function nor did not entirely empty the effectiveness of national collective bargaining rights vis-à-vis the transferee.

The second premise concerned the possibility that the CJEU interprets labour law with a purposive approach, and that the marginalisation of the emancipatory rationale of labour law derived from its reasoning is the result of its normative bias. However, the second part of the research showed that the Court's reasoning is the product of multiple dynamics and that the normative bias of the Court is at most only one of the elements at play.

Chapter 6 has shown that the evolutionary moments that have characterised the Court's jurisprudence may be attributable to a number of external pressures, especially from the national judicial context. It was also explained that even the tendency to converge with the Commission's position does not necessarily mean that the Court shares the same socioeconomic vision regarding European integration. It could also simply indicate that the Court is subject to a certain institutional subservience to the Commission. In light of these considerations, the role of the Court with respect to labour law might be that of searching for a synthesis of the various normative claims that arise from the multidimensional and heterogeneous context in which the Court exercises its interpretative activity.

The third and final insight descends from the previous two and is that the normative direction of the case law is not inexorable but can, to an extent, be influenced. In other words, the Court's case law could be one of the settings in which to counteract the erosion of the emancipatory significance of labour law. It is worth recalling that among the various elements that emerged in Chapter 6 as potentially determining for the Court's reasoning are trans-judicial dynamics and national jurisprudence. This suggests that there is room to turn to the preliminary ruling mechanism as an instrument to strategically advance labour protections. In addition to exploring this strategic avenue in areas where EU labour standards already exist, just as in the case of the directive on transfer of undertakings, this option could also prove valuable in areas where a defined regulatory approach has not yet settled, precisely because of the regulatory vacuum that the Court could fill. Examples might be those aspects of the world of work most affected by digital technologies, areas in which, moreover, existing legislative solutions are currently failing to provide adequate protection for workers.

In order to best harness the impact of trans-judicial dynamics on the CJEU, the preliminary references could draw on a number of elements that were identified in Chapter 6 as potentially significant in influencing the Court's judicial reasoning. One of these is the presence of a preemptive opinion of the referring court, especially if it is a superior court. Another potentially influential element is the reference to national jurisprudence in the request to the CJEU, again preferably from higher courts, which shows that the national judiciary has already ruled on a similar point of law in a way that supports the workers' claims.

But even before encouraging strategic litigation based on preliminary ruling references, this research revealed the need to broaden the research agenda of EU labour law studies. More understanding of how the Court approaches labour norms is needed. This book has taken some initial steps in the direction of expanding the epistemological framework with which to investigate the Court's interpretative activity vis-à-vis labour rules, and thus to better understand its role with respect to the emancipatory dimension of these norms. This research has limitations but could nonetheless show that while it cannot be completely ruled out that the Court may sometimes act as a policy actor, its role should not be reduced to that. There is more behind the Court's judicial lawmaking, and a deeper understanding of these dynamics could be highly valuable for EU labour law studies, also with a view to developing (judicial) strategies to strengthen the rights that EU law provides to workers.

Annex: Case Study Figures for Chapter 6

Author's own elaboration

Figure 15 Satisfaction of Litigants' Interests (Legal Transfer)

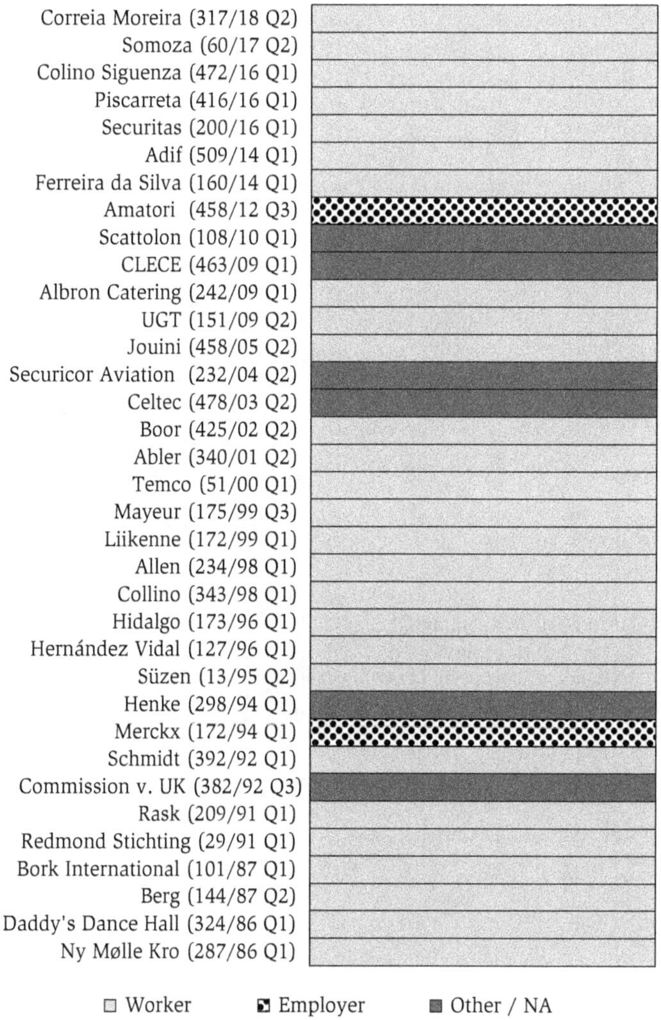

Figure 16 Satisfaction of Litigant's Interests (Transfer of a Business)

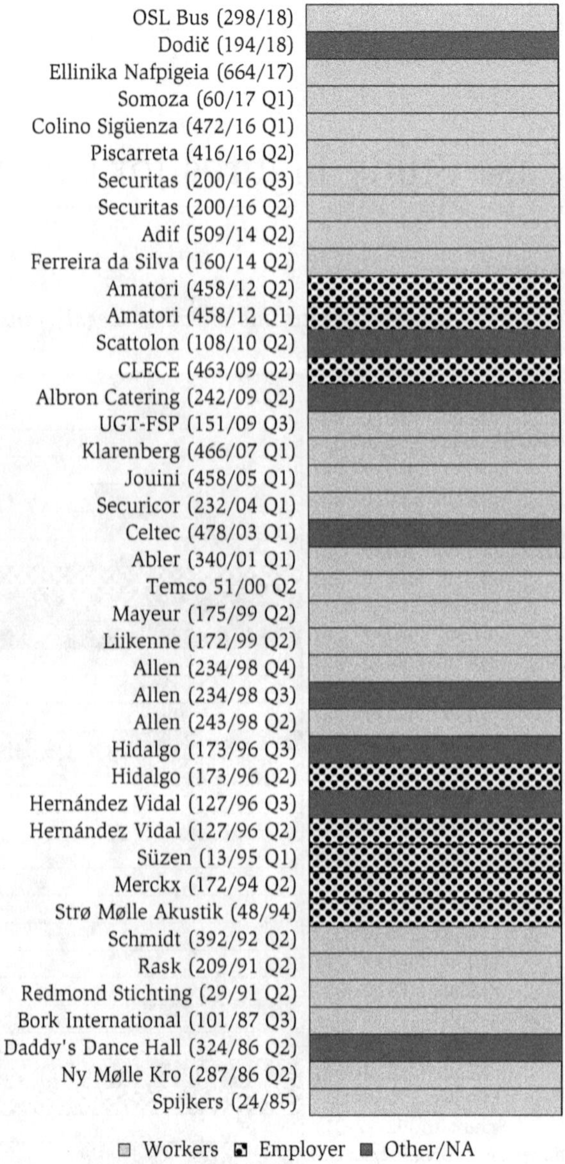

Figure 17 Satisfaction of Litigants' Interests (Workers' Rights)

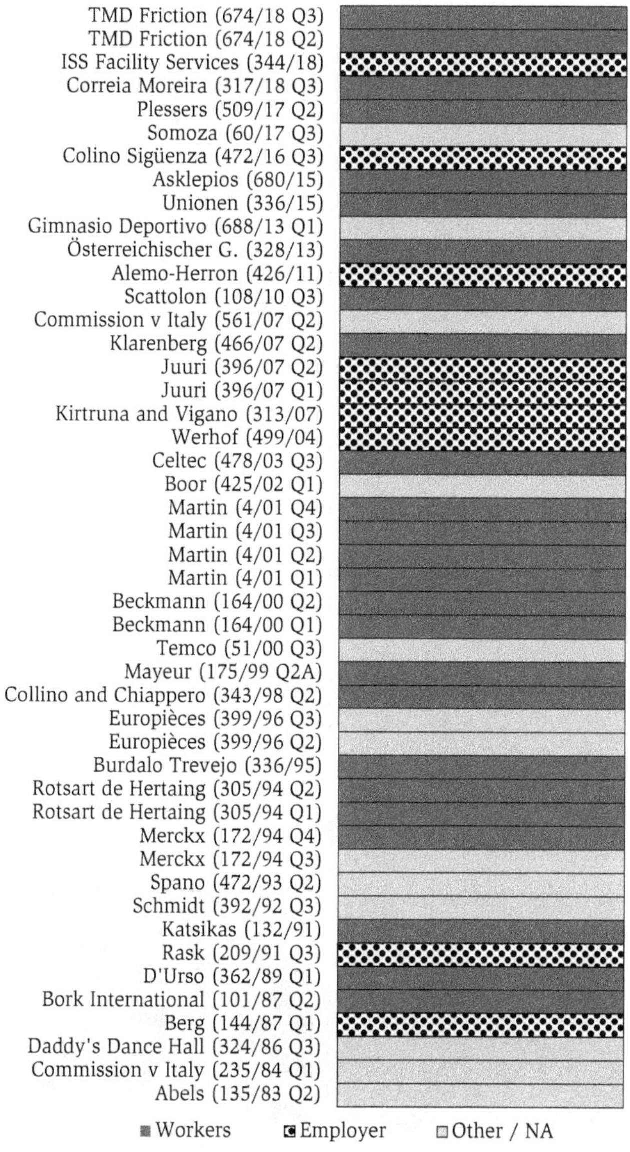

Figure 18 Conformity Between the Reasoning of the Court and the Position of the Commission (Legal Transfer)

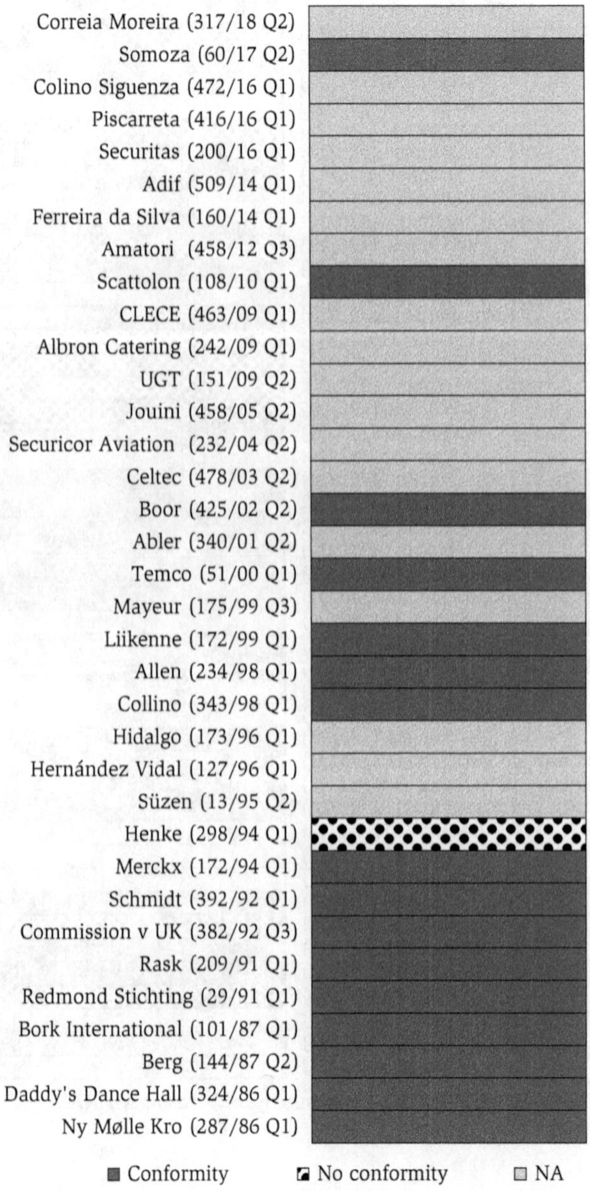

Figure 19 Conformity Between the Reasoning of the Court and the Position of the Commission (Transfer of a Business)

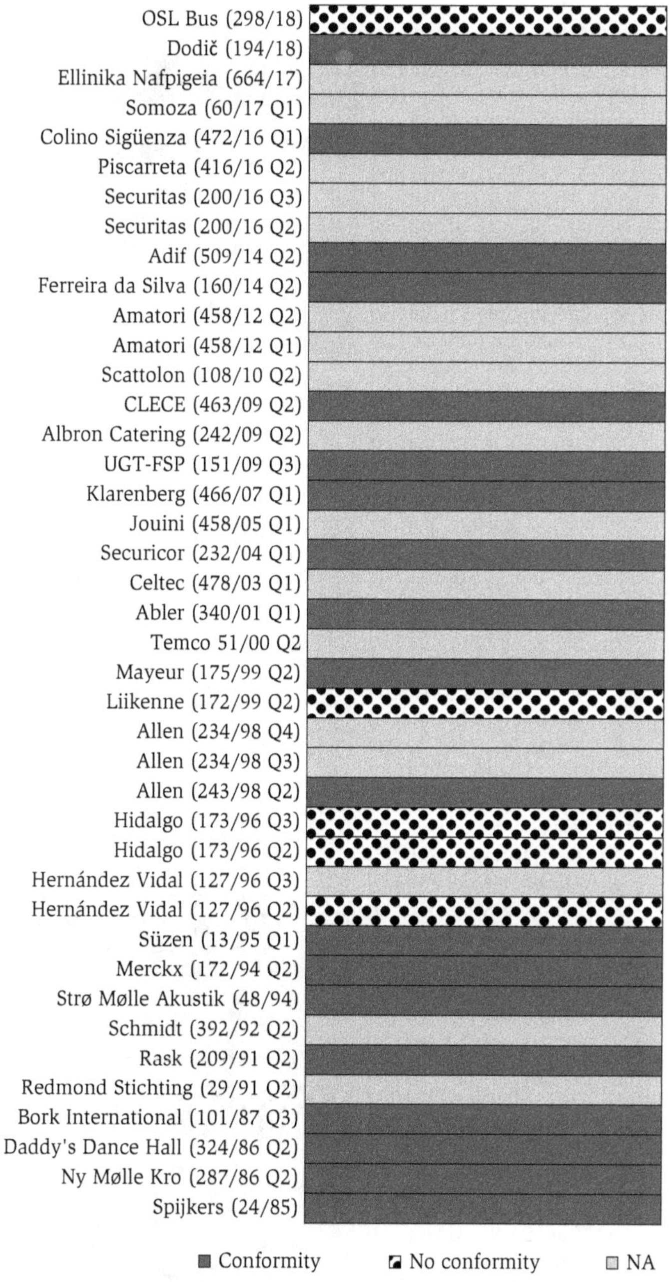

Figure 20 Conformity Between the Reasoning of the Court and the Position of the Commission (Workers' Rights)

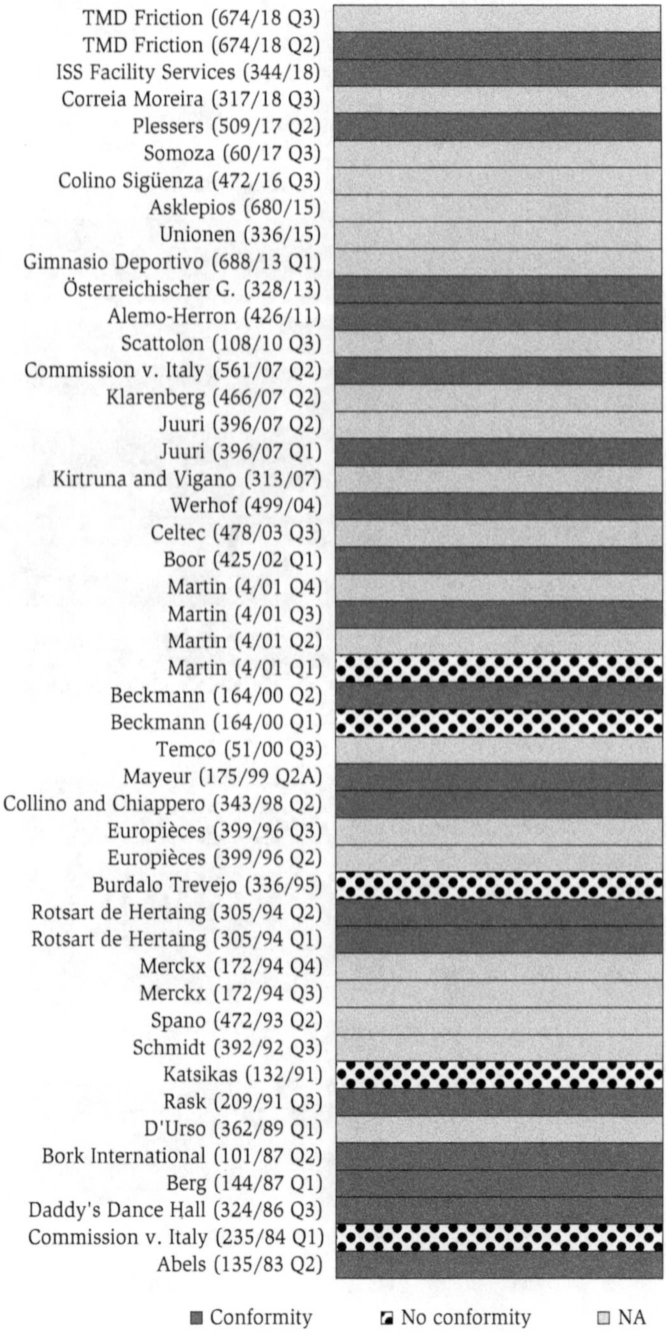

Table 7 Convergence Between the Reasoning of the Court and Amicus Briefs Submitted by National Governments

	CJEU endorses the position of one of the national governments	CJEU does not endorse the position of any of the national governments	No amicus briefs were submitted	Amicus briefs were submitted but not mentioned in the judgment or in the AG opinion
Number of questions addressed by the Court	40	24	26	65

Figure 21 Convergence Between the Reasoning of the Court and Amicus Briefs Submitted by National Governments (Legal Transfer)

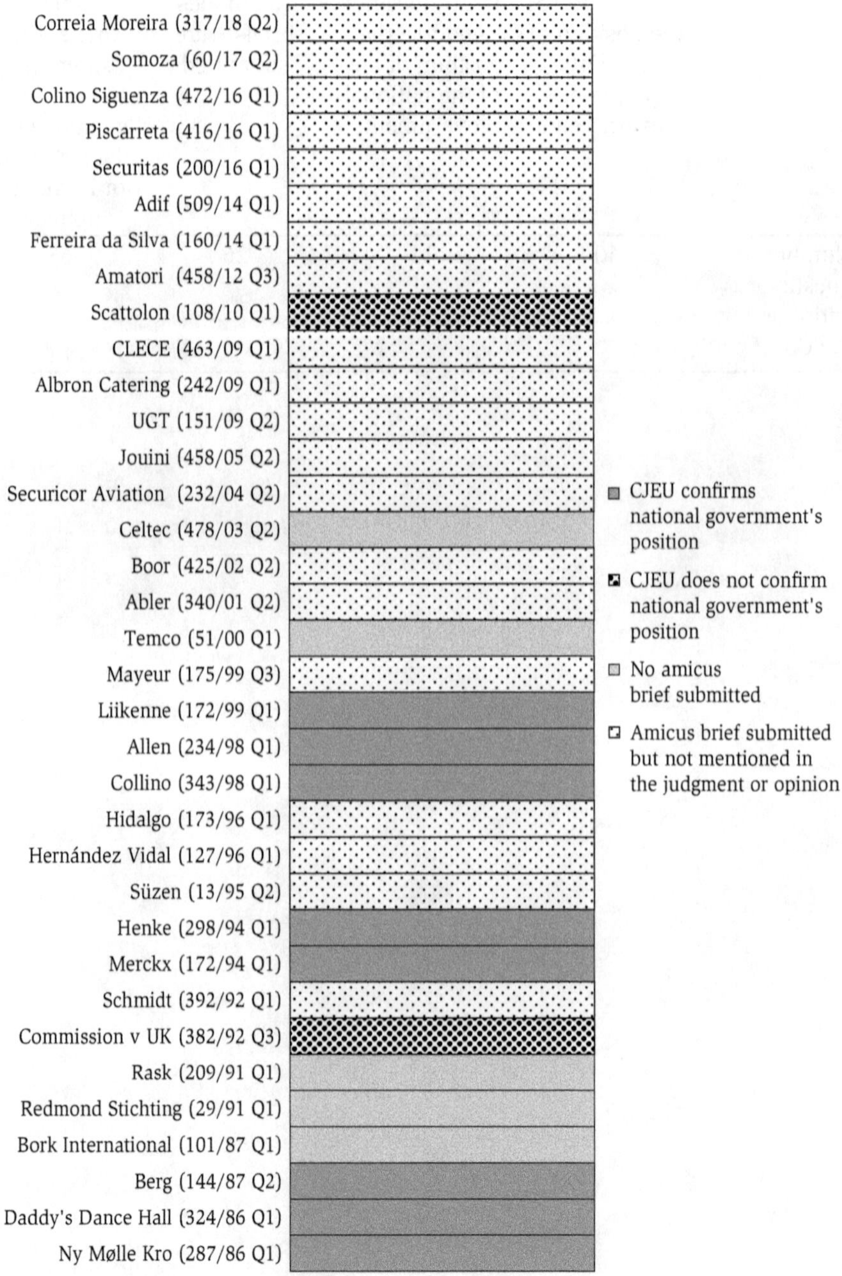

Figure 22 Convergence Between the Reasoning of the Court and Amicus Briefs Submitted by National Governments (Transfer of a Business)

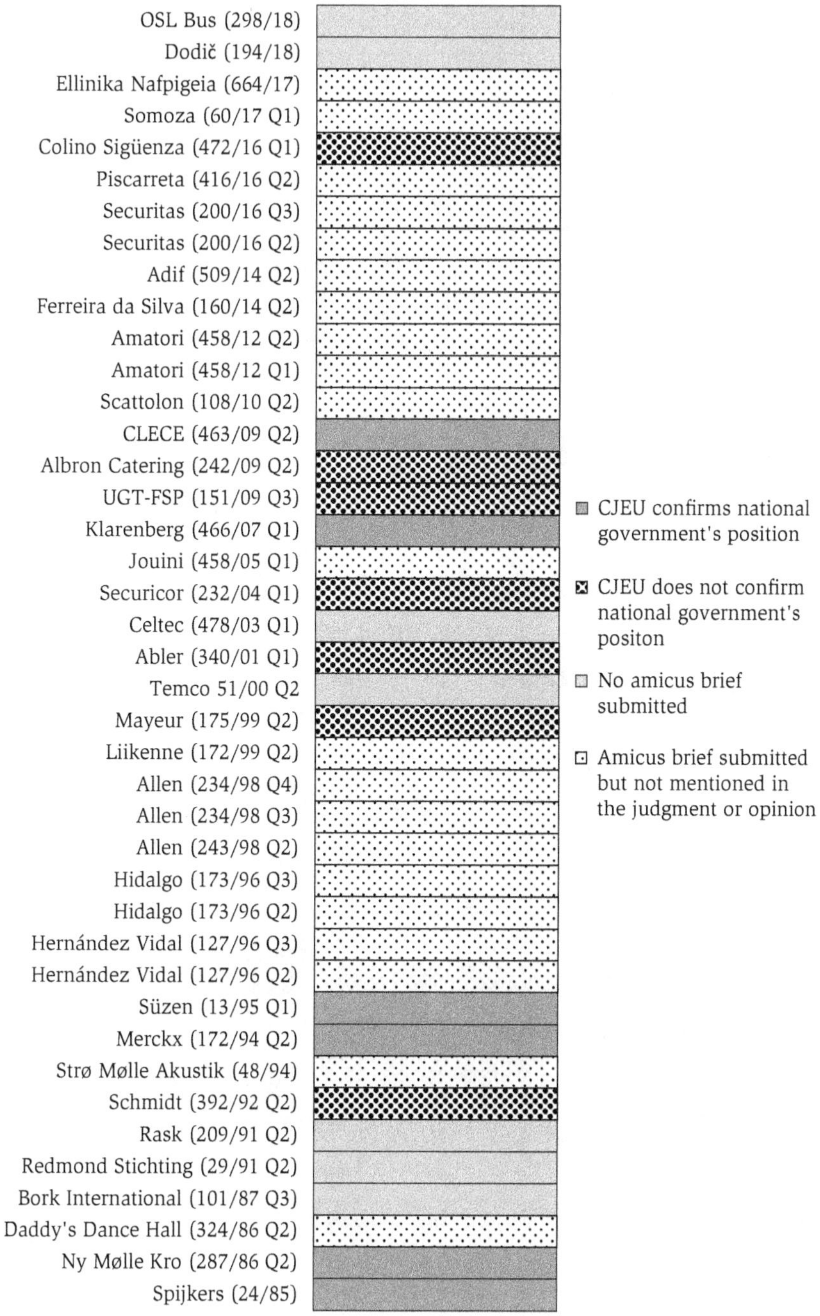

Figure 23 Convergence Between the Reasoning of the Court and Amicus Briefs Submitted by National Governments (Workers' Rights)

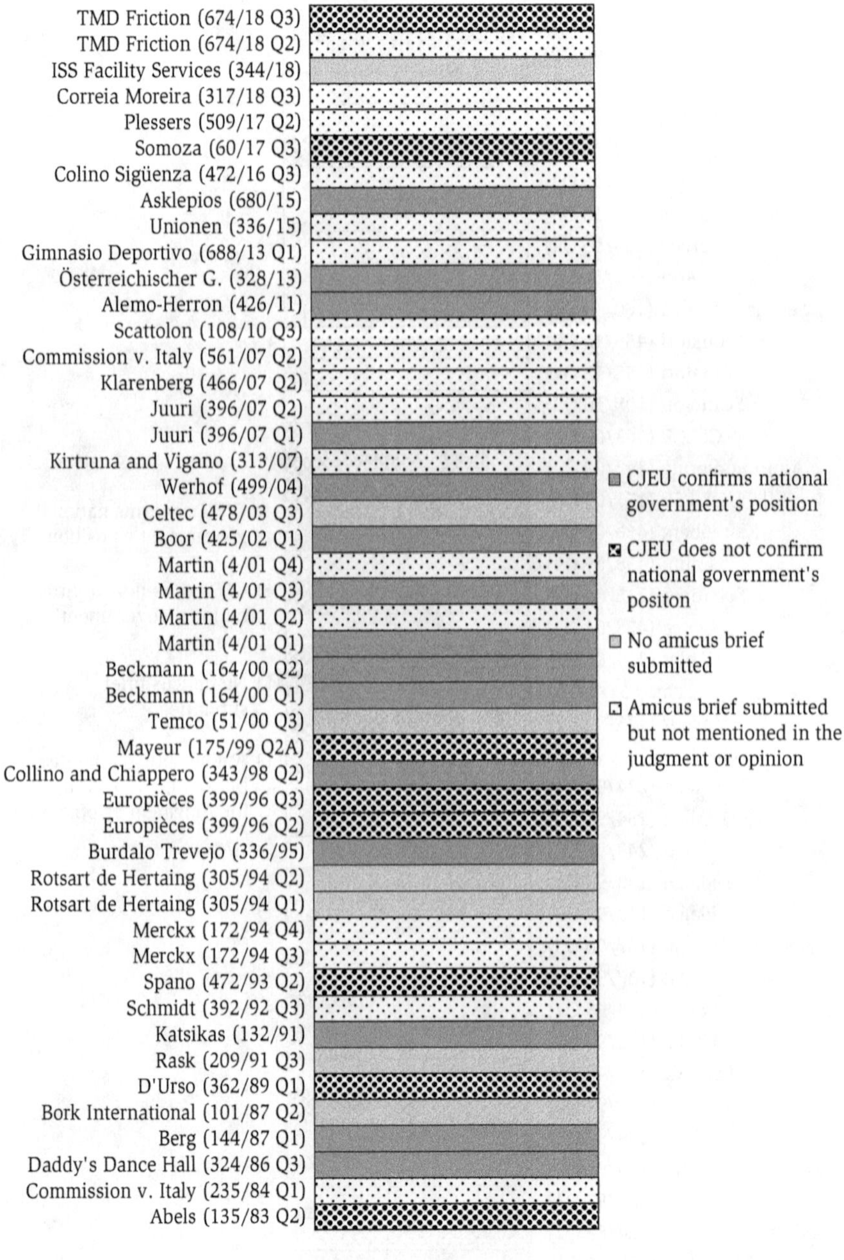

Figure 24   CJEU's Approach to National Law per Thematic Area

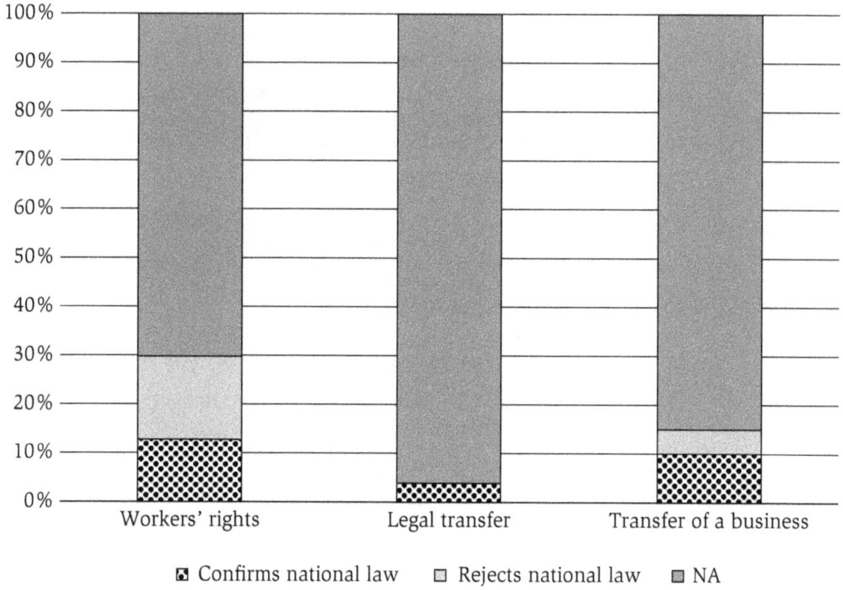

Figure 25   CJEU's Approach to National Law (Transfer of a Business)

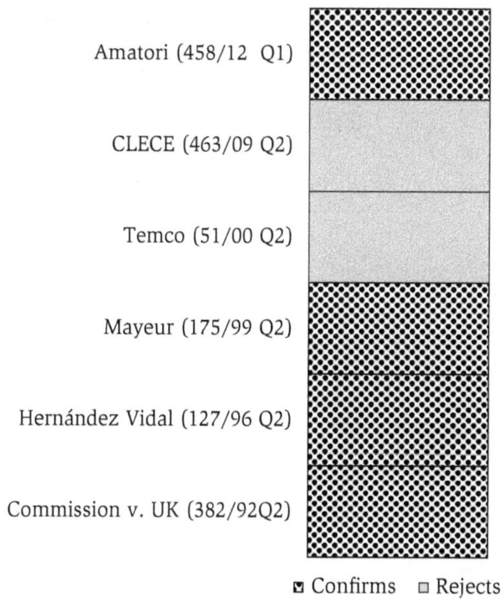

Figure 26 CJEU's Approach to National Law (Workers' Rights)

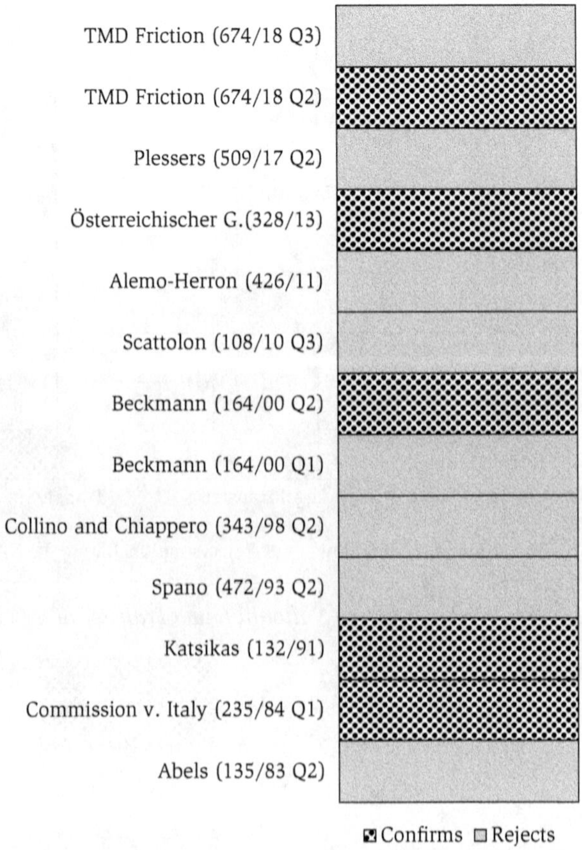

Figure 27 Margin of Discretion Left to National Referring Judges (Legal Transfer)

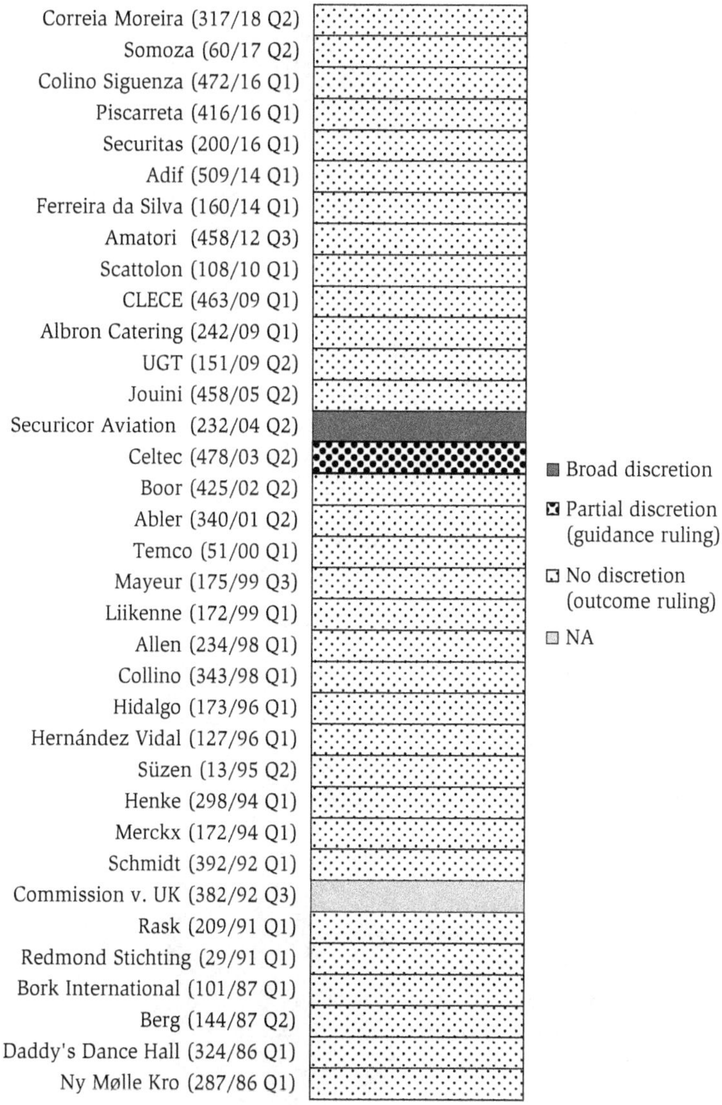

Figure 28 Margin of Discretion Left to National Referring Judges (Transfer of a Business)

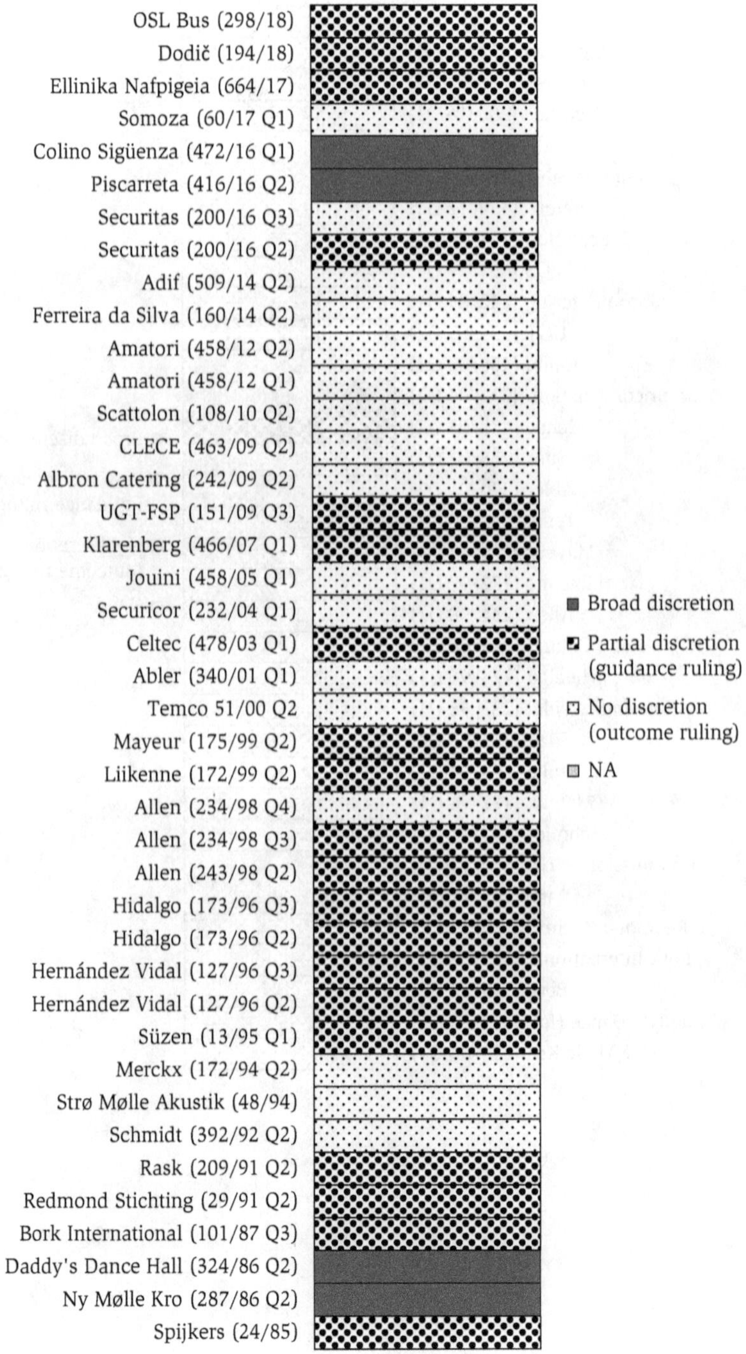

Figure 29 Margin of Discretion Left to National Referring Judges (Workers' Rights)

Figure 30 Convergence Between CJEU and the Preemptive Opinion of the Referring Judge (per Thematic Area)

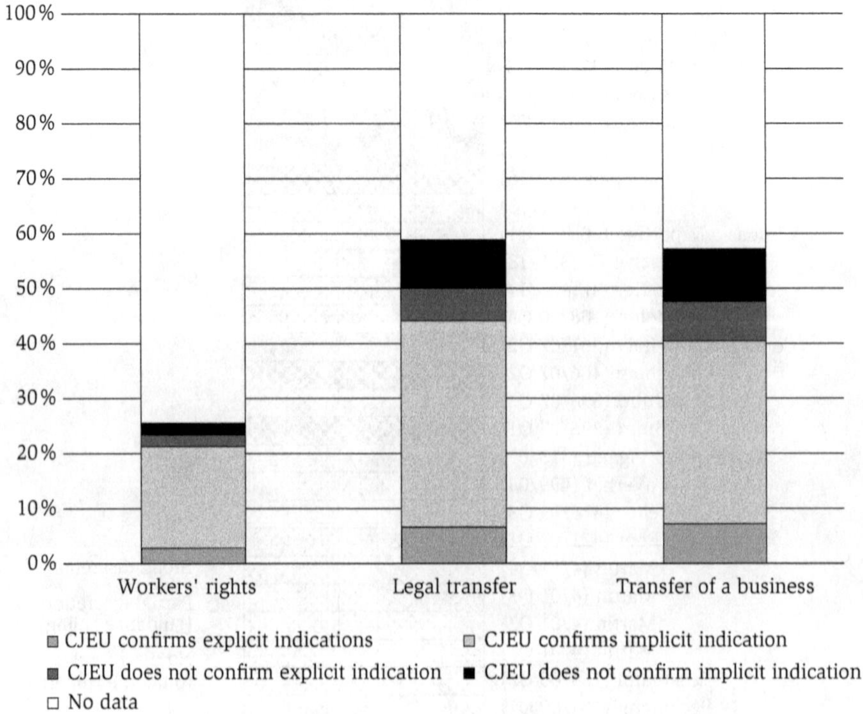

Figure 31 Convergence Between CJEU and the Preemptive Opinion of the Referring Judge (Legal Transfer)

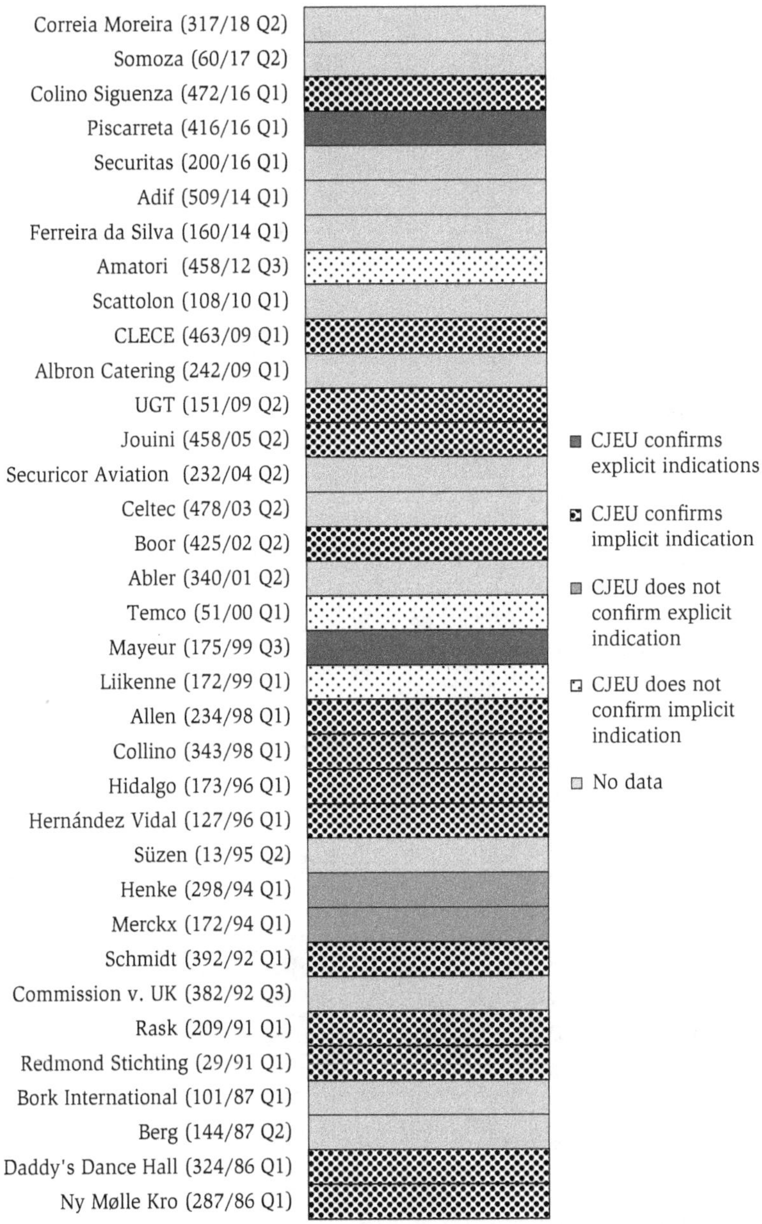

Figure 32 Type of Referring Court (Legal Transfer)

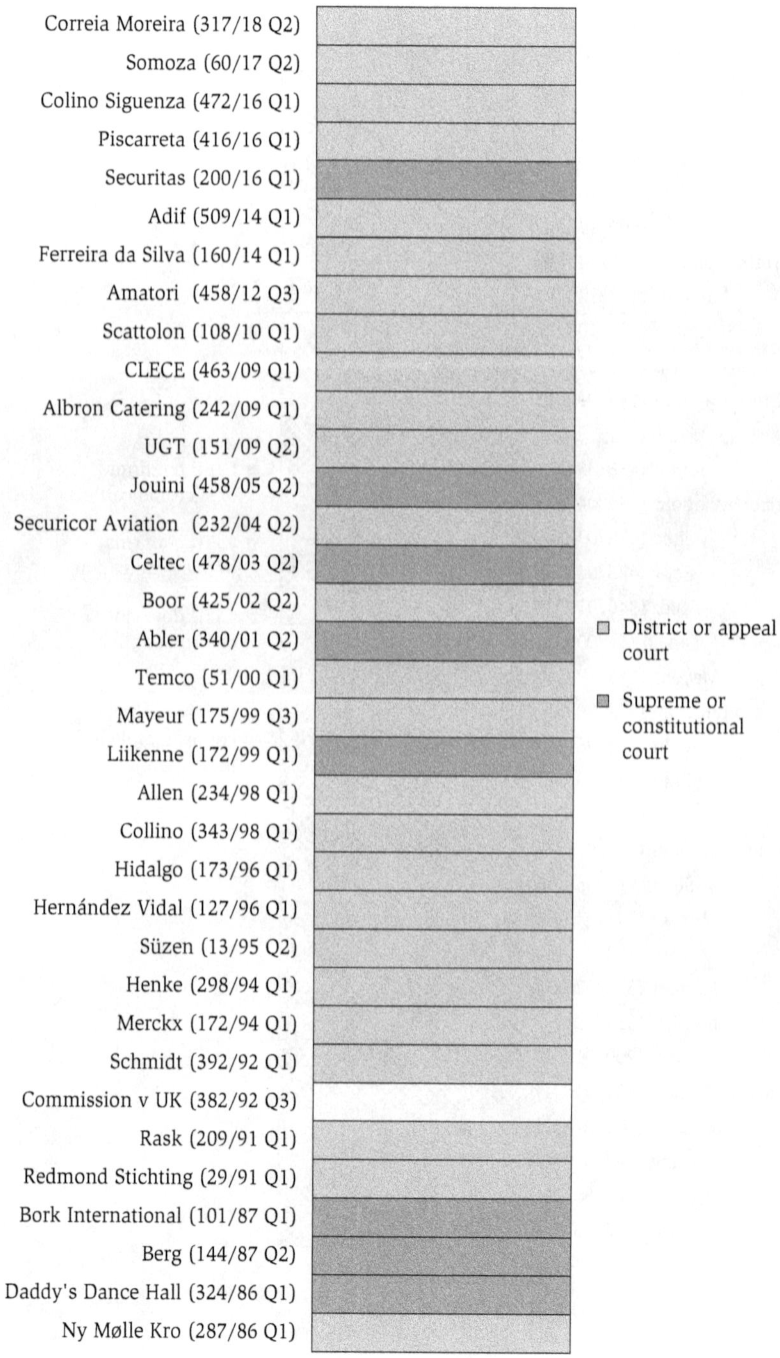

Figure 33 Convergence Between CJEU and the Preemptive Opinion of the Referring Judge (Transfer of a Business)

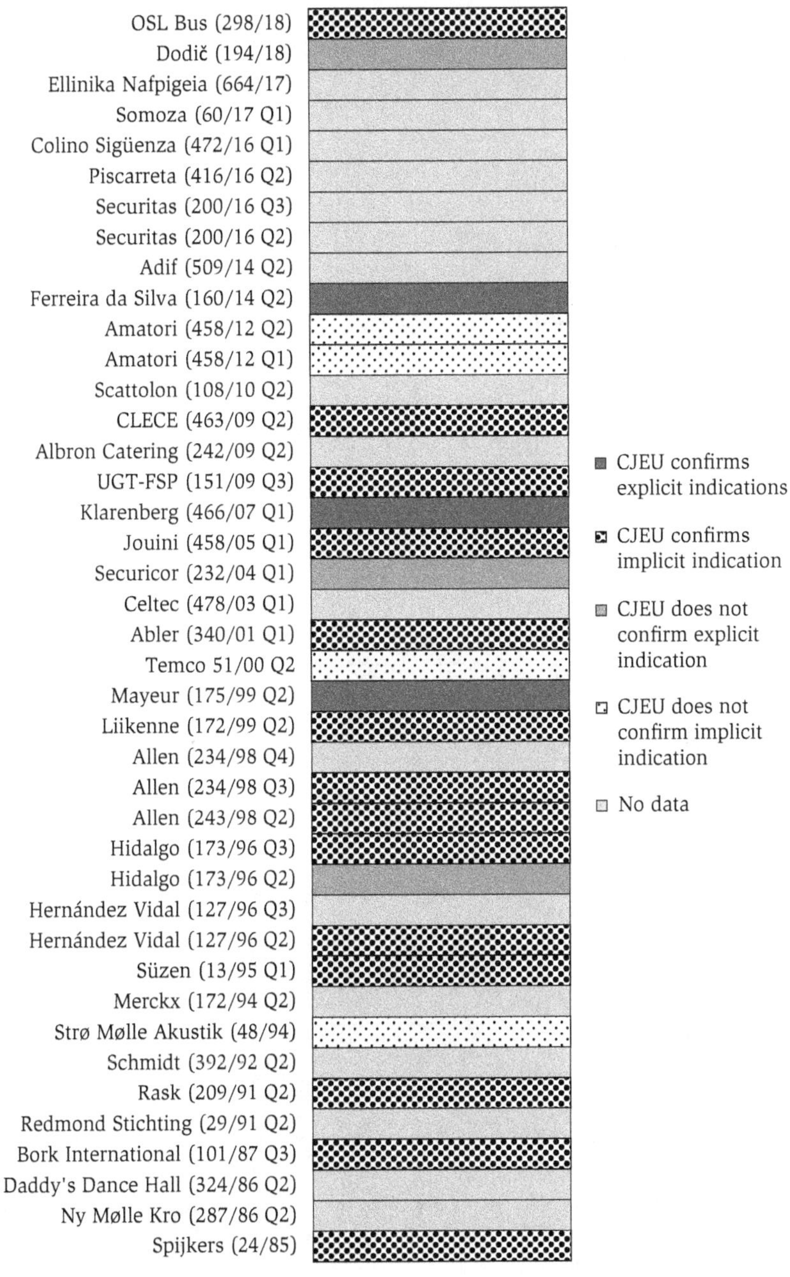

Figure 34 Type of National Court (Transfer of a Business)

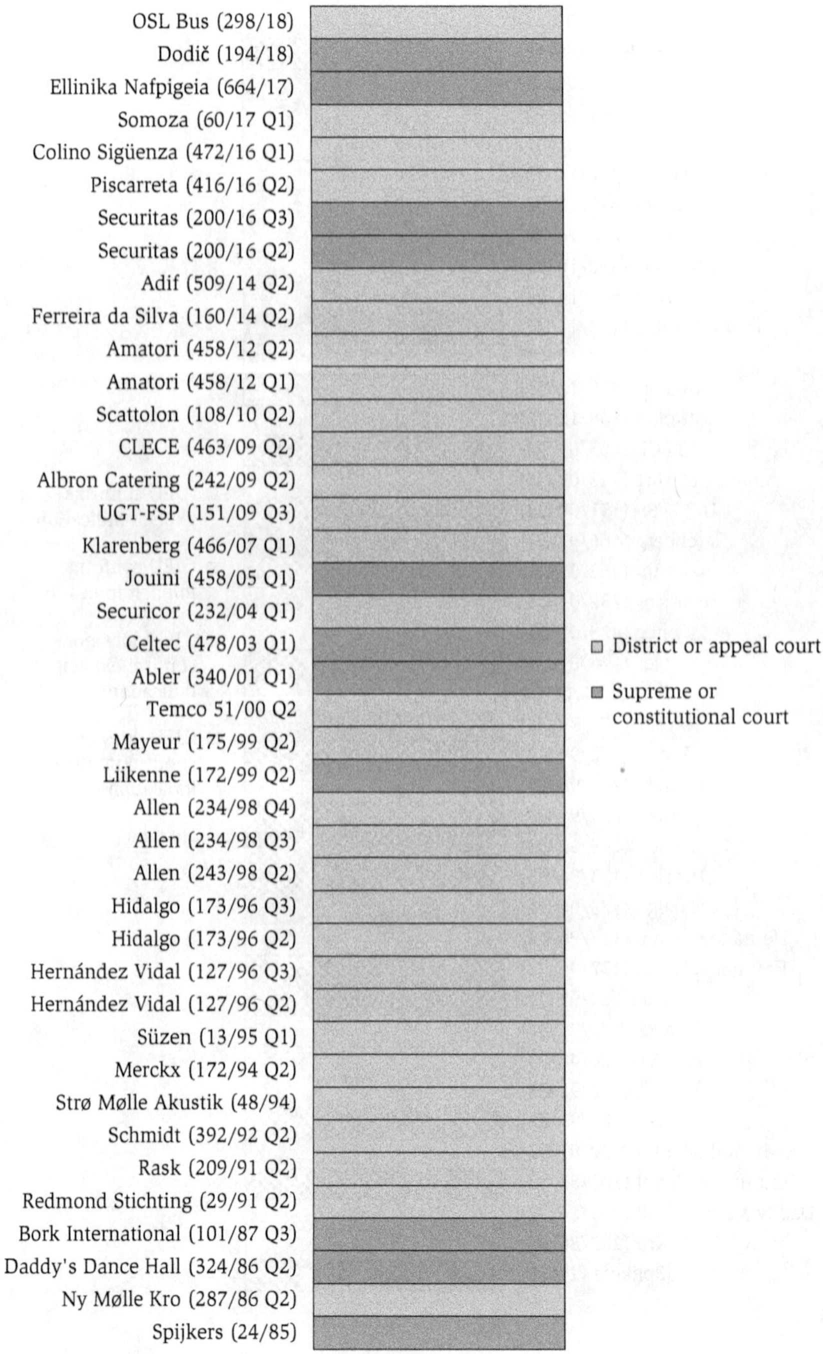

Figure 35 Convergence Between CJEU and the Preemptive Opinion of the Referring Judge (Workers' Rights)

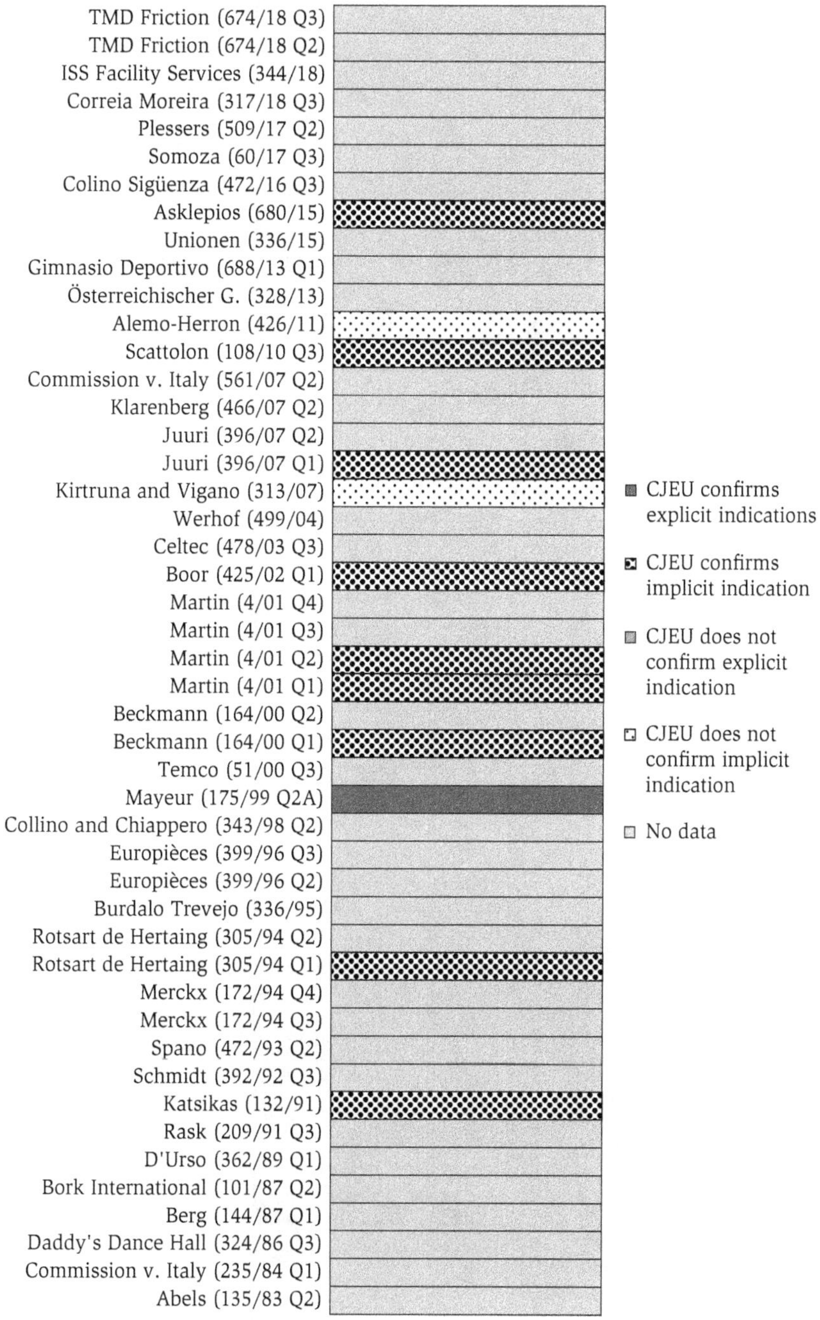

Figure 36 Type of National Court (Workers' Rights)

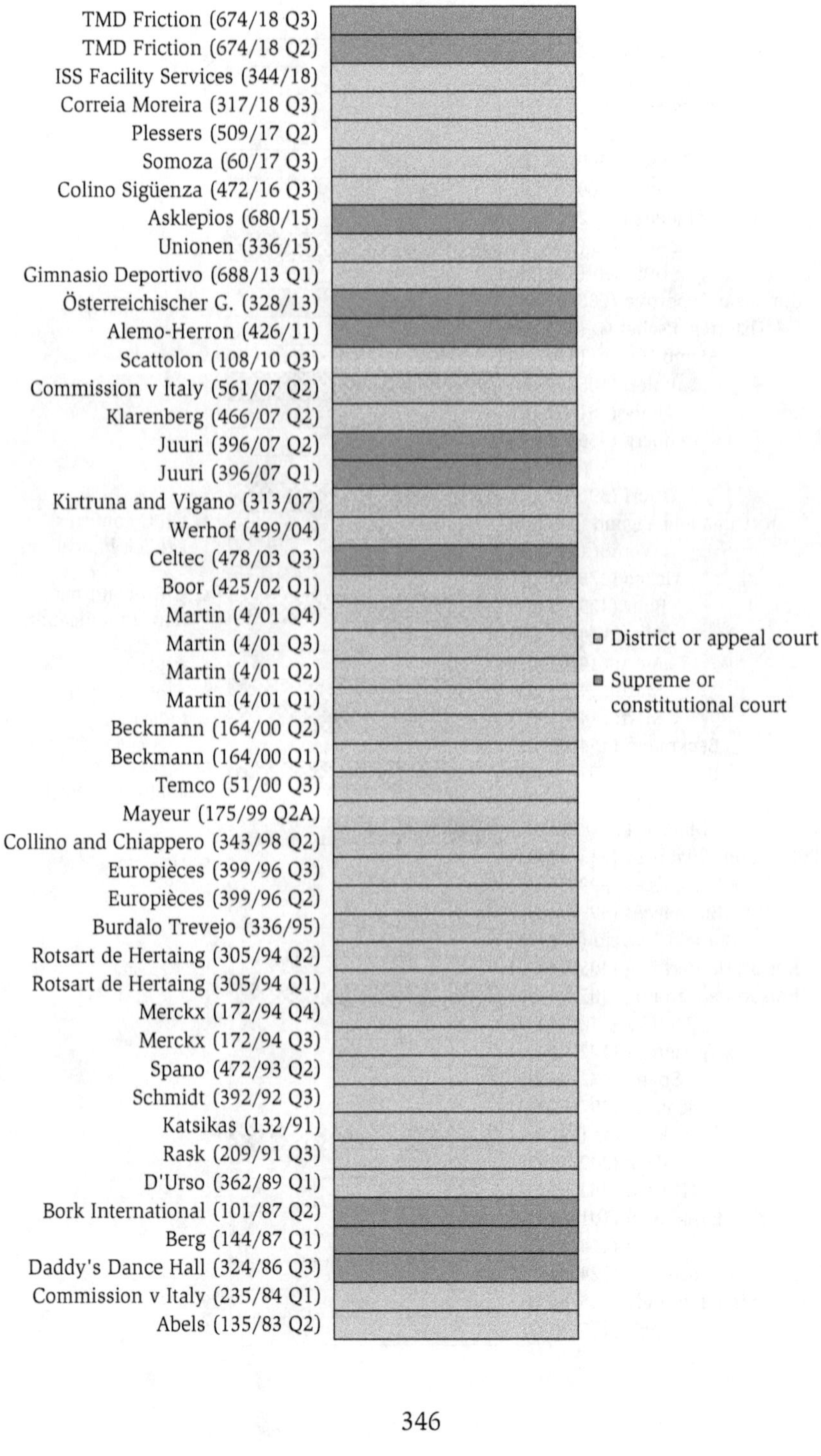

Figure 37 The CJEU's Approach to National Case Law (Legal Transfer)

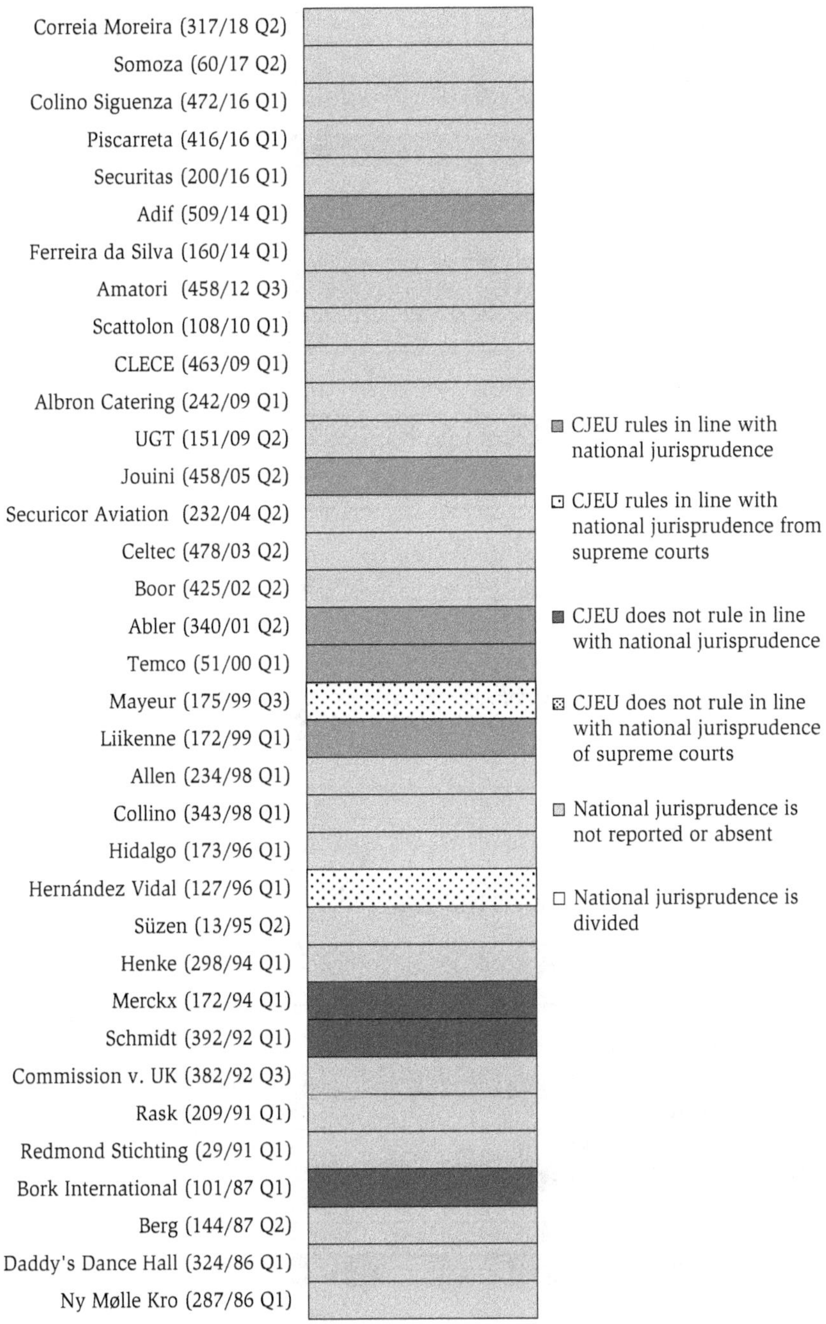

Figure 38 The CJEU's Approach to National Case Law (Transfer of a Business)

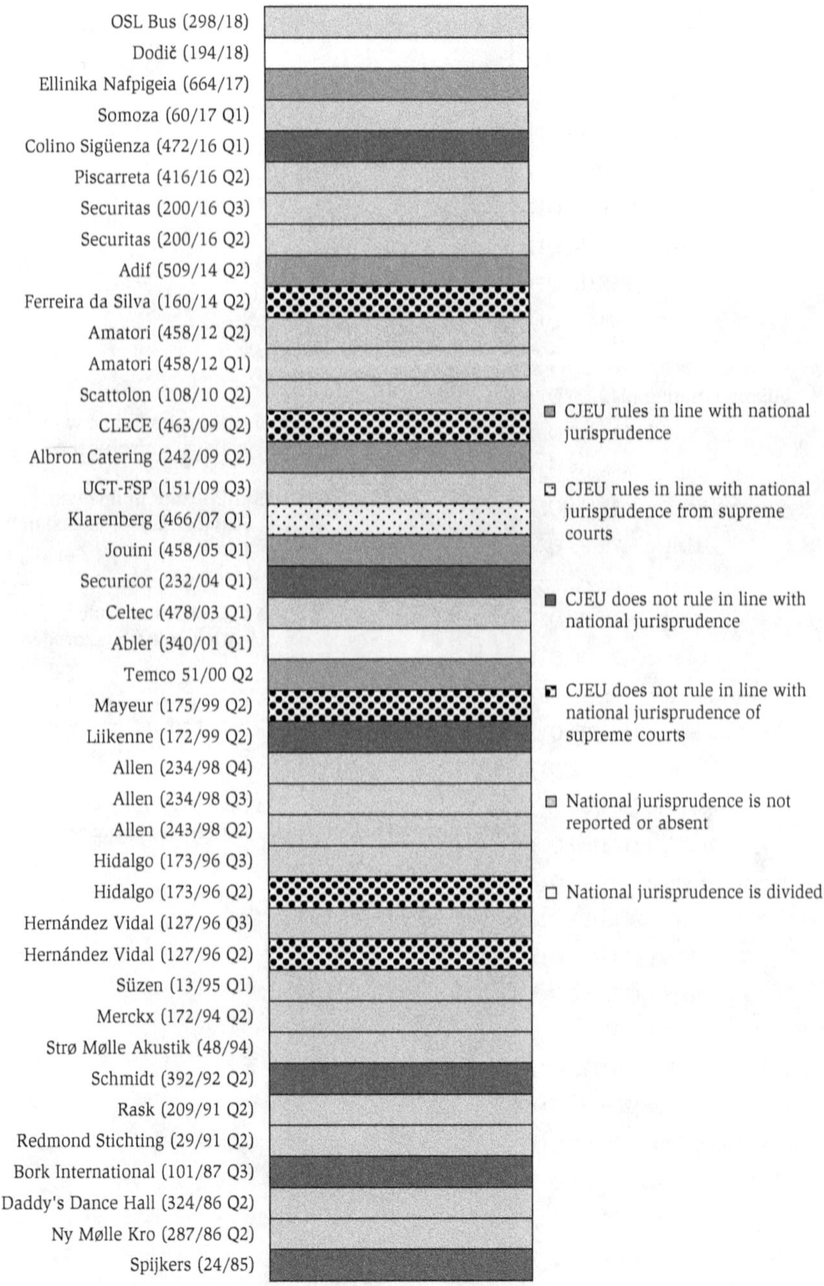

Figure 39 The CJEU's Approach to National Case Law (Workers' Rights)

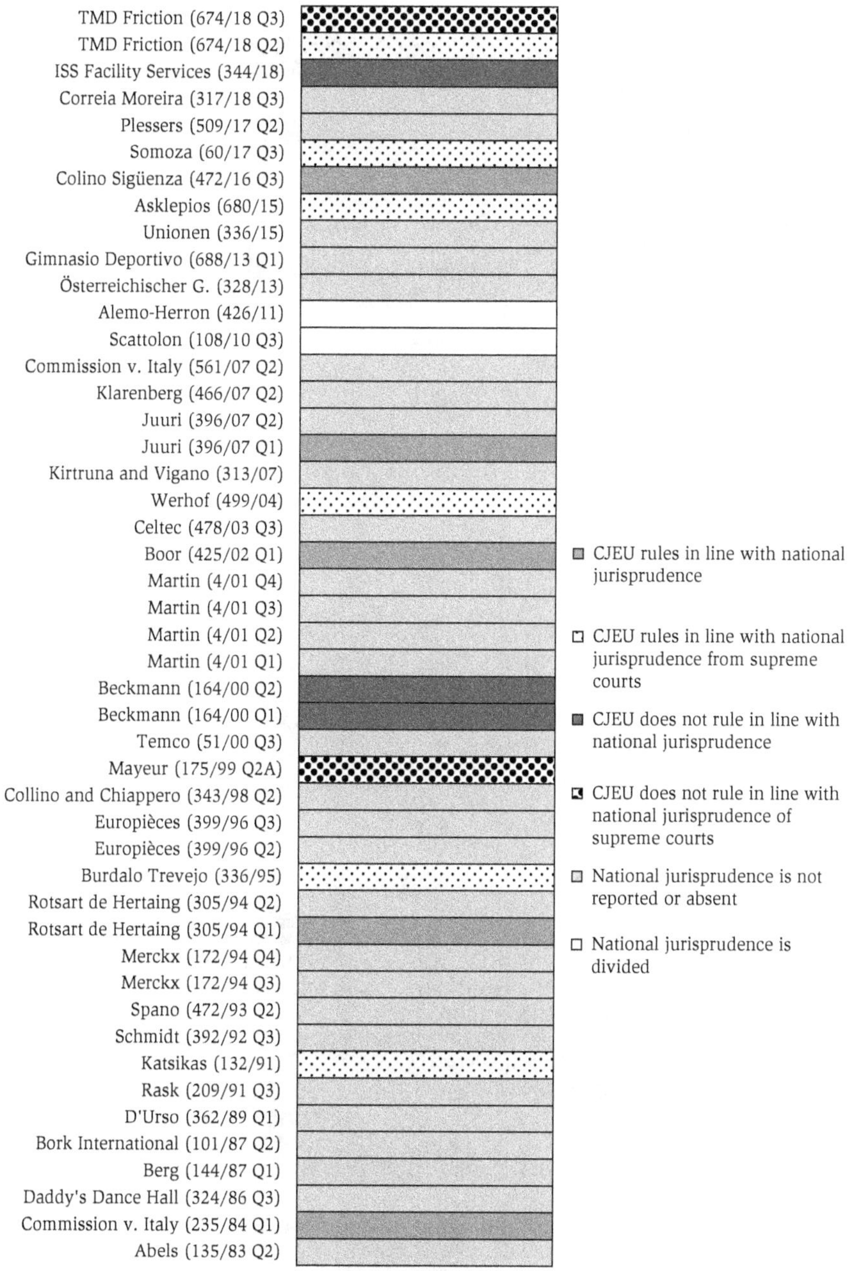

Figure 40 Convergence Between the CJEU Reasoning and the Opinion of the Advocate General (Legal Transfer)

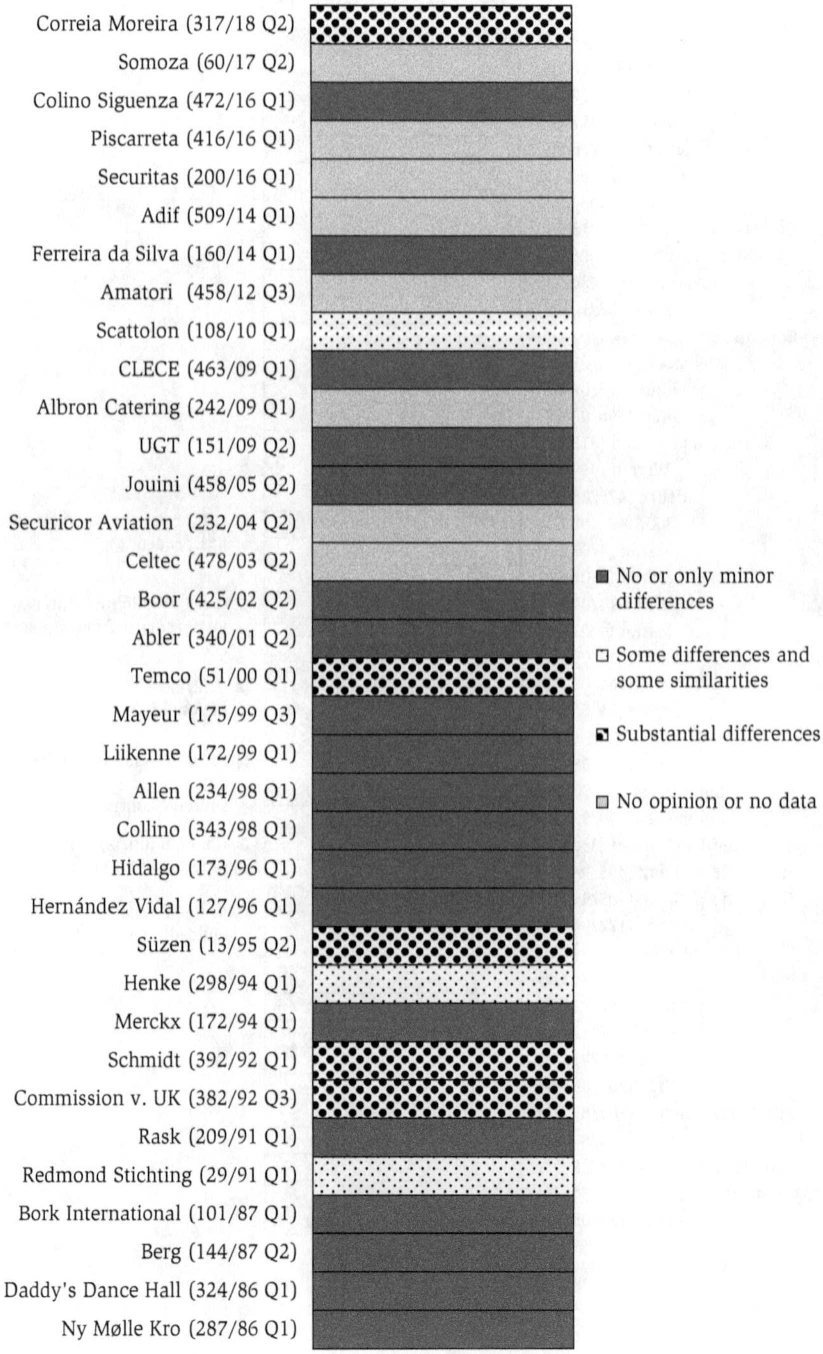

Figure 41 Convergence Between the CJEU Reasoning and the Opinion of the Advocate General (Transfer of a Business)

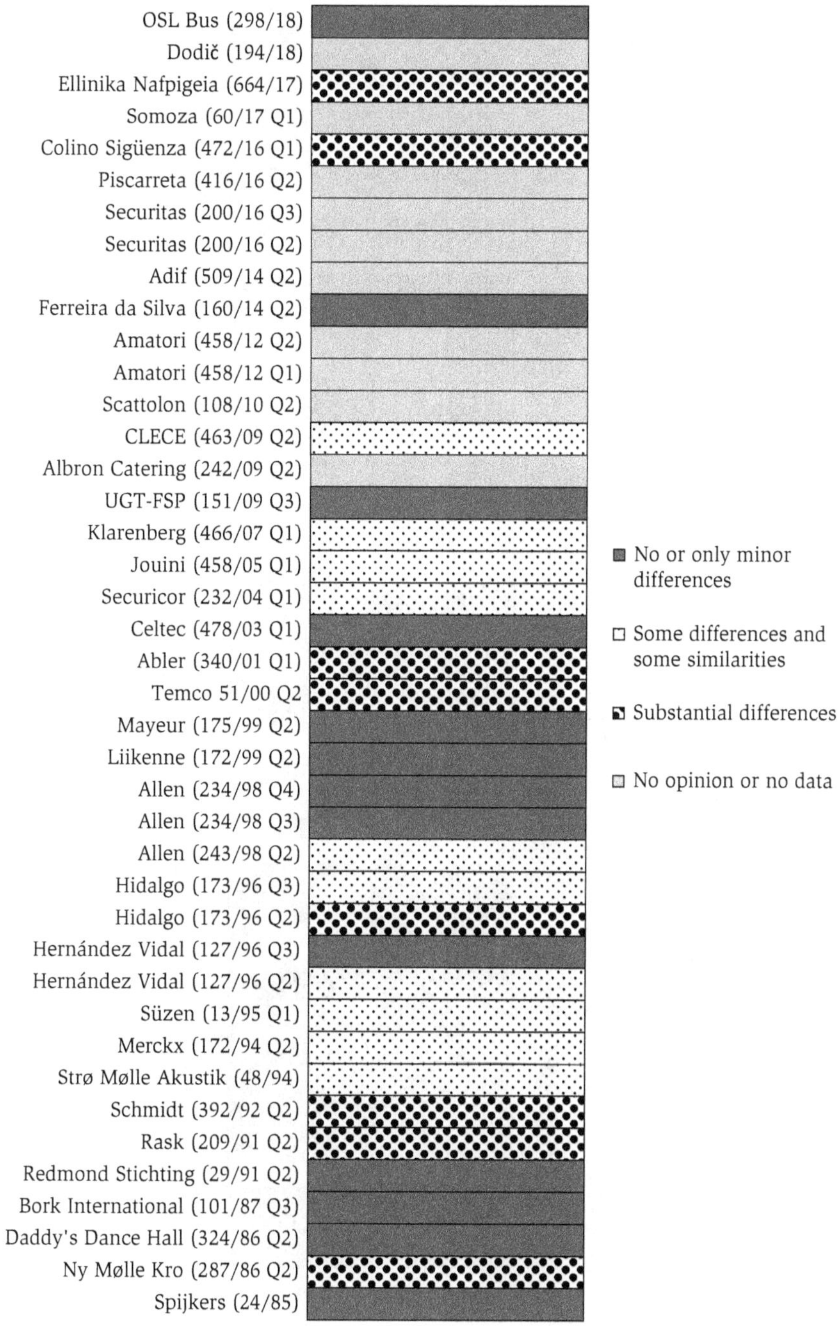

Figure 42 Convergence Between the CJEU Reasoning and the Opinion of the Advocate General (Workers' Rights)

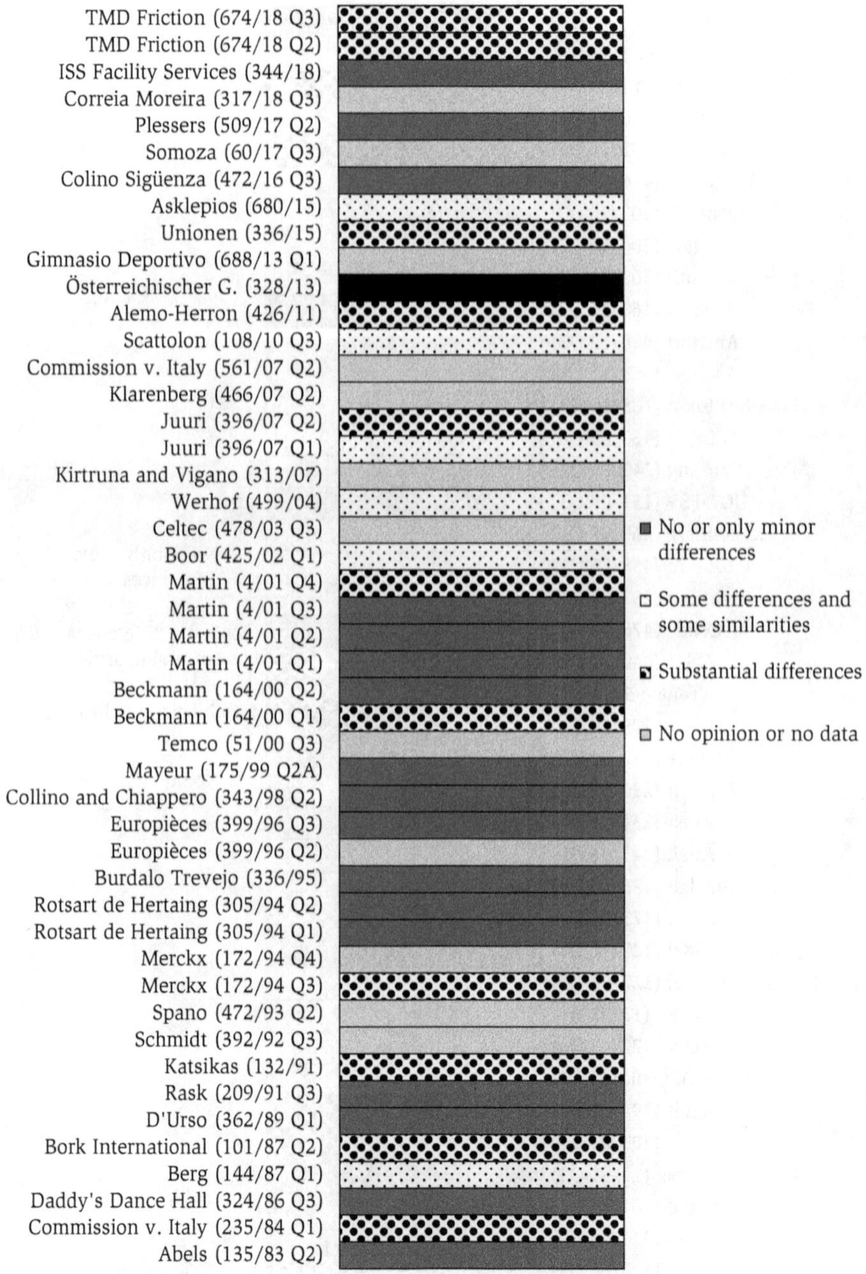

Table 8 Judge Rapporteur (Transfer of a Business)

Case	*Judge Rapporteur*
Schmidt (C-392/92)	F. Grévisse
Strø Mølle Akustik (C-48/94)	J.C. Moitinho de Almeida
Merckx (C-172/94)	F. Mancini
Süzen (C-13/95)	J.P. Puissochet
Hernández Vidal (C-127/96)	J.P. Puissochet
Hidalgo (C-173/96)	J.P. Puissochet
Allen (C-234/98)	J.P. Puissochet
Liikenne (C-172/99)	J.P. Puissochet
Mayeur (C-175/99)	J.C. Moitinho de Almeida
Temco (C-51/00)	J.P. Puissochet
Abler (C-340/01)	J.P. Puissochet
Celtec (C-478/03)	K. Lenaerts
Securicor (C-232/04)	A. Barthet
Jouini (C-458/05)	J. Malenovsky
Klarenberg (C-466/07)	J. Malenovsky
UGT-FSP (C-151/09)	J. Malenovsky
Albron Catering (C-242/09)	J. Malenovsky
CLECE (C-463/09)	J. Malenovsky
Scattolon (C-108/10)	M. Ilesic
Amatori (C-458/12)	J. Malenovsky
Ferreira da Silva (C-160/14)	R. Silva De Lapuerta
Adif (C-509/14)	F. Biltgen
Securitas (C-200/16)	A. Barthet
Piscarreta (C-416/16)	J. Malenovsky
Colino Sigüenza (C-472/16)	A. Barthet
Somoza (C-60/17)	A. Barthet
Ellinika Nafpigeia (C-664/17)	J. Malenovsky
Dodič (C-194/18)	N. Picarra
OSL Bus (C-298/18)	N. Picarra

Note: For the most dated cases the name of the judge rapporteur was not indicated in the judgment.

Table 9 Judge Rapporteur (Workers' Rights)

Case	*Judge Rapporteur*
Schmidt (C-392/92)	F. Grévisse
Spano (C-472/93)	J.P. Puissochet
Merckx (C-172/94)	F. Mancini
Rotsart de Hertaing (C-305/94)	F. Mancini
Burdalo Trevejo (C-336/95)	J.P. Puissochet
Europièces (C-399/96)	F. Mancini

Case	*Judge Rapporteur*
Collino and Chiappero (C-343/98)	J.P. Puissochet
Mayeur (C-175/99)	J.C. Moitinho de Almeida
Temco (C-51/00)	J.P. Puissochet
Beckmann (C-164/00)	J.P. Puissochet
Martin (C-4/01)	J.P. Puissochet
Boor (C-425/02)	N. Colneric
Celtec (C-478/03)	K. Lenaerts
Werhof (C-499/04)	J. Malenovksy
Kirtruna and Vigano (C-313/07)	J. Malenovksy
Juuri (C-396/07)	J. Malenovksy
Klarenberg (C-466/07)	J. Malenovksy
Commission v. Italy (C-561/07)	L. Bay Larsen
Scattolon (C-108/10)	M. Ilesic
Alemo-Herron (C-426/11)	J. Malenovksy
Österreichischer G. (C-328/13)	A. Prechal
Gimnasio Deportivo (C-688/13)	F. Biltgen
Unionen (C-336/15)	E. Levits
Asklepios (C-680/15)	J. Malenovksy
Colino Sigüenza (C-472/16)	A. Barthet
Somoza (C-60/17)	A. Barthet
Plessers (C-509/17)	J. Malenovksy
Correia Moreira (C-317/18)	J. Malenovksy
ISS Facility Services (C-344/18)	N. Picarra
TMD Friction (C-674/18)	E. Juhnasz

Note: For the most dated cases the name of the judge rapporteur was not indicated in the judgment.

Bibliography

Adler S., 'The Role of Judges in the Implementation of Social Policies', The International Journal of Comparative Labour Law and Industrial Relations, 18(4), 2002, pp. 341-376

Ahlberg K. & Bruun N. (eds), *The New Foundations of Labour Law*, Peter Lang, Frankfurt am Main, 2017

Albert M., *Capitalism vs. Capitalism: How America's Obsession with Individual Achievement and Short-Term Profit Has Led It to the Brink of Collapse*, Four Wall Eight Windows, New York, 1993

Alter K.J., 'Who Are the "Masters of the Treaty"? European Governments and the European Court of Justice', International Organization, 52(1), 1998, pp. 121-147

Alter K., 'Explaining National Court Acceptance of European Court Jurisprudence: A Critical Evaluation of Theories of Legal Integration' in A.M. Slaughter, A. Stone Sweet & J. Weiler (eds), *The European Court and National Court – Doctrine and Jurisprudence: Legal Change in Its Social Context*, Hart Publishing, Oxford, 1998, pp. 227-252

Alter K.J., *The European Court's Political Power: Selected Essays*, Oxford University Press, Oxford, 2009

Alter K., 'The European Court's Political Power: The Emergence of an Authoritative International Court in the European Union' in K. Alter (ed.), *The European Court's Political Power – Selected Essays*, Oxford University Press, Oxford, 2009, pp. 92-109

Anderman S., 'Termination of Employment: Whose Property Rights?' in C. Barnard, S. Deakin & G.S. Morris (eds), *The Future of Labour Law: Liber Amicorum Bob Hepple QC*, Hart Publishing, Portland, Oregon, 2004, pp. 101-128

Anta C.G., 'The Europe of Jean Monnet: The Road to Functionalism', History of European Ideas, 47(5), 2021, pp. 773-784

Antonaki I., 'Collective Redundancies in Greece: AGET Iraklis', Common Market Law Review, 54(5), 2017, pp. 1513-1534

Aranguiz A. & Garben S., 'Combating Income Inequality in the EU: A Legal Assessment of a Potential EU Minimum Wage Directive', European Law Review, 46(2), 2021, pp. 156-174

Arbadjieva K., 'Time to Close the Gender Pay Gap: The Need for an EU Directive on Pay Transparency', Policy Brief, 2, ETUI, Brussels, 2021

Arbadjieva K., 'Reshaping the Work-Life Balance Directive with Covid-19 Lessons in Mind', Working Paper, 1, ETUI, Brussels, 2022

Armstrong K.A., 'Mutual Recognition' in C. Barnard & J. Scott (eds), *The Law of the Single European Market: Unpacking the Premises*, Hart Publishing, Oxford, 2002, pp. 225-269

Arnull A., 'Judicial Activism and the European Court of Justice: How Should Academics Respond?' in B. de Witte, B. Muir & E. Dawson (eds), *Judicial Activism at the European Court of Justice*, Edward Elgar Publishing, Cheltenham, 2013, pp. 211-233

Azoulai L., 'The Court of Justice and the Social Market Economy: The Emergence of an Ideal and the Conditions for its Realization', Common Market Law Review, 45, 2008, pp. 1335-1356

Barak A., 'The Nature of Judicial Discretion and Its Significance for the Administration of Justice' in O. Wiklund (ed.), *Judicial Discretion in European Perspective*, Norstedts Juridik, Stockholm, 2003, pp. 11-28

Bardutzky S. & Fahey E., 'The Subjects and Objects of EU Law: Exploring a Research Platform' in S. Bardutzky & E. Fahey (eds), *Framing the Subjects and Objects of Contemporary EU Law*, Edward Elgar Publishing, Cheltenham, 2017, pp. 1-30

Barnard C. & Deakin S., 'Market Access and Regulatory Competition', Jean Monnet Working Paper 9/01, 2001

Barnard C. & Scott J. (eds), *The Law of the Single European Market: Unpacking the Premises*, Hart Publishing, Oxford, 2002

Barnard C., 'The Future of Equality Law: Equality and Beyond' in C. Barnard, S. Deakin & G.S. Morris (eds), *The Future of Labour Law: Liber Amicorum Bob Hepple QC*, Hart Publishing, Portland, Oregon, 2004, pp. 213-228

Barnard C., 'Social Dumping or Dumping Socialism', Cambridge Law Journal, 67, 2008, pp. 262-280

Barnard C., 'Internal Market v Labour Market: A Brief History' in M. de Vos (ed.), *European Union Internal Market and Labour Law: Friends or Foes?*, Intersentia, Cambridge, 2009, pp. 19-45

Barnard C., *EU Employment Law*, Oxford University Press, Oxford, 2012

Barnard C., 'EU Employment law and the European Social Model: The Past, the Present and the Future', Current Legal Problems, 67, 2014, pp. 199-237

Barnard C., 'The Calm after the Storm: Time to Reflect on EU (Labour) Law Scholarship Following the Decisions in Viking and Laval' in A. Bogg, C. Costello & A.C.L. Davies (eds), *Research Handbook on EU Labour Law*, Edward Elgar Publishing, Cheltenham, 2016, pp. 337-362

Barsotti V., et al., *Italian Constitutional Justice in Global Context*, Oxford University Press, Oxford, 2016

Bartl M. & Leone C., 'Minimum Harmonisation after Alemo-Herron: The Janus Face of the EU Fundamental Rights Review', European Constitutional Law Review, 11(1), 2015, pp. 140-154

Basilico M., *Trasferimento d'azienda e diritto dell'Unione. Le questioni aperte*, C.S.M., Roma, 2010

Bavaro V. & Pietrogiovanni V., 'A Hypothesis on the Economic Nature of Labour Law: The Collective Labour Freedoms', European Labour Law Journal, 9(3), 2018, pp. 263-286

Beblavý M., 'Protecting Employment in the Time of Coronavirus: What Is the EU's €100 Billion Going to Buy?', Policy Insights, 8, CEPS, Brussels, 2020

Bednarowicz B., 'Delivering on the European Pillar of Social Rights: The New Directive on Transparent and Predictable Working Conditions in the European Union', Industrial Law Journal, 48(4), 2019, pp. 604-623

Bekker S., 'Flexicurity in the European Semester: Still a Relevant Policy Concept?', Journal of European Public Policy, 25(2), 2018, pp. 175-192

Beltzer R.M., 'The Transfer of Undertakings and the Importance of Taking Over Personnel: A Vicious Circle', International Journal of Comparative Labour Law and Industrial Relations, 23(1), 2007, pp. 139-155

Bengoetxea J., 'The Scope for Discretion, Coherence and Citizenship' in O. Wiklund (ed.), *Judicial Discretion in European Perspective*, Norstedts Juridik, Stockholm, 2003, pp. 48-74

Bennett J. & Belgrave S.L., 'Taking Stock of Rygaard', Public Procurement Law Review, 1, 1996, pp. 16-25

Bercusson B., 'The Conceptualization of European Labour Law', Industrial Law Journal, 24(1), 1995, pp. 3-18

Bercusson B., 'Episodes on the Path Towards the European Social Model: The EU Charter of Fundamental Rights and the Convention on the Future of Europe' in C. Barnard, S. Deakin & G.S. Morris (eds), *The Future of Labour Law. Liber Amicorum Bob Hepple QC*, Hart Publishing, Portland, Oregon, 2004, pp. 179-199

Bercusson B., *European Labour Law*, Cambridge University Press, Leiden, 2009

Biagioni G., 'Norme processuali e principio di effettività: ulteriori sviluppi nella giurisprudenza comunitaria', Il diritto dell'Unione Europea, 9(1), 2004, pp. 201-212

Biernat S. & Łętowska E., 'This Was Not Just Another Ultra Vires Judgment!', Verfassungsblog, 27 October 2021, https://verfassungsblog.de/this-was-not-just-another-ultra-vires-judgment/

Blackham A., Kullman M. & Zbyszewska A., 'Introduction' in A. Blackham, M. Kullmann & A. Zbyszewska (eds), *Theorising Labour Law in a Changing World: Towards Inclusive Labour Law*, Bloomsbury Publishing, Oxford, 2019, pp. 1-16

Blanke T., 'The Principle of Subsidiarity in the Lisbon Treaty' in N. Bruun, K. Lörcher & I. Schömann (eds), *The Lisbon Treaty and Social Europe*, Hart Publishing, Oxford and Portland, Oregon, 2012, pp. 235-260

Blanpain R., *Institutional Changes and European Social Policies after the Treaty of Amsterdam*, Kluwer Law International, The Hague, 1998

Blanpain R., 'The End of Labour Law', Bulletin of Comparative Labour Law, 65, 2008, pp. 3-13

Blanpain R., 'Individual Labour Law' in *European Labour Law*, Kluwer Law International, The Hague, 2008, pp. 269-696

Blanpain R., *European Labour Law*, Kluwer Law International, The Hague, 2008

Blanpain R., 'The European Social Model (ESM): Myth or Reality?', European Labour Law Journal, 2(2), 2011, pp. 142-149

Bobek M., 'Landtová, Holubec, and the Problem of an Uncooperative Court: Implications for the Preliminary Rulings Procedure', European Constitutional Law Review, 10, 2014, pp. 54-89

Bobic A. & M. Dawson, 'Making Sense of the "Incomprehensible": The PSPP Judgment of the German Federal Constitutional Court', Common Market Law Review, 57, 2020, pp. 1953-1998

Bofinger P., 'The "Frugal Four" Should Save the European Project', Social Europe, 4 May 2020, https://socialeurope.eu/the-frugal-four-should-save-the-european-project

Bogg A., 'Beyond Neo-Liberalism: The Trade Union Act 2016 and the Authoritarian State', Industrial Law Journal, 45(3), 2016, pp. 299-336

Bogg A., Costello C. & Davies A.C.L. (eds), *Research Handbook on EU Labour Law*, Edward Elgar Publishing, Cheltenham, 2016

Bogg A., 'Brexit, Labour Law and the Twilight of Liberalism' in K. Ahlberg & N. Bruun (eds), *The New Foundations of Labour Law*, Peter Lang, Frankfurt am Main, 2017

Boitani A. & Tamborini R., 'Eurobonds and European Citizenship', Briefing, Friedrich Ebert Stiftung, 2020

Bonciu F., 'The European Pillar of Social Rights: Too Little, Too Late?', Romanian Journal of European Affairs, 18(1), 2018, pp. 60-70

Bonelli M., 'The Taricco Saga and the Consolidation of Judicial Dialogue in the European Union: CJEU, C-105/14 Ivo Taricco and others, ECLI:EU:C:2015:555; and C-42/17 M.A.S., M.B., ECLI:EU:C:2017:936 Italian Constitutional Court, Order no. 24/2017', Maastricht Journal of European and Comparative Law, 25(3), 2018, pp. 357-373

Bonica A. & Sen M., 'Estimating Judicial Ideology', The Journal of Economic Perspectives, 35(1), 2021, pp. 97-118

Börner S., 'Is the Coronoavirus Going to Reshape the European Welfare State?' in Friedrich Ebert Stiftung (ed.), *The Coronavirus Crisis and the Welfare State*, Social Europe Publishing, Berlin, 2021, pp. 20-27

Bourn C., 'When Does the Transfer of a Service Contract Constitute the Transfer of an Undertaking?', European Law Review, 23(1), 1998, pp. 59-64

Brameshuber E., 'Balancing vs. Preservation of Rights under the Acquired Rights Directive', Industrial Law Journal, 45(3), 2016, pp. 443-454

Bribosia E., et al., 'e-Nact Handbook, Module 2: The Charter's Social and Non-discrimination Provisions in the Employment Field', E-learning National Active Charter Training, EUI, 2018

Bribosia H., 'Report on Belgium' in A.M. Slaughter, A. Stone Sweet & J. Weiler (eds), *The European Court and National Court – Doctrine and Jurisprudence: Legal Change in Its Social Context*, Hart Publishing, Oxford, 1998, pp. 1-40

Brown W. & Oxenbridge S., 'Trade Unions and Collective Bargaining: Law and the Future of Collectivism' in C. Barnard, S. Deakin & G.S. Morris (eds), *The Future of Labour Law: Liber Amicorum Bob Hepple QC*, Hart Publishing, Portland, Oregon, 2004, pp. 63-77

Bruggeman F., Gazier B. & Paucard D., 'Affronter les restructurations d'entreprise en Europe, propositions pour une démarche unifiée', La Revue de l'IRES, 72(1), 2012, pp. 29-64

Bruun N., 'Employees' Participation Rights and Business Restructuring', European Labour Law Journal, 2(1), 2011, pp. 27-47

Bruun N., 'Economic Governance of the EU Crisis and Its Social Policy Implications' in N. Bruun, K. Lörcher & I. Schömann (eds), *The Lisbon Treaty and Social Europe*, Hart Publishing, Oxford and Portland, Oregon, 2012, pp. 261-275

Bruun N. & Hepple B.A., 'Economic Policy and Labour Law' in B.A. Hepple & B. Veneziani (eds), *The Transformation of Labour Law in Europe: A Comparative Study of 15 Countries, 1945-2004*, Hart Publishing, Oxford, 2009, pp. 31-57

Bruun N. & Malmberg J., 'Lex Laval: Collective Actions and Posted Work in Sweden' in R. Blanpain, F. Hendrickx, S. Bekker & A.T.J.M. Jacobs (eds), *Labour Law Between Change and Tradition: Liber Amicorum Antoine Jacobs*, Kluwer Law International, Alphen aan den Rijn, 2011

Bruun N., 'The Old and New Foundations of Labour Law' in K. Ahlberg & N. Bruun (eds), *The New Foundations of Labour Law*, Peter Lang, Frankfurt am Main, 2017, pp. 17-37

Bulletin of the European Communities, 'The First Milestone: Common Market Reaching End of First Stage', 50, 1961

Bulterman M., Wissels C., 'Strategies Developed By–And Between–National Governments to Interact with the ECJ' in B. de Witte, B. Muir & E. Dawson (eds), *Judicial Activism at the European Court of Justice*, Edward Elgar Publishing, Cheltenham, 2013, pp. 264-278

Burley A.-M. & Mattli W., 'Europe Before the Court: A Political Theory of Legal Integration', International Organization, 47(1), 1993, pp. 41-76

Burroni L. & Keune M., 'Flexicurity: A Conceptual Critique', European Journal of Industrial Relations, 17(1), 2011, pp. 75-91

Ćapeta T., 'Ideology and Legal Reasoning at the European Court of Justice' in E. Perisin & S. Rodin (eds), *The Transformation or Reconstitution of Europe: The Critical Legal Studies Perspective on the Role of the Courts in the European Union*, Hart Publishing, Oxford, 2018, pp. 89-120

Ćapeta T., 'The Weiss/PSPP Case and the Future of Constitutional Pluralism in the EU', SSRN Electronic Journal, 2020

Cartabia M., 'The Italian Constitutional Court and the Relationship Between the Italian Legal System and the European Union' in A.M. Slaughter, A. Stone Sweet & J.

Weiler (eds), *The European Court and National Court – Doctrine and Jurisprudence: Legal Change in Its Social Context*, Hart Publishing, Oxford, 1998, pp. 133-144

Cartabia M., '"Unita nella diversità": il rapporto tra la Costituzione europea e le costituzioni nazionali' in F. Donati & G. Morbidelli (eds), *Una costituzione per l'Unione europea*, Giappichelli, Torino, 2006

Cartabia M., 'Europe and Rights: Taking Dialogue Seriously', European Constitutional Law Review, 5, 2009, pp. 5-31

Cartabia M., 'Europe as a Space of Constitutional Interdependence: New Questions about the Preliminary Ruling', German Law Journal, 16(6), 2015, pp. 1791-1796

Carvalho Martins D., 'Transfer of an Economic Unit: Requirements, Effects and Recent CJEU Ruling', European Labour Law Journal, 9(1), 2018, pp. 24-49

Catalano S., 'Rinvio pregiudiziale nei casi di doppia pregiudizialità. Osservazioni a margine dell'opportuna scelta compiuta con l'ordinanza n. 117 del 2019 della Corte costituzionale', Osservatorio Costituzionale, 4, 2019, pp. 1-10

Cella G.P., 'Il Cammino Del Pluralismo: Giugni E Le Relazioni Industriali', Giornale Di Diritto Del Lavoro E Di Relazioni Industriali, Xxix(114), 2007, pp. 273-291

Chalmers D., Hadijemmanuil C. & Monti G., *European Union Law*, Cambridge University Press, Cambridge, 2006

Cichowski R.A., *The European Court and Civil Society: Litigation, Mobilization and Governance; Themes in European Governance*, Cambridge University Press, Cambridge, 2007

Claes M., 'Luxembourg, Here We Come? Constitutional Courts and the Preliminary Reference Procedure', German Law Journal, 16(6), 2015, pp. 1331-1342

Clauwaert S., The Country-Specific Recommendations (CSRs) in the Social Field: An Overview and Initial Comparison, ETUI, Brussels, 2012

Clauwaert S. & Schömann I., 'The Crisis and National Labour Law Reforms: A Mapping Exercise', Working Paper, 4, ETUI, Brussels, 2012

Clauwaert S., The Country-Specific Recommendations (CSRs) in the Social Field: An Overview and Initial Comparison, ETUI, Brussels, 2018

Clauwaert S., The Country-Specific Recommendations (CSRs) in the Social Field: An Overview and Initial Comparison, ETUI, Brussels, 2019

Collins D., *Social Policy of the European Economic Community*, Halsted Press, New York, 1975

Collins H., Davies P. & Rideout R. (eds), *Legal Regulation of the Employment Relation*, Kluwer Law International, London, 2000

Collins H., 'Regulating the Employment Relation for Competitiveness', Industrial Law Journal, 30(1), 2001, pp. 17-48

Collins H., 'Theories of Rights as Justifications for Labour Law' in G. Davidov & B. Langille (eds), *The Idea of Labour Law*, Oxford University Press, Oxford, 2011, pp. 135-154

Conant L.J., *Justice Contained: Law and Politics in the European Union*, Cornell University Press, Ithaca, New York, 2018

Conway G., 'Conflicts of Competence Norm in EU Law and the Legal Reasoning of the ECJ', German Law Journal, 11(9), 2010, pp. 966-1005

Conway G., *The Limits of Legal Reasoning and the European Court of Justice*, Cambridge University Press, Cambridge, 2012

Cosio R. & Foglia R., *Il Diritto del Lavoro nell'Unione Europea*, Giuffrè, Milano, 2011

Costamagna F., 'National Social Spaces as Adjustment Variables in the EMU: A Critical Legal Appraisal', European Law Journal, 23(2), 2018, pp. 163-190

Countouris N. & Koukiadaki A., 'The Glass Half Full: Collective Redundancies, Public Interest, and the (Unfulfilled) Potential of Europe's "Highly Competitive Social Market Economy"', Giornale di Diritto del Lavoro e di Relazioni Industriali, 153(1), 2017, pp. 193-201

Countouris N. & De Stefano V., 'The Labour Law Framework: Self-Employed and Their Right to Bargain Collectively' in B. Waas & C. Hiessl (eds), *Collective Bargaining for Self-Employed Workers in Europe*, Wolters Kluwer, Alphen aan den Rijn, 2021, pp. 3-19

Court of Justice of the European Union, Annual Report 2019: Judicial Activity, CJEU Communications Directorate, Publications and Electronic Media Unit, Luxember, 2020

Court of Justice of the European Union, Annual Report 2020: The Year in Review, CJEU Communications Directorate, Publications and Electronic Media Unit, Luxembourg, 2021

Craig P., 'Francovich, Remedies and the Scope of Damages Liability', Law Quarterly Review, 109, 1993, pp. 595-621

Craig P.P., 'Report on the United Kingdom' in A.M. Slaughter, A. Stone Sweet & J. Weiler (eds), *The European Court and National Court – Doctrine and Jurisprudence: Legal Change in Its Social Context*, Hart Publishing, Oxford, 1998, pp. 195-224

Creel J., Leron N. & Ragot X., 'Embedding the Recovery and Resilience Facility into the European Semester', Policy Brief, 14, ETUI, Brussels, 2021

Creighton B., 'The Future of Labour Law: Is There a Role for International Labour Standards?' in C. Barnard, S. Deakin & G.S. Morris (eds), *The Future of Labour Law: Liber Amicorum Bob Hepple QC*, Hart Publishing, Portland, Oregon, 2004, pp. 253-273

Dale G. & El-Enany N., 'The Limits of Social Europe: EU Law and the Ordoliberal Agenda', German Law Journal, 14, 2013, pp. 613-649

Daly M., 'The Dynamics of European Union Social Policy' in N. Lendvai-Bainton (ed.), *Handbook of European Social Policy*, Edward Elgar Publishing, Cheltenham, 2017, pp. 93-107

Davidov G. & Langille B. (eds), *The Idea of Labour Law*, Oxford University Press, Oxford, 2011

Davidov G., *A Purposive Approach to Labour Law*, Oxford University Press, Oxford, 2016

Davies A.C.L., 'One Step Forward, Two Steps Back? The Viking and Laval Cases in the ECJ', Industrial Law Journal, 37(2), 2008, pp. 126-148

Davies A.C.L., Bogg A. & Costello C., 'The Role of the Court of Justice in Labour Law' in A. Bogg, C. Costello & A.C.L. Davies (eds), *Research Handbook on EU Labour Law*, Edward Elgar Publishing, Cheltenham, 2016, pp. 114-149

Davies P., 'Transfers of Undertakings: Preliminary Remarks' in S. Sciarra (ed.), *Labour Law in the Courts: National Judges and the European Court of Justice*, Hart Publishing, Oxford, 2001, pp. 131-144

Davies P. & Freedland M., 'Changing Perspectives upon the Employment Relationship in British Labour Law' in C. Barnard, S. Deakin & G.S. Morris (eds), *The Future of Labour Law: Liber Amicorum Bob Hepple QC*, Hart Publishing, Portland, Oregon, 2004, pp. 129-159

Davies P. & Freedland M., *Towards a Flexible Labour Market: Labour Legislation and Regulation since the 1990s*, Oxford University Press, Oxford, 2007

Dawson M., 'The Political Face of Judicial Activism: Europe's Law-Politics Imbalance' in B. de Witte, B. Muir & E. Dawson (eds), *Judicial Activism at the European Court of Justice*, Edward Elgar Publishing, Cheltenham, 2013, pp. 11-32

Dawson M., 'New Governance and the Displacement of Social Europe: The Case of the European Semester', European Constitutional Law Review, 14(1), 2018, pp. 191-209

De Groof S., 'The Scope of the Transfer of Undertaking Directive Further Enlarged Through the Heineken-Case', European Labour Law Journal, 1(4), 2010, pp. 508-512

De la Porte C. & Emmenegger P., 'The Court of Justice of the European Union and Fixed-Term Workers: Still Fixed, but at Least Equal', Working Paper, 1, ETUI, Brussels, 2016

De Luca Tamajo R., 'Flexicurity: Un Improbabile Ossimoro O Un'utile Mediazione?', Il Foro Italiano, 132(4), 2009, pp. 194-197

De Schutter O., 'The CFREU and Its Specific Role to Protect Fundamental Social Rights' in F. Dorssemont, K. Lörcher, S. Clauwaert & M. Schmitt (eds), *The Charter of Fundamental Rights of the European Union and the Employment Relation*, Hart Publishing, London, 2019, pp. 9-38

De Stefano V. & Aloisi A., 'European Commission Takes the Lead in Regulating Platform Work', Social Europe, 2021, https://socialeurope.eu/european-commission-takes-the-lead-in-regulating-platform-work

De Vos M., 'Flexicurity and the European Globalisation Adjustment Fund: Propaganda or Panacea?' in M. de Vos (ed.), *European Union Internal Market and Labour Law Friends or Foes?*, Intersentia, Antwerp, 2009, pp. 105-133

De Witte B., 'Sovereignty and European Integration: The Weight of Legal Tradition' in A.M. Slaughter, A. Stone Sweet & J. Weiler (eds), *The European Court and National Court – Doctrine and Jurisprudence: Legal Change in Its Social Context*, Hart Publishing, Oxford, 1998, pp. 277-305

De Witte B., Muir E. & Dawson M. (eds), *Judicial Activism at the European Court of Justice*, Edward Elgar Publishing, Cheltenham, 2013

Deakin S. & Reed H., 'The Contested Meaning of Labour Market Flexibility: Economic Theory and the Discourse of European Integration' in J. Shaw (ed.), Hart Publishing, London, 2000, pp. 71-100

Deakin S., 'Workers, Finance and Democracy' in C. Barnard, S. Deakin & G.S. Morris (eds), Hart Publishing, Portland, Oregon, 2004, pp. 79-100

Deakin S. & Wilkinson F., *The Law of the Labour Market: Industrialization, Employment, and Legal Evolution*, Oxford University Press, Oxford, 2005

Deakin S., 'Regulatory Competition after Laval', CYELS 2007-2008(10), 2008, pp. 581

Deakin S., 'The Contribution of Labour Law to Economic and Human Development' in G. Davidov & B. Langille (eds), *The Idea of Labour Law*, Oxford University Press, Oxford, 2011, pp. 156-175

Deakin S., 'The Lisbon Treaty, the Viking and Laval Judgments and the Financial Crisis: In Search of New Foundations for Europe's "Social Market Economy"' in N. Bruun, K. Lörcher & I. Schömann (eds), Hart Publishing, Oxford and Portland, Oregon, 2012, pp. 19-43

Deakin S., 'In Search of the EU's Social Constitution: Using the Charter to Recalibrate Social and Economic Rights' in F. Dorssemont, K. Lörcher, S. Clauwaert & M. Schmitt (eds), *The Charter of Fundamental Rights of the European Union and the Employment Relation*, Hart Publishing, London, 2019, pp. 53-80

Dederke J. & Naurin D., 'Friends of the Court? Why EU Governments File Observations Before the Court of Justice', European Journal of Political Research, 57, 2018, pp. 867-882

Degryse C., 'The New European Economic Governance', Working Paper, 14, ETUI, Brussels, 2012

Degryse C., Jepsen M. & Pochet P., 'The Eurocrisis and Its Impact on National and European Social Policies', Working Paper, 5, ETUI, Brussels, 2013

Delivorias A., 'The "General Escape Clause" Within the Stability and Growth Pact: Fiscal Flexibility for Severe Economic Shocks', Briefing, Think Tank European Parliament, Brussels, 27 March 2020

Delivorias A., 'Introduction to the Fiscal Framework of the EU: The Maastricht Treaty, the Treaty on Stability, Coordination and Governance, and the Stability and Growth Pact', Study, European Parliamentary Research Service, Brussels, 2021

Di Federico G., 'Fundamental Rights in the EU: Legal Pluarlism and Multi-level Protection after the Lisbon Treaty' in *The EU Charter of Fundamental Rights: From Declaration to Binding Instrument*, Springer, Dordrecht, 2011, pp. 15-55

Dias C., Grigaité K. & Segall R., 'Recovery and Resilience Dialogue with the European Commission', In-Depth Analysis, Economic Governance Support Unit (EGOV), European Parliament, Brussels, 6,2021

Docksey C., 'Information and Consultation of Employees: The United Kingdom and the Vredeling Directive', The Modern Law Review, 49(3), 1986, pp. 281-313

Dombrovskis V., 'Budget Rules to Apply from 2023 to Avoid "Fiscal Risks"', Euroactive, 25 May 2021

Domenicucci D.P., 'Il Ruolo del Giudice Nazionale e il Procedimento Pregiudiziale', Seminario per Magistrati: Il Diritto dell'UE in Materia di Parità di Genere, ERA – Accademia di diritto Europeo, 2012

Dorssemont F., 'The Right to Take Collective Action v Fundamental Economic Freedoms in the Aftermath of Laval and Viking. Foes Are Forever!' in M. de Vos (ed.), *European Union Internal Market and Labour Law: Friends or Foes?*, Intersentia, 2009, pp. 45-105

Dorssemont F., 'Values and Objectives' in N. Bruun, K. Lörcher & I. Schömann (eds), *The Lisbon Treaty and Social Europe*, Hart Publishing, Oxford and Portland, Oregon, 2012, pp. 45-59

Douglas-Scott S., 'Subjects and Objects of EU Human Rights Law' in S. Bardutzky & E. Fahey (eds), *Framing the Subjects and Objects of Contemporary EU Law*, Edward Elgar Publishing, Cheltenham, 2017, pp. 105-123

Draghi M., 'We Face a War Against Coronavirus and Must Mobilise Accordingly', Financial Times, 25 March 2020

Dukes R., 'Hugo Sinzheimer and the Constitutional Function of Labour Law' in G. Davidov & B. Langille (eds), *The Idea of Labour Law*, Oxford University Press, Oxford, 2011, pp. 57-68

Dukes R., *The Labour Constitution – The Enduring Idea of Labour Law*, Oxford University Press, Oxford, 2014

Dukes R. & Cannon C., 'The Role of the Social Partners' in A. Bogg, C. Costello & A.C.L. Davies (eds), *Research Handbook on EU Labour Law*, Edward Elgar Publishing, Cheltenham, 2016, pp. 89-113

Dyevre A., 'European Integration and National Courts – A Strategic Analysis of Judicial Behaviour', SSRN, 2009, pp. 1-52

Dyevre A., 'Domestic Judicial Defiance and the Authority of International Legal Regimes', European Journal of Law and Economics, 44, 2017, pp. 453-481

Dyevre A., Glavina M. & Atanasova A., 'Who Refers Most? Institutional Incentives and Judicial Participation in the Preliminary Ruling System', Journal of European Public Policy, 27(6), 2019, pp. 912-930

Dyevre, A., Lampach N. & Glavina M., 'Chilling or Learning? The Effect of Negative Feedback on Interjudicial Cooperation in Nonhierarchical Referral Regimes', Journal of Law and Courts, 10(1), 2022, pp. 87-112

Ebner A., 'The Intellectual Foundations of the Social Market Economy', Journal of Economic Studies, 33(3), 2006, pp. 206-223

Eeckhout P., 'The European Court of Justice and the Legislature', Yearbook of European Law, 18(1), 1998, pp. 1-28

EULawLive, 'Polish Constitutional Court Declares EU Treaties Ultra Vires in Poland', EULawLive, 7 October 2021, https://eulawlive.com/polish-constitutional-court-declares-eu-treaties-ultra-vires-in-poland/

Eurofound, Monitoring and Managing Restructuring in the 21st Century, Publications Office of the European Union, Luxembourg, 2013

European Commission, 'The European Community's Social Policy', European Documentation, 2, Office for Official Publications of the European Communities, Brussels, 1978

Even Z., 'Distinction Asset-Intensive/Labour Intensive Not Decisive; All Spijkers Criteria Relevant', European Employment Law Cases, 6, 2014, pp. 6-10

Everling U., 'The Court of Justice as a Decisionmaking Authority', Michigan Law Review, 82, 1984, pp. 1294-1310

Evju S., 'The Right to Collective Action under the European Social Charter', European Labour Law Journal, 2(3), 2011, pp. 196-224

Ewing K., 'Laws Against Strikes Revisited' in C. Barnard, S. Deakin & G.S. Morris (eds), *The Future of Labour Law: Liber Amicorum Bob Hepple QC*, Hart Publishing, Portland, Oregon, 2004, pp. 41-61

Faraguna P., 'La Saga OMT: il Diritto all'Ultima Parola tra Corte di Giustizia e Tribunali Costituzionali', Giurisprudenza Costituzionale, 62(1), 2017, pp. 567-600

Feis H., 'International Labour Legislation in the Light of Economic Theory' in W. Sengenberger & D. Campbell (eds), *International Labour Standards and Economic Interdependence*, International Institute for Labour Studies, Geneva, 1994, pp. 29-57

Fernandes S. & Kerneïs K., 'The Porto Social Summit: Turning Principles into Actions', Notre Europe, 3 May 2021, https://institutdelors.eu/en/publications/sommet-social-de-porto-passer-des-principes-a-laction/

Figueroa A., 'Labour Market Theories and Labour Standards' in Werner Sengenberger & Duncan Campbell (eds), *International Labour Standards and Economic Interdependence,* International Institute for Labour Studies, Geneva, 1994, pp. 57-65

Fischman J.B. & Law D.S., 'What Is Judicial Ideology, and How Should We Measure It?', Washington University Journal of Law & Policy, 29, 2009, pp. 133-214

Fontanelli F., 'All's Well That Ends Honeywell', Diritticomparati.it, 2010, https://www.diritticomparati.it/alls-well-that-ends-honeywell/

Fontanelli F., 'You Can Teach a New Court Mangold Tricks – The Horizontal Effect of the Charter Right to Paid Annual Leave', EU Law Analysis, 2018, http://eulawanalysis.blogspot.com/2018/11/you-can-teach-new-court-mangold-tricks.html

Frantziou E., 'Mangold Recast? The ECJ's Flirtation with Drittwirkung in Egenberger', European Law Blog, 24 April 2018, https://europeanlawblog.eu/2020/06/23/the-commissions-proposal-for-a-european-minimum-wage-another-ultra-vires-challenge-for-the-eu/

Fredman S., 'The Ideology of New Labour Law' in C. Barnard, S. Deakin & G.S. Morris (eds), *The Future of Labour Law: Liber Amicorum Bob Hepple QC,* Hart Publishing, Portland, Oregon, 2004, pp. 9-39

Freedland M.R., 'Employment Protection: Redundancy Procedures and the EEC', Industrial Law Journal, 5(1), 1976, pp. 24-34

Freedland M. & Prassl J. (eds), *Viking, Laval and Beyond*, Hart Publishing, Oxford, 2014

Freedland M. & Prassl J., 'Viking, Laval and Beyond: An Introduction' in M. Freedland & J. Prassl (eds), *Viking, Laval and Beyond*, Hart Publishing, London, 2014, pp. 1-20

Fusco A., 'The Supreme Court of the United Kingdom and Preliminary References to the European Court of Justice: An Opencast Constitutional Lab', German Law Journal, 16(6), 2015, pp. 1529-1542

Galetta D.U., 'The European Union in the Constitutional Framework of the Member States: The Italian Case' in R. Arnold (ed.), *Limitations of National Sovereignty through European Integration*, Springer, Dordrecht, 2016, pp. 87-99

Gallo D., 'Challenging EU Constitutional Law: The Italian Constitutional Court's New Stance on Direct Effect and the Preliminary Reference Procedure', European Law Journal, 25, 2019, pp. 1-23

Garben S., 'Competence Creep Revisited', Journal of Common Market Studies, 57(2), 2017, pp. 205-222

Garben S., 'The European Pillar of Social Rights: Effectively Addressing Displacement?', European Constitutional Law Review, 14(1), 2018, pp. 210-230

Garben S., 'The European Pillar of Social Rights: An Assessment of Its Meaning and Significance', Cambridge Yearbook of European Legal Studies, 21, 2019, pp. 101-127

Garde A., 'Recent Developments in the Law Relating to Transfers of Undertakings', Common Market Law Review, 39, 2002, pp. 523-550

Gardner J., 'The Contractualisation of Labour Law' in H. Collins, G. Lester & V. Mantouvalou (eds), *Philosophical Foundations of Labour Law*, Oxford University Press, Oxford, 2019, pp. 33-47

Gárdos-Orosz F., 'Preliminary Reference and the Hungarian Constitutional Court: A Context of Non-reference', German Law Journal, 16(6), 2015, pp. 1569-1590

Garrett G., 'International Cooperation and Institutional Choice: The European Community's Internal Market', International Organization, 46(2), 1992, pp. 533-560

Garrett G. & Weingast B.R., 'Ideas, Interests and Institutions: Constructing the EC Internal Market' in *The Role of Ideas in Foreign Policy*, Cornell University Press, Cornell, 1993, pp. 173-206

Garrett G., 'The Politics of Legal Integration in the European Union', International Organization, 49(1), 1995, pp. 171-181

Garrett G., Kelemen R.D. & Schulz H., 'The European Court of Justice, National Governments, and Legal Integration in the European Union', International Organization, 2(1), 1998, pp. 149-176

Georgiou D., 'The New EU Directive on Transparent and Predictable Working Conditions in the Context of New Forms of Employment', European Journal of Industrial Relations, First Online, 2022

Gerards J., 'Pluarlism, Deference and the Margin of Appreciation Doctrine', European Law Journal, 17(1), 2011, pp. 80-120

Geyer R.R., *Exploring European Social Policy*, Polity Press, Cambridge, 2000

Gill-Pedro E., 'Freedom to Conduct Business in EU Law: Freedom from Interference or Freedom from Domination?', European Journal of Legal Studies, 9(2), 2017, pp. 103-134

Giubboni S., 'Social Rights and Market Freedom in the European Constitution: A Re-appraisal', European Labour Law Journal, 1(2), 2010, pp. 161-184

Giubboni S., 'Libertà d'impresa e diritto del lavoro nell'Unione europea', Costituzionalismo.it, 3, 2016, pp. 89-133

Giubboni S., *Diritto del lavoro europeo: Una introduzione critica*, CEDAM, Padova, 2017

Giubboni S., 'Appunti E Disappunti Sul Pilastro Europeo Dei Diritti Sociali', Quaderni Costituzionali, 37(4), 2017, pp. 953-962

Giubboni S., 'The Rise and Fall of EU Labour Law', European Law Journal, 24(1), 2018, pp. 7-20

Giubboni S., 'Freedom to Conduct a Business and EU Labour Law', European Constitutional Law Review, 14, 2018, pp. 172-190

Giubboni S., 'The Rise and Fall of EU Labour Law', European Law Journal, 24, 2018, pp. 7-20

Glavina M., 'Judicial Hierarchy in the Preliminary Ruling Procedure: Exploring the Relationship Between the First and the Second Instance Courts', European Papers, 5(2), 2020, pp. 799-823

Grimshaw D., Koukiadaki A. & Tavora I., 'Social Dialogue and Economic Performance', Conditions of Work and Employment Series, 89, ILO, Geneva, 2017

Groussot X., 'Constitutional Dialogues, Pluralism and Conflicting Identities' in M. Avbelj & J. Komárek (eds), *Constitutional Pluralism in the European Union and Beyond*, Hart Publishing, London, 2012, pp. 319-342

Groussot X., Pétursson T.G. & Pierce J., 'Weak Right, Strong Court – The Freedom to Conduct Business and the EU Charter of Fundamental Rights', Legal Research Paper Series, 1, Lund University, Lund, 2014

Guastaferro B., 'Beyond the Exceptionalism of Constitutional Conflicts: The Ordinary Functions of the Identity Clause', Yearbook of European Law, 31(1), 2012, pp. 263-318

Hansenne M., 'The European Social Model and Globalization of the Economy' in R. Blanpain, C. Engels, M. Weiss & B. Aaron (eds), *Labour Law and Industrial Relations at the Turn of the Century: Liber Amicorum in Honour of Roger Blanpain*, Kluwer Law International, The Hague, 1998

Hardy S. & Painter R., 'Revising the Acquired Rights Directive', Industrial Law Journal, 25(2), 1996, pp. 160-168

Harlow C., 'Francovich and the Problem of the Disobedient State', European Law Journal, 2, 1996, pp. 199-225

Hartley T., 'Federalism, Courts and Legal Systems: The Emerging Constitution of the European Community', The American Journal of Comparative Law, 34(2), 1986, pp. 229-247

Hartley T., 'The European Court, Judicial Objectivity and the Constitution of the European Union', The Law Quarterly Review, 112, 1996, pp. 95-109

Hatzopoulos V., 'Actively Talking to Each Other: The Court and the Political Institutions' in B. de Witte, B. Muir & E. Dawson (eds), *Judicial Activism at the European Court of Justice*, Edward Elgar Publishing, Cheltenham, 2013, pp. 102-141

Hendrickx F., 'Foundations and Functions of Contemporary Labour Law', European Labour Law Journal, 3(2), 2012, pp. 108-129

Hendrickx F. & Giubboni S., 'European Union Labour Law and the European Social Model: A Critical Appraisal' in M.W. Finkin & G. Mundlak (eds), *Comparative Labour Law*, Edward Elgar Publishing, Cheltenham, 2015, pp. 379-402

Hendrickx F., 'The European Social Pillar: Labour Law Not Only Needs Rights', Global Workplace Law & Policy, 2017, http://global-workplace-law-and-policy.

kluwerlawonline.com/2017/11/29/the-european-social-pillar-labour-law-not-only-needs-rights/

Hendrickx F. & De Stefano V. (eds), *Game Changers in Labour Law: Shaping the Future of Work*, Wolters Kluwer, Alphen aan den Rijn, 2018

Hendrickx F., 'The European Social Pillar: A First Evaluation', European Labour Law Journal, 9(1), 2018, pp. 3-6

Hendrickx F., 'European Labour Law and the Millenium Shift: From Post to (Social) Pillar' in F. Hendrickx & V. De Stefano (eds), *Game Changers in Labour Law: Shaping the Future of Work*, Wolters Kluwer, Alphen aan den Rijn, 2018, pp. 49-63

Hepple B.A., 'Introduction' in B.A. Hepple (ed.), *Social and Labour Rights in a Global Context: International and Comparative Perspectives*, Cambridge University Press, Cambridge, 2002, pp. 1-18

Hepple B.A. & Veneziani B. (eds), *The Transformation of Labour Law in Europe: A Comparative Study of 15 Countries, 1945-2004*, Hart Publishing, Oxford, 2009

Hepple B.A., 'Factor Influencing the Making and Transformation of Labour Law in Europe' in G. Davidov & B. Langille (eds), *The Idea of Labour Law*, Oxford University Press, Oxford, 2011, pp. 30-42

Hepple B.A., 'Fundamental Social Rights since the Lisbon Treaty', European Labour Law Journal, 2(2), 2011, pp. 150-154

Herezog R. & Gerken L., 'Stop the European Court of Justice', EuObserver, 10 September 2008, https://euobserver.com/opinion/26714

Herresthal C., 'Constitutionalisation of Freedom of Contract in European Union Law' in K.S. Ziegler & P.M. Huber (eds), *Current Problems in the Protection of Human Rights: Perspectives from Germany and UK*, Hart Publishing, Oxford and Portland, Oregon, 2013, pp. 89-116

Hochscheidt L., 'Social Pillar Action Plan – Longer on Aspiration', Social Europe, 9 May 2021, https://socialeurope.eu/social-pillar-action-plan-longer-on-aspiration

Holmes S., 'Climate Change, Sustainability, and Competition Law', Journal of Anittrust Enforcement, 8, 2020, pp. 354-405

Höreth M., 'The Least Dangerous Branch of European Governance? The European Court of Justice under the Checks and Balances Doctrine' in B. de Witte, B. Muir & E. Dawson (eds), *Judicial Activism at the European Court of Justice*, Edward Elgar Publishing, Cheltenham, 2013, pp. 32-56

Horsley T., *The Court of Justice of the European Union as and Institutional Actor: Judicial Lawmaking and Its Limits*, Cambridge University Press, New York, 2018

Hős N., 'The Principle of Proportionality in Viking and Laval: An Appropriate Standard of Judicial Review?', European Labour Law Journal, 1(2), 2010, pp. 236-253

Houwerzijl M.S. & Wilkinson T., 'The Effects of EU Law on the Social and Economic Goals of Europe 2020: A Decision Theoretic Approach to Wage Liability Regimes in Modern Europe', German Law Journal, 14(10), 2013, pp. 1981-2001

Howard E., 'Headscarves and the CJEU: Protecting Fundamental Rights or Pandering to Prejudice', Maastricht Journal of European and Comparative Law, 28(5), 2021, pp. 648-666

Hunt J., 'The Court of Justice as a Policy Actor: The Case of the Acquired Rights Directive', Legal Studies, 18(3), 1998, pp. 336-359

Jacobs F.G., 'Judicial Dialogue and the Cross-Fertilization of Legal Systems: The European Court of Justice', Texas International Law Journal, 38, 2003, pp. 547-556

Jacobs A., 'Collective Self-Regulation' in B. Hepple (ed.), *The Making of Labour Law in Europe*, Mansell Publishing Limited, London, 1986, pp. 193-240

Jacobs A., 'The Janus Head of the European Union: The Social Market Economy Versus Ultraliberal Policies' in J. Wouters, L. Verhey & P. Kiiver (eds), *European Constitutionalism Beyond Lisbon*, Intersentia, Cambridge, 2009

Jacobs A., 'Services of General Interest and the Treaty of Lisbon' in N. Bruun, K. Lörcher & I. Schömann (eds), *The Lisbon Treaty and Social Europe*, Hart Publishing, Oxford and Portland, Oregon, 2012, pp. 277-302

Jacobs A., 'The Future of the Charter on Fundamental Rights of the European Union' in F. Dorssemont, K. Lörcher, S. Clauwaert & M. Schmitt (eds), *The Charter of Fundamental Rights of the European Union and the Employment Relation*, Hart Publishing, London, 2019, pp. 39-53

Jaklic K., *Constitutional Pluralism in the EU*, Oxford University Press, Oxford, 2014

Joerges C. & Roedl F., 'The "Social Market Economy" as Europe's Social Model?', Working Paper, European University Institute, Florence, 2004

Johnson M. & Pulignano V., 'Editorial', Transfer, 27(Transforming Care Work Within an Era of Changing Priorities of Care Policy, 3), 2021, pp. 275-278

Jordan J., Maccarrone V. & Erne R., 'Towards a Socialization of the EU's New Economic Governance Regime? EU Labour Policy Intervetions in Germany, Ireland, Italy and Romania (2009-2019)', British Journal of Industrial Relations, 59(1), 2021, pp. 191-213

Kahn-Freund O., Davies P. & Freedland M.R., *Kahn-Freund's Labour and the Law*, Stevens, London, 1983

Kalula E., 'Beyond Borrowing and Bending: Labour Market Regulation and the Future of Labour Law in Southern Africa' in C. Barnard, S. Deakin & G.S. Morris (eds), *The Future of Labour Law. Liber Amicorum Bob Hepple QC*, Hart Publishing, Portland, Oregon, 2004, pp. 275-287

Kaufman B.E., 'Labor Law and Employment Regulation: Neoclassical and Institutional Perspectives', UWRG Working Paper, 24, Georgia State University, 2008

Kaupa C., 'Maybe Not Activist Enough? On the Court's Alleged Neoliberal Bias in Its Recent Labor Cases' in B. de Witte, B. Muir & E. Dawson (eds), *Judicial Activism at the European Court of Justice*, Edward Elgar Publishing, Cheltenham, 2013, pp. 56-75

Kennedy D., 'Proportionality and "Deference" in Contemporary Constitutional Thought', Harvard Public Law Working Paper, 179, 2016

Kilroy B., *Member State Control or Judicial Independence? The Integrative Role of the European Court of Justice, 1958-1994*, University of California, Los Angeles, 1996

Knegt R., 'Recovering the Impact of Normative Regimes on Labour Relations Practices: A Socio-Historical View of Institutional Requirements' in A. Blackham, M.

Kullmann & A. Zbyszewska (eds), *Theorising Labour Law in a Changing World: Towards Inclusive Labour Law*, Bloomsbury Publishing, London, 2019, pp. 19-36
Kok W., 'Jobs, Jobs, Jobs - Creating More Employment in Europe', Report of the Employment Taskforce Chaired by Wim Kok, Directorate-General for Employment, Social Affairs and Inclusion (European Commission), Brussels, 2003
Kokott J., 'Report on Germany' in A.M. Slaughter, A. Stone Sweet & J. Weiler (eds), *The European Court and National Court – Doctrine and Jurisprudence: Legal Change in Its Social Context*, Hart Publishing, Oxford, 1998, pp. 77-133
Kollonay-Lehoczky C., Lörcher K. & Schömann I., 'The Lisbon Treaty and the Charter of Fundamental Rights of the European Union' in N. Bruun, K. Lörcher & I. Schömann (eds), *The Lisbon Treaty and Social Europe*, Hart Publishing, Oxford and Portland, Oregon, 2012, pp. 61-104
Konstadinides T., 'Constitutional Identity as a Shield and as a Sword: The European Legal Order within the Framework of National Constitutional Settlement', Cambridge Yearbook of European Legal Studies, 13, 2011, pp. 195-218
Koopmans T., 'Comparative Law and the Courts', International and Comparative Law Quarterly, 45, 1996, pp. 545-556
Koslowski P., *The Social Market Economy: Theory and Ethics of the Economic Order*, Springer, Berlin, 1998
Koukiadaki A., 'The Evolution of Employee Involvement in European Labour Law', ERA Forum, 11, 2011, pp. 601-619
Koukiadaki A., 'The Economic Crisis and Collective Labour Rights in Europe', Revue Francaise des Affaires Sociales, 3, 2015, pp. 53-73
Krommendijk J., 'The Highest Dutch Courts and the Preliminary Ruling Procedure: Critically Obedient Interlocutors of the Court of Justice', European Law Journal, 25(4), 2019, pp. 1-22
Krunke H. & Klinge S., 'The Danish Ajos Case: The Missing Case from Maastricht and Lisbon', European Papers, 3(1), 2018, pp. 157-182
Kühn Z., 'The Czech Republic: From a Euro-Friendly Approach of the Constitutional Court to Proclaiming a Court of Justice Judgment Ultra Vires' in A. Albi & S. Bardutzky (eds), *National Constitutions in European and Global Governance Democracy, Rights, the Rule of Law*, Springer, Dordrecht, 2019, pp. 795-833
Kukovec D., 'Law and the Periphery', European Law Journal, 21(3), 2015, pp. 406-428
Kukovec D., 'Subject-Object Dialectics and Social Change' in S. Bardutzky & E. Fahey (eds), *Framing the Subjects and Objects of Contemporary EU Law*, Edward Elgar Publishing, Cheltenham, 2017, pp. 45-63
Kumm M. & Ferreres Comella V., 'The Primacy Clause of the Constitutional Treaty and the Future of Constitutional Conflict in the European Union', International Journal of Constitutional Law, 3(2-3), 2005, pp. 473-492
Kyriazis N., 'The Economic and Social Cohesion of the Community', Economic Series, 13, European Parliament Directorate General for Research, Brussels, 1988
Laagland F., 'Member States' Sovereignty in the Socio-Economic Field: Fact or Fiction? The Clash Between the European Business Freedoms and the National level of Workers' Protection', European Labour Law Journal, 9(1), 2018, pp. 50-72
Langille B., 'Labour Law Is Not a Commodity', The Industrial Law Journal, 19, 1998

Langille B., 'Labour Law's Theory of Justice' in G. Davidov & B. Langille (eds), *The Idea of Labour Law*, Oxford University Press, Oxford, 2011, pp. 101-120

Laulom S., 'The European Court of Justice in the Dialogue on Transfers of Undertakings: A Fallible Interlocutor?' in S. Sciarra (ed.), *Labour Law in the Courts: National Judges and the European Court of Justice*, Hart Publishing, Oxford, 2001, pp. 145-178

Leczykiewicz D., 'Horizontal Effect of Fundamental Rights: In Search of Social Justice or Private Autonomy in EU Law?', Oxford Legal Studies Research Paper, 38, University of Oxford, Oxford, 2013

Lenaerts K., 'Some Thoughts about the Interaction Between Judges and Politicians', University of Chicago Legal Forum, 1, 1992, pp. 93-1331

Lenaerts K., 'Interlocking Legal Orders in the European Union and Comparative Law', International and Comparative Law Quarterly, 52, 2003, pp. 873-906

Lenaerts K., 'Interpretation and the Court of Justice: A Basis for Comparative Reflection', The International Lawyer, 41(4), 2007, pp. 1011-1032

Lenaerts K., 'Le Statut de la Négociation Collective dans la Jurisprudence Européenne', Revue de Droit Social, 1, 2009, pp. 3-18

Lenaerts K., 'Discovering the Law of the EU: the European Court of Justice and the Comparative Law Method' in E. Perisin & S. Rodin (eds), *The Transformation or Reconstitution of Europe: The Critical Legal Studies Perspective on the Role of the Courts in the European Union*, Hart Publishing, Oxford, 2018, pp. 61-87

Levi Sandri L., 'Social Policy in the Common Market 1958-1965', Community Topics, 22, European Community Information Service, Brussels, 1966

Lewis R., 'Kahn-Freund and Labour Law: An Outline Critique', Industrial Law Journal, 8(4), 1979, pp. 202-221

Liso F., 'Appunti per un profilo di Gino Giugni dagli anni '50 allo Statuto dei lavoratori', Working paper, 316, Centre for the Study of European Labour Law 'Massimo D'Antona', Catania, 2016

Lo Faro A., 'Judicial Developments of EC Social Policy and Intra-Community Institutional Dialogues: How to Define a "Legal Transfer"' in S. Sciarra (ed.), *Labour Law in the Courts: National Judges and the European Court of Justice*, Hart Publishing, Oxford, 2001, pp. 210-228

Lohse E.J., 'The German Constitutional Court and Preliminary References – Still a Match Not Made in Heaven?', German Law Journal, 16(6), 2015, pp. 1491-1508

Lörcher K., 'Social Competences' in N. Bruun, K. Lörcher & I. Schömann (eds), *The Lisbon Treaty and Social Europe*, Hart Publishing, Oxford and Portland, Oregon, 2012, pp. 165-234

Lörcher K. & Schömann I., 'The European Pillar of Social Rights: Critical Legal Analysis and Proposals', Report, 139, ETUI, Brussels, 2016

Lyon-Caen A., *Droit du travail, démocratie et crise en Europe occidentale et en Amérique : Canada, Espagne, Etats-Unis d'Amérique, France, Grande Bretagne, Italie, Mexique, Pérou, République fédérale d'Allemagne : essai comparatif*, Actes Sud, Arles, 1986

MacCormick N., 'Second-Order Justification' in *Legal Reasoning and Legal Theory*, Oxford University Press, Oxford, 1978, pp. 100-128

Malo M.A., 'European Labour Law and Severance Pay Determination in Collective Redundancies', European Journal of Law and Economics, 12(1), 2001, pp. 73-90

Mancini G.F., 'The Making of a Constitution for Europe', Common Market Law Review, 26(4), 1989, pp. 595-614

Mancini G.F. & Keeling D.T., 'Democracy and the European Court of Justice', The Modern Law Review, 57(2), 1994, pp. 175-190

Marín Aís J.R., 'Freedom of Religion in the Workplace v. Freedom to Conduct a Business, the Islamic Veil Before the Court of Justice: Ms. Samira Achbita Case', European Papers, 26 April 2018

Marinelli M., 'Clausole di rinvio al contratto collettivo e libertà di associazione nella recente giurisprudenza della Corte di giustizia', Working Paper, Centro Studi di Diritto del Lavoro Europeo 'Massimo D'Antona', Catania, 2006

Markakis M., 'Can Governments Control Mass Layoffs by Employers? Economic Freedoms vs Labour Rights in Case C-201/15 AGET Iraklis', European Constitutional Law Review, 13, 2017, pp. 724-743

Marsden D., *A Theory of Employment Systems: Micro-Foundations of Societal Diversity*, Oxford University Press, Oxford, 1999

Marsden D., 'The Impact of Industrial Relations Practices on Employment and Unemployment', OECD Jobs Study Working Paper, 3, OECD Publishing, Paris, 1995

Martinico G., 'Judging in the Multilevel Legal Order: Exploring the Techniques of "Hidden Dialogue"', King's Law Journal, 21, 2010, pp. 257-281

Martinico G., 'The "Polemical" Spirit of European Constitutional Law: On the Importance of Conflicts in EU Law', German Law Journal, 16(6), 2015, pp. 1343-1374

Marzo C. & Lecomte F., 'Le refus d'être transféré: droit comparé', Droit Social, 6, 2010, pp. 698-710

Maslauskaitė K., Social Competition in the EU: Myths and Realities, https://institutdelors.eu/en/publications/social-competition-in-the-eu-myths-and-realities/

Mattli W. & Slaughter A.-M., 'Constructing the European Community Legal System from the Ground Up: The Role of Individual Litigants and National Courts', Working Paper No. 56, European University Institute, Florence, 1996

Mattli W. & Slaughter A.-M., 'Revisiting the European Court of Justice', International Organization, 52(1), 1998, pp. 177-209

Mattli W. & Slaughter A.M., 'The Role of National Courts in the Process of European Integration' in A.M. Slaughter, A. Stone Sweet & J. Weiler (eds), *The European Court and National Court – Doctrine and Jurisprudence: Legal Change in Its Social Context*, Hart Publishing, Oxford, 1998, pp. 253-276

McMullen J., 'An Analysis of the Transfer of Undertakings (Protection of Employment) Regulation 2006', Industrial Law Journal, 35(2), 2006, pp. 113-139

McMullen J., 'Some Problems and Themes in the Application in Member States of Directive 2001/23/EC on Transfer of Undertakings', The International Journal of Comparative Labour Law and Industrial Relations, 23(3), 2007, pp. 335-374

McMullen J., 'Recent Judicial Reasoning on the Acquired Rights Directive', Employment & Industrial Relations Law, 21(1), 2011, pp. 1-4

McMullen J., 'Recent CJEU Case Law on the Transfer of Asset-Reliant Undertakings', Industrial Law Journal, 45(3), 2016, pp. 455-464

McMullen J., 'Leaving a Legacy: Recent Jurisprudence of the European Court on Transfer of Undertakings', Industrial Law Journal, 50(1), 2021, pp. 130-157

Mestitz F., 'Hugo Sinzheimer e il diritto del lavoro: ieri e oggi', Scienza e Politica, 9(5), 2013, pp. 57-83

Meucci M., 'Esternalizzazione di personale tramite trasferimento di fittizi rami d'azienda', Altalex, 2015

Micklitz H.-W., 'Social Justice and Access Justice in Private Law', Working Paper, 2, European University Institute, Florence, 2011

Micklitz H.-W., *The Politics of Justice in European Private Law*, Cambridge University Press, Cambridge, 2018

Millet F.-X. & Perlo N., 'The First Preliminary Reference of the French Constitutional Court to the CJEU: Rvolution de Palais or Revolution in French Constitutional Law?', German Law Journal, 16(6), 2015, pp. 1471-1490

Millspaugh P.E., 'Employment Rights Law in Great Britain: The Thatcher Government Confronts the EEC', Arizona Journal of International and Comparative Law, 54(6), 1989, pp. 54-72

Mooij A.A.M., 'The Weiss Judgment: The Court's Further Clarification of the ECB's Legal Framework Case C-493/17 Weiss and Others, EU:C:2018:1000', Maastricht Journal of European and Comparative Law, 26(3), 2019, pp. 449-465

Moravcsik A., 'Liberal Intergovernmentalism and Integration: A Rejoinder', Journal of Common Market Studies, 33(4), 1995, pp. 611-628

More G., 'The Aqcquired Rights Directive: Frustrating or Facilitating Labour Market Flexibility' in J. Shaw & G. More (eds), *New Legal Dynamics of European Union*, Clarendon Press, Oxford, 1995, pp. 129-147

Morijn J., 'Balancing Fundamental Rights and Common Market Freedoms in Union Law: Schmidberger and Omega in the Light of the European Constitution', European Law Journal, 12(1), 2006, pp. 15-40

Morin M-L., 'Labour Law and New Forms of Corporate Organization', International Labour Review, 144(1), 2005, pp. 5-27

Morris G.S., 'The Future of the Public/Private Labour Law Divide' in C. Barnard, S. Deakin & G.S. Morris (eds), *The Future of Labour Law. Liber Amicorum Bob Hepple QC*, Hart Publishing, Portland, Oregon, 2004, pp. 159-178

Moschella M., 'What Role for the European Semester in the Recovery Plan?', In-Depth Analysis, European Parliament Directorate General for Internal Policies, Brussels, 2020

Muir E., 'Enhancing the Effects of Community Law on National Employment Policies: The Mangold Case', European Law Review, 36(1), 2006, pp. 879-891

Muir E., Dawson M. & de Witte B., 'Introduction: The European Court of Justice as a Political Actor' in B. de Witte, B. Muir & E. Dawson (eds), *Judicial Activism at the European Court of Justice*, Edward Elgar Publishing, Cheltenham, 2013, pp. 1-11

Muir E., 'The Court of Justice: A Fundamental Rights Institution Among Others' in B. de Witte, B. Muir & E. Dawson (eds), *Judicial Activism at the European Court of Justice*, Edward Elgar Publishing, Cheltenham, 2013, pp. 76-102

Müller T. & Schulten T., 'The European Social Pillar – Towards an EU Minimum Wage Policy?', Social Europe, 2017, https://socialeurope.eu/european-social-pillar-towards-eu-minimum-wage-policy

Müller-Armack A., 'The Principles of the Social Market Economy' in Peter Koslowski (ed.), *The Social Market Economy: Theory and Ethics of the Economic Order*, Springer, Berlin, 1998

Nazerali J. & Plumbley-Jones K., 'New Acquired Rights Directive – A Step in the Dark?', European Business Law Review, 6(2), 1995, pp. 31-36

Neal A., 'Comparative Labour Law and Industrial Relations: "A Major Discipline? – Who Cares?"' in R. Blanpain, C. Engels, M. Weiss & B. Aaron (eds), *Labour Law and Industrial Relations at the Turn of the Century: Liber Amicorum in Honour of Roger Blanpain*, Kluwer Law International, The Hague, 1998

Nielsen R., 'Free Movement and Fundamental Rights', European Labour Law Journal, 1(1), 2010, pp. 19-32

Nyikos S.A., *The European Court of Justice and National Courts: Strategic Interaction Within the EU Judicial Process*, University of Virginia, 2000

Nyikos S.A., 'Strategic Interaction among Courts Within the Preliminary Reference Process – Stage 1: National Court Preemptive Opinions', European Journal of Political Research, 45, 2006, pp. 527-550

Nyström B., 'Final Decision in the Laval Case', European Labour Law Journal, 1(2), 2010, pp. 276-279

O'Higgins P., 'The End of Labour Law as We Have Known It?' in C. Barnard, S. Deakin & G.S. Morris (eds), *The Future of Labour Law. Liber Amicorum Bob Hepple QC*, Hart Publishing, Portland, Oregon, 2004, pp. 289-301

Ojeda Avilés A. & Garcia Vina A.J., 'Regulation of the Labour Market' in B.A. Hepple & B. Veneziani (eds), *The Transformation of Labour Law in Europe: A Comparative Study of 15 Countries, 1945-2004*, Hart Publishing, London, 2009, pp. 59-98

Oladeinde O., 'Global Capitalism and Rise of Non-standard Employment: Challenges to Industrial Relations' in R. Blanpain (ed.), *The Global Labour Market: From Globalization to Flexicurity*, Wolters Kluwer, Alphen aan den Rijn, 2008, pp. 53-61

O'Leary S., *Employment Law at the European Court of Justice: Judicial Structures, Policies, and Processes*, Hart Publishing, Oxford, 2002

Orator A., 'The Decision of the Austrian Verfassungsgerichtshof on the EU Charter of Fundamental Rights: An Instrument of Leverage or Rearguard Action?', German Law Journal, 16(6), 2015, pp. 1429-1448

Orlandini G., 'Libertà di stabilimento versus diritto al lavoro: ancora un bilanciamento "sbilanciato" tra libertà economiche e diritti dei lavoratori', Giornale Di Diritto Del Lavoro E Di Relazioni Industriali, 153(1), 2017, pp. 203-217

Ovádek M., 'Supranationalism, Constrained? Locating the Court of Justice on the EU Integration Dimension', European Union Politics, 22(1), 2021, pp. 46-69

Pani F., 'L'obbligo (flessibile) di rinvio pregiudiziale e i possibili fattori di un suo irrigidimento. Riflessioni in margine alla sentenza Association France Nature Environnement', European Papers, 2(1), 2017, pp. 383-391

Papa V., 'The Dark Side of Fundamental Rights Adjudication? The Court, the Charter and the Asymmetric Interpretation of Fundamental Rights in the AMS Case and Beyond', European Labour Law Journal, 6(3), 2015, pp. 190-214

Papadopoulos N.A., 'Criticizing the Horizontal Direct Effect of the EU General Principle of Equality', Human Rights Law Review, 4, 2011, pp. 437-447

Pataut E., 'The Aftermath of the Laval Affair: The Swedish Lex Laval Before the Committee of Social Rights' in H. Muir Watt et al. (eds), *Global Private International Law – Adjudication Without Frontiers*, Edward Elgar Publishing, Northampton, 2019, pp. 484-492

Pavone T. & Kelemen R.D., 'The Evolving Judicial Politics of European Integration: The European Court of Justice and National Courts Revisited', European Law Journal, 25(4), 2019, pp. 1-22

Payandeh E.M., 'Constitutional Review of EU Law after Honeywell: Contextualising the Relationship Between the German Constitutional Court and the EU Court of Justice', Common Market Law Review, 48(1), 2011, pp. 9-38

Pecinovsky P., 'EU Economic Governance and the Right to Collective Bargaining: Part 2: From Imposed Restrictions of the right by EU Member States Towards a Social Economic Governance', European Labour Law Journal, 10(1), 2019, pp. 43-68

Pernice I., 'Multilevel Constitutionalismand the Treaty of Amsterdam: European Constitution-Making Revisited?', Common Market Law Review, 36, 1999, pp. 703-750

Pernice I., 'A Difficult Partnership Between Courts: The First Preliminary Reference by the German Federal Constitutional Court to the CJEU', Maastricht Journal of European and Comparative Law, 21(1), 2014, pp. 3-13

Pertek J., *La Pratique du Renvoi Préjudiciel en Droit Communautaire*, Litec, Paris, 2001

Pescatore P., 'Le recours, dans la jurisprudence de la Cour de justice des Communautés européennes, à des normes déduites de la comparaison des droits des Etats membres', Revue internationale de droit comparé, 32(2), 1980, pp. 337-359

Phelan W., *In Place of Inter-State Retaliation: The European Union's Rejection of WTO-Style Trade Sanctions and Trade Remedies*, Oxford University Press, Oxford, 2015

Piasna A. & Myant M.R. (eds), *Myths of Employment Deregulation: How It Neither Creates Jobs Nor Reduces Labour Market Segmentation*, ETUI, Brussels, 2017

Pietrogiovanni V., 'Redifining the Boundaries of Labour Law: Is "Double Alienness" a Useful Concept for Classifying Employees in Times of Fractal Work?' in A. Blackham, M. Kullmann & A. Zbyszewska (eds), *Theorising Labour Law in a Changing World: Towards Inclusive Labour Law*, Bloomsbury Publishing, Oxford, 2019, pp. 55-71

Piqani D., 'Constitutional Courts in Central and Eastern Europe and Their Attitude Towards European Integration', European Journal of Legal Studies, 1(2), 2007, pp. 1-22

Plotner J., 'Repor on France' in A.M. Slaughter, A. Stone Sweet & J. Weiler (eds), *The European Court and National Court – Doctrine and Jurisprudence: Legal Change in Its Social Context*, Hart Publishing, Oxford, 1998, pp. 41-76

Poiares Maduro M.P., *We the Court: The European Court of Justice and the European Economic Constitution: A Critical Reading of Article 30 of the EC Treaty*, Hart Publishing, Oxford, 1998

Poiares Maduro M., 'Contrapunctual Law: Europe's Constitutional Pluralism in Action' in N. Walker (ed.), *Sovereignty in Transition*, Hart Publishing, Portland, 2003, pp. 501-537

Poiares Maduro M., 'Interpreting European Law: Judicial Adjudication in a Context of Constitutional Pluralism', European Journal of Legal Studies, 1(2), 2008, pp. 1-21

Poiares Maduro M., 'Three Claims of Constitutional Pluralism' in M. Avbelj & J. Komárek (eds), *Constitutional Pluralism in the European Union and Beyond*, Hart Publishing, London, 2012, pp. 67-84

Pollack M.A., 'Principal-Agent Analysis and International Delegation: Red Herrings, Theoretical Clarifications and Empirical Disputes', Bruges Political Research Paper, 2, College of Europe, Bruges, 2007

Pollicino O., *Discriminazione sulla Base del Sesso e Trattamento Preferenziale nel Diritto Comunitario*, Giuffrè, Milano, 2005

Pollicino O., 'Dall'Est una Lezione sui Rapporti tra Diritto Costituzionale e Diritto Comunitario', Il diritto dell'Unione Europea, 11(4), 2006, pp. 819-852

Pollicino O., *Allargamento dell'Europa a est e rapporto tra Corti costituzionali e Corti europee*, Giuffrè, Milano, 2010

Pollicino O., 'Qualcosa è Cambiato? La Recente Giurisprudenza delle Corti Costituzionali dell'Est vis à vis il Processo di Integrazione Europea', Diritticomparati.it, 15 November 2012, https://www.diritticomparati.it/qualcosa-e-cambiato-la-recente-giurisprudenza-delle-corti-costituzionali-dellest-vis-a-vis-il-proces/?print-posts=print

Pollicino O., 'Corte di giustizia e giudici nazionali: il moto "ascendente", ovverosia l'incidenza delle "tradizioni costituzionali comuni" nella tutela apprestata ai diritti dalla Corte dell'Unione', 1, Consulta Online, 2015

Polomarkakis K.A., 'A Tale of Two Approaches to Social Europe: The CJEU and the Advocate General Drifting Apart in Case C-201/15 AGET Iraklis', Maastricht Journal of European and Comparative Law, 24(3), 2017, pp. 424-437

Prassl J., 'Freedom of Contract as a General Principle of EU Law? Transfers of Undertakings and the Protection of Employer Rights in EU Labour Law', Industrial Law Journal, 42(4), 2013, pp. 434-446

Prassl J., 'Business Freedoms and Employment Rights in the European Union', Cambridge Yearbook of European Legal Studies, 17, 2015, pp. 189-209

Prassl J., "The interaction of EU Law and National Law: Between Myth and Reality' in A. Bogg, C. Costello & A.C.L. Davies (eds), *Research Handbook on EU Labour Law*, Edward Elgar Publishing, Cheltenham, 2016, pp. 42-63

Přibáň J., 'The Semantics of Constitutional Sovereignty in Post-sovereign "New" Europe: A Case Study of the Czech Constitutional Court's Jurisprudence', International Journal of Constitutional Law, 13(1), 2015, pp. 180-199

Raffini L., *La Democrazia in Mutamento. Dallo Stato-nazione all'Europa*, Firenze University Press, Firenze, 2010

Rainone S., 'Labour Rights in the Making of the EU and in the CJEU Case Law: A Case Study on the Transfer of Undertakings Directive', European Labour Law Journal, 9(3), 2018, pp. 299-325

Rainone S., 'Workers' Involvement in Collective Redundancies in EU Law – What For? A Case Study', Bulletin of Comparative Labour Relations, 107, 2019, pp. 207-220

Rainone S., 'The European Pillar of Social Rights – Tell Me Where You Come from and I Will Tell You Who You Are', Zbornik Znanstvenih Razprav Letnik LXXX, Perspective on the European Pillar of Social Rights, 2020, pp. 133-178

Rainone S., 'The European Response to the Covid-19 Crisis – Where Are We Going To?', Global Workplace Law & Policy, 4 June 2020, http://global-workplace-law-and-policy.kluwerlawonline.com.tilburguniversity.idm.oclc.org/2020/06/04/the-european-response-to-the-covid-19-crisis-where-are-we-going-to/

Rainone S., 'An Overview of the 2020-2021 Country-Specific Recommendations (CSRs) in the Social Field – The Impact of Covid-19', Background Analysis, 1, ETUI, Brussels, 2020

Rainone S. & Aloisi A., 'Time to Deliver? Assessing the Action Plan on the European Pillar of Social Rights', Policy Brief, ETUI, Brussels, 2021

Rainone S., 'After the "Hairdressing Agreement", the EPSU Case: Can the Commission Control the EU Social Dialogue?', Policy Brief, 15, ETUI, Brussels, 2020

Rainone S. & Countouris N., 'Collective Bargaining and Self-Employed Workers – The Need for a Paradigm Shift', Policy Brief, 11, ETUI, Brussels, 2021

Rainone S., 'Enforcing EU Information and Consultation Rights' in Z. Rasnača, A. Joukiadaki, N. Bruun & K. Lorcher (eds), *Effective Enforcement of EU Labour Law*, Hart, Portland, 2022

Rask Madsen M., Palmer Olsen H. & Šadl U., 'Competing Supremacies and Clashing Institutional Rationalities: The Danish Supreme Court's Decision in the Ajos Case and the National Limits of Judicial Cooperation', European Law Journal, 23(1), 2017, pp. 140-150

Rasmussen H., *On Law and Policy in the European Court of Justice: A Comparative Study in Judicial Policymaking*, Martinus Nijhoff/Dr W. Junk, Dordrecht, 1986

Rasnača Z., 'Bridging the Gaps or Falling Short? The European Pillar of Social Rights and What It Can Bring to EU-Level Policymaking', Working Paper, ETUI, Brussels, 2017

Rasnača Z., *First or One among Equals? The CJEU and the Construction of EU Social Policy*, European Univerity Institute, Florence, 2017

Rasnača Z., 'Procedure: Litigating Before EU Courts in the Light of the Charter' in F. Dorssemont, K. Lörcher, S. Clauwaert & M. Schmitt (eds), *The Charter of Fundamental Rights of the European Union and the Employment Relation*, Hart Publishing, London, 2019, pp. 163-188

Ratti L., 'The European Economic Constitution and the Constitution of a Social Europe: Gleanings from the CJEUs Collective Redundancies Cases' in H.C.H. Hofmann et al. (eds), *The Metamorphosis of the European Economic Constitution*, Edward Elgar Publishing, Cheltenham, 2019, pp. 154-176

Ratti L., "To Hire or Not to Hire: The Ambivalent Impact of Social Rehire Clauses on the Transfer of Undertakings Directive', European Labour Law Journal, 11(2), 2020, pp. 225-244

Rayer C.W.G., 'European Court of Justice, 19 January 2010, C-555/07 (Seda Kücükdeveci / Swedex GmbH & Co. KG)', European Labour Law Journal, 1(2), 2010, pp. 264-268

Rémy P., 'L'arrêt "Alemo-Herron" de la CJUE et la directive transfert: faut-il encore prendre au sérieux la Cour de justice?', Revue de droit du travail, 12, 2013, pp. 789-797

Repetto G., 'Pouring New Wine into New Bottles? The Preliminary Reference to the CJEU by the Italian Constitutional Court', German Law Journal, 16(6), 2015, pp. 1449-1470

Rodgers L., 'Theorising Labour Law in the State of Exception: Political and Judicial Responses to Crisis' in A. Blackham, M. Kullmann & A. Zbyszewska (eds), *Theorising Labour Law in a Changing World: Towards Inclusive Labour Law*, Bloomsbury Publishing, London, 2019, pp. 37-54

Rodin S., 'The Subject and Object in the Interpretation of EU Law' in S. Bardutzky & E. Fahey (eds), *Framing the Subjects and Objects of Contemporary EU Law*, Edward Elgar Publishing, Cheltenham, 2017, pp. 31-44

Rodríguez-Izquierdo Serrano M., 'The Spanish Constitutional Court and Fundamental Rights Adjudication After the First Preliminary Reference', German Law Journal, 16(6), 2015, pp. 1509-1528

Rogowski R., 'The Emergence of Reflexive Global Labour Law', The German Journal of Industrial Relations, 22(1), 2015, pp. 72-90

Rosas A., 'The European Court of Justice in Context: Forms and Patterns of Judicial Dialogue', European Journal of Legal Studies, 1(2), 2007

Ross M., 'Beyond Francovich', The Modern Law Review, 56(1), 1993, pp. 55-73

Rubery J. & Piasna A., 'Labour Market Segmentation and Deregulation of Employment Protection in the EU' in A. Piasna & M.R. Myant (eds), *Myths of Employment Deregulation: How It Neither Creates Jobs Nor Reduces Labour Market Segmentation*, ETUI, Brussels, 2017, pp. 43-56

Ruggeri Laderchi P., 'Report on Italy' in A.M. Slaughter, A. Stone Sweet & J. Weiler (eds), *The European Court and National Court – Doctrine and Jurisprudence: Legal Change in Its Social Context*, Hart Publishing, Oxford, 1998, pp. 147-169

Sadl U., 'National Court and the Effectiveness of EU Law' in B. de Witte, J.A. Mayoral & U. Jaremba (eds), *National Court and EU Law: New Issues, Theories and Methods*, Edward Elgar Publishing, Cheltenham, 2006, pp. 68-105

Sadl U., 'Does the Court of Justice Make Law in Small Steps? (Circumstantial) Evidence from the Free Movement of Persons Jurisprudence', Paper presented at the EUI Faculty Seminar, EUI, 2020

Sadurski W., '"Solange, Chapter 3": Constitutional Courts in Central Europe – Democracy – European Union', European Law Journal, 14(1), 2008, pp. 1-35

Sandbu M., 'Europe Has Rediscovered the Social Market Economy', Financial Times, 19 December 2021

Sankari S., 'Constitutional Pluralism and Judicial Adjudication: On Legal Reasoning, Minimalism and Silence by the Court of Justice' in G. Davies & M. Avbelj (eds), *Research Handbook on Legal Pluralism and EU Law,* Edward Elgar Publishing, Cheltenham, 2018, pp. 309-322

Santoro-Passarelli G., 'The Transfer of Undertakings: Striking a Balance Between Individual Workers' Rights and Business Needs', International Journal of Comparative Labour Law and Industrial Relations, 23(3), 2007, pp. 311-334

Sauter W. & Schepel H., *State and Market in European Union Law: The Public and Private Spheres of the Internal Market Before the EU Courts*, Cambridge University Press, Leiden, 2009

Scharpf F., 'The Asymmetry of European Integration, or Why the EU Cannot Be a "Social Market Economy"', Socio-Economic Review, 8(2), 2009, pp. 211-250

Scheingold S., 'The Law in Political Integration: The Evolution and Integrative Implications of Regional Legal Processes in the European Community', Occiasional Paper in International Affairs, 27, Harvard University Center for International Affairs, 1971

Schepel H., 'Reconstructing Constitutionalization: Law and Politics in the European Court of Justice', Oxford Journal of Legal Studies, 20(3), 2000, pp. 457-468

Schiek D., 'Constitutional Principles and Horizontal Effect: Kücükdeveci Revisited', European Labour Law Journal, 1(3), 2010, pp. 368-379

Schmitter P.C., 'Ernst B. Haas and the Legacy of Neofunctionalism', Journal of European Public Policy, 12(2), 2006, pp. 255-272

Schoukens P. & Smets J.B., 'Fighting Social Exclusion under EU Horizon 2020. Enhancing the Legal Enforceability of the Social Inclusion Recommendations?', European Journal of Social Security, 16(1), 2014, pp. 51-72

Schoukens P., Barrio Fernandez A. & Montebovi S., 'The EU Social Pillar: An Answer to the Challenge of the Social Protection of Platform Workers?', European Journal of Social Security, 20(3), 2018, pp. 219-241

Schutze R., 'Judicial Majoritarianism Revisited: "We, the Other Court"?', European Law Review, 43(2), 2018, pp. 269-280

Sciarra S., 'Integration Through the Court: Article 177 as a Pre-federal Device' in S. Sciarra (ed.), *Labour Law in the Courts: National Judges and the European Court of Justice*, Hart Publishing, Oxford, 2001, pp. 1-24

Sciarra S., 'Market Freedom and Fundamental Social Rights', Working Paper, European University Institute, Florence, 2002

Sciarra S., 'The "Making" of EU Labour Law and the "Future" of Labour Lawyers' in C. Barnard, S. Deakin & G.S. Morris (eds), *The Future of Labour Law. Liber Amicorum Bob Hepple QC,* Hart Publishing, Portland, Oregon, 2004, pp. 201-211

Shapiro M., 'The European Court of Justice: Of Institutions and Democracy', Israel Law Review, 32(1), 1998, pp. 3-50

Shekhaway D.S., 'Rule of Law Crisis Deepens in Poland: Fresh Attack on the EU', A Path for Europe, 22 November 2021, https://pathforeurope.eu/rule-of-law-crisis-deepens-in-poland-fresh-attack-on-the-eu/

Sileoni S., 'La Corte Costituzionale Polacca, il Mandato d'Arresto Europeo e la Sentenza sul Trattato di Adesione all'UE', Quaderni Costituzionali, 4, 2005, pp. 894-896

Smit N., 'A Chronicle of Issues Raised in the Course of Dismissals by the Transferor and/or Transferee in Circumstances Involving the Transfer of an Undertaking', Industrial Law Journal, 26, 2005, pp. 1853-1895

Snyder F., 'The Effectiveness of European Community Law: Institutions, Processes, Tools and Techniques', The Modern Law Review, 56(1), 1993, pp. 19-54

Somma A., 'Il diritto del lavoro dopo i Trenta gloriosi', Lavoro e Diritto, 2, 2018, pp. 307-322

Spasova S., et al., 'Social Protection of Non-Standard Workers and the Self-Employed During the Pandemic', Report, 5, ETUI, Brussels, 2021

Staudt N., et al., 'Judging Statutes: Interpretive Regimes', Loyola of Los Angeles Law Review, 38, 2005, pp. 1909-1970

Stein E., 'Lawyers, Judges, and the Making of a Transnational Constitution', The American Journal of International Law, 75(1), 1981, pp. 1-27

Steinbeis M., 'We Super-Europeans', VerfBlog, 9 May 2020, https://verfassungsblog.de/we-super-europeans/

Stone K.W., 'Flexibilisation, Globalization and Privatization: Three Challenges to Labour Rights in Out Time', Public Law and Legal Theory Research Paper Series, UCLA School of Law, 2005

Stone Sweet A. & Brunell T., 'Constructing a Supranational Constitution', The American Political Science Review, 92(1), 1998, pp. 63-81

Stone Sweet A. & Caporaso J.A., 'From Free Trade to Supranational Polity: The European Court and Integration' in W. Sandholtz & A. Stone Sweet (eds), *European Integration and Supranational Governance*, Oxford University Press, Oxford, 1998, pp. 93-133

Stone Sweet A., 'Constitutional Dialogues in the European Community' in A.M. Slaughter, A. Stone Sweet & J. Weiler (eds), *The European Court and National Court – Doctrine and Jurisprudence: Legal Change in Its Social Context*, Hart Publishing, Oxford, 1998, pp. 305-331

Stone Sweet A. & McCown M., 'Discretion and Precedent in European Law' in O. Wiklund (ed.), *Judicial Discretion in European Perspective*, Norstedts Juridik, Stockholm, 2003, pp. 84

Stone Sweet A., *The Judicial Construction of Europe*, Oxford University Press, New York, 2004

Streit M.E., 'Has the Market Economy Still a Chance? On the Lack of a Discipline Challenge' in P. Koslowski (ed.), *The Social Market Economy*, Springer, Berlin, 1998, pp. 50-63

Strömholm S., 'Introductory Address' in O. Wiklund (ed.), *Judicial Discretion in European Perspective*, Norstedts Juridik, Stockholm, 2003, pp. 1-10

Stylogiannis C., 'Freedom of Association and Collective Bargaining in the Platform Economy: A Human Rights-Based Approach and an Over Increasing Mobilisation of Workers', International Labour Review, 138(1), 2021, pp. 1-24

Swinnen W., 'The Economic Perspective in the Reasoning of the ECJ in Age Discrimination Cases', European Labour Law Journal, 1(2), 2010, pp. 254-263

Syrpis P., *EU Intervention in Domestic Labour Law*, Oxford University Press, Oxford, 2007

Syrpis P., 'The Relationship Between Primary and Secondary Law in the EU', Common Market Law Review, 52, 2015, pp. 461-488

Tassinari A. & Maccarrone V., 'Riders on the Storm: Workplace Solidarity among Gig Economy Couriers in Italy and the UK', Work, Employment and Society, 34(1), 2020, pp. 35-54

Ter Haar B., 'Open Method of Coordination: A New Stepping Stone in the Legal Order of International and European Relations', Nordin Journal of International Law, 77(3), 2008, pp. 235-251

Terkelsen O., 'The Danish Ajos Case and the Danish Approach to International Law", European Public Law, 24(2), 2018, pp. 183-193

Tizzano A., 'Ancora sui rapporti tra Corti europee: principi comunitari e c.d. controlimiti costituzionali', Il diritto dell'Unione Europea, 12(3), 2007, pp. 734-744

Tremblay L.B., 'The Legitimacy of Judicial Review: The Limits of Dialogue Between Courts and Legislatures', International Journal of Constitutional Law, 3(4), 2005, pp. 617-648

Treu T., 'The Role of a European Social Model' in R. Blanpain, C. Engels, M. Weiss & B. Aaron (eds), *Labour Law and Industrial Relations at the Turn of the Century: Liber Amicorum in Honour of Roger Blanpain*, Kluwer Law International, The Hague, 1998

Tridimas T., 'The ECJ and the National Courts: Dialogue, Cooperation, and Instability' in D. Chalmers & A. Arnull (eds), *The Oxford Handbook of European Union Law*, Oxford University Press, Oxford, 2015, pp. 1-30

Trstenjak V., 'National Sovereignity and the Principle of Primacy in EU Law and Their Importance for the Member States', Beijing Law Review, 4(2), 2013, pp. 71-76

Tsebelis G. & Garret G., 'The Institutional Foundations of Intergovernmentalism and Supranationalism in the European Union', International Organization, 55(2), 2001, pp. 357-390

Usai A., 'The Freedom to Conduct a Business in the EU, Its Limitations and Its Role in the European Legal Order: A New Engine for Deeper and Stronger Economic, Social, and Political Integration', German Law Journal, 14(9), 2013, pp. 1867-1888

Valdés Dal-Ré F., 'Transfers of Undertakings: An Experience of Clashes and Harmonies between Community Law and National Legal Systems' in S. Sciarra (ed.), *Labour Law in the Courts: National Judges and the European Court of Justice*, Hart Publishing, Oxford, 2001, pp. 179-209

Van Gestel R. & De Poorter J., *In the Court We Trust: Cooperation, Coordination and Collaboration Between the ECJ and Supreme Administrative Courts*, Cambridge University Press, Cambridge, 2019

Van Hiel I., 'The Protection of Collectively Agreed Labour Conditions Under the Transfer of Undertakings Directive' in J. de Bruyne, M. de Potter & I. Van Hiel (eds), *Policy Within and Through Law*, Maklu, Anterpen, 2015, pp. 283-294

van Vliet O. & Nijboer H., 'Flexicurity in the European Union: Flexibility for Outsiders, Security for Insiders', Research Memorandum, 2, Department of Economics, 2012

Vanhercke B. & Verdun B., 'From the European Semester to the Recovery and Resilience Facility – Some Social Actors Are (Not) Resurfacing', Working Paper, 13, ETUI, Brussels, 2021

Vanhercke B. & Verdun A., 'The European Semester as Goldilocks: Macroeconomic Policy Coordination and the Recovery and Resilience Facility', Journal of Common Market Studies, 60(1), 2022, pp. 204-223

Vatsov M., 'European Integration Through Preliminary Rulings? The Case of the Bulgarian Constitutional Court', German Law Journal, 16(6), 2015, pp. 1591-1622

Veneziani B., 'The Evolution of the Contract of Employment' in B. Hepple (ed.), *The Making of Labour Law in Europe*, Mansell Publishing Limited, London, 1986, pp. 31-70

Veneziani B., 'The Employment Relationship' in B.A. Hepple & B. Veneziani (eds), *The Transformation of Labour Law in Europe: A Comparative Study of 15 Countries, 1945-2004*, Hart Publishing, Oxford, 2009, pp. 99-128

Veneziani B., 'The Role of the Social Partners in the Lisbon Treaty' in N. Bruun, K. Lörcher & I. Schömann (eds), *The Lisbon Treaty and Social Europe*, Hart Publishing, Oxford and Portland, Oregon, 2012, pp. 123-161

Vergis F., 'Back to the Future: Rediscovering the Non-economic Role, Value and Scope of Labour Law and Collective Labour Institutions in a Changing World' in A. Blackham, M. Kullmann & A. Zbyszewska (eds), *Theorising Labour Law in a Changing World: Towards Inclusive Labour Law*, Bloomsbury Publishing, Oxford, 2019, pp. 81-106

Vesterdorf B., 'A Constitutional Court for the EU?', International Journal of Constitutional Law, 4(4), 2006, pp. 607-617

Vielle P., 'How the Horizontal Social Clause Can Be Made to Work: The Lessons of Gender Mainstreaming' in N. Bruun, K. Lörcher & I. Schömann (eds), *The Lisbon Treaty and Social Europe*, Hart Publishing, Oxford and Portland, Oregon, 2012, pp. 105-121

Viţă V., 'The Romanian Constitutional Court and the Principle of Primacy: To Refer or Not to Refer?', German Law Journal, 16(6), 2015, pp. 1623-1662

von Bogdandy A. & Schill S., 'Overcoming Absolute Primacy: Respect for National Identity under the Lisbon Treaty', Common Market Law Review, 48, 2011, pp. 1417-1454

Walker N., 'The Idea of Constitutional Pluralism', The Modern Law Review, 65(3), 2002, pp. 317-359

Walker N., 'Late Sovereignty in the European Union' in N. Walker (ed.), *Sovereignty in Transition*, Hart Publishing, Portland, 2003, pp. 3-32

Watrin C., 'The Social Market Economy: The Main Ideas and Their Influence on Economic Policy' in P. Koslowski (ed.), *The Social Market Economy*, Springer, Berlin, 1998, pp. 13-28

Weatherill S., 'The Common Market: Mission Accomplished?' in V. Heiskanen & K. Kulovesi (eds), *Function and Future of European Law*, Helsinki University Press, Helsinki, 1999, pp. 33-57

Weatherill S., 'Use and Abuse of the EU's Charter of Fundamental Rights: On the Improper Veneration of "Freedom of Contract"', European Review of Contract Law, 10(1), 2014, pp. 167-182

Weatherill S., 'Viking and Laval: The Internal Market Perspective' in M. Freedland & J. Prassl (eds), *Viking, Laval and Beyond*, Hart Publishing, London, 2014, pp. 23-40

Wedderburn L., 'Labour Standards, Global Markets and Labour Law in Europe' in, *International Labour Standards and Economic Interdependence*, International Institute for Labour Studies, Geneva, 1994, pp. 247-253

Weiler J.H.H., 'The Community System: the Dual Character of Supranationalism', Yearbook of European Law, 1(1), 1981, pp. 267-306

Weiler J.H.H., 'The Transformation of Europe', The Yale Law Journal, 100(8), 1991, pp. 2403-83

Weiler J., 'Europe: The Case Against the Case of Statehood', European Law Journal, 4(1), 1998, pp. 43-62

Weiler J.H.H., 'Federalism Without Constitutionalism: Europe's Sonderweg' in K. Nicolaïdis & R. Howse (eds), *The Federal Vision: Legitimacy and Levels of Governance in the United States and the European Union*, Oxford University Press, Oxford, 2001

Weiler J.H.H., 'Prologue: Global and Pluarlist Constitutionalism – Some Doubts' in Gròinne de Burca & J.H.J. Weiler (eds), *The Worlds of European Constitutionialism*, Cambridge University Press, Cambridge, 2012, pp. 8-19

Weiler J.H.H., 'Van Gend En Loos: The Individual as Subject and Object and the Dilemma of European Legitimacy', International Journal of Constitutional Law, 12(1), 2014, pp. 94-103

Weiss M., 'The Future of Workers' Participation in the EU' in C. Barnard, S. Deakin & G.S. Morris (eds), *The Future of Labour Law: Liber Amicorum Bob Hepple QC*, Hart Publishing, Portland, Oregon, 2004, pp. 229-251

Weiss M., 'Re-inventing Labour Law?' in G. Davidov & B. Langille (eds), *The Idea of Labour Law*, Oxford University Press, Oxford, 2011, pp. 43-56

Welz C., 'From Val Duchesse to Riga: How to Relaunch Social Dialogue?', Social Europe, 2015, https://socialeurope.eu/val-duchesse-riga-relaunch-social-dialogue

Wije A., 'Changing Terms and Conditions Following a TUPE Transfer', Emerald Insight, 20(4), 2018, pp. 1-5

Wijtvliet W. & Dyevre A., 'Judicial Ideology in Economic Cases: Evidence from the General Court of the European Union', European Union Politics, 22(1), 2021, pp. 25-45

Wiklund O., 'Taking the World View of the European Judge Seriously' in O. Wiklund (ed.), *Judicial Discretion in European Perspective*, Norstedts Juridik, Stockholm, 2003, pp. 29-47

Wilthagen A.C.J.M., 'Flexicurity Pathways: Turning Hurdles into Stepping-Stones', Expert Report for the European Commission, Tilburg Flexicurity Research Programme, Tilburg, 2007

Windbichler C., 'Cheers and Boos for Employee Involvement: Co-determination as Corporate Governance Conundrum', European Business Organization Law Review, 6, 2005, pp. 507-537

Wolff G., et al., 'Post-Council Commentary', Podcast, Bruegel Think Tank, 24 April 2020

Wyatt D., 'Horizontal Effect of Fundamental Freedoms and the Right to Equality after Viking and Mangold, and the Implications for Community Competence', Legal Research Paper series, published in Croatian Yearbook of European Law & Policy, Oxford, 2008

Wynn-Evans C., 'TUPE, Collective Agreements and the Static-Dynamic Debate', Industrial Law Journal, 39(3), 2010, pp. 275-279

Zahn R., 'The Court of Justice of the European Union and Transfers of Undertakings. Implications for Collective Labour Rights', European Labour Law Journal, 6(1), 2015, pp. 72-85

Zekic N., 'Job Security or Employment Security: What's in a Name', European Labour Law Journal, 7(4), 2016, pp. 548-575

Table of Cases

Judgment of 2 September 2021, *European Federation of Public Service Unions (EPSU) v. European Commission*, C-928/19, ECLI:EU:C:2021:656, 67

Judgment of 15 July 2021, *European Commission v. Republic of Poland*, C-791/19, ECLI:EU:C:2021:596, 253

Judgment of 15 July 2021, *IX v. WABE eV and MH Müller Handels GmbH v. MJ*, C-804/18, Joined Cases C-804/18 and C-341/19, ECLI:EU:C:2021:594, 220, 264

Judgment of 9 September 2020, *EM v. TMD Friction GmbH and FL v. TMD Friction EsCo GmbH*, C-674/18, ECLI:EU:C:2020:682, 103

Judgment of 26 March 2020, *ISS Facility Services NV v. Sonia Govaerts and Atalian NV, formerly Euroclean NV*, C-344/18, ECLI:EU:C:2020:239, 134, 158

Judgment of 27 February 2020, *Reiner Grafe and Jürgen Pohle v. Südbrandenburger Nahverkehrs GmbH and OSL Bus GmbH*, C-298/18, ECLI:EU:C:2020:121, 120, 277, 287

Judgment of 13 June 2019, *Cátia Correia Moreira v. Município de Portimão*, C-317/18, ECLI:EU:C:2019:499, 103, 294

Judgment of 13 June 2019, *Ellinika Nafpigeia AE v. Panagiotis Anagnostopoulos and Others*, C-664/17, ECLI:EU:C:2019:496, 109, 121, 277

Judgment of 16 May 2019, *Christa Plessers v. PREFACO NV and Belgische Staat*, C-509/17, ECLI:EU:C:2019:424, 103

Judgment of 8 May 2019, *Jadran Dodič v. Banka Koper and Alta Invest*, C-194/18, ECLI:EU:C:2019:385, 300

Judgment of 11 December 2018, *Proceedings brought by Heinrich Weiss and Others*, C-493/17, ECLI:EU:C:2018:1000, 247

Judgment of 7 August 2018, *Jorge Luís Colino Sigüenza v. Ayuntamiento de Valladolid and Others*, C-472/16, ECLI:EU:C:2018:646, 278

Judgment of 11 July 2018, *Ángel Somoza Hermo and Ilunión Seguridad SA v. Esabe Vigilancia SA and Fondo de Garantia Salarial (Fogasa)*, C-60/17, ECLI: EU:C:2018:559, 277

Judgment of 17 April 2018, *Vera Egenberger v. Evangelisches Werk für Diakonie und Entwicklung e.V.*, C-414/16, ECLI:EU:C:2018:257, 261

Judgment of 5 December 2017, *Criminal proceedings against M.A.S. and M.B.*, C-42/17, ECLI:EU:C:2017:936, 224

Judgment of 19 October 2017, *Securitas - Serviços e Tecnologia de Segurança SA v. ICTS Portugal – Consultadoria de Aviação Comercial SA and Others*, C-200/16, ECLI: EU:C:2017:780, 119

Judgment of 20 July 2017, *Luís Manuel Piscarreta Ricardo v. Portimão Urbis EM SA and Others*, C-416/16, ECLI:EU:C:2017:574, 103, 109, 277

Judgment of 22 June 2017, *Federatie Nederlandse Vakvereniging and Others v. Smallsteps BV*, C-126/16, ECLI:EU:C:2017:489, 103

Judgment of 27 April 2017, *Asklepios Kliniken Langen-Seligenstadt GmbH v. Ivan Felja and Asklepios Dienstleistungsgesellschaft mbH v. Vittoria Graf*, C-680/15, ECLI: EU:C:2017:317, 130, 131, 158, 278, 298

Judgment of 6 April 2017, *Unionen v. Almega Tjänsteförbunden and ISS Facility Services AB*, C-336/15, ECLI:EU:C:2017:276, 125, 133

Judgment of 14 March 2017, *Samira Achbita and Centrum voor gelijkheid van kansen en voor racismebestrijding v. G4S Secure Solutions NV*, C-157/15, ECLI: EU:C:2017:203, 2, 158

Judgment of 14 March 2017, *Asma Bougnaoui and Association de défense des droits de l'homme (ADDH) v. Micropole SA*, C-188/15, ECLI:EU:C:2017:204, 2, 158

Judgment of 21 December 2016, *Anonymi Geniki Etairia Tsimenton Iraklis (AGET Iraklis) v. Ypourgos Ergasias, Koinonikis Asfalisis kai Koinonikis Allilengyis*, C-201/15, ECLI:EU:C:2016:972, 2, 32, 38

Judgment of 19 April 2016, *Dansk Industri (DI), acting on behalf of Ajos A/S v. Estate of Karsten Eigil Rasmussen*, C-441/14, ECLI:EU:C:2016:278, 5, 160, 223, 256

Judgment of 26 November 2015, *Administrador de Infraestructuras Ferroviarias (ADIF) v. Luis Aira Pascual and Others*, C-509/14, ECLI:EU:C:2015:781, 103, 109, 277

Judgment of 9 September 2015, *João Filipe Ferreira da Silva e Brito and Others v. Estado português*, C-160/14, ECLI:EU:C:2015:565, 118, 277

Judgment of 8 September 2015, *Criminal proceedings against Ivo Taricco and Others*, C-105/14, ECLI:EU:C:2015:555, 204, 225

Judgment of 16 June 2015, *Peter Gauweiler and Others v. Deutscher Bundestag*, C-62/14, ECLI:EU:C:2015:400

Judgment of 18 December 2014, *Opinion pursuant to Article 218(11) TFEU — Draft international agreement — Accession of the European Union to the European Convention for the Protection of Human Rights and Fundamental Freedoms — Compatibility of the draft agreement with the EU and FEU Treaties*, C-2/13, ECLI:EU:C:2014:48, 198

Judgment of 11 September 2014, *Österreichischer Gewerkschaftsbund v. Wirtschaftskammer Österreich — Fachverband Autobus-, Luftfahrt- und Schifffahrtsunternehmungen*, C-328/13, ECLI:EU:C:2014:2197, 131, 158, 278

Judgment of 6 March 2014, *Lorenzo Amatori and Others v. Telecom Italia SpA and Telecom Italia Information Technology Srl*, C-458/12, ECLI:EU:C:2014:124, 108, 278, 280

Judgment of 15 January 2014, *Association de médiation sociale v. Union locale des syndicats CGT and Others*, C-176/12, ECLI:EU:C:2014:2, 260

Judgment of 18 July 2013, *Mark Alemo-Herron and Others v. Parkwood Leisure Ltd*, C-426/11, ECLI:EU:C:2013:521, 2, 32, 130, 158, 300

Judgment of 26 February 2013, *Stefano Melloni v. Ministerio Fiscal*, C-399/11, ECLI: EU:C:2013:107, 221, 249

Judgment of 24 January 2012, *Maribel Dominguez v. Centre informatique du Centre Ouest Atlantique and Préfet de la région Centre*, C-282/10, ECLI:EU:C:2012:33, 223, 259

Judgment of 6 September 2011, *Ivana Scattolon v. Ministero dell'Istruzione, dell'Università e della Ricerca*, C-108/10, ECLI:EU:C:2011:542, 109, 120, 125, 133

Judgment of 22 June 2011, *Marie Landtová v. Česká správa socialního zabezpečení*, C-399/09, ECLI:EU:C:2011:415, 251

Judgment of 8 March 2011, *Gerardo Ruiz Zambrano v. Office national de l'emploi (ONEm)*, C-34/09, ECLI:EU:C:2011:124, 149

Judgment of 20 January 2011, *CLECE SA v. María Socorro Martín Valor and Ayuntamiento de Cobisa*, C-463/09, ECLI:EU:C:2011:24, 103, 109, 278

Judgment of 22 December 2010, *Ilonka Sayn-Wittgenstein v. Landeshauptmann von Wien*, C-208/09, ECLI:EU:C:2010:806, 219

Judgment of 21 October 2010, *Albron Catering BV v. FNV Bondgenoten and John Roest*, C-242/09, ECLI:EU:C:2010:625, 108

Judgment of 14 September 2010, *Akzo Nobel Chemicals Ltd and Akcros Chemicals Ltd v. European Commission*, C-550/07, ECLI:EU:C:2010:512, 212

Judgment of 29 July 2010, *Federación de Servicios Públicos de la UGT (UGT-FSP) v. Ayuntamiento de La Línea de la Concepción, María del Rosario Vecino Uribe and Ministerio Fiscal*, C-151/09, ECLI:EU:C:2010:452, 102-103, 109, 122, 277

Judgment of 22 June 2010, *Aziz Melki and Sélim Abdeli*, C-188/10, Joined cases C-188/10 and C-189/10, ECLI:EU:C:2010:363, 249

Judgment of 2 March 2010, *Janko Rottman v. Freistaat Bayern*, C-135/08, ECLI: EU:C:2010:104, 211

Judgment of 19 January 2010, *Seda Kücükdeveci gegen Swedex GmbH & Co. KG.*, C-555/07, ECLI:EU:C:2010:21, 5, 148, 160, 176, 255

Judgment of 19 November 2009, *Krzysztof Filipiak v. Dyrektor Izby Skarbowej w Poznaniu*, C-314/08, ECLI:EU:C:2009:719, 221, 252

Judgment of 12 February 2009, *Dietmar Klarenberg v. Ferrotron Technologies GmbH*, C-466/07, ECLI:EU:C:2009:85, 121, 277

Judgment of 16 December 2008, *Michaniki AE v. Ethniko Symvoulio Radiotileorasis and Ypourgos Epikrateias*, C-213/07, ECLI:EU:C:2008:731, 217

Judgment of 27 November 2008, *Mirja Juuri v. Fazer Amica Oy*, C-396/07, ECLI: EU:C:2008:656, 125, 133

Judgment of 3 April 2008, *Dirk Rüffert v. Land Niedersachsen*, C-346/06, ECLI: EU:C:2008:189, 221

Judgment of 1 April 2008, *Tadao Maruko v. Versorgungsanstalt der deutschen Bühnen*, C-267/06, ECLI:EU:C:2008:179, 5, 210, 221

Judgment of 14 February 2008, *Dynamic Medien Vertriebs GmbH v. Avides Media AG*, C-244/06, ECLI:EU:C:2008:85, 219

Judgment of 18 December 2007, *Laval un Partneri Ltd v. Svenska Byggnadsarbetareförbundet, Svenska Byggnadsarbetareförbundets avdelning 1, Byggettan and Svenska Elektrikerförbundet*, C-341/05, ECLI:EU:C:2007:809, 2, 35, 157

Judgment of 11 December 2007, *International Transport Workers' Federation and Finnish Seamen's Union v. Viking Line ABP and OÜ Viking Line Eesti*, C-438/05, ECLI:EU:C:2007:772, 2, 35, 157

Judgment of 13 September 2007, *Mohamed Jouini and Others v. Princess Personal Service GmbH (PPS)*, C-458/05, ECLI:EU:C:2007:512, 108, 120, 277

Judgment of 15 February 2007, *Athinaïki Chartopoïïa AE v. L. Panagiotidis and Others*, C-270/05, ECLI:EU:C:2007:101, 38

Judgment of 6 September 2006, *Portuguese Republic v. Commission of the European Communities*, C-88/03, ECLI:EU:C:2006:511, 219

Judgment of 13 June 2006, *Traghetti del Mediterraneo SpA v. Repubblica italiana*, C-173/03, ECLI:EU:C:2006:391, 156, 170

Judgment of 27 April 2006, *Sarah Margaret Richards v. Secretary of State for Work and Pensions*, C-423/04, ECLI:EU:C:2006:256, 209

Judgment of 9 March 2006, *Hans Werhof v. Freeway Traffic Systems GmbH & Co. KG*, C-499/04, ECLI:EU:C:2006:168, 125, 128, 129, 158, 300

Judgment of 15 December 2005, *Nurten Güney-Görres v. Securicor Aviation (Germany) Ltd and Kötter Aviation Security GmbH & Co. KG*, C-232/04, Joined cases C-232/04 and C-233/04, ECLI:EU:C:2005:778, 119, 277

Judgment of 22 November 2005, *Werner Mangold v. Rüdiger Helm*, C-144/04, ECLI: EU:C:2005:709, 5, 148, 159, 176, 255

Judgment of 25 January 2005, *Irmtraud Junk v. Wolfgang Kühnel*, C-188/03, ECLI: EU:C:2005:59, 38

Judgment of 11 November 2004, *Johanna Maria Delahaye, née Delahaye v. Ministre de la Fonction publique et de la Réforme administrative*, C-425/02, ECLI: EU:C:2004:706, 102, 109

Judgment of 14 October 2004, *Omega Spielhallen- und Automatenaufstellungs-GmbH v. Oberbürgermeisterin der Bundesstadt Bonn*, C-36/02, ECLI:EU:C:2004:614, 35, 218

Judgment of 23 March 2004, *Brian Francis Collins v. Secretary of State for Work and Pensions*, C-138/02, ECLI:EU:C:2004:172, 148

Judgment of 7 January 2004, *K.B. v. National Health Service Pensions Agency and Secretary of State for Health*, C-117/01, ECLI:EU:C:2004:7, 209

Judgment of 20 November 2003, *Carlito Abler and Others v. Sodexho MM Catering Gesellschaft mbH*, C-340/01, ECLI:EU:C:2003:629, 118, 277, 303

Judgment of 6 November 2003, *Serene Martin, Rohit Daby and Brian Willis v. South Bank University*, C-4/01, ECLI:EU:C:2003:594, 272

Judgment of 6 November 2003, *Criminal proceedings against Piergiorgio Gambelli and Others*, C-243/01, ECLI:EU:C:2003:597, 219

Judgment of 30 September 2003, *Gerhard Köbler v. Republik Österreich*, C-224/01, ECLI:EU:C:2003:513, 156, 170

Judgment of 12 June 2003, *Eugen Schmidberger, Internationale Transporte und Planzüge v. Republik Österreich*, C-112/00, ECLI:EU:C:2003:333, 35, 219

Judgment of 27 February 2003, *Santex SpA v. Unità Socio Sanitaria Locale n. 42 di Pavia, and Sca Mölnlycke SpA, Artsana SpA and Fater SpA*, C-327/00, ECLI: EU:C:2003:109, 237
Judgment of 17 September 2002, *Baumbast and R v. Secretary of State for the Home Department*, C-413/99, ECLI:EU:C:2002:493, 148
Judgment of 24 January 2002, *Temco Service Industries SA v. Samir Imzilyen and Others*, C-51/00, ECLI:EU:C:2002:48, 101, 277
Judgment of 26 June 2001, *The Queen v. Secretary of State for Trade and Industry, ex parte Broadcasting, Entertainment, Cinematographic and Theatre Union (BECTU)*, C-173/99, ECLI:EU:C:2001:356, 206
Judgment of 6 March 2001, *Roderick Dunnett and Others v. European Investment Bank*, T-192/99, ECLI:EU:T:2001:72, 206
Judgment of 25 January 2001, *Oy Liikenne Ab v. Pekka Liskojärvi and Pentti Juntunen*, C-172/99, ECLI:EU:C:2001:59, 107, 109, 118, 277, 280, 287
Judgment of 26 September 2000, *Didier Mayeur v. Association Promotion de l'information messine (APIM)*, C-175/99, ECLI:EU:C:2000:505, 102, 109, 134, 277
Judgment of 14 September 2000, *Renato Collino and Luisella Chiappero v. Telecom Italia SpA*, C-343/98, ECLI:EU:C:2000:441, 103, 109, 280
Judgment of 6 July 2000, *Katarina Abrahamsson and Leif Anderson v. Elisabet Fogelqvist*, C-407/98, ECLI:EU:C:2000:367, 210
Judgment of 11 January 2000, *Tanja Kreil v. Bundesrepublik Deutschland*, C-285/98, ECLI:EU:C:2000:2, 221
Judgment of 2 December 1999, *G. C. Allen and Others v. Amalgamated Construction Co. Ltd*, C-234/98, ECLI:EU:C:1999:594, 108, 277, 280
Judgment of 10 December 1998, *Francisco Hernández Vidal SA v. Prudencia Gómez Pérez, María Gómez Pérez and Contratas y Limpiezas SL*, C-127/96, Joined cases C-127/96, C-229/96 and C-74/97, ECLI:EU:C:1998:594, 119, 277
Judgment of 10 December 1998, *Francisca Sánchez Hidalgo and Others v. Asociación de Servicios Aser and Sociedad Cooperativa Minerva*, C-173/96, Joined cases C-173/96 and C-247/96, ECLI:EU:C:1998:595, 107, 109, 280
Judgment of 10 December 1998, *Horst Ziemann v. Ziemann Sicherheit GmbH and Horst Bohn Sicherheitsdienst*, C-247/96, Joined cases C-173/96 and C-247/96, ECLI: EU:C:1998:595, 107
Judgment of 1 December 1998, *Criminal proceedings against André Ambry.*, C-410/96, ECLI:EU:C:1998:578, 236
Judgment of 12 November 1998, *Europièces SA v. Wilfried Sanders and Automotive Industries Holding Company SA*, C-399/96, ECLI:EU:C:1998:532, 91
Judgment of 12 March 1998, *Jules Dethier Équipement SA v. Jules Dassy and Sovam SPRL*, C-319/94, ECLI:EU:C:1998:99, 103
Judgment of 17 February 1998, *Lisa Jacqueline Grant v. South-West Trains Ltd*, C-249/96, ECLI:EU:C:1998:63, 206, 209
Judgment of 16 October 1997, *Maria Antonella Garofalo (C-69/96), Giovanni Pagano (C-70/96), Rosa Bruna Vitale (C-71/96), Francesca Nuccio (C-72/96), Giacomo Cangialosi (C-73/96), Giacoma D'Amico (C-74/96), Giulia Lombardo (C-75/96), Emanuela Giovenco (C-76/96), Caterina Lo Gaglio (C-77/96), Daniela Guerrera*

(C-78/96) and Cesare Di Marco (-79/96) v. Ministero della Sanità and Unità sanitaria locale (USL) n° 58 di Palermo, C-69/96, Joined cases C-69/96 and C-79/96, ECLI:EU:C:1997:492, 229

Judgment of 17 September 1997, *Dorsch Consult Ingenieurgesellschaft mbH v. Bundesbaugesellschaft Berlin mbH*, C-54/96, ECLI:EU:C:1997:413, 206

Judgment of 11 March 1997, *Ayse Süzen v. Zehnacker Gebäudereinigung GmbH Krankenhausservice*, C-13/95, ECLI:EU:C:1997:141, 95, 107, 116, 277, 280, 283, 292

Judgment of 15 October 1996, *Annette Henke v. Gemeinde Schierke and Verwaltungsgemeinschaft Brocken*, C-298/94, ECLI:EU:C:1996:382, 102, 109

Judgment of 8 October 1996, *Anke Heuer v. Bundesrepublik Deutschland*, C-189/94, Joined cases C-178/94, C-179/94, C-188/94, C-189/94 and C-190/94, ECLI:EU:C:1996:375, 241

Judgment of 30 April 1996, *P v. S and Cornwall County Council*, C-13/94, ECLI:EU:C:1996:170, 176, 209

Judgment of 28 March 1996, *Accession by the Community to the European Convention for the Protection of Human Rights and Fundamental Freedoms*, C-2/94, ECLI:EU:C:1996:140, 190

Judgment of 7 March 1996, *Albert Merckx and Patrick Neuhuys v. Ford Motors Company Belgium SA*, C-171/94, Joined cases C-171/94 and C-172/94, ECLI:EU:C:1996:87, 103, 116, 277

Judgment of 5 March 1996, *Brasserie du Pêcheur SA v. Bundesrepublik Deutschland and The Queen v. Secretary of State for Transport, ex parte: Factortame Ltd and others*, C-46/93, ECLI:EU:C:1996:79, 156

Judgment of 14 December 1995, *Peterbroeck, Van Campenhout & Cie SCS v. Belgian State*, C-312/93, ECLI:EU:C:1995:437, 237

Judgment of 7 December 1995, *Luigi Spano and others v. Fiat Geotech SpA and Fiat Hitachi Excavators SpA*, C-472/93, ECLI:EU:C:1995:421, 91

Judgment of 30 November 1995, *Reinhard Gebhard v. Consiglio dell'Ordine degli Avvocati e Procuratori di Milano*, C-55/94, ECLI:EU:C:1995:411, 229

Judgment of 17 October 1995, *Eckhard Kalanke v. Freie Hansestadt Bremen*, C-450/93, ECLI:EU:C:1995:322, 210

Judgment of 19 September 1995, *Ledernes Hovedorganisation, acting for Ole Rygaard v. Dansk Arbejdsgiverforening, acting for Strø Mølle Akustik A/S*, C-48/94, ECLI:EU:C:1995:290, 95, 116, 283, 299

Judgment of 14 July 1994, *Carole Louise Webb v. EMO Air Cargo (UK) Ltd*, C-32/93, ECLI:EU:C:1994:300, 176

Judgment of 8 June 1994, *Commission of the European Communities v. United Kingdom of Great Britain and Northern Ireland*, C-382/92, ECLI:EU:C:1994:233, 109, 122

Judgment of 14 April 1994, *Christel Schmidt v. Spar- und Leihkasse der früheren Ämter Bordesholm, Kiel und Cronshagen*, C-392/92, ECLI:EU:C:1994:134, 95, 115, 283, 292

Judgment of 24 March 1994, *Her Majesty's Customs and Excise v. Gerhart Schindler and Jörg Schindler*, C-275/92, ECLI:EU:C:1994:119, 208

Judgment of 24 November 1993, *Criminal proceedings against Bernard Keck and Daniel Mithouard*, C-267/91, ECLI:EU:C:1993:905, 208

Judgment of 18 May 1993, *Schutzverband gegen Unwesen in der Wirtschaft e.V. v. Yves Rocher GmbH*, C-126/91, ECLI:EU:C:1993:191, 206

Judgment of 26 January 1993, *Telemarsicabruzzo SpA and Others v. Circostel, Ministero delle Poste e Telecomunicazioni and Ministero della Difesa*, C-320/90, Joined cases C-320/90, C-321/90 and C-322/90, ECLI:EU:C:1993:26, 233

Judgment of 12 November 1992, *Anne Watson Rask and Kirsten Christensen v. Iss Kantineservice A/S*, C-209/91, ECLI:EU:C:1992:436, 128

Judgment of 19 May 1992, *Dr. Sophie Redmond Stichting v. Hendrikus Bartol and others*, C-29/91, ECLI:EU:C:1992:220, 107, 109, 115, 280

Judgment of 19 November 1991, *Andrea Francovich and Danila Bonifaci and others v. Italian Republic*, C-6/90, ECLI:EU:C:1991:428, 156, 170

Judgment of 25 July 1991, *Giuseppe d'Urso, Adriana Ventadori and others v. Ercole Marelli Elettromeccanica Generale SpA and others*, C-362/89, ECLI:EU:C:1991:326, 91, 92, 128

Judgment of 18 June 1991, *Elliniki Radiophonia Tiléorassi AE and Panellinia Omospondia Syllogon Prossopikou v. Dimotiki Etairia Pliroforissis and Sotirios Kouvelas and Nicolaos Avdellas and others*, C-260/89, ECLI:EU:C:1991:254, 39, 170

Judgment of 13 November 1990, *Marleasing SA v. La Comercial Internacional de Alimentacion SA*, C-106/89, ECLI:EU:C:1990:395, 170

Judgment of 27 June 1990, *Maria Kowalska v. Freie und Hansestadt Hamburg*, C-33/89, ECLI:EU:C:1990:265, 176

Judgment of 17 May 1990, *Douglas Harvey Barber v. Guardian Royal Exchange Assurance Group*, C-262/88, ECLI:EU:C:1990:209, 175, 196

Judgment of 7 March 1990, *GB-INNO-BM v. Confédération du commerce luxembourgeois*, C-362/88, ECLI:EU:C:1990:102, 206

Judgment of 8 November 1989, *Elisabeth Johanna Pacifica Dekker v. Stichting Vormingscentrum voor Jong Volwassenen (VJV-Centrum) Plus*, C-177/88, ECLI:EU:C:1990:383, 176

Judgment of 13 July 1989, *Hubert Wachauf v. Bundesamt für Ernährung und Forstwirtschaft*, C-5/88, ECLI:EU:C:1989:321, 170, 241

Judgment of 13 July 1989, *Ingrid Rinner-Kühn v. FWW Spezial-Gebäudereinigung GmbH & Co. KG*, C-171/88, ECLI:EU:C:1989:328, 176

Judgment of 11 May 1989, *Commission of the European Communities v. Federal Republic of Germany*, C-76/86, ECLI:EU:C:1989:184, 207

Judgment of 14 July 1988, *3 Glocken GmbH and Gertraud Kritzinger v. USL Centro-Sud and Provincia autonoma di Bolzano*, C-407/85, ECLI:EU:C:1988:401, 206

Judgment of 14 July 1988, *Criminal proceedings against Zoni*, C-90/86, ECLI:EU:C:1988:403, 206

Judgment of 15 June 1988, *P. Bork International A/S, in liquidation v. Foreningen af Arbejdsledere I Danmark, acting on behalf of Birger E. Petersen, and Jens E. Olsen and others v. Junckers Industrier A/S*, C-101/87, ECLI:EU:C:1988:308, 107, 280

Judgment of 5 May 1988, *Harry Berg and Johannes Theodorus Maria Busschers v. Ivo Martin Besselsen*, C-144/87, ECLI:EU:C:1988:236, 109, 128, 295

Judgment of 10 February 1988, *Foreningen af Arbejdsledere i Danmark v. Daddy's Dance Hall A/S*, C-324/86, ECLI:EU:C:1988:72, 107, 128, 280, 282

Judgment of 17 December 1987, *Landsorganisationen i Danmark for Tjenerforbundet i Danmark v. Ny Mølle Kro*, C-287/86, ECLI:EU:C:1987:573, 282

Judgment of 22 October 1987, *Foto-Frost v. Hauptzollamt Lübeck-Ost*, C-314/85, ECLI:EU:C:1987:452, 245

Judgment of 29 September 1987, *Giménez Zaera v. Instituto Nacional de la Seguridad Social and Tesorería General de la Seguridad Social*, C-126/86, ECLI: EU:C:1987:395, 51

Judgment of 12 March 1987, *Commission of the European Communities v. Hellenic Republic*, C-176/84, ECLI:EU:C:1987:125, 206

Judgment of 12 March 1987, *Commission of the European Communities v. Federal Republic of Germany*, C-178/84, ECLI:EU:C:1987:126, 206

Judgment of 4 December 1986, *Commission of the European Communities v. Federal Republic of Germany*, C-179/85, ECLI:EU:C:1986:466, 206

Judgment of 15 May 1986, *Marguerite Johnston v. Chief Constable of the Royal Ulster Constabulary*, C-222/84, ECLI:EU:C:1986:206, 204

Judgment of 13 May 1986, *Bilka - Kaufhaus GmbH v. Karin Weber von Hartz*, C-170/84, ECLI:EU:C:1986:204, 175

Judgment of 17 April 1986, *State of the Netherlands v. Ann Florence Reed*, C-59/85, ECLI:EU:C:1986:157, 206

Judgment of 18 March 1986, *Jozef Maria Antonius Spijkers v. Gebroeders Benedik Abattoir CV and Alfred Benedik en Zonen BV*, C-24/85, ECLI:EU:C:1986:127, 115, 282

Judgment of 11 July 1985, *Foreningen af Arbejdsledere i Danmark v. A/S Danmols Inventar, in liquidation*, C-105/84, ECLI:EU:C:1985:331, 103

Judgment of 7 February 1985, *Abels v. Bedrijfsvereniging voor de Metaalindustrie en de Electrotechnische Industrie*, C-135/83, ECLI:EU:C:1985:55, 91

Judgment of 7 February 1985, *Knud Wendelboe and others v. L.J. Music ApS, in liquidation*, C-19/83, ECLI:EU:C:1985:54, 103

Judgment of 7 February 1985, *Industriebond FNV and Federatie Nederlandse Vakbeweging (FNV) v. The Netherlands State*, C-179/83, ECLI:EU:C:1985:57, 103

Judgment of 10 April 1984, *Sabine von Colson and Elisabeth Kamann v. Land Nordrhein-Westfalen*, C-14/83, ECLI:EU:C:1984:153, 234

Judgment of 13 March 1984, *Criminal proceedings against Karl Prantl*, C-16/83, ECLI:EU:C:1984:101, 206

Judgment of 21 September 1983, *Deutsche Milchkontor GmbH and others v. Federal Republic of Germany*, C-215/82, ECLI:EU:C:1983:233, 207

Judgment of 17 March 1983, *Criminal proceedings against De Kikvorsch Groothandel-Import-Export BV*, C-94/82, ECLI:EU:C:1983:85, 206

Judgment of 6 October 1982, *Srl CILFIT and Lanificio di Gavardo SpA v. Ministry of Health*, C-283/81, ECLI:EU:C:1982:335, 230

Judgment of 9 December 1981, *Commission of the European Communities v. Italian Republic*, C-193/80, ECLI:EU:C:1981:298, 207

Judgment of 5 February 1981, *Officier van justitie v. Koninklijke Kaasfabriek Eyssen BV*, C-53/80, ECLI:EU:C:1981:35, 207
Judgment of 16 December 1980, *Criminal proceedings against Anton Adriaan Fietje*, C-27/80, ECLI:EU:C:1980:293, 206
Judgment of 26 June 1980, *Criminal proceedings against Herbert Gilli and Paul Andres*, C-788/79, ECLI:EU:C:1980:171, 206
Judgment of 13 December 1979, *Liselotte Hauer v. Land Rheinland-Pfalz*, C-44/79, ECLI:EU:C:1979:290, 204
Judgment of 8 November 1979, *Firma Denkavit Futtermittel GmbH v. Minister für Ernähung, Landwirtschaft und Forsten des Landes Nordrhein-Westfalen*, C-251/78, ECLI:EU:C:1979:252, 206
Judgment of 20 February 1979, *Rewe-Zentral AG v. Bundesmonopolverwaltung für Branntwein*, C-120/78, ECLI:EU:C:1979:42, 156, 157, 172
Judgment of 9 March 1978, *Amministrazione delle Finanze dello Stato v. Simmenthal SpA*, C-106/77, ECLI:EU:C:1978:49, 156, 170
Judgment of 19 October 1977, *Albert Ruckdeschel & Co. and Hansa-Lagerhaus Ströh & Co. v. Hauptzollamt Hamburg-St. Annen ; Diamalt AG v. Hauptzollamt Itzehoe*, C-117/76, ECLI:EU:C:1977:160, 159
Judgment of 8 April 1976, *Gabrielle Defrenne v. Société anonyme belge de navigation aérienne Sabena*, C-43/75, ECLI:EU:C:1976:56, 2, 148, 159, 160, 175, 241
Judgment of 12 December 1974, *B.N.O. Walrave and L.J.N. Koch v. Association Union cycliste internationale, Koninklijke Nederlandsche Wielren Unie and Federación Española Ciclismo*, C-36/74, ECLI:EU:C:1974:140, 178
Judgment of 11 July 1974, *Procureur du Roi v. Benoît and Gustave Dassonville*, C-8/74, ECLI:EU:C:1974:82, 156
Judgment of 21 June 1974, *Jean Reyners v. Belgian State*, C-2/74, ECLI:EU:C:1974:68, 149
Judgment of 14 May 1974, *J. Nold, Kohlen- und Baustoffgroßhandlung v. Ruhrkohle Aktiengesellschaft*, C-4/73, ECLI:EU:C:1974:51, 170, 241
Judgment of 2 December 1971, *Aktien-Zuckerfabrik Schöppenstedt v. Council of the European Communities*, C-5/71, ECLI:EU:C:1971:116, 206
Judgment of 25 May 1971, *Gabrielle Defrenne v. Belgian State*, C-80/70, ECLI: EU:C:1971:55, 175
Judgment of 17 December 1970, *Internationale Handelsgesellschaft mbH v. Einfuhr- und Vorratsstelle für Getreide und Futtermittel*, C-11/70, ECLI:EU:C:1970:114, 170, 240
Judgment of 17 December 1970, *Einfuhr- und Vorratsstelle für Getreide und Futtermittel v. Köster and Berodt & Co*, C-25/70, ECLI:EU:C:1970:115, 206
Judgment of 12 November 1969, *Erich Stauder v. City of Ulm – Sozialamt*, C-29/69, ECLI:EU:C:1969:57, 181, 203
Judgment of 30 June 1966, *G. Vaassen-Göbbels (a widow) v. Management of the Beambtenfonds voor het Mijnbedrijf*, C-61/65, ECLI:EU:C:1966:39, 229
Judgment of 15 July 1964, *Flaminio Costa v. E.N.E.L.*, C-6/64, ECLI:EU:C:1964:66, 32, 155, 169

Judgment of 27 March 1963, *Da Costa en Schaake NV, Jacob Meijer NV, Hoechst-Holland NV v. Netherlands Inland Revenue Administration*, C-28/62, ECLI: EU:C:1963:6, 229

Judgment of 5 February 1963, *NV Algemene Transport- en Expeditie Onderneming van Gend & Loos v. Netherlands Inland Revenue Administration*, C-26/62, ECLI: EU:C:1963:1, 32, 155, 169

Table of AG Opinions

Opinion of Advocate General Tanchev of 6 May 2021, *European Commission v. Republic of Poland*, C-791/19, ECLI:EU:C:2021:366, 313

Opinion of Advocate General Pikamae of 20 January 2021, *European Federation of Public Service Unions (EPSU) v. European Commission*, C-928/19, ECLI:EU:C:2021:38, 313

Opinion of Advocate General Tanchev of 5 March 2020, *EM v. TMD Friction GmbH and FL v. TMD Friction EsCo GmbH*, C-674/18, ECLI:EU:C:2020:180, 313

Opinion of Advocate General Szpunar of 26 November 2019, *ISS Facility Services NV v. Sonia Govaerts and Atalian NV, formerly Euroclean NV*, C-344/18, ECLI:EU:C:2019:1009, 313

Opinion of Advocate General Sharpston of 11 July 2019, *Reiner Grafe and Jürgen Pohle v. Südbrandenburger Nahverkehrs GmbH and OSL Bus GmbH*, C-298/18, ECLI:EU:C:2019:593, 313

Opinion of Advocate General Szpunar of 7 February 2019, *Ellinika Nafpigeia AE v. Panagiotis Anagnostopoulos and Others*, C-664/17, ECLI:EU:C:2019:105, 313

Opinion of Advocate General Szpunar of 23 January 2019, *Christa Plessers v. PREFACO NV and Belgische Staat*, C-509/17, ECLI:EU:C:2019:50, 313

Opinion of Advocate General Tanchev of 6 December 2017, *Jorge Luís Colino Sigüenza v. Ayuntamiento de Valladolid and Others*, C-472/16, ECLI:EU:C:2017:943, 313

Opinion of Advocate General Mengozzi of 29 March 2017, *Federatie Nederlandse Vakvereniging and Others v. Smallsteps BV*, C-126/16, ECLI:EU:C:2017:241, 313

Opinion of Advocate General Tanchev of 1 February 2017, *Unionen v. Almega Tjänsteförbunden and ISS Facility Services AB*, C-336/15, ECLI:EU:C:2017:77, 313

Opinion of Advocate General Bot of 19 January 2017, *Asklepios Kliniken Langen-Seligenstadt GmbH v. Ivan Felja and Asklepios Dienstleistungsgesellschaft mbH v. Vittoria Graf*, C-680/15, ECLI:EU:C:2017:30, 37, 132, 312

Opinion of Advocate General Wahl of 9 June 2016, *Anonymi Geniki Etairia Tsimenton Iraklis (AGET Iraklis) v. Ypourgos Ergasias, Koinonikis Asfalisis kai Koinonikis Allilengyis*, C-201/15, ECLI:EU:C:2016:972 41

Opinion of Advocate General Bot of 11 June 2015, *João Filipe Ferreira da Silva e Brito and Others v. Estado português*, C-160/14, ECLI:EU:C:2015:390, 313
Opinion of Advocate General Wahl of 11 September 2014, *FNV Kunsten Informatie en Media v. Staat der Nederlanden*, C-413/13, ECLI:EU:C:2014:221, 313
Opinion of Advocate General Cruz Villalon of 3 June 2014, *Österreichischer Gewerkschaftsbund v. Wirtschaftskammer Österreich — Fachverband Autobus-, Luftfahrt-und Schifffahrtsunternehmungen*, C-328/13, ECLI:EU:C:2014:909, 313
Opinion of Advocate General Cruz Villalon of 19 February 2013, *Mark Alemo-Herron and Others v. Parkwood Leisure Ltd*, C-426/11, ECLI:EU:C:2013:82, 305
Opinion of Advocate General Trstenjak of 8 September 2011, *Maribel Dominguez v. Centre informatique du Centre Ouest Atlantique and Préfet de la région Centre*, C-282/10, ECLI:EU:C:2011:559, 260
Opinion of Advocate General Léger of 10 July 2011, *J. C. J. Wouters, J. W. Savelbergh and Price Waterhouse Belastingadviseurs BV v. Algemene Raad van de Nederlandse Orde van Advocaten*, C-309/99, ECLI:EU:C:2001:390, 313
Opinion of Advocate General Bot of 5 April 2011, *Ivana Scattolon v. Ministero dell'Istruzione, dell'Università e della Ricerca*, C-108/10, ECLI:EU:C:2011:211, 313
Opinion of Advocate General Trstenjak of 26 October 2010, *CLECE SA v. María Socorro Martín Valor and Ayuntamiento de Cobisa*, C-463/09, ECLI:EU:C:2010:636, 313
Opinion of Advocate General Sharpston of 30 September 2010, *Gerardo Ruiz Zambrano v. Office national de l'emploi (ONEm)*, C-34/09, ECLI:EU:C:2010:560, 313
Opinion of Advocate General Mazàk of 7 June 2010, *Aziz Melki and Sélim Abdeli*, C-188/10, Joined cases C-188/10 and C-189/10, ECLI:EU:C:2010:319, 313
Opinion of Advocate General Bot of 3 June 2010, *Albron Catering BV v. FNV Bondgenoten and John Roest*, C-242/09, ECLI:EU:C:2010:317, 313
Opinion of Advocate General Sharpston of 6 May 2010, *Federación de Servicios Públicos de la UGT (UGT-FSP) v. Ayuntamiento de La Línea de la Concepción, María del Rosario Vecino Uribe and Ministerio Fiscal*, C-151/09, ECLI:EU:C:2010:255, 313
Opinion of Advocate General Trstenjak of 14 April 2010, *European Commission v. Federal Republic of Germany*, C-271/08, ECLI:EU:C:2010:183, 223
Opinion of Advocate General Bot of 29 October 2009, *Ingeniørforeningen i Danmark v. Dansk Arbejdsgiverforening*, C-405/08, ECLI:EU:C:2009:675
Opinion of Advocate General Mengozzi of 6 November 2008, *Dietmar Klarenberg v. Ferrotron Technologies GmbH*, C-466/07, ECLI:EU:C:2008:614
Opinion of Advocate General Maduro of 8 October 2008, *Michaniki AE v. Ethniko Symvoulio Radiotileorasis and Ypourgos Epikrateias*, C-213/07, ECLI:EU:C:2008:544, 214
Opinion of Advocate General Ruiz-Jarabo Colomer of 4 September 2008, *Mirja Juuri v. Fazer Amica Oy*, C-396/07, ECLI:EU:C:2008:471, 313
Opinion of Advocate General Maduro of 23 May 2007, *International Transport Workers' Federation and Finnish Seamen's Union v. Viking Line ABP and OÜ Viking Line Eesti*, C-438/05, ECLI:EU:C:2007:292, 222
Opinion of Advocate General Bot of 22 March 2007, *Mohamed Jouini and Others v. Princess Personal Service GmbH (PPS)*, C-458/05, ECLI:EU:C:2007:182, 313

Opinion of Advocate General Ruiz-Jarabo Colomer of 15 November 2005, *Hans Werhof v. Freeway Traffic Systems GmbH & Co. KG*, C-499/04, ECLI:EU:C:2005:686, 305
Opinion of Advocate General Geelhoed of 20 October 2005, *Portuguese Republic v. Commission of the European Communities*, C-88/03, ECLI:EU:C:2005:618, 313
Opinion of Advocate General Léger of 11 October 2005, *Traghetti del Mediterraneo SpA v. Repubblica italiana*, C-173/03, ECLI:EU:C:2005:602, 313
Opinion of Advocate General Poiares Maduro of 16 June 2005, *Nurten Güney-Görres v. Securicor Aviation (Germany) Ltd and Kötter Aviation Security GmbH & Co. KG*, C-232/04, Joined cases C-232/04 and C-233/04, ECLI:EU:C:2005:395, 284-285
Opinion of Advocate General Poiares Maduro of 27 January 2005, *Celtec Ltd v. John Astley and Others*, C-478/03, ECLI:EU:C:2005:66, 313
Opinion of Advocate General Tizzano of 30 September 2004, *Irmtraud Junk v. Wolfgang Kühnel*, C-188/03, ECLI:EU:C:2004:571, 313
Opinion of Advocate General Léger of 17 June 2004, *Johanna Maria Delahaye, née Delahaye v. Ministre de la Fonction publique et de la Réforme administrative*, C-425/02, ECLI:EU:C:2004:376, 313
Opinion of Advocate General Ruiz-Jarabo Colomer of 10 July 2003, *Brian Francis Collins v. Secretary of State for Work and Pensions*, C-138/02, ECLI:EU:C:2003:409, 313
Opinion of Advocate General Geelhoed of 19 June 2003, *Carlito Abler and Others v. Sodexho MM Catering Gesellschaft mbH*, C-340/01, ECLI:EU:C:2003:361, 313
Opinion of Advocate General Alber of 17 June 2003, *Serene Martin, Rohit Daby and Brian Willis v. South Bank University*, C-4/01, ECLI:EU:C:2003:351, 313
Opinion of Advocate General Léger of 10 April 2003, *Commission of the European Communities v. Italian Republic*, C-145/01, ECLI:EU:C:2003:223, 313
Opinion of Advocate General Alber of 13 December 2001, *Katia Beckmann v. Dynamco Whichloe Macfarlane Ltd*, C-164/00, ECLI:EU:C:2001:693, 313
Opinion of Advocate General Geelhoed of 27 September 2001, *Temco Service Industries SA v. Samir Imzilyen and Others*, C-51/00, ECLI:EU:C:2001:496, 313
Opinion of Advocate General Geelhoed of 5 July 2001, *Baumbast and R v. Secretary of State for the Home Department*, C-413/99, ECLI:EU:C:2001:385, 313
Opinion of Advocate General Tizzano of 8 February 2001, *The Queen v. Secretary of State for Trade and Industry, ex parte Broadcasting, Entertainment, Cinematographic and Theatre Union (BECTU)*, C-173/99, ECLI:EU:C:2001:81, 313
Opinion of Advocate General Léger of 12 October 2000, *Oy Liikenne Ab v. Pekka Liskojärvi and Pentti Juntunen*, C-172/99, ECLI:EU:C:2000:563, 313
Opinion of Advocate General Léger of 13 June 2000, *Didier Mayeur v. Association Promotion de l'information messine (APIM)*, C-175/99, ECLI:EU:C:2000:313, 313
Opinion of Advocate General Jacobs of 23 March 2000, *Pavel Pavlov and Others v. Stichting Pensioenfonds Medische Specialisten*, C-180/98, ECLI:EU:C:2000:151, 313
Opinion of Advocate General Alber of 18 January 2000, *Renato Collino and Luisella Chiappero v. Telecom Italia SpA*, C-343/98, ECLI:EU:C:2000:23, 313
Opinion of Advocate General La Pergola of 26 October 1999, *Tanja Kreil v. Bundesrepublik Deutschland*, C-285/98, ECLI:EU:C:1999:525, 209

Opinion of Advocate General Ruiz-Jarabo Colomer of 8 July 1999, *G. C. Allen and Others v. Amalgamated Construction Co. Ltd*, C-234/98, ECLI:EU:C:1999:383, 313

Opinion of Advocate General Jacobs of 28 January 1999, *Albany International BV v. Stichting Bedrijfspensioenfonds Textielindustrie*, C-67/96, ECLI:EU:C:1999:28, 313

Opinion of Advocate General Cosmas of 24 September 1998, *Francisco Hernández Vidal SA v. Prudencia Gómez Pérez, María Gómez Pérez and Contratas y Limpiezas SL*, C-127/96, Joined cases C-127/96, C-229/96 and C-74/97, ECLI: EU:C:1998:426, 284

Opinion of Advocate General Cosmas of 24 September 1998, *Francisca Sánchez Hidalgo and Others v. Asociación de Servicios Aser and Sociedad Cooperativa Minerva*, C-173/96, Joined cases C-173/96 and C-247/96, ECLI:EU:C:1998:426, 313

Opinion of Advocate General Mischo of 14 May 1998, *Criminal proceedings against André Ambry.*, C-410/96, ECLI:EU:C:1998:227, 313

Opinion of Advocate General Cosmas of 7 May 1998, *Europièces SA v. Wilfried Sanders and Automotive Industries Holding Company SA*, C-399/96, ECLI:EU:C:1998:207, 313

Opinion of Advocate General Ruiz-Jarabo Colomer of 26 June 1997, *Maria Antonella Garofalo (C-69/96), Giovanni Pagano (C-70/96), Rosa Bruna Vitale (C-71/96), Francesca Nuccio (C-72/96), Giacomo Cangialosi (C-73/96), Giacoma D'Amico (C-74/96), Giulia Lombardo (C-75/96), Emanuela Giovenco (C-76/96), Caterina Lo Gaglio (C-77/96), Daniela Guerrera (C-78/96) and Cesare Di Marco (-79/96) v. Ministero della Sanità and Unità sanitaria locale (USL) n° 58 di Palermo*, C-69/96, Joined cases C-69/96 and C-79/96, ECLI:EU:C:1997:330, 313

Opinion of Advocate General Cosmas of 20 February 1997, *Pedro Burdalo Trevejo and Others v. Fondo Garantía Salarial*, C-336/95, ECLI:EU:C:1997:80, 313

Opinion of Advocate General La Pergola of 15 October 1996, *Ayse Süzen v. Zehnacker Gebäudereinigung GmbH Krankenhausservice*, C-13/95, ECLI:EU:C:1996:385, 292

Opinion of Advocate General Lenz of 11 July 1996, *Jules Dethier Équipement SA v. Jules Dassy and Sovam SPRL*, C-319/94, ECLI:EU:C:1996:29, 313

Opinion of Advocate General Lenz of 4 July 1996, *Claude Rotsart de Hertaing v. J. Benoidt SA, in liquidation and IGC Housing Service SA*, C-305/94, ECLI: EU:C:1996:269, 313

Opinion of Advocate General Lenz of 11 June 1996, *Annette Henke v. Gemeinde Schierke and Verwaltungsgemeinschaft Brocken*, C-298/94, ECLI:EU:C:1996:230, 313

Opinion of Advocate General Tesauro of 14 December 1995, *P v. S and Cornwall County Council*, C-13/94, ECLI:EU:C:1995:444, 209

Opinion of Advocate General Cosmas of 17 October 1995, *Luigi Spano and others v. Fiat Geotech SpA and Fiat Hitachi Excavators SpA*, C-472/93, ECLI:EU:C:1995:323, 313

Opinion of Advocate General Lenz of 6 July 1995, *Albert Merckx and Patrick Neuhuys v. Ford Motors Company Belgium SA*, C-171/94, Joined Cases C-171/94 and C-172/94, ECLI:EU:C:1995:227, 313

Opinion of Advocate General Léger of 20 June 1995, *Reinhard Gebhard v. Consiglio dell'Ordine degli Avvocati e Procuratori di Milano*, C-55/94, ECLI:EU:C:1995:194, 313

Opinion of Advocate General Cosmas of 10 May 1995, *Ledernes Hovedorganisation, acting for Ole Rygaard v. Dansk Arbejdsgiverforening, acting for Strø Mølle Akustik A/S*, C-48/94, ECLI:EU:C:1995:130, 285

Opinion of Advocate General Tesauro of 1 June 1994, *Carole Louise Webb v. EMO Air Cargo (UK) Ltd*, C-32/93, ECLI:EU:C:1994:215, 313

Opinion of Advocate General Van Gerven of 2 March 1994, *Commission of the European Communities v. United Kingdom of Great Britain and Northern Ireland*, C-382/92, ECLI:EU:C:1994:78, 313

Opinion of Advocate General Van Gerven of 23 February 1994, *Christel Schmidt v. Spar- und Leihkasse der früheren Ämter Bordesholm, Kiel und Cronshagen*, C-392/92, ECLI:EU:C:1994:61, 313

Opinion of Advocate General Van Gerven of 10 November 1992, *Grigorios Katsikas v. Angelos Konstantinidis and Uwe Skreb and Günter Schroll v. PCO Stauereibetrieb Paetz & Co. Nachfolger GmbH*, C-132/91, ECLI:EU:C:1992:422, 313

Opinion of Advocate General Van Gerven of 8 October 1992, *Anne Watson Rask and Kirsten Christensen v. Iss Kantineservice A/S*, C-209/91, ECLI:EU:C:1992:377, 313

Opinion of Advocate General Van Gerven of 24 May 1992, *Dr. Sophie Redmond Stichting v. Hendrikus Bartol and others*, C-29/91, ECLI:EU:C:1992:144, 313

Opinion of Advocate General Van Gerven of 30 May 1991, *Giuseppe d'Urso, Adriana Ventadori and others v. Ercole Marelli Elettromeccanica Generale SpA and others*, C-362/89, ECLI:EU:C:1991:228, 313

Opinion of Advocate General Lenz of 23 January 1991, *Elliniki Radiophonia Tiléorassi AE and Panellinia Omospondia Syllogon Prossopikou v. Dimotiki Etairia Pliroforissis and Sotirios Kouvelas and Nicolaos Avdellas and others*, C-260/89, ECLI:EU:C:1991:26, 313

Opinion of Advocate General Darmon of 28 March 1990, *Maria Kowalska v. Freie und Hansestadt Hamburg*, C-33/89, ECLI:EU:C:1990:152, 313

Opinion of Advocate General Darmon of 14 November 1989, *Elisabeth Johanna Pacifica Dekker v. Stichting Vormingscentrum voor Jong Volwassenen (VJV-Centrum) Plus*, C-177/88, ECLI:EU:C:1989:424, 313

Opinion of Advocate General Darmon of 18 April 1989, *Ingrid Rinner-Kühn v. FWW Spezial-Gebäudereinigung GmbH & Co. KG*, C-171/88, ECLI:EU:C:1989:158, 313

Opinion of Advocate General Darmon of 4 May 1988, *P. Bork International A/S, in liquidation v. Foreningen af Arbejdsledere I Danmark, acting on behalf of Birger E. Petersen, and Jens E. Olsen and others v. Junckers Industrier A/S*, C-101/87, ECLI:EU:C:1988:229, 313

Opinion of Advocate General Mancini of 9 February 1988, *Harry Berg and Johannes Theodorus Maria Busschers v. Ivo Martin Besselsen*, C-144/87, ECLI:EU:C:1988:70, 313

Opinion of Advocate General Darmon of 9 December 1987, *Foreningen af Arbejdsledere i Danmark v. Daddy's Dance Hall A/S*, C-324/86, ECLI:EU:C:1987:537, 313

Opinion of Advocate General Mancini of 28 October 1987, *Landsorganisationen i Danmark for Tjenerforbundet i Danmark v. Ny Mølle Kro*, C-287/86, ECLI:EU:C:1987:471, 313
Opinion of Advocate General Mancini of 11 June 1987, *Giménez Zaera v. Instituto Nacional de la Seguridad Social and Tesorería General de la Seguridad Social*, C-126/86, ECLI:EU:C:1987:278, 313
Opinion of Advocate General Slynn of 17 April 1986, *Commission of the European Communities v. Italian Republic*, C-235/84, ECLI:EU:C:1986:156, 313
Opinion of Advocate General Slynn of 18 February 1986, *Commission of the European Communities v. Kingdom of Belgium*, C-237/84, ECLI:EU:C:1986:61, 313
Opinion of Advocate General Slynn of 22 January 1986, *Jozef Maria Antonius Spijkers v. Gebroeders Benedik Abattoir CV and Alfred Benedik en Zonen BV*, C-24/85, ECLI:EU:C:1986:24, 313
Opinion of Advocate General Darmon of 15 October 1985, *Bilka - Kaufhaus GmbH v. Karin Weber von Hartz*, C-170/84, ECLI:EU:C:1985:410, 313
Opinion of Advocate General Slynn of 30 April 1985, *Foreningen af Arbejdsledere i Danmark v. A/S Danmols Inventar, in liquidation*, C-105/84, ECLI:EU:C:1985:162, 313
Opinion of Advocate General Slynn of 8 November 1984, *Abels v. Bedrijfsvereniging voor de Metaalindustrie en de Electrotechnische Industrie*, C-135/83, ECLI:EU:C:1984:338, 313
Opinion of Advocate General Slynn of 8 November 1984, *Knud Wendelboe and others v. L.J. Music ApS, in liquidation*, C-19/83, ECLI:EU:C:1984:337, 313
Opinion of Advocate General Slynn of 8 November 1984, *Industriebond FNV and Federatie Nederlandse Vakbeweging (FNV) v. The Netherlands State*, C-179/83, ECLI:EU:C:1984:339, 313
Opinion of Advocate General Rozès of 31 January 1984, *Sabine von Colson and Elisabeth Kamann v. Land Nordrhein-Westfalen*, C-14/83, ECLI:EU:C:1984:37, 313
Opinion of Advocate General Trabucchi of 10 March 1976, *Gabrielle Defrenne v. Société anonyme belge de navigation aérienne Sabena*, C-43/75, ECLI:EU:C:1976:39, 313
Opinion of Advocate General Dutheillet de Lamothe of 29 April 1971, *Gabrielle Defrenne v. Belgian State*, C-80/70, ECLI:EU:C:1971:43, 313

Table of Policy Documents

Council of the European Union, Recommendation on access to social protection for workers and the self-employed, 2019/C 387/01, Brussels, 8 November 2019, 74

Court of Justice of the European Union, The Year in Review – Annual Report 2020, Luxembourg, 2021, 162

Court of Justice of the European Union, Annual Report 2020 – Judicial Activity, Luxembourg, 2021, 189, 233, 235

Court of Justice of the European Union, Press Release Following the Judgment of the German Constitutional Court of 5 May 2020, 58/20, Luxembourg, 8 May 2020, 248

Court of Justice of the European Union, Recommendations to national courts and tribunals, in relation to the initiation of preliminary ruling proceedings, 2016/C 439/01, 25 November 2016, 233, 234

Denmark, Austria, Sweden and The Netherlands, Non-Paper – EU Support for Efficient and Sustainable Covid-19 Recovery, Brussels, 26 May 2020, 78

Economic and Social Committee, Opinion on the proposal for a Council Directive on the approximation of the laws of the Member States relating to the safeguarding of employees' rights in the event of transfers of undertakings, businesses or parts of businesses, 95/C 133/07, Brussels, 31 May 1995, 285

Economic and Social Committee, Opinion on a draft Council Resolution on a Social Action Programme, 74/C 37/09, Strasbourg, 29 November 1973, 49

European Central Bank, Report, Monthly Bulletin October, Frankfurt, 2012, 246-247

European Commission, Proposal for a Directive of the European Parliament and of the Council to Strengthen the Application of the Principle of Equal Pay for Equal Work or Work for Equal Value Between Men and Women Through Pay Transparency and Enforcement Mechanisms, COM (2021) 93 final, Brussels, 4 March 2021, 65, 76

European Commission, Proposal for a Directive of the European Parliament and of the Council on Improving Working Conditions in Platform Work, COM(2021) 762 final, Brussels, 9 December 2021, 65, 76

European Commission, Collective Bargaining Agreements for Self-Employed – Scope of Application of EU Competition Rules, Inception Impact Assessment, Brussels, 6 January 2021, 76

European Commission, automat the Application of EU Competition Law to Collective Agreements Regarding the Working Conditions of Solo Self-Employed Persons – Approval of the Content of a Draft for a Communication from the Commission, Annex, C(2021) 8838 final, Brussels, 9 December 2021, 76

European Commission and European Council, A Roadmap for Recovery – Towards a More Resilient, Sustainable and Fair Europe, Brussels, 21 April 2021, 78

European Commission, Staff Working Document, Guidance to Member States on Recovery and Resilience Plans, Commission Staff Working Document, SWD(2021) 12 final, Brussels, 22 January 2021, 83

European Commission, The EU Economy after Covid-19: Implications for Economic Governance, COM(2021) 662 final, Strasbourg, 19 October 2021, 83

European Commission, Staff Working Document, In-Depth Review for Italy, in Accordance with Article 5 of Regulation (EU) No 1176/2011 on the Prevention and Correction of Macroeconomic Imbalances, SWD(2021) 407 final, Brussels, 2 June 2021, 84

European Commission, Press Release: Rule of Law: European Commission refers Poland to the European Court of Justice to Protect Independence of Polish Judges and Asks for Interim Measures, Brussels, 31 March 2021, 253

European Commission, Press Release: Independence of Polish Judges: Commission Asks European Court of Justice for Financial Penalties Against Poland on the Activity of the Disciplinary Chamber, Brussels, 7 September 2021, 253

European Commission, Press Release: European Commission Reaffirms the Primacy of EU Law, Brussels, 7 October 2021, 254

European Parliament, Report, Commitments made at the hearings of the Commissioners-designate Von der Leyen Commission 2019 – 2024, PE 629.837, Brussels, October 2020, 64

European Commission, A Strong Social Europe for Just Transitions, Communication, COM(2020) 14 final, Brussels, 14 January 2020, 75

European Commission, Proposal for a Directive of the European Parliament and of the Council on Adequate Minimum Wages in the European Union, COM(2020) 682 final, Brussels, 28 October 2020, 64, 76

European Commission, Coronavirus: The Commission mobilises all of its resources to protect lives and livelihoods, IP/20/582, Brussels, 2 April 2020, 78

European Commission, Activation of the General Escape Clause of the Stability and Growth Pact, COM(2020) 123 final, Brussels, 20 March 2020, 79

European Commission, Proposal for a Council Regulation on the Establishment of a European Instrument for Temporary Support to Mitigate Unemployment Risk in an Emergency (SURE) Following the COVID-19 Outbreak, COM(2020) 139 final, Brussels, 2 April 2020, 79

European Commission, Proposal for a Council Decision on the System of Own Resources of the European Union, COM(2020) 445 final, Brussels, 28 May 2020, 82

European Commission, Proposal for a Council Regulation establishing a European Union Recovery Instrument to Support the Recovery in the Aftermath of the COVID-19 Pandemic, COM(2020) 441 final, Brussels, 28 May 2020, 82

European Commission, Commission Welcomes Political Agreement on Recovery and Resilience Facility, Brussels, 18 December 2020, 82

European Commission, Economic Governance Review, COM(2020) 55 final, Brussels, 5 February 2020, 83

European Commission, Annual Sustainable Growth Strategy 2020, COM(2019) 605 final, Brussels, 17 December 2019, 70

European Commission, More efficient Decision-making in Social Policy: Identification of Areas for an Enhanced Move to Qualified Majority Voting, COM(2019) 186 final, Strasbourg, 16 April 2019, 74

European Commission, European Pillar of Social Rights: Statement by President Juncker, Vice-President Dombrovskis and Commissioner Thyssen one year following its proclamation, STATEMENT/18/6390, Brussels, 13 November 2018, 64

European Commission, Monitoring the implementation of the European Pillar of Social Rights, Communication, COM(2018) 130 final, Strasbourg, 13 March 2018, 65, 71

European Commission, State of the Union 2018: Letter of intent to President Antonio Tajani and to Chancellor Sebastian Kurz, Strasbourg, 12 September 2018, 74

European Commission, Infosheet on the Roadmap for the Future Commission's Initiative on 'More Efficient Law-making in Social Policy: Identification of Areas for an Enhanced Move to Qualified Majority', Brussels, 20 December 2018, 74

European Commission, Reflection Paper on the Social Dimension of Europe, Communication, COM(2017) 206 final, Brussels, 26 April 2017, 66, 67

European Commission, Memorandum on Directive on Transparent and Predictable Working Conditions, establishing EU rules on the extension of social and labour protection to casual workers and other forms of atypical workers, COM(2017) 797 final, Brussels, 21 December 2017, 62

European Commission, Delivering on the European Pillar of Social Rights – Commission adopts first concrete initiatives, IP/17/1006, Brussels, 26 April 2017, 70

European Commission, Staff Working Document, Social Scoreboard, SWD(2017) 200 final, Brussels, 26 April 2017, 71

European Commission, Commission Proposal for a Council Decision on guidelines for the employment policies of the Member States, COM(2017) 677 final 2017/0305 (NLE), Brussels, 22 November 2017, 72

ETUC, Directive on Transparent and Predictable Working Conditions: A First Major Step Forward but Weaker than Expected, Brussels, 21 December 2017, 62, 74

Council of the European Union, Recommendation on the establishment of National Productivity Boards, 2016/C 349/01, Brussels, 20 September 2016, 62

European Commission, New start for social dialogue – one year on, MEMO/16/823, Brussels, 16 March 2016, 63

European Commission, Speech by M. Thyssen, European Commissioner for Eurostat and Employment, Social Affairs, Skills and Labour Mobility, First outline of the

European Pillar of Social Rights and reform of the Posting of Workers Directive, SPEECH/16/682, Brussels, 8 March 2016, 44, 64, 65

European Commission, Launching a consultation on a European Pillar of Social Rights, Communication, COM(2016) 127 final, Strasbourg, 8 March 2016, 65

European Commission, Report, A new start for Social Dialogue, Brussels, August 2016, 68

European Commission, Staff Working Document, Key Economic, Employment and Social Trends Behind a European Pillar of Social Rights, SWD (2016) 51 final, Strasbourg, 8 March 2016, 68

European Commission, Report, Completing Europe's Economic and Monetary Union ('The Five Presidents' Report'), In close cooperation with Donald Tusk (President of the European Council), Jeroen Dijsselbloem (President of the Eurogroup), Mario Draghi (President of the European Central Bank), and Martin Schulz (President of the European Parliament), Brussels, 22 June 2015, 59

European Commission, Preparing for Next Steps on Better Economic Governance in the Euro Area, In close cooperation with Donald Tusk, Jeroen Dijsselbloem and Mario Draghi, 12 February 2015, 61

European Commission, Strengthening the Social Dimension of the Economic and Monetary Union, Communication, COM(2013) 690 final, Brussels, 2 October 2013, 56, 62, 63

European Commission, A Blueprint for a Deep and Genuine Economic and Monetary Union, COM (2012) 777 final, Brussels, 28 November 2012, 58, 59

European Commission, Towards a Single Market Act for a Highly Competitive Social Market Economy (50 Proposals for Improving our Work, Business and Exchange with One Another), Communication, COM(2010) 608 final, Brussels, 27 October 2010, 56, 57

European Commission, Europe 2020: A Strategy for Smart, Sustainable and Inclusive Growth, COM(2010) 2020, Brussels, 3 March 2010, 57

European Commission, Reinforcing economic policy coordination, COM(2010) 250 final, Brussels, 12 May 2010, 80

European Commission, Towards Common Principles of Flexicurity: More and Better Jobs Through Flexicurity and Security, Communication, COM(2007) 359 final, Brussels, 27 June 2007, 54

European Commission, Modernising Labour Law to Meet the Challenges of the 21st Century, COM(2006) 708 final, Brussels, 22 November 2006, 56

European Commission, Social Agenda, COM(2005) 33 final, Brussels, 9 February 2005, 30

European Commission, Integrated Guidelines for Growth and Jobs (2005-2008), Communication, COM(2005) 141 final, Brussels, 12 April 2005, 56

European Commission, The Social Dimension of Globalisation – The EU's Policy Contribution on extending the benefits to all, Communication, COM(2004) 383 final, Brussels, 18 May 2004, 56

European Commission, Social Policy Agenda, COM(2000) 379 final, Brussels, 28 June 2000, 30

European Commission, Proposal for a Council Directive on the Approximation of the Laws of the Member States Relating to the Safeguarding of Employees' Rights in the Event of Transfers of Undertakings, Businesses or Parts of Undertakings or Businesses (codified version), COM(2000) 259 final, Brussels, 2 May 2000, 91

European Commission, Medium Term Social Action Programme 1995-1997, COM(95) 134 final, Brussels, 12 April 1995, 53, 54

European Commission, Green Paper - European Social Policy, Options for the Future, COM(93) 551, Brussels, 17 November 1993, 53

European Commission, Community Charter of Fundamental Social Rights, COM(89) 471 final, Brussels, 2 October 1989, 52

European Commission, Communication on the action programme relating to the implementation of the Community Charter of Basic Social Rights for Workers, COM(89) 568 final, Brussels, 29 November 1989, 53

European Commission, Social Dimension of the Internal Market, Working Paper, SEC (88) 1148 final, Brussels, 14 September 1988, 52

European Commission, Completing the Internal Market, White Paper, COM(85) 310 final, Brussels, 14 June 1985, 51, 61, 180

European Commission, Speech by H. Vredeling, Vice-President of the Commission of the European Communities, to the London Europe Society and Confederation of British Industry, The Community role in the field of social and employment policy, London, 9 February 1979, 49, 50

European Commission, Speech by P.J. Hillery, Vice-President of the Commission of the European Communities, to the Financial Times and Irish Times conference 'Europe after the Referendum', Does the Community need a social policy?, Dublin, 24 July 1975, 49, 50

European Commission, Speech by P.J. Hillery, Vice-President of the Commission of the European Communities, to the Royal Irish Academy, European social policies: problems and prospects, 98/75, Dublin, 28 April 1975, 50

European Commission, Proposal for a Directive of the Council on harmonisation of the legislation of Member States on the retention of the rights and advantages of employees in the case of mergers, takeovers and amalgamations, COM(74)351 Final/2, Brussels, 29 May 1974, 37, 93

European Commission, Social Action Programme, COM(73)1600, Brussels, 25 October 1973, 48

European Commission, Speech by M. Shanks, Director-General for Social Affairs at the European Commission, to the European Institute for Social Security, Towards a Community social action programme, X/417/73-E, Cambridge, 10 September 1973, 49

European Commission, Preliminary guidelines for a community social policy programme, SEC (71) 600 final, Brussels, 17 March 1971, 48

European Commission, Speech by L. Levi Sandri, Member of the Commission of the European Economic Community, to the General Meeting of the Belgian Association for Social Progress, The Role of Social Policy in European Integration, 1820/PP/64-E, 10 February 1964, 46

European Commission, Speech by Lionello Levi Sandri, EEC Commissioner, at the 47th International Labour Conference, IP (63) 109, Brussels, 14 June 1964, 46

European Commission, Interview sur les objectives de la Communauté Européenne, February 1963, 46

European Commission, Speech by G. Petrilli, Member of the Commission of the European Economic Community, The Social Tasks Facing the E.E.C., X/2613/60-E, April 1960, 46

European Council, Report, Towards a Genuine Economic and Monetary Union ('The Four Presidents' Report'), In close collaboration with: José Manuel Barroso, President of the European Commission, Jean-Claude Juncker, President of the Eurogroup, Mario Draghi, President of the European Central Bank, Brussels, 5 December 2012, 58, 59

European Council, Presidency Conclusions, Lisbon strategy, Lisbon, 23 March 2000, 54, 55

European Council, Concerning a Community medium-term social action programme, 84/C 175/01, 22 June 1984, 50

European Council, Resolution concerning a Social Action Programme, Brussels, 21 January 1974, 48

European Parliament and Council of the European Union, Directive on transparent and predictable working conditions in the European Union, 2019/1152, Brussels, 20 June 2019, 64, 73, 78

European Parliament and Council of the European Union, Directive on work-life balance for parents and carers and repealing Council Directive 2010/18/EU, 2019/1158, Brussels, 20 June 2019, 64, 74, 163

European Parliament, Legislative resolution embodying Parliament's opinion on the proposal for a Council Directive on the approximation of the laws of the Member States relating to the safeguarding of employees' rights in the event of transfers of undertakings, businesses or parts of businesses, C4-0151/94 94/0203(CNS), Brussels, 3 February 1997, 285

European Parliament, Opinion of the European Parliament on the 1972 Report of the Commission on the development of the social situation in the Community, 30 April 1973, 48

European Parliament, Report, Rapport fait au nom de la commission politique sur les résultats de la Conférence au sommet des Chefs d'État ou de gouvernement des Etats membres de la Communauté élargie, Paris, 19 October 1972, 48

European Trade Union Confederation, ETUC Submission on the European Commission Roadmap 'More efficient law-making in social policy: identification of areas for an enhanced move to qualified majority voting', Brussels, 19 January 2019, 75

Presidency of the Council of the European Union, European Semester 2015: Contribution to the European Council (25-26 June), 9304/15, Brussels, 10 June 2015, 63

Index

1974-1976 Social Action Programme, 48, 50, 88
1985 White Paper, 51, 180
1989 Social Action Programme, 52
1995-1997 Social Action Programme, 53
1998 Amending Council Directive, 119

A

Abler, 118, 303
Abrahamson, 209
Achbita, 2, 220, 263, 264, 265
Action Plan to implement the Pillar, 73
Advocate General Bot, 37, 132
Advocate General Maduro, 5, 166, 179, 201, 204, 205, 207, 208, 210, 212, 214, 216–218, 222
Advocate General Villalòn, 35, 36
Aget Iraklis, 2, 19, 32, 38–42, 158, 221, 223
Ajos, 223, 256–260
Akustik Süzen, 142, 311
Albron, 108
Alemo-Herron, 2, 32–38, 40, 42, 96, 97, 129–132, 135, 136, 142–143, 158, 221, 223, 263-265, 277–279, 286, 292, 294, 296, 300, 302, 304–308, 311, 313, 314, 319, 321,
Allen, 108
Amatori, 108
Amicus briefs, 193
AMS, 259–261, 263, 264
Amsterdam Treaty, 54
Article 16 CFREU, 37–39, 96, 158, 220, 263–265, 269, 281, 306
Article 117 TEEC, 137
Article 118 TEEC, 46
Article 119 TEEC, 159, 175, 196
Article 177 TEEC, 162, 189
Article 4(2) TEU, 214, 215, 217, 219, 295
Article 267 TFEU, 161, 162, 226–228, 231, 297, 300
Asklepios, 37, 130–132, 135, 278, 286, 304–306, 308, 311, 314, 321
Asset-based business, 111, 117, 118
Austerity, 65, 78, 83

B

Bananenmarket, 245
Barroso, 30, 44
Barber, 175, 196, 197, 288
Barber Protocol, 196, 288
Berg, 109, 128, 295
Bilka, 175
Bougnaoui, 2, 220, 263, 264, 265
Brasserie du Pecheur, 156

C

Capital intensive business, 287
Cassis de Dijon, 156, 157, 164, 172, 173, 179–181, 192, 193, 199, 200, 208, 245
Charter of Fundamental Rights (CFR), 34

Cilfit, 229
Collective redundancies, 38, 48, 49, 85, 88, 108
Collective dismissals, 38
Collective laissez faire, 26
Collino, 109
Commission v Italy, 207
Common constitutional traditions of the Member States, 171, 202–205
Community Charter of Fundamental Social Rights of Workers, 52
Concession by a public body, 99, 100, 109
Constitutional pluralism, 216–222, 224, 307
Contrapunctual law, 216–218, 222
Costa v. Enel, 32, 154–156, 239
Counterlimits, 250
Country Reports, 70–72
Country Specific Recommendations (CSRs), 70–72, 79, 82
Covid-19, 44, 45, 72, 77–85, 319
Czech Constitutional Court, 250–252, 258

D

D'Urso, 128
Daddy's Dance Hall, 107, 128, 133, 272, 282
Danish Supreme Court, 256, 258
Dassonville, 156, 157, 164, 172, 173, 208, 245
Defrenne I, 175
Defrenne II, 2, 159, 175
Dekker, 176
Delors, 51
Deference case, 236
Direct effect, 96, 148, 155, 157, 159, 162, 169, 170, 175, 176, 181, 198, 239, 242, 255, 256, 258–262, 264, 265
Direct horizontal effect, 159, 255, 260, 263, 264
Directive 77/187/EEC, 8, 88–91, 99–101, 110, 122, 128, 283, 284, 318
Directive 98/59/EC, 38, 40
Directive 2001/23/EC, 8, 9, 13–14, 33, 34, 88–91, 99, 102, 131, 143, 185, 267–315
Dodič, 299, 300, 302
Dominguez, 223, 259–261, 263, 264
Dual polity, 43, 45–47, 84
Dynamic clauses, 34–37, 130, 132, 301, 304–306, 308, 311

E

Egenberger, 259, 261–264
Ellinika, 109, 121
Employment guidelines, 56, 63, 70–72
EMU *See* European Monetary Union (EMU)
European Pillar of Social Rights, 12, 44, 66
EPSR, 12, 44, 58, 60, 61, 63–77, 83–85, 87, 318, 319
Equal pay, 76, 159, 160, 175, 196, 197
Erga omnes, 34, 37, 93, 130, 226, 235
ERT, 39
Escape clause, 78, 80, 83
Eurocrisis, 57
Europe 2020 strategy, 85
European Monetary Union (EMU), 58–61, 63, 70, 85
European Semester, 57, 60, 62, 63, 70–73, 78, 82, 85
Executive regime, 286

F

Ferreira, 118
Five presidents report, 59, 62, 65
Flexicurity, 4, 30, 54–56, 68, 69, 85, 318
Foto-frost, 257
Four presidents report, 59
Francovich, 156, 211
Freedom of contract, 20, 34, 36, 96, 125, 128, 131, 132, 286, 305, 306

Freedom to conduct a business, 25, 31, 35, 37, 38, 97, 99, 130, 132, 158, 204, 220, 263–265, 269, 270, 281, 306
Frontini, 240

G

German Federal Constitutional Court, 240, 242, 257, 259, 260
Giugni, 27
Golden Period, 48, 84
Granital, 205, 240, 242
Grant, 82, 88, 176, 209, 210, 220, 240, 250, 296, 297
Guardian of the Treaties, 167–169
Guidance case, 236
Guidelines on competition law and collective bargaining, 76

H

Haas, 153
Hauer, 204, 241
Hernandez Vidal, 119
Hidden dialogue, 229–231
Hidalgo, 109
Hillery, P. J., 50
Holubec, 251, 252
Honeywell, 257, 259
House of Lords, 33, 300, 302, 305

I

Informal partnership, 151, 177–181, 183, 279, 320
Intangible assets, 115
Integrationalist theory, 166–185, 281, 287, 312
Inter-court competition, 232
Intergovernmentalism, 11, 166, 189–201, 266, 269, 271, 272, 287–293, 311, 314
Internationale Handelsgesellschaft, 203, 240
Inviolabile constitutional principles of the national legal system, 239–244
ISS, 134, 135, 142, 143, 286
Italian constitutional court, 224, 239, 240, 242, 243

J

Jouini, 108, 120, 313
Judicial activism, 37, 148–152, 159, 166, 174, 176, 181, 182, 192, 197, 205, 212, 224, 231, 235, 240, 250, 254–257, 259, 264, 281, 297
Judicial restraint, 222, 224, 263, 264
Juncker, 44, 58, 64, 65
Juuri, 133–135

K

Kalanke, 209
Kahn-Freund, 25, 27
Keck, 208
Klarenberg, 116, 120, 121
Kobler, 156, 162, 230
Kompetenz-kompetenz, 238, 239, 244–248, 251, 252, 257, 259, 297
Kowalska, 175
Kücükdeveci, 176, 182, 221, 223, 255–257, 260, 261

L

Labour intensive business, 120, 292
Landtová, 251, 252, 258
Laval, 2, 4, 5, 32, 97, 157, 174, 176, 182, 221, 223
Liikenne, 109, 118, 120, 287, 308
Lisbon Agenda, 85
Lisbon Strategy, 55–57
Lissabon Urteil, 244, 245
Luxembourg Compromise, 173
Luxembourg Strategy, 54

M

Maastricht Treaty, 53, 80, 171, 196, 204, 214, 217, 219, 245, 288
Maastricht Urteil, 243–245
Macroeconomic imbalance procedure, 60
Maduro, 5, 166, 179, 201, 204, 205, 207, 208, 210, 212, 214, 216–218, 222
Majoritarian activism, 205, 207, 210–212, 307
Majoritarian approach, 188, 205–212, 221, 293
Mangold, 159, 160, 176, 182, 221, 254–258, 260–262
Maruko, 210, 221
Meanwhile ruling, 242
Merckx, 115, 116
Michaniki, 217, 218
More favourable clause, 90
Moreira, 294, 295, 301
Mutual recognition, 148, 157, 172, 179–181, 193, 199
Muller Armack, A., 47, 49, 84

N

National constitutional identities, 215, 217–219
National Reform and Resilience Plans (NRRPs), 72, 73, 83
Negative freedom of association, 93, 129, 300
Neofunctionalist theory, 152–166, 174, 183–185, 271, 273, 274, 279, 307, 320
Next Generation EU (NGEU), 70, 72, 73, 81–85, 87, 319
Nold, 204, 241
Non contractual employer, 108

O

Omega, 218
OMT, 245–247
Open method of coordination (OMC), 54, 57
Opinion 2/94, 199
Opinion 2/13, 198, 199
Ordoliberalism, 23, 47
OSL Bus, 120, 287
Österreichischer Gewerkschaftsbund, 130–132, 135, 278, 286
Outcome case, 237

P

Paris Summit, 48
Partnership judicial regime, 180, 183
Petrilli, 45, 46
Piscarreta, 109
Platform work, 85
Pluralistic approach, 212–225
Polish constitutional court, 252, 253
Preemptive opinion, 233–235, 266, 271, 297–301, 303, 308, 321, 324
Preliminary ruling mechanism, 155, 161, 162, 184, 189, 198, 226–228, 232, 234, 297, 323
Principle of primacy of EU law, 223, 227, 238, 250
Public procurement, 109, 217, 280
PvS, 209

R

Rask, 128
Recovery and Resilience Facility, 82
Reorganisation of public administrative authorities, 102
Ruckdeschel, 159

S

Satisfaction of the litigants' interests, 274
Scattolon, 120, 132
Schindler, 208, 218, 219
Schmidberger, 219
Schmidt, 115, 117, 118, 270, 274, 283, 284, 286, 292, 296, 311, 313, 314
Securitas, 118
Securicor, 119
Simmenthal, 156, 162, 169, 232, 239, 242
Single European Act (SEA), 51, 164, 173, 174
Sinzheimer, 24, 27
Social market economy, 23, 41, 44, 47, 49, 55–58, 84
Social triple A, 60–63
Solange I, 205, 241, 242
Solange II, 242, 251
Sophie Redmond Stichting, 107, 109, 115
Spijkers, 111, 115, 117, 276, 282, 286
Stability and Growth Pact (SGP), 78–80, 83, 84
Static clause, 131, 132, 300
Stauder, 203
Strø Mølle Akustik, 95, 116, 117, 121, 143, 270, 274–277, 280, 283–286, 292, 296, 299, 307, 311, 313,
SURE, 79, 80

T

Taricco I, 224, 225, 243
Taricco II, 224, 225, 243
Traghetti del Mediterraneo, 156, 162, 230
Trans-judicial dialogue, 7, 16, 163, 188, 217, 224–265, 269, 287, 297–306, 312, 314, 320, 321
Treaty establishing a Constitution for Europe, 55, 174, 177, 182, 281

U

Ultra vires, 245, 247, 252, 253, 257, 258
Unionen, 133

V

Van Gend en Loos, 32, 154–156, 162, 169
Viking, 2, 4, 5, 32, 221–223, 255
Von on der Leyen Commission, 64, 75, 85, 318

W

Wabe, 220, 264, 265
Webb, 176
Weiss, 246–248
Werhof, 128–131, 135, 270, 274, 276–279, 281, 286, 288, 292, 296, 300, 301, 304–308, 311, 313, 314, 321

BCLR - BULLETIN OF COMPARATIVE LABOUR RELATIONS

Vol. Author/Title/Year/ISBN

1. Roger Blanpain, *Individual Employment Contracts: Collective Agreements*, 1970.
2. Roger Blanpain, *Social Planning*, 1971 (ISBN 90-312-0018-2).
3. Roger Blanpain, *Guaranteed Income Funds*, 1972 (ISBN 90-312-0019-0).
4. Roger Blanpain, *Employee Participation at the Level of the Enterprise*, 1973 (ISBN 90-312-0020-4).
5. Roger Blanpain, *Vastheid van Betrekking: Staking en Bezetting*, 1974.
6. Roger Blanpain, *Labour Law and Industrial Relations (International Bibliography)*, 1975 (ISBN 90-312-0023-9).
7. Roger Blanpain, *Multinational Enterprises*, 1976 (ISBN 90-312-0024-7).
8. Roger Blanpain, *Worker's Participation in the European Company*, 1977 (ISBN 90-312-0044-1).
9. Roger Blanpain, *Women and Labour*, 1978 (ISBN 90-312-0077-8).
10. Roger Blanpain, *European Conference on Labour Law and Industrial Relations: Multinational Enterprises*, 1979 (ISBN 90-312-0091-3).
11. Roger Blanpain, *Job Security and Industrial Relations*, 1980 (ISBN 90-312-0147-2).
12. Roger Blanpain, Greg Bamber & Russell Lansbury, *Technological Change and Industrial Relations: An International Symposium*, 1983 (ISBN 90-312-0205-3).
13. Roger Blanpain, James Janssen van Raay & A. Moulty, *Worker's Participation in the European Community: The Fifth Directive*, 1984 (ISBN 90-654-4187-5).
14. Roger Blanpain, *Equality and Prohibition of Discrimination in Employment*, 1985 (ISBN 90-654-4215-4).
15. Roger Blanpain, *Restructuring Labour in the Enterprise: Law and Practice in France, F.R. of Germany, Italy, Sweden and the United Kingdom*, 1986 (ISBN 90-654-4283-9).
16. Roger Blanpain & E. Kassalow, *Unions and Industrial Relations: Recent Trends and Prospect: A Comparative Treatment*, 1987 (ISBN 90-654-4294-4).
17. Roger Blanpain & Marco Biagi, *Trade Union Democracy and Industrial Relations*, 1988 (ISBN 90-654-4394-0).
18. Roger Blanpain & Jelle Visser, *In Search of Inclusive Unionism*, 1990 (ISBN 90-654-4439-4).
19. Roger Blanpain, *Flexibility and Wages: A Comparative Treatment*, 1990 (ISBN 90-654-4461-0).

20. Roger Blanpain, Stephen Frenkel & Oliver Clarke, *Economic Restructuring and Industrial Relations in Industrialised Countries,* 1990 (ISBN 90-654-4488-2).
21. Roger Blanpain & Friedrich Fürstenberg, *Structure and Strategy in Industrial Relations,* 1991 (ISBN 90-654-4559-5).
22. Roger Blanpain, Amira Galin & Ozer Carmi, *Flexible Work Patterns and Their Impact on Industrial Relations,* 1991 (ISBN 90-654-4572-2).
23. Roger Blanpain, *Workers' Participation: Influence on Management Decision-Making by Labour in the Private Sector,* 1992 (ISBN 90-654-4600-1).
24. Roger Blanpain, Brian Brooks & Chris Engels, *Employed or Self-Employed,* 1992 (ISBN 90-654-4613-3).
25. Roger Blanpain & Tiziano Treu, *Industrial Relations Developments in the Telecommunications Industry,* 1993 (ISBN 90-654-4642-7).
26. Roger Blanpain & Marco Biagi, *Industrial Relations in Small and Medium Sized Enterprises,* 1993 (ISBN 90-654-4696-6).
27. Roger Blanpain & Marco Biagi, *Participative Management and Industrial Relations in a Worldwide Perspective,* 1993 (ISBN 90-654-4769-5).
28. Roger Blanpain, Jacques Rojot & Hoyt N. Wheeler, *Employee Rights and Industrial Justice,* 1994 (ISBN 90-654-4804-7).
29. Roger Blanpain & Ruth Ben-Israel, *Strikes and Lock-Outs in Industrialized Market Economies,* 1994 (ISBN 90-654-4841-1).
30. Roger Blanpain, Kazuo Sugeno & Yasuo Suwa, *The Harmonization of Working Life and Family Life,* 1995 (ISBN 90-411-0064-4).
31. Roger Blanpain & Laszio Nagy, *Labour Law and Industrial Relations in Central and Eastern Europe,* 1996 (ISBN 90-411-0298-1).
32. Roger Blanpain, *Labour Law and Industrial Relations in the European Union,* 1997 (ISBN 90-411-0527-1).
33. Taco Van Peijpe, *Employment Protection under Strain,* 1998 (ISBN 90-411-0528-8).
34. Roger Blanpain, Takashi Araki & Ryuichi Yamakawa, *The Process of Industrialization and the Role of Labour Law in Asia,* 1999 (ISBN 9-041-1104-7-X).
35. Roger Blanpain & Marco Biagi, *Non-standard Work and Industrial Relations,* 1999 (ISBN 90-411-1117-4).
36. Roger Blanpain, *Private Employment Agencies: The Impact of ILO Convention 181 (1997) and the Judgment of the European Court of Justice of 11 December 1997,* 1999 (ISBN 90-411-1118-2).
37. Roger Blanpain, *Multinational Enterprises and the Social Challenges of the XXIst Century: The ILO Declaration on Fundamental* Principles *at Work, Public and Private Corporate Codes of Conduct,* 2000 (ISBN 90-411-1280-4).
38. Roger Blanpain, Ryuichi Yamakawa & Takashi Araki, *Deregulation and Labour Law: In Search of a Labour Concept for the 21st Century,* 2000 (ISBN 90-411-1370-3).
39. Roger Blanpain, *The Council of Europe and the Social Challenges of the XXIst Century,* 2001 (ISBN 90-411-1543-9).

40. Roger Blanpain, *On-Line Rights for Employees in the Information Society, Use & Monitoring of E-Mail & Internet at Work*, 2002 (ISBN 90-411-1626-5).
41. Roger Blanpain, *The Evolving Employment Relationship and the New Economy: The Role of Labour Law & Industrial Relations*, 2001 (ISBN 90-411-1691-5).
42. Roger Blanpain, *Involvement of Employees in the European Union, Works Councils, Company Statute, Information and Consultation Rights*, 2002 (ISBN 90-411-1760-1).
43. Michele Colucci, *The Impact of the Internet and New Technologies on the Workplace: A Legal Analysis from a Comparative Point of View*, 2002 (ISBN 90-411-1824-1).
44. Roger Blanpain, *White Paper on the Labour Market in Italy: The Quality of European Industrial Relations and Changing Industrial Relations*, 2002 (ISBN 90-411-1841-1).
45. Roger Blanpain, Russell D. Lansbury & Young-Bum Park, *Impact of Globalisation on Employment Relations: A Comparison of the Automobile and Banking Industries in Australia and Korea*, 2002 (ISBN 90-411-1850-0).
46. Roger Blanpain & Antoine Jacobs, *Employee Rights in Bankruptcy: A Comparative-Law Assessment*, 2002 (ISBN 90-411-1942-6).
47. Roger Blanpain, Takashi Araki & Shinya Ouchi, *Corporate Restructuring and the Role of Labour Law*, 2003 (ISBN 90-411-1949-3).
48. Roger Blanpain, *Collective Bargaining, Discrimination, Social Security and European Integration*, 2003 (ISBN 90-411-2010-6).
49. Roger Blanpain & Luis Aparicio-Valdez, *Labour Relations in the Asia- Pacific Countries*, 2004 (ISBN 90-411-2239-7).
50. Roger Blanpain & Ronnie Graham, *Temporary Agency Work and the Information Society*, 2004 (ISBN 90-411-2252-4).
51. Roger Blanpain, *The Actors of Collective Bargaining: A World Report*, 2004 (ISBN 90-411-2253-2).
52. Roger Blanpain & Michele Colucci, *The Globalisation of Labour Standards: The Soft Law Track*, 2004 (ISBN 90-411-2303-2).
53. Roger Blanpain, Takashi Araki & Shinya Ouchi, *Labour Law in Motion: Diversification of the Labour Force & Terms and Conditions of Employment*, 2005 (ISBN 90-411-2315-6).
54. Roger Blanpain, *Smoking and the Workplace*, 2005 (ISBN 90-411-2325-3).
55. Roger Blanpain, *Confronting Globalization: The Quest for a Social Agenda*, 2005 (ISBN 90-411-2381-4).
56. Roger Blanpain, Thomas Blanke & Edgar Rose, *Collective Bargaining Wages in Comparative Perspective: Germany, France, the Netherlands, Sweden and the United Kingdom*, 2005 (ISBN 90-411-2388-1).
57. Roger Blanpain & Anne Numhauser-Henning, *Women in Academia & Equality Law: Aiming High - Falling Short?*, 2006 (ISBN 978-90-411-2427-6).
58. Roger Blanpain, *Freedom of Services in the European Union: Labour and Social Security Law: The Bolkestein Initiative*, 2006 (ISBN 978-90-411-2453-5).
59. Roger Blanpain, Frans Pennings & Nurhan Sural, *Flexibilisation and Modernisation of the Turkish Labour Market*, 2006 (ISBN 978-90-411-2490-X).

60. Roger Blanpain & Boel Flodgren, *Corporate and Employment Perspectives in a Global Business Environment*, 2006 (ISBN 978-90-411-2537-X).
61. Roger Blanpain, Shinya Ouchi & Takashi Araki, *Decentralizing Industrial Relations and The Role of Labor Unions and Employee Representatives*, 2007 (ISBN 978-90-411-2583-3).
62. Roger Blanpain, *European Framework Agreements and Telework: Law and Practice: A European and Comparative Study*, 2007 (ISBN 978-90-411-2560-4).
63. Roger Blanpain, Jim Kitay, Leanne Cutcher & Nick Wailes, *Globalization and Employment Relations in Retail Banking*, 2007 (ISBN 978-90-411-2620-1).
64. Roger Blanpain, Russell Lansbury, Jim Kitay, Nick Wailes & Anja Kirsch, *Globalization and Employment Relations in the Auto Assembly Industry: A Study of Seven Countries*, 2008 (ISBN 978-90-411-2698-6).
65. Roger Blanpain & Michele Tiraboschi, *The Global Labour Market: From Globalization to Flexicurity*, 2008 (ISBN 978-90-411-2722-8).
66. Roger Blanpain, Michele Colucci & Frank Hendrickx, *The Future of Sport in the European Union: Beyond the EU Reform Treaty and the White Paper*, 2008 (ISBN 978-90-411-2761-7).
67. Roger Blanpain, Linda Dickens, *Challenges in European Employment Relations: Employment Regulation, Trade Union Organization, Equality, Flexicurity, Training and New Approaches to Pay*, 2008 (ISBN 978-90-411-2771-6).
68. Roger Blanpain, Hiroya Nakakubo & Takashi Araki, *New Developments in Employment Discrimination Law, 2008* (ISBN 978-90-411-2782-2).
69. Roger Blanpain, Andrzej Marian wiątkowski, *The Laval and Viking Cases: Freedom of Services and Establishment v. Industrial Conflict in the European Economic Area and Russia*, 2009 (ISBN 978-90-411-2850-8).
70. Roger Blanpain, William Bromwich, Olga Rymkevich, Silvia Spattini, *The Modernization of Labour Law and Industrial Relations in a Comparative Perspective*, 2009 (ISBN 978-90-411-2865-2).
71. Roger Blanpain, Juan Pablo Landa & Brian Langille, *Employment Policies and Multilevel Governance*, 2009 (ISBN 978-90-411-2866-9).
72. Roger Blanpain, European Works Councils; *The European Directive 2009/ 38/EC of 6 May 2009, 2009* (ISBN 978-90-411-3208-6).
73. Roger Blanpain, William Bromwich, Olga Rymkevich & Silvia Spattini, *Labour Productivity, Investment in Human Capital and Youth Employment: Comparative Developments and Global Responses*, 2010 (ISBN 978-90-411-3249-9).
74. Greg J. Bamber & Philippe Pochet, *Regulating Employment Relations, Work and Labour Laws: International Comparisons between Key Countries*, 2010 (ISBN 978-90-411-3199-7). General Editor: Roger Blanpain.
75. Roger Blanpain, Desislava Nikolaeva Dimitrova, *Seafarers' Rights in the Globalized Maritime Industry*, 2010 (ISBN 978-90-411-3349-6).
76. Roger Blanpain, Hiroya Nakakubo & Takashi Araki, *Regulation of Fixed- Term Employment Contracts*, 2010 (ISBN 978-90-411-3356-4).

77. Roger Blanpain, William Bromwich, Olga Rymkevich & Iacopo Senatori, *Rethinking Corporate Governance*, 2011 (ISBN 978-90-411-3450-9).
78. Roger Blanpain & Frank Hendrickx, *Labour Law between Change and Tradition: Liber Amicorum Antoine Jacobs*, 2011 (ISBN 978-90-411-3424-0).
79. Roger Blanpain, Thomas Klebe, Marlene Schmidt & Bernd Waas, *Trade Union Rights at the Workplace*, 2012 (ISBN 978-90-411-3460-8).
80. Roger Blanpain, William Bromwich, Olga Rymkevich & Iacopo Senatori, *Labour Markets, Industrial Relations and Human Resources Management: From Recession to Recovery*, 2012 (ISBN 978-90-411-4004-3).
81. Roger Blanpain, Hiroya Nakakubo & Takashi Araki, *Systems of Employee Representation at the Enterprise: A Comparative Study*, 2012 (ISBN 978-90-411-4080-7).
82. Roger Blanpain & Frank Hendrickx, *Temporary Agency Work in the European Union and the United States*, 2013 (ISBN 978-90-411-4769-1).
83. Roger Blanpain, Toker Dereli, Y. Pınar Soykut-Sarıca & Aslı en-Tabaı, *Emerging Patterns of Work and Turkish Labour Market Challenges under Globalization: Readings on Labour and Employment Relations*, 2014 (ISBN 978-90-411-4983-1).
84. Roger Blanpain, Pablo Arellano Ortiz, Marius Olivier & Gijsbert Vonk, *Social Security and Migrant Workers: Selected Studies of Cross-border Social Security Mechanisms*, 2014 (ISBN 978-90-411-4770-7).
85. Roger Blanpain & Nikita Lyutov, *Workers' Representation in Central and Eastern Europe: Challenges and Opportunities for the Works Councils' System*, 2014 (ISBN 978-90-411-4746-2).
86. Roger Blanpain, Ulla Liukkunen & Chen Yifeng, *China and ILO Fundamental Principles and Rights at Works*, 2014 (ISBN 978-90-411-4984-8).
87. Roger Blanpain, *The Use of Languages and Employment Relations*, 2014 (ISBN 978-90-411-5606-8).
88. Roger Blanpain, Hiroya Nakakubo & Takashi Araki, *Protection of Employees' Personal Information and Privacy*, 2014 (ISBN 978-90-411-5608-2).
89. Roger Blanpain, Jan Wouters, Glenn Rayp, Laura Beke & Axel Marx, *Protecting Labour Rights in a Multi-polar Supply Chain and Mobile Global Economy*, 2015 (ISBN 978-90-411-5662-4).
90. Roger Blanpain & Stefania Marassi, *Globalization and Transnational Collective Labour Relations: International and European Framework Agreements at Company Level*, 2015 (ISBN 978-90-411-4748-6).
91. Roger Blanpain, Frank Hendrickx & Petra Herzfeld Olsson, *National Effects of the Implementation of EU Directives on Labour Migration from Third Countries*, 2016 (ISBN 978-90-411-6257-1).
92. Roger Blanpain, Frank Hendrickx & D'Arcy du Toit, *Labour Law and Social Progress: Holding the Line or Shifting the Boundaries?* 2016 (ISBN 978-90-411-6747-7).

93. Roger Blanpain & Frank Hendrickx, *Reasonable Accommodation in the Modern Workplace: Potential and Limits of the Integrative Logics of Labour Law*, 2016 (ISBN 978-90-411-6258-8).
94. Roger Blanpain, Frank Hendrickx & Bernd Waas, *New Forms of Employment in Europe*, 2016 (ISBN 978-90-411-6239-7).
95. Roger Blanpain, Frank Hendrickx, Hiroya Nakakubo & Takashi Araki, *The Notion of Employer in the Era of the Fissured Workplace: Should Labour Law Responsibilities Exceed the Boundary of the Legal Entity?*, 2017 (ISBN 978-90-411-8470-2).
96. Elena Sychenko, *Individual Labour Rights as Human Rights: The Contributions of the European Court of Human Rights to Worker's Rights Protection*, 2017 (ISBN 978-90-411-8629-4).
97. William Bromwich & Olga Rymkevich, *Improving Workplace Quality: New Perspectives and Challenges for Worker Well-Being*, 2017 (ISBN 978-90-411-8628-7).
98. Sarah De Groof, *Work-Life Balance in the Modern Workplace: Interdisciplinary Perspectives from Work-Family Research, Law and Policy*, 2017 (ISBN 978-90-411-8630-0).
99. Sylvaine Laulom, *Collective Bargaining Developments in Times of Crisis*, 2018 (ISBN 978-90-411-8999-8).
100. Frank Hendrickx & Valerio De Stefano, *Game Changers in Labour Law: Shaping the Future of Work*, 2018 (ISBN 978-90-411-9953-9).
101. Ivana Palinkaš, *The Legal and Institutional Framing of Collective Bargaining in CEE Countries: Between Europeanisation and Decentralisation*, 2018 (ISBN 978-90-411-9199-1).
102. Jeremy Waddington, *European Board-Level Employee Representation: National Variations in Influence and Power*, 2018 (ISBN 978-90-411-9202-8).
103. Jan Pichrt & Kristina Koldinská, *Labour Law and Social Protection in a Globalized World: Changing Realities in Selected Areas of Law and Policy*, 2018 (ISBN 978-94-035-0093-5).
104. Matthew W. Finkin, *American Labor and the Law: Dormant, Resurgent, and Emergent Problems*, 2019 (ISBN 978-94-035-0654-8).
105. Giuseppe Casale & Tiziano Treu, *Transformations of Work: Challenges for the Institutions and Social Actors*, 2019 (ISBN 978-94-035-0891-7).
106. Miguel De la Corte-Rodríguez, *EU Law on Maternity and Other Child-Related Leaves: Impact on Gender Equality*, 2019 (ISBN 978-94-035-1452-9).
107. Valeria Pulignano & Frank Hendrickx, *Employment Relations in the 21st Century: Challenges for Theory and Research in a Changing World of Work*, 2020 (ISBN 978-94-035-1764-3).
108. Matteo Bottero, *Posting of Workers in EU Law: Challenges of Equality, Solidarity and Fair Competition*, 2021 (ISBN 978-94-035-2860-1).
109. Bernd Waas & Christina Hießl, *Collective Bargaining for Self-Employed Workers in Europe: Approaches to Reconcile Competition Law and Labour Rights*, 2021 (ISBN 978-94-035-2373-6).

110. Mathias Wouters, *International Labour Standards and Platform Work: An Analysis of Digital Labour Platforms Based on the Instruments on Private Employment Agencies, Home Work and Domestic Work*, 2022 (ISBN 978-94-035-4024-5).
111. Luca Ratti, *In-Work Poverty in Europe: Vulnerable and Under-Represented Persons in a Comparative Perspective*, 2022 (ISBN 978-94-035-4996-5).
112. Silvia Rainone, *The Role of the Court of Justice in EU Labour Law: A Case Study on the Transfer of Undertakings Directive*, 2023 (ISBN 978-94-035-2896-0).

www.ingramcontent.com/pod-product-compliance
Lightning Source LLC
Chambersburg PA
CBHW071411230926
51846CB00001B/51
* 9 7 8 9 4 0 3 5 2 8 9 6 0 *